A Just and Righteous Cause

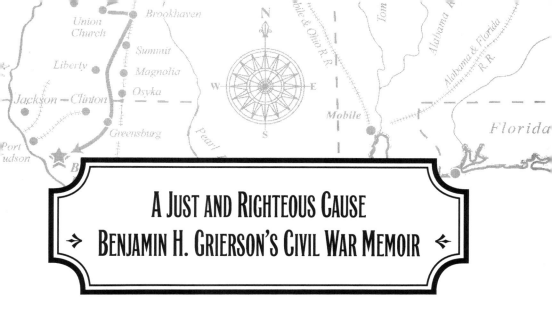

A Just and Righteous Cause
Benjamin H. Grierson's Civil War Memoir

Edited by Bruce J. Dinges and Shirley A. Leckie

Southern Illinois University Press
Carbondale

Southern Illinois University Press
www.siupress.com

Copyright © 2008 by the Board of Trustees,
Southern Illinois University
Printed in the United States of America
First printing in paperback, 2016

19 18 17 16   4 3 2 1

Cover illustration: "Triumphal Procession of Colonel
Grierson, Commanding Sixth and Seventh Illinois
Cavalry, through Baton Rouge, May 2, 1863 (detail)
from a sketch by J. R. Hamilton, *Harper's Weekly*,
June 6, 1863, p. 356.

Library of Congress Cataloging-in-Publication Data
Grierson, Benjamin Henry, 1826–1911.
  A just and righteous cause : Benjamin H. Grierson's
Civil War memoir / edited by Bruce J. Dinges and
Shirley A. Leckie.
      p. cm.
  Includes bibliographical references and index.
  ISBN-13: 978-0-8093-2859-8 (cloth : alk. paper)
  ISBN-10: 0-8093-2859-3 (cloth : alk. paper)
  1. Grierson, Benjamin Henry, 1826–1911. 2. United
States—History—Civil War, 1861–1865—Personal
narratives. 3. United States—History—Civil War,
1861–1865—Cavalry operations. 4. Generals—
United States—Biography. 5. United States. Army—
Biography. I. Dinges, Bruce J. II. Leckie, Shirley A.,
date. III. Title.

E467.1.G8A3 2008
973.7'3092—dc22
[B]   2007051047

  ISBN: 978-0-8093-3512-1 (paperback)
  ISBN: 978-0-8093-8709-0 (e-book)

Printed on recycled paper. ♻

Dedicated to the memory of
William H. Leckie
and
Wilbert and Julia Dinges

Contents

Illustrations

Acknowledgments

The editors thank, first and foremost, the Morgan County (Illinois) Historical Society for its advocacy and unstinting support of this project, in particular: Dr. Frank and Mrs. Frances Norbury (for their wonderful hospitality during General Grierson Days); Rand and Patricia Burnette; John R. Power, publisher emeritus of the *Jacksonville Journal-Courier*; Ron Gray; Greg and Pam Olson; and Robert Sibert. We also thank Lonnie Johns for his unflagging interest in this work and its eventual publication. The late William H. Leckie and Frank E. Vandiver provided encouragement and inspiration, along with their own sterling examples of the historian's craft. Aaron Cohen and Shelly Dudley of Guidon Books in Scottsdale, Arizona, repeatedly rode to the rescue with hard-to-find volumes. Mary L. Williams of Fort Davis National Historic Site, Texas, furnished photographs, advice, and good cheer. Sylvia Rodrigue, of Southern Illinois University Press, has been a gentle guide and an encouraging force throughout the editorial process. Finally, our heartfelt appreciation to the anonymous reviewers who painstakingly read the manuscript, catching errors, identifying sources we had overlooked, asking perceptive questions, and pointing us in new directions. The book is much improved by their diligence. Ben Grierson has been an enduring and enriching presence in our lives. We hope that he would approve of this edition of his Civil War memoir. Any errors or other shortcomings are strictly our own.

Southern Illinois in 1861. Map drawn by George Skoch.

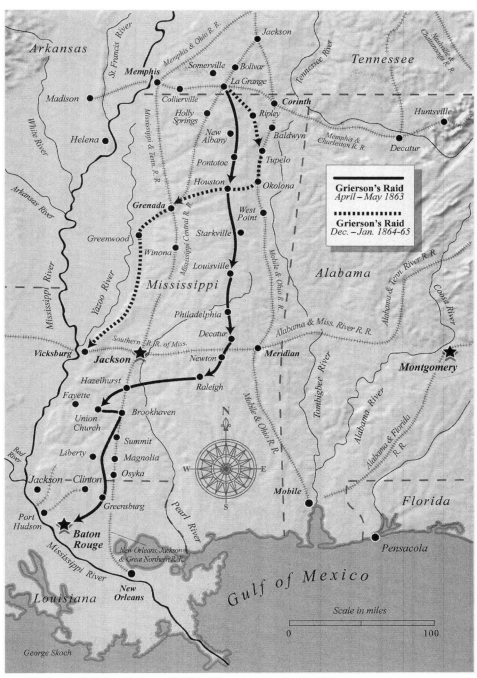

Benjamin H. Grierson's Area of Military Operations in the Civil War.

Map drawn by George Skoch.

➜ A Just and Righteous Cause

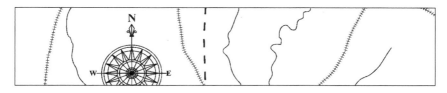

Editors' Introduction

Benjamin H. Grierson and his wife, Alice Kirk Grierson, were living in St. Louis, Missouri, in 1873, enjoying a respite from Ben's military service in the Indian Territory (present-day Oklahoma). As colonel of the 10th Cavalry, one of the U.S. Army's two black cavalry regiments, Ben had been stationed in the Trans-Mississippi West since 1866. After the Cheyenne defeat at the battle of the Washita in 1868, he had overseen the building of Fort Sill. Most recently, he and his family had been stationed at Fort Gibson, also in the Indian Territory. In St. Louis, the family resided at the "Old Arsenal" while Ben was involved in recruiting duty. He described their quarters as "comfortable and commodious," a far cry from the cramped and often primitive accommodations that officers' families usually endured at frontier posts.

While visiting the Griersons in St. Louis, Ella L. Wolcott, an old friend from Elmira, New York, began arranging their voluminous correspondence to create a record of Ben's achievements during the Civil War. In 1875, Ben was recalled to the frontier—this time to duty at Fort Concho in west Texas. He continued working on his record in his spare time, while commanding the post and the District of the Pecos. Ben went on to serve in Arizona and New Mexico before retiring as brigadier general and commander of the Department of Arizona in Los Angeles in 1890. Alice died of cancer in 1888. Four years later, in 1892, Ben completed his memoirs.[1]

Grierson notes in the preface that, initially, he intended the autobiography for his family and *not for publication.* This assertion may have been somewhat disingenuous, as sometime later he revised it in the hope that, as "a faithful record of events connected with a remarkable and sanguinary conflict for the advancement of human liberty," it would give "pleasure to those who fought, or gave their earnest support to our Government[,] when the life of the Nation was imperiled and furnish such a story as will become of interest to their descendants." He even hints that if the memoir received a favorable reception, he might produce another volume covering his quarter century of service in command of buffalo soldiers on the Western frontier. Grierson died on August 31, 1911, at age eighty-five, without making good on that promise. Very likely his increasing fragility as he aged sapped his energy for the hard work of writing and his marriage in 1897 to the Jacksonville widow Lillian King gave him the comfort of a companion and, thus, less need to reminisce about the past.[2]

Like most army officers of his generation, Ben Grierson viewed the four years of excitement and bloody fighting during the Civil War as the defining period of his life and career, against which subsequent decades of tedious and unrewarding duty at far-flung frontier outposts paled in comparison. Grierson certainly had a remarkable story to tell. The youngest son of Scots-Irish immigrants who had followed the westward route of migration from Pittsburgh, Pennsylvania, to Youngstown, Ohio, and Jacksonville, Illinois, he had grown up along the vibrant and sometimes turbulent Middle Border, where free enterprise, religious enthusiasm, and abolitionist agitation eventually gave birth to the Republican Party. While his father made a respectable living as a merchant and real estate speculator, material success seemed to elude Ben. A musical prodigy, he played in various bands and taught music, but his one business venture—a mercantile partnership—floundered and eventually collapsed in the national panic of 1857.

At the outbreak of the Civil War, Ben Grierson was a thirty-four-year-old husband and father of two small boys, with no military experience and few civilian prospects. His energetic efforts on behalf of the Republican Party in heavily Democratic Morgan County, however, opened the door to military service. Through his connections with his Jacksonville neighbor, now Republican governor, Richard Yates, Grierson obtained an appointment as volunteer aide on the staff of another Republican politician-turned-soldier, Benjamin M. Prentiss, holding the strategic junction of the Ohio and Mississippi rivers for the Union. In those critical months, Grierson learned the soldier's trade, and in the spring of 1862, Yates commissioned him colonel of the 6th Illinois Cavalry.

Described by Maj. Gen. Henry Halleck as "active and wirey [sic] enough to make a good cavalry-man," the 5 foot 11½ inch tall, 175 pound Grierson established his competence in the West under the appreciative eyes of Generals William T. Sherman and Ulysses S. Grant. After Grierson spent six months chasing guerrillas in western Tennessee and northern Mississippi, Sherman recommended him to Grant as "the best cavalry officer I have yet had." Grant observed Grierson's abilities firsthand during his aggressive pursuit of Confederate general Earl Van Dorn's raiders following the destruction of Grant's supply base at Holly Springs, Mississippi, at Christmastime 1862.[3]

Grierson catapulted into the front ranks of Union cavalrymen with his remarkable raid down the length of Confederate-held Mississippi. Leaving La Grange, Tennessee, on April 17, 1863, with 1,700 horsemen and six small artillery pieces, he employed a dazzling combination of speed and deception that left his pursuers stunned and confused. Covering 600 miles in sixteen days, Grierson emerged at Baton Rouge, Louisiana, on May 2, leaving in his wake torn up rails and telegraph lines and smoldering supply depots. Most important, the raid diverted Confederate attention while Grant's army crossed the Mississippi River to attack Vicksburg from the rear. Grant called it "one of the most brilliant cavalry exploits of the war" and predicted that "it will be handed down in history as an example to be imitated." It earned Grierson national acclaim and a brigadier general's star. A century later, Grierson's exploit inspired Dee Brown's classic history *Grierson's Raid*, Harold Sinclair's popular novel *The Horse Soldiers*, and a John Ford film based on the novel starring John Wayne and William Holden.[4]

Grierson's moment in the spotlight was short-lived, however. For the remainder of the war, he served competently, but unspectacularly, in support of Union operations commanded by other generals, many of whom proved much less competent, ranging from mediocre to abysmal. Maj. Gen. Nathaniel Banks snared Grierson's cavalry to guard the Union rear during the siege of Port Hudson in mid-1863. In February of 1864, Grierson accompanied Brig. Gen. William Sooy Smith's abortive expedition toward Meridian, Mississippi, and in June he commanded the cavalry that staved off disaster for Brig. Gen. Samuel Sturgis's retreating army when it was assailed by Nathan Bedford Forrest at Brice's Cross Roads. He played a minor role in Brig. Gen. A. J. Smith's defeat of Forrest near Tupelo, Mississippi, in July. Grierson was then given command of the Cavalry Corps, District of West Tennessee, only to be removed in November when twenty-seven-year-old Bvt. Maj. Gen. James Harrison Wilson assumed command of the newly constituted Cavalry Corps of the Military Division of the Mississippi.[5]

Grierson's talents, however, were not wasted. Between December 21, 1864, and January 5, 1865, he hammered Confederate general John Bell Hood's lines of communication, cutting a 450-mile swath through Mississippi and destroying tracks, telegraph lines, moving stock, factories, warehouses, and supplies. The following month, Grant assigned him to organize the cavalry in Maj. Gen. E. R. S. Canby's Department of the Gulf, explaining to the latter that Grierson would serve him well. "I am satisfied you would either find him at the appointed place in time or you would find him holding an enemy." The end of the war found Grierson at the head of 4,000 cavalry at Troy, Alabama. He organized cavalry at New Orleans for service in Texas but was disappointed when Maj. Gen. Philip Sheridan replaced him with Generals Wesley Merritt and George A. Custer. Grierson completed his military service with Reconstruction duty in command of the Northern District of Alabama at Huntsville. He was mustered out on January 15, 1866. Called to testify before a subcommittee of the Joint Committee on Reconstruction, he successfully lobbied for reinstatement and discharge on April 30, 1866, as major general of volunteers.[6]

Grierson held high cards in the intense competition to fill regimental commands created by the 1866 Army Reorganization Act. In addition to his war record, he had earned the friendship and respect of Generals Grant and Sherman. Moreover, he had impressed Congress with his outspoken support for the Radical Republican platform. It was no surprise, therefore, that he was selected to organize and command the 10th U.S. Cavalry, one of the postwar army's two mounted regiments composed of white officers and black enlisted men. Over two decades, he molded the 10th Cavalry buffalo soldiers into one of the finest regiments on the frontier.[7]

Grierson's reminiscence occupies a unique niche in the crowded field of Civil War memoirs. Biographers of military figures often complain of the dearth of personal correspondence that, were it available, would enable them to paint vivid, three-dimensional portraits of their subjects. As William Leckie and Shirley Leckie demonstrate in *Unlikely Warriors: General Benjamin H. Grierson and His Family*, Ben and Alice were prolific writers, corresponding with each other when separated and carrying on intimate correspondence with members of their extended families. And they saved everything. Today, extensive and important collections of Grierson papers reside at Texas Tech University's Southwest Collection, the Illinois State Historical Library, and the Newberry Library.

Just as this treasure trove of material has been a boon to twentieth- and twenty-first-century historians, it also informs and enlivens Grierson's autobiography, lending a warmth and immediacy that is rarely found in military memoirs. Like most military memoirists, Grierson relied heavily on his official reports to reconstruct events in camp and field. Thanks to Miss Walcott's archival skills, he was also able to dip into his letters home to rekindle the feelings of thirty years past. The fact that many of the principal Union commanders had passed on by the time he sat down to write afforded him the luxury of freely expressing his judgments and opinions—although his occasional criticisms pale in comparison with other (especially Confederate) memoirists who wielded their pens to settle old scores.[8]

Although less well known than John A. Logan and Nelson Miles, Grierson belongs among the ranks of volunteer soldiers whom the war molded into competent military commanders. His autobiography explains how that process occurred and adds evidence to the debate over why men fought. In Grierson's case, the overriding motivation was patriotism and his firm commitment to preserving the Union.[9]

This memoir also throws fresh light on mobilization and important campaigns in the Western theater of the Civil War so often ignored by historians. Through Grierson's observant eyes, we see the scramble to secure the strategic river port of Cairo, Illinois, for the Union, early campaigns in southeastern Missouri, the rise of Ulysses S. Grant and William T. Sherman, army politics, the seasoning of Union cavalry in operations against Confederate guerrillas, Grierson's great raid through Mississippi, the siege of Port Hudson, and subsequent operations in Mississippi and the Gulf states. Equally important, because Grierson was a passionate Republican who owed his commission to political connections, we gain insight into the important relationship between politics and command during the Civil War and Reconstruction.

It is instructive to observe that Grierson begins his memoir with a description of his family and boyhood on the westward-expanding Middle Border. The Griersons were part of the great migration of people fleeing poverty, warfare, and religious persecution in the northern British Isles that began in the eighteenth century and continued well into the nineteenth century. In Ben's memoir, readers follow the family's fortunes as Robert Grierson embarks on a path well trod by previous Scots-Irish immigrants from western Pennsylvania to northeastern Ohio and finally the Mississippi River valley. At each stop, he builds the family's modest fortune by engaging in mercantile pursuits, farming, and real estate speculation. The long odyssey ends in the mid-1850s, with the Griersons sinking deep roots in the central Illinois community of Jacksonville.[10]

Jacksonville, as the seat of Morgan County, was an attractive city. Thirty miles west of Springfield, the state capital, and set in the midst of green rolling hills, it had been founded in the 1820s by transplanted New Englanders, who laid it out with broad streets extending from a central town square. A group of ministers and teachers, known as the "Yale Band," had arrived in 1829 to establish Illinois College as a center of learning and civilization in the West. By the 1840s, the town boasted a female seminary, various reading and discussion groups, and musical societies, which were especially attractive to Ben. Finally, the townfolk had established three asylums—one for deaf-mutes, one for the blind, and another to treat the insane. The Griersons, as abolitionists and Free-Soilers, were comfortable in this community wedded to learning, uplift, and charitable endeavors. The family home at 852 East State Street, affectionately nicknamed "the old homestead," was Ben's lodestar throughout his life and a military career that eventually took him as far away as the West Coast and the far Southwest.[11]

Family was the supreme concern and greatest joy of Ben Grierson's life. In a marriage that spanned more than three decades, Ben and Alice demonstrated a rare devotion that surmounted quarrels, tragedy, and long separations. When apart, the couple exchanged loving letters in which both expressed their eagerness to be reunited and pledged themselves to strive to become more loving and thoughtful spouses. Together, they endured much. Careful readers of this memoir will find hints of future tragedy. Given the high infant mortality rate in the nineteenth century, it is not especially unusual that only four of the Griersons' seven children survived to adulthood. Grierson's allusions to his mother's and his sister Mary's bouts with depression, however, foreshadow still more heartbreak.

Although undiagnosed at the time, manic depression, or what is now referred to as bipolar disorder, stalked three of the four Grierson boys. Charlie, the eldest, succumbed while a cadet at West Point in 1877, recovered to graduate in 1879, married and fathered three children, served with the 10th Cavalry, and was a lieutenant colonel when he suffered a relapse in 1915 that compelled his confinement at Letterman General Hospital in San Francisco and then at St. Elizabeth's Hospital in Washington, D.C., until his death in 1928. Robert suffered a breakdown in a Chicago hotel while he was a medical student at the University of Michigan. He recovered to run the family's ranch at Fort Davis, Texas, until his commitment in the 1890s to the Oak Lawn Retreat at Jacksonville and later to the state mental hospital, where he died in 1922. Theodore McGregor (George), the youngest Grierson child, exhibited similar signs of mental illness while he and his brother Benjamin Henry Jr. (Harry) managed the Fort Davis property but remained at the ranch until his death in 1950. Harry, who married briefly and then divorced, died in 1934.[12]

Finally, Grierson's racial attitudes merit some discussion. Readers familiar with his long association with black troops and his articulate advocacy of fair and equitable treatment for blacks and Indians may be surprised by Ben's casual and repeated stereotyping of freed slaves, and African Americans in general, as buffoonish "darkies." The only explanation is to acknowledge that he was a man of his time who expressed the prevailing racial attitudes of his day. In Grierson's case, those attitudes undoubtedly were further molded by his experiences as a young musician in minstrel shows that were then popular. Race in America was, and is, a complex phenomenon. As Grierson's memoir amply demonstrates, it was possible in nineteenth-century America to champion abolitionism and civil rights intellectually, while at the same time denigrating African American life and culture.[13]

This edition has been prepared from an original typescript in the Benjamin H. Grierson Papers at the Illinois State Historical Library, Springfield. The typescript consists of 888 double-spaced pages, arbitrarily divided into two, roughly equal parts (which accounts for why Grierson refers to "these *volumes*" in his preface). In preparing it for publication, we have eliminated the opening chapters in which Grierson traces the family genealogy back to the ancients lairds of Scotland, letters to and from family members, poetry, extraneous military correspondence, newspaper articles and puffery, and the text of Grierson's congressional testimony. We have also removed descriptive headings and combined chapters to improve narrative flow. Otherwise, we have exercised a light editorial hand. To improve readability, we have broken up run-on sentences (of which Grierson was inordinately fond) and long paragraphs. Occasionally, we have corrected syntax where it confuses meaning. We have also corrected spelling, modernized capitalization, and standardized the way in which Grierson cites dates, unit numbers, and so on (e.g., *May 7* instead of *the seventh of May*; *6th Illinois Cavalry* instead of *Sixth Illinois Cavalry*; *XIV Corps* instead of *Fourteenth Corps, First Brigade* instead of *1st Brigade*). Wherever possible, first names have been furnished for persons Grierson only identifies by surname. These and other insertions are indicated by brackets. Our guiding principal has been to retain the engaging informality of the original.

A note on the title of this book. Grierson christened his autobiography "The Lights and Shadows of Life: Including Experiences and Remembrances of the War of the Rebellion." Although "lights and shadows" was a popular nineteenth-century allusion, its resonance for modern readers has dimmed. For that reason, and to better convey Grierson's patriotism and his passionate commitment to the Union and to the principles of the Republican Party, the editors have retitled his memoir *A Just and Righteous Cause.* The phrase is from Grierson's reflection on his political activities during the 1858 and 1860 Lincoln campaigns: "it is probable . . . that the experience thus gained in sustaining what I deemed a just and righteous cause was absolutely necessary to enable me to put forth greater efforts in the memorable struggle which was so soon to follow."[14]

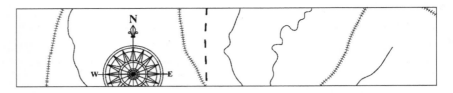

Preface

To at once acknowledge my indebtedness to others, and show what has led to the writing of these volumes, it is proper to state that in 1873, when stationed at Fort Gibson in the Indian Territory, and comfortably fixed in excellent quarters, I received the following telegram:

Washington, D.C., Jan. 3rd, 1873.

To—

Col. B. H. Grierson, 10th. Cavalry:—Do you want the detail for recruiting service?

W. T. Sherman,
General

Being at that time so pleasantly situated, and not having applied for the position, the question flashed upon me so unexpectedly by the General of the Army was rather hard to answer, but upon consulting Mrs. Grierson, it was decided that the change to St. Louis, Missouri, then the station of the Superintendent of the General Mounted Recruiting Service, and only ninety miles from our home at Jacksonville, Illinois, would for many reasons be advantageous. Therefore my acceptance was telegraphed, the necessary orders issued, and the move made without delay.

The change proved a pleasant relief, gave opportunities to visit home, and enabled us to entertain friends, residents of the States, a pleasure of which we had been deprived while at distant stations on the frontier. Our quarters at the "Old Arsenal" were comfortable and commodious, and among other friends who accepted our hospitality was Miss Ella L. Wolcott of Elmira, New York. During her stay, two ladies residing in the city of St. Louis, who proved to be connections, called and made some inquiries in regard to the Griersons in Europe. Miss Wolcott was present at the interview and became much interested in the conversation, which naturally led to the looking up of family records.

It so happened that about that time I had occasion to overhaul my papers for the purpose of furnishing information required by the Adjutant

General of the Army, and while thus engaged, some of my reports were read by Miss Wolcott, who inquired if my papers were all safe and in good order. I replied that they were partially arranged, that I burned some now and then, but that the quantity did not seem to diminish. Mrs. Grierson, who in the meantime had taken part in the conversation, quaintly asked Miss Wolcott if she would not like to see her records, humorously pulling out of drawers and trunks numerous packages of letters. Miss Wolcott, in high glee, indicated that they were the very papers she would prefer to examine. The letters referred to, which were hastily written by me during the war, had long been tied in bundles and carefully preserved, notwithstanding my frequent requests to Mrs. Grierson to destroy them. Invariably, she quietly gave me to understand that they were her private property, that I need not worry about them, and in changing station, no matter how limited our transportation, they, by her supervision and management, were sure to be taken with us. The examination of the letters began and continued from day to day with increasing interest and much merriment, until finally Miss Wolcott proposed to compile them, with official papers and statements, into a fuller record of my services during the war. At that time I was of the opinion the object to be gained would hardly justify the labor required. But, consent being given, the work was begun in earnest and persistently pursued until the troublesome task which finished as designed.

Subsequently, when stationed at Fort Concho, Texas, after many years of active scouting and campaigns against hostile Indians, I found myself with less official duty to perform than at any time after my entry into the regular army. Having at my headquarters a printing press, I concluded to revise a synopsis of my services for file at the War Department, and that was so quickly done I decided to undertake the revision and printing of the longer record, prepared as already stated. That, too, was satisfactorily accomplished under my direct supervision. A few letters written by my father, sister, brother, Mrs. Grierson, and myself were inserted, and some corrections made in statements of incidents, where it seemed I had failed to make myself fully understood by Miss Wolcott in our hurried interviews. But the record, in its entirety, is mainly as she left it. It was printed only for the *information of my family*, and *not for publication*. In the following pages I have made free use of the compilation referred to, placing the facts into a more connected form, adding such things as have since come to my mind, and excluding some unimportant matters in order to make this work more complete and satisfactory as a narrative.

It was my good or ill fortune to participate in the War of the Rebellion. And since those memorable years, I have been frequently urged by zealous friends to write my memoirs or recollections of the occurrences which then came under my observation. But having entered the regular army at the close of the war, and serving thereafter almost continuously on the frontier, my time was so fully occupied with official duties that I found little leisure for private affairs or recreation. Now, however, being retired from active service, and actuated by a desire to gratify those who have a right to expect that their wishes should be favorably considered, I have rather reluctantly yielded to their oft-repeated solicitations.

I am conscious of the difficulties to be encountered and not unmindful of my inability to satisfactorily accomplish the work. But I will simply make a plain statement of the facts that have come to my knowledge, in my usual manner of writing, without seeking after adornment or a faultless style of expression, believing that the information so imparted will be more acceptable to those likely to be interested in the subject. If I can thus succeed in giving any pleasure to those who fought, or gave their earnest support to our government, when the life of the nation was imperiled and furnish such a story as will become of interest to their descendants, it will be the most gratifying compensation I can receive. Possibly, the time will come when those for whom this work is more especially intended will be glad to have it in their possession. For however incomplete or imperfect, it will at least embrace a faithful record of events connected with a remarkable and sanguinary conflict for the advancement of human liberty, which although crowned with success, tested to the utmost the strength of the Republic.

B. H. Grierson
Jacksonville, Illinois

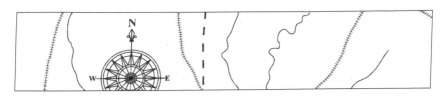

1. An American Boyhood

The Griersons who emigrated from Scotland to Ireland first settled in the Province of Ulster about the middle of the 17th Century, and subsequently removed to Dublin and other parts of that country.

Captain John Grierson, my grandfather, the eldest son of Robert Grierson of Smithfield Street, Dublin, Ireland, was a strong loyalist and was in command of cavalry during the Irish Catholic Rebellion of 1798. He took part in the battles of Tara and Repih, and was actively engaged throughout the war. He married a Miss Margaret Clare, daughter of Joshua Clare of Claremount. They had five children: Benjamin Henry, Robert, Joshua, Susan, and Margaret. The family residence was at a place called Peacockstown, about ten miles from the city of Dublin.

Robert Grierson, my father, was born near the city of Dublin on August 23, 1789. He first came to this country when quite a young man, previous to the War of 1812. The voyage was made in a merchant trading vessel belonging to a friend of his father's family. The captain gave such glowing accounts of the United States that he induced young Robert, who was fond of adventure, to accept the invitation to visit the Republic of which he had heard such favorable reports. Having a thorough knowledge of navigation, he made himself useful in taking charge of the "log-book," and being an excellent penman and accountant, assisted the captain in various other ways. The vessel first touched at Newfoundland, and sailed thence to Boston and New York, and afterwards coasted as far southward as Savannah, Georgia. Delaying a few weeks at the latter port, the vessel sailed to Liverpool and thence to Dublin, the entire journey occupying nearly one year.

This visit to America filled young Grierson with a desire to return, and was no doubt the main cause of his subsequent emigration to this country. On June 4, 1815, Robert Grierson married Miss Mary Sheppard, daughter of Mrs. Mary Sheppard of the city of Dublin, and in a few years thereafter prevailed upon his wife—although she was devotedly attached to her friends and country—to give up all and seek with him a new home in the United States. On November 17, 1818, their arrangements were perfected and preparations made for their departure. Relatives were assembled at the house of Mrs. Sheppard to bid the voyagers good-bye, and some of the party accompanied the family, then consisting of Robert and Mary Grierson and their two children, Louisa and Susan, to the ship, where in the midst of a violent storm, they hurriedly embarked, bidding farewell to their friends and their native land as the vessel put to sea.

They encountered unfavorable weather, heavy gales prevailed, and strange to relate, after many attempts to get the vessel out to sea, it was driven about the Irish Channel for nearly a week, and finally back to the port of Dublin, where the would-be emigrants went on shore and again visited for a night the home of Mrs. Grierson's mother. It was occasion for mingled emotions of pleasure and pain. The second parting proved much harder to endure than the first, as with tearful eyes and throbbing hearts the last warm embraces were received and given by those endeared by family ties—all realizing the sad fact that they were separating to meet no more on earth.

A voyage from Europe to this country at that time, in a sailing vessel, was a very different undertaking compared with the ready manner in which the same journey can be made in a steamship with all the modern improvements and comforts of the present day. Then the voyage occupied weeks, and often months, instead of the few days in which the trip can now be made. The second attempt was successful. The ship weathered the gale and cleared the Irish Channel, but the voyage was dangerous, as violent storms prevailed and adverse winds were encountered. The vessel was very old and soon leaked badly, and much time was spent by the sailors in pumping out the water. The captain and seamen were rough and profane men, and the alarmed and anxious look of the passengers tended to make them violent and unreasonable.

After being driven about on the ocean for over two months, the vessel was found to be not a great distance from the island of Bermuda, and on account of its bad condition, the captain was prevailed upon to endeavor to make that port. The water arose to such an extent in the vessel that Mrs. Grierson—the only woman on board—had to be brought upon deck with her children, where they were long exposed to inclement weather, enduring mental and bodily suffering and the terrible suspense and horrors of castaways. All the men on board were obliged to work the pumps to keep the ship from sinking, which was finally wrecked near Bermuda, the passengers and crew barely making their escape with the assistance rendered from the shore.

The population of the island at that time consisted of a few white officials and soldiers and a large number of colored people. Among the latter, there was constant drinking and turbulence, and there was no quiet retreat from the discordant elements that reveled in publicity. After nearly three months' delay in the midst of such deplorable surroundings, the family took passage on board a staunch vessel for New York, arriving there in safety on April 6, 1819.

While in New York another child, named Robert, was born. But, being weak and sickly, he lived only about a month, the early death of the child no doubt being mainly due to the exhausting sea voyage endured by the mother. After five or six months' residence in New York, the family proceeded to Philadelphia and thence across the Allegheny Mountains to Pittsburgh, Pennsylvania. The journey, which occupied about a month, was made in a large covered wagon such as in those days conveyed the traffic and much of the travel between those cities. The mountain scenery must, notwithstanding the clumsy mode of locomotion, have had charms for them, though it was not then what it now is. The towns that now nestle in picturesque beauty among the mountains, images of repose and homes of peace, did not then delight the eye of the wayfarer. There was a rude highway ascending and descending, bending now this way and now that through the mountains, and endless reaches of super-abounding vegetation— a scene of wild natural grandeur. The travelers were impelled, however, to emphasize the weariness they felt, more than to extol the wonders of the way.

They reached Pittsburgh on Tuesday, October 5, 1819, and soon after their arrival proceeded to take a general view. At the end of the excursion, Mrs. Grierson asked if that was the whole of the city. It probably appeared to her as if she had been journeying to the end of the rainbow for much less than the fabulous pot of gold. The fame of its prosperity had drawn them to the infant city, and then its littleness was the only noteworthy consideration. The mirage vanished as it does at some time to every ardent, imaginative, beauty-loving soul, and grim reality sat in the house and walked in company by the way, darkening the world until the mind, seizing and wrestling with the grimness, evolved its latent power and accepted existence with its bitter and its sweet.

My mother had become in some degree acclimated, physically and socially, but in the beginning was truly an exotic in a harsh clime. Reference is here made to both the social atmosphere and the rude external conditions in which she and my father found themselves, where so much was to be learned painfully, amid almost entire privation of all that embellished their previous life. They had neither leisure nor opportunity to recreate their minds with the pleasures and the refining influences that were vibrant in the very air of their native city. The new sphere was narrow and uncongenial, and to her nothing appeared to compensate for lost friends and the brightness, beauty, and widely varied interests of her former home. For Pittsburgh was at that date a very diminutive and unpolished city, and even prompt access to the very best life it afforded would not have indemnified them for what had been relinquished.

They were not entirely without means, but it was necessary for the head of the family at once to establish a business and pursue it with persistent energy, which he did. He was ambitious, intelligent, and conscious; of fine natural powers, of which his expressive, prepossessing features were the index. Those characteristics were also legible in the tall form, where strength and grace were combined in the entire body, even to the large, but exquisitely formed, hands and feet. Whatever his personal discouragements and regrets may have been, they at least became silent and apparently extinguished in cheerful manly endeavor.

He saw his wife trying to bear her share of the burden and of the responsibility for the children; the tender unpracticed hands toiling in her domestic affairs, with her heart too full of cherished memories drooping visibly; all events and circumstances of the weary days serving by sharp contrasts to remind her of the past. It did not change the current of her thoughts to see the plain kind people with whom acquaintance was made plodding contentedly and feeling no vacuum in existence. Perhaps it only aggravated her sense of unfitness, for her environment impelled her, it may be, more and more to take refuge in the recollections of the circle in which she had moved beyond the sea, in homes where ease and comfort were made the measure of appropriateness and where the most strenuous efforts she had shared were those put forth to adorn life and add to its joyousness.

The depression amounting to homesickness did not, however, continue long. The oppressed mind seemed to free itself from bonds and find strength sufficient for its lot. Doubtless time, too, that heals wounded hearts and helps all dutiful aspirations, was not without its usual efficacy. Regret became submerged in sympathy with her children, who like all children, were happy and even more unconscious of deficiency in life than were the plodding people above spoken of. However admirable is the strong man who uncomplainingly puts his shoulder to the wheel, tender regard is due the woman by whom the first experiences in hardship were so severely felt, and in whom unfavorable circumstances interacting on delicate health untuned for a time a naturally cheerful mind.

During their residence in Pittsburgh, four children were born to Robert and Mary Grierson: John Charles, Robert Henry, Mary, and Benjamin

Henry. By the varied experience gained during that period, my father and mother had learned to grasp life in a new country with firmer hands, and recollections of the years they had lived in their native land, with the scenes and associations so sacred and dear to memory, were gradually relinquishing their power as the past was withdrawing into the distance.

———

I was born at 3 o'clock in the morning of July 8, 1826, at the Grierson residence on Market Street. During eight years' residence at Pittsburgh, my father was engaged in the mercantile business; accumulated considerable wealth, and owned valuable property in the city and in Allegheny Town, as [it was] then called. But for some reason, he became dissatisfied with his surroundings, sold out, and removed west to Youngstown, Ohio, arriving there in the early part of the year 1829, when I was between two and three years old. Of course, I have no recollections of the journey, beyond a vague impression of being the center of care and attraction, while clinging to my mother to avoid the proffered attention of strangers. The noise and confusion of the change, strange objects, and the mingling of unknown with familiar voices tended more to disturb and amaze than to quiet or comfort me, and left nothing tangibly fixed in my memory. But when my thoughts revert to our dear old home in Youngstown, in the Mahoning Valley, a world of pleasant memories is revived.

The quaint old town, as I when a boy saw it, stands forth to view with its familiar houses on either side of Federal Street, scattered along from Judge Raynes' residence at the western end to that of Lawyer Hines at the eastern extremity, those prominent structures facing each other portentously under the dominating influence of their well-known proprietors. A conspicuous feature of the village in those early days was the big pond near the public square, between McCoy's Hotel and Heslip's Store, where in summer the boys sailed their improvised ships and in winter skated the idle hours away. The fields, pastures, pine or hemlock and other woods in the distance, filled with rabbits and squirrels ready to be trapped and hunted; the beautiful Mahoning River, with its quiet nooks for fishing and bathing; the two branches, Crabb and Mill creeks, with their rapid current, rocky beds, cascades, placid pools, and picturesque banks—all those, in addition to the dear good people of the town and country, so well known to me, now pass in review, although the scenes have changed amazingly and the names of nearly all those once-living actors will be found engraved in the cold marble within the graveyard on the hill.

Were it possible, gladly would I be placed back to live over in reality those happy and memorable boyhood days. To attempt, however, to record minutely the experiences of over half a century, which has since intervened, would be an undesirable effort for memory, and if accomplished, too great a tax on the time of the most admiring friends of my acquaintance. But a rapid glance over that period of my life prior to the War of the Rebellion, giving an incident here and there, may be of some interest to my kith and kin in connection with the record of more important events to follow.

When about eight years old, I received a very serious injury from the kick of a young horse. There was a log-rolling, brush-burning, and general clearing up of what was known as the three-cornered pasture of my father's farm, one mile south of Youngstown. I had urged my mother to let me go to see the men work and witness the big blazing bonfires that were to be lighted that day. She rather reluctantly gave permission, having a sort of presentiment of disaster. I went away, however, in high glee for the holiday and stuck quite close to my father and brother for a time, as admonished. But during the day, noticing that the latter was getting ready to go on an errand to Michael Vatter's place half a mile distant southward from the farm, I followed with the intention of getting a ride on horseback returning.

I arrived at the gate, or bars, leading into Mr. Vatter's house as my brother came out from there, and when ready to get on the horse, he kindly consented to let me ride. He had already unhitched the horse and thought first of mounting and pulling me up behind him, but at the last moment concluded to lift me on first and then mount behind me for my greater security, not wishing to trust to my holding on to him. But no sooner had I touched the horse's back than my heels were punched recklessly into his sides and away went the animal, with myself alone, like a flash before my brother could mount. The young horse was without saddle or even blanket.

I kept my position quite well for a time and was enjoying the ride hugely, laughingly chirping at the horse and looking back at my brother's fruitless attempt to overtake me. I had gotten nearly a quarter of a mile away when suddenly the horse became frightened and jumped to one side, jostling me in the opposite direction. My brother screamed to me to hang on, and I did like a good fellow, with my hands clinched firmly into the mane. But my arms finally tired out, I dropped upon the ground, rolled over unhurt, and was just turning my head as I raised up to look back at my brother, when the horse kicked with full force, striking me squarely in the face.

Before my brother could reach me, Mrs. James McKinney, who witnessed the occurrence, ran out from their place, clasped me in her arms, and hurriedly carried me into the house. My brother followed, caught the horse, and dashed off to town for medical assistance, not letting my mother know what had really happened. But my sister Susan, judging correctly as to the trouble, quickly saddled her horse and was among the first to enter the room where I lay mangled and bleeding. I was cautiously removed towards our home, but the doctors fearing that I would die before reaching there, I was taken into another house, on the Manning farm, on the south side of the river, a quarter of a mile away, having been unconscious all of that time. Upon awakening from my stupor and hearing my sister's voice, I at once commenced to tell her how the accident occurred, and when in the midst of my story again became unconscious, remaining so nearly two weeks without speaking as I lay hovering between life and death. When I again came to my senses, strange to relate, I began the recital of my story to my sister just where I had left off so long before, and finished the tale.

The skill of the doctors, good nursing, and the prayers of my dear mother finally brought me through to health again, but it was a long time before I recovered. I remember my great desire to see. I could hear distinctly, and recognized not only the voices of the members of our own family but also those of my playmates and our neighbors. At first all the doctors of the town were summoned to my assistance. Young Dr. Tylee, who was a great favorite of the family, gave up his practice and remained constantly with me, night and day, during that doubtful period of my existence. About eight weeks after the occurrence, the doctor submitted to the earnest appeals of myself and my family and removed, or raised, the bandage from one of my eyes sufficiently to enable me to try to open it. I remember the circumstances as if it was but yesterday and just what I said on that occasion, when with delight to myself and astonishment of all present, I exclaimed, "by gum I can see." But only a glance or two were permitted me, during which, however, I had the satisfaction to behold, surrounding the bedside with the doctor, [were] my father, mother, sisters, and brother.

It was many months before I could see out of the other eye, and finally when I could again enjoy the light of day—for I was for a long time kept in a darkened room—I was one of the happiest mortals on earth. My face was cut open from my forehead to my chin and my right cheek badly mangled, and I still carry the scars from the injuries then received. There was not one person excepting my mother who believed that I could possibly live. How much her prayers, which were fervent and almost constant, had to do with my recovery God alone knows. I at least shall, while life lasts, remember her sweet voice in earnest supplication. My brother John felt terribly about the matter, and some were so thoughtless as to blame him for not using greater precautions. But he was entirely innocent of any fault, for the calamity was brought upon myself by my reckless desire for a free and unencumbered ride on that wild horse. The thought of danger never entered my head, anymore than it has since then at many other critical periods of my life.[1]

Among my early recollections, I recall listening with astonishment to my sister Louisa relating wonderful tales, legends and incidents of history, and repeating from memory the poetry of Shakespeare and Byron. The story of William Tell shooting the apple off his son's head in the public square in Altorf interested me greatly, and I determined to learn to shoot in like manner. I succeeded in obtaining a crossbow, quite well constructed, with quiver for arrows, etc., and became quite an expert in its use. But the possession of the gun proved unfortunate.

I had among my playmates a girl by the name of Harriet Woodruff, the daughter of one of our nearest neighbors, and I decided to shoot an apple off her head. She seemed not to fear my making the attempt, was anxious for me to try my skill, and willingly consented to stand against my father's warehouse, while I fired at the apple placed on the top of her head. I was a little fearful of hitting her, and several of the shots struck too high. Finally, I took deliberate aim and fired away, expecting to see the arrow pierce the apple, but it unfortunately struck her in the center of the forehead. She screamed, and I hesitated whether to pull the arrow out or run off.

Just at that moment, my father appeared at the corner of the warehouse, coming from the alley leading out from the stables. He had a riding bridle in his hand, and seeing to his great surprise what had taken place, quickly took in the situation. He rushed at me with the bridle. The first stroke hit and broke my gun into pieces as I pushed it out to ward off the blow. I was very active on foot, and it did not take me long to get away from that place. I darted into the open store door, out through the back hall into the yard and garden, and thence climbed over the fence and, like a flash, ran away through our back lot to Raynes' Hill, my father's pursuit serving to hasten my speed, for he succeeded in punishing me some, as from time to time the end of the bridle would hit me on the back, legs, or heels. But, I finally outran or out-winded him, and he gave up the chase.

I did not see him again for several days, as he was occupied with business matters, and I, through the intercession of my kindhearted mother, was kept out of sight, quietly making my way upstairs to bed for several nights. I finally had to meet him, but as he had gotten over his anger, my forlorn look so overcame him that I observed a smile gathering at the corner of his eyes and lips. Despite his efforts to look serious, I got off with a good scolding instead of whipping. I never saw the gun afterwards and had to seek out some other source of amusement.

My sister Louisa was always getting up entertainments of some sort for myself and sister Mary. I remember she had a contrivance poked through a broken pane of a front window of her bedroom, which in due time we learned was a *camera obscura*, by means of which, with the room darkened, we were enabled to see on the opposite wall the images of persons and animals that passed along the street in front of our house, much to our amazement and delight.

My mother had a very retentive memory and remarkable talent for music. All the old Scotch and Irish ballads were known to her and she could sing or repeat them with ease and clearness, recalling either the music or words without hesitation. She possessed a wonderful fund of information and a most happy faculty of expressing it. She was always entertaining in conversation and in relating incidents from history or those connected with her past life. Her thoughts would often revert to the scenes and occurrences of bygone days, and she frequently alluded to her old home to which she ever remained devotedly attached. Often have I seen her weep when thinking of her departure from Ireland and separation from the dear relatives and friends of her native land.

From my earliest remembrance I had a great love and talent for music. Long before I played on any instrument, I used to amuse myself and others by singing and whistling, and had a peculiar way of drumming an accompaniment on anything I could get hold of in the shape of a drum. Before I could speak plainly, I wanted a "vass rum," which seemed to me a wonderful instrument. First a toy drum was procured, but to beat on a large one was my delight and ambition. I became, at an early day, an excellent drummer on both the bass and snare drum. I disliked the snares on the small drum and preferred to have them muffled, as they grated upon my ears and nerves. In time, I learned to play on all kinds of musical instruments and was a skillful performer on many, particularly the flute, clarinet, and bugle. I became the leader of the Youngstown Band when between twelve and thirteen years old.[2]

I well remember the first lesson I ever received in music from my teacher, Professor Isaac White, who was also the first instructor of the Youngstown Band. Money had been raised to purchase instruments, and the day Professor White left for Pittsburgh to obtain them, he wrote for me "Scotts wa hae" and "Life let us Cherish" on a slip of paper, while resting his hands upon the counter of my father's store. I had him whistle those tunes and then went upstairs into the room over the store, got into the middle of the bed, and never left it until I could play both pieces. My father had borrowed a flute for me from Dr. Bayne —a large yellow box-wood instrument with numerous keys. It was very difficult to stretch my fingers far enough apart to cover up the holes, but I managed somehow to accomplish it and astonished everybody by playing, not only the tunes Mr. White had written, but many others which I had heard my mother and sisters sing.

I was so infatuated with music that I could think of but little else, being unwilling to give up playing the flute even to eat or sleep.

When Professor White returned, he brought me a small octave flute, which suited my small hands much better than the larger one. He was greatly pleased with my proficiency and at once wrote off what was to be number one for the band. I played it for him before he left the store, so that number two had to be written on the opposite side of the music paper. By the time the twelve lessons for the band were over, I had played on all the band instruments, and especially well on George Tod's E-flat clarinet. He was a brother of David Tod, who during the war became famous as the governor of Ohio.[3]

George Tod was the first leader of the Youngstown Band, but he held that position for only a short time. During the intermissions from practice, I would plead for permission of the band members to use their instruments and, seemingly by intuition, could play with ease on all. The band met for practice in the upper rooms of the old Youngstown Academy, where I so long attended school. Before the commencement of the second term of lessons, the citizens of the town furnished money to purchase a fine cocoa [cocuswood] clarinet for me, and I at once, by unanimous vote, became the leader of the band.

I well remember going about serenading in those days and subsequently playing during the Log Cabin and Hard Cider, "Tippecanoe and Tyler, too," political campaign of 1840.[4] The band went everywhere throughout eastern Ohio, attending political meetings. On one occasion, at a very large gathering at Warren, as the band was marching along, the crowd was very large and the streets filled with people, but the tones from my clarinet were audible above all the din and confusion. I was so small that few could see where the music came from, but I was finally observed by two enthusiastic individuals, large tall men, who rushed into the column and lifted me upon their shoulders. In that position, I continued to play as long as the procession moved, being an object of interest both on account of my music and my comical appearance, as I had on my brother's coat, which hung down to my heels, it being much too long and large in the skirts and sleeves.

Soon after that time, I began to take music lessons on the piano from Mrs. Rockwell of Youngstown, and rapidly became proficient on that instrument, and also on the guitar and violin. I also procured through Dr. Theodatus Garlick of Youngstown, who was a warm friend of mine, a very old reed instrument which was called a "Bass Clarion." It was large, mostly wood, with numerous keys, a copper bell, and shaped somewhat like a bassoon, but different. I never saw another instrument like it. It came apart in several pieces so that it could be placed in a box when not in use, and originally belonged to the old Coneaut Band of Ohio. The music I got out of it was astonishing. George King,[5] who played well of the violin; Charley Thorn, a skilled performer on the flute; and myself used to often go out serenading, and the trio of performers became quite famous. We were great friends and practiced together constantly. All those still living who ever heard us play will be very apt to retain a pleasant remembrance of the exquisite harmony we produced with those three instruments.

Long ago I gave up music entirely and turned over my instruments to my son, B. H. Grierson, Jr., who bids fair to excel me in their use. I made music my profession for many years and was quite successful, having besides many pupils, numerous bands under my instruction throughout Ohio and Illinois.

I was the youngest member of our family. My brother Robert Henry died at Pittsburgh, when about two years old. My sister Mary was next to me and the older by about two years. We were almost constant companions. She was bright, cheerful, sprightly, and of a happy disposition as a rule, but at times became greatly depressed in spirits. She was clearheaded and intelligent, a fine letter-writer, and when at school wrote excellent compositions and was always highly complimented by her teachers for her ability and success in all such undertakings. She had many warm friends among her schoolmates, and attachments thus formed always proved enduring.

My sister Louisa received an excellent education, had fine natural abilities and a remarkably clear and graceful manner of expressing herself, either in speaking or writing. Her life has been one of thought and study, and there are few subjects of interest in regard to which she is not well informed. My sister Susan was taller, stronger, and more robust than Louisa. While the latter resembled my mother, the former bore a striking resemblance to my father and possessed much of his vigor and activity. I remember Susan's looks. She was supple and graceful as a deer and was one of the handsomest girls in Youngstown, passionately fond of outdoor exercises and sports, but did not care for books and studies like her sister Louisa. She was remarkably fond of horseback riding and became at an early age an excellent equestrienne, and could ride and manage with ease and skill the wildest and most unruly horses that could be found. She took pleasure in seeking out unbroken colts, and her great success in taming and riding such animals soon became well known. She was often seen dashing through the town on a fiery steed, and when people would be brought to their doors and windows to see the runaway, they found it was Susan Grierson who was out for a ride. They would manifest no further uneasiness as they felt sure she was not in danger, as she could not be thrown off.[6]

I remember my father's fondness for a good horse. He at times owned many fine ones, and Susan would always select the wildest and most spirited to ride. Among my father's horses was a young sorrel called "Grit." Many persons who were considered good horsemen had tried to ride him without avail. My brother John, who was fearless and successful in the management of horses, determined to ride "Grit," and after much effort succeeded in saddling him. But for some reason he failed to control the horse, which ran off and in some manner got away from him. Fortunately, he was not injured.

The occurrence provoked my father, who caught the horse returning to the stable. He at once mounted and rode off towards the river, and finally down the back street, quietly enough for a time, but suddenly the horse became frightened and unmanageable and threw my father. Again the horse returned to the stable, where Susan got John to help change the saddle and assist her to mount. When well seated, while John and another man held the horse, she told them to "let him go," and off went "Grit" as if he had been shot from a cannon. But he did not throw Susan, as every effort made by the horse failed to get her off his back. She would not let him stop when tired of jumping and running, but gave him the whip until she had taken all the "grit" out of him. When she returned to town from her long ride, the horse was perfectly subdued, and she never found any difficulty in riding him thereafter.

For many years after his arrival in this country, my father was a strong Democrat. But, being an ardent lover of liberty, when the encroachments of the slave power made that institution a national as well as sectional sin and disgrace to the Republic, he became an earnest "Free-Soiler," or "Abolitionist" as then called, although he did not advocate any unlawful interference with slavery where it existed. He was a warm friend of Wendell Phillips[7] and Lloyd Garrison,[8] and took an active part in politics during that exciting period, expressing his sentiments freely and fearlessly on all occasions, and often facing large mobs, regardless of all threats of violence from the maddened advocates of slavery.

My brother John was always a hard worker. From the time I can first remember him as a boy, he was never so miserable as when he was out of employment. He generally spent his summers in working on the farm, hauling wood, etc., and going to school during the winter. He was very active and sturdy, both as a boy and man, and when not over fifteen years old used to load and haul, without assistance, large logs, which many men could not lift or handle, from the farm to town. I remember my father saying that he would rather have one boy like John to work than a ten-acre lot full of such boys as myself. I presume he put a proper estimate upon us. I do not remember ever having any remarkable talent or desire for work of any kind, but always had an extraordinary ability for all sorts of play and games, such as ball playing and kindred sports.

I quickly became an expert in any game I undertook to learn, and do not remember ever getting tired of such occupation when a boy. I often used to play truant from school in order to gratify my inordinate desire for games, but always managed to keep up with my studies and was generally at the head of my classes. I was very fond of backgammon and have often played with my father and old Dr. Dutton of Youngstown, and frequently beat them, although they were considered experts at the game. I always played cards well, but never gambled at that or any other game during my life.

My brother was a good hunter and an excellent shot with the rifle. I have known him to shoot more squirrels and other game in a day than both of us could carry home. He was also an excellent skater, and there was but one person that could excel him in the town, a Mr. Fordam Burnett, who was the most rapid and skillful person on skates in that entire section of country.

John was perfectly fearless even when a boy, and I have known him, with the assistance of a few other boys, to attack desperados and run them out of town. One was a man by the name of Henry Cherry, who was very quarrelsome and who had, without just cause or reason, brutally beaten some friend of my brother. My brother's plan was to accumulate a good supply of rocks as ammunition at certain points, piled up in readiness near where it was known that Cherry would pass in going in or out of town, and when least expected John and his allies would make the attack. Cherry would turn upon, but could not catch, them as they always kept a sharp watch of his movements and well out of his reach.

My brother grew up to be an excellent businessman, but the larger part of his life was spent in the employment of others. He was an excellent bookkeeper and accountant and was physically very powerful. Once, when clerking for Mr. Stoddard Stevens of Gustavus, Ohio, he lifted a half-barrel of white lead which weighed 625 pounds. It happened that while passing into the store or warehouse one day, he saw two men tugging at the half-barrel of white lead, making much ado about getting it into the store. He reached out his hand and took hold of the rim of the barrel to heft it, but did not move it much. When the men laughed, this aggravated him and he at once offered to bet that he could lift it himself. Accordingly, it was rolled near the counter, where he grasped it in his arms and lifted it from the floor to the top of the counter. There was not another man in the town or surrounding country who could do so. And, although many came from a distance to try their strength, all failed in the attempt to lift such a heavy weight.

John once made the journey to Dublin, Ireland, to obtain money that was due on property belonging to my mother. I remember running after the stagecoach as it was leaving the town and waving my hat on his departure. He wrote quite a funny letter home from New York City, which concluded as follows:

> On Yankee soil I take my stand,
> And cast a wishful eye
> Far o'er the sea to Erin's land,
> Where our possessions lie.

He made a successful voyage and transacted the business satisfactorily. When he returned to his home from the trip, he was so fleshy that he could not cross his legs and could scarcely see out of his eyes through the accumulation of flesh surrounding them.

John used to have a peculiar way of dropping himself down suddenly as he walked along. With knees bent up and close to the body, he would in that way reduce his height nearly one-half. If he had on a frock coat, his head and body erect with his broad shoulders, he would look very funny indeed. He thus became a perfect dwarf, and had such strength that he would continue to walk in that singular manner for quite a distance. Suddenly rising to an erect position, he seemed to almost pop up out of the ground. He never failed to create amazement and was sure to raise a laugh when performing the feat.

At a later period of my residence in Youngstown, I was one among other persons—mostly members of the band at that time—who organized one of the first troupes of minstrels in this country.[9] George King, who was the teacher of the Presbyterian Choir, led in the singing. Among the members were Henry Holcomb, Henry Manning, Shelden Medberry, Andrew Gardner, Frank Le Roy, and Henry McKinney. Dr. Ike Barclay, youngest brother of Frank and Joseph Barclay, was the violinist. When blacked up with burnt cork, the habitual smile on his handsome face gave him the appearance of a genial yet dignified darky. Nate Holland, who was very comical, in fact a natural clown, played the castanets and I the banjo. We two also did the dancing, and the music we got out of our heels was extravagantly ludicrous. The minstrels confined their exhibitions to Youngstown and vicinity, simply for their own amusement and that of their friends. Their entertainments were highly characteristic and enjoyable.

Over fifty years ago, when only a boy, I became devotedly attached to Alice Kirk(patrick). She was in like manner fond of me and decidedly interested in my music. In those early times, she was the frequent recipient of serenades, not only from the band, but from instruments on which I excelled as a performer. Frequently at night, when all was still, I would open the window of my bedroom and point my clarinet in the direction of the Kirk mansion, and play the tunes I knew she most admired. Of course, my warm feelings towards her enabled me to execute with precision and give that kind of expression so essential to the proper rendering of music. I used to often meet her in those days at school, parties, and elsewhere, and frequently walked by her father's house in the evening, with the hope of meeting or seeing her.

On one of those occasions, which I had good reason to remember, she was on the upper porch with her aunt, and I stopped at the gate to chat with them. While enjoying ourselves in this manner her aunt, Louisa, whom I knew very well, proposed that I should climb up on the porch and do my talking there. I jumped over the gate instanter and, by the aid of the slats and grape vines, was quickly beside them. It was a thoughtless movement accomplished on the spur of the moment, without due reflection. Our conversation at short range was enjoyable and prolonged.

The noise of our laughing and talking attracted the notice of Thomas Kirk, the brother of Alice, who happened to come out of the house and saw the three of us on the porch together. He at once ran into the house and told his mother, who soon thereafter came up into the room adjoining the porch and called Alice into the house. Of course, I clambered down off the porch as quickly as I had gotten up and, although no thought of wrong had entered my head, the feat of climbing upon the porch was never repeated.

In due time, Mrs. Kirk reported the circumstance to Alice's father, who became unreasonably offended at the occurrence. His anger got the better of his judgment, and while enraged, he injudiciously forbade me from ever entering his house and told his daughter that she should have nothing more to do with me. To separate us still further, she was soon after sent away to school at Milan and subsequently to Hudson, some fifty miles distant. I remember the day she left Youngstown—September 5, 1845. I had the satisfaction, however, of seeing her as she started off in a buggy with a Mr. Richard Garlick, a good friend of mine who stopped to afford us an opportunity to bid each other good-bye. I was quite distressed at our separation, as she was absent most of the time for three years.

Sometime after her departure, Mr. Kirk decided to give me a talking to on account of my injudicious action and came to see me at Mr. Brander's store, at which establishment I was employed as a clerk. As he passed toward the warehouse at the back of the store, he indicated that he desired me to follow him, which I did and listened respectfully and attentively to all he had to say on the subject. I made the best apology I could and gave a truthful statement of the occurrence. I told him that his daughter was in no way to blame and that the fault, whatever it might have been, must rest with myself and his own sister, who had urged me to make the ascent of the porch at the time I became an unfortunate trespasser upon his premises. That, while I could not justify my action, I believed he took a wrong view of the matter, as I was sincerely attached to his daughter and could never think less of her and hoped that he could see some way by which our friendly relations, which had so long existed, could be continued. In short, I asked his forgiveness, which he would not grant, and we parted.

For a long time, a remarkable coolness was manifested between us. So far as I know, all of our friends and acquaintances in Youngstown sympathized with Alice and myself in our trouble, and earnestly hoped that we would soon be brought permanently together. In time, Mr. Kirk relented so far as to invite me to his house in response to a request of his daughter, Alice. But his letter was couched in such language, and contained such restrictions, that after full consideration, I deemed it best under all the circumstances to respectfully decline the indulgence and wrote him accordingly. The letter was a good one, a copy was furnished to Alice, and my action met her approval. She managed to be present in the room when her father received and opened the letter, which he hastily read, tore up, and threw into the fire, indicating by his manner and dissatisfaction that our friendly relations were ended forever.[10]

It was not long after this occurrence that I took my departure for the West. Before going away, I managed to see Alice, and we had a long talk together. On that occasion, our manifestations of regard were intense and sufferings great, and had I urged her to do so, she would have left her home and friends to share my fortunes whatever they might have been. But, after a full discussion of the subject, we finally decided to separate. I had made up my mind that it was wrong, under all the circumstances, to hold her to any engagement; could not advise her to disobey her father; and, before my departure, left her unbound by any pledges, free to act in the future as she judged best for her own welfare and happiness. I felt quite sure that I would never marry anyone else, and told her that if in time matters so changed as to enable us ever to be united, it must be with the free and proffered consent of her father. I returned the letters she had written to me, received those I had written to her, and in writing verified my statements made to her when we last met, after which our correspondence entirely ceased and we only heard of each other indirectly and at long intervals for several years.

A year or so after I left Youngstown, my father and his family moved to Jacksonville, Illinois. In course of time, it so happened that in our case it proved "that all things come to those who know how to wait," for Alice Kirk came to Springfield, Illinois, to visit relatives and while there was induced to take the position of teacher in the Springfield Academy, or Seminary, for Young Ladies. Singularly enough, I was at the same time teaching a band in that city. I did not know of her contemplated visit, nor that she was there, until some days after her arrival.

Casually calling at Mr. Post's store, the proprietors being intimate friends of mine, I there accidentally saw a notice of the opening of the seminary and, among the teachers, read the name of *Alice Kirk*. The name instantly sent a thrill through my heart, reviving associations of bygone days, and I wondered if it were possible that there could be another person of that name besides the dear "girl I left behind me" in Youngstown, Ohio, some years before. I asked Mr. Herbert Post if he knew anything about the young lady, pointing to her name on the notice referred to. He informed me that she was a cousin of Dr. Lord's of that city and was visiting at his house. I knew Dr. Lord very well, and was also aware that he was Alice's cousin. That settled the matter as to the identity of the person in question.

I had arranged to go to my home in Jacksonville that day, and upon looking at my watch, found that I had about half an hour to reach the train. I walked rapidly to Dr. Lord's, and upon entering his office, which adjoined his house, asked him if it was true that Alice Kirk was stopping with them. He informed me that she was there. It did not take long for me to enter his parlor, and soon afterwards Miss Kirk entered from an adjoining room. She had learned from Dr. or Mrs. Lord that I was, or had been, in Springfield, and presumed that sooner or later we would meet again. She had determined, in such an event, to address me as Mr. Grierson. But, immediately upon her appearance, I sprang towards her and blurted out, "Alice how are you?" She at once exclaimed, "Ben Grierson," and clasped my extended hand.

Well, to make a long story short, I asked her to put on her wraps and come with me to Jacksonville to visit our folks. My sister Mary, who loved her sincerely, would be delighted to welcome her, as would also other members of the family. She hesitated for a moment and looked towards Mrs. Lord to see what she thought about her acceptance of the invitation. Mrs. Lord said, "You'll be safe in Ben's hands, Alice," and advised her to accompany me as requested. Therefore, she hurriedly put on her things and we started for the station.

Her reception at our home was all she could wish. My sister Mary, with her full generous heart, flew out of the house upon our approach, clasped Alice in her arms, and kissed her affectionately. Other members of the family received her most kindly. Alice remained with us several days, until obliged to return to Springfield so as to be there at the opening of the seminary. I escorted her on her return, and we frequently met during the time she remained at Springfield.

After finishing her engagement there, she returned to Youngstown, to which place, a few months later, I proceeded, where, on September 24, 1854, we were married at her home, the ceremony being performed by her father, who was not only a good elder in the church,[11] but who had during the few years we had been separated, grown older and perhaps wiser. In any event, he had recovered from the effects of his temporary anger and, being in reality a noble-hearted man, regained his former friendship for me, which I have good reason to believe he retained in full force until the day of his death.

After our marriage, so long doubtfully held in abeyance, but which was finally consummated to the entire satisfaction of all parties interested, we made a delightful visit with our many friends at Youngstown and elsewhere in Ohio. Mrs. Grierson accompanied me to Illinois, and stopping a few days en route with my brother and family, then residents of Cincinnati, we arrived safely at my father's residence, now No. 852 East State Street, Jacksonville, Illinois, where we found kind friends awaiting our arrival.

———

During my residence in Jacksonville previous to my marriage, my musical attainments had brought me into favorable notice, and among my intimate acquaintances were the professors and teachers of the Illinois College, seminaries, and other institutions located in that place. Mrs. Grierson, therefore, upon arrival, found herself surrounded by warmhearted friends of mine and, in due time, became much attached to them. Our own family circle was large and my father and mother's home, which for a time was also ours, became very attractive. It was a place where anyone included among our acquaintances could come at all times, with certainty of receiving a welcome. My father, mother, and sister Mary, being extraordinarily genial in disposition, gladly received visitors and heartily joined in their amusements. The house was frequently filled with joyous revelers, who virtually took possession. And, the more noise made or hilarity manifested, the better the old folks were pleased. Although the time flew rapidly away, it made a vivid impression on our minds, and I cannot see how we could have been made more happy than during the early days of our married life.

Although Mrs. Grierson had been separated from a large number of relatives and connections in Ohio upon her departure for Illinois, yet the loss thus incurred was at least partially compensated for by the generous warmth of her reception at Jacksonville. In those memorable days, on all occasions, whether at home or abroad, music occupied our thoughts and took a prominent part at all entertainments, and the busy hours passed pleasantly and fleetly away.

During my residence in Ohio, I had composed and arranged a considerable amount of music for bands and orchestras, and after my arrival in Illinois much additional music was written and arranged for the excellent band and orchestra in Jacksonville, of which I was the leader. Among the musicians who took a prominent part in college commencements and on other occasions were Mr. Robert Hockenhull, Professor Harrington, Mr. Burdett, Mrs. Thomas Smith, Mr. Stryker, Mr. John King, Dr. Haines, and others. Miss Murdock, now Mrs. Smith, was the pianist, and many of the older residents will remember with satisfaction the successful concerts and musical gatherings of those days. While residing at Jacksonville, I wrote for our Christmas family meetings and other private entertainments several comic operas, the rendering of which on those happy occasions proved, to say the least, enjoyable. I never published any music, although urged to do so. Much of it is stowed away in the big attic room in the old homestead at Jacksonville. In time I may overhaul it and bring to light some of the music now almost forgotten even by myself.[12]

The extent and value of our happiness during the Christmas gatherings were not fully realized at the time. The manner of getting up those meetings was for members of the family and connections to form groups a month before the time for assembling, comprising those residing near each other, out of which someone was usually selected to determine upon some combined action towards arranging special things in the way of entertainments to be perfected and brought out during the holidays. The action of the various groups as to what they would do was kept a profound secret from all the others, and thus a general surprise was sure to meet the eyes and ears of all attendants.

Within our family and connections there was quite a variety of talent. My sister Louisa usually furnished a poem, besides assisting in arranging for other less thoughtful productions. My parts were generally connected with musical compositions, operas, comic songs, etc. Pieces were spoken by others of an extravagant nature, either in rhyme or prose, and all took interest enough in the work undertaken to insure a most hearty reception from the constantly changing audience. There was loud, side-splitting laughter and frequent encores were insisted upon. Often after the holidays, as chance meetings of the family occurred with some intimate friends and acquaintances, those productions were reproduced, much to the surprise and merriment of all present.

In the fall of 1855, I gave up my profession and removed to Meredosia, a small town situated on the Illinois River, six miles north of Naples and about twenty miles from Jacksonville, in the extreme western part of Morgan County. I formed a co-partnership there with Mr. John Walihan, and engaged for five years in the mercantile and produce business. Mr. Walihan formerly lived in Youngstown, Ohio, and had at one time worked on my father's farm. He had considerable experience in business, and although it was new to me, we were quite successful until after the general financial crash of 1857. We had made considerable money on grain and merchandise, but unfortunately instead of restricting our business when so many were breaking up, we extended it too widely and sold largely on credit. Just at that time, my partner went to New York City and purchased an overstock of goods, which we sold out with too little care to "Tom, Dick, and Harry," and for most of the goods never received any pay. When our payments came due, they had to be met. And, although we worried along until 1860, we were finally obliged to close up our business. In the settlement of our indebtedness we both gave up our homesteads, although not obliged to do so, and were virtually left without a dollar.

While residing in Meredosia, I came near losing my life in a rather singular manner during an overflow on the Illinois River. It happened that I, with a suitable party, had gone some miles up the stream on a small steamboat and tows, after corn which was in danger of being washed away by the high water. Being delayed in securing the grain, we did not start back until after dark. Before reaching Meredosia, a most violent storm arose and obliged us to stop and tie up the boat for the night. Thinking our families would be alarmed at our absence, my partner, myself, brother, and one or two employees started in the storm for the town in a skiff.

We had proceeded but a short distance when it became evident that we could not reach the landing in safety by the river, and we endeavored to make our way through an overflowed point of land, or thickly wooded peninsula, back of which was a wide bay or inlet. Upon nearing the outer shore of the bay, we came near being capsized and had to again enter the woods. Even there, the waves rolled so high as to rapidly fill up the boat with the splashing waters. So, we were compelled to get under a tree, where the overflow was about ten feet deep. There, grasping hold of the overhanging limbs, we hung on for our lives until morning.

The lightning flashed, the thunder rolled, trees were uprooted and washed away during the terrific storm and flood by which we were surrounded. To add to our discomforts, the woods were covered with green worms which fell upon us in swarms, getting into our clothing next to our skins and wet and disordered apparel. But we dare not let go of the tree, and altogether passed a night of absolute horrors, being apprehensive that we would at every moment be drowned.

When day finally came, after the long and interminable night of darkness, we were in a most awful plight, and it took all our combined strength and careful management to enable us to reach the mainland. When it became known how our lives had been endangered, there was much rejoicing at home upon our return, as our escape under the circumstances was very miraculous. With myself and party, "Hang to the willows" became a byword ever after, suitable to all occasions of danger or apprehensions of calamity.

During the political campaign of 1856, I took an active part for [John C.] Fremont and [William L.] Dayton.[13] I was for a time the only man in the town and precinct who openly declared himself a Republican. After the nomination of Fremont, Murray McConnel and his son, John,[14] together with Mr. [Thomas L.] Harris, the Democratic congressman from that district, came to Meredosia, stopping in front of our store upon their arrival. Young McConnel jumped from the carriage and shouted out to those assembled to receive them: "Thank God, we are in a place where there is not a man who dare say he is a Republican or will vote for Fremont." I was in the store at the time, and upon hearing his exclamation, I jumped over the counter, ran out to the front of the store among the assembled Democrats, and shouted at the top of my voice, throwing my hat in the air: "Here is a man, who if The Almighty lets him live until the election, will surely vote for John C. Fremont and who glories in the fact that he is a Republican." "Hip, Hip, Hurrah" was given with a will by myself alone, to the astonishment of the unterrified Democrats present. Previous to this I had been very quiet and said but little on politics. The political discussion which followed was maintained by myself, alone, against the three politicians mentioned.

A ludicrous scene which occurred at the time soon put us all in good humor. One of the leading Democrats of the town, who was full of whiskey, endeavored to take part in the discussion, but was finally prevailed upon to desist. In attempting to take a seat, which was some little distance behind him, he sat down as he supposed upon a chair, but instead of reaching it, dropped suddenly in the middle of the floor. Grunting with the pain of his unexpected fall, he looked towards the chair and exclaimed, "My God, McConnel, I missed it about four feet." After much laughter at this occurrence, quiet and good humor prevailed, and among others, I extended a welcome to those leading lights of the Democracy.

By spending much time and money attending political meetings, about thirty-two votes were obtained for the Republican ticket, out of a poll of about 400 votes, which under the circumstances was deemed a remarkable success where the Democratic majority was so great, and I was heartily congratulated by leading Republicans for my efforts in the cause. A considerable vote was polled for [Millard] Fillmore by the old Whigs, many of whom could not get over their prejudices and could not make up their minds to vote for Fremont. The campaign was a hot one and I, nearly single-handed and alone, from the time the nominations were made until the elections took place, continued to put forth my utmost exertions in the cause of Republicanism.

As an illustration of the feeling that existed against me on account of my political views, it is only necessary to refer to one single occurrence. The night before the election, my partner, John Walihan, who, although a very strong Democrat, was a warm personal friend, came quietly to my house to plead with me not to risk the great danger of going to the polls the next day. He stated that he knew positively that, in the excitement of the occasion, it was the intention to attack and probably fatally injure me. He manifested a great deal of feeling, and tears came to his eyes as he insisted on my remaining quietly at home on election day.

My course of action had been firmly resolved upon, and while I thanked him for the interest manifested in my safety and thus placing me upon my guard, I requested him as a favor to go back to his good Democratic friends and inform them for me that "If God let me live until the next day I would be present at the polls to do all in my power towards protecting the purity of the ballot; that while I would not in any manner infringe on the right of anyone, I should not hesitate to challenge and prevent the registration of illegal votes in that precinct; that I would go armed to protect myself and would not permit any man to improperly interfere with my rights as a citizen."

It is hardly necessary to state that I was there from the opening until the closing of the polls, the only Republican continuously present outside, as others who voted for Fremont were, by our opponents, supposed to have been voting for Fillmore or [James] Buchanan.[15] Two out of three Republicans who had agreed to share the danger with me at the polls were inside as judges, and the other I had to hunt up and bring there to vote. Despite all the threats that had been made, I was not molested, as even the most noisy and drunken Democrats gave me a wide berth, and never during the most heated campaign thereafter was any effort made to interfere with my privilege of citizenship.

During the Lincoln-Douglas contest[16] I continued my efforts for the Republican cause, frequently speaking, and also writing for our party papers.

I composed a great many songs which were widely sung and published throughout the country, and often met and was intimately acquainted with

Mr. Lincoln. He was at Meredosia during the campaign and stopped at my house the night after making a speech at that place. After the speaking was over and Mr. Lincoln had retired, I went back to the building in which the meeting took place to assist in quelling a disturbance which might otherwise have arisen. I worked earnestly and persistently until after the election of Mr. Lincoln to the presidency—a result which no person in the land rejoiced over more than myself.

In the fall of 1860 I returned to my father's house, with wife and family my only possessions, and for a time resumed my profession of music as a means of sustenance. I have often wondered since why I spent five years of my life in Meredosia. It is probable, however, that the experience thus gained in sustaining what I deemed a just and righteous cause was absolutely necessary to enable me to put forth greater efforts in the memorable struggle which was so soon to follow.

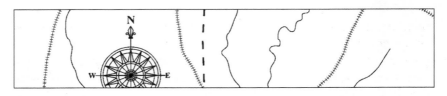

2. Rallying around the Flag

For several years previous to the political campaign which resulted in the election of Mr. Lincoln to the presidency, my brother, John C. Grierson, had been a resident of Memphis, Tennessee. By the full correspondence kept up between us, I was well advised as to the true condition of the South and the settled determination of the southern people to precipitate war upon the country. During the winter of 1860–61, my brother judged from information received from the most reliable sources that it was highly important that the North should at once prepare to meet the conflict soon to come, as the South was terribly in earnest and preparing to arm on an extensive scale for a long war.

He felt sure that civil strife would be the result of the secession tragedy and that, before the last scene of the last act was over, the problem would still have to be solved by the people as to which would be the best for humanity and civilization—slave or free labor. He clearly perceived from the evidence by which he was surrounded that that was really the pith of the question to be decided by the war and judged that, even if the North would quietly submit to a peaceable secession of the slave states, it would still be doubtful if war could be avoided. Living as he did in a southern city on the Mississippi River, that great commercial artery alone appeared to him to be an everlasting barrier to the quiet consummation of a peaceable separation, as the North could never give up to the South the control of that important stream.

Early in the spring, it was believed throughout Tennessee and adjoining states that Jeff Davis would have possession of Washington City within a short time, and that immediately upon the breaking out of hostilities all the border states would join the South, or able-bodied men therein be enrolled in the rebel army, and that when the ball was once set in motion, the South would gain the control of the entire government. My brother had many warm friends in the South, and they used every available influence to induce him to take the side of the rebels. Although he would regret to have to fight against them, as they too were Americans, he had determined that if he had to engage in war, his name would never be found enrolled among the traitors of his country.

People living at the North were not able to judge correctly as to the difficulty by which northern men who had removed into the South to reside were at that crisis surrounded. Many thus situated were unable to resist the pressure brought to bear upon them by personal friends in that section, as they found the friendships formed and attachments strengthened by their residence among the southern people irresistible. Great credit is therefore justly due to the men who had the nerve to cut loose from all such ties when the hour of trial came.

My brother was in Memphis when Fort Sumter was fired upon and when the information was received there of President Lincoln's proclamation calling for 75,000 men. In the midst of the wild and ungovernable excitement, [and] rapid enrollment of troops aroused by inflaming speeches hurled forth by desperate men bent on the destruction of the government, he felt the full force of the sad and deplorable condition of affairs. The sentiment of the people was all one way and exclamations every moment came to his ears, such as "War to the Knife," "Extermination," "No quarter," etc. Seeing that bankruptcy, poverty, and distress would be the natural result to many, and not knowing which side would win, his mind, thank the Lord, was at once made up to leave for his old home in the North. Without regarding the difficulties in the way or the losses to be incurred, he gave up his business and quickly arranged matters for his departure.

It is probable that he could not have gotten away had it not been for the quiet assistance of warm friends who had already entered the rebel army, and who notwithstanding their strong southern proclivities, in view of their friendship, helped him off and out of the difficult position in which he was unavoidably placed. The Union men who were situated as he was realized clearly the great terrors of the coming struggle in a degree impossible to be understood by those living in the comparatively quiet North. It will be remembered that many distinguished citizens at that period, like Secretary [of State William H.] Seward,[1] allowed but ninety days for the closing of the war with an army of 75,000 men, and judged [General William T.] Sherman[2] crazy for saying it would take 200,000 men to put down the rebellion. Certainly few, if any, realized that the government would require over 1,000,000 men to successfully end the war.

Stephen A. Douglas[3] was one of the few men in the North who, from his former close relations with the South, was able to put a correct estimate upon the magnitude of the impending conflict. Although his action previously as a politician precipitated the war, his noble conduct when the test came cannot be too highly commended, for notwithstanding his strong party affiliations, his patriotism shone forth in magnificent grandeur. I heard him say when Lincoln's proclamation was issued for 75,000 men that the call should have been made for 500,000 men; that in his judgment the more stupendous the effort made by the North, the sooner the war would be brought to a close. The result proved how farsighted he was, and I have always thought it was a great pity that he could not have lived to see the government victorious.

Being able to clearly estimate the magnitude of the conflict in which the government was soon to be involved, the firing upon Fort Sumter on April 13 [12], 1861, was not so great a surprise to me as to many others who had not so favorable an opportunity of gaining the definite and reliable information which I had received. The alacrity with which the people of the North responded to the call of the president and sprang to arms in defense of our flag was a spontaneous manifestation of patriotism rarely if ever equaled in the world's history. Having been an ardent Republican since the organization of the Republican Party in 1854, and believing that the treacherous attack of the audacious rebels made war inevitable, I immediately did all in my power to sustain the right and to hasten the enrollment and organization of troops.

A company of infantry was promptly formed in Jacksonville, then my residence, and my departure with the company was only prevented by the sudden dangerous illness of my mother. When she had sufficiently recovered to enable me to leave her bedside, I hastened to Springfield in response to a notice from my friend, Governor [Richard] Yates,[4] and proceeded thence to Cairo with dispatches for Colonel B. M. Prentiss[5] of the 10th Illinois Infantry, to which regiment the Jacksonville volunteers had been assigned. I was well acquainted with the colonel, we having frequently met during the political campaigns of 1856 and 1860, and when he passed Jacksonville with troops from Quincy, he expressed a cordial wish that we might serve together.

Immediately upon my arrival at his headquarters at the St. Charles Hotel in Cairo, at 11 o'clock P.M., May 8, 1861, finding that he had retired, I was shown to his room, awoke him, and placed within his outstretched hand the dispatches entrusted to my care, with his commission from Governor Yates as brigadier general of Illinois state troops. He was delighted to see me, and understanding from the letters received that his command was already viewed as a brigade and realizing the near approach of further promotion, he offered me the position of aide-de-camp, with the nominal rank of lieutenant and the promise of assistance to secure for me a commission at as early a date as possible.

I had already been informed that the infantry company from Jacksonville had, the day previous to my arrival at Cairo, been mustered into the service with the full complement of enlisted men and officers by Captain John Pope[6] (now a retired major general U.S. Army), he having rejected eighteen volunteers for that company, they being over the number authorized by law. Although disappointed at the information, I determined to go into the army in any event, either as an aide to a general officer; an officer of the line; chief musician of a regiment or brigade, for which my musical attainments well fitted me; or as a private soldier in the ranks. Therefore, the general's kind offer was thankfully received and accepted.

Finding that the hotel was full to overflowing and not being able to procure a bed elsewhere, the general insisted upon my taking a share of his, which I rather reluctantly did. We conversed together until after midnight, and the good understanding and mutual confidence then so singularly and firmly established continued uninterruptedly thereafter. The full force of our strong attachment is still well understood, as chance affords us an opportunity to grasp each other by the hand in friendly greeting.

During my residence in Youngstown, Ohio, I [had] served as trumpeter in a troop of cavalry of which Samuel Gibson was captain. Subsequently, myself and George King became the buglers of the regiment to which Gibson's troop belonged. John Clark, who for many years worked for my father, was the colonel of the regiment. We continued five years in that position and received certificates for services thus rendered.

At that time, according to state law, all able-bodied men between the ages of twenty-one and forty-five years, except musicians, were obliged to serve in the militia. The militia, however, came into disrepute, mainly for the reason that neither the state nor the general government furnished suitable arms or equipments. At certain periods, all organizations were obliged to turn out for drills and encampments. The regiments in that portion of the state not being properly armed, the rank and file generally appeared on parade with cornstalks, brooms, rails, poles, or anything that would answer as a substitute for arms. The officers, selected by ballot, were well-known drunkards possessing peculiar characteristics. Among the successful candidates were Captains Hughes, Bellard, Colwell, and Spencer—all of whom were droll and natural oddities.

During muster days, the men worked systematically to get the officers drunk, and the maneuvers usually wound up by marching to the tow-path of the canal, where sooner or later they managed to charge upon and plunge the officers into the water to sober them. There was a good deal of fun on such occasions, followed in due time by the arrest and burlesque court-martial of the alleged offenders. Many funny speeches were made by parties implicated, but in some manner they always managed to get off "scot-free." While witnessing those proceedings, I little thought that the time would ever come when I would be called upon to serve in earnest with troops battling for the Union during a great rebellion. Of course, the knowledge and experience gained by service with the Ohio militia was not essentially beneficial in aiding me to command successfully in serious warfare.

At the beginning of the war, the volunteers called for so largely and responding in such haste were not heedful as to the strict requirements of the Adjutant General's Department at Washington. Like many others zealous in the cause of their country, I saw work to be done and did it, leaving the question of rank and pay to be settled afterwards, relying upon the justice of the government to set me right in a degree corresponding to my generous efforts in its behalf. I did not receive a commission until long afterwards, and many months of hard and tedious work—covering the time of my constant and faithful service as aide-de-camp on the staff of General Prentiss, from May 8 to October 24, 1861—is still unpaid for and unrecognized officially on the Army Register.

Although obliged to borrow money necessary for the support of my family during that period, it is gratifying to know that the services were thus rendered, as it proved that my patriotism was strong enough to enable me to discharge my duty, although suffering from embarrassments greater than deprivation of rank, pay, or substantial position. It is also a satisfaction to remember, and for others to know, that in my case "a good name was better than riches"—for during the uncertain period of work without wages an old friend of the family, Mr. A. B. Safford,[7] a banker at Cairo, took my individual note without other security and advanced thereon sufficient money to meet my wants and those of my thrifty wife and two children. The duties devolving upon me were performed to the best of my ability, and when not otherwise engaged, I studied the tactics of the various arms of the service, army regulations, military science, law, strategy, and especially the topography of the country southward. The knowledge thus gained was useful to me as a staff officer, and became of great benefit when actively engaged in command of troops.

It will be remembered that Kentucky and Missouri claimed to be neutral at the commencement of the war. But it was a very one-sided neutrality, which enabled most of the citizens of those states to go into the rebel army, while their families and property were protected by the federal government. It so happened that I took part in the first expedition into the so-called sacred soil of Kentucky, which at the time created a great deal of excitement. The governor [Beriah Magoffin][8] protested against the invasion of that commonwealth, and the occurrence resulted in much correspondence between General Prentiss and the authorities in Washington.

Information had been received to the effect that an organization of secessionists, numbering about 100 men, were assembled at a point known as Elliot's Mills, about midway between Cairo and Columbus, Kentucky, five miles inland from the Mississippi River, much to the annoyance of Union men in that vicinity and those who passed that point on the way to the North. Many had been arrested and suffered from the loss of property, and in some cases had to submit to being searched and whipped, to have their heads shaved, and to suffer other indignities. Those outrages were frequent and General Prentiss decided that they must be stopped.

Two companies of infantry under command of Captain [Charles H.] Adams were sent by boat down the Mississippi to a point on the Kentucky shore nearest the rebel encampment. I was specially selected by General Prentiss to accompany the command and, about June 1, we left Cairo accordingly. Upon arrival at the point indicated, the troops were disembarked and proceeded inland, arresting every man met on the way, surrounding houses, awakening inmates to obtain information, and placing guards over them until our return.

Arriving at Elliot's Mills just before daylight, the troops surrounded the place, but it was found after a thorough search that the rebels had retreated towards Columbus, leaving their camp fires burning. After scouting throughout the woods in the immediate vicinity of the mills, the command returned to the boat and thence to Cairo. Although we failed to capture or destroy the rebels, their camp was broken up by the movement and the result gave much satisfaction to the Union men.

The usual precautions were taken on the expedition to guard against surprise or ambush. There was an advance and rear guard, flankers, scouts, etc., the same as if a real invasion of the country had been contemplated. Upon arrival at the point where the rebels were presumed to be encamped, in the dim light objects could be seen stirring about and lights also observed. The troops approached cautiously, and when near enough, charged impetuously and completely routed the enemy, which proved to be a drove of hungry hogs that were eating the forage left by the rebels. Our onslaught stirred them up decidedly and they, being alarmed fully as much as the attacking party, scattered wildly in all directions, making much confusion, accompanied by the explosive grunts usual to such animals when suddenly disturbed. That memorable encounter, however, was omitted from the official report.

Early in June, another expedition was organized and proceeded on the *City of Alton* to a point about four miles below the town of Columbus, Kentucky. The command consisted of a portion of the 8th and 10th regiments of Illinois infantry and a section of artillery, under command of Colonel [Richard] Oglesby, subsequently major general of volunteers, U.S. senator, and recently governor of Illinois, and familiarly known as "rare Old Dick Oglesby."[9] Strict orders were given by General Prentiss not to land on the Kentucky shore unless attacked by the rebels. I also accompanied that expedition.

As the boat approached the town of Columbus, many persons could be seen passing to and from the shore. By the aid of a field glass, I noticed a rebel flag near the river and pointed it out to Colonel Oglesby. It made my blood boil to see that contemptible piece of bunting floating in the breeze, and I asked permission to capture it, if anyone was allowed to land.

It was reported that the rebels had erected a battery of artillery near the shore for the purpose of making any boat that passed round to [turn back]. Therefore, going down the stream, we kept close to the Missouri shore, although in hopes that the rebels would fire upon us so that we could land and have the satisfaction of cleaning out the town. Returning, we kept close to the Kentucky shore, and when nearly opposite the flag which was hoisted on a large pole near the bank of the river in front of the town, Colonel Oglesby shouted to the people and asked, "Is there a Union man on shore within the sound of my voice, among the large crowd assembled who will take down that flag?" But no one responded. He then said, "If you don't take it down I'll have it shot down," and Colonel [James D.] Morgan directed Captain [Caleb] Hopkins of the artillery to try the range of his pieces to see if he could shoot down the pole. He found that he could, but from the position of his guns would be likely to hit some of the houses in the town. As that would not answer, another plan must be adopted, for to go back without the flag would never do.

The boat had passed the flag, and the crowd on the shore, thinking it would not be taken, became bold and defied us. I then asked Colonel Oglesby to have the boat run near the shore so that I could jump off, without stopping the boat, and cut down the flag. He informed me that neither I nor anyone belonging to the command could leave the boat. I informed him that I was not mustered into the United States service; that I was only acting as volunteer aide and was willing to run the risk if he would let me undertake the capture of the flag. But he would not give his consent.

Colonel Oglesby, Colonel Morgan, and myself then consulted together, all determined that the flag must be taken in some way. After a few minutes' talk, the machinery got out of order and the boat drifted ashore. Captain Barnes of the steamer *Alton*, a large, handsome, athletic man, with two of his boatmen jumped off, ran up the bank, cut the rope and hauled down the flag, clasped it in their arms as it fell, and ran with it onto the boat. The troops on board were ready to fire in case of any resistance, but none was made except by a squad of drunken men, who after much bluster and noise, fell back, cursing as they moved away. After the captain returned on board, the machinery was soon in order, and away we steamed for Cairo, giving three cheers for [the] Stars and Stripes, three for Abraham Lincoln, three for General Prentiss, and three for Colonels Oglesby and Morgan, as we went on our way rejoicing. Just as we were leaving the upper part of the town, a cowardly rebel fired a rifle, but the shot did not take effect. If it had injured any of our men, we would have turned and given them a few rounds.

We arrived at Camp Defiance about 4 P.M. in high glee, the Stars and Stripes floating to the breeze with the rebel flag inverted and placed underneath. Our approach to the camp was the cause of no little commotion, for thousands were assembled on the shore, cheering loudly as our boat reached the landing, and the artillery was firing a salute. The flag was placed in charge of Captain Barnes and myself to march up with it to headquarters. It was almost impossible to keep the soldiers from tearing it to pieces. The whole command marched to the St. Charles Hotel, in front of which we were met by General Prentiss, who upon receiving the flag, got upon the balcony, holding the flag in his hand while making a speech to the soldiers in the midst of great excitement and enthusiasm. I was directed by Colonel Oglesby to cut up the flag and give a piece of it to each soldier who took part in the expedition, a duty I performed to the entire satisfaction of all concerned.

On June 13, General [George B.] McClellan[10] arrived at Cairo, and in the afternoon we had a grand review of all the troops in the brigade, which passed off in a very satisfactory manner. I was immediately in the rear of Generals McClellan and Prentiss, and had a fine opportunity to witness the display. After the troops passed in review and formed again into line, General Prentiss put them through the Manual of Arms, Major Baldwin and myself repeating the commands to the right and left so that all could hear them. On the 14th, we visited the camps of the brigade and had a very pleasant time. On returning to headquarters, dispatches were received which required General McClellan to leave for Springfield and St. Louis. I presented the general with the center star of the secession flag (which I had intended for General Prentiss), and also gave him a piece of the flag showing the width of the three stripes. The flag was nine feet wide by twenty feet long, and was the first rebel flag captured in the state of Kentucky.

———

Notwithstanding the annoyances and difficulties encountered in endeavoring to live without means, it is noteworthy to observe that Mrs. Grierson, to whom I wrote almost daily, always answered encouragingly, and in one of her letters significantly said, "Do not be troubled about sending money at present, I have still five dollars left." She manifested a remarkable amount of patience, enduring privations without murmur or complaint, steadfastly proffering that kind of support which was, under the circumstances, not only highly gratifying, but invaluable to me. I believe, therefore, and have repeatedly stated, that for any success I may have gained during the war she is justly entitled to at least half the credit. Even the reverses of the Army of the Potomac, which sent such a thrill of dismay through the homes of so many people of the North, did not shake my faith in the final outcome or triumph of our cause. Although obliged to borrow money and work without pay, such troubles only stimulated me to put forth greater exertion.

The time was approaching when the "three months' men" would be mustered out and a larger army enrolled into the service to meet coming emergencies. Soldiers partially drilled and disciplined were discharged and returned to their homes, and raw recruits enlisted in their stead. Therefore, none of the regiments were efficient. Additional troops arrived at Cairo and vicinity, and a brigade was formed and placed at Bird's Point under the command of Colonel W. H. L. Wallace of the 11th Illinois Infantry. He was a very gallant officer and was subsequently killed at the battle of Shiloh.

Exaggerated reports had been circulated in regard to the force and movements of the rebels, but from the best information obtained it was believed that they would confine their movements, for a time at least, to the vicinity of New Madrid and some of the islands in the Mississippi River. There was little rest, however, for the troops either at Cairo or Bird's Point, and false alarms were frequent. At the former station, we were often aroused at night by the report of an attack on Bird's Point; and at the latter place, the same excitement prevailed nightly for fear an attack would be made on Cairo. Soldiers had not then learned to recognize the difference between the random firing of a picket, or a few scattered shots, and a regular volley. The troops were constantly called out, often to wait for hours at the wharf for transportation, only to be dismissed as the excitement allayed, to return to their beds to make up for the loss of sleep, when any time was left to them to do so. It was expected that complete equipments, including improved muskets, rifles, cannon, mortars, and in short everything needed, would be forthcoming without delay, but it was a long time before our forces were properly armed and equipped.

About the middle of July, I took part in a reconnaissance into Missouri, back of Bird's Point, with General Prentiss, Colonel Oglesby, Quartermaster [Reuben B.] Hatch,[11] Major [Thomas E. G.] Ransom[12] and a number of other officers, and a few soldiers of Colonel Wallace's command. When about five miles out we observed fresh horse tracks, and as none of the troops had been there from camp, we knew the tracks must have been made by horses of the rebels. A squad of twenty or thirty horsemen had been seen at a point ten miles away the evening before, but our observations were extended that far without finding the enemy.

Upon returning, when we reached the place where the horse tracks had been observed, our minds naturally reverted to the subject. General Prentiss, always full of fun, concluded to have a little, and told me quietly that he would hold the detachment back while I went some distance ahead. The arrangement was that I should return after riding a half mile or so, and report to him that there were some fifteen or twenty horsemen in advance to cut us off.

After going the required distance, I returned on the run, making my horse, which was a very good and fast one, fly over the ground with great rapidity, really outdoing himself. Just as I approached the group, I made him jump a treetop which happened to be in the way, rode up to the officers pale as a sheet with hair fairly standing on end, saluted the general, and made my report with trembling voice and in a greatly excited manner. I played my part so well I almost fooled the general and Colonel Oglesby, also in [on] the secret, as both were so deceived by my manner that they quickly asked me in an undertone, "Did you really?" A consultation was immediately held, and it was decided that we should advance until we came near the place where the horsemen were reported to have been seen. I stated that some had turned to the left, others to the right, and that a few were still left in the road where first observed.

When we arrived at the place indicated, I started off to the right and Colonel Oglesby and some of the others proceeded to the left. After riding into the woods about 300 hundred yards, I drew my revolver and fired four or five times in quick succession. The shots were answered by General Prentiss, which brought back the party that went to the left, they of course not seeing anyone. They proposed to start to my relief at once, supposing that I was fighting the rebels all alone. Captain Hatch, in particular, was extremely excited and difficult to restrain from rushing in alone to my aid. He exclaimed, "My God, they are murdering Ben Grierson. It's an outrage to leave him there without help."

After I had fired the first few shots, I changed my position, going farther off, and fired a few more, having two revolvers. That added to the excitement, and it was as much as the general could do to keep the entire party from going to my rescue. Finally, he told them it was all "a sell," and they at once grew very merry over the adventure.

I soon returned to where they were halted and found them considerably excited, but laughing ready to split their sides. They all said it was the best joke of the season, and were unanimous in the opinion that my part was played to perfection. It would not do, and was really unlawful, to play such tricks on soldiers, but our party were mostly officers who enjoyed it hugely and declared that it added very much to the pleasure of the trip. We returned to camp in fine spirits. The apparent fight was a real one to most of the party, and no one showed the white feather. They named the engagement "Grierson's retreat," as the most striking feature of the performance was when I brought in the news in such haste and amazement.

The concentration of the rebel forces continued. Jeff Thompson,[13] it was reported, had encamped with troops on the New Madrid road south of Charlestown, about twenty miles from Bird's Point. Other large encampments of rebels were near at hand, and with those at New Madrid the enemy numbered, it was said, 10,000 men. The reports were exaggerated but generally from information received at that time presumed to be reliable.

The heat at Cairo and vicinity during the latter part of July was excessively oppressive and many were prostrated with sunstroke, General Prentiss and some other officers among the number. The fleet of steamboats bearing General Fremont and several regiments of troops for Bird's Point arrived in the midst of much excitement and enthusiasm on July 29. It was a grand sight to witness the approach of reinforcements so much needed and a soul cheering scene for the soldiers already stationed there, who were thus enabled to get rest and sleep securely at night. General Fremont approved the assignment of Colonel Wallace, who was the senior officer present, to the command of the brigade now further enlarged, thus making General Prentiss command a division of two brigades. General Fremont indicated very plainly that General Prentiss should have command of the forward movement, which it was evident must soon take place. Of course the intimation was very gratifying to General Prentiss, who was extremely anxious to enter upon an active campaign without unnecessary delay.

The general introduced and commended me very warmly to General Fremont, whom I found to be very approachable. I was also pleased to meet Mrs. [Jessie Benton] Fremont,[14] who had accompanied her husband. I distinctly remember her saying that she was hardly presentable, as she had left St. Louis unexpectedly and in such haste that she did not take along a change of clothing, and therefore had to wear for a collar one of her husband's shirt collars. She was at that time a robust, good-natured, fine-looking woman, and I judged her to be possessed of a considerable amount of good common sense. It was a great satisfaction to me to shake them by the hand. On doing so, I could not but think of the stirring times during the presidential campaign of 1856, in which I felt so much interest.

Recently, I had the pleasure of meeting Mrs. Fremont at her home in Los Angeles, California, and took occasion to refer to the foregoing incident, and was pleased to find she remembered the circumstances and conversation. She laughingly remarked to me, when I told her of the statement in regard to being obliged to use one of the general's shirt collars, "Yes, that is very true, but not all of the story." For, said she, "The collar I wore at that time was fastened to one of General Fremont's shirts, and besides, I may as well tell you, I also had to wear the general's socks and underwear, however uncomfortable and unsuitable, as a change of clothing became a necessity. The greatest trouble I encountered was in keeping the socks from slipping down over my ankles. But, everything considered, I got along quite well until my return to St. Louis, although then glad to rehabilitate myself in more suitable garments."

She related, in a most interesting manner, how she came to make up her mind to share the danger of the trip with the general. She had learned through a staff officer that the rebels contemplated placing batteries on the Mississippi River, with a view of sinking the boat on which the general was to embark. Without his knowledge and unaccompanied, she proceeded to the steamboat and quietly hid herself in a stateroom until after the boat had proceeded some distance down the river, when much to the general's surprise and apparent annoyance, she made her appearance in the cabin. But her persuasive faculties proved sufficiently powerful to carry the point in sharing the danger with which the commander of the Department of the West was threatened. Her visit to Cairo, however, was not devoid of substantial good, for it was on her special plea to the general that some of the steamboats were utilized as hospitals, which resulted in so much comfort for the sick who had up to that time been so illy provided for.

On August 7, information was received at division headquarters at Cairo to the effect that the rebels had attacked the United States troops at Cape Girardeau. Colonel [C. C.] Marsh[15] reported the enemy 5,000 strong, and he had only two regiments and a battery under his command. Therefore, Colonel [John] McArthur,[16] with six companies of infantry and four cannon, was sent immediately to Colonel Marsh's assistance, and troops were also ordered there from St. Louis. The rebels continued to threaten Bird's Point, and troops had been advanced eight or ten miles inland to check their approach. The demonstration against Cape Girardeau was probably intended to draw off troops from Bird's Point and Cairo, with a view to favor the opportunity for successful attack on those places. The fortifications at Cairo and Bird's Point were being strengthened, and a feeling of security prevailed throughout both encampments.

On August 7, news was received from Cape Girardeau, by way of Jonesborough [Jonesboro, Ill.], that all was quiet at the Cape and no immediate prospects for a fight. The enemy, instead of being near at hand in large force as reported, was fully twenty-five miles inland from that place. What alarmed Colonel Marsh was a troop of rebel cavalry attacking and driving in his pickets, from which occurrence he inferred that the entire force of rebels were advancing. His hasty action in reporting an attack caused trouble and expense and the sending of troops from Cairo and St. Louis to his assistance.

All being quiet and serene again at Cairo and vicinity, General Prentiss telegraphed to General Fremont for leave to visit his home for a few days and received an answer that he could go, but to do so at once and make his stay as short as possible. As the steamer *Memphis* was then at Cairo and no train going out that day, he concluded to make the trip by boat as far as St. Louis. He desired me to go with him, and of course, I obeyed the order with alacrity, hoping that I might thereby be enabled to reach my home at Jacksonville. We, therefore, hastily embarked just as the steamer was about to leave the wharf and had a delightful trip up the Mississippi River, and enjoyed the scenery which was varied and beautiful.

Arriving at St. Louis, we took a carriage and drove rapidly to the Planter House for dinner, after which we called on General Fremont, with whom we had a very pleasant interview. General Prentiss was assured of the great confidence reposed in him and given to understand that he would soon be assigned to an important command for a forward movement down the Mississippi. General Fremont remarked that he had no fear for the safety of Cairo with General Prentiss in command there, and indicated that he was not so well pleased with some other generals he might mention. Although he gave no names, he said sufficient to give us to plainly understand to whom he referred.

Our stay in St. Louis was short, and we were soon on the steamer again bound for Quincy. Upon arrival at Hannibal, Missouri, we found part of a regiment there waiting for transportation south. The general made a short speech to the soldiers, which seemed to please them very much. At its conclusion, they gave him three cheers with a will. At St. Louis, the general received dispatches which indicated a forward movement of the rebels from New Madrid. On reaching Quincy, he received a telegram from General Fremont directing him to return forthwith to St. Louis, and he made arrangements for a special train which took us back there in quick time. Upon arrival again at Fremont's headquarters, it was found that General Prentiss was needed for an important movement which was contemplated through eastern Missouri from Ironton, where troops were already concentrating for that purpose. We immediately departed for Ironton, arriving there on August 17, where we found ourselves in a beautiful valley surrounded by mountains of iron. Among other troops, we found a company of the 2nd Illinois Cavalry under the command of 1st Lieutenant James K. Catlin, who was intimately known to me, being a resident of Jacksonville.

The frequent change of commanders of the Union forces had been detrimental to the interests of the government, but it now seemed that the active measures for the protection of the loyal people by the effective warfare which was so energetically inaugurated by General [Nathaniel] Lyon[17] some months before in Missouri were about to be resumed, and further dilly-dallying, or unnecessary delays, abandoned for an earnest prosecution of the war. It was very unfortunate that General Lyon could not have lived to see the consummation of the work he so vigorously began. His great decision of character and ability in overcoming obstacles had been severely tested, his efforts recognized and crowned with eminent success. And his early death was truly an irreparable loss to the Union cause.

General Prentiss, who was anxious to have me continue with him during the war, had endeavored to obtain, by the assistance of General Fremont, a commission for me from the War Department with the rank of captain. He was assured by General Fremont that he should have command of the troops both at Cairo and in southeast Missouri. Being the commander, as he understood it, of even more than a division, he thought himself entitled to an aide-de-camp with the rank of major, and was determined that I should have that grade, if he could obtain it for me. So soon as the troops could be equipped and properly supplied with transportation, it was the intention to move southward to Greenville, Wayne County, Missouri, to attack the rebels said to be there under command of General [William J.] Hardee,[18] and supposed to be 6,000 in number.

With so much to do at headquarters and daily letters to write to comfort a faithful wife at home, it is not to be wondered at that other correspondents had to suffer. My brother John, who was left back at Cairo as clerk in the office of Quartermaster Hatch, wrote rather spicily complaining at my neglect. Leaving Cairo so hastily for what was expected to have been but a brief and temporary absence instead of a change of base, everything I had there, except the contents of a satchel, was left unpacked and scattered about in confusion. Having given directions for them to be gathered up and sent to me, my brother wrote that he had shipped accordingly, "One box, one trunk, one package (two foils) all plainly marked B. H. Grierson, care of General B. M. Prentiss, Ironton, Mo." He further stated, "I hesitated about sending the foils but concluded to let 'the tail go with the kite' especially as you have not been man enough to write me since you left. Please remember and do not fail—when you get over the fright of being called into active service and your knees have ceased trembling—to write me a few lines for it might be the last opportunity you'll have, as you may be fool enough, if in an engagement, to jump in the way of a chunk of secession lead. All I have to say is, be careful and if you must be hit let it be not in the back." Soon afterwards, my brother was ordered to Ironton as assistant to Quartermaster Hatch.

On arrival of General Prentiss at Ironton, he found General [Ulysses S.] Grant[19] pushing things as well as he could with the force available. Fremont, liking Prentiss, had resolved to increase his command, and on the promises heretofore mentioned, had sent him to Ironton. Grant supposed himself relieved. But Prentiss claiming superiority under Fremont's orders, Grant asked leave to go to St. Louis to consult with Fremont on the subject. Prentiss, of course, cheerfully gave his consent. General Fremont finally ascertained that Grant did rank Prentiss, and saw that it was a great blunder to have brought these two officers into collision. Grant, not wishing to go back to Ironton to supersede Prentiss, was sent temporarily to Jefferson City, and soon afterwards assigned to Prentiss' old command at Cairo and vicinity, a change which proved fortunate for the former and correspondingly detrimental to the interests of the latter.

Being detained at Ironton longer than was expected, there appearing to be no prospect of an immediate movement and having been disappointed in making a contemplated visit to my family, I wrote to Mrs. Grierson to come if possible to see me, believing she would have time to do so before our departure. If she had considered her own wishes only, she would have needed no urging. But to go in the intense heat of mid-summer from Chicago to Ironton was too great a risk for the health of our young children. Only those who have had dear friends at the front expecting battle can appreciate the self-denial of remaining at home when inclination would have taken them away in the face of their better judgment. The wisdom of Mrs. Grierson was clearly proven by the event and handsomely acknowledged by me, as I was almost immediately ordered away and had to leave before she could have possibly reached that place. The sudden move was occasioned by an unexpected order which directed General Prentiss to proceed without delay with his command to Jackson, Missouri, a town about ten miles inland from Cape Girardeau.

On August 22, I was ordered to inspect all the outposts, and to extend my observations as far as Mineral Point and Potosi, to ascertain the condition and effective strength of the troops, exact location of detachments situated along the line of the Iron Mountain Railroad—the Potosi branch thereof—and to report the result with the least practicable delay. Having accomplished the work assigned me, all grand guards, outposts, and available detachments were promptly concentrated in the vicinity of Ironton. And on August 25, the entire available force began the march to Jackson in compliance with orders received.

I was a little uneasy for fear Mrs. Grierson had, in view of the wish repeatedly expressed in my letters, left Chicago to join me. But her good sense prevented the impracticable undertaking. I concluded there might be "a good time coming," but that we would have to "wait a little longer" for its realization, and departed on the expedition resolved to do my duty without being unguarded or rash, bearing in mind that the blood of brave and loyal men must necessarily flow in the coming struggle for freedom, the end of which no one at that time could foresee.

By permission of General Prentiss, I for the first few days accompanied the extreme advance, composed of a detachment of the 2nd Illinois Cavalry under command of Lieutenant Catlin. On one occasion, we with six cavalrymen and two infantry foragers, picked up on the way, had gotten a few miles ahead of the main column and probably a half mile or more in front of the advance proper. When passing over a brow of a hill, we observed on a slope below us rebel soldiers, some forty in number. Further on, a larger force was discovered.

If the rebels had not run, perhaps we would [have done so] in the face of such great odds. But, putting on a bold face and turning our heads toward the rear, we shouted, "come on boys, here they are," as if the main army, miles behind, were in reach of our voices, and thus charged impetuously down the long sloping hillside. There was mounting in hot haste and hurrying to and fro, without a look behind them, as the panic-stricken rebels scattered and flew away before that army of eight horsemen and reserve of two infantrymen.

We chased the flying foe until we came to a pleasant-looking plantation and large house situated some distance from the foot of the hill, which belonged to one "Dougherty," a member of the Missouri State Legislature with secession proclivities. The family at once made for the woods, and only the grinning darkies remained as we dashed up and carefully reconnoitered the place, placing pickets on the flanks to observe and give warning of the approach of any of the rebels.

We then dismounted and entered the premises. The black eyes of the slaves twinkled and their white teeth shone as we asked them for something to eat. "Don't spect dars nothing in de house massa. Soldiers done took it all." "Where is the cellar?" we demanded. "Cellar done locked up massa. Dunno where de keys is." "Well, find the keys or we'll find the cellar without them." They were soon produced, nor did it take long to go through the house.

The finding of rebel uniforms, letters, etc., removed all scruples concerning confiscation, and the darkies, nothing loath, were obliged to set the contents of the cellar cupboards upon the dining table. Cold meats, ham, eggs, chickens, fruits, pickles, jellies, pies and cakes of all kinds, all that a lavish plantation kitchen provided for the master's table and his friends, were forthcoming in abundance. The soldiers relieved each other, and by turns feasted to the top of their bent.

Catlin and myself sat jolly at the bountiful table and layout, when up dashed a detachment from General Prentiss at full gallop. The officer in charge said the general was provoked at the advance for venturing so far away, that we might be killed or taken prisoners as a thousand rebels were reported within reach, and that we and our squad must return at once to the column. The newcomers looked appreciatingly at the "spread" before them, of which they were cordially invited to partake. And they, after all, were not so prompt in returning themselves as in giving their orders. Of course, such a reckless way of advancing on the march in the midst of enemies was a foolhardy proceeding, and General Prentiss had good reason to be annoyed at us. As he had information to the effect that the enemy intended to make a stand at or near Dougherty's plantation, the approach, under the circumstances, should have been more cautious. But when we observed the panic-stricken and astonished rebels, we could not resist the fun of making a dash at them.

Marching through the so-called neutral state of Missouri, efforts were made to prevent depredations by soldiers. But there were some Dutch regiments in the command that were irrepressible and impossible to control, [Colonel John B.] Turchin's and [Colonel Frederick] Hecker's, in the order named, being the most ungovernable.[20] Colonel Turchin's regiment was in advance when I was sent forward to select a camp and order a halt for the night. The place chosen was near a well-stocked farm surrounded by rail fences. After the assignment of grounds were made to the various regiments, the line formed, arms stacked and men dismissed, the soldiers with whoops and bounds, like boys let loose from school, exploded in shouts of merriment and quickly scattered in all directions. In five minutes, not a panel of fence was left on the place, as all the rails were appropriated for camp fires. Chickens, ducks, geese, and pigs were proclaiming themselves, cackling, quacking, hissing, and grunting, as they were chased over the place—an enclosure no longer—run under and into the house, barns, and other buildings; caught by the head, the tail, the ear, the wing, the foot; shot, bayoneted, sabered, or strangled, as occasion might serve. In vain did women scream or children cry. In vain did officers swear or put forth efforts to stop the slaughter. And in vain did Prentiss himself ride up and vociferate at the top of his voice to quiet the disorder. Where one man was arrested ten started for his quarry, and if one screaming fugitive was released, it was but to chase after other incorrigible depredators. The cows were milked on the run; eggs [were] rifled from every nest and absolutely squeezed from the hens as they were ruthlessly and unceremoniously removed from their quiet resting places. The scene was indescribable and very ludicrous, but quite unappreciable by the residents of the ranch, even when the destructive whirlwind occasioned by the invaders had swept onward. The march from Ironton to Jackson occupied a week or more, and many other amusing incidents might be related were the time available.

When General Prentiss was ordered on that expedition, he supposed it was to head the great movement southward. But when he arrived at Jackson he found Colonel Marsh with troops already there, who upon receiving his orders, informed him he already had them from General Grant and could not, of course, obey two commanders. General Prentiss was appointed a brigadier general of Illinois state troops on May 8, 1861, and received his commission on that day. His appointment of brigadier general of volunteers was dated May 17, the same date as General Grant's, and General Prentiss believed himself entitled to precedence on account of his commission as brigadier general received from the governor of Illinois. But, on account of General Grant's previous service in the United States Army, he was by the War Department placed above him in the order of appointment and was therefore superior to General Prentiss in rank, as well as many other officers who were appointed general officers at that time.

General Prentiss immediately proceeded to Cape Girardeau to meet General Grant. It was early in September when the interview herein related took place, which resulted in a wide breech between those two officers and the subsequent removal of General Prentiss to a distant command. I was the only other person present on that occasion. I did my utmost to maintain peace between those gallant and ambitious officers. I believed my friend and commander, General Prentiss, to a certain extent justifiable in his cause, but could not be insensible to the intemperance with which he urged his claims. Seeing that General Prentiss was laboring under great excitement, I had determined at all hazards to prevent any serious collision between him and General Grant.

At the commencement of the interview, a staff officer who accompanied General Grant, hearing loud talking in the room, opened the door as if to enter. General Grant, turning towards him, raised his hand and indicated that he wished him to remain outside. Seeing this, I at once proposed to General Grant to withdraw also, as I then presumed he might prefer to be alone with General Prentiss. General Grant, however, immediately said that he desired me to remain. I had already been endeavoring to quiet General Prentiss and to secure an understanding and an arrangement which would be satisfactory to both officers. Although my position was, under the circumstances, an embarrassing one, I believe my coolness and presence of mind was a fortunate thing for all parties immediately concerned, as well as for the cause in which we all felt so deep an interest.

General Prentiss, having a reasonable expectation of being the first in command in that part of the country and leader of the main expedition southward, was exceedingly exasperated at finding himself subordinate to General Grant. General Grant, however, offered the most favorable arrangement possible to General Prentiss, promising him opportunities to do and troops to do with. But nothing could assuage General Prentiss, who became very violent and abusive. General Grant was very patient and magnanimous; told General Prentiss he did not want to interfere with him; offered to place him in command of the movement southward and to let him have all the men necessary, and in short, aid him to the utmost in every way in his power to insure the success of the expedition.

General Prentiss persistently refused to be appeased, and relying on General Fremont's regard for him, believed he could carry his point. He refused absolutely to take orders from General Grant; returned to Jackson in great anger; turned over his command to Colonel John Cook of the 7th Illinois Infantry; and then went to his tent, laid down on his bed, and there dictated a letter to General Fremont, giving a statement of the whole transaction and interview between himself and General Grant, and sent me to deliver it to General Fremont at St. Louis.

I started immediately to carry out instructions, but on my arrival at General Fremont's headquarters I found that the general was just starting to make a call on Prince Napoleon.[21] I succeeded in presenting the papers to his private secretary, however, and arranged to return in the afternoon for an answer. Upon so returning, I unfortunately found that Prince Napoleon was there returning General Fremont's call, which of course made it necessary to arrange for the interview to take place the next morning. Before leaving headquarters, I learned from the secretary that General Prentiss had already been ordered to St. Louis, where he arrived at 6 o'clock A.M. the next day. His presence, of course, relieved me from further action in the matter. He called on General Fremont at the hour fixed upon, but found him so much occupied in giving orders for the shipment of troops that he had to make a further appointment to meet him later in the day. While he was having that interview, I occupied my time in writing an account of those extraordinary occurrences to Mrs. Grierson.

General Prentiss had, under excitement, on the spur of the moment, tendered his resignation. But, after the conference with General Fremont, he was induced to withdraw it on the assurance that he would be assigned to an adequate command. The whole affair was unfortunate for General Prentiss, and in my judgment, it was a very great mistake, under all the circumstances, for him to refuse to receive orders from General Grant. Had he remained at his post he would have had every opportunity afforded him for distinction. Fremont could not sustain him against a higher power, and Prentiss was finally ordered into north Missouri, where the rebels carried on a sort of guerilla warfare which amounted to nothing. He had a large section of country and a large number of troops, but they were so scattered and the rebels so disinclined to concentrate and attempt any great movement, that the command was a very undesirable one, as nothing but the most petty and desultory warfare was possible.[22]

My remonstrances with General Prentiss were earnest, and for a time seemed persuasive, but unfortunately failed in the end, and it is probable that the result was afterwards regretted by General Prentiss himself. My relations with General Grant during this unfortunate quarrel were perfectly satisfactory, notwithstanding my loyalty to my superior and friend, General Prentiss. I first met General Grant early in the summer of 1861 on the cars between Decatur and Springfield, when he was on his way to offer his services to Governor Yates, and he told me during our conversation that he felt doubtful about being able to obtain a commission in the volunteer service.

———

While General Prentiss was arranging to go to his new command in northern Missouri, I obtained permission and made a short visit to my family then at Chicago and brought Mrs. Grierson and the children from that place, where they were spending the summer, to Jacksonville, where they again took up their abode with my parents at the old homestead. I rejoined General Prentiss at Quincy, Illinois, on September 21 and made a trip with him over the Hannibal and St. Joseph Railroad as far as the Missouri River, the general having already assumed command of north Missouri.

Upon returning to Quincy on September 26, we found the report current there that we had been cut off and taken prisoners in Missouri by some of [Sterling] Price's men,[23] which might have been the case had they made an attack upon us, as our force at St. Joseph was less than 1,000 and the reported strength of the rebels in that vicinity estimated at over 5,000. Apprehension was felt that an attack would be made upon St. Joseph while we were there, but the rebels did not put in an appearance. From the latest information received, it was believed that Price was moving southward with his entire force, and doubts were entertained as to Fremont's ability to overtake the enemy in the vicinity of Lexington, as had been deemed possible. Our troops, as usual since the war began, were too slow in their movements to get into close contact with, or to gain any decisive victory over, the rebels.

About the last of September we were ordered to Chillicothe, on the Hannibal and St. Joseph Railroad, to make that place our headquarters, but had no indication as to how long we would be required to remain in that desolate-looking and uninteresting town. Upon arrival, a report was received to the effect that the rebels were marching on the place from the south and mustering their forces in the surrounding country for the purpose of joining in the attack, nearly all the people in the neighborhood being bitter secessionists. Our force consisted of about 1,200 men, including the home guards, without cannon.

Everything considered, we were not very well prepared to make an effective resistance. Scouts were ordered out to thoroughly scour the country in every direction and efforts were made to procure reinforcements in the event of an engagement. If the rebels made a stand at Lexington, as reported, General Prentiss would probably be required to lead a column southward to join in an attack on them, provided a suitable force could be gotten together at Chillicothe for that purpose.

I was much in need of my horse and equipments and some other property I had been obliged to leave upon my hasty departure from Cape Girardeau. But my efforts to get the horse and other things shipped to me so far had failed. In the emergency, I had appealed to my brother, who had returned to Cairo, to use his utmost efforts to have the animal and my effects forwarded to me with the least possible delay. He, after a good deal of trouble, succeeded in accomplishing the work, but wrote home, so Mrs. Grierson informed me, that "Benjamin had a screw loose in his bump of order" and that he, John, "always did have to pick up his things after him."

At Chillicothe, we made our headquarters at the "Harry House" and gave the proprietor the very suggestive and appropriate name of "The Old Harry." Anyone who noticed him closely would be apt to conclude, from his sullen appearance and peculiar odor, that he came near "filling the bill," or suiting the appellation, as any mortal left outside of the lower regions. He was a rank secessionist, like nearly all others in that place, and whenever he passed any of us he looked as though he would enjoy cursing us out loud, as no doubt he did inwardly.

On October 7, information was received to the effect that Price had gone from Lexington with his whole force, without being attacked or meeting any serious opposition. On the evening of the same day, a telegram was received from General Fremont ordering General Prentiss to Jefferson City, there to await further orders. We left on the 8th for Quincy, Illinois, intending to proceed to St. Louis and thence to the capital city of the state, which was to be the center of our operations for a time. Thus we were pushed about from "post to pillar," unable to accomplish anything of service to ourselves or anyone else.

We were delayed twelve hours in going from Chillicothe to Quincy by a collision on the railroad, which occurred about eighty miles west of Quincy. Our train, while passing round a curve and moving very rapidly, ran into another train, causing a great smash-up. Some of the passengers on both of the trains were killed and others badly injured. One of the locomotives ran up on top of the other, tearing both to pieces. Fortunately, neither the general nor myself, nor any of our staff officers, were much injured, but all were bruised more or less and decidedly astonished at the sudden and unexpected stop.

General Prentiss' colored servant, who was sitting on the platform of our car when the collision occurred, was jammed in between the ends of the cars, and we had to push them apart to get him out from the place where he was fastened. He seemed to be dead or insensible for some time after being released. His head was knocked all out of shape; his tongue was hanging out as if in search of the dinner which had been discharged from his stomach. After rolling his apparently lifeless body about, he came to with a most terrific groan and was afterwards sufficiently recovered to be sent with others of the injured to Brookfield, still alive. The proverbial thickness of the African skull proved too much for even a railroad crash, as he in due time recovered.

In the course of events we reached Quincy and left on the 9th for St. Louis, arriving there on the 10th and reaching Jefferson City on the 11th of October. From instructions there received, it was found that General Prentiss' command had been enlarged by the addition of central Missouri. But the assignment to such an indefinite scope of country, with a lot of troops scattered about in all directions, was not satisfactory to General Prentiss, as I could readily observe.

The Secretary of War [Simon Cameron] and Adjutant General of the Army [Lorenzo Thomas] arrived in St. Louis on October 12 and left there on a special train to confer with General Fremont, for whom it appeared there was a storm brewing.[24] By prompt and judicious management, it was thought he might succeed in repelling the attack made upon him from the rear and yet succeed in pitching in to give the rebels "Jessie." "It never rains but it pours," it is said, and troubles seemed to be accumulating around Fremont, whose advanced views on the slavery question did not suit the more conservative element which for the time seemed to control the government and cripple the movements of the army by a misconception of the true necessities of the hour—foolishly trying to conciliate rebels who were in arms, endeavoring by every means in their power to destroy the nation. The result of this misguided policy soon became apparent by the issuing of General [Henry W.] Halleck's[25] remarkable General Order No. 3, directing the return of slaves to their masters, which utterly failed in its design and execution, was laughed at by the rebels, and met the supreme disgust and contempt of a large majority of the officers and soldiers of the Union army.[26] I determined to quit and go to my home before I would be forced into the position of a slave catcher for the rebels of our country, who were totally unworthy of such acts of conciliation when in open war and rebellion.

On October 14, General Prentiss received a telegram from General Fremont stating that he wished to see him immediately at his headquarters at Tipton, which indicated another change of base. Yet what it would be was then of course all conjecture, but I earnestly hoped that something might be done to enable me to be nearer home or to get there for a short time, at least, in the near future. I had about that time received a number of letters from Mrs. Grierson and relatives which brought to my mind the unsatisfactory condition of my private affairs, and it was hard to determine what my real duty was under the circumstances. In the uncertain position then occupied, and the belief that I could not be of much service to the government or to anyone as then engaged, the future looked uninviting, and gloomy forebodings at times took possession of me, in spite of all efforts to cast them aside. However, it is said that "the darkest hour is just before the dawn," through which daylight enters as the gloom fades away. It proved so in my case.

If it had not been for the thought of being separated from my wife, family, and relatives, I would have really liked to have gone into a fight with the rebels of my country. I never thought that I was cowardly but, nevertheless, my thoughts at times did make me quake and shudder. If I had had no wife and children, father, mother, brothers or sisters; in short, if I had none of those ties and joys that make life dear to human beings, I think I could have walked in, rode in, or pitched in to a fight with traitors without the blink of an eye, quiver of a limb, or the least thought of fear. But I now have to acknowledge that, in view of all my connections and surroundings at that time so plainly in my mind, in the event that I should have had the necessity forced upon me to walk up, or come up on double quick, to the mouth of cannon, I would have much preferred to have had them spiked or not loaded. In view of the extraordinary patience and power of endurance manifested by Mrs. Grierson, I took occasion to write to her that I truly believed that she was the most economical, generous, self-sacrificing, noble-hearted woman in the world. And I desire here to renew that statement, considering it to be no more than she justly merited.

Upon the return of General Prentiss from his interview with General Fremont, the necessity for an immediate trip for both of us to Illinois became important in view of coming changes then foreshadowed. Having the permission of General Fremont, we left that same day for St. Louis, where we separated, the general going direct to Quincy and thence to Springfield and I to Cairo, with the understanding that we were to meet in a few days at the latter place.

General Prentiss had up to that time hoped by General Fremont's inclination and influence to procure such position and command in the army as desired. But he probably learned at his recent interview that Fremont would be superseded. In his perplexity, he determined to make an effort to regain his old brigade, and therefore sent me to Cairo that I might sound the officers who commanded regiments under him previously on the subject. Most of those colonels, however, were looking to the augmentation of the army, with the hope of becoming brigadiers themselves, as indeed most of them did shortly afterwards. They were, therefore, not very earnestly desirous of General Prentiss' return, though without any personal prejudice against himself. They promised to consider the matter and write, but the arrangement came to nothing. I had also expected Fremont's influence to obtain a commission from Washington so as to insure my retention as a staff officer with General Prentiss, but saw that it would be utterly useless to depend upon any such arrangement. I, therefore, decided to make application direct to Governor Yates of Illinois for an appointment.

I reached St. Louis on the evening of October 16, 1861, en route to Cairo, where I arrived the 18th, and was detained longer than expected. Finding that I could not arrange to get to Jacksonville by Saturday as contemplated, I telegraphed to Mrs. Grierson to meet and spend the Sabbath with me at Decatur, as I would be detained there for a day while on my way to Springfield. She obeyed the summons, and there was one day of sunshine in the midst of the gloom which had so long surrounded us.

Arriving at Springfield the next day, I there met the general, who had made a longer stay at Quincy than he had at first contemplated. We at once had an interview with the governor relative to procuring a commission, as it had become a pressing necessity in order to maintain the rank of the position I had been filling and to enable me to draw pay for service I was rendering to the government. It was ascertained that there was a vacancy of major in the 6th Illinois Cavalry, which had been offered to several persons but refused for the reason that it was that of the 3rd battalion, too far in the rear for those ambitious individuals who wished to be appointed major of the 1st battalion, or to a higher grade. I informed the governor that the position would be acceptable to me, and upon my direct written application to the adjutant general of the state, endorsed in the governor's office by General Prentiss, I was appointed and the adjutant general directed to make out my commission for Governor Yates' signature, a document which was thankfully received and placed in my pocket with no small amount of satisfaction. In view of the fact that I had not then received any pay for services as aide-de-camp, by direction of the governor my commission was made to rank from August 28, 1861, which was prior to that given to the other two majors of the regiment. I reported at once to the colonel and obtained his permission to remain temporarily on duty with General Prentiss. The general having no objection, I stopped off at Jacksonville for a short visit with my family and friends.

I arrived at Jefferson City toward the last of the month, on the eve of the general's departure on an expedition up the Missouri River. Having left my horse and equipments with Dr. [William] Varian, our brigade surgeon, I found the doctor on board ready to start. Not wishing to deprive him of the use of the animal, I asked the general if I could be of any service to him if left there, being dismounted. He decided that it was best for me to remain to assist Captain [Henry] Binmore with the work of the headquarters until further orders. The general had a number of volunteer aides for the occasion—Ed Eno of Jacksonville among the number, who was subsequently an officer of volunteers.

During my short stay at Jacksonville, I had been admonished by my relatives and acquaintances to be cautious. That evening I wrote Mrs. Grierson that "staying behind might prevent a stray bullet from the gun of some rebel taking effect on my person and robbing me of the 'mortal coil' by which my soul was surrounded." Seeing the troops embarking made me desire to go, but remembering my promise to be careful and to not needlessly put myself into danger, I concluded that it was best to accept the situation as presented and quietly obey the orders received to remain.

In the parlor of the hotel, temporarily used as an office, there was a piano. In the evening Colonel [Gustav] Waagner,[27] who used to be at Cairo during the "three months' service" and who was then on General Fremont's staff as chief of artillery, came to call, and seeing the instrument referred to, said that he used to play when a young man. Upon my request, he played and sang several old favorite songs last sung at his home in Hungary. I do not know why, but the playing and singing stirred me up amazingly, and when he got up from the piano, I sat down to play, much to his surprise and to that of Captain Binmore. I pitched into the music as it happened to come into my mind, with a satisfaction appreciated by all present, myself among the number.

A necessity having suddenly arisen to communicate with General Prentiss, I left Jefferson City on November 1, 1861, on board the steamer *J. D. Perry* for Providence, twenty miles up the Missouri River, with a view to proceed thence to Columbia, the seat of Boone County, ten to twelve miles inland from the river, where it was presumed General Prentiss would be found. I had an escort of sixteen mounted men, and although I did not apprehend any trouble, I could of course not know what would occur, as the country in all directions was reported to be full of skulking guerillas.

During the night previous, reports were received at headquarters to the effect that several places to the west on the line of the railroad were threatened by the rebels and a simultaneous attack on all seemed imminent. No troops could be spared from Jefferson City, as General Prentiss had departed with all the available force. Beside the foregoing necessity for the general's presence, we had received important dispatches for him relative to the reorganization of his old brigade, which it was deemed best that he should see with the least delay practicable.

I returned safely from the trip after a hard ride and no sleep for two days and nights, traveling nearly 100 miles through the rebel lines with a squad of twelve poorly equipped and badly mounted men, having had to leave four men as guard at the steamboat. We charged through Columbia and other towns, dispersing the rebels estimated from 50 to 100 strong. We proceeded rapidly to a point ten miles beyond Fayette, Howard County, without finding General Prentiss or his command, and passed through more real danger than did those who went on the expedition with the general—and without loss or injury, only what naturally follows want of sleep and great fatigue.

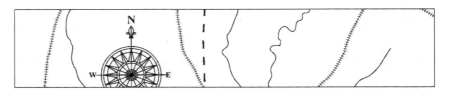

3. Colonel of the 6th Illinois Cavalry

The weak and vacillating policy of the government, while being gradually drawn under the influence of politicians, was discouraging and deplorable. When efforts were put forth to turn the army into slave catchers for the South, there was unmistakable evidence of coming trouble. Had Halleck's order been strictly enforced, there would have been serious opposition by officers and soldiers, who never could be forced into such a mistaken and ignoble occupation. There was a general reaction against the manifest change of policy. And, although Fremont's removal had for some time been foreshadowed for both political and military reasons, the efforts put forth by McClellan to impress upon the people of the so-called neutral states of Missouri and Kentucky that we were fighting solely to uphold the integrity of the Union and power of the national government did not satisfy the people throughout the East and North, who saw clearly that much more was involved in the conflict; that not only would the rebellion have to be put down, but that slavery, the real cause of the war, must necessarily be destroyed before peace could be restored.

General Fremont, upon relinquishing command of the Western Department on November 2, 1861, bid farewell to the army in a short, manly, and feeling address, and with his staff, departed for St. Louis, passing Jefferson City on November 8, where I had the pleasure of again meeting him. He looked careworn and appeared to be considerably depressed in spirits at being deprived of his command and the opportunity, as he thought, to move onward and force the enemy into action and gain a victory, which he then believed to be within his reach. Had he been as capable of equipping, commanding, and maneuvering an army in the field, as he was in grasping the keynote of the problem, which was finally solved by striking off the shackles of nearly 4,000,000 slaves—the only feasible measure which made success for the Union cause possible—the end of the terrible conflict might have been hastened, and thereby thousands of lives and millions of dollars saved. Although premature and inoperative, his bold attempt to confiscate the property and free the slaves of those found in arms against the government of the United States was correct in theory, as subsequently fully demonstrated, and possibly might have been successfully inaugurated at an earlier date than that established by the Emancipation Proclamation, which proved so humane, beneficent, and far-reaching in its results.[1]

Let this be as it may, it was at the time referred to a great satisfaction for me to meet the general, as I considered him in the midst of his misfortunes as being, with all his failings, head and shoulders above many of his enemies and traducers. I believed then that he merited, and still think he deserved, a warm place in the hearts of all lovers of freedom, of which he was an earnest, constant, and fearless advocate. His reception at St. Louis, upon return to that city, was a grand affair and must have proven a source of great gratification to the general in the face of his deprivation of an important command. Major General David Hunter[2] succeeded temporarily to the command of the Western Department, but soon after assumed that of the Department of Kansas, being relieved at St. Louis by General Halleck, who was given the "Department of Missouri," as at that time designated in orders, of which he took command on November 19, 1861.

About that time, the receipt of letters from Mrs. Grierson was a source of great comfort, and only those who have been similarly situated can fully realize the pleasure and benefit they afforded me. Had I been unfortunate enough to have had a complaining, fault-finding, and disconsolate wife, I would have been driven to despair and out of the army. But nothing came to me from home but the clearest manifestations of patient endurance and loving kindness, which encouraged and enabled me to successfully cope with disappointments and deprivations. The contents of such communications were devoured with avidity and responded to instanter, when the opportunity was afforded.

Usually at such times, for the amusement of the younger ones of the family, I had a way of making words, either double or single, flow out in a sort of a musical jingle. I humorously wrote to Mrs. Grierson that:

> These lines are by twos and will give you no news; they're scratched o'er the sheet by the foot or by feet, and according to pleasure just tuned off in measure. To light a cigar might prove better far, or a rusty old pipe with tobacco so ripe, that when fired not blazing would be so amazing that if it didn't provoke would sure end in smoke curled in clouds short or long, either mild or too strong, for palate or nerves that for smelling one serves; which if sensitive might be offensive quite, but to the more vulgar taste would be sweet; yours in haste. To go by night's mail my letter did fail, I good morning will say and send it today. This is the eighth of November if I correctly remember and just six months ago I

arrived at Cairo; full six months to a day I have served without pay, living on expectation with some hesitation, fighting under vexation to help save the nation.

The first news received of the engagement of Belmont[3] was rather discouraging and created the impression that our forces had met with defeat and disaster. Later information, however, gave assurance that General Grant had been successful in gaining a victory over the rebels there, which was more important for the reason that it was the most noteworthy success gained in the West since the death of General Lyon, and a fair triumph to offset the inglorious defeat and mortifying surrender at Lexington, Missouri.[4]

On November 9, a request was made to Colonel [Thomas] Cavanaugh of the 6th Illinois Cavalry that I be detached from the regiment and ordered to report to General Prentiss for duty on his staff. On November 15, the detail was made by the colonel, subject to the approval of the general commanding the Western Department. General Hunter, who was in command at that time, would probably have permitted the arrangement, but General Halleck, who soon after relieved General Hunter, following precedent more strictly, refused his consent on technical grounds. Such refusal, at the time, was greatly regretted by both myself and General Prentiss. But, like many other dreaded things, it proved a blessing in disguise, for had I remained a staff officer, it is probable that I would never have had an opportunity for further advancement.

As a rule, many officers preferred the chance for good quarters, easy living, and the greater freedom from responsibility of a staff position—especially if, as in my case, they had the personal friendship and confidence of their chief—to the routine drudgery of drill and the tedium of camp life. But the true apprenticeship to military science is in direct command of troops in the field, and the royal road to success is not friendly patronage but self-reliant hard work. I always felt diffident about attempting "to paddle my own canoe," but if inevitable, I usually paddled it "like thunder." I, therefore, made arrangements to meet the coming emergency and join my regiment on the receipt of orders.

General Halleck's refusal to approve my detail to remain on detached service was good-humored, but very decided. In our conversation on the subject, he said that "the new regiments were much in need of officers, and especially field officers." And, referring to me jocularly, remarked that I looked active and wiry enough to make a good cavalryman; that the information I had gained as a staff officer would be of great assistance to me; and that it would be best for the service and my own advancement to join my regiment—facts which time fully verified.

General Prentiss was at that time virtually without command. It was well understood that many changes would be made by General Halleck, and as he had said but little as to what those changes would be, many officers in command of districts, brigades, and divisions were in great suspense as to what orders they would receive or to what duty they would be assigned. Whatever the orders might be, it was evident that Halleck would not permit any hesitation upon the part of those to whom they were issued.

General Prentiss still earnestly desired to be sent without delay southward towards the land of "Dixie." And, under all the circumstances, it seemed only just that his claims should be favorably considered. My position was so indefinite and doubtful in its look that it was certainly hard to see what was really best to do. For, although commissioned major of a cavalry regiment by the governor of Illinois, yet I could not get any pay until the regiment was mustered into the service of the United States, and no information was at that time obtainable as to when such muster would take place. The headquarters of the regiment had been ordered to Shawneetown from Camp Butler near Springfield, Illinois, as most of the companies were recruited in the southern part of the state. It was no wonder that I was disgusted with soldiering where it was all work and no pay, with no certainty as to when, if ever, I would get any; with starvation or the poor house constantly before my eyes and no prospect of employment at home or elsewhere.

By selling my horse and disposing of some other things from my scanty supply, deemed essential for the comfort of a soldier, I managed to reach home and there arranged for the necessary means to proceed to join my regiment via Springfield and Cairo, stopping off at the former place to see Governor Yates and some others, and at the latter to meet my old friend [A. B.] Safford and my military acquaintances still there. I proceeded thence on the steamer *Chancellor* for Paducah, Kentucky, where I met Colonel [Eleazer A.] Paine,[5] [John] McArthur, and other officers, all of whom were glad to see me and to know that I was a major of cavalry. They kindly saw me safely on board the steamer *Golden Gate* bound for Shawneetown, where I found work enough to do with the battalion to which I had been assigned and where my patience, energy, and ability were soon thoroughly tested.

I arrived at Shawneetown early in December, and as it was late in the afternoon, stopped overnight at the hotel and the next day proceeded to the camp of the regiment, which was situated about two miles back from the town, in the woods in the midst of farms mostly fenced off in cornfields, with the dead stocks standing or piled in shocks on the uneven furrowed ground, which, when not frozen, was soft and muddy from the recent rain and snow. Some of the snow could still be seen in drifts about the fence corners and among the corn shocks, and altogether the scene presented a dreary and uninviting appearance. Until arrangements could be made to procure tents, I occupied, by direction of the commanding officer, those of Major [John] Wood, he having gone to his home in Quincy, Illinois.

I found everything connected with the command in great confusion, with but little signs of discipline or system. The regiment had never been drilled since its organization, except a very little on foot. In fact, there was no suitable place for either drills or parades. Efforts had been made, without avail, to secure any eighty-acre cornfield, which seemed to be the only place at all suitable in the vicinity. Three of the companies of my battalion had been at Camp Butler and two were mustered there. One was not full and the captain was away with a detachment, endeavoring to enlist the requisite number of men to insure the muster of the company into the service.

The colonel was about taking his departure for Springfield to arrange for the final muster of the regiment, which he thought he would be able to have date from October 1, 1861. If he succeeded in doing so, it might result in enabling me to draw pay from that date, which on the principle of "half a loaf being better than no bread," would leave me still without any pay for my services previous to that date. I had about made up my mind that, unless I was paid from at least October 1, I would quit and go home, where if I was obliged to starve, I possibly might have the satisfaction of dying in my wife's arms.

To add to my uneasiness, I found that there was considerable dissatisfaction and grumbling among the officers and men. At least five of the captains of the regiment had been applicants for the position to which I had been appointed. But I met them cordially and indicated quite plainly that if, after a fair trial, it was found that I was not a suitable person for the position, I would surrender it to anyone else for whom the officers and men might signify their preference. On better acquaintance, they all seemed to be better pleased with me. I was frequently in command, as the colonel and other field officers spent their time in going to, remaining at, and returning from their homes, instead of attending to their proper duties with the regiment.

It only took a few days for me to obtain the true inwardness of the situation. The more I investigated the matter the more I became aware of the unsatisfactory condition of affairs, and saw the general confusion which seemed to reign supreme and which gave the encampment more the appearance of a camp meeting than that of a regiment presumed to be preparing for serious warfare. The colonel was in great disrepute, and he never attempted to drill the regiment. None of the companies had been drilled mounted, although all had horses, and both officers and men were ignorant of the simplest movements. It was seldom that there was a full company in the camp, the men being permitted to wander about the town and go to their homes to stay as long as they felt inclined. Instead of the officers drilling the men as their duty required, they had brought a drillmaster from Camp Butler, and he spent his time in guzzling beer at the sutler's and talking loudly about what great things he expected to accomplish. He tried to look wise, but failed to demonstrate what he could do, excepting in the way of eating, drinking, and swaggering around, emphasizing his boisterous talk by frequent oaths. Knowing that the regiment was not entitled to a drillmaster and that one could not be paid except by the officers and men, I determined that he should not have anything to do in the way of giving instruction to my battalion. Drillmasters were only allowed to regularly organized camps of instruction and not furnished to a regiment supposed to be near the enemy's lines in readiness for service.

Neither the officers nor men had any confidence in the colonel and plainly stated that they did not place any reliance in anything he told them, simply saying, "it was all talk and no cider." His son was adjutant and totally unfit for the place; was pompous and offensive to the whole command; did not stay in camp at all but stopped in the town playing billiards and riding on horseback with young chits of girls. The nearest drill ground that could be obtained was over a mile away, and the companies had to go twice a day to Shawneetown to water the horses. There was no good drinking water to be had. In short, the camp was the worst that could have been selected in that entire section of country, and was evidently occupied without proper examination. As for getting any news, we might as well have been on top of the Rocky Mountains. I was greatly disgusted and discouraged, but began at once with squad and company drills and made preparation for battalion drills to be had with the least possible delay. The regiment was called the "Bloody Sixth," but the "Bloodless Sixth" would have been a more appropriate name for it at that stage of its organization.

I at once determined to stay in camp and take my share of roughing it and, as guard duty was loosely performed, placed a separate guard around my own battalion and permitted no one to be absent without permission. I organized a school for the officers, and gave theoretical and practical instruction daily. As there was no officers' mess established, I had to take my meals with a family near the camp, and permitted other officers to do so. The house was a wretched, open, almost doorless and windowless double log cabin. The living was of the plainest, yet the people, although very poor, were respectable and obliging, and the food was placed on the table in generous style. I always ate heartily and relished my meals, for my time was so much occupied with work that I was sure to be hungry, and the exercise made me tired enough to sleep at night. The drills were kept up every day when the weather would permit, and inspection and dress parades held on Sundays. The morning reports were required to be in my office by 8 o'clock A.M., and everything so far as related to my immediate command was soon moving along in good order.

About December 15, the weather grew quite cold. It snowed nearly all day, and during the night and next day, it turned into sleet and rain. On the 20th, I had a fine battalion drill and wound up by an inspection and parade, although the command was only armed with sabers and a few old musketoons. Just after forming the battalion into close column, I made a speech to the officers and men, and quite astonished myself as well as the soldiers, after which I received three cheers from the entire battalion. We then marched back to camp, passing through the "City of Shawnee," so-called. Upon our return to camp, before breaking ranks, three more cheers were given with a will. It was evident that I had struck the right chord in the hearts of the officers and men, and I made up my mind that the 3rd battalion of the "Governor's Legion," although the third in number, should be second to none in the regiment as to drill and efficiency.

Colonel Cavanaugh returned from Springfield on December 22 and reported that he had arranged for the muster in of the regiment to take place on the thirty-first of the month, to date from October 1, 1861. He also had much to say about his success in getting everything required to fully equip the command, stating that "the arms and accouterments were all on the way." So they had long been, according to his statements, and might be for months to come. At that time, I did not make any great pretensions as to my knowledge of military affairs, being well aware of my inability to properly impart instruction. But I had devoted much time for several months to hard study, and although not satisfied with my acquirements, I probably knew more in regard to military matters than any other field officer of the regiment.

The speech I had made a few days before established a good feeling towards me throughout my command. Among other things, I stated that I could readily understand the sensitiveness that some of the officers might feel at having a strange officer placed over them, when it might be reasonable to expect that the captains who recruited and organized companies should have their claims for advancement favorably considered. Nevertheless, I had been legally commissioned by the governor of the state and had reported for duty in compliance with orders from proper authority, and if I remained would certainly do everything in my power to make them good soldiers. But if they did not want me to stay, they had only frankly to say so, and I would at once resign in favor of any officer whom they might select for appointment in my stead.

The response was spontaneous and decisive. Captain [Reuben] Loomis of Company I—one of the officers who had been disappointed in not getting the place—sprang forward and, turning toward the soldiers, exclaimed: "We do not want Major Grierson to resign. We prefer to have him remain with us." Raising his hat in the air, he shouted, "three cheers for Major Grierson." And they were loudly given in the midst of much enthusiasm. The earnest expression of regard so cheerfully made was very gratifying to me. I never thereafter lost the confidence of my officers and soldiers, and feel that I did my whole duty towards them while serving as major, and afterwards as colonel, of the 6th Illinois Cavalry.

The year 1861 was drawing to a close without anything of great importance being gained by the operations of either the Federal or so-called Confederate armies. The government and its opponents had made the mistake to enlist soldiers into the service for too short a time, and both armies had been crippled by the discharge and return of soldiers to their homes when they were needed in the field. Both contestants were obliged to make greater exertions to enlist soldiers for a greater period, and it was more clearly understood throughout the whole country that the coming struggle must be fought out until victory should rest with one side or the other.[6]

I had accepted an invitation to dine in town on Christmas. The morning was clear and cold, and after having a battalion drill, I proceeded thence to take part in the proffered festivities. I would have greatly preferred to have gone to my home in Jacksonville to join our family gathering there, but as that was impracticable, I made a virtue of necessity and endeavored to make myself comfortable as possible among comparatively newly made acquaintances. I had been getting but little in the way of variety in food and was quite hungry enough to enjoy a change. The fine large turkey and savory delicacies which covered the table of the generous host and hostess, Mr. and Mrs. Docker, looked very inviting and proved very palatable. The result was that I ate right through the bill of fare and relished the meal hugely.

On the night of December 26, I attended a large party at the house of Mr. Richardson, a prominent citizen and wealthy merchant of the town. During the evening, I added somewhat to the entertainment by playing on the piano, violin, and guitar. A very nice supper was served about 10 o'clock, and the assemblage broke up about midnight, with many manifestations of enjoyment. I, for the first time, remained in town until morning, sleeping in the quartermaster's storehouse, on a bundle of blankets, with some of the same comfortable articles over me obtained through kindness of the obliging and popular quartermaster, Lieutenant John M. Snyder of the 6th Illinois Cavalry.

General Grant arrived at Shawneetown on December 27, and Colonel Cavanaugh came to camp and ordered the troops out for review. I laughed to myself at the idea of the regiment being reviewed by the general. But, feeling confident that the 3rd battalion could "pass muster" with the others, I promptly obeyed the order, and we were the first in readiness to march. When the regiment arrived in town, General Grant had already left for Cairo. The reputation of the 6th Illinois Cavalry did not suffer by the general's timely departure. The colonel, although apparently disappointed at the result of his futile efforts to trot out his command, courageously decided to review it himself. The performance excelled any farce I ever saw. All commands were improperly given by the colonel. The officers and soldiers were disgusted, and I could not help having the same feeling, with all due regard and respect for my commanding officer.

The last few days in December were mild and sunny, and I continued to drill my command effectually while the weather permitted. The officers and men were greatly encouraged at the progress made, and manifested a commendable zeal to excel the other battalions. I cheered them on to the best of my ability and found, much to my surprise, that I could command more self-possession than I had believed myself capable of, and succeeded without embarrassment in talking to nearly 400 soldiers when it became necessary. But I was cautious to not get it into my head that I could talk so well as to talk too much or too often. I looked forward to the future with more confidence and had stronger faith in the belief that I would live through and beyond the war, and began to appreciate the fact that if I could only be contented under the circumstances, I would in any event be independent of riches or well off without the things which usually represent wealth in this world. I realized with more clearness that there was a power above to bring all things even in the end and determined, in any event, to trust in the Lord and "to keep my powder dry." I did not anticipate any great or sudden change in myself and was aware that good resolutions not carried into effect were, as a rule, likely to do more harm than good. But, without any fear of danger to myself or others, I determined to aim higher, however much I might fall below the mark, having an abiding faith in the hope that I might climb up the ladder a round or two as I got on in years.

It being the last chance in the old year, I determined to pitch my tents and to procure some necessary articles for my comfort, so as to occupy them on the first day of the new year. I wondered if I should have to work another year without pay and borrow money to pay expenses. But I still had faith in the integrity and stability of the government, and could not help believing that honest, faithful work would in the end be recognized and paid for. In any event, it was creditable that my devotion to the cause enabled me to steadfastly continue on in the service of my country under such adverse circumstances.

———

The 6th Illinois Cavalry was mustered into the service on January 7, 1862, the officers being sworn in on that evening by the mustering officer, Captain Watson, U.S. Army. The payrolls were made out for the regiment and arrangements made for the payment to take place the following week, which would be a great relief to all the officers and enlisted men. No one in the entire command was probably in such need of money as myself. The colonel, who was figuring for a brigadier generalship, had gone again to Cairo and Springfield for the purpose of pushing his claims. He felt so sure he would get it that he provided, and had no better taste than to appear in, the uniform of that grade. The display proved to be decidedly premature, for he ingloriously failed to receive the appointment, which was subsequently conferred upon Colonel John M. Palmer of Illinois, subsequently a major general of volunteers, governor of Illinois, and at present U.S. senator of that state.[7]

Besides the knowledge that my long-delayed pay was needed for the immediate support of my family, I was also harassed by anxieties connected with [my] late business co-partnership. We had been recklessly pressed by a leading creditor at a time when our assets were more than sufficient to pay every claim, if judiciously handled. We had given up all the property we possessed, homesteads and all, and made an assignment which would have enabled us within one year to pay all debts in full, and have several thousand dollars left. The assignment had been broken through a technical flaw; our goods and effects placed in the hands of a receiver and sold for a mere nominal price. For instance the receiver, himself, bought for $30 a carriage and double-harness which cost $500, and other things were sacrificed in the same reckless manner. Having thus given up all and more than enough, we did not feel in honor bound to do more. Still, the continual pressure of the affair was exasperating in the extreme. Yet, one very common annoyance in such cases was spared—there were no reproaches from home.

Mrs. Grierson wrote on January 15:

I have seventy-five cents left, and Charlie a dollar and five cents; we am [sic] in no great need of anything, but I think your father will be wonderfully glad to receive some money. You speak of your youth being passed, but I scarcely think we are middle-aged yet. I certainly feel very young, and do hope, as you say, that we both will try to make the future, so far as is in our power, such that memory will love to recall it. I can say truly that I enjoy life now, with all its sorrows, privations, cares, and responsibilities, and am thankful that I have been allowed to live so long.

On January 18, 1862, the 6th Illinois Cavalry was paid to include December 31, 1861. Major Whitney, who made the payment, got out of money and had to pay some of the officers besides myself by draft on Cairo, where he had funds deposited. He would not pay the field officers further back than October 1, and refused at first to pay either Major Wood or myself at all. But we showed him our commissions, and by considerable talk, he finally concluded to pay us from that date. He would not pay the battalion adjutants or quartermasters, and as those officers were going to Cairo to see if they could not get their pay there, I concluded to send my draft by Lieutenant [Samuel] Docker to draw the money for me. The colonel would not give any of the majors permission to go to Cairo. He and his son, however, could both go home and that without leave of General Grant, the boy leaving immediately upon the receipt of his pay, by the way of Cairo, and the colonel the next morning, via Evansville, Indiana. I had but little time to arrange matters but wrote hastily to my father and brother, one letter to be mailed at Cairo and the other to be enclosed in an express package with money sent home. Out of the $594.60 received, $400 were forwarded to Jacksonville by express—$250 for my father; $100 for my brother; and $50 for Mrs. Grierson, not because she deserved less than the others, but that it would be well understood why such division was made. One hundred ninety-four dollars and sixty cents was returned to me at Shawneetown, out of which amount, after paying debts, I expected to purchase a horse, if a suitable one could be found in that vicinity.

In a day or two after receiving his pay, Major John Wood, who was much dissatisfied with the way affairs were conducted in the regiment, resigned and left for his home. And it looked as if other resignations would soon be made unless a change for the better could be brought about within a reasonable time. It was rumored that a brigade was to be formed of the 6th Cavalry and other regiments. Colonel Cavanaugh with his man Friday—Parson [James F.] Jaquess—was at Springfield pressing his claims with the governor for command of the brigade. It was thought that if he did not succeed in his aspirations, he would return and growl around "like a bear with a sore head," until his overbearing conduct towards his officers and men would result in displacing him from command of the regiment.

The latter part of January, the Ohio and tributaries became very high and overflowed their banks, making the roads almost impassable. The rise facilitated the movements of troops in some places and retarded them in others. But, altogether, it proved more advantageous to the Federal forces than the rebels. All communication between the town and our camp was by a roundabout way, as the water came within a few hundred yards of the encampment. I was in command most of the time, as the other field officers persisted in absenting themselves in town and elsewhere. It was a pleasure for me to remain in camp, as going to town would be sure to result in spending more or less money. The responsibility of taking possession of a meadow near the camp for a drill ground was assumed by me, although it was against the orders of the colonel, who was still away. But there was no other suitable place in the neighborhood, and the regiment was much in need of drill. If court-martialed for disobedience of orders for such an offense, it would at least look well on the record.

Since the regiment was paid off, there had been considerable drinking of whiskey, and it seemed almost impossible to keep the men from getting it. There had also been some gambling among officers and men. I, therefore, ordered the captains of the different companies to arrest and place under guard any soldier found gambling. They had a game of cards called "chuck a luck," which they had been playing using grains of corn, the value of which was understood between themselves. Some of the men had lost at that game nearly all the money they had drawn on payday. If seen playing, they would say they were only playing for fun, and the only way to stop it effectually was to have no card playing in camp. Many of the men had families at home, actually suffering for the necessaries of life, and it was well that the gambling should be stopped, at least while I was in command.

In the early part of January, some successes were reported by Colonel James A. Garfield[8] of [Brig. Gen. Don Carlos] Buell's[9] command, near the boundary line between Virginia and Kentucky. Subsequently, General George H. Thomas gained a substantial victory at Mill Springs,[10] which resulted in the death of General [Felix] Zollicoffer[11] and several hundred other rebels. Successful reconnaissances were also made by Generals C. F. Smith[12] and [John A.] McClernand[13] towards Fort Henry and Columbus, Kentucky, which opened up the way for more extensive operations. The capture of Fort Henry quickly followed, and soon thereafter the unconditional surrender of the rebels at Fort Donelson to General Grant took place.[14] Those great successes sent a thrill of joy throughout the entire North and dismay all over the so-called Confederacy. The Federal troops left back for want of proper arms and equipments were impatient, and it was with great satisfaction that we learned that the 6th Cavalry would soon be sent farther south, where they would at least be near the field of active movements.

The latter part of January, I received leave of absence from General Grant for seven days for the purpose of going home to visit and comfort my aged and invalid mother, who had again been dangerously ill. By permission of the general, I returned from Jacksonville by the way of Hamilton, Ohio, for the purpose of securing arms if possible, having learned that Gwyn and Campbell of that place had carbines on hand on an uncompleted contract previously made with General Fremont. By pushing the matter through the influence of Governor Yates with the War Department, the regiment was armed much sooner than if affairs had been left to the ordinary methods.

Upon return to Shawneetown, I found almost open war in the regiment on account of the great dissatisfaction existing towards Colonel Cavanaugh, and I had to listen to the complaints of the two factions. Nearly every commissioned officer of the regiment, but myself, had signed a petition to the colonel to resign, a copy of which had been forwarded to the governor. The colonel locked me in his room for three hours after my arrival and gave me his version of the story, which was verified by his friend Parson Jaquess, after which other officers of the regiment gave me their views on the subject.

Not having had any trouble with the colonel, nor anything whatever to do with the controversy, I deemed it best for the regiment and myself not to mix up in any manner with personal or official quarrels. The colonel had previously been editor of a Democratic newspaper and had secured the appointment of colonel through political or pecuniary motives, and utterly ignored its duties and responsibilities. In the interview with him, I urged the necessity, even at that late day, of his entering energetically into the work required, admonishing him that he should promptly acquire a knowledge of those duties of which he was deficient. Had he tried to do so, it would have afforded me pleasure to assist and befriend him to the utmost. But, he continued to skulk in his tent or spend his time in running to Shawneetown and Springfield, and hoped by political maneuvering to obtain a higher grade and thereby separate and relieve himself from his embarrassments.

On February 19, in compliance with instructions from Brigadier General W. T. Sherman, orders were issued by Colonel Cavanaugh for myself and battalion to proceed to Smithland, Kentucky, which, much to my relief, separated us for a time from the deplorable regimental entanglements. The instructions received, however, showed that the colonel was so ignorant of his command that he did not know or take the trouble to find out, even for official communications, the names of the captains of his regiment. Immediately on receipt of the orders referred to, we left camp, marched to Shawneetown, and embarked on a steamer for Smithland during a heavy rain which continued during the day and night. As there was a battery of artillery on board for Paducah and we reached Smithland about midnight in a violent storm, the boat continued on to Paducah and brought us back to Smithland on its return, as it was understood that the same boat was to take the remainder of the regiment to Paducah.

Many of the soldiers procured liquor at Shawneetown and got drunk. After we were under way, I made an examination of the canteens and emptied twenty or thirty which were filled with whiskey, and ordered the captains of the different companies to spill out all they could find. We had our hands full to govern the men, but succeeded very well. It was found that the barkeeper on the boat, who had been forbidden to sell any liquor of any kind to the men, was dealing it out on the sly. But when he was advised that the contents of his bar would be thrown overboard if the sale was continued, he was induced to quit his nefarious traffic. [Still,] it was necessary to place a guard around the bar to keep the soldiers from tearing it open.

To get the drunken soldiers aboard the boat at Shawneetown was no easy task, as they were running about the place swearing they would not go. A squad of the most sober men that could be found, armed with musketoons, was sent out to drive them on board. But they were very violent and boisterous, and the captains who had been ordered to empty the canteens shrank from any interference with so crazy a lot of men. It was important that they be thoroughly controlled at once, and a confiscation and emptying out of the whiskey was promptly carried into effect under my own supervision. The men bullied, threatened, and swore that neither the major nor any other officers should destroy their whiskey; that they would throw them overboard and take the boat. When their canteens were emptied, they started in a body for the bar. But by firmness and judicious management, the victory was won over them at last, and of course, they respected their commanding officer the more when their drunken spree was over. By morning, they became reasonably sober and were disembarked at Smithland in tolerably good order. As that town was under martial law, whiskey was scarce there and hard to obtain.

On the evening of our arrival at Smithland, I started up the Cumberland by boat for Fort Donelson to endeavor to procure carbines or pistols for my command from General Grant, presuming that he had taken some from the rebels, which would of course be given to the first who called for them if in need of arms. I returned well pleased with the trip, although no arms were obtained. The only well-armed rebel cavalry regiments at Fort Donelson made their escape during the fight. I rode all over the battleground and completely around the fortifications, which were very strong and evidently laid out by a good engineer. It was certainly astonishing that the rebels surrendered as soon as they did, and I judged they must have lacked proper discipline or courage. It seemed to me that our Illinois troops, alone, could have held the place against the whole combined force of the southern Confederacy.[15]

The boat upon its return was crowded with the wounded and sick, so that there was scarcely space in the cabin large enough to put one's foot down. Some of the poor fellows were terribly mangled, and it was a dreadful sight to see them in the depths of their suffering. Colonel John A. Logan—subsequently a distinguished major general of volunteers and U.S. senator from Illinois—was among the wounded.[16] One man, who had been shot through the head, died soon after the boat left the landing. Others were so badly wounded that it was evident they could live only a short time. It was impossible to find a place to sit down, except upon the upper deck. Finally about 3 o'clock in the morning, feeling very sleepy, I went below and luckily reached the back part of the ladies' cabin and slept on the top of the piano until daylight.

———

Soon after my return from Fort Donelson, I proceeded to Paducah, Kentucky, to procure blank reports and muster and payrolls for the use of the battalion. The troops at Cairo, Smithland, and Paducah were under command of General Sherman, who had his headquarters at the latter place. Upon arrival, I called to pay my respects, and found him to be a very courteous and agreeable gentleman. It was the first time we had met, and in view of all the stories that had been in circulation as to his being "crazy," I naturally scrutinized him quite closely.[17] [I] judged him to be a man of marked ability, and it was a real pleasure to me to hear him talk. He walked back and forth across the floor in a rather nervous manner during our conversation, occasionally stopping abruptly to give some orders to his staff officers. He was greatly pleased in view of the victory at Donelson, but said that the battle would cause the rebels to put forth greater exertions and that the war would be apt to last several years. Yet, he had no doubt as to the final result. At the time, I thought it would be well if the government had a few more such officers.

In response to the general's kind invitation, I again called at his office before returning to Smithland. While there, Captain [John A.] Rawlins[18] of General Grant's staff came in, having been sent there to confer with General Sherman in regard to the movement of troops. From what was said, it was evident that General Grant supposed he might be superseded by General Sherman, the latter being the senior brigadier general. But General Sherman promptly answered: "Tell Grant to do whatever he thinks best. He knows more about matters up the Tennessee than I do. I am not here to raise the question of rank with Grant. Tell him to go ahead and I'll send him troops as rapidly as possible." This occurred soon after the battle of Fort Donelson, but before Grant had received his appointment as major general of volunteers. That was the beginning of the pleasant acquaintance between myself and General Sherman, under whose command I subsequently served for a long time. Our relations from first to last were [in] every way most agreeable and satisfactory.

I also found Colonel Cavanaugh at Paducah with the 2nd battalion of the 6th Illinois Cavalry. He was stopping at a hotel, as large as life and twice as natural, and the officers and men were scattered about the town, apparently doing as they pleased. The colonel was still in bad repute, and it was reported that he would be tried by court-martial. He certainly could, to my certain knowledge, have been tried and convicted of absence without leave and neglect of duty. Smithland, although rather quiet and lonely to anyone whose time was not actively employed, proved to be a much more pleasant station than Shawneetown.

The battalion was mustered for pay on February 28 by the post commander, Major [Christian] Thielemann. My commission antedated his, but I did not raise the question of rank, believing my time would be more profitably employed if devoted entirely to my own battalion, instead of being fritted away with the details of post duty. So Major Thielemann continued to attend to the monotonous business at the post of Smithland. Upon completion of the matter, the payrolls were promptly made up, but from information received from the paymaster it was doubtful as to when we would be paid, as many of the regiments had not been paid for several months and it appeared only just that they should first receive their money before the troops who had been paid to include December 31, 1861.

In the meantime, I had made a scout up the country between the Tennessee and Cumberland rivers. Although the expedition was not of sufficient magnitude to call for [a] special report, it proved successful as we captured some property belonging to the rebels and brought in between fifteen and twenty prisoners. Upon return, I found myself in command, Major Thielemann having been ordered to Cairo or elsewhere on some special duty. I, however, let the adjutant attend to routine matters, merely examining papers to which my signature appeared to be indispensable.

Early in March, hearing that there were 400 carbines at Cairo, I proceeded there to obtain them, but upon investigation found, instead of the desired arms, some worthless muzzle-loading Austrian muskets, which of course would be of no service to cavalry. Upon return to Smithland, I proceeded to Hamilton, Ohio, to urge forward the shipment of arms promised from there. From thence, upon telegraph received from Governor Yates, I went to St. Louis and Springfield, but found no suitable arms at either place. The most satisfaction gained by those efforts was in seeing my family. Mrs. Grierson met me at Springfield and accompanied me to Tolono, Illinois, where I turned southward to rejoin my command, while she with the children went northward to make another visit with her parents in Chicago. With renewed hope in the belief that arms would soon be received for my command, I energetically resumed the duties which devolved upon me. As it was doubtful when we would receive any more pay, all the money saved from the amount first received was sent to Mrs. Grierson at Chicago.

On March 25, orders were received for all the troops at Smithland to proceed up the Tennessee River to report to General Grant. All was excitement and bustle as preparations were made for our departure, presuming that we would have to leave at once. But transportation could not be procured for several days and we did not get started until March 27. That day, however, the 3rd battalion, 6th Illinois Cavalry, embarked on board the steamer *Planet* for Pittsburg Landing, with instructions to report at Paducah to the commanding officer for further orders. On our arrival there, we found a messenger from General [William K.] Strong,[19] General Sherman having been ordered up the Tennessee River, with written instructions to stop the troops which had embarked at Smithland, unless they were fully armed and equipped for the field. As we had no arms but what God had given us naturally, except a few old sabers and musketoons, we had to disembark at Paducah, where the remainder of the regiment was detained for the same reason. We had been highly delighted at the prospect of getting into the field and, of course, felt greatly distressed at finding ourselves deprived of the long-wished-for privilege of entering within the belt of active operations. However, we were obliged to obey orders. Upon reporting at headquarters of the post, I obtained permission to place my battalion in camp on the bank of the Ohio River, about a mile below the town, where we soon pitched our tents and where I placed a strong guard around the camp to keep the soldiers from the town, where the officers and men of the other battalions were idling the time away wandering about in aimless confusion.

About the middle of March, it was reported that Colonel Cavanaugh had resigned, or forwarded his written resignation to General Halleck.

But, subsequently, he stated that the general would not accept it, so that doubts were entertained in regard to the matter, and most of the officers believed that he did not resign as stated. The feeling became more bitter than ever against him. It would have been a fatal mistake for the regiment to have entered the field under the command of a man whose conduct had rendered him totally unfit for the position and whose acts bore marked evidence of insanity. On March 31, there was a review ordered for all the troops at the post. My battalion was the only one of the regiment which put in an appearance on time, but it passed through the ordeal of inspection and review alright, and I was highly complimented by the commanding officer of the post.

The pressure became so great against Colonel Cavanaugh for not having his regiment ready for review that he again tendered his resignation. I learned that over thirty officers of the regiment had signed a petition to the governor of Illinois recommending me for colonel of the regiment. It was thought that nearly all other officers of the 6th Illinois Cavalry would join in the request, if Colonel Cavanaugh went out. I had made no effort whatever to obtain the position although ex-Governor [John] Wood[20] was very active in trying to force his son, John Wood, formerly major, on Governor Yates for the colonelcy.

Early in April, Emerson Etheridge[21] arrived at Paducah, en route to his home in Tennessee, and it was thought that a large force would be sent with him as escort. He visited our camp and made a speech to the soldiers and was very bitter against the secessionists. The lack of arms and equipments which detained my battalion at Paducah may have been the circumstance which kept it from disaster and reserved the 6th Illinois Cavalry for future success and distinction. It is very probable that I would have been captured with General Prentiss' division[22] had we been permitted to go on up the Tennessee, as we would have no doubt been ordered to report upon arrival at Pittsburg Landing to the general on account of the knowledge he had gained of me while I served with him as a staff officer.

Our food in camp was of the plainest kind, as it was almost impossible to obtain anything in the way of variety from the country to better the bill of fare. On April 4, I wrote to Mrs. Grierson: "Have not had anything good to eat lately and can almost smell the food cooking at home. Have some crackers, cheese, and pickles near at hand to nibble at occasionally, also a few chips left from the dried beef you put in my carpetbag, and the latter is greatly relished." Dried beef had become a byword in the family. I was very fond of it, and on a former occasion Mrs. Grierson had playfully enclosed some "Chips" of it in a letter which she gave to Master Charlie to post, instructing him not to tell anybody. He stopped by the way at his aunt's and, childlike, said, "there's something good to eat in papa's letter," whereupon the whole family smelled it out and said, "it's dried beef Charlie." The betrayal of the secret almost broke his boyish heart, and it was a long time before he would be consoled.

The high water in the Cumberland and Tennessee rivers, which had proved advantageous to the Federal forces during the advance upon and capture of Forts Henry and Donelson, became detrimental to the movements of our troops toward Corinth and the Memphis and Charleston Railroad. The first expeditions made in that direction proved fruitless, beyond giving some further information in regard to the enemy. It appeared that the rebel forces were concentrating in the vicinity of Corinth with a determination to prevent, by every possible means, an invasion of the Federals into the cotton states.

In the meantime, as the waters abated, our forces effected a landing from transports at various places up the Tennessee River and began to concentrate at Pittsburg Landing, deemed the most available point from which to make a forward movement then contemplated into the country occupied by the enemy. From all information obtained, it was evident that the rebels would make a desperate effort to recover the ground lost, or to prevent, as far as possible, a further advance of the Federal troops. General Buell's army was preparing to move to Savannah, on the Tennessee River, and everything indicated that a great battle would soon be fought near Corinth, Mississippi. Nothing of much importance had occurred throughout other parts of the West, and the Army of the Potomac was, "Macawber-like," waiting for something to turn up, probably for an advance of the enemy, and little was doing in that army beyond the routine duties of camp life. Altogether, the successes gained by our troops towards the heart of the so-called Confederacy were highly encouraging to the loyal people throughout the country, and many were led to believe that the end of the war was near at hand.

From the first information received at Paducah of the battle of Pittsburg Landing, or Shiloh, it appeared that our army had been badly repulsed or, if the victory was ours, it was very dearly won.[23] It was evident that our troops had been too much scattered in front of the rebels to concentrate promptly to repel their sudden and unexpected attack, which brought about the disaster of the first day's fight. It was said that General Lew Wallace failed to come [in] time with his division when expected and greatly needed; that he lost his road in making a nine-mile march, when it would seem that the cannonading might have guided him to the battlefield.[24] It was thought at the time by many that the delay was intentional and that he expected to win laurels by coming into the fight and whipping the rebels after General Grant was repulsed and beaten. Subsequent reports greatly modified the first received, but it appeared that there was serious trouble between Generals Grant and Wallace in regard to the matter, which was not adjusted for a long time afterwards. Previous to General Grant's death the difficulty was arranged to the satisfaction of both officers, General Wallace being exonerated from blame and the serious strictures which were at the time cast upon him. When more was known about the battle, and full reports received, it became quite evident that the victory was gained in the end by the Union forces, although the rebels had the best of the engagement during the first day of the fight.

I have heard hundreds of officers and men who were engaged in the battle of Shiloh give their versions of the fight and I do not think any two are alike, but all different in many particulars. The rebels claimed that the Federals were surprised, which is indignantly denied by the Union generals engaged. From all the information gained on the subject, I am of the opinion that, if our troops were not surprised when they found that the whole rebel army was in their front and making an attack in earnest, they were certainly very greatly embarrassed. The battle of Shiloh has ever since been a matter of controversy, and it is probable that it never will be satisfactorily settled in the minds of the contending parties.

On April 13, 1862, Governor Yates, his adjutant general, and the secretary of state of Illinois arrived at Paducah en route to Pittsburg Landing. With other officers, I went on board the steamer to pay my respects to the governor and, much to my surprise, came off soon after colonel of the 6th Illinois Cavalry, with my commission in my pocket received without any effort on my part, notwithstanding the great exertions made by several other persons to obtain the position. Besides Lieutenant Colonel [John] Olney of the regiment, who was doing everything possible to obtain promotion, Lieutenant Colonel Harvey Hogg of the 2nd Illinois Cavalry and a captain in the regular army recommended by General Pope and others were actively engaged seeking the appointment. And Major Wood pressed his claims to the last, having several friends on the boat making the trip with the governor on purpose to obtain for him the colonelcy. But it was all without avail. It was a big jump from the position of junior major to that of colonel of the regiment, but it was made by me without self-seeking or outside influence, and purely upon my recognized fitness for the place. The lieutenant colonel was said to be inefficient. Major Wood was strongly backed by outside influence, his father being an old politician of great wealth—lieutenant governor and governor of the state—but the major had previously abandoned his position in the regiment in disgust at difficulties which I had patiently and successfully encountered.

Governor Yates proposed that I accept the lieutenant colonelcy of the 2nd [Illinois] Cavalry, so that he could make his friend, Lieutenant Colonel Hogg of that regiment, colonel of the 6th [Illinois] Cavalry. The latter had been a very active politician, and had been of service to the governor, and was really a promising officer and very talented man. The proposition was probably offered as a compromise. But I had once before tried entering a strange regiment over the heads of other offices. And, although I had then made a success of it, I did not wish to repeat the experiment. The majors of the 2nd Illinois Cavalry, in the event of a vacancy above them, were really entitled to promotion in preference to any outsider. And besides, I had become attached to the officers and men of my battalion, and had gained the confidence of my command, and disliked to be separated therefrom. I, therefore, thanked the governor for his great kindness, but declined to accede to his proposition and, kindly bidding all good-bye, turned to leave the boat. I had just reached the shore when the governor called to me, saying that he had forgotten to introduce me to some of his friends on the steamer, among whom were several ladies, who were musicians like myself. Upon his invitation, I returned on board and walked back to the ladies' cabin where, approaching the party assembled, he exclaimed, "Colonel Grierson of the 6th Illinois Cavalry, ladies and gentlemen, a very young colonel, just five minutes old," at once taking from his pocket and presenting to me my commission, it having been filled in with my name and signed by the governor while I was leaving the boat.

The regiment was still unarmed. The 300 carbines I had procured at Hamilton, Ohio, were shipped but not received. While going on board a steamboat at Paducah and by chance meeting General Sherman there, having heard that there were some arms at Cairo, I asked of him an order for carbines from the quartermaster in whose possession they were said to be stored. The general quickly answered: "No use, Grierson, no use at all. There are no arms there." But I persisted, and the general went to the bar of the boat and wrote the desired order. Upon handing it to me, [he] said, "there, there you won't get any."

Proceeding at once to Cairo, I presented the order to the quartermaster, who said, "no carbines here, issued the last yesterday." But assuring him that my information made it clear to my mind that the desired arms were there, I prevailed upon him to go with me. Upon search, we found 150 new Sharps carbines that had in some manner been shoved aside and overlooked in the issue made the day before. The quartermaster hesitated about letting me have them, but was finally prevailed upon, being assured that they were greatly needed and would be taken up on my papers and properly accounted for.

It did not take me long to get them on board the boat. Upon reaching Paducah that evening, meeting the general again, I told him of my success. "How did you find out they were there?" said he. "By keeping my eyes and ears open" was the reply. The general smiled and extended his hand, which was warmly grasped. From the look he gave, it is evident that he judged I would succeed in getting arms for my regiment.

Having been appointed colonel of the regiment, many applications were received soliciting the appointments of battalion adjutants and quarter-masters, some of those positions having been vacated by the resignation of the officers who had filled them, who not being able to draw pay, were not inclined to serve under such conditions; there being also doubt as to the legality of their appointments, although commissioned by the governor of the state. Among the applications received was one from my brother, John C. Grierson. In answer, I wrote him:

> By letter from the Adjutant General at Springfield, Illinois, it ap-pears that according to law, or order from the War Department, no extra lieutenants are allowed in cavalry except the adjutant and quartermaster. Battalion adjutants and quartermasters are only allowed where the battalions are separated, and they must be lieutenants of the line, selected from one of the companies of the battalion. I therefore have no power to appoint anyone outside of the regiment to those positions. Of course, there are many appli-cants for every place to be filled and I must act in such manner as will in my judgment give satisfaction to the regiment. I would be glad to have you with me as adjutant and know you would fill that position much better than anyone who is likely to get the appoint-ment. But I cannot now, under all the circumstances, satisfy my own mind that it would be best for you to accept such a position, even if it were in my power to appoint you. It would be hard for both of us to be away and far better that my life be risked for the good of all concerned than that you be placed in a position where yours would be more or less in danger and both of us be away from home at the same time. You may not, it is true, be making much money in your business, yet it is better that you remain where you are for the sake of the old folks. Although my pay now as colonel is $253 per month, and we are much in need of money, still nothing on earth can repay anyone who has a heart in the right place for being away from the loved ones at home. It is almost impossible to obtain leave of absence and will most likely be so until the end of the war.

Before the end of April, I had succeeded in securing sufficient carbines and pistols to arm my command quite well. On the 30th of the month, I was ordered by the commanding officer of the post to muster my regiment, which was for the first time since its organization done according to regulations, the muster being preceded by a review and minute inspection. The post commander complimented me highly on the very marked change in the appearance of the officers and men. I was tolerably well pleased with my management of the regiment, and was rather surprised to find that the responsibility did not weigh very heavily on my shoulders. Nearly 200 of my men had returned the day previous from a five-days' scout, all safe after having captured a number of rebels, with their arms and equipments. Another scout was ordered out for the day following the muster.

I remained constantly in camp. As usual, for want of better, [I] wore my old clothes, and [on] the whole, some may have thought me a rather common-looking colonel. But I felt just as well as if I had fine clothes on and was occupying a fine house for headquarters, like the post commander and some other officers of less rank.

It required both moral and physical courage to bring about the marked improvement in the rough western men of my regiment, who were [more] inclined to fight than to obey orders. The officers and soldiers of the 1st and 2nd battalions had scattered themselves throughout the town. I issued orders for them to come into camp. The "bullies" vowed they would not. Captain [George W.] Peck, who had been a soldier in the Mexican War, went around and found his men, and brought them in at once. Other captains quickly followed his example. Captain [James B.] Morray, however, who had gained a reputation as a great fighter and bully, swore he wasn't going into camp until he got ready. I sent him word to come at once or he would be made to come, and ordered Captain Peck with 150 men to find Captain Morray, with his company, and bring them in. Captain Peck was keen to go for the fun of the thing. But just as they mounted, Captain Morray and his company made their appearance in no gracious mood. When told where to camp, he blustered out that it wasn't a fit place, and his men wouldn't go there, and he would take them where he thought best. I told him on the spot that he should camp there and nowhere else, and that at the first sign of mutiny in his company the captain would be the first man shot down in their presence. Captain Morray gave no further trouble after that.

On May 5, I received two months' pay, part of which was for service as major and part for that of colonel, amounting to $392.20, all of which was sent home, excepting enough to square my indebtedness at Paducah and pay my friend Safford, banker at Cairo, one hundred dollars which he had kindly loaned me in an emergency. On the previous day, nearly all the Union people in the town and adjoining country were frightened out of their wits by a portion of the 5th Iowa Cavalry, about 150 in number, rapidly making their way into the town, having been attacked the night before, near Dresden, by a large body of rebel cavalry. A number were killed, some taken prisoners, and all others put to flight. Some stragglers arrived on the morning of the 6th and others came in during that day. Great numbers of Union men from northern Tennessee and southern Kentucky also came into town, saying that they thought the rebels intended to attack that place.

I sent two companies, under command of one of my best officers, at once in the direction from which the rebel force was said to be advancing. Captain Loomis, who was soon to be commissioned major to fill the vacancy occasioned by my promotion, was directed to watch the movements of the enemy and to give timely warning of their approach in order that the balance of the regiment and all troops could be placed in readiness to repel any attack that might be made. The entire force consisted of one company of artillery and [the remainder cavalry],[25] amounting in all to nearly 1,000 men. It was found that the rebels had retreated southward, upon which information the usual quiet was restored.

I greatly wished to have Mrs. Grierson visit me in Paducah before we should be yet more widely separated. Notwithstanding the liability of my being ordered away, she came with our oldest son [Charlie], a boy six years old. She, for some forgotten reason, did not telegraph to me from Cairo as directed, and was annoyed there somewhat by the officious attentions of some unknown officer, who expatiated about the trouble of getting through the lines and offered to procure passes for her. She finally got rid of him and reached Paducah on the steamboat about 3 o'clock in the morning.

The hotel was a dirty, vile-smelling place, the sleepy clerk rough as such hotel clerks usually are, and certainly it was an uninviting place to rest. The moon was shining full and bright without, and she knew my camp was about a mile below the town on the river bank. She reasoned that rogues and vagrants would be housed at that hour, and taking her child by the hand, walked down the river shore. When she found the ground soft and muddy, she went up the bank and took the road which seemed to keep nearest the river.

She walked on in the moonlight until the child exclaimed: "Why mama there's the fort. Don't you see the big guns?" They went a little further, until they came upon the sentinel's beat, and walked up to him and said: "I'm Colonel Grierson's wife. Can you tell me where his camp lies?" He answered, "Just beyond that little hill." A few steps further, she met the guard coming to relieve the first sentinel. He being relieved followed her and said, "Mrs. Grierson, I will show you the colonel's tents." And so, without the least trouble whatever, they reached them.

She knew them by description, passed [from the] first one to the sleeping tent beyond, lifted the flap, and said, "Ben?" I started up with a spring and a word, not yet recognizing her voice in my sleep. But she knew mine and, turning to the guide, said, "All right, thank you," and entered. Imagine the pleasure with which I ate breakfast next morning, [and] told of my surprise and capture. She remained at Paducah about three weeks, boarding at a house near the camp, and during the visit spending an hour or two with me every morning at the headquarters of the regiment.[26]

There was another incident of that Paducah visit which clearly showed Master Charlie's Irish descent. One day, while watching the artillery firing across the river, he saw a skiff with two men in it hastily making for the shore, apparently greatly alarmed by the firing over their heads. Speaking of the occurrence afterwards, he said: "Why mamma, they just took to their heels and rowed as fast as they could."

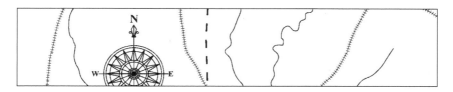

4. Scouting after Guerillas in West Tennessee

About the middle of May two men, citizens of Illinois appointed judges for the purpose, came to Paducah, to take the vote of the Illinois troops for or against the new constitution, which was deemed by the Republican administration to be very faulty in its construction.[1] I took the trouble to inform the soldiers of my regiment in regard to its imperfections and the necessity for voting it down. It was quite satisfactory to observe, after the poll was taken, that only two votes were recorded for it out of the entire vote of the officers and men belonging to my Egyptian Democratic regiment.[2] It required some talk in the right direction to bring about such a satisfactory result.

A Masonic Lodge had been formed in my regiment, and I had become a Master Mason and expected by dispensation from the Grand Lodge of the State of Illinois to become a Royal Arch Mason. But, owing to movements southward and the fact that the regiment for a time became separated, I never succeeded in carrying out the design as contemplated. The 2nd battalion of the 6th Illinois Cavalry had some time previously been ordered to Columbus, Kentucky, and it was thought it would march from there by the most practicable route to Memphis, or to the line of the Memphis and Charleston Railroad. Towards the end of May, reports reached us of fighting in the direction of Corinth and it was thought that we would all soon be ordered farther south.

On May 30, Mrs. Grierson took her departure for the North. Her visit had proven a great satisfaction to both of us and, although I wished her to remain longer, she had become almost as anxious to see Robert, our youngest son, as she was previous to her arrival to see me with Charlie—but had really determined in her mind before leaving home that she would not be likely to prolong her stay at Paducah for more than two weeks. I hoped that on the next visit she would be able to bring both of the children with her, and thus be better contented than if separated from one of them.

Subsequently, my letters, as usual, spoke of the routine duties of camp life, movements of troops, etc., while hers from home, not only then but always, told of the little daily incidents of domestic life. The children are sick with the measles; the servant falls down stairs and is helpless for a few days; the walk to church; the chat with the neighbors; the new things the baby learns are the events noted. But the soldier in camp hungers for those trifling details as the stayers-at-home hearken for news from the seat of war.

And the motive power of that great machine of destruction of the army was really generated at home. Mrs. Grierson would cheerfully forego every luxury and endure any fatigue or privation to come to see me whenever a favorable opportunity offered, but she never, under any annoyances or discomforts, asked me to quit the army and come home. In all transactions, whether of the miserable Meredosia business, which still hung over us, or in the tiresome delays or dangers of military experiences, she never appealed for one single moment to any other consideration than the one idea of duty and the highest nobleness of character.

The stories of poisoning our men during the war were usually regarded as merely sensational newspaper reports, but it was true that at Paducah soldiers were poisoned by milk, buttermilk, and provisions which were sold to them by rebels. Skiffs and flatboats were moved along the shore near the camp for that purpose and the soldiers were frequently tempted to purchase something to better the army ration, but at the peril of "death in the pot." Attempts were also made to poison the wells and springs in the neighborhood, from which the soldiers obtained water for drinking purposes.

The secessionists of Paducah were very bitter and violent, and before the place was occupied by our troops, fiendish outrages were perpetrated on Union men. The family of Mr. Woodward were well-known residents and much esteemed there, and the seniors of the family were not much molested. But S. L. Woodward,[3] one of the sons—a young man who was not slow to express his patriotism and his detestation of rebels—was threatened with tar and feathers and given twenty-four hours to leave the city as he valued his life. It was no unmeaning threat with them, as many Union men had been tarred and feathered and sent adrift down the river with their hands tied behind them. And young Woodward, knowing that his life was not safe, took the first favorable opportunity to proceed to Cairo for the purpose of reporting the matter to General Prentiss, who was in command there. The general, being busy at the time, referred the matter to me to confer with Mr. Woodward to ascertain the facts and decide what action should be taken. After hearing all he had to say on the subject, and finding that we were at the time powerless to render him any assistance,

I advised him to enlist in the Union army, so that he could have a chance to retaliate on the rebels for the ill treatment received at their hands. There were some troops of cavalry then organizing in Illinois, opposite to Paducah. He soon after went there and enlisted in Captain [John M.] Boicourt's company of the 6th Illinois Cavalry. Some months later, he was detailed as clerk at General Sherman's headquarters and was with the general at the battle of Shiloh.

The two battalions from Paducah were ordered to Columbus, Kentucky, about the middle of June, and the regiment concentrated there, excepting two companies, which to the best of my recollection, had been sent to Bird's Point, Missouri. On June 17, I embarked on the steamboat *Crescent City* for Memphis, Tennessee, with five companies of my regiment, the other five companies being ordered southward on a scout. We arrived at Memphis at 4 o'clock on the afternoon of June 18. We had to leave our wagon transportation at Columbus, as there was not room on the boat for it. Upon disembarking, [we] could not procure teams to take our camp equipage out that night, but had to haul it out the next day to an enclosure known as the race track, where we were directed to encamp.

Four of the five companies were ordered on a day's scout to the southwest, while I reported in person to Colonel [James B.] Slack, the post commander, who in turn ordered me to report to General Lew Wallace. I had an hour's talk with the general and found him very pleasant. He had only arrived in Memphis the night before, with part of his division, and had only one battalion of cavalry under his command. [He] said he would have plenty of work for us and hoped the remainder of the regiment would soon arrive. Two regiments of rebel cavalry were reported in the vicinity of Hernando, Mississippi, about twenty miles south, said to be the advance of a large force moving northward with a view of attacking the Union forces at Memphis. I slept in the open air the night of our arrival, and did not feel any the worse for the exposure.

We found Memphis to be a decidedly "secesh" city—saw but one Union flag in the place, besides that at General Wallace's headquarters. We found the dear ladies very bitter in their feelings and particularly displeased at the arrival of the Union troops. They would spit and turn their backs upon us as we marched through the city. The wife of a rebel officer, who was driven in a very nice carriage by a darky, stopped and asked me if I was a Federal officer, to which I responded, "Yes." She then asked what we intended doing with the "secesh" ladies. I told her we expected to treat them as they deserved. She said she supposed we would allow them to be savage and do as they pleased. I told her that no lady would conduct herself in that way. She said that she understood we intended to take all their servants away and allow the people no privileges at all. I told her that none but very ignorant persons could possibly believe so. "Well," said she, "I think you should allow the ladies to do as they please." I told her we expected to do so, as long as they pleased to do right and behave like ladies; that all traitors, whether male or female, would be treated as rebels to the government; that the rebellion would surely be put down and that the sooner she and all others like her were making peace with God and our country the better. She then waved her hand to me and directed her servant to drive on. I returned the salute, thinking she was perfectly welcome to all she made out of me.

On June 19, we received orders from General Wallace to proceed southward to Hernando, and left immediately with five companies of the 6th and two of the 11th Illinois Cavalry, numbering in all 315 men, on a forced march to attack rebels reported at that place. We arrived at Hernando at 5 o'clock in the morning of the 20th and found that the rebels had departed and that the telegraph wire had been taken down; that Jeff Thompson, who was in command of the rebels, had retreated to Coldwater Station, twelve miles south. Upon making a thorough search of the town, we succeeded in arresting some stragglers from [Colonel William H. "Red"] Jackson's cavalry.[4] We concluded to move immediately on Coldwater Station and bridge to attack the forces reported there, some 400 strong. Lieutenant [Frank] Lindsey of the 1st Illinois Cavalry, who reported to me half an hour after my arrival at Hernando with a detachment of twenty-five men of his regiment, was left in Hernando as a rearguard, with instructions to follow us in half an hour after our departure.

We pushed forward to Coldwater Station, hoping to reach that place before the cars would leave. When within three quarters of a mile and to the right of the station, hearing the locomotive, we dashed on to a point south and beyond the station, sending at the same time thirty men to attack the guard said to be at the bridge two miles north. Unfortunately, we were a few minutes too late to capture the train on which Jeff Thompson was leaving, but soon enough to charge with impetuosity upon the rebels who were assembled at the station to attack us. We succeeded in killing three, wounding seven, and capturing nine with their horses, arms, and equipments. Among those was a lieutenant who was endeavoring to escape on Jeff Thompson's horse, which was killed in the engagement.

In the meantime, the detachments which had been sent to the railroad bridge, upon their arrival there, found the bridge burning, capturing one man upon the bridge, whom it was presumed fired the incendiary match. Finding it impossible to subdue the flames or pursue the enemy further in that direction, the detachment rejoined my command at the station.

Upon searching the depot, we found 15,000 pounds of bacon, a quantity of lard, and forage, which we rolled out, set on fire, and totally destroyed. At the same time we burned the car, which was evidently to be used in transporting the stores above mentioned to A. M. West, quartermaster general of Mississippi, to whom they were marked. In the mail captured was a letter dated June 19, directed to Major Ben Bynum, which indicated his movements, [and] also a copy of notice by T. J. Morris to the citizens of DeSoto County, north of the river, to have their cotton prepared for burning, which had been thoroughly carried into effect so far as we could judge from our scout.

Receiving from various sources information, which we deemed reliable, that Jackson was approaching Coldwater Station with 800 cavalry and was expected that day, and that larger forces of rebels were stationed below Senatobia on the railroad—having accomplished the object of our expedition as far as possible, our horses unfit for further rapid travel, and the men being in the saddle sixteen hours without rest—we started on our return and camped for the night three miles north of Hernando. During the night, our pickets were fired upon but promptly returned it, compelling the rebels to retire without venturing an attack on our camp.

The face of the country which we passed over between Memphis and Hernando was flat and heavily timbered. Numerous small creeks interspersed the country, over which were thrown corduroy bridges, poor in construction and not very safe. Beyond Hernando for about eight miles the country is hilly and broken, until within three miles of Coldwater Station, where it becomes suddenly flat and the creeks running through it are small and winding with steep banks, the timber very heavy, and the soil deep and miry, the streams being almost impassable for cavalry without the aid of bridges. During the expedition, the officers behaved coolly, bravely obeying orders [and] cheerfully and gallantly charging what they supposed to be a much larger force than their own. The command returned to Memphis on the evening of the 22nd, having accomplished the object of the expedition without the loss of a man.

On June 23, after writing my report of the scout, I was sent for to report in person at General Wallace's headquarters. [I] immediately obeyed the order, presuming that I was required for another scouting expedition. Upon arrival at headquarters, the message proved to be for an entirely different purpose, as much to my surprise, I found General Grant there with General Wallace. Saluting those officers upon entering the room where they were sitting, I handed my report to General Wallace, who glanced it over and then gave it to General Grant, at the same time instructing me to report to the latter officer for further orders. There was a very marked coolness manifested by the two generals towards each other. General Grant appeared to be not only dissatisfied with General Wallace for his failure to come [in] time with his division at the battle of Shiloh, but also apparently for his entering Memphis without proper orders or authority.

General Wallace asked if a leave could be granted him. General Grant inquired how long a leave was desired, was informed, and merely said he would issue the necessary orders. General Grant then turned towards me and said: "I will read your report attentively, but am already informed in regard to your successful expedition into Mississippi and will soon have other important work for you and your command; will send for you again to come and see me, perhaps this evening or tomorrow morning. I must write a letter now to General Halleck." I had a very pleasant interview with General Grant the next day, in which he stated that he would get up an expedition to move eastward along the line of the Memphis and Charleston Railroad and that he would give me command of some regiments of infantry, in addition to my cavalry; that he had read the report of my expedition, and complimented me highly on my success and promised to give me plenty of work for the future.

In a subsequent expedition southward into Mississippi, a rebel mail was captured by our advance, which in addition to information gained in regard to movement of the rebels, contained a letter written by the wife of General [James R.] Chalmers,[5] which makes reference to, and gives some amusing incidents of, my first raid southward from Memphis, from a southern point of view:

I received your letter yesterday when I had despaired of ever hearing from you again. The Yankees have been to town. Father got here Friday evening and said he expected that they would be here the next day. So he came to help me out. Sure enough, Saturday morning about 5 o'clock Mary Jane came bolting in: 'Mrs. Becker, the Yankees is coming.' I immediately rushed to the window, and there they were in splendid style in full gallop.

As soon as they got in town they separated and went to every house in which there were soldiers staying. They rushed up to Jim Tate's house and were upstairs before anybody had time to turn around except Mrs. Tate. She pushed three soldiers in her pantry. The other one she pretended was her young brother and went on terribly when they insisted upon taking him, and even kissing him at parting. She acted her part so well that they turned him loose, but a little boy told on him.

They went to Dr. Temple's looking for Jeff Thompson, who was not there, but Major Woodford and a captain passed off for citizens and were not suspected. Clate Jones and Pad Smith were at home and had to run. They chased some of our cavalry down to Coldwater, and if they had taken all of Jackson's cavalry, the people in this country would have been glad, for they are playing the wild generally. One of the Yankees told Mr. Jones that the war would end when we killed ourselves running off, and they killed them- selves running after us. They took Dr. Temple's horse. He went to see if he could get it back. The colonel told him he didn't see how it could make any difference with him as he was a good Union man. Whereupon Dr. Temple told him he would as soon be the devil, for which insolent language he was taken and carried to Coldwater and back down to Memphis.

The cars would have been taken, but Sally heard they were at Coldwater, and as the train was coming up, she ran out with some- thing white and waved them back. They took Colonel White's car- riage and horses. Mrs. White told them they were her horses and they ought not to make her suffer for what Mr. White did. I would not say that to them. They did not come near this place, I suppose they knew there was no one here but me, as they knew everything else, even the names of the soldiers. They said if they could catch you they'd hang you so high the birds would not get you.

They say Mr. Dean is the one who informed them. Mr. Ford told them he was a Union man. They told him to go off, he was a d——d liar. They asked Mr. Meriwether for the key of General Chalmers' safe and if he did not have Confederate bonds in it. He told them there was none in it and offered them the key, which they did not take. But the funniest thing was their going to see Mrs. Waller. They asked her where her husband was. She said, 'I have none.' 'Then where is your sweetheart?' 'I have none.' Then, in a very insinuating voice, 'Where is the Doctor?' Whereupon she cursed them good. They told her that they would take her to Memphis. They made her give [them] the doctor's clothes. The Cairo papers and [Memphis] *Avalanche* say McClellan is whipped and 30,000 prisoners taken by us.

While the capture of Tuscumbia and Huntsville, Alabama, in April, by troops from Buell's command was looked upon as an important matter, as it gave the Federal forces possession and control of over 100 miles of the main artery of communication of the rebels and deprived them of the means to concentrate their forces, it was also thought that had General Halleck, in his advance on Corinth, displayed less technical science of the theory and art of war and substituted therefore a little of the brute force and native stupidity accredited to the volunteer officers of the army at that time, and forced the rebels into a general engagement, instead of letting them escape as he did, the end of the war might have been hastened. His exaggerated reports, giving the impression that what was really almost a defeat for us was a tremendous victory, were decidedly misleading and injurious to our cause. Even had prompter measures been taken to rapidly capture the lines of communication from the rebels, far greater successes would have been gained. At the same time, it appeared also that the slow, methodical movements of the Army of the Potomac afforded another example of too much time spent in preparation and display of military knowledge, instead of taking greater risks with the greater chances for that success which is rarely attained except by prompt and decisive action of an army in the field in the face of a vigilant enemy.

On June 27, 1862, I was ordered by General Grant to proceed with the effective force of the five companies of the 6th Illinois Cavalry then at Memphis to Germantown, Tennessee. To enable me to carry out his instructions, the 52nd Indiana and 58th Ohio Infantry regiments were added to my command. Those regiments were considerably depleted, but the whole force amounted to about 1,200 officers and men.

Upon arrival at Germantown, scouting expeditions were sent out in all directions without finding the enemy, reported to be 2,000 strong and marching upon that place. We encamped three miles east of the town, near the Memphis and Charleston Railroad, where the track had been torn up and a bridge and train of cars burned by the rebels, who hunted down with bloodhounds the Union soldiers on the train when it was wrecked [and] as they attempted to escape. In view of that manifestation of barbarity, the bloodhounds in that section of the county were promptly reduced in number. Over twenty bloodhounds were killed, and if the savage owners who set them on our men could have been caught, they would have been treated in the same summary manner. Some arrests were made of persons said to be implicated, and the prisoners sent to the provost marshal at Memphis. The darkies in the neighborhood were jubilant at the appearance of Union troops and relished the reduction made of the number of dogs, which were kept especially for hunting them down and preventing their escape to parts occupied by Federal troops. The cavalry was out night and day, scouting in all directions, and the detachments began to return without being able to capture prisoners or make arrests.

The Fourth of July we celebrated to the best of our ability, by speaking and hurrahing for the heroes of 1776 and the defenders of the Republic and for everybody engaged in fighting to perpetuate the Union. In the afternoon, in obedience to summons, I proceeded with a small escort to Memphis to see General Grant, who expressed himself highly pleased with my successful operations around Germantown. By his direction,

Colonel [Joseph D.] Webster[6] sent out a battery of artillery to be added to my command.

For greater convenience, and in order to attend to matters which came before me for decision, I had to make my headquarters in town instead of in camp, and the railroad depot was taken possession of for the quartermaster's and commissary departments. The position I then held was similar to that of post commander, and my duties became much more varied without being more agreeable. I constantly came in contact with various grades of secessionists, and had many cases new to me to decide. I got along very well, did not hear of any complaints from headquarters, and gave as good satisfaction to the rebels as could be expected under the circumstances.

Nearly all of the cotton in southwestern Tennessee and northern Mississippi had been burned by order of General [P. G. T.] Beauregard.[7] Small lots, however, that had been hidden away by some of the planters, were quietly hauled inside of the lines at night to be taken to Memphis for sale. In accordance with instructions received, many wagon and dray loads, which belonged to men who would have been for the Union if they dared, were passed through the lines. Many of the planters were exasperated at the burning of their cotton, and it was thought that Beauregard's action in causing its destruction would work to the advantage of the Union cause. The people gradually became aware that our troops were not there to disturb the persons or property of peaceably disposed citizens. Their eyes were opened to the true state of affairs, and they began to see that they had been misled by misrepresentations as to the intentions of the Northern army and the Federal government.[8]

There were large numbers of Negroes in that section of the country, and many were giving "leg-bail" whenever an opportunity was afforded. Although no encouragement was given them by our troops to leave their homes, when they came inside of the lines they were not molested or driven back again and were simply given passes and no questions asked in regard to which way they were going. Hearing that the Episcopal minister in that place was going to pray for Jeff Davis, I took occasion to attend church to listen to his utterances, but he did not make use of any disunion sentiments. If he had, my instructions would have obliged me to arrest and expel him from the sacred desk and remove the congregation from the church, cause it to be closed up and the keys delivered at headquarters.

For a time, I arranged to board at the hotel in the town, where a comfortable room could be had for office purposes which opened on the front porch on the lower floor. There was a large yard about the house, filled with trees and shrubbery, where at almost any hour of the day or night, the guards could be seen walking their beats in front and rear of the building. General Grant had ordered a telegraph line to be erected between that point and Memphis, and it was thought the cars would soon be running again between the two places.

The people of the town and vicinity were beginning to find out that the Yankees were not such terrible savages as they understood them to be. The ladies in particular, who were not to be seen for several days after our arrival, began to promenade the streets of the town again, and many of them even called and found me to be, as I learned afterwards, according to their statements, "a very pleasant, intelligent and agreeable gentleman." I took particular pains to let a little light into their darkened minds. Nearly all had brothers or husbands in the rebel army, and several promised that they would use their influence to have them come home and take the oath of allegiance.

On July 8, reports were received from various sources that the rebels were concentrating some fifteen miles southward for the purpose of attacking the troops at Germantown. The pickets and guards were increased and scouts sent in the direction that the rebels were reported to be advancing. It was reported that a larger force was concentrating at or near Coldwater Station, where we previously had a fight, and rumors had also reached Memphis that we were fighting the rebels at Germantown.

That night, about 12 o'clock, a messenger arrived from General Grant with an escort of about thirty cavalrymen, which had to remain outside as they could not get through the pickets. The messenger was brought in, and was quite surprised to hear we had not been attacked. I got out of bed and wrote a long letter to General Grant, giving him information in regard to the movements of the rebels, their whereabouts, etc., which I afterwards learned was very satisfactory to the commanding general. I received a reply from him the next day, giving instructions for my guidance. He also informed me that he wanted about 100 able-bodied Negroes, in addition to those already there, to work on the fortifications at Memphis, and directed me to forward them by the next wagon train which was to be sent to Memphis for supplies. Detachments were pushed out at daylight to gather the Negroes up at the different plantations in the vicinity, with instructions to take those of the planters who were known to be the strongest secessionists. The Negroes were promptly obtained and were on their way to Memphis by 12 o'clock that day. General Grant was greatly pleased with the promptness with which the order was carried into effect.

He also sent another messenger, with the information that the rebels were concentrating at a point some twelve or fifteen miles south from Germantown to surprise and attack my command. It was gratifying to be able to inform the general in return that I had already sent sufficient force to that place to attack the rebels and prevent them from concentrating, so that it was impossible to surprise or attack us. We had scoured the country in every direction and knew for certain that there was no force sufficiently strong, from which danger need be apprehended, within a distance of forty miles of Memphis, notwithstanding there were numerous reports of overwhelming forces of rebels gathering to gobble up my command and take possession of that city. General Grant had a hearty laugh over the receipt which I gave for the levied Negroes, of which the following is a copy:

Germantown, July 10th, 1862.

Received of Mr. —— this 10th day of July, 1862, —— negroes, who are to be used on works at Memphis, in pursuance of instructions received from Major-General U.S. Grant, Commanding District of West Tennessee; said negroes to be returned when the work is completed, unless in the opinion of the Commanding General, the conduct and bearing of their owners should not justify or render such a course advisable.

B. H. Grierson,
Colonel, Commanding United States Forces

Having received a receipt for 106 Negroes from the commanding officer at Memphis, it might be surmised that I was running a rather extensive plantation. It was quite astonishing to see how happy those darkies were after they were gathered together [and] before they started for Memphis. They put in the time singing and dancing, and had a good time generally. It put me in mind of the old song: "A nigger will be nigger whether slave or free." The poor souls, so little did they know, that they imagined that they were absolutely free. They were all very anxious to go, and did not need a guard to keep them from running away. In less than two days after I sent those to Memphis, fully fifty more came in to know if they were not wanted too. But as I had filled the order and a little over, of course I could not accommodate them with an escort, but merely passed them out to make their way home again or to their "new Jerusalem."

Soon after, General Grant left Memphis for Corinth, leaving Brigadier General [Alvin P.] Hovey[9] in command of the troops at Memphis, to whom we were to report for further orders. I had selected a new camp for my command and moved my headquarters to the depot building, which we found much cooler and more suitable for the purpose.

After Memphis was in [the] possession of the Union troops, so that it was thought loyal men could be safe there, my brother John C. Grierson, whom it will be remembered had been obliged to leave Memphis at the breaking out of the war, sold out his business in Jacksonville and returned to Memphis, hoping to again find more profitable occupation. The following is a quotation from a letter written by him to Mrs. B. H. Grierson, dated July 17, 1862:

> This morning I was very agreeably surprised by Colonel Grierson walking into the office of the Gas Light Company, where I was sitting. He and nearly all of the command are in tolerably good health. He visited Memphis under orders and was in town but a short time. It was his first visit after his departure from Memphis and I was lucky in meeting him, and both of us were very agreeably surprised as he had not heard of my arrival here. I thought he would shake the arm off me. The shirts and collars you sent, I delivered to him personally, and as he had not time to do so himself, he desired me to write to you and send you many thanks and love to all at home. It may be that he will be ordered to Memphis with his force, as the general talk here, street talk of course, is that the rebels intend to take Memphis. But, in my opinion, should the attempt be made, the city will be a mass of ruins before it is effected.

This visit of mine to Memphis was at the time that General Hovey, alarmed at exaggerated reports, sent orders out to me to return at once to Memphis with my command. From the information obtained, knowing that it was entirely unnecessary to do so, I rode into the city with a citizen, in a buggy [and] without escort, to thus prove the entire security of the vicinity, and succeeded in prevailing on General Hovey to delay or rescind the order. But soon after my return to Germantown, he again became anxious about the rumored attack and, to my intense disgust, issued orders for our immediate return. We arrived at Memphis on the 18th, as an attack was expected to be made upon the city that day. At the time we left Germantown, we had about three days' rations and forage on hand for the whole command, all of which General Hovey ordered me to destroy. Knowing that to be unnecessary and unwise, I did not obey the order. Instead of doing so, I pressed in teams, wagons, and darky drivers from the neighboring plantations and brought everything safely to Memphis. I told the general about this when we arrived, and he was very well pleased and said it was much better than to have destroyed the provisions and forage or to have left it there for the rebels.

We marched through the city in good order, with the band of the 58th Ohio discoursing fine music. The column consisted of five companies of the 6th Illinois Cavalry, the 58th Ohio and 52nd Indiana regiments of infantry, and one battery of artillery, followed by the train belonging to each regiment, with a suitable rearguard. We stirred up quite an excitement and let the rebel sympathizers know that, should the city be attacked, there would be more Yankees to whip before the place could be taken. For several days, my time had been so much occupied with the various official matters which required my personal attention that I had slept but little and had been almost constantly in the saddle for forty-eight hours.

We had been almost lost among the different changes of commanders since our first arrival at Memphis five weeks before, having passed in that brief period through the hands of Colonel Slack, Generals Wallace, Grant, [and] Hovey, and finally came under General Sherman, who arrived in Corinth with his division and assumed command. None of those officers claimed that the 6th Illinois Cavalry belonged to their commands, although they all wanted us badly. General Grant was at Corinth in command of the Western Department, General Halleck having gone east.

In my judgment, had the latter not been placed in command of the western army after the battle of Shiloh, the end of the war would have been materially hastened. Even after his great failure at Corinth, had he made judicious use of his large army and moved promptly southward into central Mississippi and Alabama and opened communication with the Union forces in Louisiana, the sieges of Port Hudson and Vicksburg would have been obviated, the Mississippi River opened without a struggle, and the Confederacy effectually cut in twain. And, thus, very great advantages would have been gained. Instead of doing so, however, he foolishly scattered his large and effective command, which resulted in placing the Federal troops in Tennessee, Mississippi, and Alabama on the defensive for a long time, and consequently led to the sacrifice of many thousands of lives and much treasure.

On July 27, we were ordered out on a four-days' scout with my entire effective force of cavalry, from which we returned in due time alright, having had three successful skirmishes with the rebels, killing two, wounding several, and taking twenty prisoners, among them one lieutenant colonel, one major, and two lieutenants. Our advance received the fire of the enemy several times while charging, but none of our men were killed and only one or two slightly wounded. General Sherman was greatly pleased with the result of the expedition.

We had marched over 100 miles and returned to Memphis on August 1, where we moved into a new camp in a beautiful grove about one and a half miles from the city. The place belonged to Old Doctor Gilbert, a well-known resident who lived in a large house, well furnished with more pictures than I ever saw in a private residence, including a fine piano and an organ, which cost $2,000, from which the doctor ground out music in abundance. He had kindly asked me to dine with him and the invitation was accepted. The food proved to be palatable, everything being gotten up in fine style. The doctor informed me that his daughters were all married and his sons in the rebel army; that he had taken the oath of allegiance and was probably about as good a Union man as the majority in that vicinity. He had no one at home with him then except his wife. Both were kind to me, and upon their request, I placed a guard at the house to prevent any depredations from the soldiers.

My brother, John C. Grierson, was still at Memphis, and the following extract from a letter written by him to Mrs. Grierson, will show the rash manner in which he sought amusement:

> Last Friday night Matt Star[r],[10] myself, and a man named Benham went out scouting a distance of twenty miles back of Memphis into the hot-bed of guerillas and were gone all Friday night and all day Saturday. We obtained much valuable information and captured three prisoners, one of whom was a Confederate spy. We were fired upon several times and our man Benham shot one scamp through the bridge of the nose. We had a good time generally and got back safe and well and are the lions of the regiment. Now that it is all over I must admit that I would not like to make the same trip again.

This scout was made without my knowledge, and the three adventurers were severely reprimanded by me for their recklessness in venturing so far outside of the lines.

——

It quickly became evident that General Sherman did not intend to permit the grass to grow under the feet of the cavalry horses, or to let their riders suffer for want of suitable exercise. Besides the picket duty we had to perform, detachments were kept scouting in the vicinity, and whenever more than a company left camp for that purpose, I was sure to go along. The entire country was soon known so well that our troops could travel night or day with facility, regardless of roads; were always sure to reach any point started for unobserved; rarely traveled the same route twice in succession, and were thus enabled to pounce down upon, surprise, capture, or scatter the rebels without loss or injury to our command. The general [Sherman] was pleased to state that: "The rebels quickly learned to fear Grierson's cavalry and were soon obliged to keep a full day's march distant from Memphis."

About the middle of August, a court-martial was convened by General Sherman for the trial of Colonel [Thomas] Worthington for drunkenness and other offenses. The court consisted of three brigadier generals and nine colonels. General S. A. Hurlbut[11] was president and I the junior member of the court. I had no acquaintance with Colonel Worthington, but had seen him riding about the streets of the city in a drunken condition. He was very talkative at such times and would, in a boasting manner, assert that he was more competent to command the army than either Halleck, Grant, or Sherman. He was cruel to his men, arrogant to his officers, and insolent at times to General Sherman. He had a supreme contempt for the volunteers, while he showed his own incapacity by building a fort out of cordwood at Collierville, Tennessee, only fit for Indian warfare, as the splinters of wood from artillery fire would be as dangerous to his own command as the shot and shell of the enemy. General Sherman was the first witness who testified before the court-martial, which was in session about two weeks. During intervals, or adjournment, I went out scouting as usual.

About this time the government, as a means of retrenchment, reduced the pay of officers of the army, and my pay was thus lessened about forty dollars per month. As cigars were high in price and poor in quality, I concluded that it would be well to quit paying out any money for them. Mrs. Grierson wrote me that she thought it a very sensible conclusion. Although I smoked before and during the war, I was not really a slave to the habit, but dallied with the luxury now and then. Mrs. Grierson, as all good wives usually do, urged gentle objections—said it spoiled my kisses, etc. And I, as most men do, answered with occasional serious thoughts, which however depended very much upon whether or not the cigars obtained were really worth the smoking.

Letters from home were so slow and irregular in reaching me that arrangements were made to address them in care of "Secretary of the Gas-Light Company," which seemed to avail for more prompt delivery. It must be remembered that the residents of Memphis were strong secessionists. The secretary of the Gas-Light Company was Mr. William Fitch, whose first wife was a sister of Mrs. Grierson.[12] His second wife was wholly Southern, but he was strongly for the Union. When the Union men were driven out of the city, he was permitted to remain, as he was the only person there capable of managing the gas business. He stayed to protect his property, but afterwards said that he would not pass through such an experience again for any amount of money.

The 6th Illinois Cavalry had been separated at Paducah and Columbus, Kentucky, and it was only by the most strenuous efforts that it was gotten together again. But, by repeated applications to Generals Grant and Sherman, it was finally, by General Grant's orders, concentrated at Memphis. Some companies of the 4th Illinois Cavalry, which had been temporarily with General Sherman's division, left on August 25 to relieve the five companies of my regiment at Trenton [Tennessee]. The arrangement was very gratifying to me, as it had been rather hard to do the work required with only five companies. Five companies of the regiment had been stopped at Trenton, when en route to Memphis from Columbus several months before. One company had been left at Paducah and one sent to Bird's Point. Three companies of the seven absent [were] being used as escorts to brigadier generals. I wished the detached companies to receive the same drill and discipline which had made those under my eyes so efficient, and thus have a larger force for longer enterprises. It was by such means that the 6th Illinois Cavalry was brought together and enabled to gain its subsequent brilliant reputation. About that time, I was appointed chief of cavalry by General Sherman, who hoped to retain me permanently with his division, although he feared that General Grant had given the order for the regiment to be concentrated for special service with his own immediate command.

On the last day of August, I was directed to inspect and muster for pay Thielemann's Cavalry, in addition to my own. When I was a major at Smithland, Kentucky, Major Thielemann mustered my battalion for pay, and it seemed as if turn about was only fair play. Ten companies of my regiment were present for muster on August 31, and the other two were expected to join my headquarters early in September.

In compliance with [a] letter of instructions from General Sherman dated September 4, I left camp quietly on the same evening, with 160 men, on another scout southwestward into Mississippi for the purpose of breaking up some rebel organizations said to be concentrating in that section of the country. We returned on the evening of the 6th , having had a hard fight with the rebels who outnumbered us four to one, but over whom we gained a complete victory. During the expedition we killed twenty-three, wounded between forty and fifty, and captured over thirty prisoners with their arms, horses, and equipments.

The hardest fight took place near Olive Branch, about fourteen miles from Memphis. We had been beyond Hernando and had a skirmish there the day before, capturing twelve prisoners, after which we swooped around to the westward and encamped near the Pigeon Roost road, which leads southwestward into Mississippi. The rebels collected about 600 mounted men and followed us from 11 o'clock that day until 7 o'clock next morning, when they suddenly drove in our pickets and attacked us while part of our command were engaged in eating breakfast. They advanced two dismounted companies upon us, holding the remainder of their force in reserve. I promptly ordered my men into line, just back of a slight rise in the ground opposite to the corrals where most of our horses were feeding, and [threw] out skirmishers along the fences on the right and left, from which our men poured volley after volley into the ranks of the advancing foe. At this time I did not have over sixty men in line, but they firmly held their ground and the rebels in check. Noticing that their lines began to waver, I ordered about twenty men to mount and led them in a charge, chasing the rebels in confusion to their reserve.

Our rations having been exhausted, I had sent the balance of my command under Major [James D.] Stacey to a plantation about a mile distant to take breakfast. Upon the first alarm, I dispatched a messenger with an order to the commanding officer to attack the rebels in rear and flank. After our charge upon the enemy, our position was very critical for a few moments, as they opened fire upon us and sent more men to the right and left than we had engaged, with the evident intention of surrounding and capturing us. We were within pistol shot of the rebel line, and I saw that we must fall back unless the force under Major Stacey should immediately attack their rear, which they then failed to do. But they had heard our firing and did the best they could to reach the scene of action.

I ordered the men to fall back slowly to our first position, sending skirmishers to the right and left to ascertain if the rebels were really flanking us. Finding that they were not, and seemed to be hesitating about advancing, we wheeled to the right about and moved steadily upon them, driving them back. Just at that moment, we heard the firing of the guns of the force under Major Stacey. Thereupon, [we] promptly charged upon the rebels again, scattering them in every direction as they, in hot haste, used guns as whips to urge away their horses. We followed the larger part of the retreating enemy several miles, everywhere finding traces of their hasty retreat.

After pursuing as far as prudent, [we] returned to the battle ground and gathered up their scattered arms, horses, and equipments. We found that some civilians had been busy carrying the dead and wounded into neighboring houses. In the house where some of the wounded men had been taken, they had washed and taken care of their dead, but had not touched our living wounded men. One of them had his mouth and eyes so filled and covered with clotted blood and mud that it was almost impossible for him to breathe. So much for the humanity of secession sympathizers. The darkies were the only persons who showed any good feeling towards us, and they were happy over the result of the fight.

All the officers and men behaved with coolness and courage, with the exception of one sergeant and two men who, at the commencement of the fight, became so much alarmed that they ran away to Memphis and reported to the commanding officer of our camp, and also to General Sherman, that I and my entire command had been taken prisoners. A force was immediately sent to our assistance and soon met a detachment of our men with the prisoners, when the truth became known. General Sherman expressed himself as highly delighted with the result of the expedition and presented me with a beautiful carbine with silver mountings, which had been captured from the rebels. The clothing of many of the men was completely riddled by balls, and five or six of them had their horses killed from under them. But I soon mounted them again on captured horses.

During this expedition, I sent from Hernando, Mississippi, to Memphis fifteen men of my command, whose horses were unfit for further rapid travel, in charge of prisoners under the command of Lieutenant Nathanial B. Cunningham of the 6th [Illinois] Cavalry. When within about twelve miles of the city, he was fired upon from ambush by a party of guerillas. [Cunningham was] instantly killed and a number of his men wounded. His death, however, was soon avenged by a detachment that was sent out by order of General Sherman, under command of Major [Reuben] Loomis of the 6th Illinois Cavalry, who pursued, captured, or destroyed the murderers.[13]

In the entire expedition, we had one officer killed and seventeen men wounded, not including myself. I received slight wounds on the ends of my first and second fingers of the left hand. Two balls passed through my coat, a linen duster with a cape, and one through my pants just above the knee. Three balls took effect on my horse. We fought against great odds. During the thickest of the fight, a runaway from Stacey's detachment reported to us that the major and his men had all been taken prisoners. That was discouraging information, but we still fought on and won in the end. After this encounter with a superior force, which warranted my immediate return to Memphis by the shortest route, I traveled some ten or fifteen miles out of the way to make the arrest of several citizens in the vicinity of White's Station, on the Germantown road, in order to complete in full the instructions that had been received from General Sherman.

In a subsequent expedition, the rebel report of this engagement was captured. In it, the commanding officer stated that he had dismounted two companies to move forward to take in the Yankee colonel and his party, while a detachment was sent north on another road from Olive Branch to ascertain where the larger portion of the command had gone; that in the midst of the fight an overwhelming force came suddenly upon their flank and rear; and that he then discovered it was a trap to surround and capture them. But, fortunately, he succeeded in getting away with the larger part of his command. It also stated that a man in a linen coat, who was evidently giving orders, was especially singled out. Several sharp-shooters [were] sent along the fence to reach him, but their aim failed to take effect.

In a letter referring to this scout, written by my brother to Mrs. Grierson, after giving the main incidents of the engagement, he stated that:

> Ben's clothes are perfectly riddled with bullets but he was not hit save on the ends of his fingers; he is well and safe, thank God. You can imagine my feelings yesterday about noon when I received a line from M. H. Starr saying that Ben and his whole command were that morning taken prisoners, and you can readily understand how rejoiced I was about five o'clock P.M., to hear that the report was false and that he was victorious in the fight. Ben is in a fair way to become a lion. He was in front of his men during the whole engagement, which lasted about one hour; he pursued the enemy southward several miles and made them skedaddle beautifully. There appears to be a mutual satisfaction between Ben and his men as to his and their conduct. They say they have a brave colonel and that he has the best fighting regiment of cavalry in the service.

In conversation with General Sherman relative to further movements, he stated that he thought it was General Halleck's plan to remain on the defensive in the West and not to commence aggressive operations until late in the fall. When out on the last scout I learned by the capture of a rebel mail that Price and [Maj. Gen. Earl] Van Dorn[14] were moving towards Corinth, with the evident intention of attacking that place. General Grant's forces had been much reduced by sending troops to General Buell, who was being driven northward into Kentucky by [General Braxton] Bragg's army.[15] The Confederates were also inaugurating an active campaign in Virginia, forcing our armies to fight on the defensive, and the outlook everywhere was decidedly discouraging to the Union cause. Frequent changes of commanders were being made, and General Halleck, under whose control all were operating, was demonstrating the fact that sooner or later, to insure success, someone must be found to command the armies of the United States who had sufficient ability to combine the Union forces and cause such concert of action as would result in marching onward and southward to victory.

The mails became more regular to and from the North and it was very gratifying to be able to hear from home more frequently. I wrote to Mrs. Grierson whenever an opportunity afforded, always sending messages for the children.

On September 8, orders received from General Sherman directed me to have the entire effective force of my command, excepting suitable details for picket duty at Memphis, ready for inspection by himself at any time between 3 and 5 o'clock that day, after which I was directed to proceed with it to a point beyond the Nonconah where it crossed the Pigeon Roost road, and there report to Brigadier General Morgan L. Smith,[16] commanding expedition, who had received full instructions in regard to its object. In compliance with the orders received, I left camp accordingly about 6 P.M. that evening, marched to the place designated, reported to General Smith, and by his direction encamped for the night about three miles beyond the Nonconnah. On the morning of the 9th, we proceeded to Olive Branch, where a number of arrests were made and the prisoners sent back to General Smith. Two miles further on, my advance surprised a detachment of rebels, killed one and captured several, pursuing the fleeing enemy several miles in a southerly direction. After a forced march of five miles, [we] came up with them again and continued the pursuit beyond the Coldwater in the direction of Cockrum's Crossroads. When within about two miles of the latter place, we suddenly came upon a large force of the enemy consisting of parts of Jackson's and [Colonel R. A.] Pinson's regiments of cavalry and two companies of Mississippi Mounted Infantry, numbering in all between 800 and 1,000 men, strongly posted in a well-chosen position, protected by heavy timber, broken ground, and deep gullies or ditches, which were in places filled with mud and water. We were so close upon the rebels that retreat would have led to disaster, and I instantly saw that there was but one thing to do to insure success and that was to attack them vigorously, which we did. Directing portions of my command to the right and left, [I threw] out skirmishers, rapidly moving at the same time forward to the ditches and gullies in front of the rebels, who poured volley after volley upon us as we advanced. Their shots, however, passed harmlessly over our heads.

We, upon gaining the protection of the ditches and gullies above mentioned, opened a vigorous fire upon the enemy from all points, which proving destructive, they soon fell back. We pressed them closely through the woods for a mile to a large field, at the edge of which they rallied, endeavoring to make a stand. That portion of my force which was dismounted and fighting on foot having remounted, with our entire force I directed an impetuous charge upon their flanks, preventing them forming into line, and drove them in a confusion across fields a distance of quite a mile. Here gaining the protection of heavy timber and fences and the advantage of rising ground they, by gathering their scattered forces, attempted to make another stand. Pushing forward the center, frequently admonishing my men to keep in good order and fire low, the rebels yielding under this movement on their left and center made a desperate effort to flank our left. I then ordered the main portion of my force against their right, resulting in the complete rout of their whole command, which scattered and fled in every direction.

We pursued as far as we could see any of them. Then halting, [we] reformed, congratulated each other upon our signal success, sent three rousing cheers for the Stars and Stripes reverberating through the woods after the skedaddling foe, and returned through the battle ground, gathering up the arms, horses, and equipments, which in the rout and disorder the enemy had abandoned, bringing with us our few wounded to Coldwater Bridge.

The enemy were well armed with breech-loading carbines and revolvers—a portion, the mounted infantry, having muskets and rifles—but they failed for some reason to use them to advantage. We killed of the enemy during the engagement forty-one; wounded between seventy and eighty; took forty prisoners with their horses, arms, and equipments; and killed fifteen of their horses. Fortunately, we had but one man killed and four wounded, and seven horses killed in the engagement. We moved from the battle ground in good order, taking our wounded with us.

[As] we were re-crossing Coldwater, an alarm was caused by stragglers reporting the enemy moving in force to attack us. I soon got my men in position on the right and left of the bridge, and advanced with one squadron mounted and one dismounted. After scouring the woods and finding no enemy, we returned and moved on until we came to a road leading to Robinson's Crossroads, from which point I sent a messenger to General Smith with a report of our successful engagement. Subsequently, I learned that an officer of my command, for some unaccountable reason, became so bewildered during the fight as to take the responsibility to send, without my knowledge, a report to General Smith to the effect that a large force of infantry was in our rear and that we were in danger of being cut off, which caused both his command and mine considerable extra and unnecessary marching, the responsibility for which was placed where it should properly rest, the officer referred to being obliged to resign his commission in order to avoid court-martial.

Joining General Smith on the morning of the 10th, by his order I afterwards took the advance, proceeded to Hernando, and camped for the night. During the day, a detachment of my cavalry had a skirmish with a party of mounted rebels, resulting in the killing of one man and horse and the capture of twenty rebels by the infantry, among whom they were driven.

On the morning of the 11th, after scouring the country in every direction, we followed the infantry southwards toward Coldwater, passing them and pressing to the front when within two miles of the bridge over that stream, which upon approaching we discovered to be on fire and guarded by a force of rebel cavalry stationed on the opposite side. Of those, we killed one and succeeded in driving away the balance and saving the bridge from destruction. From that point, the bridge having been repaired, upon the arrival of General Smith, by his direction, I proceeded to Coldwater Station on the Mississippi and Tennessee Railroad, and upon arrival there, found that the enemy were retreating in the direction of Senatobia. After burning the depot and contents and three railroad cars, we pushed on after the retreating rebels, driving them before us, kicking up a big dust, to within two miles of Senatobia. But, not having time under my orders to pursue them further, we returned and rejoined the infantry at Coldwater Bridge.

One of the men who had straggled behind was fired upon between Coldwater Station and the bridge by guerillas and wounded, and one man accidentally shot himself after our return to the bridge, causing his death in a short time. Returning to Hernando, we encamped for the night. On the morning of the 12th, after the departure of the infantry and artillery for Memphis, I, by direction of General Smith, proceeded eastward on the Holly Springs road, where we came upon the enemy's pickets, fired upon them, and drove them towards Coldwater. Returning through Hernando, I learned that the enemy had felled trees in a number of places across the road we had marched over in our approach to that place the day previous.

Passing General Smith on the Hernando and Memphis road, I left a portion of my force with him and pushed on to Memphis. During the day's march, we were twice fired upon by guerillas, but without injury. Where all acted so praiseworthy, it is here deemed invidious to particularize, as all officers and men obeyed orders cheerfully and promptly, bearing themselves gallantly, and bravely fighting against superior numbers.

While I was scouting south of Coldwater, General Smith with his infantry took and destroyed the large railroad bridge over that river, including the trestle work on both sides of the stream, which was the main object of the expedition. In speaking of my command, General Smith was pleased to state in his official report that: "The 6th Illinois Cavalry, under command of Colonel Grierson, behaved admirably throughout the expedition."

From prisoners captured on this expedition, I learned of Captain Peck's gallant attack, with fifty-three men of the 6th Illinois Cavalry, on [Captain W. W.] Faulkner's command near Dyersburg.[17] He completely surprised them, killing twenty-five, [and] taking fifty-three horses with arms and equipments. It appears that [Faulkner's] company had crossed the Tennessee River, with orders to go into Kentucky and burn cotton. They traveled in the night and encamped to sleep during the day. Captain Peck learned of their whereabouts from two Negroes, who guided them around their pickets. They had at that time received recruits from Dyer, Lauderdale, and Hickman counties. Some of the men of Faulkner's command who made their escape were in the fight at Cockrum's Crossroads and assisted in getting up the ambush to retaliate and destroy my command in the fight near that place, which resulted so disastrously to themselves.

My official report of the expedition was handed to General Smith on September 13, and on the same day, in a letter to Mrs. Grierson, I wrote:

> The rebel cavalry that attacked us is considered the best the South could produce, being armed with carbines and revolvers and well mounted. As we approached the enemy, finding difficulty in getting flankers across the ditches and gullies on the left near which the road crossed, I had for better protection led my column some distance to the right of the road, through uneven ground. I was immediately in rear of the advance and at the head of the column, which was well closed up and marching by fours. With a view to look back towards the rear of the column, I had wheeled my horse to the left, and just as I did so, the rebels raised up from the opposite side of the ditches referred to, where they had been screened by fences, and fired upon us without effect, except the terrific noise which reverberated through the woods and echoed from the surrounding hills. Not a man left his position in the column, which I immediately wheeled to the left and ordered to charge. Thereupon, the men passed over the ditches and gullies, which had before seemed impassable, as if they had not been there at all. The fences beyond the ditches, behind which the rebels had been posted, disappeared as if they had been struck by a cyclone, as our men charged mounted against them, firing volley after volley from their carbines as they dashed on in pursuit of the retreating foe through the woods for nearly a mile. During the engagement, a carbine ball passed just over my right ear so close as to cause the ear and head to be swollen and painful for a few days. During the expedition, we reached a point farther south than any Federal troops had been inland at that time southward into Mississippi.

Learning through a staff officer at General Sherman's headquarters there was a probability of Mrs. Sherman visiting the general before the active movement southward would take place, I arranged for Mrs. Grierson to visit me. She arrived in Memphis, with Masters Charlie and Robert, on September 20, 1862.

The camp of my regiment was still at Gilbert's Grove, some distance out of town. Mrs. Grierson accepted the invitation of her brother-in-law and his hospitable, but southern, wife to visit them, and with our two children remained for several weeks at their house. In the meantime, General

Sherman assigned the depot of the Memphis and Charleston Railroad to me for headquarters. Upon leaving Mr. Fitch's, we occupied two rooms in the depot formerly used for office purposes, where we found an old bedstead for which we bought a mattress and borrowed some bedding from Mrs. Fitch and also a crib for Robert, using a camp bed for Charlie. Our cooking was done over the open grate, and we bought only just enough dishes and kitchen utensils to answer for such limited apartments. Occasionally, Mrs. Grierson would prepare some little delicacy and take it over to Mrs. Fitch's stove to bake. Altogether, we relished the food and got along quite well.

Sometime in October, my brother, John C. Grierson, was appointed quartermaster of the 6th Illinois Cavalry. His office and quarters [were] also in the Memphis and Charleston depot. There, his wife and young daughter joined him from the North, so that after a time quite a family party gathered at the common table. One evening, while at the theater, General Sherman received information which brought him suddenly to my quarters. Upon arrival, he bolted in unannounced, as he had repeatedly done before, but a change had come upon the scene. The housekeeping was just begun, the night was cool, and a bright fire was burning in the grate. The children were asleep in the corner and Mrs. Grierson sat on the floor paring apples for mince pies. The bed was wheeled out before the fire to serve as a table, whereon I had spread my maps and was as usual studying the face of the country.

General Sherman had never heard or thought whether or not I had a family, and was quite surprised on his entrance. "Why what's all this?" said he half retreating. But I, in my shirt sleeves, quickly answered: "Come in, come in General, don't be alarmed." [I] introduced Mrs. Grierson, explained about her recent arrival, [and] told him I was studying up the surrounding country and the whereabouts of the rebels. "Alright," said the general, "that is the place I want you to go," pointing the place out on the map as he approached the bed. He chatted in a pleasant manner for some time with us, showed us an intercepted letter, perhaps that from which he obtained his information, written by a rebel woman and with which he was highly amused. She spoke of the different commanders that had been at Memphis, mentioning the names of Slack, Wallace, Grant, Hovey, and others, and then said: "Now we have Sherman and he is the wiriest rat of them all. He keeps the Yankees raiding around in every direction so that the people in the surrounding country can't have a minute's peace or rest." [She] stated that, if she could only buy, borrow, or steal a postage stamp, she would write again, soon. It was evident that the general would cheerfully furnish her stamps for the pleasure of reading such letters.

Within an hour after General Sherman left the room, I with 250 men of my command left Memphis for a scout across Wolf River to the place designated, between Collierville and Summerville. By daylight, we reached the vicinity of the rebel camp and found that they had picketed a bridge about a mile in front, on the road by which we were advancing. As we neared the bridge, we came upon a wagon load of forage which was being taken into their camp by a darky driver. We took possession of the wagon, driver and all, turned out the forage, put men into the wagon, covered them with fodder, and then had them driven over the bridge where, upon arrival on the opposite side, the soldiers jumped from their hiding place upon the rebel pickets and took them all without firing a shot. My whole force then crossed and surprised and attacked the rebel camp, killing four, wounding many, and capturing about twenty prisoners and scattering the remainder in every direction. If we had fallen from the skies, they could not have been more surprised. This success was accomplished without loss or injury to my command.

My mother had been in feeble health for many years, and during the summer months had had a stroke of partial paralysis. My wife had remained at the homestead taking care of her until the middle of September when, thinking it was probable that the invalid would live without much change for several months longer, she joined me with the boys at Memphis. My mother, Mrs. Robert Grierson, died on October 8, 1862. I had sometime previously endeavored to obtain leave of absence to go and see her again, thinking I could bring my family back with me to Memphis. But the leave could not be granted me, and only those who have been placed in a similar position can fully realize my feelings on learning, or hearing, of her death. She was one of the best mothers, kindhearted and loving, and greatly revered by her children. The gradual decay of her faculties, both physical and mental, during the year preceding her death had, however, in some measure prepared us all for her final release.

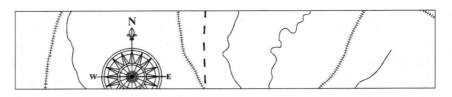

5. From Iuka to Holly Springs

The battle of Iuka,[1] fought in September [1862], demonstrated the fact that the rebels were concentrating their forces to make vigorous effort to regain the territory they had lost. From their movements, it was plain to see that Corinth was their objective point. The attack of Van Dorn, on October 3, was precipitated with a view of gaining that important position before General Grant could succeed in getting reinforcements there. Although the defeat of the rebels at Corinth was not followed up as vigorously as it should have been, yet in my judgment General [William S.] Rosecrans deserves great credit for his decisive victory in repulsing the desperate attacks of the rebels.[2] The result was of great importance. His achievement was not fully appreciated at that time, but the general's assignment to an important command in middle Tennessee soon thereafter was only a just reward for the services he had rendered. The necessity for an aggressive movement of the Union forces into Mississippi became imperative. General Grant, who had been assigned to the command of the Department of the Tennessee in the latter part of October, soon proceeded to make his arrangements accordingly, and the inspiriting effect upon the troops so long kept fighting on the defensive was readily observable.

From the middle of October until the latter part of November, numerous scouts were made in West Tennessee by myself and command, all of which were successful. General Sherman, when he took command at Memphis, was somewhat inclined to undervalue the service of the cavalry and, in a general way, looked upon it as more expensive than useful. But, seeing was believing with the general, and he was soon led to recognize its worth when he saw that it could be effectively handled.

A much larger force of rebels had been ordered for duty in the vicinity of Memphis and greater efforts were being made to organize and recruit their forces in northern Mississippi and western Tennessee. During that time, much was done by my command, under the direction of General Sherman, to "nip in the bud" those rebel organizations. I well remember an expedition made [during] the latter part of October.

Information had been received of a regiment forming northeast of Memphis, in the direction of Covington, Tennessee. The general did not like to risk sending me with the cavalry alone so far, lest I might be intercepted and cut off from return. In looking over the map, I proposed that instead of returning direct to Memphis, we make for Randolph on the Mississippi River, if boats could be sent there to transport my command back to the city. "The very thing," said the general, delighted. For, by such arrangement, I could get along with less men and accomplish the object without loss or serious injury to my command.

To disguise the movement, a large force of infantry under command of Colonel [David] Stuart was sent out on the Somerville road while I, with 150 picked men, marched rapidly east from Memphis some twenty-five miles, where we had a broken skirmish with the enemy a few miles north of Collierville. [We] then swooped around, joining the infantry about fifteen miles from Memphis, on the Somerville road, where we encamped for the night. The next day, after making a forward demonstration, Colonel Stuart with the infantry returned leisurely to Memphis, while I moved on northward across the Loosehatchie.

While carefully approaching and preparing to cross that stream, I rode forward to the bank to reconnoiter. [I] was recognized by the enemy as the commanding officer, and suddenly received the concentrated fire of a company of rebels that had been screened behind a bank that lined the opposite shore. It seemed a miracle that I was not shot and, fortunately, did not lose my presence of mind. My men, who were near at hand, charged upon and drove the pickets from the bank. In less time than it takes to relate it, we were on the other side of the stream in pursuit of the retreating foe. We proceeded rapidly to Wythe's Station, where we had another skirmish. Moving forward at a gallop, we captured and destroyed their camp, and chased the amazed and disgruntled rebels for miles in every direction, killing a few, wounding a good many, and taking over twenty prisoners.

Meanwhile, the enemy had assembled in considerable force between my command and Memphis, and had taken possession of all the bridges and crossings of the streams and gotten into readiness to capture myself and command upon our expected return. But, instead of returning as they had been led to suppose, I moved on northward, making demonstrations with small detachments in the direction of Memphis. I halted my command about midway between Randolph and Somerville, on a large plantation well stocked with everything necessary for our wants, until the return of all detachments. Among other good things, we found several smokehouses well filled with sugar-cured hams and bacon. The soldiers had earned their supper and regaled themselves on the hams, notwithstanding the proprietress tried to put them off with "sides."

The same night, we moved on towards Randolph and crossed a long corduroy bridge through a swamp, which a handful of men might have defended against an army. The tread of the horses was heard for miles. At the farther end of the bridge, a rebel force had gathered en route to join the regiment which had been just dispersed. They heard our approach, but never even dreamed that the noise could possibly be made by any but their own soldiers crossing to join them. Lieutenant [Charles W.] Whitsit, with the advance of my men, was among them before they discovered the mistake. When their surrender was demanded, they laughed and said "that joke's played out." When I rode up a few minutes later and asked the lieutenant, "How many have you got?" he replied, "I don't know but by Jove it's all of them."

In due time, we pushed on to Randolph and found boats awaiting our arrival, on which we embarked with our prisoners, while the largest force of the enemy was quietly waiting to ambush us on our return by the route on which we had taken our departure. The general was so greatly pleased with the result of the expedition that he sent out, under a flag of truce, a jug of whiskey or basket of champagne to the rebel commander, with General Sherman's compliments and message to the effect that Colonel Grierson had returned to Memphis and that he would soon be sent again to pay his respects to the Confederate forces.

In a few days after my return to Memphis, another expedition was made to and beyond Somerville, first moving southward and swinging around the city, leaving it in an almost opposite direction, [at] about 10 o'clock at night. The next morning, reaching the camp of the rebels unexpectedly, we surprised and scattered them in every direction. Upon reporting again to General Sherman, he having learned of another reorganization in northern Mississippi, near the Coldwater, I proceeded thence with about 300 picked men, first marching rapidly as far east as Lafayette. From there swinging around to the south in the direction of Holly Springs, [I] came in rear of the rebel camp, which was situated near Byhalia, some distance south of the Pigeon Roost road. [We] charged upon them at daylight on the second day out, so unexpectedly that we captured many of their horses, arms, and equipments. We traveled almost day and night for three days and, on that expedition, killed four of the enemy, wounded several others, took thirty prisoners, and destroyed the rebel camp.

In the early part of November, another expedition was made by order of General Sherman across to La Grange, Tennessee, fifty miles east of Memphis, to communicate with General Grant, taking dispatches to the general and bringing back others from him to General Sherman relating to the forward movement soon to take place. The enemy had concentrated quite a large force in the vicinity of Holly Springs, and General Sherman, fearing that if I attempted to return direct to Memphis I might be intercepted, instructed me to swing around when on return by the way of Somerville.

After reaching La Grange and reporting to General Grant and receiving his dispatches, I expressed faith in my ability to return direct, feeling reluctant to make such a long detour to the right as required by General Sherman's instructions. The general smiled and said: "These dispatches should be delivered to General Sherman soon as possible. The direct route is the best, unless an absolute necessity exists for you to go by a round-about way." I caught at the words and said: "Backed by your opinion, general, I will endeavor to return by the most direct practicable route."

Leaving La Grange at night, first making a demonstration northward, we wheeled westward, striking the direct Memphis road some distance from La Grange, and by noon the next day, were back in the city. Without waiting to go to camp, I reported at once to General Sherman. The general was considerably amazed at my sudden appearance, as he did not expect to see me for several days. He exclaimed, "Thunder and guns, Grierson, are you here? Couldn't you get through?" He was greatly delighted at receiving the dispatches which I placed in his extended hand. While we were talking, Mrs. Sherman,[3] who had joined the general sometime previously, sent a message to the effect that she wished to see Colonel Grierson of whom she had heard so favorably. I tried to excuse myself, being covered with dust and dirt, but the general would take no denial. Rough and unkempt as I was from riding night and day, he made me walk in and join them at dinner.

By such constant and active scouting, the country from forty to fifty miles around Memphis was kept well scoured, and no rebel organization could be formed within that distance and remain in safety for any length of time in one place. General Sherman, while we were dining, stated in answer to a question of Mrs. Sherman, that: "Colonel Grierson always goes with his men wherever sent; is invariably successful in accomplishing orders and bringing in his command safely; worries the rebels to death and is just the sort of a cavalryman I have been hunting for." As for my own views on the subject, I looked upon the work performed during those few months under command of General Sherman as an excellent school of instruction for myself and command, which was subsequently of great advantage—being just that kind of experience that resulted in a fitting preparation for more extended and important operations.

Soon afterwards, General Sherman indicated to me the probable date he would leave Memphis, so that I might make the necessary arrangements for my departure on an expedition which was such that it was then impossible to indicate with any certainty when my command would return to Memphis. While preparations were going on for the coming movements, I happened to be at headquarters one day to see the adjutant general about some matter, when General Sherman came into the office and commenced talking to his quartermaster in regard to transportation, which it appeared was not available so soon as General Sherman had expected.

He walked back and forth across the floor, talking rapidly and indicating plainly that it was the quartermaster's business to see that transportation was ready when it was required and that there must be no failure about it. [He] wanted to know why it was not ready, that it had been ordered, that the whole movement depended upon it. The quartermaster defended himself to the best of his ability—stated that he did all he could; that he had made timely requisitions for the mules and other animals, but that they had not arrived; that he could not create them; that it was impossible to obtain them until the arrival of the steamers upon which he had been notified the animals had been shipped.

I listened a few minutes to their conversation and, turning away from the adjutant general with whom I had been conversing, I approached General Sherman and the quartermaster and said: "There is no need of any trouble in regard to the matter, for I can get you 2,000 mules and horses by tomorrow night, and more if you want them." General Sherman and his quartermaster—J. Condit Smith—turned toward me in amazement, exclaiming: "How? Where in the world can you get them?" "Take them from the rebels wherever they may be found," I replied. General Sherman smiled and, turning to the quartermaster, said: "We must have them. Do it, Grierson. Get them." "All right," I responded. "I will do so by your order."

It happened that, in my recent scouting expeditions, I had kept my eyes open and knew just where the animals could be found. I sent my men throughout the country and swept them in by tens, twenties, fifties, and hundreds. I stopped wagons and carriages and took the mules and horses from the traces, and scoured the plantations and thus quickly obtained the animals from barns, corrals, and pastures and, in fact, wherever they could be found. It was a military necessity. I caused receipts to be given for the animals taken, as a guarantee for payment to their owners on satisfactory proof of loyalty.

There was soon a hornet's nest about headquarters. Men and women besieged General Sherman with protestations of loyalty and special pleas that their property should be respected, though in nineteen cases out of twenty the real owners were in the rebel army. The general stood it as long as he could, then locked himself up and answered all demands by the exclamation: "Send them to Grierson. Let them go to Grierson." Of course, there were some cases which, upon hearing the circumstances, the animals were returned. But the transportation was ready when wanted as a result of this mode of procedure, and General Sherman had no further trouble in regard to leaving Memphis at the time arranged between himself and General Grant.

Years afterward, J. Condit Smith, the quartermaster, would laugh when he met me and smilingly ask if I was still in the mule business. For in the long march through the enemy's country which followed, if I was within reach, he had only to send word that the animals were exhausted and that he wanted fifty fresh mules to quickly obtain them by detachments of cavalry, which were promptly sent out from my command for that special purpose.

In October, the building on the southeast corner of Beale and Lauderdale streets, Memphis, known as the Hunt property, was assigned to my command for use as a hospital. It was a good house, with fine, large grounds filled with trees and shrubbery. The owner was a noted rebel, and the place had been previously confiscated for government use. As the depot buildings would probably be required for other troops after the headquarters of the 6th Illinois Cavalry were removed from Memphis, and it would be neither prudent nor pleasant for Union ladies to remain there after we had gone, arrangements were made, in view of the information received from General Sherman, to have quarters in the hospital building above referred to assigned to my family. Mrs. Grierson, our two children and colored servant, Vernon, who was too sick to go along but afterwards joined me; my brother's wife and little daughter; and a brother of Mrs. John Grierson, a Mr. George Cook, were, a few days before we left, moved to the Hunt house.

It was subsequently found that the place was not very suitable for the purpose, as after the soldiers were gone and the force at Memphis so much reduced, the house became unsafe from its isolated position and there was much disorder in the neighboring streets. The owner of the house, who had returned to the city, offered $300 to anyone who would burn it down over the heads of the Yankees, although among the occupants there were several sick persons. Therefore, in the latter part of December, my wife and children returned to the homestead in Jacksonville, while my brother's wife and child went to board at Mr. Fitch's, as nothing could be definitely learned at that time in regard to when the expedition in which we were soon to take part would terminate, or whether or not the 6th Illinois Cavalry would again return to Memphis.

Early in November 1862, General Grant began his forward movement from Tennessee southward against the rebel army under [Lt. Gen. John C.] Pemberton,[4] then mainly in position south of the Tallahatchie River in Mississippi, with a smaller force at Holly Springs and detachments as far north as Grand Junction and La Grange, Tennessee. The Federal troops marched simultaneously from Bolivar and Corinth to La Grange and vicinity, and soon after pushed on to Holly Springs, the rebels falling back to the line of the Tallahatchie upon their approach. General [James B.] McPherson[5] commanded the center corps under General Grant's immediate supervision, General Sherman the right, and General [Charles S.] Hamilton[6] the left wing of General Grant's army, which numbered in all over 30,000 men.

On November 26, our preparations having been perfected, the 6th Illinois Cavalry left Memphis in advance of General Sherman's corps, marching southward on the Pigeon Roost road in the direction of Holly Springs, Mississippi. The troops did not do much more than get started the first day, and camped some eight or ten miles from the city. On the morning of the 27th, the march was resumed at daylight, the cavalry encamping the second night out some distance south of Coldwater River, on a well-stocked plantation. Our wagons having been in the rear of the infantry upon our departure from Memphis and the rations which the men had carried in their haversacks having been exhausted, the fodder, poultry, pork, and potatoes, all of which were found in abundance, were duly appropriated for the command, as much to the discomfort of the owners as to our satisfaction.

General Sherman made an unexpected entrance upon us after we had bivouacked, although we were some miles in advance of the main column. As he dismounted, he got a savory whiff of the cooking victuals and exclaimed: "Where do you fellows get all your good things to eat?" Glancing at the bountiful supper placed before us, I referred him to our excellent commissary, Lieutenant [Commissary Sergeant George] Redfern, for the desired information. The latter, although he had the sober look of a sedate judge or minister, was nevertheless something of a wag and was equal to the occasion, as he answered: "We buy them of our neighbors. Please sit down, general, and take supper with us," as a fresh chicken was gracefully placed on a stump by our obliging commissary. The general was hungry and ate heartily, and asked no more questions then. After the meal was over, we walked about and, when giving me orders for the next day's march, the general pointed towards Lieutenant [sic] Redfern and remarked: "What a solemn looking liar that commissary of yours is. I wonder if he thinks I believed what he said?" I answered: "He is a very sedate looking soldier and certainly is an efficient commissary, and really a good fellow to have along on a trip like this." The general laughed, lighted a cigar, and with his staff officers and orderlies rode back to his camp in excellent humor.

On the 28th, we skirmished with the enemy, about 100 strong, one mile south of Byhalia. [We] renewed the fight on the 29th, and entered the town of Chulahoma on the 30th, about noon, driving out the largest force of rebels yet encountered, [and] pursuing them four miles southward in the direction of the Tallahatchie River. We remained one day at Chulahoma, during which time, however, one battalion of the 6th Illinois Cavalry was sent with the 8th Missouri Infantry to the Tallahatchie River at Wyatt, where the enemy were presumed to be in force. The command returned at night and reported no enemy to be found north of that river.

On December 1, we left Chulahoma at 10 o'clock P.M., [and] marched the balance of the night, arriving at Wyatt at daylight the next morning, where two companies—E and G of the 6th Illinois Cavalry—were dismounted and crossed on a broken ferry boat, which had only been partially destroyed by the enemy. The dismounted cavalry marched out on foot two miles, where they found fortifications of considerable extent on the high ground bordering the river bottom, which however were found to be deserted, with the exception of a few stragglers who immediately skedaddled on the appearance of our men. The companies returned to Wyatt, where General Sherman had just arrived with the advance of the infantry.

An attempt had been made to cross some of the cavalry by sending over the equipments on the ferry boat and swimming the horses through the swollen stream. This being found to be impracticable, I placed myself at the head of the regiment and swam across the stream, the entire command promptly following and swimming to the opposite shore, from which point we proceeded at once to Oxford, Mississippi, fifteen miles distant, where we arrived next morning, December 3, after marching in a terrible rain storm until after midnight.

At that place was the beginning of some little trouble or dissatisfaction. The command of a brigade and the conduct of subsequent expeditions to lead, find, and fight the enemy, at least in front of General Sherman's corps, was intended for and had been assigned to me by the general, who had endorsed me as the best cavalry officer he had yet had. General Grant was quite ready to appreciate General Sherman's recommendation and to assure me that I would have an increased command. But when the cavalry officers met at Oxford, it was discovered that by commission Colonel [John K.] Mizner[7] of the 3rd Michigan Cavalry, whose regiment I understood to be in my brigade, outranked me seven days. He, therefore, at once assumed command of my regiment and ordered me to furnish 200 dismounted men for patrol duty in the town.

I knew that that was not what General Sherman expected or intended and, therefore, went at once to Colonel [T. Lyle] Dickey,[8] General Grant's chief of cavalry. Being intent on active service instead of patrol duty, I asked to be sent out at once with my regiment, alone, in quest of the enemy, indicating where the general desired me to scout upon returning to join his command. Colonel Dickey willingly acceded to the proposition, as it relieved him for the time from another still greater irregularity. It was found that Colonel [A. L.] Lee[9] and Colonel [Edward] Hatch[10] had been placed in command of brigades, although I outranked them both and, therefore, was better entitled to command a brigade than either of them. Had I pushed my claims at that time, I could have compelled a reorganization of the brigades there, as Colonel Dickey gave me privately to understand.

The whole matter, however, appeared to me at that time as a repetition in another degree of a similar difficulty which had arisen between General Grant and General Prentiss. But, unlike my former chief, I made the best of the circumstances. Although chafing under the delay, without bothering myself further about rank or command of a brigade to which I was entitled, I good-humoredly shook hands with the officers present, including Colonel Dickey, and bid them all good-bye. I then quickly rejoined my command and galloped beyond the limits of the town, being determined to get away before any message would reach me countermanding the order for my departure.

From Holly Springs, we scouted the country west of Oxford and south of the Tallahatchie River. Although we found only a few stragglers of the enemy here and there, we captured over 100 head of beef cattle which had been left by the rebels in their hurried retreat, which was at once sent by the most direct road to General Sherman's command, while we returned by a circuitous route to within five miles of Wyatt, where we arrived and encamped that night and the next day, during which time the infantry constructed a bridge across the Tallahatchie, on which General Sherman's troops crossed over to the south side of the river. On December 5, the regiment moved forward to Toby Tubby Creek, two and a half miles southwest of College Hill and seven miles west of Oxford, where we pitched our tents on a plantation belonging to Mr. Buford, while General Sherman's corps closed up and occupied College Hill and vicinity. By direction of the general I proceeded that night to Panola, thirty-seven miles southwest. We marched until midnight and again took the road at daylight, arriving at Panola about noon the same day. Dashing into town, we drove out some cotton burners and saved several hundred bales of cotton from destruction.

While at Panola, a woman came to me weeping and begging me to release her husband from jail, where she said he had been confined on account of his Union tendencies. This led to an investigation and release of all the prisoners confined there, as the result proved that they had all been arrested for similar reasons. Subsequently, the man first referred to became a spy for our army, but afterwards [was] discovered selling our secrets in return to the rebels, thus becoming a spy for both sides. The jail delivery caused much excitement among the citizens, who gathered in knots in the streets. Threats were uttered especially against Lieutenant Woodward, through whom, as acting adjutant, the order for the release of the prisoners was given, and who was not backward in its execution.

Hearing that troops had been sent by General [Frederick] Steele[11] from Helena [Arkansas] to the Yocknapatalfa [Yacona] River,[12] fourteen miles southward, I ordered the regiment into camp three miles west of Panola, while with a detachment of forty men I proceeded southward with a view to communicate with the Federal troops. Arriving at the point I indicated, I found that they had already retraced their steps to Helena, whereupon I returned and rejoined the command before daylight the next morning.

When I was about starting southward the night before, Woodward could not be found, and it was feared that the citizens to whom he had made himself so obnoxious by releasing the prisoners before referred to had spirited away the handsome lieutenant, the favorite of the regiment. His friends began "every tower to search and each nook to scan." But, like Lord Lovell's bride,[13] they might have "sought him that night, sought him next day and sought him in vain when a week passed away," if he had his will. For here it may be observed that his favorite amusement was flirting with the pretty girls. And, having found one, wherefore should he himself be found. But the cry went forth: "Where is Woodward?" And echo answered, "Where?" "Where is Woodward?" was asked in louder tones, and soldiers began to cast gloomy looks upon citizens who, with blank and sullen faces, retired from the street corners. Captain [Thomas G.] Herod, who took charge of the search, began to grow decidedly excited on the subject. [He] swore that the citizens had murdered Woodward—had foully assassinated him—[and] that he, Herod, would retaliate. If Woodward was not soon found, he would burn every house in the town over the occupants' heads; would kill every man, woman and child; would give them two hours, one hour, half an hour, ten minutes, five minutes to find Woodward. Or that he would make a slaughter of the innocents worthy of his great namesake, Herod of olden time. While the town and regiment were thus buzzing like a hive when the queen bee is lost, Woodward coolly walked up and asked what all the fuss was about. Suffice it to say that

Panola was not burnt and the innocents were not destroyed. But Captain Herod found out the secret and knew better how to manage next time when Woodward happened to be absent on a similar adventure.

On December 7, we resumed our march back to our camp on Toby Tubby Creek, where we arrived at 9 o'clock P.M. the next day, having marched without stopping to feed men or horses. By that rapid march to the southwest, we obtained the first reliable information in regard to the whereabouts of the troops from Helena, which were known to have left that point, marching on an expedition into Mississippi, about the time we started from Memphis. It was the expedition made under command of Generals Hovey and [Cadwallader C.] Washburn,[14] the object of which was to strike and destroy the railroad south of Pemberton's encampment on the Tallahatchie. They reached the railroad, but only destroyed a small bridge and then retreated back to the Mississippi River in much greater haste than they had advanced, without accomplishing the real object of the expedition, as it was evident that the advance of Grant's army was the real cause of Pemberton's retreat from the Tallahatchie River.

On December 9, I received orders from General Sherman to proceed to Helena, Arkansas, with dispatches from General Grant to General Steele. The following extract is from a letter received from General Sherman covering my instructions:

> I hand you in person two communications from General Grant, which he desires should be delivered to General Steele at Helena, Arkansas, and the commanding officer of the cavalry force which we expect you will find at Friars Point. Your route of travel is left to yourself, but let what may befall you the dispatches must not fall into the enemy's hands, as they contain the outlines of plans which will take months to fully accomplish. As soon as your horses recover from the fatigue, you will return to College Hill and report to General Grant at Oxford. If, on crossing the Coldwater, you judge the road to be open, you might leave a part of your command and proceed to Helena with the dispatches. Tell General Steele that I will reach Memphis Friday night and expect to be on board five days afterwards, viz.: the 18th instant, and that Hovey's forces should be embarked by that date ready to follow. Tell him General Grant bases his calculations on 12,000 infantry and 2,000 cavalry. Hoping to meet you soon again down in the Yazoo. . . .

On the same date, General Sherman wrote and handed me another letter addressed to General Grant, Oxford, Mississippi, which was to be delivered to the general upon my return from the expedition on which I was about starting:

Colonel Grierson is about to start for Helena with your dispatches
and I also towards Memphis. When he returns he will report to
you in person. Colonel Grierson has been with me all summer and
I have repeatedly written to you and spoken in his praise. He is the
best cavalry officer I have yet had. I commend him specially to your
consideration. He has already had assigned to him a brigade, but
the cavalry has been so busy that he has not yet had his command.
I ask for him anything you can do for his benefit and the good of
the service. I know that you will soon appreciate his merits.

The day before these communications were written, General Sherman
had received orders from General Grant directing him to proceed without delay to Memphis, and from thence down the Mississippi River, to
organize and take command of an army with a view to the reduction and
capture of Vicksburg and the opening up of the Mississippi River. The
expedition made up the Yazoo by General Sherman resulted in disaster
to the Union forces.[15]

Accordingly, on December 9, with the effective force of my regiment,
numbering 600 men, I started on an overland trip to Helena, Arkansas,
leaving the least effective portion of my regiment as a camp guard at Toby
Tubby Creek. As usual on such expeditions, we started after dark, traveled
until midnight, and again took the road about daylight the next morning.
We crossed the Tallahatchie River at Panola on the morning of the 11th
and traveled a road which had been obstructed in every possible way by
the falling of timber and destruction of bridges. The enemy had expended
much labor at such work, they no doubt believing that the army of General
Sherman would cross the Tallahatchie River at Panola instead of Wyatt.

After moving northward some distance, we turned westward toward
Helena and found also that the roads in that direction had been obstructed
by the rebels in the same manner, they expecting that the forces from
Helena would move eastward to join the main expedition southward into
Mississippi. After a hard day's ride, we struck the famous Mississippi River
bottom[16] about dark, penetrating it about two miles and a half, where we
encamped for the night and sent out scouting parties to attack two rebel
camps and captured a considerable quantity of camp equipage, arms,
ammunition, and a number of prisoners.

Early in the morning of December 12, we resumed the march through
an almost impassable canebrake, where we were frequently exposed to the
deadly fire of the enemy in ambush. We arrived at Coldwater about noon
that day, where I left the main part of the regiment and, with seventy-
five men, crossed the river and proceeded to Helena, twenty-five miles
distant, where I arrived about 9 o'clock that night with the dispatches

for General Steele, which I delivered to the general in person. I was detained at Helena until 2 o'clock P.M. on December 13, when I re-crossed the Mississippi, joined my detachment, and proceeded some distance out. [We] encamped for the night on the Yazoo Pass, in the midst of a country infested by rebels.

The same night, the regimental pickets were fired upon by the enemy from the opposite side of the Coldwater River. On the next morning, not having made my appearance and it being feared that I had been intercepted, an expedition was organized, and was on the point of starting to my relief, when wild shouts of joy rang through the woods announcing my safe return from Helena. During my absence, the regiment had encamped on a plantation belonging to Jacob Thompson, who had been secretary of the interior under Buchanan's administration.[17] The plantation was a large one and was well supplied with Negroes, stock, corn, fodder, etc. In addition to these, on first arrival there we also found forty hogs butchered, hanging up ready for use. It is needless to say they had entirely disappeared during my march to Helena, and the food obtained at that plantation was of great use in subsisting my command. The supplies could not have been obtained from a more despicable rebel or one who, as is well known, did so much to aid the rebellion while serving as a cabinet officer under the president of the United States.

Immediately on my arrival at Thompson's plantation from Helena, we started our return, marching until about 11 o'clock P.M., when we bivouacked for the night and again took up the march at daylight. Passing through the town of Sardis, we crossed the Tallahatchie at Belmont, in the midst of a terrible storm on the afternoon of the 15th, and proceeded thence to our old camp on Toby Tubby Creek, where we learned that all the troops had moved southward. After resting for the night, we marched to our new camp below the Yocknapatalfa [Yacona], arriving there on the night of the 16th, I having that morning delivered to General Grant in person at Oxford the dispatches entrusted to my care by General Steele.

———

During the expedition to Helena, we carried neither tents nor camp equipage, and subsisted men and horses almost entirely on the country through which we passed. We had to destroy the tents and camp equipage, arms, etc., captured from the rebels on our outward march, it being impossible to take them with us, as the roads through the canebrake bottoms were almost impassable even for horses. In some places, the mud was over knee deep, and frequently the cane would bend over and meet above our heads, and we were obliged to stoop while mounted to pass through the narrow roadway. Altogether, the march was a very fatiguing one, which tried the power of endurance of the whole command. But the troops bore the hardships without murmur or complaint, and upon return, joined Grant's army in the best of spirits, where we as usual found plenty of work awaiting us.

Although we had just returned from such a long and tiresome march, yet we continued to actively scout the country to the west and southward of our camp on December 17, 18, and 19. On the 20th, [we] started in pursuit of the enemy under command of Van Dorn, who was then threatening Holly Springs, being thus hastily called upon with a view to protect the vast supplies at that point, on which the whole movement southward into Mississippi depended. The emergency brought the 6th Illinois Cavalry again under Colonel Mizner.

In obedience to orders received, we left our camp at 1 o'clock P.M., and reported to him at Springdale, five miles to the northwest, in the direction of Oxford. Arriving there at 3 o'clock A.M., we halted until nearly 6 o'clock, awaiting the arrival of the colonel and the balance of the forces, consisting of the 4th Illinois, 7th Kansas, and 3rd Michigan Cavalry, which with the 6th Illinois Cavalry made a force of about 1,600 men. We then forded the Yocknapatalfa [Yacona] and proceeded to Oxford, arriving at 1 o'clock P.M., marching a portion of the way through an almost impassable swamp. Another delay of three hours was made at Oxford, when the march was resumed. We arrived at the Tallahatchie at 8 o'clock P.M., where by direction of Colonel Mizner we bivouacked for the night until about 2 o'clock in the morning of the 21st, when we again moved forward, arriving at Waterford, nine miles south of Holly Springs, shortly after daylight.

At that point, Colonel Mizner was relieved from command by order of General Grant on account of the slow manner in which the movement was conducted. Colonel Mizner, although ordered to proceed with all possible speed, failed to satisfactorily comply with his instructions, having delayed three hours at Springdale, three hours at Oxford, and six hours at the Tallahatchie River. Colonel Lee of the 7th Kansas immediately assumed command, presuming himself to be the senior officer. But, upon investigation, it was found that I outranked him several months, whereupon the command devolved upon myself.

In conjunction with a force of infantry under Colonel [C. C.] Marsh, we immediately proceeded against Holly Springs, where we arrived at noon the same day. The cavalry traveling by parallel roads on the flanks, the whole force [arrived] simultaneously, but found the rebels had left the evening previous. There we were detained by Colonel Marsh, much to our chagrin, until 10 o'clock at night when, by his order, I put the regiment on the backward march toward Oxford. The 6th Illinois Cavalry, however, had only proceeded about one mile northward from Holly Springs, when a dispatch was received from General Grant, addressed to myself, directing me to "follow Van Dorn until he was caught or west Tennessee so completely exhausted as to render it impossible to support an army." In the meantime, the 3rd Michigan Cavalry had been sent northward toward Grand Junction by order of Colonel Marsh.

Upon the receipt of General Grant's dispatch, I immediately countermarched the 6th Illinois Cavalry and proceeded with it and the first brigade of Colonel Lee, marching at night to Grand Junction, arriving there at 7 A.M., December 23, having passed the 3rd Michigan Cavalry during the night, that regiment having gone into camp midway between those two points. While halting to feed men and horses, I obtained information to the effect that the whole force of the enemy had gone in the direction of Bolivar.

After three hours rest, the 3rd Michigan Cavalry having again joined us under command of a major, I started the column northwest, arriving at Bolivar, twenty-two miles distant, at 11 o'clock that night, where we found General [Mason] Brayman[18] in command and glad to see us. He was much alarmed at reports of Van Dorn's approach and determined to retire to the fort, and feared that he would be compelled to surrender the town. When awakened in the night by the arrival of my command, he at first supposed it to be a summons to surrender, or a night attack on the place. On the road during the previous night, I distinctly saw the camp fires of the enemy about six miles to the southeast of Bolivar. Having sent out scouts to reconnoiter and ascertain their position, I moved my command into the town and bivouacked for the night.

About daylight the following morning, December 24, the enemy, having made a circuitous march of eleven miles, attacked the town on the west, capturing some pickets of the 1st Tennessee Cavalry and some stragglers of the 3rd Michigan, driving in others, and coming within easy range of the fortifications. I immediately put my command in position and sent out skirmishers to ascertain their strength and movements. The scouts were fired upon and returned the fire, killing two of the enemy, but fell back to our lines, reporting the enemy in large force. I at once moved out on them by the Brownsville road, skirmishing and driving them back for over two miles. They, not knowing before that we had succeeded in reaching Bolivar, became considerably confused at our attack and, falling back some distance, struck off southward toward the Middleburg road.

Not knowing their purpose and fearing they intended making a circle to our rear for the purpose of attacking the fort, I with the main body of my force dropped back to Bolivar, sending two companies on their trail to watch their movements. The companies pursued the rebels closely, crossed the Somerville road and proceeded on toward the Middleburg road, where it was ascertained that the enemy made this flank movement without reference to any traveled road.

Having thus definitely ascertained their intentions, I immediately started with my whole force in pursuit, again coming upon their rear at Middleburg, where they had attacked a small force stationed there under command of [Lieutenant] Colonel [William H.] Graves of the 12th Michigan Infantry but were repulsed with considerable loss. We engaged them briskly when they again retreated, we following them closely to Van Buren, and thence to Saulsbury, and arrived at the latter place shortly after dark, where we bivouacked for the night, without campfires, close to the enemy, and fed men and horses for the first time since the night before, having while en route forwarded dispatches to General Grant from both places, indicating the position and movements of the enemy and our progress southward.

The enemy becoming aware of our close proximity soon made preparations for retreat, while I, by sending scouts into their camp, was apprised of their movements and was again on the road in pursuit before daylight. Colonel Lee with his brigade, to whom I had sent repeated orders to close up, having failed to do so, I sent him a written order to move forward at once, which still found him five miles in the rear, with skirmishers on the flanks and front, on ground over which I had passed with all due caution several hours previously. Continuing the pursuit during the day, I halted on the main road leading to Grand Junction and awaited the arrival of Colonel Lee, sending out scouts to watch the movements of the enemy.

During the night, I received dispatches from General Grant acknowledging receipt of mine from Middleburg and Van Buren, copies of which I learned had been sent to Colonel Hatch in command of the Federal forces at Salem. My scouts returned at 2 o'clock A.M., and reported the enemy preparing to move southward. At 4 o'clock A.M., I was again on the road in close pursuit. At about 4 o'clock P.M., we again overtook the rebels about one mile south of Ripley, where we attacked vigorously and drove them southward. In the last engagement, Van Dorn commanded in person with three full regiments and made several desperate attempts to repulse us. But his lines were as often broken and his men fled in confusion. At this junction, I ordered one battalion of the 6th Illinois Cavalry, under Major Loomis, to mount and charge the rebels should they again attempt to form.

In the meantime, Colonel Mizner had joined the column about eight miles south of Saulsbury and assumed command. When within eight miles of Ripley, the 3rd Michigan being in advance and their horses appearing fatigued, I asked permission of Colonel Mizner to move the 6th Illinois to the front, which after some hesitation was granted. Moving forward on the gallop we proceeded rapidly to Ripley, as stated, where we met a detachment of the 2nd Illinois Cavalry under command of Major [John J.] Mudd, who just arrived from Holly Springs.

By direction of Colonel Mizner, I moved with my brigade through town to select a camp a mile or two south. But, encountering the enemy within a short distance of the town, I pursued them seven miles without finding any camp, as previously stated. It is due to the 6th Illinois Cavalry to remark that, although there were three other regiments accompanying us in the pursuit, yet none of them took any part in the engagements with the enemy, nor did they join us south of Ripley until darkness had compelled us to give up the pursuit and we had dropped back two miles and fed our horses after a sharp encounter in which we captured a lieutenant and twenty men and scattered the rebels in every direction.

Upon arrival of Colonel Mizner, I proposed to follow the enemy and make a night attack, which however was not approved. We again took up the line of march on the morning of the 26th, Colonel Lee's brigade taking the advance. The whole force proceeded in a cautious and leisurely manner to New Albany on the Tallahatchie River and halted for two hours, when it moved to a point about six miles south, toward Pontotoc, without again coming upon the enemy. There, by command of Colonel Mizner, the pursuit was abandoned and the command turned to the right with a view to cross the Tallahatchie at Kings Bridge. But, by some mistake, the wrong road was taken and we did not arrive at Kings Bridge until after dark, when we were obliged to stop in the Tallahatchie bottom in the midst of a terrible storm. A larger part of the command was halted on the south side of the river in a dismal swamp, but the 6th Illinois Cavalry crossed Kings Bridge and proceeded two miles beyond, on to the higher ground, and bivouacked for the night. The rain fell in torrents and the whole command was completely drenched, but not a word of complaint was uttered and our men proved that they were well worthy the name of soldiers. On December 27, at 7 o'clock A.M., we took up the line of march back toward Holly Springs and camped for the night at Potts' plantation. Resuming the march in the morning, [we] arrived at Holly Springs at 2 o'clock P.M. on December 28.

During the trip, we captured about 100 of the enemy and killed a good many. [We] also captured a large number of horses and mules, which were turned over to the provost marshal at Holly Springs. Our camp equipage was still below the Tallahatchie River, some twenty miles distant. But, being ordered forward, it joined us the next evening, December 29. We remained in camp in the vicinity of Holly Springs for five days when, on January 3, 1863, we were ordered to Waterford, nine miles south.

In the meantime, the cavalry was reorganized into two brigades. I was assigned to the first brigade, composed of the 6th and 7th Illinois and 2nd Iowa Cavalry. It will be remembered in the former organization of the cavalry that there were three brigades: one commanded by Colonel Mizner, one by Colonel Lee, and the other by Colonel Hatch, I being placed in Colonel Mizner's brigade. In the reorganization, two brigades were formed: one commanded by myself and the other by Colonel Lee, Colonel Mizner being ordered northward toward Jackson, Tennessee, with his regiment alone. General Grant directed Captain Rawlins, assistant adjutant general, to give me my choice of the cavalry regiments and to arrange to place it all under my command, if I so desired. I thought the three regiments selected were a large enough force for me at that time and, thanking General Grant for his kind offer, I declined to take command of the whole of the cavalry as proffered. We remained in camp at Waterford about one week, scouting the country to the east, west, and south, when information being received that the enemy had left the line of the Tallahatchie and fallen back southward into central Mississippi, we formed the rearguard of General McPherson's corps and proceeded to Holly Springs, where we remained until the last division of the infantry had moved northward.

During the evacuation of Holly Springs, a desperate attempt was made by several regiments of Federal infantry to burn the town. But the 6th Illinois Cavalry, having arrived there from a scout from the southeast, received orders to patrol the town, which they did, effectually driving out many stragglers and incendiaries. A number of buildings were fired but, by extraordinary vigilance, the town was saved from destruction.

Early in the morning of the following day, we proceeded to Coldwater Creek where we encamped, remaining there until all the artillery and baggage trains had passed northward. Rumors having reached us that the rebel force had again occupied Holly Springs, we made a dash into it, driving out a few stragglers, but found no large force of the enemy. We recovered, however, by the movement, a large quantity of ordnance stores, which during evacuation had by some mistake been left at the depot. After remaining for a day or two scouting in all directions, we again left Holly Springs and took up the march for La Grange, Tennessee, where the last detachment of my brigade arrived on January 12, 1863.

Meeting with different commanders during the expedition after Van Dorn gave me a great deal of trouble, as I was thus thrown in the presence of officers who outranked me and who assumed control over my command. Colonel Mizner being relieved at Waterford, Colonel Lee was very anxious to get me out of the way that he might himself command a brigade. He, therefore, arranged through Colonel Marsh with General Hamilton, who was in command at Holly Springs at that time, for my departure. By order of Colonel Marsh, and in accordance with instructions from General Hamilton, I with the 6th Illinois Cavalry was ordered back to Oxford, while the other cavalry regiments were sent forward toward La Grange and Grand Junction.

The road to Oxford was blocked by our troops and trains. Besides, I knew that was not the way I should be sent. Still, I obeyed the order and put the command on the march toward Oxford. But, feeling confident that it was wrong under the circumstances to send me southward again, contrary to military etiquette I returned to the telegraph office and there, over the heads of both Colonel Marsh and General Hamilton, telegraphed direct to Major General Grant, stating that I had been ordered to Oxford, that I did not know why I should go there when the enemy was known to be going in an opposite direction, and asked the general to give me direct orders to take the pursuit.

The men of the 6th Illinois Cavalry would march with the snail when their backs were toward the enemy, and Grant's peremptory order, sent direct to me, to follow Van Dorn reached the 6th Illinois Cavalry only one mile away on the backtrack. They countermarched with speed and alacrity, passed Mizner's Michiganders in the night, and fought on wherever fate happened to place them to the end of the chapter, while the disappointed cable [cabal] digested its wrath as best it could, notwithstanding Lee sulked and dillydallied five miles in the rear, that Mizner after resuming command quickly gave up the pursuit, and that Hamilton nursed his spite against me for use on future occasions. At one time during the pursuit of Van Dorn, the 6th Illinois Cavalry, alone, bivouacked without campfires within a mile of the enemy, although we had but six hundred men while Van Dorn had nearly as many thousand. We did not light campfires because we did not wish to reveal the smallness of our numbers nor, by making known our proximity, to frighten away the enemy too soon. If Lee had come up as repeatedly ordered, we might have made a night attack without much risk. As it was, we bivouacked so near the enemy at times that many of Van Dorn's foragers came by mistake to our camp, bringing in pigs, geese, chickens, etc., supposing they were within their own lines. Of course, our men gave them a very pleasant and polite welcome as they led the amazed rebels to the rear and placed them under guard.[19]

During the active service and almost constant travel for nearly two months preceding our arrival at La Grange in the rear of the army returning from the unsuccessful campaign into Mississippi, the mails were very irregular. Consequently, both Mrs. Grierson and myself had to suffer from the perplexing delays in the transmission of letters in common with thousands of other lonely, anxious, and expectant persons in like situation at times during the war. Mrs. Grierson, who had given up the hope of seeing me again during the winter, being uncomfortably situated with her two children in Memphis, had left that city late in December for the north and, after numerous delays, had reached the old homestead in Jacksonville early in January 1863. She arrived there in the night in the midst of rain, sleet, and mud, which a dray could hardly be pulled through, to find the gate chained [and] the house locked, dark and vacant. My father, who had become tired of living there alone, had left the premises to spend some weeks in Concord, ten miles distant, with his daughter, Mrs. Louisa Semple.

For days after my arrival at La Grange, I anxiously awaited the receipt and opening of the mails, hoping to hear from home, not having heard either directly or indirectly from Mrs. Grierson since I had left her at Memphis in November, 1862, upon departure of Sherman's army into Mississippi. As complaints and worry could be of no avail, I had to put up with the disappointment and tried to content myself with the hope that we might be permitted to remain quietly at La Grange for sufficient time to arrange for my family to visit me before being obliged to again take the field. I really felt, too, as if a rest would do me good and knew it would be of great benefit to the entire command.

We had selected a comfortable camp and had obtained a pleasant room, for office purposes, in a private house belonging to pleasant and accommodating people. Our tents were pitched in the front yard, surrounded by evergreens and shrubbery. Lieutenant Woodward of the 6th Illinois Cavalry had become my acting assistant adjutant general and J. C. Grierson brigade quartermaster. [I] was entitled to a commissary, surgeon, and two aides, but had decided to only appoint them as their services were needed. I found it much pleasanter to have command of a brigade than only a regiment, as it removed me from the everlasting noise and confusion of horses, mules, and soldiers. But, of course, I found that the position had its drawbacks for, although exercising a brigadier general's command, I was not a general, [and] yet [was] obliged to perform the work without being able to draw the pay of that grade.

Mrs. Grierson, being deprived of the power to communicate with me for weeks, had heard as she passed north through Cairo that there were train loads of delayed mails for Grant's army, which was not calculated to encourage her to write to me when there was so little prospect that letters would, in any reasonable time, reach their destination. The few that are now left of her writing at that period manifest more real abject loneliness and discouragement than those written at any other time during the war, which then seemed would be so indefinitely prolonged. I well remember my great disappointment at finding no letters from her when I reached La Grange from the south to go into winter quarters with my command, and in letters then written home, my discomfort and discontent is manifest throughout their contents.

There came about that time, too, a lull from the excitement of active pursuit—a sort of breathing time to prepare for another struggle with the enemy, filled with suspense as to the future, saddened by the fact that the movements of our armies had in a measure failed to attain decided successes so long hoped for by the people of the land, and in the midst of all, the old exasperating difficulty of long-delayed payments to hard-worked troops who had thrice earned the pittance due them by the government for services rendered during the summer and fall campaign.

For several days after our arrival at La Grange, it rained almost incessantly and looked as though it would continue to pour down for days to come, with but little prospect of clear skies appearing in the near future. However, gloomy days can be endured where there is some prospect of good arising. It soon became evident that it would be impossible to move troops through the accumulations of mud, which was almost impassable for men and animals, and it seemed hardly probable that we would be called upon at such a time for active service in the field. Therefore, the troops were almost sure of a rest during the continued wet weather. The thought would arise, however, that the rest thus obtained would be to me far from perfect without my family to comfort me in the lonely hours deprived of their cheering and much-desired presence. In fact, it brought vividly before me the picture of our home far away where, if only present to enjoy its comforts, to sit of an evening by a good cheerful fire talking, reading, singing, discoursing music or listening to well-known melodies dear to all at home, sweet home of bygone days, the pleasure would have been memorably great.

Only a day after such reflections, from information received it appeared that my brigade might be ordered back to Memphis and thence southward down the Mississippi River to join Grant in his operations against Vicksburg, After General Sherman's failure to capture that stronghold, he had fallen under the command of General McClernand in the expedition against Arkansas Post. Soon after, General Grant assumed command of all the troops operating down the Mississippi, placing McClernand in command of the XIII Corps. The transfer of my brigade was contemplated, but the difficulty of getting steamboat transportation prevented the movement. And it really seemed unnecessary to take the cavalry from

Tennessee when there was a large force at Helena, Arkansas, in the event that the services of mounted troops could be made effective, which appeared rather improbable on account of the continued heavy rains and consequent overflow of the Mississippi River.

I made up my mind to be ready for marching orders, judging that if the most of the troops, infantry and artillery, should be taken from Memphis, we might be called upon at almost any time to move there, however much mud we might be obliged to pass through while making the dismal march back to that city, fifty-one miles distant from our camp at La Grange. So long as Memphis remained the base of operations in West Tennessee, it would have been well if enough troops could be kept there to permit with safety an outpost as far west as La Grange. But, if the force was to be still further decreased, it would be absolutely necessary to draw in our military horns towards the Mississippi River, while the operations were being pushed forward against the rebel position at Vicksburg.

A report also reached us to the effect that half a dozen paymasters were in Memphis awaiting the receipt of funds to make the payments to the troops which had been so long deferred. The money was much needed as everyone in the army in that section was, as the saying is, "flat broke." I was at that time unfortunate enough to burn the toes off my new boots, the pair costing only a few days before $15. It became absolutely necessary to buy others in order to keep my feet dry. Therefore, I had to exhaust the contents of my pocketbook in paying $12 for another pair, that amount being every cent I had excepting a $20 Confederate bill given me as a curiosity, being the reflection of a shadow representing the imaginary solidity of the Confederate Treasury, but which would not buy anything at La Grange or within our lines, although a poor meal of victuals might have been obtained for it farther south. At that time, the government was indebted to me in the sum of $1,400. The best I could do was to write encouragingly to Mrs. Grierson that, so soon as paid, "I'll send you some money, my honey."

The first letter received from Mrs. Grierson, after bidding her good-bye at Memphis in November, reached me at La Grange [on] the evening of January 17. Of course, I was delighted upon receiving it, read it over and over again, handled and looked upon it as a remarkable curiosity. It was received and read first in General McPherson's office. The general left that day for Memphis with a view of going thence south to join General Grant in the campaign against Vicksburg. In bidding me good-bye, he shook my hand very warmly and complimented me and my command on the service we had rendered, saying that he intended to make application for my brigade to be ordered to join his corps in central Mississippi so soon as a movement thence became practicable.

By the authority of the general, I moved my office to a building nearer the center of town, just opposite to the building that the general had occupied for office purposes, that building having been taken by the post commander, Colonel [John M.] Loomis of the 26th Illinois Infantry. Colonel [Brig. Gen. James W.] Denver's[20] division was still at La Grange but held in readiness for marching orders, which were then daily expected. The general was an old acquaintance and a tip-top jolly man—"the biggest toad in the puddle" in every sense of the word, as he was very large and weighed nearly 300 pounds. Just before departure, General McPherson turned over the band of the 2nd Iowa Cavalry to me for use at my headquarters. The band had been with the general for some time but, as he was going away, he had no further use for it and it was placed at my disposal. The general was very pleasant and genial, and I disliked to part with him. He was a gallant, promising officer, his worth was highly appreciated by General Grant, and had he lived longer would no doubt have risen to still higher rank and command in the army.

On January 23, orders were received for my brigade to guard the Memphis and Charleston Railroad from La Grange to Lafayette, a bothersome and unsatisfactory duty for cavalry. The order plainly indicated that the infantry, or most of it, would be withdrawn from that line and that the cavalry would be held there pending the operations of troops moving southward via the Mississippi River. It seemed probable that one regiment of cavalry from my brigade would have to be sent to Moscow Station, ten miles east, but my headquarters would remain at La Grange.

The withdrawal of so many troops from Memphis and the line of the Memphis and Charleston Railroad soon brought about a change in the position and movements of the rebels. The information received from my scouts showed that Van Dorn was again moving northward. After threatening demonstrations in our direction, [he] flanked off towards Savannah, Tennessee. Notwithstanding the continued wet weather, the cavalry was occupied in scouting southward, watching the movements of the enemy. But my brigade was in condition to give the rebels a warm reception in the event that they came within striking distance. Price was at the same time reported to be occupying and fortifying Granada, Mississippi, and the indications were that we would soon have active work to keep the advancing rebels in check, as marked activity among them was plainly observable.

On January 30, information was received to the effect that a paymaster would start [from] Memphis for La Grange to pay my brigade. The news was very acceptable and the money, when obtained, would be more so, as it would afford the officers and soldiers the means to obtain many things necessary for the comfort of their families and those depending upon them for support.

Towards the end of January, the weather changed somewhat for the better. The clouds would break away and occasionally let the warm face of the sun shine out brightly as ever. But, on January 30 the skies were again darkly clouded, indicating that another storm was brewing, and by night the rain poured down as wet as usual. As the old saying is, "There is no rest for the wicked," and I often wondered if the cavalrymen did not belong to that class. Few have any clear idea of the amount of work that constantly falls to their lot during a protracted war and the very little credit gotten, as a rule, for doing it. Between scouting, picket duty, and patrols, the cavalry soldiers were almost constantly on the move. It was hard service for both men and horses, and seldom that there was any real quiet or rest for either the one or the other.

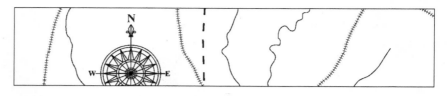

6. Grierson's Raid

On February 3, [1863,] I was ordered to Memphis to confer with General Hurlbut relative to [an] expedition southward into Mississippi.[1] While there, I received some maps and other papers giving information of the country over which the contemplated march would probably be made. I also arranged for the pay of my command for the two months ending August 31, 1862. I returned to La Grange on February 4, and on the 5th received pay for July and August 1862, amounting to $449.10, all of which was sent home, excepting enough to pay to William Fitch of Memphis the money he had kindly loaned me in an emergency.

On February 8, I received a letter from Governor Yates of Illinois, advising me that he had strongly recommended my promotion to brigadier general of volunteers. I was also advised that Generals Prentiss, Grant, and Hurlbut had, or would, forward like recommendations for my advancement. Nearly every officer of higher rank of my acquaintance told me that I was justly entitled to promotion for services rendered during the fall campaign in Mississippi. It was gratifying to have them think me deserving of the place, even if the appointment should not be conferred upon me at the time.

On February 9, General Sherman, from his camp before Vicksburg, wrote to the secretary of war as follows:

> I take pleasure in inviting your attention to the services of Colonel
> B. H. Grierson, 6th Illinois Cavalry, now commanding a brigade of
> cavalry back of Memphis. During the time of my command there
> I had the 6th Illinois Cavalry Regiment, the only cavalry near,
> and Colonel Grierson by his rapid, intelligent and decisive move-
> ments beat the enemy in every case and compelled them to keep
> a full day's march distant. I cannot now enumerate the instances
> but recall two, one on the Coldwater and another from Wolf River
> over to Randolph. Although the expeditions were not of sufficient
> magnitude to call for special reports yet they made the enemy fear
> "Grierson's Cavalry." General Grant has spoken to me in high terms
> of Colonel Grierson who had served near him since I left the regi-

ment at Oxford, Mississippi, in December. I consequently endorse his claims for promotion to Brigadier General of Volunteers.[2]

In enclosing a copy of the foregoing letter to me, the general writes:

General Grant speaks to me in the highest terms of you and ratifies all I have written, so you have the good will of your late and present commanders. You have seen that the newspapers are after me again and the correspondents admit that they must write me down because I am the inveterate enemy of their class. I certainly do consider them as much the enemy of the United States as the secesh and a great deal more contemptible. The former, the secesh, openly take up arms and declare hostility, the latter publish all they can to keep the enemy advised of our plans, purposes and designs and also enter our camps as spies, sowing sedition and ill feeling. It was and is all nonsense that our troops were demoralized. As usual, many get tired of the war when they hear the whistle of the bullet and put it off on any popular excuse. We are now laying on shore, digging canals, and trying to turn the channel of the Mississippi, but sooner or later we must get on to the high dry land and fight it out.[3]

Timely and frequent requisitions had been made for everything necessary to fully reequip my command and every effort possible taken to secure fresh horses, arms, and equipments as were needed, but great delay had arisen in their delivery. The troops were very destitute of clothing and the men were growing very impatient at its non-receipt. The weather was simply abominable and, altogether, it had been a very gloomy winter. It still continued to rain nearly every day and the sun seldom shone. There were many cases of small-pox in the command, besides more than usual of other sickness. The hospitals were filling up and it was thought that, unless the weather soon cleared, one-half of the soldiers in the command would soon be on the sick report. Under all the circumstances, I came about as near having the blues as I wished to, and a trifle nearer, and earnestly hoped that it would dry or freeze up, or that the sun would shine long enough to drive dull care away.

On February 14, I received orders to hold my whole effective force in readiness for a long and dangerous trip, and presumed that I would receive marching orders within a few days thereafter. From information received, it was evident that the expedition could not be made in less than twenty days, and perhaps thirty would be required to accomplish the undertaking, during all of which time I would not probably be in a position to communicate with my friends or anyone outside of my command, although circumstances might arise to change the design as then agreed upon or arranged. I had sometime previously made application for a twenty-days' leave of absence. But, even if received, under marching orders I would not have taken advantage of it.

On February 17, eight tons of quartermaster stores for my brigade were received at Memphis and arrangements made to forward the same at once to La Grange, in order that the cavalry might be equipped and supplied with everything necessary to place it in thoroughly excellent condition for the field. The intended scout, however, came to nothing at that time. General Hamilton, then in command at La Grange, had some intention of sending out [a] cavalry expedition into Mississippi, which according to his design I should merely be called upon to cover and protect with my brigade. If any such expedition was really made, I should have by right commanded the entire force. Hearing of the presence of a large rebel force on the proposed route gave the general an excuse for postponing the hazardous attempt, although I would willingly have undertaken it had I been placed in command. General Hamilton apparently hoped by a little delay to get me out of the way, as he still held a grudge against me on account of the way I wiggled myself out of his command while in pursuit of Van Dorn. He hoped that I would be ordered elsewhere so that he could give Colonel Lee, or some other favorite officer, an opportunity for distinction by carrying out his designs for his contemplated expedition.

The following, written by General Grant to General Hurlbut, indicates what the general thought of General Hamilton's maneuvers. On March 9, 1863, Grant wrote to Hurlbut: "I look upon Grierson as being much better qualified to command this expedition than either Lee or Mizner." On February 13, he [had written] to General Hurlbut: "It seems to me that Grierson with about 500 picked men might succeed in making his way south and cut the railroad east of Jackson, Mississippi. The undertaking would be a hazardous one but would pay well if carried out. I do not direct that it shall be done but leave it for a volunteer enterprise." On February 21, I wrote to Mrs. Grierson: "I was just about to write to you to bid you good-bye for sometime to come as I had marching orders for my brigade to take part in a long expedition and it was expected that we were to start this morning, but have this moment received a telegram countermanding the order for the present." The next few letters written home were decidedly homesick in tone.

Hearing nothing of my application for leave nor of my chances for promotion, the proposition received soon after from General Hurlbut was very acceptable. Upon visiting his headquarters, the general told me that he intended to transfer my brigade to his immediate command and that we would probably move to the vicinity of Memphis. He said that he was determined to hold me closely under his control until the design of the long expedition into Mississippi, which had been talked over, should be carried into effect; that he had no power to grant a leave of absence except upon surgeon's certificate approved by a medical director—a thing which I could not expect to get considering my vigorous health—yet he promised that, before the move was made, he would detail me on some special service northward and thus give me an opportunity to visit my family.

That much-deserved visit home was not merely a special favor granted without good reason. The great raid made two months later, [that] thrilled throughout the nation from Maine to California, had for some time been contemplated, although unknown except to General Grant, Rawlins, Hurlbut, and myself. It was deferred for some time on account of unexpected delays in the movements against Vicksburg, but it was thought that before attempting the hazardous undertaking for which I had volunteered my services, I should be afforded an opportunity to visit my family, though of course the true reason could not be made public. But all this is anticipating the event. Yet in reading over my letters of the next few weeks, the fact is brought to my mind that, while plans and hopes were uncertain, the expedition was, during that period, always looked forward to as among the possibilities.

On March 5, I was ordered to hold the effective force of two regiments of my brigade in readiness for a five-days' scout to break up some rebel organizations reported to be northwest of La Grange. On March 13, I wrote to Mrs. Grierson:

> I returned safely yesterday after a successful expedition in which we cleaned out the noted guerilla [Colonel Robert V.] Richardson. The fight took place about three miles south-east of Covington; we killed twenty-two, wounded a great many, took about seventy prisoners and scattered the remainder of the rebels in every direction. The attack was a complete surprise and we captured the entire outfit of the rebels; their camp, tents, commissary and quartermaster stores; powder, ammunition, arms, wagons and teams; all regimental and company books and papers; all records and paroles of Federal officers; all company muster rolls, valuable maps, papers, letters, etc. Our entire loss in the engagement was four missing, not having one killed or wounded. General Hamilton complimented me highly on my success and informed me that I was to be called upon very soon for another big scout.

In that expedition, made between March 8 and 13, I had with me about 900 men of the 6th and 7th Illinois Cavalry. Not finding Richardson in camp where he had been reported, and obtaining information as to the

exact location of his camp, I marched to the point indicated to make the
attack, proceeding rapidly onward towards the northwest, making a forced
march of thirty-five miles in seven hours over roads almost impassable from
recent heavy rains. We came suddenly upon the enemy's camp at Big Creek,
three miles southeast of Covington. The surprise was complete and our
troops dashed impetuously against the rebels from all sides. They could not
have been more surprised if we had fallen upon them from the clouds.[4]

On March 15, orders were given to abandon the railroad line from
Columbus to Jackson, in consequence of which the mails from the north
were sent from Cairo to Memphis by steamboat and thence by rail to
La Grange. The time was not so quick by three days as when brought by
the other route. March 15 was the day I had fixed upon in my mind to
be at home, but at that date really saw little prospect of getting there, as
I received notice that day to hold my entire command in readiness for
speedy and heavy service on which we were to be sent by order of General
Grant. Consequently, we were every day expecting instructions to march.
It seemed to me then, when thinking of home and my long-hoped-for visit
there, that if not obtained the disappointment would be too great to bear.
Under the worry of mind, I felt like resigning in order to get home and stay
while permitted to live—the hope of going I could not give up, although
the prospects then seemed so dark and uncertain.

My disappointment at not being able to get leave to go home was partially compensated for by receiving numerous letters from Mrs. Grierson
and friends in the North, among which was one from Governor Yates of
Illinois, who advised me that he had recently been to Washington and
had again recommended to the president, in person, my promotion to
brigadier general, and thought the appointment would soon be received.
This was encouraging and, having been successful in every fight so far had
with the rebels, I felt that my record justly entitled me to promotion. On
the same day, too, the sun shone out brightly, the roads were drying up
rapidly, [and] the buds on the trees were beginning to swell. There were
many other indications of an early spring, and the farmers in the vicinity
of La Grange who had any fencing left were plowing up ground for crops
of cotton and corn.

———

General Orders No. 14, issued at Holly Springs, December 22, [1862,] by
General Grant, assigned my command, the First Brigade of Cavalry, to the
XVII Army Corps, commanded by Major General McPherson. So many
changes occurred during that winter that it was hard to tell to whose
command troops belonged. Upon General McPherson's departure from
La Grange on January 17, I fell under command of General Hamilton.

Great confusion was caused by the various designations of commands; that of General Hamilton at that time was the District of West Tennessee. On March 25, another change took place at La Grange, occasioned by the resignation of General Denver and the removal of General Hamilton to Helena, Arkansas, to report to General McClernand. My relations with General Denver during the time I was under his command were very pleasant and satisfactory in every respect. On the contrary, General Hamilton was the most disagreeable man I had served under. He lacked many things which I had been taught to believe were essential to a gentleman. He was tyrannical, dogmatic, and repulsive in his manner and seemed to arrogate to himself the assumption of being one of the great men of the age; was always dissatisfied with the commands assigned to him and had few friends among the officers of the army in the District of West Tennessee or XVI Army Corps, as it was also designated in orders.

It was, therefore, gratifying to receive on March 24 a telegram advising me that he had been relieved from the XVI Army Corps and that I would thereafter report direct to General Hurlbut or to one of his division commanders. On the same date, General W. Sooy Smith,[5] who had arrived to take the place of General Denver, told me that for the present I was to be assigned to his division. Thus the changes occurred, and it would not have astonished me to have found myself under command of someone else the next day. But, in no event could I have been placed under a more disagreeable person than General Hamilton.

General Smith was an entire stranger to me. He had been commanding a division in General Rosecrans' army, [but] was relieved from that and ordered to report to General Grant, by whom he was sent to La Grange to take the place of General Denver. On March 25, I had a long talk with the general on military matters and found him to be a very intelligent and agreeable gentleman. He expressed great satisfaction at finding a person with such thorough knowledge of the country as myself, and at once said he wished me to take entire charge of the cavalry, without waiting to receive orders from him; to constantly keep out patrols and scouts in all directions; and not to let any force of the enemy approach La Grange without giving timely warning—all of which I accomplished to his satisfaction.

The evening previous to our conversation, the pickets on the road leading southeast from our camp were attacked and some of them captured. Upon notification of the occurrence, I started fifty men immediately in pursuit, who came up with the enemy a few miles out. [They] killed three, captured three, recaptured our own men, and scattered the rebels in all directions. I determined to make it equally hot for them [the rebels] whenever they put in an appearance in that vicinity.

Only a few days before, I had sent out a scout under Colonel [Edward] Prince[6] in a northwesterly direction from La Grange. [Prince] came upon a band of guerillas, killed and wounded several, and captured and brought in a number of prisoners. On the 17th, I ordered a hundred men in an easterly direction beyond Saulsbury, where they attacked another band of guerillas and widely scattered them. A few days after Major [Horatio C.] Nelson, 7th Illinois Cavalry, and Lieutenant Colonel [Reuben] Loomis, 6th Illinois Cavalry, were sent out with about 200 men each. The latter had a hard fight two miles south of Belmont, where his command was suddenly attacked in the night by the rebels under Richardson and [W. A.] Dawson, who out-numbered our men three to one. But our plucky cavalry were jumped from their sleep and dashed into the fight. [They] whipped and drove the enemy away in great confusion. Our loss was eight killed and over twenty wounded. Lieutenant Jessie B. Wilson of Company K, 6th Illinois Cavalry, a very brave and gallant officer, was among the killed. The rebels left seven dead in the hands of our men and thirty prisoners, among whom were a major, [a] captain, and [a] lieutenant of Richardson's command. Some of our wounded men were left at a house near where the fight took place. On information of the engagement, I started on the night of the 30th, with 500 men, to bring them in and determined that, if I got on Richardson's trail, to make it as lively for him as usual. [I] expected to be gone several days. [Lieutenant] Colonel Loomis and his gallant command were highly complimented in orders.

I returned from my scout on April 3, 1863, having accomplished the orders received from General Smith, in compliance with whose instructions I had previously, on March 28, dispatched 200 men of the 7th Illinois Cavalry, under command of Major Nelson, to proceed westward toward Moscow and strike the trail of a party of rebels who had attacked a train of cars that day near Moscow. At the same time, [I] sent a force of 200 men of the 6th Illinois Cavalry, under command of Lieutenant Colonel Loomis, to proceed toward Somerville, thence rapidly westward, with instructions to endeavor to intercept the enemy with the prisoners from the train and form a junction with the expedition under Major Nelson. This latter officer proceeded westward, got upon the trail, and followed the rebels to Macon where, although they were but a few hours in advance and encumbered by prisoners, he gave up the pursuit and returned to camp, utterly failing to comply with his instructions to form a junction with [Lieutenant] Colonel Loomis.

The expedition from the 6th Illinois Cavalry proceeded to Somerville, thence westward as directed, struck the trail, overtook and skirmished with the rebels, killed and wounded a number, and captured some prisoners, among whom was a captain of Richardson's command. Having pursued and dispersed the enemy, the command went into camp on the night of March 29, where they were attacked while in bivouac by a largely superior force under Colonel Richardson. Although they were in a manner surprised and had a number killed in their beds, yet they firmly stood their ground, drove the enemy from the field, and remained in full possession. It would be impossible to award too much honor to the officers and men present on that occasion for their unprecedented coolness and gallantry. The death of Lieutenant Wilson was an irretrievable loss to his friends and the country. He was a very deserving officer and had rendered most effective service in the field at all times, wherever his services were required.

I arrived near the scene of the engagement [at] about 11 o'clock on the morning of the 31st, and rapidly pushed two companies forward to dash into the place with a view to capture any rebels that might be there. Upon our approach, they fled precipitately. We pursued them closely and succeeded in killing three, wounding several, and capturing twenty prisoners. Having buried the dead and properly disposing of such of the wounded as could be moved in ambulances, we proceeded to the plantation of Lewis P. Wilkinson and bivouacked for the night.

The following morning, the wounded and prisoners were sent to La Grange under proper escort. Dividing the rest of my command into two parties, we followed the enemy. Major [Lt. Col. William] Blackburn was sent to Mason's Depot with one party, where he captured a quantity of secesh clothing, trimmings, and other supplies, which were destroyed. With the balance of the force, I proceeded westward, forming a junction with him at Concordia.

After feeding, we again started in different directions in pursuit of the enemy and encamped for the night on the plantation of Mr. Montague, north of the Loosehatchie River, where we found a quantity of cavalry saddles and a shop for their manufacture. The shop and saddles were destroyed and the employees engaged in the business taken into custody. The next morning, I crossed the Loosehatchie with part of my force at Quinn's Bridge and sent another force eastward to cross at Cameron's Bridge, after which small parties were scattered over the by-roads and lanes, with instructions to meet the main column at Macon. The whole command arrived there almost simultaneously, having succeeded in capturing a number, among whom were the quartermaster of Richardson's regiment and his private secretary, with important papers. While in Macon, a portion of the mail captured on the train near Moscow was retaken, and the man with whom it was found, resisting when an attempt was made to capture him, was killed. It was afterwards ascertained that he was a member of [Captain Ed E.] Porter's guerilla band.

Having camped for the night about three miles to the southeast of Macon, we returned to La Grange, via Moscow, on April 3, arriving about noon. The expeditions under Lieutenant Colonel Loomis and myself succeeded in killing twenty of the rebels; wounding between forty and fifty, many of them mortally; and taking over fifty prisoners. Our entire loss was fifteen killed and thirty-seven wounded. When it is remembered that the engagement on the night of March 29 did not last over twenty minutes, the desperation of the conflict can be readily imagined.

When the movement down the Mississippi River was first contemplated, troops were organized and sent forward from Illinois, Iowa, and Indiana, in which General McClernand was specially empowered by the War Department to assist, with some kind of tacit understanding that he should have command of the movement for the opening of that important commercial highway, for which troops were also withdrawn from Missouri, Arkansas, and elsewhere. Later, the forces were divided into four army corps and General Grant placed in command of all, with a request from the president that General McClernand's corps should be given the advance of the down river expedition.[7] The final arrangement of the army [corps] for the Vicksburg campaign was as follows: XIII Corps, General McClernand; XV, General Sherman; XVI, General Hurlbut; and XVII, General McPherson. Some friction had been occasioned by General McClernand taking command over General Sherman and the troops which had been placed under the latter for the Yazoo expedition, which resulted in the assumption of immediate command by General Grant of all troops operating against Vicksburg.

The movement of Grant's army into central Mississippi from La Grange, Sherman's expedition up the Yazoo and attack on Haynes Bluff [Chickasaw Bayou], efforts to construct canals on the west side of the Mississippi River, and other attacks and attempts to take Vicksburg were all failures. During all the time our troops floundered about in the mud and mire, it was evident that, sooner or later, they must get upon firm ground on the east side of the Mississippi River and fight it out with the rebels, who from the first were determined to tenaciously hold on to that important position. General [Nathaniel P.] Banks[8] had been directed to co-operate with General Grant by coming up the Mississippi River from New Orleans, and the gunboats from Admiral [David] Farragut's[9] fleet passed the rebel batteries of Port Hudson and moved up the river between Natchez and Vicksburg. Of course, all was conjecture as to what would be the final result, but it was generally conceded that the high ground below Vicksburg must be gained before successful operations could be insured.

General McClernand's expedition, which resulted in the capture of Arkansas Post with its troops and munitions of war, was a most important matter. Getting his corps across the country to a point below Vicksburg before the passage of the gunboats and transports was timely, and aided materially in the forward movement to Port Gibson and rear of Vicksburg. General Grant did not at first appreciate the importance of General McClernand's movement against Arkansas Post, although General Sherman was fully aware of its necessity. It would have been a fatal mistake to have left the enemy in that position with so strong a force in rear of the army operating down the Mississippi.[10]

The passage of the fleet of gunboats and transports, magnificently accomplished in the face of the terrific fire from the rebel batteries, and the safe foothold attained by Grant's army on firm land on the east side of the Mississippi River, which made possible the movements to the rear of Vicksburg, in conjunction with and facilitated by the great cavalry expedition through the state of Mississippi, from La Grange, Tennessee, to Baton Rouge, Louisiana, were achievements that astonished the Union and Confederate governments, and the first really effective demonstrations against the rebel strongholds of Vicksburg and Port Hudson.

The notice given in September 1862, that a proclamation would be issued in January, 1863, declaring all slaves in the states in rebellion to be free, maddened the people of the South, and particularly the slaveholders of the cotton states. When January 1 came and the great Emancipation Proclamation was issued by President Lincoln, the Confederacy was from that day doomed to destruction. The people of the South, however, were moved to greater exertion, and at once put forth greater efforts to gain the advantage by activity and persistent attacks upon the Union forces wherever favorable opportunities were presented. The battle of Stones River was a striking example of their temerity. And although the victory was claimed by Rosecrans, it was dearly bought, as the losses to the Union troops under his command were terribly severe.[11] In the Army of the Potomac, few if any advantages were gained by our troops, and there was a general feeling of despondence throughout the North and an earnest desire for some decided success that would be readily recognized over the entire country.

Before the great movements referred to above, which foreshadowed success, great distrust was entertained by the people of the North as to General Grant's ability, and much clamor was raised for a change of commanders. But the president stood by him faithfully and rendered him every assistance possible. All of Grant's corps commanders doubted the propriety of the movements he was making and prophesied disaster. But, with great firmness, that great general adhered to his plan and, although weighted down with care and responsibilities, he never let go his bull-dog grip until grandly victorious in the face of all opposition.

———

It was fortunate for me that my brigade had been paid during the latter part of March for the months of September and October 1862, as I was thus provided with the means to pay my expenses north to Illinois and to leave some money with my family for use during my prolonged scout through the Southern Confederacy, so soon to begin without any absolute certainty as to when, where, or how it would end. I shall never forget the considerate action of General Hurlbut in answer to my application for some kind of an order that would enable me once more to see my wife and family before entering upon that perilous expedition, the result of which no living mortal could foresee. Quickly the wires flashed back to me the following order from the kind and noble-hearted general [Special Orders No. 57, April 3, 1863]: "Colonel B. H. Grierson, Commanding 1st Brigade of Cavalry, will proceed without delay to Springfield, Illinois, as bearer of dispatches. Having accomplished the mission set before him he will return forthwith."

Of course it did not take long to get ready for my departure on such a welcome mission. I left La Grange in high glee on a special train and in a few hours reached Memphis. [I] called to pay my respects to General Hurlbut and to thank him for the great favor he had conferred upon me. Upon presenting myself before him, he sprang up from the chair on which he sat diligently at work at his desk in the discharge of his duty and, clasping both my hands, said: "God bless you, Grierson. Go home at once. I'll give you all the time possible and telegraph you when to return." I could not speak, but encircled my arms around the general's waist and gave him in return a genuine hug, which I dare say he never forgot. There were two pair of moist eyes in that room before I left it on my mission of love.

That visit home was one of the most enjoyable experiences of my life. It was an oasis of love in the midst of a desert of doubt, darkness, and uncertainty. A person only who has determined upon some perilous adventure, beyond which the dimmest ray of light could not be made out in the shadowy distance, can realize the extreme rapture that filled my heart at being once more surrounded by the kind, loving hearts of home. And no place ever looked more enchanting to the eyes of any soldier than that one to mine.

But the time passed fleetly away and, on a quiet April morning, there came a sudden flash of lightning and thunder clap, after which the rain poured down in torrents for a few moments and then stopped. The clouds quickly cleared away and the sun shone brightly again. While I was romping helter-skelter about the hall, like a big boy, with Charlie and Robert, all in high glee, their mother looking on approvingly, there came a rap on the front door, which was opened by Mrs. Grierson as a boy handed her a telegram. Without opening it, she turned towards me and said: "Ben, here are your orders." And sure enough, upon opening the envelope it proved to be a message dated: "Army Headquarters, Memphis, Tenn., April 13th, 1863."

Colonel B. H. Grierson, Jacksonville, Ill., via Cairo.

Return immediately. By command of General Hurlbut.

H. Binmore, Assistant Adjutant General

That short but glorious visit was the only home preparation for an enterprise considered so desperate that it was not ordered, but only accepted as a volunteer service. Whatever I may have told my wife of the plans matured before I visited her, not one word was breathed aloud, even to my relatives. It was our first meeting since November 1862, when I started from Memphis on nearly two months of constant travel and danger throughout northern Mississippi. What was our parting may be imagined but cannot be fully realized by any person not placed in a similar situation.

Upon reaching General Hurlbut's headquarters at Memphis, I learned that a locomotive was in readiness to take me to La Grange and was to start at 1 o'clock P.M. My command had already been instructed to be prepared to start next morning. I wrote a hurried note to Mrs. Grierson and spent the remainder of my short stay talking with General Hurlbut, from whom I learned as nearly as possible the condition of affairs as to the whereabouts of General Grant and his army, the probable operations of our troops for the future, and all that could be given me as to the whereabouts and movements of the rebel forces. I was particularly advised verbally as to the general's [Grant's] wishes—that while he considered the expedition I was about to undertake a measure of great importance and one which he very much desired to have made, he looked upon it as too hazardous to take the responsibility to give definite or written orders for its execution. As I had volunteered for the service, he hoped and believed I would be successful, and with General Hurlbut wished me God's speed. I parted with General Hurlbut with much feeling, but a most determined will to do my whole duty to accomplish the desired object.

Upon arrival at La Grange, I found General Smith very glad to see me. He gave every possible aid and some additional verbal instructions, together with some important papers covering information in regard to movements of the enemy. I had a busy night of it and found myself too much engaged with official duties to gain time enough to write another note to Mrs. Grierson. My command was in readiness to move at daylight, and as it was marched off, I stopped for a moment to speak to General Smith. We shook hands cordially, and mounting my horse, I rode away waving my hat and shouting: "Once more, good-bye General."

———

With a view of occupying the rebels in northern Mississippi and attracting their attention from General Grant's movement against Vicksburg and my cavalry expedition made in conjunction therewith southward through the so-called Confederacy, General Hurlbut ordered out troops from Memphis and various points along the line of the Memphis and Charleston Railroad to make demonstrations towards the Coldwater and Tallahatchie rivers, all of which returned to the camps after complying with their instructions in a satisfactory manner. Those movements, of course, aided materially in giving me a better opportunity of getting a good start within the rebel lines and assisted in giving the enemy the impression that my command would, like all others, return again to Tennessee, and had a tendency to hold a larger force of the enemy in northern Mississippi than would have otherwise remained there if not held by the timely advance of troops of the XVI Army Corps then under General Hurlbut's command.[12]

In accordance with the desire of General Grant and instructions of General Hurlbut, received through Brigadier General W. Sooy Smith at La Grange, I marched from that place at daylight on the morning of April 17, 1863, with the effective force of my brigade, consisting of the 6th and 7th Illinois and 2nd Iowa Cavalry and [Captain Jason B.] Smith's battery of Woodruff guns, numbering in all about 1,700 officers and men, those regiments in the order mentioned being commanded respectively by Lieutenant Colonel R. Loomis [and] Colonels Edward Prince and Edward Hatch. As the sun rose bright and clear and tinged with golden hues the tops of the trees and high ground in the vicinity of the town, and while a most refreshing breeze swept diagonally across the column, we moved southward into Mississippi. No person other than myself and Lieutenant S. L. Woodward, a.a.a. [acting assistant adjutant] general of the brigade, knew the probable extent of the expedition on which we had started.

A most cheerful spirit prevailed throughout the entire command, and both officers and men had plainly observable on their manly countenances a stern and determined look which presaged devotion to duty and gave assurance of success. The vigor of the soldiers was conveyed to the noble animals they rode, as they felt the pressure of the thighs of their riders, as gracefully they bore themselves and adapted their motion to that of their horses. As the column wound about through the open road, the invigorating atmosphere and the buoyant spirits of the moving force plainly indicated the strength and power of the command, as fearlessly it entered upon an important expedition, the extent and destination of which was really not fully known to myself. The flowers of spring in all their freshness of beauty added to the fragrance and variety of the scenery which surrounded us as we went marching on into and through the domain of the South.

The first day's march was almost entirely without interruption or interference from the enemy, and the command reached and passed the Tallahatchie River, on the afternoon of April 18, at three different points. One battalion of the 7th Illinois Cavalry, under Major [John M.] Graham, crossing at New Albany, over fifty miles south of La Grange, found the bridge partially torn up and the rebels near at hand, attempting to set it on fire. As our cavalry approached the banks of the river, they were fired upon from the opposite side but at once dismounted, threw out skirmishers, quickly drove the enemy from their position and, repairing the bridge, crossed to the south side of the Tallahatchie. The balance of the 7th Illinois and the whole of the 6th Illinois crossed at a ford two miles above and the 2nd Iowa about four miles still further up the stream. After crossing, the 6th and 7th Illinois Cavalry moved southward on the Pontotoc road and encamped for the night on the plantation of Mr. Sloan. The 2nd Iowa also moved southward from their point of crossing and encamped about four miles south of the river.

The rain fell in torrents all night, and on the morning of the 19th, I sent a detachment eastward to communicate with Colonel Hatch and make a demonstration towards Chesterville, where a regiment of cavalry was reported to be organizing. I also sent an expedition back to New Albany and another northwestward towards King's Bridge to attack and destroy another force of cavalry organizing there under Major [Alexander] Chalmers. I thus sought to create the impression that the object of our advance was to break up and scatter those rebel organizations.

The expedition eastward found Colonel Hatch still moving southward, parallel to the other columns. The one to New Albany, under command of Captain [George W.] Trafton of the 7th Illinois Cavalry, came upon twenty rebels near the town [and] engaged them, killing and wounding a number. The one sent northeast [northwest] found that Major Chalmers' command, hearing of our proximity, had suddenly left in the night, going west.

When the 6th and 7th Illinois Cavalry, on a previous expedition from La Grange, cleaned out the noted guerilla Richardson, we encamped the night before the engagement on a large plantation near Covington, Tennessee. Upon arrival there, I with some of my staff officers rode up to the front of the house near the entrance and called for the owner. He came out and proved to be quite a deaf and irascible old gentleman, whose sons were in the rebel army. We advised the proprietor of our intention to stop for a short time on his place and asked for food for our horses.

Just then, the old rebel spied the little cannon as they were wheeling off to enter the barnyard. Whether he heard us or not, he told us that "there is the barn and there are the hay stacks. We could, and we no doubt would, and we might take what we wanted." But ripping out a tremendous oath, he exclaimed that he wished he had the power to turn our own guns on us, for if he could, "he would blow every damned Yankee to hell." Whatever we called for he gave promptly and handsomely, saying it was no use to deny anything, for "the damned Yankees would have it anyhow." And, of course, they were welcome to it, "certainly, certainly gentlemen take anything you please"; and then in the next breath would curse and confound us all for a set of "villains and scoundrels." Said he would give everything he had that we wanted and "to the devil with you, damn you. I only wish I could blow you all to thunder."

After the troops were supplied, we asked the old gentleman if we could have some supper. In answer, he said that he did not suppose there was much in the house to eat, but there were the cellar, pantry, and cupboard. "Might every mouthful poison us," but we could help ourselves. We did help ourselves, and set the servants to cooking a capital supper, and had the best dishes set out and the table loaded with all the delicacies the cellar, pantry, and cupboard afforded. And when all was ready, we politely invited the proprietor to eat with us. He said he thought it was rather a cool piece of business to invite him to dinner in his own house, off his own chickens and wines in such grand style, but that it was no use at all to refuse. For the whim of the thing, he would go out and eat with us, but we might rest assured that, if he had the power, he'd serve us all up in a very different style. So, he took one end of the table and I the other, and with alternate civility and curses, the supper was in due time concluded. On our departure, we thanked him for his hospitality and bade him good-bye. He, in turn, said he did not thank us "a damn bit" and would not be glad to have us come again, but said that, everything considered, we had behaved tolerable well for Yankees. Still, he wished he had the power to shoot or hang us all, for there wouldn't be one left if he had his way.

We found quite a different stamp of man at the Sloan plantation south of New Albany, Mississippi, where and near which the brigade encamped the second night of the great raid. As usual on such occasions, we rode up to the place and demanded the keys of the smokehouse and barns, and asked food for men and horses. Mr. Sloan, the proprietor, wanted in a small way to resist, where effective resistance was of course impossible. He would not give his keys until the locks were about to be broken, and when he saw his stores issued out, he was completely beside himself, alternately going to cut my throat and apparently desirous of having his own throat cut. I tried to reason [with] and pacify him, to cool him off.

He acknowledged to having furnished the Confederates with supplies, and was told that the least he could do was to contribute to the old Union cause. He would moderate a little for a moment, when the sight of some new depredation would set him in a tantrum again. No plea of necessity, or usage of war, or crime of treason would avail to quiet him. Once he congratulated himself aloud, saying that we hadn't got his horses anyhow; they were safely hidden away where no Yankee in the world could find them. He had hardly finished speaking, when up came a squad of soldiers driving all his horses and mules into the barnyard. Then he fairly foamed, rushed towards me, and for the fiftieth time demanded that we should "take him out and cut his throat and be done with it"; that he did not want to live a minute longer; that all his property had been taken, eaten up, and destroyed.

I concluded to take him at his word, as nothing I could say or do would suffice to quiet him. With a wink to those who comprehended, I called for one of my orderlies—an immense, athletic, heavily bearded man—and upon his reporting told him that Mr. Sloan was very desirous of having his throat cut, that I had tried to reason him out of his strange wish, but that he persisted and that the orderly might take him out into the field near by and "cut his throat and be done with it," according to his oft-repeated and urgent request. The huge orderly never smiled or hesitated, but deliberately taking a large knife in one hand, with the other seized Mr. Sloan and moved off with him as if he had been a kitten.

Then a general hub-bub began. Mrs. Sloan, who all along had been more self-possessed than her husband—telling him not to be a fool. That if the Yankees took ten times as much as they did, that if they took all they could, there would still be the plantation left and there was no use in howling over what could not be helped—pleaded in vain with the infuriated man. Upon seeing him taken out by the orderly, she began to scream in chorus with the servants and beg me not to mind what her husband had said; that he did not know what he was about. The man himself, before the orderly had gotten him out of the house, was hollering lustily for the commanding officer and begging for dear life of the strong hand which held him. He was finally allowed to reach my presence again, and having, before everybody present, avowed that he did not want to have his throat cut—that he did not want to die—was released. Thereafter during our stay, he remained comparatively quiet. The next morning, when I showed him the tired stock, horses, and mules we would leave in place of the fresh animals we had taken from him, he was quite appeased and said he was not so sure but he had the best of the trade with the Yankees after all.

After return of the various detachments sent out to mislead the enemy in regard to the real design of the expedition, I moved on southward with the whole force to Pontotoc. Colonel Hatch, with the 2nd Iowa Cavalry, joined us about noon of the 19th, reporting having skirmished with about 200 rebels the afternoon before and that morning, killing, wounding, and capturing a number. Upon reaching Pontotoc about 5 o'clock P.M., the advance dashed into the town, came upon some guerillas, killed one and wounded and captured several more. There we also captured a large mail, about 400 bushels of salt, and the camp equipage, books, papers, etc. of Captain [John T.] Weatherall's command, all of which were destroyed. After a short delay, we moved out and encamped for the night on the plantation of Mr. Dagget, five miles south of Pontotoc, on the road to Houston [Miss.].

At that point, I gave orders to the regimental commanders to cause a close inspection to be made, with a view of selecting all men and horses [in] anyway disabled or not fit for further hard marching, in order that they might be sent back to their camp at La Grange, thus freeing the command of any encumbrance or what might become such in our onward movements. When the detachments were brought together, I personally inspected every man as to his fitness for further active duty. By such judicious action, about 200 men and animals, constituting the least effective portion of the command, were separated from the main force and were in readiness to move at 1 o'clock A.M., on the 20th. After feeding, the detachment moved northward a little before 3 o'clock A.M., under the command of Major [Hiram] Love of the 2nd Iowa Cavalry, with orders to proceed to La Grange, marching in column of fours before daylight through Pontotoc, thus creating the impression that my whole force had returned. The major had orders also to send off a single scout to cut the telegraph wires south of Oxford on the Central Railroad.

I found it absolutely necessary, to insure celerity of movements, to reject and separate myself from all but the most serviceable material. Some of the soldiers who had first been selected to join those returning northward asked permission to speak to me and plead so as not to be sent back. Upon looking at them more closely, [I] decided that their disability was only temporary and, satisfying myself that they were of the right kind of stuff to recuperate, consented to their request and permitted them to remain with the main column. And they made the long journey all right. The detachment sent back was long afterwards, when the brigade was united in Tennessee, dubbed by their more fortunate comrades who made the trip successfully as "The Quinine Brigade."

Sending them by night through Pontotoc was a good ruse. Making all the spread they could with their led horses, mules, prisoners, and one gun of the battery, the people of that place believed and quickly reported that the whole command had gone back north, while two hours after Major Love's departure I proceeded south with the main force on the Houston road, passing around that place about 4 P.M., marching thence in a southeasterly direction and halting at dark on the plantation of Mr. [Benjamin] Kilgore, about twelve miles from Houston on the road to Starkville. The passing around the town of Houston with the main column was for a similar purpose—to avoid having our numbers counted. By going through fields and making a wide track, our force was greatly overestimated. And that gave us more time, as the rebels, before following when they found out the direction we were traveling, waited to amass larger numbers.

The following morning, April 21, at 6 o'clock, we resumed the march southward and, at about 8 o'clock A.M., reached the road leading southeast towards Columbus. There, I detached Colonel Hatch, with the 2nd Iowa Cavalry and one gun of the battery, with orders to proceed to the Mobile and Ohio Railroad, in the vicinity of West Point, to destroy the road and telegraph lines; thence move south, destroying the railroad and all public property as far south as Macon; thence to cross the railroad, making a circuit northward, take Columbus and destroy all government works at that place, and again strike Okolona and, destroying it, to return to La Grange by the most practicable route. Of that expedition and the one previously sent back, I of course heard nothing definite until long afterwards, except vague and uncertain rumors through secession sources. Those detachments were intended as diversions, and even should the commanders not have been able to carry out their instructions, yet by attracting the attention of the enemy in other directions, they would in any event be of service. And they did assist us much in the accomplishment of the main object of the expedition.

The officers in command were carefully selected with a view to their fitness. Major Love, although willing to go on, was not strong or in good health, but was well suited to look closely after the safety of his command and, as the result proved, conducted his march in an admirable manner, reached La Grange in due time, and brought reliable information to Generals Smith and Hurlbut of our whereabouts and progress southward. Colonel Hatch had served under my command since the organization of my brigade in December 1862, and I looked upon him as a brave, discreet, and capable officer; one whose whole heart was thoroughly aroused in the cause of his country. And, although I regretted to part with him and his gallant regiment of officers and men, yet his horses, on account of the hard and constant work they had been performing, were not in my judgment as suitable as those of the 7th Illinois Cavalry, nor were the officers and men so well known to me at that time as those of the 7th Illinois, which was from my own state.

In addition to his other instructions, I directed Colonel Hatch to follow the trail of the main column about four miles and then return. As we were bidding each other good-bye, he suggested that the sending of one battalion would afford more rest for his tired animals, and I assented to the proposition. Major Datus E. Coon's[13] battalion was selected for the duty. He was a brave and most gallant officer, and I well remember the look of regret he gave me as he warmly shook my hand when the column halted to enable him to counter-march his command. I would gladly have taken him and his brave troops with me, if it had been practicable to do so.

It had lately rained considerable throughout that section of the country, and the fact that the freshest tracks pointed northward led the rebels, when they examined the trail three hours afterwards, to believe that the whole command had marched eastward from Clear Springs towards Columbus. They, therefore, followed Colonel Hatch's command and apparently took him somewhat by surprise, but were gallantly repulsed.[14] The colonel did not follow up his advantage and reach Macon as I had hoped and directed, but did make a skillful retreat to La Grange, doing what damage he could by the way and drawing the enemy after him as far north as practicable. It would appear that after having stampeded the enemy at Palo Alto, without the loss of a man, he might have dashed down to Macon and destroyed it before the rebel reinforcements, which afterwards protected it, had arrived. He, however, no doubt did what he deemed best, considering the condition of his horses and the distance he had to march through the enemy's country in returning to La Grange, where he in due time arrived after a successful expedition.

———

After starting Colonel Hatch on his expedition and securing half an hour's rest, with the remaining portion of my command, consisting of the 6th and 7th Illinois Cavalry and four guns of Smith's battery, in all less than 1,000 officers and men, I continued my hazardous journey southward, still keeping [to] the Starkville road, arriving at that place about 4 o'clock P.M., where we captured a mail and a quantity of rebel government property, which was destroyed. From that place, we took the direct road to Louisville and, after marching about five miles through a dismal swamp nearly belly-deep in mud and water [and] sometimes swimming our horses to cross swollen streams [until] finally reaching high and suitable ground, we encamped for the night in the midst of a violent rain storm.

From that place, I detached a battalion of the 7th Illinois Cavalry, under Major Graham, to proceed to Bankston to destroy a large tannery and shoe

manufactory in the service of the rebels.[15] The detachment returned safe[l]
after having accomplished the work most effectual[ly]. A large number of
boots and shoes and quantity of leather and machinery were destroyed,
amounting in value to about $20,000, and a rebel quartermaster from Port
Hudson was captured, who was laying in a supply for General [Franklin]
Gardner's[16] command.

Up to that time, I had by the use of my orderlies [and] by occasional
small detachments sent out as foragers and select scouts for special services managed to obtain all necessary information of the country and
the movements of the enemy. But as we approached the heart of the rebel
country, I felt the need of a larger and more effective force of scouts and
arranged to secure them from among the most venturesome and daring
soldiers, to be selected with great care. Of course, the duty was so hazardous and the difficulties so great in the work desired that the service
had necessarily to be voluntary. I talked with some of the officers on the
subject, and soon after a number of suitable men were found willing to
volunteer for the duty. The 7th Illinois being in advance at the time, the
first scouts selected were from that regiment.

Lieutenant Colonel Blackburn, a very energetic and capable officer,
entered into the spirit of the thing at once, [and] said he knew the very
men to select for such perilous duty. Sergeant Richard W. Surby[17] was one
of the first to offer his services. His character being excellent, being the
quartermaster sergeant of the regiment, [he] was placed in charge of the
scouts—well-known, reliable men, from five to ten in number, who were
to be kept in advance and upon the flanks of the column to gain information as to the movements of the enemy, the character of the country, the
different roads, streams, bridges, the products of the country, the whereabouts of forage and other supplies. In short, anything which would be
of interest or importance to know was to be promptly reported. Sergeant
Surby proved to be a most excellent man for the position, and the services
of himself and scouts were invaluable and aided materially to the success
of the expedition. They could not be at the time fully reported, as it would
have insured their hanging had they been taken prisoners during the war.
After the war, Sergeant Surby published a narrative of these adventures,
under the title of *Grierson Raids*, in which many amusing incidents and
narrow escapes here omitted were related.

The scouts were soon habilitated [in] "butternut," or rebel, uniform
and their appearance was well calculated to deceive. In fact, they were for
some days taken for rebels by our own men and presumed to be prisoners, as they would at times pass the column to the rear or front. But the
officers and soldiers soon came to know them. Their singular appearance
always brought forth smiles, and Surby and his squad were soon dubbed

"The Butternut Guerillas," their quaint citizen's dress, saddles, long rifles, shotguns, pouches, and general make up completing their admirable disguise. Of course, the advance had to be particularly advised and cautioned daily about their movements. Below Starkville, the scouts made their first capture, a lieutenant from Vicksburg with a spanking team of gray horses with which he was cutting a dash with his lady love while home on leave. The horses were turned over by me to the battery.

The three days' cooked rations in haversacks and saddle pockets with which the command had left La Grange had all disappeared, and we were living entirely off the country. Foraging parties became a necessity and besides, when we stopped at a plantation for the night or to feed during the day, a detail for guard was immediately placed at the smokehouses, kitchens, and dwellings, with instructions not to allow anything to be taken without permission of a commissioned officer. The commissary and quartermaster sergeants issued out the supplies pro-rata to the various companies, giving them their proper allowance. If there was not enough for all the men and command at one plantation, part would be sent to another, but always within supporting distance. Still, the rapid marches made were such that the command seldom got more than one good meal per day. We were getting a long way from our own base of supplies, but managed to live quite well off the products of the country.

Upon entering a town, we were surprised to find ourselves at times ahead of information and were, therefore, often taken for Confederate soldiers going to intercept the Yankees, of whom all had received more or less exaggerated reports. The consternation occasioned by the sudden appearance of our detachments in conjunction with the main column, apparently so widely scattered and traveling in opposite directions, caused reports of our force to be greatly overestimated. I always had rather a remarkable faculty for judging correctly as to where supplies could be obtained, readily determining from the character of the country where a large plantation or mill ought to be located, and was sure to reach them unerringly. Sometimes, after a hard day's ride in a desolate looking country, night would approach with no apparent prospect of supplies or food for men or animals. But, by what seemed to the men an unfailing instinct, orders would be given to flank off on some by-road or across a field to an unknown or unsuspected foraging place, till the command learned to trust to my discretion or judgment without complaint.

Upon return of the detachment from Bankston [sic], we resumed our march to Louisville distant about twenty-eight miles, mostly through a dense swamp—the Noxubee River bottom. For miles, it was belly-deep to the horses, in mud and mire, so that at times no road was discernable.

The inhabitants through that part of the country generally did not know of our coming and would not believe us to be anything but Confederates. We arrived at Louisville about dark. Upon approaching the place, I sent a battalion of the 6th Illinois Cavalry, under Major [Matthew H.] Starr, rapidly in advance to picket the town and remain until the column had passed, when they were relieved by a battalion from the 7th Illinois Cavalry under Major Graham, who was instructed to remain until we should have been gone an hour, to prevent persons leaving with information of the course we had taken, to drive out stragglers, and quiet the fears of the people. They had heard of our coming a short time before we arrived, and some in great alarm had left, taking only what they could hurriedly move. The column proceeded quietly through the town without halting, and not a thing was disturbed. Those who remained at home acknowledged that they were greatly surprised. They had expected to be robbed, outraged, and to have their houses burned. On the contrary, they were protected in their persons and property.

Before our arrival at Louisville, Captain [Henry C.] Forbes,[18] with his Company B, 7th Illinois Cavalry, was detached to proceed to Macon on the Mobile and Ohio Railroad, to take the town if possible, and to destroy the railroad and telegraph and any government property that might be found there and to rejoin the main column soon as possible. Fearing that he might not be able to reach the line of the railroad with so large a force, I soon after sent Captain [John] Lynch, Company E, 6th Illinois Cavalry, and one man, Corporal [Jonathan W.] Ballard of his company, who had gallantly volunteered for the purpose, disguised as citizens, to proceed to the Mobile and Ohio Railroad and to cut the wires if possible, as it seemed important that it should be done to prevent the information of our presence and movements from flying along the wires on the railroad from Jackson and other points.

It was the sending out of these expeditions, with Colonel Hatch's regiment previously detached, together with the judicious movement of the main column so rapidly southward, that so disconcerted the enemy. General Daniel Ruggles of the Confederate Army, then commanding a district in Mississippi, referring in his official report to the conflicting rumors, states that: "a report received at 8 P.M. on the 25th of April from Lieutenant J. P. Shaw at Macon, conveyed the startling information that from reliable sources Bankston [sic] factory was burned by a large force of Federals that morning said to be 20,000 infantry and 6,000 cavalry, making their way to the Southern Railroad via Louisville and Kosciusko. While the day before a dispatch received by him from Major Hewlett of the Confederates then at Aberdeen, reported that 1,500 of the enemy's forces were between

Okolona and Aberdeen threatening an immediate attack on the latter place." Subsequently, he states that "while we were confronting the enemy at one place, another column marching westward had proceeded to the Southern Railroad between Meridian and Jackson."

After leaving the town of Louisville we struck another swamp. In crossing it, as we were obliged to do in the dark, we lost several animals drowned, and some of the men narrowly escaped the same fate. Marching until midnight, we halted until daylight at the plantation of Mr. Estus, about ten miles south of Louisville. After crossing the Big Black [Pearl] River and the swamps and reaching the rolling country beyond, the troops were taken for Van Dorn's rebel cavalry and complimented on their fine appearance. One would suppose the uniform would be known, but the men were so covered with mud and dust that at a short distance they might pass for gray. When the blue was perceived, it was supposed to be captured clothing, which it seems the rebels not unusually at that time wore. While passing a school house, the teacher gave the pupils a recess. They flocked to the roadside, hurrahing for Beauregard, Van Dorn, and the Confederacy. One little girl thought she recognized one of the men and, running up, asked him how John was, and if her uncle was along with the soldiers.

At one place, we stopped at a mill for meal. The old miller grumbled loudly when I informed him that we would receipt for what we got. "Yes, I've met your sort before. You always say you'll pay and you give receipts, but they ain't worth a damn. I wish the Yankees would come along and clean you out. They might give a fellow something. But you, you eat up everything in the country without keeping them out. Why don't you go after Grierson instead of hanging around here. Yes, I know you. You say you'll pay, but I never got a cent for what I gave you before. The Yanks might as well have it as you." By the impression that we were Confederates we readily gained much valuable information, besides misleading the enemy into many contradictory reports as to our force and movements. By information obtained by Surby and his scouts and from Negroes, many good mules and horses were secured for the command to replace those lost while crossing swamps or worn out by fatigue.

On the morning of April 23, at daylight we took the road southward to Philadelphia, a town six miles south of Pearl River, to cross which we must take or recover the bridge, which we had learned was guarded by a party of rebels. Our scouts were pushed forward and the column followed rapidly, for the bridge must be captured before it could be set on fire or destroyed, as its destruction would be fatal to our progress. The river was very high and unfordable, and before we caught sight of the gleaming water, we could hear the rushing of the turbulent flood. We were all well aware of the necessity of gaining the bridge at all hazards, and no time was lost in reaching it. The rebels had torn up some of the planks and had piled them on the bridge, with kindling, in readiness to be set on fire on notice of the approach of the Yankees. Our scouts dashed forward, followed by the troops, and reached the bridge so suddenly and unexpectedly that their well-laid plan was disconcerted, and they all fled without firing a shot or lighting the incendiary match. The planks which had been removed were quickly replaced, and very soon the tread of the horses' feet was heard as the command crossed to the south side of the swollen river. A few minutes delay or hesitation would have cost us trouble, and that delay might have proved fatal to the success of the expedition.

On our march southward from Pearl River to Philadelphia, our advance caught sight occasionally of a mounted rebel. When approaching near to the town, the force in our front gradually increased until, finally, quite a number of mounted and dismounted men were observed stretched in line across the road, apparently in readiness to dispute our passage. The scouts, with a small detachment, dashed forward and stampeded the party who, after firing a few shots, fled precipitately, six of their number being captured with their horses, equipments, etc.

One of [them] proved to be the county judge, under whose fatherly lead it seemed his citizen neighbors had armed for resistance. He was no doubt a very worthy man, and one who would naturally be looked to for advice in an emergency, but he was decidedly out of his element in command of those would-be soldiers. At first, he and his misguided followers were greatly agitated and alarmed, thinking perhaps that they would be shot or hanged by the Yankees. They acknowledged that they had sent some men to destroy the bridge, but that their hearts had failed them on our sudden approach. Seeing that they were not regular Confederate soldiers, I soon quieted their apprehensions by good-humoredly informing them that we were not there to interfere with private citizens, or to destroy their property, or to insult or molest their families; that we were after the soldiers and property of the rebel government. After some further conversation and the administration of an informal parole, they were all turned loose, a wiser if not better lot of men.

While bidding them good-bye, we moved quietly on through the town, where nothing was disturbed, passing that point about 3 o'clock P.M. on April 23, without further interruption. We proceeded about five miles southeast on the main road to Enterprise, where we rested until about 10 o'clock at night, keeping scouts well out in every direction with a view to prevent any information as to our whereabouts or movements reaching the enemy. The command being refreshed and strengthened by those few hours' recuperation, I detached two battalions of the 7th Illinois Cavalry, under command of Lieutenant Colonel Blackburn, to proceed rapidly as practicable to Decatur and thence to Newton Station on the Southern Railroad to capture the place and to inflict all the damage possible upon the enemy. I followed, with the main force, about one hour later.

It was near that point that Captain Lynch and his comrade, Corporal Ballard, rejoined the command after his perilous adventure. He had succeeded in reaching the rebel pickets near Macon. But finding that the bridge over the Noxubee had been destroyed, so that it was impossible to reach the railroad, he ascertained the disposition and numbers of the rebel forces and much other valuable information, giving in return exaggerated accounts of the force and movements of the Yankees. [He] told them that he had been sent out from Enterprise to ascertain the whereabouts and movements of the Yanks. The guard at once responded, "You need not go any further for they are now within two miles of here. The commanding officer sent out a squad of cavalry to reconnoiter, and they all returned but one, who was either killed or taken prisoner." Thus, he was at once made aware of the movement of Captain Forbes' command. Having gained all the knowledge he could as to rebel forces and position, he made an excuse to withdraw, stating that he had left two men at a plantation about a mile back; that he would go for them and return and stop with the pickets for the night. The guards thought it alright and allowed him to depart. Of course, they were not troubled by another visit from the captain, who made good his escape and, by hard riding, with his comrade rejoined the command.

The advance under Lieutenant Colonel Blackburn passed Decatur before daylight and struck the railroad about 6 o'clock A.M. I arrived there one hour after with the main column. Lieutenant Colonel Blackburn dashed into the town after first reconnoitering the place with his scouts, took possession of the railroad and telegraph, and succeeded in capturing two trains in less than half an hour after his arrival. One of those contained twenty-five cars loaded with ties and machinery. The other thirteen cars [were loaded] with commissary stores and ammunition, among the latter several thousand loaded shells. Those, together with a large quantity of commissary and quartermaster stores and about 500 stands of arms stored in the town, with much other government property, were destroyed. About 100 prisoners were captured there, and in that vicinity, and paroled. The locomotives were exploded and otherwise injured and rendered completely unserviceable. There also, the track was torn up and a bridge half a mile west of the station destroyed. I at once detached a battalion of the 6th Illinois Cavalry, under Major Starr, to proceed eastward to destroy such bridges as he might find over Chunky River.

Having damaged as much as possible the railroad and telegraph and destroyed all government property in the vicinity of Newton, I moved about four miles south of the railroad and fed men and horses. The forced marches which I had been obliged to make in order to reach the railroad successfully very much fatigued and exhausted my command. Rest and food were absolutely essential for its safety.

From captured mails and information obtained by my scouts, I knew that large forces had been sent out to intercept our return. Having instructions from Major General Hurlbut and Brigadier General Smith to move in any direction from that point, which in my discretion and judgment would be for the welfare of my command and further success of the expedition, I at once decided to continue on south in order to secure the necessary rest and food for men and horses and then return to La Grange through Alabama or make for Baton Rouge, as I might thereafter deem best. Major Starr had in the meantime rejoined us, having destroyed most effectually three bridges and several hundred feet of trestle work and telegraph from eight to ten miles east of Newton Station.

After resting about three hours, we moved south towards Garlandville. During our march that day, we overtook quite a number of citizens who were fleeing from the Yankees, having with them only such things as they most valued, fearing that they would be robbed. We at once enlightened their minds on the subject by advising them to return to their homes; that they would not be molested. At times, guards were placed to protect such persons until the column had passed, and nothing whatever was taken from them. Of course, they were greatly astonished at such kind treatment when they had been led to believe that they would be mistreated, insulted, beaten, and even murdered on sight by the so-called villainous Yankees.

Upon nearing the town of Garlandville, we found the citizens, many of them venerable with age, armed with shotguns and rifles [and] organized to resist our approach. As the advance entered the town, those citizens fired upon our soldiers and wounded one of our men and one horse. We at once charged upon and captured nearly all of them. After disarming, we showed them the folly of their action and turned the poor deluded creatures loose again without further punishment. Without an exception, they all acknowledged their mistake and declared that they had been greatly deceived as to our character. One volunteered his services as guide and, upon leaving us, declared that thereafter his prayers should be for the old Stars and Stripes and the Union army. I mention these things as a sample of the feeling which existed and of the good effect which our presence produced among the people in the country through which we passed. Hundreds who were skulking and hiding to avoid conscription were only waiting for the presence of our arms to sustain them, when they would rise up and declare their principles, and thousands who had been deceived, upon the vindication of our cause, would at once return to loyalty.[19]

During our stay at Garlandville, Lieutenant Woodward, my acting assistant adjutant general, while looking for forage and provisions, entered a house where the lamps were lighted, the supper on the table, the corn bread actually steaming hot from the stove, and everything else correspondingly fresh. Not a soul was to be seen, nor would come for calling, nor could be found about the premises. He stepped to the door and called me in to observe the condition of affairs. When informed of all the facts, having a very decided relish for such savory food, we could not resist the temptation and sat down to the table and ate the supper at our ease. But we never learned for whom it was prepared.

After such delay as was deemed advisable, we moved southwest from Garlandville about ten miles and encamped at night on the plantation of Mr. [C. M.] Bender, about two miles west of Montrose. Our men and horses having become gradually exhausted, I determined upon making a very easy march the next day and to look more to the recruiting of my little command than to the accomplishment of any more important object. Consequently, I marched at 8 o'clock the next morning taking a west, and varying to a northwest, course. After proceeding about five miles, we halted to feed and rest at the plantation of Mr. [Elias] Nichols. There we rested until about 2 o'clock P.M., during which time I sent detachments north to threaten the line of the railroad at Lake Station and other points, after which we moved southwest toward Raleigh, making about twelve miles during the afternoon, and halted at dark on the plantation of [Dr.] Mackadora. From that point I sent a single scout to proceed northwest to the line of the Southern Railroad to cut the telegraph wires and, if possible, fire a bridge or trestle work.

His name was [George] Steadman, one of the men selected from among Sergeant Surby's scouts. He was a medium-sized, muscular man [with] sandy complexion [and] reddish hair. He sometimes was as honest and harmless-looking as a Presbyterian deacon. He had a peculiar impediment, or sort of stutter, in his speech which enabled him to think twice before he answered once any question put to him. Altogether, his makeup—with his long hunting rifle, powder horn, etc.—was most admirable. He started on his journey about midnight and, as I shook hands with him on his departure and bid him God's speed, I thought to myself that in any event the rebels would not get the best of that singular-looking, but bright and sharp, individual.

He made his way without interruption to a point within seven miles of the railroad, where he suddenly came upon a regiment of rebel cavalry from Brandon, who were out in search of the Yankees. Passing himself off for a citizen of the country, he conversed with the commanding officer, and answering all the questions put to him in a satisfactory manner considering the impediment in his speech, he succeeded in effectually misdirecting the rebels as to the place where he had last seen us. Having seen them well on their wrong road, he immediately retreated his steps to camp with the news of his adventure. When he first met the rebels they were on the direct road to our camp and, had they not been turned from their course, would have come up to us before daylight.

From information received through my scouts who were kept out in all directions and from other sources, I found that Jackson and the stations east as far as Lake Station had been reinforced by infantry and artillery. Hearing that a fight was momentarily expected at Grand Gulf, I promptly decided to make a rapid march, cross Pearl River again, and strike the New Orleans, Jackson, and Great Northern Railroad at Hazlehurst. After destroying as much of the road as possible, [I would] endeavor to get upon the flank of the enemy and cooperate with our forces and join them, if practicable, should they be successful in the attack upon Grand Gulf and Port Gibson.

Having obtained during the day and night plenty of forage and provisions, and having had a good rest for my command, we were invigorated and strengthened to such an extent as to be again ready for any emergency that might arise. Accordingly, at 6 o'clock in the morning of April 26, we continued our march, crossed Leaf River, burning the bridge behind us to prevent the enemy who might be in pursuit from following, then moved through Raleigh, where we captured the sheriff of that county with $3,000 in Confederate government funds. [We] then proceeded to Westville, reaching that place soon after dark.

Near Pineville, a small place passed through that day, we came upon a large plantation, the owner of which was in the field with his whip driving the Negroes. Being summoned to the house, he readily complied but was vexed to see the soldiers helping themselves to fodder without even asking leave. He said that "he had none to spare. Not[hing] but the Confederate vouchers were good enough, and he was willing to loan his share, but he had fed several squads already and had no more left than he wanted for his own use." He complimented the soldiers upon their fine looks, saying how well they were dressed and how healthy they looked and what superb arms they had. He gave us all the information he could but probably made a very wry face when the men, in searching the outbuildings, found and released an imprisoned Negro slave, manacled and chained to a ring in the floor for trying to run away. The irons, an inch thick, had worn the flesh to the bone, inducing gangrene and almost mortification. The poor fellow went through with us to Baton Rouge and never tired of serving his deliverers.

The slaves had heard all manner of stories about the hated Yankees. They were represented to be a "kind of beast, had horns, hooves and claws; were like the devil and would eat people up, would run the blacks off to Cuba and sell them, etc." Few of them, however, believed those kinds of yarns. Among themselves they imagined God was sending the Yankees, like angels, on purpose to make them free. Not a word could be pumped out of them in the presence of their masters. But out of sight of the manor house, from under bushes or logs or fence corners or tall weeds or swamp grass, a wooly head and shambling figure would crawl slowly out, look carefully about, and then tell with grinning lips or point with dusky finger "whar massa's horses done be hid," or "whar spec de secesh soldiers is," followed by the restful query: "When are you uns gwine to make we uns free?"

Passing on through Westville, we halted to feed again about two miles beyond the town, in the midst of a heavy rain, on the plantation of Mr. [George W.] Williams, a major in the rebel army home on leave and then living near Pearl River. He was quietly sitting in his house when I rode up and halted before his door in the midst of the storm. Being so far inland from Port Hudson, Port Gibson, and Vicksburg, he never dreamed of the presence of Yankees. He came quietly to the door and asked whose command it was. No one seemed to pay attention to him. The soldiers rode through his gate and tied their horses to the trees. He became furious. [He] swore that he would report the commanding officer to General Pemberton; that he would not stand such abuse and insult on his own premises; they were ruining his garden and feeding up his corn and fodder. He became cooler, however, when to his great surprise he found out with whom he had to deal.

———

After feeding and resting the command at the plantation of Major Williams, Colonel Prince of the 7th Illinois Cavalry, with two battalions, was sent immediately forward to Pearl River to secure the ferry and landing. He arrived in time to capture a courier, who had come to bring intelligence of the approach of the Yankees and orders for the destruction of the ferry. With the main column I followed as rapidly as practicable, in about two hours.

When Colonel Prince reached Pearl River early in the morning of April 27, the ferry boat was on the opposite side. Not daring to arouse the citizens by hailing it, the colonel called for a volunteer to swim the swollen river.

One man undertook the perilous task, but the current was so strong [that] he was carried down and nearly lost his life. Presently, a man came to the shore on the other side and asked if they wanted to cross. The colonel answered promptly, with an imitation of the southern accent, manner, and voice: "A few of us would like to cross, but it was harder to wake his nigger ferryman than to catch the conscripts." The man at once woke up the ferryman and sent him over with the boat. We ferried and swam our horses and succeeded in crossing the whole command by 2 o'clock P.M. As soon as Colonel Prince had crossed his two battalions, he was ordered to proceed immediately to the New Orleans, Jackson, and Great Northern Railroad, striking it at Hazlehurst. Our troops were taken for the 1st Alabama Cavalry coming from Mobile. I receipted to the ferryman for the passage of the command in the name of that regiment.

As the crossing was necessarily slow, only twenty-four horses at a time, myself and staff officers accepted an invitation to breakfast at a fine house near the ferry. The meal was well served [and] the ladies were all smiles. But in the midst of our enjoyment, and before the repast was finished, up came some blunder head of a soldier and blurted out to me something about the "6th Illinois Cavalry" and what they were doing. The countenances of the hosts changed, and some persons at once left the room. I knew very well that every effort would be made to give information. Bidding the ladies good-bye rather hastily, and without waiting to finish the breakfast, I instantly dispatched a messenger to hurry up my scouts previously sent to Hazlehurst [and] with a written dispatch in the name of the rebel colonel to General Pemberton at Jackson to say that "the Yankees had advanced to Pearl River and finding the ferry destroyed they could not cross and had left, taking a north-easterly course."

The scouts reached Hazlehurst, ten miles distant, taking prisoners by the way several citizens with arms who were gathering to exterminate the invading Yankees. They also destroyed a gunsmith shop with twenty-five guns of all descriptions—muskets, rifles, pistols, old shotguns, etc. They captured [as well] a rebel courier, who was hurrying to the river with a warning that the Yankees were crossing and that the ferry boat must be destroyed.

Two of the scouts reached the telegraph office in Hazlehurst with my feigned dispatch. It tallied with the orders already sent to destroy the ferry. The operator was seated, with six or eight Confederate officers and soldiers standing around. They had not the least idea that the Yankees were [on] that side of Pearl River. The dispatch was examined, canvassed, and sent in their presence. The scouts then complained of hunger and mounted their horses to ride to the hotel, when up came a prisoner who had managed to escape the night before. He at once recognized the scouts and shouted for help to arrest them. But they were mounted and at full gallop. Several persons tried to stop them, but the crack of revolvers warned them off. They soon met the rapidly advancing column and re-entered the town. When they went to the depot again, not a soul was there but two old men. The rest had absconded and the telegraph operator had taken his instrument with him. He had not succeeded in countermanding the false dispatch, for judging accurately when it would be sent, we had cut the wires between the offices and Jackson immediately afterward.

It was at Georgetown, after crossing Pearl River, that the gallant Captain Forbes rejoined us. He had fortunately reached the river just as the last of the command were crossing and soon after came up with the column, having had a most exciting and wonderfully successful expedition. It will be remembered that he was sent off from the main command near Louisville to proceed to Macon on the Mobile and Ohio Railroad. I had hoped that Colonel Hatch, previously sent to destroy that railroad, would have succeeded in reaching it at that place. But, hearing no rumors of his proceedings since being detached from the command, and wishing to break the road at Macon if possible, I had offered to Captain Forbes, through Colonel Prince, the dangerous but necessary service of seeing what could be done.

Captain Forbes, with his little company of thirty-five men, volunteered for the doubtful attempt. Finding that he could not reach [the railroad] for the same reason that prevented Captain Lynch, [and] meeting with the same barriers in the destruction of the bridge over the Noxubee River, he turned back to our trail [but] was thrown off at Newton Station by the very success with which he had fooled the rebels. He had to go through swamps, [cross] swollen streams, [and] travel through timber, often regardless of roads, for hours at a time in order to avoid forces that were patrolling the country in quest of the Yankees.

He reached Enterprise and marched his little squad into town, but found instead of myself and command 3,000 rebels just getting off on the cars. Quick as thought, he raised a flag of truce and riding forward demanded that they surrender in the name of Colonel Grierson. It seemed that my name was a host on that occasion. I have still the soiled scrawl so hastily penciled by the commanding officer, which is as follows: "Colonel [Edwin] Goodwin's compliments to Colonel Grierson, commanding United States Forces, and asks permission to consider his demand for one hour." Captain Forbes gravely promised to carry the report "back to the reserves" and made good use of the hour. Whether he was pursued, or how long the rebel colonel with his 3,000 men waited for the expected reply or to consider the proposition, was never known. But by rough riding at the rate of sixty miles per day, he re-joined the column without loss. Surprising by the way a party of guerillas, [he] destroyed their arms and carried off their horses and captain.

At Hazlehurst, we found a number of cars containing about 6,000 loaded shells and a large quantity of commissary stores and quartermaster stores intended for Grand Gulf and Port Gibson. They were all destroyed, together with as much of the railroad and telegraph as possible. Upon the first arrival of the troops at Hazlehurst, it was learned that a train was soon due from the north. The usual precaution was taken by Colonel Prince to capture it, but waiting a proper time for its appearance and presuming that it was not coming, the soldiers again became scattered about the town when suddenly the train hove in sight around a corner from which the engineer caught the sight of the "Blue Coats." By quickly reversing his engine, he succeeded in retreating safely with, so it was said, several Confederate officers and a large amount of Confederate money. The depot was not destroyed on account of its proximity to other buildings in the town. Several barrels of eggs, [together with] a lot of sugar, flour, ham, and bacon, were found at the station, which with other supplies appropriated proved sufficient for a hearty meal for the entire command.

Despite all efforts to prevent it, a drug store near where the cars were burned took fire. That and several other buildings adjoining were consumed. But the officers and men worked energetically and, by great exertion, saved the town from destruction. The citizens who had arrived to resist us, hearing of this, returned and were greatly astonished at our action and complimented us upon our good conduct. They were not the first nor the last of the citizens of Mississippi who were surprised at our gentlemanly bearing and leniency towards those who might have been treated as foes to the general government and Union cause.

After several hours' rest, we moved out from Hazlehurst in good order, taking a northwesterly [westerly] course to Gallatin four miles, thence southwest three and a half miles to the plantation of Mr. Thompson, where we halted until the next morning. Directly after leaving Gallatin we captured a sixty-four-pound gun and a heavy wagon load of ammunition and machinery for mounting the gun, all on the road to Port Gibson. The gun was spiked and carriage and ammunition destroyed. During the afternoon it rained in torrents, and the men were completely drenched.

At 6 o'clock the next morning, April 28, we moved westward. After proceeding a short distance, I detached a battalion of the 7th Illinois Cavalry, under Captain Trafton, to proceed back to the railroad at Byhala [Bahala] to destroy the road, telegraph, and all government property to be found there. With the rest of the command I moved southwest towards Union Church. We halted to feed at 2 o'clock P.M., on the plantation of Mr. [Adam] Snyder, about two miles northeast of the town. While feeding, our pickets were fired upon by a considerable force of the rebels. I immediately moved out upon the rebels, skirmished with and drove them through the town, wounding and capturing a number who proved to belong to Wirt Adams' Alabama Cavalry. After driving them away, we held the town and bivouacked for the night.

After accomplishing the object of his expedition, Captain Trafton returned to us about 3 o'clock in the morning of the 29th, having come upon the rear of the main body of Adams' command. The enemy having a battery of artillery, it was his intention to attack us in front and rear about daylight. But the sudden appearance of Captain Trafton with a force in his rear changed his purpose, and quickly turning to the right, he flanked off and took the direct road towards Port Gibson.

After leaving Hazlehurst, the greatest generalship [and] the utmost care and vigilance was necessary for the safety of my command. We were within twenty-five miles of the capital of the state; could hear the great guns from the fleet and the rebel strongholds on the Mississippi; could make no communication with General Grant's forces, nor cooperate with him, as I had hoped, in an attack on Grand Gulf. I had hurried forward fearing that I might be too late, but unfortunately had traveled a little too fast and was a few days ahead of time. It was impossible to wait or remain quietly there, for the rebels were all round us.

In spite of all my precautions, one courier had escaped from Georgetown to General Gardner at Port Hudson. The enemy had every advantage—a knowledge of the country; of every road, public or private; every stream of water, large or small, with its fords and bridges. They had forces above and below on the railroad, in front from Port Hudson to Vicksburg on the river, and in rear everywhere in all directions. Their scouts were watching; their couriers flying; their troops concentrating to capture us. What should hinder them from annihilating myself and small command? One thing only was in the way, and that was there were two parties to that little transaction. I, too, understood the runways and the shortest route to reach them. I also knew the rebels, their whereabouts, and the surest way to blind and lead them astray. I thought subtly through the difficult problem. I considered what Generals Gardner and Pemberton and other rebel commanders would do as capable military men, and what they would expect me to do. Then I did not do what was expected of me.

My first duty and business was to destroy the railroad, and I did it first for fifty miles from Bahala to Summit, so thoroughly that it was not repaired till long after the war was over. We thus effectually broke up the railroad connection between Port Hudson and Vicksburg and rendered the rebel strongholds unable to communicate with, or support each other, besides starving them out by cutting off their supplies and so forcing them to an earlier surrender. Meantime, I fooled the enemy by a strong feint against Natchez and Port Gibson. While Captain Trafton was behind, destroying the railroad at Bahala, the main column, by a zigzag route, was making its way to Union Church. Even our men supposed we were going to the Mississippi. None but myself and my adjutant were in [on] the secret.

A prominent citizen who had been taken prisoner was treated with such consideration and courtesy as to be brought into the house with us and led to believe that I did not know how great a rebel he was or how much he was devoted to the Southern cause. He was rather carelessly placed in an adjoining room to the one I occupied and within earshot of myself and adjutant, where he could hear our conversation. He heard the conclusion of our conversation and heard me clearly articulate the remark that I was determined to go to Natchez and then cross the Mississippi. The rebel citizen was then slyly suffered to make his escape without being paroled, that he might carry the information thus obtained to the enemy who surrounded us.

General Gardner reckoned from military reasons that our troops would not go to Natchez and had instructed his forces to close in behind me at Union Church. He did so once, but Captain Trafton's detachment, returning to the command, came unexpectedly in his rear and alarmed them. They went off on a side road and swung round to ambush myself and command on our way to Natchez. Meantime, our men were resting and getting into true fighting trim and mood. The cavalry went through the village of Union Church by sheer might. Whole lines of picket fences were torn up and overturned by a mere rush. Right and left went everything that came in their way, scarcely breaking their onward step. The enemy they had to do with were part of Wirt Adams' Cavalry. No wonder they retreated to their reserve to ambush.

That night our scouts, riding in disguise, captured a rebel picket who informed them that "we belong to old Wirt Adams' Cavalry and tomorrow we intend to give the Yankees under Grierson hell," adding that Colonel Adams had gone to Fayette to be reinforced from the river and would meet the Yanks between Union Church and that place; that the Yanks intended to make Natchez but would get slipped up; that their pickets were at the crossroads to notify all forces coming up where to find Colonel Adams. But on the next day those men, instead of helping to "give the Yanks hell," were riding along with our column [as] prisoners of war. Therefore, from

Union Church I of course made a strong demonstration towards Fayette, with a view to impress upon the enemy the belief that we had certainly determined to go to Natchez or Port Gibson, in accordance with the plan revealed to our citizen prisoner who was allowed to escape to thus report our intentions, while we quietly took the opposite direction to Brookhaven on the railroad.

Before we arrived at that place, we ascertained that about 500 citizens and conscripts had organized to resist us. Upon [our] charging into the town, however, they fled, making but little resistance. Thus, while the befooled Colonel Adams was waiting in ambush till 2 o'clock P.M., his game was "over the hills and far away," tearing up railroads, burning Confederate property [and] bridges, and capturing rebels. So bewildered were the people of the country that, while on the way to Brookhaven, we actually met loaded trains of wagons which were running off provisions and other property to save it from the Yankees.

We were received in Brookhaven with terror and confusion. There was much running and yelling as our cavalry dashed into the place, but it soon quieted down into almost a welcome. The landlord of the hotel, being well paid in captured Confederate money for his dinners, said he wished "the Yanks would come every day, if they all paid like you uns do." The private houses and property of the citizens were guarded and their families protected. The depot and other buildings [were] saved from burning by the exertions of the soldiers under my direct supervision.

I recently passed through Brookhaven, going northward from New Orleans. The scenes here described were brought vividly to mind, as were also those at other stations enacted nearly thirty-five years ago—by my command. Little did the citizens, when passing to and fro about the streets, suspect that the modest-looking individual who sat in the sleeper quietly gazing at the place was the man who had created such a stir in their midst so long ago. All of the towns referred to looked about as they did in 1863, leaving out the bustle and excitement then caused by the presence of the Federal cavalry.

———

We captured over 200 prisoners at Brookhaven [and] a large and beautiful camp of instruction, comprising several hundred tents, [together with] a large quantity of quartermasters and commissary stores, ammunition, arms, etc. After paroling the prisoners and destroying the railroad and all government property, we moved southward about dark and encamped for the night at Mr. Gill's plantation, about eight miles south of Brookhaven.[20] The following morning, we moved directly south along the line of the railroad, destroying all bridges and trestle-work to Bogue Chitto Station, where we burned the depot and contents—fifteen freight cars—and captured a large secession flag.

From thence we still moved along the railroad, destroying every bridge, trestle-work, water tank, etc., as we passed to Summit, which place we reached soon after noon. There we destroyed twenty-five freight cars and a large quantity of government sugar. We found much Union sentiment in that town and were kindly welcomed and fed by the citizens, who had heard from Brookhaven and elsewhere of our kind and considerate action towards the people. They were less alarmed than at other places, feeling that their persons and property would not be molested or interfered with. It was simply the old story over again and a sample of the effects as to what kindness could do. I suddenly found myself an object of special interest, and it seemed as if the inhabitants of that section of the country, as a rule, could not do too much for us. I became as great a favorite as General Pemberton.

At that place, however, we met an enemy more dangerous just then than Wirt Adams' Cavalry and other rebel troops. Some forty barrels of Louisiana rum were hidden under the sidewalks, as if soldiers could not nose them out. I discovered them before it was too late to save my men, and emptied the vile stuff as remorselessly as I did the canteens of whiskey of my soldiers at Shawneetown two years before.

Hearing nothing more of our forces at Grand Gulf and not being able to ascertain anything definite as to General Grant's movements or whereabouts, I concluded to make for Baton Rouge to recruit my command, after which I could return to La Grange through southern Mississippi and western Alabama, or by crossing the Mississippi River, move through Louisiana and Arkansas. Accordingly, after resting two hours the call for "Boots and Saddles" was sounded, just as the sun was setting. Amid the waving of handkerchiefs and much genuine good feeling of the citizens, we started again on our march southward [southwest] to Liberty, where we camped for the night on the plantation of Mr. [Alten] Spurlack.

As the column filed out, a lady came down to the gate in front of her house and asked for the commanding officer. I was told of her wishes, and as the troops moved on I presented myself, apparently much to her gratification. She was very ladylike, polite and courteous, and her civility met a suitable response from me as she apologized for occupying a few moments of my time. I dismounted to listen in a most respectful manner to what she had to say. She told me that her husband was an officer in the Confederate Army and that her whole soul, like his, was enlisted in the Confederate cause; that she was a Southern woman through and through, but that she was amazed at my great success; that the whole thing from beginning beat anything she had ever heard of or read in history; that if the North should win in the end and I should ever run for president, her husband should vote for me or she would certainly endeavor to get a divorce from him. Thanking her in a suitable manner for her appreciation of my efforts and the exploits of my command, we tendered each other an adieu as we separated and I galloped off to take my place at the head of the column. After traveling about fifteen miles in a southeasterly [southwesterly] direction, we encamped in the vicinity of Liberty.

Perhaps some of the Louisiana rum had not yet worked off, or it may have been that the name of the man that owned the plantation (Spurlack) had proven suggestive and some of the men were "spread up" in their search for food to a lack of proper regard for their hungry comrades. In any event, there was played a "maneuver" not set down in the tactics. There had been all those fourteen days of hard work scarcity of rest and rations, wherein the officers had scarcely fared so well as the men and especially the scouts, who were feasted on the fat of the land. Being taken for Confederates, they were well supplied and the men were usually first served.

That night, I had determined that myself and staff should have a good supper, or at least be as well provided for as the soldiers. I accordingly had a guard placed at a well-filled chicken coop, while the storehouses and smokehouses were opened as usual and their contents dealt out to the men. But while superintending the necessary arrangements of a camp in the face of the enemy and looking in person to the details upon which our safety depended, I was suddenly made aware that the men, either by hustling away or by conniving with the guard, were devastating the hen coop. I hastened to the spot, looked in, and saw the last chicken and a hand grasping for it. Now, I am tall and of such a figure that when in full uniform and on dress parade, like many another officer, I make quite an imposing appearance, so it has been said. In any event, my soldiers sprung from lounging or careless positions to do me reverence as military etiquette and occasion required, which was answered with gracious politeness as behooved a dignified soldier or commanding officer.

In my travel-stained uniform, I cannot say just how I looked, nor did I stop to consider. I neither called for a guard nor for help, but drew my saber and went for that private like a flash of lightning. I jumped clean over the hen coop, around the pig sty, through the stable, behind the smokehouse, between the horses and under the horses. Dodging the trees and shrubbery, hopping over briers [and] up and down steps, smashing the trellis, and vociferating in language more forcible than polite, I closely pursued that soldier and squeaking hen, while the laughing officers, whose attention had been attracted by the novel scene, were clapping their hands and cheering on the lively chase, until finally the soldier went scrambling and tumbling over a high rail fence, dropping the fowl on my side under a stroke of the saber. I grasped the fluttering, cackling thing with a firm hand and held it up in triumph. It did not need much picking by that time. The victory was gained, and the cook and bystanders declared that I had surely earned my "fricassee."

That night we held the forks of several important roads, on all of which the rebels were closing in upon us. Besides myself and adjutant and a few of the scouts, our dangerous situation was unknown to the command. I knew just where the rebel forces were and decided just how to avoid them and outwit them. The next morning, detachments were sent out to make demonstrations towards Magnolia, Osyka, and other points, while I led the main column through fields, woods, and by-lands southward.

Coming upon an old but well-defined ridge road, within a few miles we met an old man going to mill. He took us for rebel troops and asked how in thunder we got in there. Said we were on the "old Kentucky trail," which he thought nobody knew but himself. I asked him how much he knew about the roads and country. He said that he knew every inch within ten miles, but beyond that he did not know much. I told him he was just the man we wanted as a guide; that he must go with us. He said no, he'd enough of that work; that the fellows had taken him before and never given him a cent for his trouble. He wanted to go about his own business; he had enough to do without fooling his time away with us. He asked why we didn't go to fight the Yankees instead of riding around the country in that way. Where did we get our good clothes? They were better than any clothes he had seen us fellows wear before. He was told that we got our clothes from the Yankees at Holly Springs. On being offered a horse to keep for his own use and some Confederate money, he concluded that he would go along with us for awhile. He filled the desired position as guide, through wood and plantations, in an admirable manner.

On coming into the main road from Clinton to Osyka, fresh horse tracks showed that a considerable force of the enemy had passed but a short time before. It proved to be the 9th Tennessee Cavalry going to guard the bridge over the Tickfaw River. The column was halted and the scouts sent forward in Confederate uniform. They rode straight up to the first picket, shouting out: "Hello, boys on picket." The rebels were deceived as usual and answered: "Yes, been on about an hour and feel devilish tired. Been traveling night and day after the damned Yanks, and I'll bet my horse that they'll get away yet." "That is just our case," answered the scouts, "but where is your command?"

While the conversation was going on, the column was hidden from view behind the trees which intervened by a bend in the road. But an officer, with a few men from the rear of our command, took advantage of the halt to go to a house nearby, where unexpectedly they met some straggling rebels. Upon discovering each other, a few shots were unfortunately fired, our men capturing two prisoners and four horses in the skirmish. The firing alarmed those in front and, although the first pickets were speedily taken and passed to the rear, yet our scouts riding forward soon came upon a rebel officer, Captain [E. A.] Scott and his orderly, who riding slowly towards them asked: "What in hell does all that firing mean?" The ready scout answered that reinforcements were coming up and your pickets fired on our advance, but no one was hurt and it was all right. "Is that all?" they said with a laugh and galloped forward. They were also quietly taken and passed to the rear.

The passage of the Tickfaw might have been a complete surprise and accomplished without loss, but for the accident of the firing and alarm. Unfortunately, Lieutenant Colonel Blackburn, calling on the scouts to follow him, dashed forward to the bridge without waiting for the column to come into supporting distance. Colonel Blackburn had asked specially for command of the advance that day, the 7th Illinois being in front, and I had given it, admonishing him particularly to make a cautious approach. The little squad that made the gallant dash with Colonel Blackburn were, of course, quickly repulsed and compelled to retreat and wait for reinforcements to dislodge the enemy from his strong position. Had the colonel been as discreet and wary as he was brave, it is very probable that not a man would have been wounded, and very likely most of the rebels would have been captured, as our approach was not expected from that direction.

As it was, the enemy was quickly driven off in great disorder by dismounting two companies that were pushed forward as skirmishers and flanked the bridge by getting into position on the banks of the stream, followed speedily by the column. It was all accomplished so quickly that the old man citizen, who had not yet discovered his first mistake, was in high glee. [He] turned round to our men and exclaimed: "Why you can fight. I thought you were a lot of dandies in your fine clothes. But, Moses, didn't you clean those Yanks out nicely." Finding that he knew nothing about the country beyond the Tickfaw, he was dismissed on the horse that had been given to him, departing northward in blissful ignorance as to who we really were. In due time, it is safe to presume, he found that he had been for a time in the clutches of the dreadful Yankees. Our loss in that engagement was one man killed and Lieutenant Colonel Blackburn and four men wounded—Sergeant Surby, who had rendered such faithful and efficient service, among the number.

As the column passed, the brave Colonel Blackburn tried to rise from the ground where he had fallen mortally wounded, with his dead horse lying partly on him, and said to me: "Onward, Colonel. Onward, men. Whip the rebels. Onward and save your command. Don't mind me." Thus heroically urging us on to victory, when he knew he was being separated from his comrades forever.

The 6th Illinois Cavalry charged, routing the rebels [and] dispersing them in all directions. We captured, in all, over thirty prisoners. While the 7th Illinois looked after and cared for the wounded, the 6th Illinois pushed on in pursuit of the enemy. Everything possible was done for the comfort of those left behind. They were all taken to the plantation of Mr. [Thomas] Newman, about one mile distant beyond the bridge. Their horses, equipments, and arms were taken through with us. I dismounted, turned back, and bid Colonel Blackburn and the other wounded men farewell, knowing that we could not all meet again on earth. A doctor and nurse were left to take charge of the wounded. We all deeply regretted the loss met with at the Tickfaw, which might have been avoided.[21]

Colonel Prince was at first considerably excited over the loss which fell upon his regiment. He wished to go into camp there. But that under the circumstances was not advisable, as he quickly saw on reflection. Three more rivers were yet to be crossed. The enemy were gathering thick and fast behind us. We were near their strongholds, and delay would have been fatal to success. Leaving our comrades behind, I ordered the column to advance and on we marched.

At 2 o'clock that afternoon, we had a race with about fifty rebels for another bridge over the Tickfaw River, which we re-crossed on our way to Greensburg. The rebels were on a parallel road, but our men got to the bridge first. After crossing, with one battalion of the 6th Illinois Cavalry and two guns of the battery flanked off to the right, I drove the enemy away without halting the column. At about 4 P.M., we passed through Greensburg, taking prisoner the county clerk who, armed with a shotgun, was waiting at the crossroads for a courier with information. At that place Lieutenant [George W.] Newell, Company G, 6th Illinois Cavalry, overtook the command, having been ordered out early that morning with a view to procure some horses and provisions. He was not aware of our fight until he had passed over the battleground, and had a narrow escape from capture.

We were again ahead of information, and it was of vital importance to move rapidly in order to secure the bridge over the Amite River, a large stream swollen by recent rains into a rapid torrent. We had captured that day two couriers from Port Hudson, who were on their way to Osyka. One courier, despite all our vigilance, had escaped us, taking the most direct route from a point near Liberty to Port Hudson. I had calculated the time that he would reach General Gardner's headquarters and the probable time that would elapse before he could send a force to Williams Bridge, the only place we could cross the Amite River on our way to Baton Rouge. That a large force would be sent there was very evident to my mind, and we must reach that important point before them.

On, then, by moonlight over the level roads and through the beautiful pine forests, when the enemy was sleeping and tarrying by the way. Large forces were in pursuit behind us; large forces were moving to our front. Our scouts, who were kept well ahead to give information, learned that a company was stationed near the bridge about one mile away, while a detachment of ten men was kept on the bridge by day and all but two recalled at night. The two guards were taken as usual. The scouts advanced, with letter in hand, as couriers on the way to Port Hudson. A cocked revolver [was] quickly placed at the heads of the guards. No words were spoken above a whisper, and both were readily captured. On notice that the bridge was ours, it was not long until the welcome sound of our horses' hooves were heard reverberating as we went gaily marching on over the raging torrent. Over the long bridge we passed at midnight, while other watchers were sleeping a half mile and mile away.

Without halting the command—for another large river was still to be crossed before rest could be obtained for my weary command—I sent a company of the 6th Illinois Cavalry to fire into the camp of the bridge guard. If an earthquake had occurred, or lightning struck them from the cloudless, starlight heaven above, they could not have been more surprised or more bewildered. They jumped from their sleep and departed. Those who could get away, it was thought, never would stop running. Some were killed and some captured, and the troop rejoined the column.

The enemy were but a few hours behind us, [and] a large force of infantry and artillery reached the bridge early the next day. We could still hear the booming of our own heavy guns from the Mississippi. All night we rode and made good speed, although nearly the entire command were much of the time asleep on their horses. Often, as the officers and men would be nodding, their horses would flank off and stop to eat grass. The shock given by the occasion of the inaction or momentum would waken up the rider, when the horse and man would re-enter the column. A few officers and men who believed they could keep awake were kept on the flanks to route up the sleepy horses and men. Besides myself, few of the command were awake that night.

———

About daylight on May 2, while the command was marching on towards the Comite River, information was received that a large rebel camp had been discovered and was then only a short distance ahead. At the time this news reached us, nearly the entire command of officers and soldiers were asleep on their horses. The prospect of a fight, however, quickly awakened all the sleepers, who began to tighten up their reins, grasp their carbines and revolvers, and prepare for a charge, the order for which was soon given. It was wonderful to observe what life and vigor was stirred up as the order went back to the rear to prepare for a rapid advance upon the foe which, to judge from the size of the camp, must be a considerable force.

The order "trot march" was given, soon followed by the "gallop" and then the "charge," as into the camp we dashed, down through the long rows of tents, with a tremendous yell, firing right and left, waking the sleepers, who felt so secure that they had no pickets out. Only one of the entire outfit escaped. Being subsequently captured, [he] told his story of that night: At the first shots and yells, he rushed from his tent, reached his horse, hastily untied and mounted him barebacked without any bridle, [and] with nothing on but his shirt, drawers, and socks. He never stopped until he reached his home, "sixty miles away." It turned out that there was only a guard left at the camp. The entire effective force had gone north toward Natchez or Brookhaven to intercept "Grierson and his raiders." A few were killed during the charge and about forty prisoners captured. The 6th Illinois Cavalry destroyed the camp, while the 7th Illinois marched on.

Soon an officer appeared in the road coming towards us. It proved to be the rebel lieutenant colonel [Lieutenant Joseph Hinson] going towards his camp to see what the firing meant. He wheeled his horse and dashed on towards our scouts, who had already passed the advance. He took them for his own men and shouted: "Get like hell boys, the road is full of Yanks in our rear." "Yes," they answered, and "here you are among them," as they closed around and captured him.

On we rode towards the last large river, which was reported to be high, with bridges destroyed and stream unfordable. It was also ascertained by the scouts that Stuart's Cavalry [Miles Legion] were stationed there, in happy ignorance of the fact that the Yankees were in their rear and near at hand. They were picketing the last station towards Baton Rouge. When the scouts came up to the picket, the rebels said: "How are you, gentlemen? Have you come to relieve us?" "Yes our company will soon be up," the scouts replied. "It's about time, for we have been here four days and are nearly out of rations."

The camp of the enemy and river not being far off, I had ordered one battalion to the right and another to the left. So soon as they had gained the river bank, they both wheeled and moved forward, while the balance of the command were so disposed as to fill up the entire space between the two battalions. Thus we closed up upon the enemy and, when near enough, charged. So complete was the surprise that only one made his escape and that was the rebel captain [B. F. Bryan], who had climbed up into a tree and thus escaped observation, he being hid behind the thick Spanish moss which encircled it. No more than a dozen shots were fired. One sergeant took over a dozen rebels out of a hole in the bank of the river, all of whom surrendered to him on demand. The confusion was indescribable. Shotguns, rifles, saddle blankets, camp kettles, coats, and hats were scattered in all directions, while men, horses, and mules were stampeding from all quarters but could not get through our lines. We captured forty men with their horses, arms, and equipments. Everything in their camp that could not be taken along was destroyed, together with tents and all government property, same as at the camp at the Big Sandy.

Although the river had been very high and unfordable for some time previous to our arrival, and the bridge had been destroyed, by a little search we found a place where it could be forded. In due time, the entire command reached the opposite side of the stream where, knowing that no enemy in sufficient force could possibly be between us and Baton Rouge, I ordered the entire command, excepting a suitable guard for prisoners, to take a good rest. It was not long until every officer and soldier but myself, Lieutenant Woodward, and the guard were enjoying a sound and refreshing sleep.

Finding a house nearby, I astonished the occupants by sitting down and playing upon a piano which I found in the parlor. In that manner, I managed to keep awake while my soldiers were enjoying themselves by relaxation, sleep, and quiet rest. Only six miles then to Baton Rouge, and four miles would bring us inside of the lines guarded by the soldiers of the Union. Think of the great relief to the overtaxed mind and nerves. I felt that we had nobly accomplished the work assigned us, and no wonder that I felt musical. Who would not under like circumstances?

When the command was halted to rest on the south side of the Comite River, one of my orderlies, who happened to be asleep and therefore did not hear the order, went moping on, nodding to the motion of his horse. The tired steed, realizing that a town was near and a better resting place, walked on to the Federal picket line adjoining the town. There the horse was stopped by the pickets and the soldier awakened. He rubbed his eyes in astonishment and answered all the questions put to him in a sort of a dazed manner. When he finally told the Federal guards that he belonged to Colonel Grierson's command from La Grange, Tennessee, [and] that the colonel with the 6th and 7th Illinois Cavalry were only a few miles outside, he was not believed. They thought it was some sort of a trap to draw their troops out to ambush.

It should be remembered that intelligence of the starting of the expedition had not yet traveled from La Grange to Baton Rouge, by the way of the New York and New Orleans route. The Union scouts, in the meantime, reported to General [Christopher C.] Augur[22] that a large force had crossed the Comite River to attack the place. Upon receipt of the strange reports and hearing the tale of the orderly, who had been arrested and sent to his headquarters, the general sent out two companies of cavalry under command of Captain [J. Franklin] Godfrey to reconnoiter and ascertain the facts in the case, and to meet us if there as reported.

Thinking it might be well to have someone else awake besides myself and Lieutenant Woodward, I had directed him to wake up a couple of orderlies and place them on each flank of the command. In an hour or two after the command had halted, the orderly sent towards the town rode back to the house where I had stopped to play on the piano and informed us that the enemy was advancing on the command with a line of skirmishers. Feeling confident that there must be some mistake about the matter and that no enemy could possibly come against us from that direction, I rode out alone to meet the troops, without waking up my command.

Upon approaching the troops who were continuously advancing, being firmly convinced that they must be Federal soldiers, I went towards them alone [and] dismounted, while the orderly held my horse. It was hard to convince the Union soldiers under Captain Godfrey that we were really and truly "bona fide" Illinois troops from Tennessee. The captain had his men dismounted behind fences and apparently [was] not at all satisfied with the looks of things. I, however, approached waving my handkerchief and, so soon as near enough, shouted out my name. The captain then climbed up on the fence, while I kept walking on towards himself and command. Soon thereafter, he jumped off to the ground. When we met and shook hands, his soldiers sprang up and clamored onto the fence and gave a shout. The captain ordered his men to mount, and we walked to where I [had] left my horse. Upon his being brought, we rode to our camp. He [Godfrey] was glad to hear of our success and especially well pleased to know that, among our prisoners, we had gotten all of Stuart's Cavalry, except the commanding officer. The Stuart prisoners were rather jubilant than otherwise. They twitted the Baton Rouge soldiers, saying that they never could have captured them; that the United States government had to send Illinois soldiers clear from Tennessee into their rear before they could be taken.

It is proper here to state that during the last few days large numbers of Negroes—men, women, and children—had flocked from all quarters to join our column and march on to freedom and glory. I tried at first to

prevent them, knowing how rapidly we would have to march and fearing that they would not be able to keep up, and that they would be made
to suffer if caught by their masters. But it was no use. Come they would
and come they did. They were mounted on all sorts of horses, mules, etc.
[They] had come with all sorts of vehicles—carriages, wagons, carts—with
their bundles tied about their persons and piled up and mixed in among
their wooly heads. With their white teeth and the whites of their eyes
shining—all grinning or singing, playing, and shouting—they presented
the most wonderful appearance imaginable. Sometimes there would be
a whole family on one mule or old horse. Every carriage, wagon, buggy,
and cart was filled to overflowing, besides the more able-bodied men who
marched along, all going to "Glory Halleluiah" and making all sorts of
characteristic remarks, singing all sorts of plantation melodies.

I never before during my life saw such a medley or motley crowd. To
describe it would be an impossibility. Those who beheld the strange crowd
fording the Comite River will never forget the picture presented to view.
When once across that stream they believed themselves free, and alternate
shouts of rejoicing and prayers for deliverance they put in while the command was sleeping. They may not have been very handsome individually
or collectively, but they added to the variety and picturesque appearance
of the strange cavalcade which was to soon enter the city of Baton Rouge
in triumph.

Captain Godfrey having departed to report to General Augur that we
would reach the city that afternoon, the command was gotten in readiness for the final march about 11 A.M., May 2, 1863, in the following order:
the 6th Illinois Cavalry in advance; the battery, the prisoners, and the 7th
Illinois Cavalry; the Negroes, with the led horses and mules; and, lastly,
about fifty vehicles of every description, from the finest carriage to the
commonest cart or wagon. For nearly a mile before entering the city,
the road was lined with wondering spectators—old and young, male and
female, rich and poor, white and black, citizens and soldiers—all mixed up
indiscriminately. Amid the wildest shouts and cheers and waving of banners and flags, heralded by bands of music, the [tired] and travel-stained
troops marched in triumph through the city, around the public square,
down to the river to water their horses, and then out to Magnolia Grove,
the trees of which were in full bloom and deliciously fragrant, situated two
miles south of the city, where at sunset, scarcely waiting to partake of the
refreshment provided for us by the kind-hearted soldiers of the 116th New
York and 48th Massachusetts infantry regiments, we laid down to sleep
amid flowers and perfume, beside the deep waters of the great Mississippi
River, without guard and without danger.

During the expedition, we killed and wounded over 100 of the enemy; brought in nearly 200; captured and paroled nearly 1,000, including conscripts, many of them officers; destroyed over 60 miles of railroad and telegraph; captured and destroyed over 500 stands of arms and other army stores and government property, amounting in value to millions of dollars. We also captured over 1,000 horses and mules. Our loss during the entire journey was three killed and seven wounded, five left en route sick, the sergeant major and surgeon of the 7th Illinois Cavalry left with Lieutenant Colonel Blackburn, and nine men missing, supposed to have straggled. We marched over 600 miles in sixteen days. The last twenty-eight hours, we traveled seventy-six miles, had four engagements with the enemy, and forded the Comite River, which was deep enough to swim many of the horses and mules. During that time, the men and animals were almost entirely without food or rest. Much of the country through which we passed was almost destitute of forage or provisions, and it was but seldom during the journey that we obtained more than one meal a day. Many of the inhabitants were in a suffering condition for the want of the necessaries of life, which had reached almost fabulous prices. Altogether, nearly 38,000 troops were sent out from various parts to intercept and capture us, without avail. Colton's pocket map of Mississippi, which though small was very correct, was all I had to guide me. But, by the capture of couriers, dispatches, and mails, and the invaluable aid of my scouts, we were always able by rapid marches to evade the enemy when they were too strong and whip him when not too large.

General Grant landed his troops at Bruinsburg below Grand Gulf, advanced upon the enemy, and drove him back towards Port Gibson. On May 2, the same day I entered Baton Rouge with my command, he entered Port Gibson with the XIII Corps and Logan's division of the XVII Corps. It was there he first learned from a southern newspaper of my great success. The next day, [he] wrote to General Halleck: "Colonel Grierson's raid from La Grange, Tenn., through the State of Mississippi, has been the most successful thing of the kind since the breaking out of the war. . . . The southern people and southern papers regard it as one of the most dashing exploits of the war. I am told the whole state is filled with men paroled by Grierson."

The illustrated papers of New York pictured us riding trimly and daintily, as if on dress parade.[23] But the Baton Rouge correspondent, who witnessed our entry into that city, stated that:

> We were exceedingly surprised to-day by the arrival of a brigade
> of cavalry from the interior of the country, dust covered to an

extent that made it nearly impossible to judge from appearance whether they were Federals or Confederates; their horses blown and loaded down with miscellaneous plunder. Several thousand grinning contrabands, mounted and loaded helter skelter into vehicles of all kinds were in the rear of the cavalcade, a large number of prisoners, only distinguishable from their capturers by being less travel stained and riding in fatigue dress without arms. Judge of the general astonishment and delight, when we learned that the brigade was no other than the cavalry force that has for weeks been the terror of central Mississippi; heard from occasionally in rebel prints as destroying a train here and a bridge there; terrifying a town in the morning and burning a camp forty miles away in the evening; cutting telegraph wires and keeping, like "Tam O' Shanter's witches" the country side in fear!

The same writer states that:

General[s] Pemberton and Gardner used every means in their power to surround, surprise and capture Colonel Grierson's command; but by incessant vigilance, rapid movement and the most ingenious stratagem, their efforts were completely foiled. The mails and couriers of the enemy which were frequently captured, kept the commanding officer well posted in regard to the designs of the enemy. Over 20,000 rebel troops were sent out from various points with a view to intercept or capture the bold raider but they always fell in the rear, when they concentrated at different points to await the return of Grierson and his command supposing that they would go back to La Grange.

The rebel newspapers tried to account for their humiliation by some strange stories. One account was to the effect that: "Grierson himself had been recognized by many persons of Hinds County as a Kentucky horse-drover, well acquainted with the country." It was also said that: "Parties in east Mississippi recognized him as having gone through the country the preceding summer in the uniform of a Confederate officer bargaining for cattle, which he said another officer coming after him would collect and pay for."

But even the rebels had to praise the behavior of the command to the people they met and the towns they passed through. Once a wealthy planter watching the Yankee soldiers feed at his own stables broke out suddenly: "Well, boys, I can't say I have anything against you. I don't know but on the whole I rather like you. You have not taken anything of mine except a little corn and fodder for your horses and that you are welcome to. You are doing the boldest thing ever undertaken. But you'll be trapped though. Yes you'll be caught yet, mark me." Considering for a moment, and remembering no doubt the protection that had been given to himself and family, he added: "But I really trust that no harm will come to you in any event."

———

The great raid was over. The 6th and 7th Illinois Cavalry woke up refreshed after a long night's sleep and, by authority of General Augur, to whom I reported my command for duty, were granted a few days of recreation and harmless frolic. In fact, they were given the freedom of the city by the kindhearted inhabitants. Whatever saloon or restaurant they entered, they were sure to be well-served and smilingly told that "there was nothing to pay." That they should indulge in some "skylarking," on finding themselves such privileged characters, was not strange to be wondered at.

Once, they took possession of the provost marshal's office, turning him out of doors. Again, they went into a saloon and, finding the proprietor absent, took possession and refused him admittance when he returned. He applied for redress to the provost marshal, who advised him to compromise the matter and shut up his shop, as it was no use to try to do anything with those "terrible raiders." He had tried it once when they were rather noisy in an ice-cream saloon. They charged the soda fountain with gas and got it in position at the door, and he had surrendered rather than receive the salute. They entered an eating house, where the landlady requested them to interfere between two eastern officers who were engaged in fisticuffs, and in a moment the combatants lay sprawling on the street. They captured a Negro crier, with his banner and bell, and cried through the streets: "Concert tonight at Magnolia Grove by the 6th and 7th Illinois Cavalry."

The two regiments stuck to each other as sworn comrades, so that when two of the soldiers in their cups were brawling and a bystander said, "What, 6th and 7th fighting each other?" they stopped and, arm in arm, started to the nearest saloon to again pledge their friendship. All that disorder, however, was but the natural effervescence of a few days' relaxation. When the bugle call summoned them to duty and work was laid out for those true, tried, and efficient soldiers, they promptly responded and were ready for action whenever their services were required.

Yet the great raid was over, and I woke from my tired sleep and weariness to suddenly and unexpectedly find myself famous. I did not know and could not realize the extent of my success. In fact, I did not then think we had accomplished anything wonderful. But the whole nation woke up to more fully know its strength, to learn what it could do, for the "great raid" had demonstrated the fact as to the internal weakness of the Confederacy.

I had never been in New Orleans. Mentioning the fact to General Augur, he advised me to jump aboard the packet and run down to see the city. I did not care to go alone and was authorized to take a few of my officers with me. Accordingly, I selected Colonel Prince, Lieutenant Woodward, and a few others who expressed a desire to accompany me. My main object in going was to have the battery of little "Woodruff Guns" repaired, there being no means available at Baton Rouge. The wheels of the gun carriages had all been broken to pieces coming through from La Grange, and we were obliged to substitute carriage and wagon wheels in their stead. I wished to get new wheels and have the carriages and caissons put into good order again, and thought it best to superintend the matter myself. I found the battery quite useful on our late expedition and hoped to get it repaired without delay, as it was my wish and intention then to soon move northward with a view of joining General Grant's army in the advance on Vicksburg.

We proceeded to New Orleans and, upon arrival, reported to the headquarters of General [George F.] Shepley, who was then in command there.[24] Our presence soon became known throughout the city, and wherever we went we were warmly greeted. In a few hours, the streets were crowded with people and there seemed to be some very unusual excitement. Many persons were shouting: "Hurrah for Illinois." I innocently asked what all the fuss was about. I did not then have the least idea it was on account of our arrival or about myself and the officers who were with me. But we were literally surrounded by crowds and were soon captured by citizens, gunboats, school children, photographists, reporters, and everybody in general, and made the subject of a continuous ovation for several days.

On the day after our arrival, a number of officers and citizens kindly escorted us about the city to all places of interest and, among others, to a large assembly of the various schools, where several thousand pupils [had gathered] with their teachers and superintendents. Walking into the large building, we took a back seat near the entrance, to look upon the scene and to witness the proceedings for a few moments. Soon our presence became known. Some gentleman was speaking, or preparing for some exhibition in which some of the pupils were to take part. The heads of many of the audience were turned towards the seat we occupied, and some arose and even got upon the seats and benches, and a general hub-bub began. Finally, the president of the meeting learned the cause of the excitement and at once suspended the ceremonies and, in a loud voice, said that he had been informed that Colonel Grierson and some of his bold raiders, of whom they had been hearing, was at that time inside the building. On behalf of those assembled, he trusted that the colonel would come forward to the stand, in order that all might have the pleasure of seeing him and hearing from him something as to the exploits of his command, most urgently repeating the request.

Now, to tell the truth, I was astonished at such proceedings and felt like crouching under the seats, and did endeavor to get out of the door to avoid being such a conspicuous object. But it was simply no use. The whole congregation insisted by the waving of fans, scarves, and handkerchiefs and [by] loud appeals. So, up I got and passed forward to the stage, and was introduced in an appropriate manner. I had not the slightest idea I would be called upon formally for a speech and had no thought whatever as to what I should say. But, while the earnest faces of those present were turned towards me, many of them those of children—young ladies—mixed in with those of their parents or older persons, by some means I was fully prepared to make a suitable reply. To the utter surprise of myself and those present who knew me best, [I] made a most appropriate and happy response, and luckily stopped at the right time and waved myself away from the platform, shaking hands with hundreds of people I never set eyes on before or since.

Lieutenant Woodward had never heard me attempt to speak to so large an audience, and was trembling and in fear that I would break down. [He] was as much astonished as myself at the result of that adventure, but we managed to keep out of such places for the remainder of the day. That night, however, there was still a larger crowd gathered at the St. Charles Hotel where we were stopping, filling the rotunda and galleries to their utmost capacity long before the appointed time. The occasion was the presentation of a magnificent horse to myself and a saddle, bridle, and equipments to Colonel Prince. The presentation was made by a speech by L. Madison Day, Esq., after which I was obliged to make my appearance upon the stand, where I was hailed by the most deafening cheers, three times repeated. The band of the 47th Massachusetts Regiment played "Hail to the Chief," then two little girls prettily dressed in white, each bearing in one hand a flag and in the other a bouquet of magnolias and other tropical flowers, were lifted on the table beside me and presented their offerings, which I smilingly accepted with a kiss proffered in return. Just then I would have given a good deal to have been away from there, or to have someone else take my place, with the honors and all. However, I finally mustered up sufficient courage to respond to the flattering remarks of the orator and the other demonstrations.

Under the circumstances, I trust I may be pardoned for saying "that our passage through the Confederacy was not a difficult one" and for understating the strength of the enemy and the time it would take to conquer the rebellion. We did not then know what we had really accomplished. We had expected to meet serious opposition at the Pearl, the Tickfaw, the Amite, and the Comite rivers, and did not fully realize, perhaps, that the passage would have been more difficult if we had not outfought, outmarched, outmaneuvered, and outwitted the enemy. It was not until long after that time that we knew how large were the forces sent out to intercept us; how the rebels were astonished and chagrined at our daring achievements, and that there were two years more of hard fighting and active service in the field before the war could be brought to an end.

On May 9, 1863, after a delightful visit, we left New Orleans on the steamer *Sally Robinson* for Baton Rouge where, soon after our arrival, plenty of hard work was assigned to myself and command by Generals Augur and Banks during the advance upon, investment of, and siege of Port Hudson.

———

It was my earnest desire and intention upon return from New Orleans to Baton Rouge to make speedy arrangements to join General Grant's army, then reported in the vicinity of the Big Black River, moving to the rear of Vicksburg. The route of travel had not been fully determined upon, but I felt quite sure that it would be practicable to go either on the west side of the Mississippi or [the] east side of that stream, crossing the railroad leading from Port Hudson to Clinton at such point as would seem best to facilitate our march, and where we could inflict the most damage upon the enemy without endangering the safety of my command. But General Augur, who had only a small force of cavalry, detained us by authority of General Banks for service with an expedition towards Port Hudson, for which preparations were then being perfected.

Soon thereafter, we came under the direct control of General Banks, by whom we were detained in face of the efforts made by General Grant to have us relieved so that we might join his forces operating in rear of Vicksburg, where on account of the scarcity of federal cavalry our services were greatly needed.[25] Many direct and urgent applications were made by General Grant for us to report to him without delay. But General Banks seemed to think that he could not get along without the cavalry which arrived so suddenly and opportunely within his department, and in some manner managed to hold onto us. Although General Banks was always kind and considerate, and our relations were in every way satisfactory during the time we were under his command, yet our detention caused me much worry and annoyance, and I have always regretted my inability to comply with the wishes and appeals of General Grant, for I felt that the services of myself and command properly belonged to and should have been rendered with General Grant and his army at that critical period, notwithstanding there may have been a military necessity for our presence and service during the same time in the Department of the Gulf.

From Grand Gulf, on May 6, 1863, General Grant wrote to General Halleck:

> I learn that Grierson with his cavalry has been heard of; first, about ten days ago, in Northern Mississippi, he moved thence and struck the railroad thirty miles east of Jackson at a post called Newton Station. He then moved southward towards Enterprise, demanded the surrender of the place, and gave one hour's grace, during which Gen. [William W.] Loring[26] arrived. He left at once and moved towards Hazlehurst, on the New Orleans and Jackson Railroad. At that point he tore up the track; thence to Bahalia [sic] 10 miles north [south] on same road, thence eastwards [westward] on the Natches [sic] road, where he had a fight with Wirt Adams' Cavalry. From thence he moved back to the New Orleans and Jackson Railroad to Brookhaven 20 miles south of Bahalia. When last heard from he was 3 miles from Summit, 10 miles south of the last named point, supposed to be making his way to Baton Rouge. He had spread excitement through the state, destroying railroads, trestle-works, bridges; burning locomotives and railway stock, taking prisoners, and destroying stores of all kinds. To use the expression of my informant, "Grierson had knocked the heart out of the state."

No wonder General Grant felt greatly elated when he heard of our great success, and that he subsequently stated that: "Grierson's raid was of great importance, as it had attracted the attention of the enemy from the main movement against Vicksburg." It is an established fact that not much over 1,000 rebels could at first confront General Grant's forces back of Bruinsburg, increased, of course, in a day or two to 3,500. But even at the battle of Port Gibson, the enemy could only muster, or bring together in line of battle, a little over 5,000 troops, with 2,000 at Grand Gulf, making in all about 7,000 officers and enlisted men. The rebels had been widely scattered and drawn to distant points throughout Mississippi and actively occupied in endeavoring to intercept and destroy myself and little command, magnified by the reports they had received, into an army of from 10,000 to 20,000 men. They had been worn out by their many prolonged marches and movements, and discouraged by their fruitless attempts to capture us, until they were demoralized and rendered almost useless as an effective force to oppose the advance of General Grant's army into position back of Vicksburg.[27]

The report of rebel officers, from General Pemberton down, all show that they had been completely deceived in regard to the strength of my command and constantly misled by our remarkable movements, from the start of the expedition to the close. They became so excited, bewildered, and amazed that they could not judge what was best to do, being so mixed [up] and perplexed by the apparently reliable but false and contradictory reports received by them that they went blundering along in a haphazard sort of fashion, without gaining any satisfactory advantage or results. We were reported at so many different places at the same time, and our forces so greatly overestimated, that really but little correct information reached the enemy at all in regard to us until it was too late to be of any service.

All reports made by the rebel officers sent out against us, or those in any way connected with or responsible for their movements, are simply apologies for their mistakes and failures made in not being able to overhaul, injure, or even seriously interfere with our movements, from want of proper information and misconception of the real design of the expedition. Nothing beyond their own written statements are required to plainly show their great chagrin and discomfiture upon learning definitely of our safe arrival at Baton Rouge and fully realizing the fact that we had succeeded, in such an audacious and almost uninterrupted manner, in traversing the entire state of Mississippi. The detachments sent off under Major Love and Colonel Hatch of the 2nd Iowa Cavalry misled the enemy, as intended, into the belief that the whole command had gone back northward towards the Mobile and Ohio and Memphis and Charleston railroads. The movements made by Major Graham [and] Captains Lynch, Forbes, and Trafton led them widely off the track of the main column and gave rise to greatly exaggerated reports as to our numbers, intentions and destination.

The first reports of the Confederate general, Daniel Ruggles, commanding a district in northern Mississippi, estimated our strength at 6,000 men, and the reports of junior officers under him, made some days afterward, placed our force at over 20,000. At many other times and places, it was represented varying from 2,000 to 10,000. Not until we were approaching Baton Rouge did the enemy even approximately estimate or ascertain the number of men in my command.

To have to report his failure to capture myself and my bold raiders, General Gardner informed me upon being introduced by General Banks after the surrender of Port Hudson, annoyed and worried him more than anything that had occurred in his military service up to that time; that the destruction of his communications prevented him from obtaining supplies which were greatly needed during the siege of Port Hudson; and that our successful expedition, coming so unexpectedly, hastened materially, in his judgment, the surrender of both Vicksburg and Port Hudson.

Benjamin's father, Robert Grierson. Courtesy Fort Davis National Historic Site, Fort Davis, Texas.

Left to right: The Grierson brothers, John Charles and Benjamin Henry, and their wives, Elizabeth and Alice Kirk, ca. 1854. Courtesy Fort Davis National Historic Site, Fort Davis, Texas.

"The Old Homestead" at 852 East State Street, Jacksonville, Illinois.
Courtesy Fort Davis National Historic Site, Fort Davis, Texas.

Brig. Gen. Benjamin M. Prentiss.
Courtesy National Archives, Washington, D.C.

Lt. Gen. Ulysses S. Grant. Courtesy of the Ohio History Connection.

Illinois governor Richard Yates.
Abraham Lincoln Presidential Library
and Museum.

Maj. Gen. William Tecumseh
Sherman. Courtesy of the Ohio
History Connection.

Capt. Samuel L. Woodward.
Abraham Lincoln Presidential Library
and Museum.

Bvt. Maj. Gen. Edward E.
Hatch. Courtesy National Archives,
Washington, D.C.

Grierson's Raiders outside Baton Rouge, Louisiana. From Francis T. Miller, ed., *The Photographic History of the Civil War: The Cavalry*. New York: Review of Reviews, 1912.

Brig. Gen. William Sooy Smith. Courtesy National Archives, Washington, D.C.

Brig. Gen. Samuel D. Sturgis.
Courtesy National Archives, Washington, D.C.

Bvt. Maj. Gen. Benjamin H. Grierson.
Courtesy Fort Davis National Historic Site, Fort
Davis, Texas.

Alice Kirk Grierson at the end of the Civil War.
Courtesy Fort Davis National Historic Site, Fort Davis, Texas.

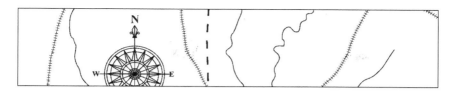

7. The Siege of Port Hudson

By the middle of May, my command was again in condition for the field, and I was exceedingly anxious to leave Baton Rouge and start northward to join General Grant. The general [was] equally desirous to have me do so. He wrote to General Banks on May 10, 1863: "Grierson's cavalry would be of immense service to me now, and if at all practicable for him to join me, I would like him to do so at once." General Banks answered May 12, regretting his inability to join General Grant, and stated that he had written me on the subject, but the letter never reached me. I was then under the command or control of General Augur, and of course he, no more than General Banks, relished the thought of our departure, as he was then preparing for a reconnaissance in the direction of Port Hudson. [He] was anxious to retain us and did so.

General Grant states in his *Memoirs*, that up to May 12, the movement of his army had been made without serious opposition. He was then near the Jackson and Vicksburg Railroad, with his line almost parallel thereto. On the night of May 13, General [Joseph E.] Johnston arrived at Jackson and assumed command of all Confederate troops in Mississippi, virtually relieving General Pemberton.[1] Soon after, the Confederate troops began to put forth greater efforts to impede the advance of the Federal army.

On the same day, in compliance with instructions from General Augur, I moved out towards Port Hudson with about 500 of the most effective portion of my cavalry and was absent three days, during which time we were actively scouting. [We] had several skirmishes and some brisk fights with the rebels, in all of which we were fortunate and successful. A detachment approached within two miles of Port Hudson and drove in the enemy's pickets. We also drove a considerable force of the enemy from rifle pits at Redwood Bridge, about nine miles east of Port Hudson, at the point where the Redwood road, which runs almost directly east from Port Hudson, joins the road from Baton Rouge to Clinton. On the night of May 15, I returned to Baton Rouge to hasten the completion of the shoeing of horses and the re-equipment of my entire command, placing the troops then out under Lieutenant Colonel [Reuben] Loomis, 6th [Illinois] Cavalry, who continued the active scouting. At that time we had only about a dozen men sick in hospital, including two officers, notwithstanding the great exertion the command had so recently passed through.

Soon after [my] return to Baton Rouge, I accompanied General Augur to New Orleans to meet General Banks with whom we dined, there being several general officers, the collector of the port, and other notables present. It was quite refreshing to sit down to so good a meal after the scanty fare we had so long been getting. General Banks, I remember, made on that occasion a very neat and complimentary speech in which he alluded to our late expedition in the most flattering terms, and in an enthusiastic manner proposing, and with all present drinking, my health, under all of which I became rather too embarrassed to respond in a manner satisfactory to myself—although in view of the confusion and noise of the glasses, it may not have been so noticeable to others.

The next day, I also dined with Admiral Farragut at the St. Charles Hotel and found him to be a most agreeable gentleman, thoroughly absorbed in the duties of his profession. Upon his special invitation, I visited the principal ships of his fleet—the *Richmond*, *Monongahela*, [and] *Pensacola*—and several of the gunboats then moored near the city. The admiral was also kind enough to arrange for me to visit that part of the fleet then near Port Hudson, which I subsequently did, when the commanding officer, for my special benefit and amusement, bombarded Port Hudson for an hour. The bombardment took place about 10 o'clock at night and was a most magnificent sight. Altogether, I was most generously feasted there, as well as at New Orleans, [and] treated with the utmost courtesy and consideration by General Banks, Admiral Farragut, and the officers of the army and navy under their command.

On May 20, the balance of the cavalry was moved out to take part in the expedition against Port Hudson. A brigade of infantry had already been sent to the support of the cavalry, which had been operating under command of Lieutenant Colonel Loomis. Most of General Augur's division moved the same day, and it was thought, with the troops to be sent from New Orleans and those near the mouth of Red River, that General Banks would have an army of 20,000 men altogether, with which the fleet under Farragut would cooperate for the attack upon and reduction of Port Hudson. The largest part of Banks' forces were to land at Bayou Sara and, soon thereafter, form a junction with the cavalry and General Augur's division [in] back of Port Hudson.

I remained at Baton Rouge to finish my report, which I then presumed would be delivered to General Grant by myself within the next ten days, as an aide-de-camp of the general's was then endeavoring to have General Banks relieve myself and command so that we would report to the Department of the Tennessee. On the same day, May 21, the advance of General Augur's division and a portion of my cavalry had a brisk fight with the enemy near Plains Store, five miles from Port Hudson, beyond which we [had] passed three miles when I was out with the cavalry a week previous and tore up the Clinton Railroad.

I left Baton Rouge on the morning of May 22, 1863, with the expectation that I would not return to that place, thinking that, after meeting with General Banks' army, in view of General Grant's earnest solicitations, we would be permitted to move onward in the direction of Vicksburg. I felt so sure of this that I had written Mrs. Grierson to address me care of General Grant's headquarters. Both myself and Adjutant Woodward, who accompanied me, were considerably elated as we rode out that day, feeling at least that we were once more moving in the right direction, where we would be nearer to and more likely to hear from our friends at home. It seemed to me then that our armies were again moving with the right kind of spirit and energy; that with proper management the Mississippi River—that great commercial artery of the West—would be freed from the hand of the traitor foe within one month.

Upon reaching General Augur's headquarters, I was advised as to the disposition of our troops, the advance of General Banks' forces, and the route by which they would come, and was directed to move out and communicate with them. This was done the next day. And in a few days, the army had taken up its position for the advance upon and investment of the enemy's works. General Banks felt quite sure at that time that but little resistance would be made, and that Port Hudson would soon be in our possession. Having made all his arrangements and disposition of troops for an attack, on the morning of May 27 orders were issued accordingly, although the movement was deemed premature by some of the division commanders. It was generally expected, however, that if the assault was made simultaneously at all points, the rebel works would be taken. It proved otherwise, and the result was disastrous to the Union forces—they meeting with a very decided repulse, which clearly demonstrated the fact that hard fighting would be required to insure the desired success. This led to a more cautious advance, and finally into a regular siege.[2]

It will be remembered that my brother, Lieutenant J. C. Grierson, my brigade quartermaster, had been left back at La Grange—I preferring to do without his services, rather than to risk the lives of both when so many were depending upon us for assistance, and for another reason. It is well he was where he could communicate with home, as about this time the old

Meredosia business entanglement had involved the property of a brother-in-law. My brother had to send $500, which he could not well spare out of his small salary, to my father to be applied as part payment of the claim. Mrs. Grierson applied in the same manner $1,000 I had furnished her. Of all which, I was fortunately for the time ignorant.

On May 25, General Grant again wrote to General Banks: "Col. Grierson would be of immense value to me now. If he has not already started, will you be kind enough to order him immediately. He should come up the Louisiana shore to avoid delay." The letter was sent by Colonel [John] Riggin [Jr.], one of General Grant's staff officers, who urged upon General Banks the necessity of complying with General Grant's request, and explained the emergency for the presence of myself and command at that time in rear of Vicksburg.

It was all of no avail, as General Banks refused to give us up, and at once wrote the following answer, under date of May 29, in which he stated: "Col. Grierson's cavalry is of great importance. It is now the only cavalry force we have. He had rendered us great service and his immediate departure will entirely cripple us. I hope to avoid a separation from him, by joining you at the same time he moved, upon the plan I have suggested."

On June 2, I wrote Mrs. Grierson: "I leave here in the morning with about 1,000 men, cavalry, mounted infantry, and artillery, on an expedition to Clinton; will probably be gone a couple of days, and hope to find that Port Hudson has been taken upon return. The rebels are becoming somewhat troublesome on our rear and flank, and I am sent out by Gen. Banks to attack them. Some of the cavalry are getting short of ammunition, and there is none in the Department to suit their carbines."

On the evening of June 4, I again wrote to Mrs. Grierson: "Have just returned from Clinton. We had a hard fight there yesterday, lasting from three o'clock to 5 P.M. The rebels outnumbered us nearly two to one. I had only 1,100 men and they over 2,000. We lost in the engagement about 50 killed and wounded, and the rebel loss was fully double our own. The balls flew around me thick and fast; three through my clothes. I am unhurt, but exhausted and worn out, and have 2½ miles yet to ride to camp. Col. Riggins [sic], of Gen. Grant's staff is again here after myself and command, and will leave for Vicksburg in the morning."

The same evening, General Banks wrote to General Grant: "There is a force of 2,000 or 3,000 in our rear, which is being strengthened daily, by such additions as can be gathered from the country about us, that will in a short time give us much trouble. Col. Grierson had a sharp engagement with them yesterday, in which we sustained some loss, and the enemy lost heavily."

I had made timely requisitions and other repeated efforts to obtain ammunition for the Smith's carbines, with which about one-half of my command were armed, but without avail, and there was no suitable ammunition within the department. Upon learning that there were 500 Sharps carbines at New Orleans, on June 2 I made official application for them to replace those for which ammunition could not be obtained. The constant scouting and picket duty in rear of General Banks' army had so exhausted our ammunition that a large part of the 6th and 7th Illinois Cavalry had only about eight rounds per man.

Notwithstanding this, I moved out promptly at 5 o'clock on the morning of June 3, in obedience to orders received, to attack a force of the enemy at Clinton reported to be 2,000 strong. In addition to the 6th and 7th Illinois Cavalry, I had detachments from the 2nd Massachusetts, 1st Louisiana, 4th Wisconsin Mounted Infantry, and one section of Nims' battery,[3] in all about 1,200. Taking the Jackson road, we proceeded without interruption to within three miles of Jackson, where I detached Captain Godfrey, with 200 men of the Massachusetts and Louisiana cavalry, to go by the way of Jackson, while with the main column I proceeded on the direct road towards Clinton. Captain Godfrey dashed into Jackson [and] captured and paroled a number of prisoners—convalescents and stragglers. Thence, taking the Clinton road, [he] rejoined the column two miles from Jackson.

Moving on, we encountered and drove in the enemy's pickets six miles from Clinton, capturing one man and five horses. We did not again encounter the enemy until we arrived at the Comite River, one mile from Clinton, when the advance guard were fired upon from ambush. Pushing across the bridge over the stream and the following ones, we arrived at a small plain, where we encountered a considerable force of the enemy ambushed on either side of the road. I immediately dismounted the whole of the 7th Illinois Cavalry, which was in advance, deployed them as skirmishers, and drove the enemy to Putty Creek, where their whole force was posted in a strong position. The 4th Wisconsin was deployed with the 7th Illinois along the creek, and a section of two-pound guns and section of Nims' battery placed in position on the right and left of the road in the plain. One battalion of the 7th Illinois Cavalry had already been posted on our right flank, across the railroad, and two companies of the 2nd Massachusetts Cavalry, commanded by Lieutenant [Solon A.] Perkins, to guard our left flank.

It soon became evident that the enemy in our front far outnumbered us, besides having a strong position, while we, in addition to the disparity of numbers, were posted in dense swamps, to and from which we had access to the open country in our rear only through a narrow defile leading across four narrow bridges, over which we had already passed in our advance upon the enemy. A portion of the 7th Illinois Cavalry who were in front were armed with the Smith's carbine, the ammunition for which we had been unable to obtain in the department. Their ammunition becoming exhausted, they were obliged to fall back. I immediately sent Captains Godfrey and [Reuben F.] Yeaton, of the two companies of the 1st Louisiana Cavalry, to take their place. The troops in front held their ground and pressed the enemy nobly against a great disadvantage, both in numbers and position.

Observing that the enemy was still moving forces to our right and left, I brought up the 6th Illinois Cavalry, which had composed our rearguard during the march, and, dismounting, posted them to the right and left to thus further strengthen our flanks. It soon became evident, however, that the enemy's numbers and position were too strong for us to carry, and our ammunition becoming scarce, I decided to fall back. Acting on this decision, I ordered the section of Nims' battery which had been brought up, but owing to the lowness of the ground could obtain no advantageous position, to fall back to the brow of a hill nearly one mile in our rear, and there come into battery until further orders. I then withdrew the 4th Wisconsin and 1st Louisiana, and such part of the 7th Illinois as still remained in front, they tearing up a bridge as they returned, and posted the 2nd Massachusetts and 1st [Louisiana] in a bayou in the right and left of the road to hold the enemy until the infantry could mount their horses and withdraw from the swamp, after which they were ordered to fall back, mount, and retreat.

In the meantime, I had one battalion of the 6th Illinois Cavalry and two guns of our little battery organized to bring up the rear. The section of Nims' battery, most of the 7th Illinois, the 4th Wisconsin, the 2nd Massachusetts, and Yeaton's company of the Louisiana cavalry had all withdrawn and gained a good position of the high ground in our rear when the enemy, with a yell, charged in solid masses upon our front and flanks. Captain Godfrey, for some unknown cause, had not obeyed the order to fall back and mount after the infantry had withdrawn. When the enemy charged, they found him still dismounted. All his horses having gone to the rear, he took to the bushes and along the railroad when the enemy, coming upon his left, cut off a number of his men. The two-pounder battery poured canister into the column advancing on our front, with telling effect, until those on our left had come within fifty yards of the guns, when they were limbered unto the rear. The battalion of the 6th Illinois, falling in between them and the enemy, beat back the advancing host and retreated in good order from the narrow defile. Having crossed the last bridge, they filed to the right and left of the road, and forming in the edge of timber, awaited the approach of the enemy until they had advanced within easy range, when they poured volley after volley into them, repulsing them with considerable loss. Under cover of the consternation created in the ranks of the enemy, the battalion fell back to the brow of the hill, where the light battery and a line of battle had already been formed.

The enemy, recovering from his repulse, again advanced to the bridge [and] crossed, but was met by repeated volleys from our guns and from our troops formed on either side of the road to support them. Being again repulsed with loss, they did not deem it prudent to follow us further. My command being almost destitute of ammunition, I withdrew and returned to camp, arriving at about 12 at night. Our loss in the engagement was eight killed, twenty-eight wounded, and fifteen missing. That of the enemy between twenty and thirty killed, over sixty wounded, and about twenty taken prisoners. The officers and men all acted with the utmost coolness and bravery. Among the slain was the lamented Lieutenant Perkins, a brave and gallant officer, commanding a squadron of the 2nd Massachusetts Cavalry. The action lasted between three and four hours, and we succeeded in bringing off all but three of our dead and seven wounded.[4]

On the morning of the 5th, we again started for Clinton, in connection with a brigade of infantry and a battery of artillery under General H. E. Paine,[5] taking a road leading from Bayou Sara to Clinton and Olive Branch. We encamped on the night of the 5th at Redwood Creek. On the 6th, [we] made an easy march to Comite River, nine miles from Clinton, where we halted until 12 m., when we again marched, reaching Clinton at early daylight on the morning of the 7th. The enemy had pickets at Olive Branch and again at the Comite, but fired and fled upon our approach. Arriving at Clinton, we found that the enemy hearing of our approach had left the day before, taking the Jackson road until within two miles of Jackson, where they turned off towards Liberty. We found in the town two hospitals, containing seven of our wounded and about twenty sick and wounded of the enemy. All of the sick and wounded which could be moved, to the number of several hundred, were sent to Osyka the day before. We paroled about thirty prisoners [and] destroyed the railroad depot, machine shops, a locomotive, woolen and cartridge manufactories, a large quantity of ammunition, several hundred hides, and much other public property, which in their haste the enemy had failed to take away. We also destroyed all the bridges on the road leading towards Jackson, over the Comite River and the numerous small streams and bayous in the vicinity.

Having accomplished as nearly as possible the object of the expedition, we returned to the Comite River, where we rested until 5 P.M., and from there returned to camp, arriving at 9 P.M. Up to this time, our loss in men since entering the Department of the Gulf had been small, but heavy in animals, having had in the two Illinois regiments nearly 100 horses killed and badly wounded. Our information concerning the loss of the enemy in the battle of Clinton was received from our own and the rebel wounded and prisoners, and confirmed by reports of rebel wounded and prisoners found in the hospitals on the second expedition to Clinton.

During all our operations in the vicinity of Port Hudson, myself and command were in rather a forlorn condition. Having left our baggage, records, and everything necessary for our comfort and convenience back in Tennessee, we were compelled to forage for such things as we could find to make our destitute condition endurable. We were for nearly two months obliged to live in a swamp and without proper shelter. Myself and Adjutant Woodward had, in lieu of tents, some old canvas spread out as kind of awning for office purposes and sleeping apartments, and were obliged to get what rest we could by spreading blankets on ammunition boxes instead of beds and bedsteads. Not hearing from home during all of that time, the prospect was to say the least decidedly discouraging for both of us, as well as all others of the 6th and 7th Illinois Cavalry situated in a similar manner.

It was not until June 16 that I received my appointment as brigadier general, and which I began to fear would not come at all. My commission was not received until nearly a year afterwards, being forwarded from point to point and delayed in the mails. On the same day, I wrote to Mrs. Grierson: "Have delayed writing, thinking that I would by this time be near Vicksburg, or at least have an opportunity of sending to you by that route. Have been disappointed as usual, and cannot now see any immediate prospect of getting away from here. Gen. Banks' forces have twice stormed the works of Port Hudson, and been repulsed with considerable loss."

Towards the last of June, I wrote again to Mrs. Grierson: "It will soon be three months since I saw you, or have heard from you directly or indirectly. Had I supposed we would have remained here so long, I would not have directed you to write me care of Gen. Grant, and no doubt would have received quite a number of letters. You can scarcely realize my anxiety in regard to you, and all at home; it is almost beyond endurance."

Subsequently, in referring to General Banks' efforts and plans, I wrote that: "Gen Banks is doing all in his power; all, perhaps, any general could do with the same materials. He has about twenty regiments of eastern nine-months men, whose term of service soon expires and who cannot be depended upon in an assault on the enemy's works."

The Massachusetts "nine-months men" were quite a contrast to the western troops, the 6th and 7th Illinois Cavalry. The latter had a trick of being absent from the rear picket duty without leave, but it was winked at because it was well known that their desertion was to the rifle pits in front, in order to be in a fight. In the attack of May 27, the 116th New York gallantly distinguished itself, while a Massachusetts regiment of nine-months men threw down their arms and ran. This left a gap in the line, whereupon General Banks sent a hasty pencil order to me: "Send forward one of your regiments if you have no enemy in your immediate front." The cavalry instantly moved forward, dismounted, and supported the 116th New York. During one of the assaults on the enemy's works, a detachment of the 6th Illinois, under command of Captain [Lucius B.] Skinner, charged mounted in front of General T. W. Sherman's[6] division, in which charge the general was wounded. A number of Captain Skinner's men were killed and wounded, his horse killed, and the scabbard of his saber shot in two. These movements of the Illinois cavalry occasioned much surprise, as many of the officers and soldiers [had] never heard of such a thing as cavalry, either mounted or dismounted, attacking forts.

Having an opportunity to communicate with Mrs. Grierson by a staff officer of General Grant's, via Vicksburg, on July 7 I wrote: "We are just in receipt of information of the surrender of Vicksburg, to Gen. Grant.[7] Port Hudson must fall within a day or two. One hundred guns from our batteries are now being fired in honor of the great victory. The Rebels have blocked the Mississippi River below New Donaldsonville, but they cannot hold it long. As soon as Port Hudson surrenders, Gen. Banks will launch his forces upon the rebels there, and clean them out. The General will dislike to have us leave, as he is much in need of cavalry, but I am determined to go North after the capture of this place."

On July 8, 1863, the thirty-seventh anniversary of my birth, General Gardner surrendered Port Hudson, with its garrison and munitions of war, to General Banks. The cessation of hostilities then was a great relief to all concerned, the enemy as well as ourselves, and the great Mississippi River was again open from its source to its mouth. General Gardner asked to see me and, when presented, congratulated me highly. In a very pleasant social manner, he talked over the events of my raid, showing at the time a handful of conflicting telegrams and letters he had received. "Grierson was here." No, "he was there, sixty miles away." Again, "he had marched north." No, "south." And again, "west." All at the same time. The general laughingly claimed, however, that "had his orders been obeyed," I would have been trapped. But, his troops ambushed us where we did not go and waited for us until morning, while we passed on unmolested during the night. Those who slept while we rode did not catch us. Much of the time during the advance upon, investment, and siege of Port Hudson, my cavalry was so active, and at times scattered, on a line so extended that it was a difficult matter to report the 6th and 7th Illinois Cavalry separately, as detachments were frequently with all the different divisions and could not be separated therefrom on the returns.

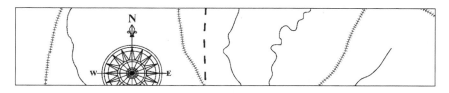

8. Reorganizing the Cavalry in West Tennessee

Our long service before Port Hudson was not without some minor annoyances. Colonel Edward Prince of the 7th Illinois Cavalry apparently became envious of the reputation gained by myself and command, and acted in an unwarranted and unsoldierly manner. Such manifestation seemed to me the more ungrateful for the reason that I always treated him with the utmost kindness and consideration, and had at a time when he was unpopular among the officers of his regiment, strongly recommended him for promotion to the colonelcy of his regiment. I then believed, and so stated, that in my judgment Prince's education, ingenuity, activity, and resolution would enable him to become a valuable officer to the government, and had therefore so commended him for advancement to Governor Yates. I was afterwards informed by some of Prince's college classmates that sooner or later his true inwardness would be shown, and it did appear in the following manner.

Knowing General Banks' wish to have more cavalry permanently attached to his command, Colonel Prince in an underhanded manner proposed to the general to detach the 7th Illinois Cavalry from my brigade, so that he (Prince) might have an independent command within the Department of the Gulf. Upon learning of this secret maneuver on his part, I promptly assembled the company commanders and other officers of the 7th Cavalry, and indicating to them the information regarding the colonel's intentions, assured them that if it was their wish to be thus taken away from my brigade I would make no opposition to such arrangement, although I should greatly regret such a separation. They responded at once, unmistakably, that they, with their men, wanted to stay in my command and go back with me to the Department of the Tennessee. Colonel Prince had rendered efficient service during our operations in rear of Port Hudson and had exercised at times a separate command; had assisted in the construction of fortifications and had succeeded in capturing two steamboats from the enemy.[1] I was greatly pleased at his success, and so was General Banks. But the latter, much to his credit, although so much in need of cavalry, would take it in no such way. When he learned that Colonel Prince's proposal was without my knowledge, he at once returned him to my control and promptly informed him that all correspondence must pass through the headquarters of the commanding officer. That was not the last time, however, that Colonel Prince attempted to circumvent and deprecate officers whom he could not rival.

Soon after the surrender of Vicksburg, General Sherman wrote to General Grant: "Can't Grierson join me by land." And again, "I will destroy the railroad, certain, but the cavalry has not the dash to do the work, cannot Grierson be brought up here. In a month he could make the state of Mississippi forever useless to the rebels." Subsequently, he states: "A prisoner was sent in with a written order on his person, dated Brookhaven. He states, the place contained but two companies, and that Grierson was reported coming. I do hope Grierson will come by land with his cavalry, and with what I have, I can clean out all middle Mississippi." On July 13, General Grant wrote in answer to General Sherman: "I have written to Banks to send up Grierson, but do not believe he will send him." The general's application to General Banks was: "I will ask that Grierson be sent here as soon as possible. I am very much in want of cavalry, and of Grierson to command them." General Grant had promised to send a division of the infantry to General Banks, and on July 12 he wrote to General Grant that: "I shall be very glad if you send down, with the division a small force of cavalry, as I made arrangements, which will enable you to expect the return of Brig. Gen. Grierson, with his command to join your headquarters within a week from this time." Although Port Hudson surrendered on July 8, it was not until the 18th of the month that sufficient transportation was furnished for my command to Memphis.

I succeeded in getting a portion of my command started for Vicksburg on the steamer *Planet* on July 16, as guard to about 200 prisoners, Confederate officers. The arrangements were perfected through General [Charles P.] Stone,[2] who was an efficient officer and one of the most agreeable gentlemen socially I ever met in my service during the war. He was remarkably well informed in regard to all branches of the service, particularly the staff departments. It was a great treat to listen to his anecdotes and reminiscences of life in the old army, especially during the Mexican War. He was familiar with the records of all the old army officers of that time, and their most striking characteristics. He was very kind and considerate in assisting us, and did everything in his power to facilitate our departure.

I left Port Hudson with the remainder of my command on the steamer *Imperial*, having in charge twenty-two prisoners, Confederate officers,

among whom were General [William N.] Beall[3] and staff. The trip up the
Mississippi River on a steamer was a pleasant change and recreation for
myself and the cavalry after so many months of constant active service. We
stopped long enough at Natchez to enable me to meet [Thomas] Ransom,
who had been promoted to brigadier general and, only a few days before,
occupied that place, and had been successful in capturing a large herd of
Confederate beef cattle. I had not met him since we were at Cairo, when
he was major of the 11th Illinois Infantry. He was a brave, gallant officer
and most agreeable gentleman, and our short interview was a great pleasure for both of us. He died not long afterwards from wounds received in
battle during General Banks' Red River campaign,[4] much to the regret of
all who knew him. Had he lived longer, no doubt he would have risen to
higher rank and command.

We stopped several hours at Vicksburg, where I was most warmly received by General Grant and staff. I had a long talk with the general, who
happened to have a little leisure time at his disposal. We congratulated
each other on our success and promotion. The general was pleased to say
that my advancement, like his own, came without asking. He was greatly
impressed with the importance of a prompt movement upon Mobile;
thought the place could, and should, be taken without delay. He had advised General Halleck of his view on the subject, but had not at that time
learned the general-in-chief's decision in regard to the matter. General
Banks took the same view, and General Sherman had also recommended
an attack on Mobile. General Grant told me that General Sherman was
then anxious to have the services of myself and command, but that Hurlbut wanted us also. In view of our long, hard, and active work, and the
scattered condition of my brigade, he would order us on to Memphis.
The general sent a staff officer with me to assist in pointing out the most
important fortifications surrounding Vicksburg. Upon my return to the
general's headquarters, I requested permission to accompany him in the
event of an advance upon Mobile. He responded at once approvingly, and
we shook hands and bade each other good-bye.

As I approached the steamboat, passing down a very narrow way among
huge piles of stores at the landing, my own New Orleans gift horse kicked
at the horse on which I was mounted and struck me severely on the knee.
Had it not been for the high-topped, heavy-legged boots that I was wearing, my leg would no doubt have been badly broken. As it was, it proved to
be a severe sprain which crippled me for many months, and was the most
annoying and serious injury received by me during the war. I could not
keep still or refrain from using my limb, and thus weakened and sprained
it anew. On arrival at Memphis, however, General Hurlbut received me

with open arms, crippled leg and all, and was greatly delighted at the return of myself and command.

I informed the general in regard to General Grant's desire to make a speedy advance on Mobile. We talked for a long time on the subject, and looked upon such a movement as of the greatest importance. General Hurlbut was at that time remarkably well informed in regard to the true condition of Mississippi. He had been corresponding with the president on the subject. He showed me a number of reports he had received through spies and numerous loyal citizens, who urged the occupation of the entire state by Federal troops and who believed the state could be readily held. The people were amazed at our successes. The rebels were paralyzed, and the consternation, which began during my raid, continued to increase in force and intensity up to and until after the surrender of Vicksburg. General Hurlbut was not only enthusiastic but eloquent in his advocacy of the prompt capture of Mobile, and also believed our lines could readily be extended eastward to the Tombigbee River, over which at that time it seemed that the people of Mississippi were stampeding and fleeing eastward with their Negroes and plunder. Had Halleck said "yes," instead of "no," to General Grant's proposition, there is no doubt in my mind that the movement would have been most successfully executed, and much of the hard work which subsequently followed in Mississippi during the latter part of 1863 and through 1864 would have been to a great extent obviated. Such action would have drawn the rebels away from Rosecrans and afforded him timely relief, without injury or serious detriment to our armies, and in many other ways proven beneficial to the cause and hastened the downfall of the Rebellion. Unfortunately, the condition of affairs in Mexico at that time made it necessary to make a demonstration and obtain a better foothold in Texas. At least Mr. Lincoln was desirous of impressing the invaders of Mexico as to the warmth of our feelings against the permanent occupation of that country by Maximilian.[5]

The cavalry of the XVI Army Corps was widely scattered along the line of the Memphis and Charleston Railroad, and virtually under the control of district commanders. The detachments of the 6th and 7th Illinois Cavalry left at La Grange and those sent back from Pontotoc, Mississippi, during the raid were soon united with their regiments again, and the cordial greeting of the soldiers was both amusing and affecting. The usual shake of the hand or nod of recognition was not sufficient for such an occasion. They not only grasped each other warmly by the hands, but frequently embraced, shook, pounded, and in some instances almost tore the clothes off each other, not in anger, but in the midst of the warmth of their heartfelt greeting and overflowing exuberance of the genuine joy of their union after so many months' separation. Those who had been left in Tennessee were proud of the success of the raiders who had so gallantly traversed the state[s] of Mississippi and Louisiana.

Colonel Edward Hatch of the 2nd Iowa Cavalry, from the time of his return to the line of the Memphis and Charleston Railroad, had been actively at work with his command against the rebels on either side of that line, and had only a few days before my return to Memphis gotten back from a most successful expedition to Jackson, Tennessee, during which he with his gallant troops inflicted severe injury upon the enemy, with slight loss to his command. Hatch was then commanding a brigade of cavalry in Colonel Mizner's division. I had been assigned as chief of cavalry [XVI Corps], relieving Colonel W. H. H. Taylor, 5th Ohio Cavalry, and had a general supervision of all the cavalry. Although unable to mount or ride a horse, I made frequent trips as far out as La Grange and Corinth, inspecting and doing all in my power under the circumstances to equip and place the troops in good condition.

Upon return to Memphis, I had hoped to obtain a short leave in order to see and bring my family south again. I had received at Vicksburg, on July 20, the first letter from Mrs. Grierson since leaving La Grange, and it is not to be wondered that I was anxious to enjoy the pleasures and comforts of home again, if even only for a brief time. General Hurlbut, however, thought that, although crippled, I had better remain with him, as he felt much in need of my services at that time. So I made arrangements and, at the general's suggestion, wrote at once to Mrs. Grierson to join me at Memphis with the children. He designated a Confederate house that could be set aside for my family as quarters. Allowing a reasonable time to enable Mrs. Grierson to reach Memphis, presuming that she would leave Jacksonville at once upon receipt of my letter, and while I was anxiously hearing the whistle and awaiting the arrival of every boat that came down the Mississippi River from the north, a letter came, much to my disappointment, which advised me that she was on a visit to her brother's in Chicago, and indicated that she did not receive my letters as quickly as I had hoped and would, therefore, be considerably delayed. So I hobbled again to Corinth on another inspecting tour, trusting that I might find my family at Memphis upon return. I got back on August 16 and, instead of meeting them, received another letter from Mrs. Grierson, in which I was advised not to expect her until she put in an appearance.

It had been nearly a month since my arrival at Memphis from Baton Rouge, and I was still obliged to use a crutch or cane in order to move about at all. While in the city, I remained quietly at my brother's house, either in bed or with my injured leg stuck up on a chair, endeavoring to amuse myself and occupy my time by fighting mosquitoes, reading, writing, and living on the hope and expectation of soon seeing my family. But each day only brought me disappointment. In a long letter to Mrs. Grierson on August 17, 1863, I wrote that: "Our little snarl will still keep snarling, instead of straightening out, my darling, but I'll not, my dear, be such a fool, as to grow vexed when I should keep cool."

My letter was abruptly brought to a close by the receipt of [a] message from General Hurlbut, who wished to see me at once at his headquarters. Upon [my] arriving there, the general said that he wished me to take command of the left wing XVI Army Corps, in place of General [Grenville M.] Dodge,[6] who was going away on leave of absence. Such a change would have made it necessary to have my headquarters at Corinth, or at least as far out as La Grange, which would not, under all the circumstances, have been at that time very pleasant. Although it was very kind in [of] General Hurlbut to think of me in that connection, I was glad to learn soon afterwards that General [Eugene A.] Carr,[7] who was my senior by commission as brigadier general of volunteers, was placed in temporary command while General Dodge was absent.

As usual, in time the "little snarl" was straightened out at last. In July, weary of home cares and the wearing anxiety and suspense occasioned by my absence and the uncertainty of my return, Mrs. Grierson [had] accepted the invitation of her brother and his wife to visit them in Chicago, and arrived there the very day Port Hudson was taken. Remembering what I in previous letters had said about obtaining leave of absence, she supposed I would do so, come to Chicago for a few days, and return with her to Jacksonville. [She] was so prepossessed with that idea that she fancied, should she start for Memphis, we would probably pass each other on the way. The mails were irregular and letters frequently delayed. The one I had written from Memphis was detained by my father in Jacksonville, he daily expecting Mrs. Grierson there on her way to Memphis and thinking that, if [it were]forwarded to Chicago, she would not be there to receive it. But Mrs. Grierson's plans were all made and carried out on the preconceived idea of my return to the North. And thus it happened that I received her letter from Chicago, in which she spoke of a contemplated visit to relatives in Michigan while awaiting for my appearance at Chicago. When she returned from Michigan and found my later letter, she started for Memphis at once. At Jacksonville, she was detained by the illness and death of children in the family of my sister, and by preparations for the southern journey.

When at last she reached Cairo, in the morning, she found the regular Memphis packet would not be there until in the afternoon, while a boat at the wharf was advertised to leave at 10 o'clock A.M. She was then so impatient that she embarked on that boat, with her two children, and paid the passage. But the boat lay at the wharf, and she had to endure seeing the regular Memphis packet come in and steam out before her eyes. Finally, the boat she was on started, went twenty miles, and laid up for the night. The next day it went some miles further, to Fort Pillow, and again tied up for the night. The third day it ran on a sand bank and remained thirty hours, till a tug came out and took the passengers off. All that time she was tormenting herself with the idea that I might change my plans, and suddenly going to Jacksonville, pass her on the way. It certainly is to be hoped that when she did get to the end of her journey, and found me on my crutches at the wharf, that the long waiting and the consequent disappointment was quickly forgotten in our joyful meeting.

———

The detached and widely separated situation of the cavalry, being scattered as it was from Memphis east along the line of the Memphis and Charleston Railroad to Corinth, was perplexing and unsatisfactory. Guarding such a long line, it was impossible to concentrate a sufficient force at any one point rapidly enough to make any effective demonstration into the enemy's country. And being compelled to constantly fight on the defensive was discouraging when so little good could be accomplished. I was determined, however, to do the best I could under the circumstances. Although unable to get about except by the use of crutches, I made frequent trips as far east as Corinth. And although repeatedly advised by the surgeons not to do so, I found it impossible to keep quiet, being so worried by my want of ability to ride on horseback.

The latter part of August, I reorganized the cavalry into three brigades, placing Colonels Mizner, [Lafayette] McCrillis,[8] and Hatch in command, with the hope of getting the troops more directly under my own control. But it was at times found to be impracticable, as local commanders would manage to gobble regiments whenever opportunity offered. I continued to work, notwithstanding my disability, until late in September, during which time the cavalry had frequent engagements with the enemy on either side of the railroad, and occasionally penetrating some distance southward into Mississippi. I found it impossible to refrain from superintending in person whatever seemed to be essential for the good of the service, and was obliged to make long and painful journeys on the railroad. Guerillas again made their appearance in numerous parts of the country, and to break up and drive them away gave constant employment to detachments of the cavalry. About the middle of September, three regiments were withdrawn from my command and ordered to Vicksburg, and General Hurlbut had been obliged to send a considerable force of infantry and artillery to the assistance of General Rosecrans, who was threatened with an attack by Bragg's army. Soon after this, the disastrous battle of Chickamauga was fought.[9] General Rosecrans' army [was] defeated and driven back to Chattanooga in a badly demoralized condition, where it was virtually besieged by the enemy.

At last the division surgeon went to General Hurlbut and told him that unless I was compelled in some way to rest, there was danger of my losing my leg, and probably my life. I was then at Corinth on crutches. On the appeal of the surgeon and recommendation of the medical director, General Hurlbut issued an order for thirty days' leave on [a] surgeon's certificate of disability; all this being done without my application or knowledge, the order being sent out to me with a note from the general to cease my work for awhile and go home for rest and recuperation. Under such circumstances I improved the opportunity to proceed with my family to Jacksonville, where upon arrival we found ourselves not without honor in our own country. We journeyed northward by boat to Cairo, from there to St. Louis by rail, and thence via Springfield to Jacksonville, arriving at our home on September 25. At Springfield, we visited the County Fair with Governor Yates and General [Joseph D.] Webster, the latter being then there on his way back to Memphis from leave of absence.

I telegraphed from Springfield to my father, but he did not receive the telegram until just before our arrival. Notwithstanding this, there were many people at the station to welcome us. Major [John N.] Niglas[10] had been sent north with me, and after our arrival at home he went on to Peoria for a short visit with his people, our old family physician, Dr. Hiram K. Jones, taking his place to give me such medical attention as might be necessary. The children enjoyed the change and joining those of the different families from whom they had been separated. When all together, they had a regular spree, with much noise and merriment.

I had been so well known at Jacksonville before the war that, although I remained quietly housed at our old homestead, many people came to see me there on September 26 and daily thereafter, as my presence became known. A public reception was not only tendered, but insisted upon in the strongest manner by the leading citizens of the place. Although naturally inclined to decline, as I did not relish being placed in such a conspicuous position, it was finally more readily accepted for the reason that, in the political condition of the country at that time, Copperheadism had become rampant.[11] And the prolonged war calling for further reinforcements of men and appropriations for money, the enthusiasm created by such a gathering would really be serving the country as faithfully as by active work in the field. On account of my crippled condition, the reception was arranged to take place October 9, 1863. The time soon came, however, and still found me unable to put in an appearance except by the aid of a stout cane and crutch. A full account of the proceedings on that occasion was published in the *State Journal* at Springfield [on] Thursday, October 13, 1863.

———

Although still suffering from the injury to my knee and unable to walk, or ride on horseback, I returned to Memphis at the expiration of my leave of absence in October to do what I could towards superintending the movements of the cavalry. Mrs. Grierson and the children accompanied me to that place. About the same time, General Grant was assigned to the command of the Military Division of the Mississippi, General Sherman to the Department of the Tennessee, and [George H.] Thomas succeeded Rosecrans. General Sherman had, previous to my arrival, passed eastward from Memphis with part of the XV and XVII Army Corps, and troops from the XVI Corps were being pushed forward to join his forces en route to Middle Tennessee. The day after the general arrived at Memphis from Vicksburg, his little son, "Willie," a bright boy about ten years old, whom I knew quite well, died of fever contracted while the general's family was in camp with him near the Big Black River in Mississippi.[12] General Dodge had returned from leave of absence and had resumed command at Corinth, relieving General Carr. It was expected that troops would arrive from Arkansas to take the place of those removed by General Sherman. The rebel force in Mississippi had been considerably increased and was actively at work endeavoring to counteract the loyal sentiment of the people by hunting down deserters, [as well as] conscripting and seizing upon all horses, mules, and other property that could be obtained throughout that section of the country.

Guerillas again made their appearance on either side of the Memphis and Charleston Railroad, and the duty devolving upon the cavalry, in its scattered condition, was most trying and arduous, and required the utmost vigilance and energy. General [*sic*] Hatch was very active at this time and had driven the rebels under Chalmers, who had attacked the troops at Collierville and had been repulsed, southward beyond the Tallahatchie at Wyatt.[13] It had been reported that General Sherman, who was passing westward with his troops, had been captured at Collierville, he being there when that place was attacked. But that was soon contradicted by the general [in] a telegram to General Hurlbut from La Fayette. In speaking of that affair, General Sherman said that the attack was very weak. For although the enemy had artillery, the fire did but little execution, as no enfilading was attempted when one or two solid shots sent tearing through his train might have destroyed it.

From information received from scouts, it was quite evident that the enemy would make a great effort to regain territory lost in Mississippi and Tennessee, or as much of it as possible, and by taking advantage of the occasion, whilst so many of General Hurlbut's troops were absent, would endeavor to recruit and strengthen their forces, and obtain all the supplies and material possible. They concentrated their troops south and along the line of the Tallahatchie, and at points parallel thereto westward, well out towards Corinth. Serious apprehensions were felt for the safety of Chattanooga and other points in Middle Tennessee, and Generals Thomas and [Ambrose] Burnside had all they could do to hold their ground with the reinforcements being sent to them against the advance of the enemy, excited and elated with their recent brilliant success.[14] General Hurlbut could have advantageously used a much larger force for guarding so long a line against the attacks of the rebels and properly look[ing] to the security of so important a point at this juncture as Memphis. Scouts were constantly kept out to watch the movements of the enemy, so as to guard as effectually as possible against attack, which from information received, I judged might be made at any time on the railroad along which our troops were kept moving on the alert.

In a little over a month after assuming command of the Military Division of the Mississippi, General Grant had succeeded under difficult circumstances in supplying the Army of the Cumberland, left almost destitute by General Rosecrans of clothing, rations, and transportation, besides providing for the wants of the large reinforcements quickly concentrated from distant points to the vicinity of Chattanooga. His troops had successfully fought numerous battles, including that of Missionary Ridge, that was mainly won by the uncontrollable enthusiasm, gallant dash, and bravery of the enlisted men of the Union army who voluntarily made the charge on the enemy's works, and the battle of Lookout Mountain, where [Maj. Gen. Joseph] Hooker victoriously fought the rebels above the clouds, which all together has been generally designated as the battle of Chattanooga, that important point thereby being made secure to the Federal cause.[15] The rebels had been driven pell-mell southward from positions deemed impregnable, with their forces broken, scattered, and demoralized. Timely relief, too, had been given to the Army of the Ohio under General Burnside at Knoxville, greatly to the delight of President Lincoln and cabinet, the great satisfaction of the loyal people of the land, and [the] dismay [of] the enemies of the country. Surely the right man had been placed in the right place, and the importance of those victories can hardly be overestimated, following as they did the capture of Vicksburg and the important battle of Gettysburg, so gallantly won by the Army of the Potomac under General Meade.[16] The results thus attained foreshadowed the early downfall of the Confederacy and clearly demonstrated the fact that General Grant was the man to bring the war to a successful close, if placed in absolute command of the armies of the United States.

In compliance with orders from headquarters XVI Army Corps, dated November 24, 1863, I ordered the brigade commanded by Colonel Edward Hatch to move on the morning of the 26th, by separate columns north of the railroad, and to scout around and assemble at Somerville, Tennessee, for the purpose of covering the taking up of the material upon the Somerville Branch Railroad. At the same time, I suggested the propriety and was authorized to order the brigade commanded by Colonel J. K. Mizner to move southward from Corinth as far as he deemed safe, without risking his command. Colonel Mizner, after marching southward about forty miles, encountered and captured some of the enemy, and ascertained the rebels were moving in large force, evidently to attack the railroad and possibly pass northward into West Tennessee. This information was promptly communicated to General Hurlbut, and in accordance with instructions, I immediately sent couriers to Colonel Hatch with orders to move as quickly as possible with his brigade to La Grange. As the enemy advanced northward, they were met by Colonel Mizner's command and several times repulsed. They, however, overpowered and drove back his brigade to Pocahontas, when they turned and moved southward again, probably as a feint, and taking another road, moved upon Saulsbury.

Colonel Hatch arrived at La Grange and was immediately ordered to move east along the railroad, scouting towards Ripley. He met the enemy at Saulsbury, after they had succeeded in destroying the railroad at that point and starting a portion of their command north. Colonel Hatch fought and drove the remainder of the enemy's force some distance south, and returned with his command to La Grange.

The next morning I sent scouts south, and information was soon obtained that the rebels were moving west, evidently with the intention of again making an attack on the railroad. I at once ordered Colonel Hatch west with his command. He arrived at Moscow simultaneously with the enemy, when a brief but severe engagement ensued in which Colonel Hatch was severely wounded and the enemy repulsed and forced southward, with a loss of about 100 in killed, wounded, and prisoners, they having left their dead on the field. Our loss was four killed and nineteen wounded. The gallantry displayed by Colonel Hatch and his brigade, and the colored regiment of infantry stationed as a guard to the railroad bridge at Moscow, under command of Colonel Frank Kendrick, was highly commendable and duly acknowledged.

The 6th Illinois Cavalry was in advance when the charge was made by Hatch's brigade over the bridge at Wolf River. Although they were under the direct fire of infantry and artillery concealed in the woods and high ground beyond, their impetuosity carried them through alright, although their loss in horses was heavy. They were quickly followed by the other regiments of the brigade, and the rebels [were] gallantly routed and driven southward for a considerable distance, in great confusion. The force of the enemy which had passed northward from Saulsbury proved to be about 1,500 strong under command of General [Nathan Bedford] Forrest,[17] who had gone north of the railroad for the purpose of conscripting and plundering in West Tennessee, as had been foreshadowed by reports previously received from my scouts.

Immediately upon receipt of news of this fight, I proceeded with Major Starr and Captain Woodward of my staff on a handcar from La Grange, starting in the dark for Moscow ten miles distant [and] leaving orders for an engine which I had directed to be sent from Grand Junction to La Grange to follow as quickly as possible. When we had made about half the distance Captain Woodward, who happened to be looking backward, saw and announced the approach of the engine, and we were obliged to hurriedly stop our handcar and hustle it and ourselves off the track, when the bright headlight of the locomotive hove in sight. We had only barely gotten off the track when the engine rushed by. We hailed the engineer and he checked speed, stopped, ran back to where we were, and picked us up. In a few minutes, we were at Moscow and listening to the account of the engagement from Colonel Hatch, who lay wounded upon his cot in a tent furnished by Colonel Kendrick. I at once recommended through official channels to the War Department the promotion of Colonel Hatch to brigadier general of volunteers. The rebels were pursued to a point near the Tallahatchie, and as the enemy returned to their camp south of that stream, my troops resumed their former status along the line of the Memphis and Charleston Railroad.

About the middle of December 1863, in pursuance of orders from General Hurlbut, Colonel Mizner was ordered to move with his command, except the 6th Tennessee Cavalry, in connection with a brigade of infantry and battery of artillery under General [Joseph] Mower,[18] from Corinth north to Purdy, while I prepared to concentrate at the same time the balance of my command at La Grange for the purpose of moving north to operate in conjunction with General Mower and General A. J. Smith,[19] who was to move south from Union City towards the position of the enemy at Jackson,

Tennessee. Information was received, however, that General Smith was not ready to start. Accordingly, my movements were postponed, with the exception of that of Colonel Mizner, who was directed to proceed to Purdy with General Mower [and] there to await further developments.

Upon arriving at La Grange on December 22, I was informed by General [James M.] Tuttle[20] that a considerable force of the enemy under General Chalmers was posted near Salem. This information having been tele-graphed to the major general commanding at Memphis, it was thought best to remain at La Grange for a time to watch the movements of the rebels and ascertain more definitely their purpose. Accordingly, at daylight the next morning I started Colonel Prince with about 500 men of the 7th Illinois Cavalry north, with instructions to cover all crossings of the Hatchie River, and if pressed by the enemy, to fall back towards Grand Junction, at the same time sending about twenty men south to feel [out] Chalmers.

Colonel Prince proceeded to Bolivar, thence northward along the Hatchie, destroying all boats as he advanced. When near Estenoba, he came upon a considerable force of the enemy under [Col. Robert V.] Rich-ardson crossing the Hatchie at that point. He attacked and drove the rebels back until night compelled him to suspend operations, when he fell back to secure a safe position in which to encamp. Upon receipt of this news, I immediately dispatched Colonel [Major Henry B.] Burgh with the 9th Illi-nois Cavalry to reinforce Colonel Prince. It being the belief that the enemy would attempt to cross the railroad between La Grange and Pocahontas, I disposed my command as well as possible to intercept him.

That night Forrest succeeded in crossing his whole command at Es-tenoba. To avoid being flanked, Colonel Prince fell back to Somerville, where he remained all day on the 25th and communicated with me at La Grange. I immediately ordered him to move east to Newcastle, where Major Burgh had by that time arrived. He started on the morning of the 26th on the road to Newcastle, and about four miles from Somerville met the enemy in force and engaged him. But, being attacked vigorously in the rear, his command was thrown into disorder and compelled to retreat. He arrived at La Grange with his command, as did also Major Burgh the same evening.

On the morning of the 27th, I learned that the enemy had moved west. Telegraphing at once the information to General Hurlbut, [I] suggested the propriety of starting a regiment of cavalry in that direction. This was approved, and Major Burgh was immediately ordered to Collierville with his regiment and instructed to report to the major general commanding upon arrival at that point. Scarcely had he started, when the operator at La Fayette stated that the enemy was coming. A few moments after, the wires were cut. The bridge at that point had repeatedly been ordered destroyed. When passing there upon the railroad on December 22, I [had] sent a staff officer to inquire if it had been done. He was told by Lieutenant [Sidney O.] Roberts of the 9th [Illinois] Cavalry, who was in command there, that it was entirely destroyed.

The information of the approach of Forrest was received about fifteen minutes after 2 o'clock P.M. on the 27th. I immediately telegraphed to Colonel [William H.] Morgan, who was at Grand Junction with his brigade and a train of cars which he had been ordered to hold in readiness to move at a moment's notice, to embark his command and run to La Fayette as speedily as possible, as the enemy had attacked at that place. Considerable delay occurred before Colonel Morgan reached La Grange, at least two hours being consumed in embarking his command and going two and a half miles. I then gave him written instructions to attack the enemy vigorously wherever he might be found [and] sent with him Major Starr, one of my staff, for the purpose of sending me information. In the meantime, I suggested to Brigadier General Tuttle that the force of white troops under Major [Samuel] Henry stationed at Moscow be sent to Grissom's Bridge until the arrival of Colonel Morgan. The suggestion was approved and acted upon.

When Colonel Morgan arrived at Grissom's Bridge, he found Major Henry there and his advance already skirmishing with the enemy. Major Henry was ordered to advance with his command, which he did with alacrity and briskly engaged the enemy, driving him back successfully. Colonel Morgan finally advanced his train within a mile and a half of La Fayette, when he disembarked and formed line of battle, although Major Henry was still in advance for some distance with skirmishers and reserves still engaging the enemy. Colonel Morgan, finding it impossible to get through the swamp where he had disembarked and first formed his line, formed column and deployed into line several times, consuming fully an hour in that manner, during which time the enemy was rapidly crossing Wolf River and succeeded in crossing his whole command before Colonel Morgan had fired a shot.

In the meantime, Major Burgh with the 9th Illinois Cavalry, who had marched by wagon road from La Grange, met the enemy about one and a half miles from Moscow, skirmished with and drove them in connection with the troops under Major Henry's command, until he arrived at La Fayette, when the enemy divided, part going west along the railroad and the rest south. Major Burgh pushed forward again and came up with the enemy near Collierville before midnight. He immediately dispatched to Colonel Morgan, who had gone into bivouac at La Fayette. At 3 o'clock

A.M. on the 28th, Colonel Morgan moved out his command, but before he reached Collierville the rebels had gone. From that point Colonel Morgan communicated with General Hurlbut, stating that his command was worn out, when he and his troops had marched only 8½ miles in two days and had not succeeded in getting within shooting distance of the enemy. The last order he received at 6 o'clock P.M. on the 28th, but [he] did not move until 3 o'clock the next morning, although ordered by both General Hurlbut and myself to start in pursuit of the enemy. Had Colonel Morgan evinced as much enterprise in pursuing and attacking the enemy as he did in making excuses for his tardy movements, success would undoubtedly have attended our efforts. In the meantime, Colonel Mizner's brigade had returned to Corinth from Purdy and was brought by rail to La Grange.

On the morning of the 28th, I started the Second Brigade (Hatch's) under command of Major [Datus E.] Coon southwest to Mt. Pleasant and thence to Hudsonville. As soon as Colonel Mizner arrived at La Grange, I proceeded with his brigade to Hudsonville. At midnight on the 28th, I sent scouts to ascertain the whereabouts of the enemy, who had passed southwest from Hudsonville the night before. At daylight on the 29th, I started the Second Brigade in pursuit, but soon received information from Major Coon that Forrest had been joined by Chalmers and that another movement on the railroad was contemplated by their combined forces. Taking that information, in connection with a dispatch received from General Hurlbut that a considerable force of the enemy had crossed Coldwater River going north to reinforce Forrest, I deemed it best to move to Mt. Pleasant, sending detachments to Olive Branch and farther west to completely cover the line of the railroad; sending expeditions also to all the fords and crossings of the Coldwater and as far west as Byhalia.

The next morning I received information from all the scouts that the enemy had passed rapidly southward. A cold rain with snow setting in, I ordered Colonel Mizner to proceed with his command to La Grange, sent the 6th Illinois Cavalry via Olive Branch to Germantown, and with the rest of the command fell back to Collierville. Before the troops reached the line of the railroad it commenced snowing furiously, and the thermometer quickly fell below zero. Colonel Mizner's column was caught out all night in the snow and, being without camp equipage or even axes to cut wood, suffered severely. We arrived at Collierville late in the afternoon on December 31, and proceeded thence by train to Memphis so as to be in readiness for New Year's dinner the next day with Mrs. Grierson and the rest of our military family.

During all these operations, although our headquarters were permanently established in Memphis, I and my staff went frequently to La Grange, and the movements were generally directed by telegraph from that point. I was still very lame from the effects of the hurt received in July previous, and at the end of the year [was] barely able to ride for a short time on horseback, having to carry a crutch to assist me in mounting and dismounting. [I] did not entirely recover the use of my limb for several months thereafter.

———

The winter of 1863–64 was spent by myself and family at Memphis. We resided at what was known as the "Davey" house in the suburbs of the city, nearly three miles from headquarters. The mud at last made the distance from the office such an inconvenience that we removed to Exchange Street, near Main, boarding with a Mrs. Hammond at a house that had been confiscated for General [James C.] Veatch.[21] The inclement weather and muddy roads prevented any army movements on any extended scale. My duties as chief of cavalry consisted mainly in inspection, re-organization, and careful preparation for the spring campaign. General Sherman arrived at Memphis on January 10, and at once began to make his arrangements for active operations to take place in February. It was the first time the general and I had met after the close of the Vicksburg campaign, and he grasped my hand warmly and congratulated me on my successful expedition through Mississippi. The general was extremely fond of amusements, and while he remained at Memphis we frequently met at the theatre, where we usually were seated together, to enjoy a laugh at the not-very-well-performed comedies which were brought upon the stage. But they served as a sort of diversion or relaxation from official duties.

The brilliant ovations of 1863 did not altogether spread my bed with rose leaves. I had been called upon for perilous duty, for which I had volunteered, [and] had performed what was deemed impossible. There were those who looked for greater achievements at every turn. If I had won the heights, it was to find them perilous. I had labored for nearly six months on crutches, suffering all the time from the pain of the injury received, yet the cavalry under my command had been kept actively at work rendering important service. There was no task performed by me during the war at which I feel more satisfaction than that rendered under such trying circumstances. But even my successes proved detrimental to my advancement.

Possibly I had been treading too near the toes of someone more ambitious, for I unexpectedly found myself during the year 1864 placed subordinate to and under the control of officers with less experience and not so capable of conducting a separate or independent command successfully as myself. But I submitted as gracefully as possible under the circumstances,

[and] kept on in the even tenor of my way, obeying with promptitude the orders of those placed over me, although I felt that an injustice was being done me and the best interest of the service disregarded. This fact is as gratifying to me now as any other experience or vicissitude endured during the war. I realized that the main thing to be considered was the putting down of the rebellion, regardless of the instruments used in its accomplishment, and never failed to feel the full force of the oath I had taken nor its most important injunction that "the first duty of a soldier was to obey orders." The treatment I received was often meted out to many another worthy and successful soldier during the war.

When in the spring of 1863 I started on my perilous way, I had received orders from General Grant through the hands, successively, of General S. A. Hurlbut and General W. Sooy Smith. Upon the brilliant success of that doubtful enterprise, General Smith may have conceived the idea that he had sent it out, or that the cavalry arm of the service was that wherein he might win fame and promotion. During the summer he had gone to Middle Tennessee and in some way obtained the place of chief of cavalry in the Military Division of the Mississippi. One main feature of General Sherman's Meridian campaign was to have a large force of cavalry pushed rapidly down the central and eastern part of the state to join his troops at Meridian, from whence the cavalry could be so disposed as to do incalculable injury to the enemy. It was expected by both Generals Grant and Sherman that I would command the cavalry. But another brigade was wanted from Middle Tennessee, and General W. Sooy Smith, instead of sending, accompanied it. In view of his rank and position as chief of cavalry, soon after his arrival [he] assumed control of all the cavalry concentrating at Memphis or Union City, without any direct orders that I ever saw or could find on record from General Grant. General Smith thus seized upon the opportunity, believing he had found the chance to satisfy his ambition and aspirations.

I spoke to General Sherman about the matter, and offered to go down and join him with one brigade, or to go out from Vicksburg with whatever cavalry he might find there, feeling that there was certainly no need for me at Memphis if General Smith was to be assigned over me, two brigadier generals being unnecessary. But General Sherman thought, as he had upon his arrival at Memphis found General Smith, Grant's chief of cavalry, already there, although he had expected me to command the cavalry column, that it would not do to rebuff Smith without manifest cause. And that as I knew the country and General Smith did not, it would be better for the success of the expedition that we should both go together. He promised me that after the cavalry reached him at Meridian, he would relieve General Smith and send him back to Nashville, giving me my own independent command again; that he would cut me loose there to create as much havoc as possible among the rebels throughout that section of the country.

General Smith had left Nashville on December 28, 1863, with a brigade of cavalry composed of Tennessee and Kentucky regiments, and had been scouting westward through the country in a haphazard sort of fashion, hunting guerillas and ostensibly looking after General Forrest. He arrived with his command at Corinth on January 8, and proceeded thence to Collierville. The regiments he brought through were comparatively new and reached Collierville in poor condition. I did all that was possible to render them more effective, with the least practicable delay.

A brigade of cavalry had been ordered by General Hurlbut from Union City, Tennessee, under command of Colonel George E. Waring, 4th Missouri Cavalry, who was expected with his brigade, on the line of the Memphis and Ohio Railroad,[22] before the end of January. But he did not reach Collierville until February 8, much to the annoyance of General Smith, who had been directed to start southward to join General Sherman at Meridian by February 10. His waiting for Waring's brigade at Collierville, and subsequently for several days south of the Tallahatchie, proved fatal to the success of the expedition.

I did everything in my power to prepare for and to hasten the departure of the troops, and my relations with General Smith were most friendly and in every way satisfactory during the entire time I was serving under his command. I had gained a tolerably thorough knowledge of the country through which it was expected we would travel, and had taken special pains to obtain still more minute and specific information from Union men who had reached Memphis previous to our departure. From one who did not want his name divulged, facts were ascertained that would have been of great assistance, had General Smith gone through as contemplated.[23]

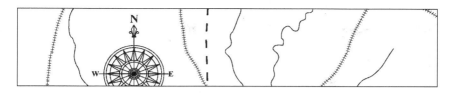

9. The Meridian Expedition

On January 27, 1864, all the cavalry of the Department of the Tennessee was, by the orders of General W. T. Sherman, assigned to the command of Brigadier General W. Sooy Smith, U.S. Volunteers. The latter did not issue any orders formally assuming command of the cavalry, but took direct control or general supervision, giving such verbal or written instructions from time to time as he deemed necessary. In accordance with General Smith's wish, the orders for the movement of the brigades and the necessary instructions to the officers of the quartermaster's, commissary, and ordnance departments were issued from my headquarters. I started on the expedition, however, with the feeling that I was really a supernumerary, as General Smith's presence prevented me from controlling the movements of the division as a whole.

By direction of General Smith, I with the officers of my staff accompanied the Third [Second] Brigade (Hatch's), which was commanded by Lieutenant Colonel William P. Hepburn, 2nd Iowa Cavalry, and which composed the column marching on the right. The First Brigade, commanded by Colonel Waring, was on the left, and the Third Brigade, consisting mainly of the troops brought through from Nashville by General Smith, formed the center column and was assigned to the command of Colonel LaFayette McCrillis, 3rd Illinois Cavalry, the total strength, including the 4th U.S. Cavalry—escort for General Smith—being about 7,500 enlisted men and officers.

The Second Brigade, with which I marched, was in readiness to move on February 1, but by direction of General Smith it remained in camp at Germantown until the 11th day of that month. The Third Brigade started from Collierville, Tennessee, on the 10th and encamped that night near Byhalia, Mississippi, where it remained during the day and night of the 11th, and then moved on southward on the morning of February 12 towards Holly Springs. The First Brigade, Colonel Waring's, which left Union City, Tennessee, January 22, 1864, and for which General Smith waited, did not reach Collierville until February 8, being eighteen days on the way. Nor did it leave the latter point and start on the expedition until the afternoon of the 11th. The First and Third brigades were kept almost constantly under the direct orders or control of General Smith.

The Second Brigade left Germantown at 3 o'clock A.M. on February 11, marched southward keeping up communication with the Third Brigade, and without meeting any opposition from the enemy worthy of notice, crossed the Tallahatchie River on February 14 and encamped five miles south of New Albany, where it was joined the same day by the Third Brigade. By direction of General Smith, both brigades were thus held from five to ten miles south of the Tallahatchie until the morning of February 17 to await the tardy movements of the First Brigade under the command of Colonel Waring, reported lost in the woods and hills of Tippah County, Mississippi.

While thus delayed, we had heavy rains. But, as we had no wagons with us, that need not have detained us. At that point we overtook a Mrs. Dunlop with her family and servants, with an outfit of one or two ambulances, moving southward. Not deeming it prudent to allow anyone to pass through our lines towards the enemy, I caused her detention. She stopped at a house near our headquarters. During the delay, we received two notes from her: the first, thanking us for kindness, stated that she fully appreciated our motives in detaining her and would make the best of the situation; the second stating that the lunch she had prepared on leaving Holly Springs had been exhausted and the family with whom she was stopping was about out of provisions, and requesting assistance. As we were living to some extent on the country, we sent out a foraging party and abundantly supplied her and the family which was entertaining her with such provisions as the country afforded. She was an agreeable little lady. We sympathized with her and did all we properly could to render her any needful assistance. When we left there, we moved south some distance, and then east to the Memphis and Charleston [Mobile and Ohio] Railroad. Not wishing Mrs. Dunlop to proceed until we had unmasked our own movements, we advised her to remain quietly where she was a day or two after our departure.[1]

On February 17 the cavalry, joined by Waring's brigade, proceeded southward through Pontotoc towards Houston, and thence eastward to Okolona on the Mobile and Ohio Railroad, without meeting any force of the enemy excepting the state troops under General [Samuel J.] Gholson,[2] which stampeded and ran away at our approach. The advance, consisting of the 9th Illinois Cavalry under command of Lieutenant Colonel Burgh, upon reaching the vicinity of Okolona, dashed forward into that place, where he captured a large rebel mail and a Lieutenant Barber, the rebel depot quartermaster. From Okolona, Colonel Burgh was sent rapidly on to Aberdeen, by my order, where two companies of state militia were encountered and driven away. Captain Rogers, commissary of subsistence, C.S. Army, was killed. One major, three other officers, and thirteen enlisted men [were] captured. Also, a considerable amount of Confederate government property [was] destroyed, and a large number of Negroes, mules, and horses which had been brought into the column were sent back to Okolona and turned over to the proper officers. From a point about four miles east of Okolona, I ordered Lieutenant Colonel Starr, 6th Illinois Cavalry, on towards Aberdeen to communicate with and support if necessary Colonel Burgh, and to secure the cotton-gin ferry over the Tombigbee River, ten miles north of that place. The same night, the balance of the Second Brigade encamped four to five miles east of Okolona.

At a late hour, after issuing orders for the next day's march to Aberdeen, I received a note from General Smith stating that he desired the work of destroying the railroad to proceed at once. So, [he] had ordered Colonel Waring to move out on the road four or five miles and commence. [Smith] had sent one regiment down to Egypt Station, eight miles distant, to destroy a lot of Confederate corn. [He] stated that McCrillis was in camp with his brigade, three miles back on the Pontotoc road; that the general movements for the next day were pretty nearly determined upon; that he must see me to talk them over fully; [and] that he had sent for McCrillis.

I started at once to the midnight conference and found that [Smith] had become alarmed by reports that the rebels were concentrating at West Point. The general seemed already in doubt about the feasibility of crossing the Tombigbee to join Sherman by that or any other route. I urged him to go on. [I] advised him of the orders already issued and showed him on the map the straight road from Aberdeen down through Columbus to Demopolis. I inspirited him with my own ideas as far as possible, assuring him of what could still be done by rapid movements, stating that I felt confident that I could readily effect a crossing of the Tombigbee and join General Sherman with one brigade, no matter where he was. General Smith approved of what I had done and authorized me to go on to Aberdeen, and thereafter to be guarded [guided?] in my movements by my judgment and discretion.

I returned to camp, and before daylight the Third [Second] Brigade was on its march and reached Aberdeen before noon, when we soon secured boats enough to construct a pontoon by which to cross the Tombigbee River for a dash with my single brigade to join Sherman. I thought General Smith, with two brigades, would surely take care of the enemy at West Point and go down on the east side of the river through Mississippi to

Meridian. But a messenger arrived from the general with instructions not to cross, and to proceed at once with my command towards West Point. Greatly disappointed, and sorely against my will, I started by an indirect movement the main portion of my brigade. But before leaving Aberdeen myself, [I] made an active demonstration for crossing the Tombigbee, which caused great consternation on the east side of the river and a hasty evacuation of Columbus. Before night, when marching on the direct road from Aberdeen to West Point, I received another message from the general to flank round to Prairie Station "to support" the two brigades he had with him, at a cost of ten miles extra marching for the one I was with—after the hard and fatiguing work it had already performed. The Second Brigade, however, was at once moved toward Prairie Station and encamped the night of the 19th within two miles of that point.

On the morning of February 20, the entire command marched in the direction of West Point—the Second Brigade in front, with the 2nd Iowa Cavalry in the advance. I ordered Lieutenant Colonel Starr to proceed with his regiment, the 6th Illinois Cavalry, and pioneer corps on the left flank, along the line of the Mobile and Ohio Railroad southward to Loohattan Station; to destroy all bridges, culverts, railroad buildings, or C.S. property of any kind found en route. He destroyed eleven bridges and culverts and 500,000 bushels of corn, and finding the enemy in force one and one-half miles east of Loohattan Station, communicated with me. I proceeded there at once with two battalions of the 7th Illinois Cavalry. The enemy under Forrest, with two brigades and artillery, seeing the movement and probably observing the column on the main West Point road, moved rapidly towards the Sakatonchee. I then moved forward, marching directly on the right flank of the rebels, until they hastily disappeared in the direction of West Point.

When within about half a mile of that place, we came upon them again advantageously posted in timber and behind rail fences, where they were vigorously attacked by the 2nd Iowa Cavalry supported by other regiments, and driven rapidly to West Point, where it was presumed another determined stand would be made. But they were soon routed by the Second Brigade, alone, and we promptly occupied the place, picketing all roads leading therefrom, and encamped for the afternoon and night on the battleground. This engagement was the first serious conflict [we] had with the enemy, and the gallant bravery of the officers and enlisted men of the old Second Brigade was quickly made manifest as they charged and routed the surprised and fleeing foe.

The force discovered by Lieutenant Colonel Starr, and subsequently flanked off, was in addition to that first encountered by Major Coon with the 2nd Iowa Cavalry. [This] consisted of Colonel [Jeffrey] Forrest's[3] brigade to the assistance of which General Forrest moved with his two brigades and artillery, making his first appearance on our left flank, instead of uniting with Colonel Forrest, as contemplated. For once, in my judgment, General Forrest was badly rattled, and his weak demonstration and subsequent movements with so large a force plainly showed it. Had General Smith followed up the advantage thus gained by pushing his whole force against the enemy, the bridge over the Sakatonchee could have been taken and securely held for our forward movement the next day, as General Forrest states that he would have avoided a general engagement until joined by General [Stephen D.] Lee's forces.[4] There was ample time for the forward movement, as General Smith's troops were encamped in the vicinity of West Point by 3 o'clock P.M. on February 20.

From General Forrest's own statements it will be seen that he re-crossed his entire force over [the] Sakatonchee. That he moved hurriedly, and without contemplating serious resistance, is very evident. In his report he states:

> On the morning of the 20th Col. Forrest met the enemy in force and fell back towards West Point, skirmishing with them but avoiding an engagement; in repelling the attacks he lost two men killed and several wounded and captured. I moved over to his assistance with Gen. Chalmers and his remaining brigade taking with me also Richardson's brigade and two batteries of artillery, joining Col. Forrest within three miles of West Point. Finding the enemy in large force, and having been informed that Gen. Lee was moving to my assistance and desiring to delay a general engagement as long as possible, I determined at once to withdraw my forces south [west] of Sakatonchee Creek, which I did, camping a portion near Ellis' Bridge and the remainder at Siloam.

Continuing, he states: "After crossing the river a courier reported the enemy as having crossed the river eight miles above Ellis' Bridge, destroying and taking horses and wagons. With five companies of Falkner's [sic] regiment[5] and my escort, I moved rapidly to the point clearly designated by the smoke of the burning mill." He further [states] that: "he gained the bridge and succeeded in capturing the squad, which proved to be a Lieutenant and 22 privates of the 4th regular U.S. Cavalry." This shows that General Forrest had, after crossing the Sakatonchee, traveled a distance of over sixteen miles before rejoining his main command; that he could not have gotten it together before the next day; and that he plainly did not contemplate any determined resistance at the Sakatonchee on the afternoon of the 20th.[6]

The night of February 20 was one of disquiet for General Smith. I was aware that he had been greatly annoyed on account of the delay occasioned by the slow movements of Waring's brigade. But it was not until after our arrival at West Point that the general seemed to fully realize he had gotten so much behind time, or that he became depressed by the weight of the responsibility devolving upon him in not being able to comply with his instructions to join General Sherman as directed. Up to that time, he had probably presumed that General Sherman might also be considerably delayed in his movements. But, on the night of the 20th it was rumored that he had entered Meridian and was probably on his way back to Vicksburg. General Smith had also received exaggerated reports in regard to the strength of the enemy in our front, and of General Lee's approach to join Forrest with cavalry, infantry, and artillery. All this—with the excitement, worry, and fatigue undergone in his march southward to West Point—had worked upon his nervous system to such an extent as to render him absolutely sick and unable to properly command in such an emergency. I had talked over the situation with him during the evening, [and] had urged the necessity of going on, or at least making a bold and persistent attack on the enemy the next day. From what he had said, [I] judged that such action would be taken. Therefore, my arrangements were made accordingly.

I had learned from Negroes of a crossing over the Sakatonchee Creek some miles below Ellis' Bridge, where trees had fallen into the stream and where the Negroes had been in the habit of crossing back and forth. I had directed a further investigation to be made, and had been advised by Colonel Starr that the 6th Illinois Cavalry, with the pioneers, could construct a safe crossing in a few hours, which would have been of much advantage in our forward movement and attack on the enemy.

About midnight, however, in response to a message from General Smith, I went to see him and found that he had determined to go no further south, and that he deemed it necessary under the circumstances to return to Memphis in order to get out of the trap set for him by the rebels. I said and did all in my power to discourage him from such a course; assured him of the confidence I felt in my ability to join General Sherman no matter where he might be, and that I would do so with one brigade if permitted; that the force he had was, in my judgment, ample to go anywhere and to fight the enemy successfully. I believed then, and do now, that it would have been better and much easier to go in any other direction than to fall back over the same road upon which we had advanced. For so long as we by maneuvers and operations against the enemy kept him in doubt as to our intentions, even if we must finally return, we would have a certain advantage, which would be quickly lost when our plans were plainly revealed by a direct movement to the rear. That, in any event, it would be best to attack the enemy at daylight and then shape our course as circumstances might require; that we could go on south or swing eastward, cross the Tombigbee, destroy ferries and bridges over that stream, march into central Alabama and thence northward to our own lines, inflicting all possible damage upon the enemy and thus insure a successful termination for the expedition. It was of no avail. General Smith had resolved upon returning and gave his orders accordingly. I then asked to be left in the rear with the Second Brigade, and to that proposition he assented.

On the morning of the 21st, he started for Okolona with the 4th U.S. Cavalry and the First and Third brigades. I remained at West Point with the Second Brigade, picketing all approaches thereto while, with a suitable detachment, I directed a vigorous attack on the enemy at Ellis' Bridge, successfully driving him back and maintaining our position for several hours, during all of which time Forrest supposed that the attack was made by General Smith's entire force. After withdrawing my command leisurely and in good order, it was sometime before Forrest became aware that a retreat was being made, and fully two hours before he came by cautious movements upon our rearguard. Of course, we knew that there was nothing else for us to do but to fight the rebels in our rear and on our flanks, so long as they had any ammunition left or ability to pursue. The records show that, so far as the officers and soldiers of the Second Brigade are concerned, they did so gallantly and successfully.

It was not until long after night that we reached the vicinity of the camp selected by General Smith [and] joined the other brigades that had left us that morning at West Point. On the 22nd, the Second Brigade, which had been so actively engaged scouting and fighting the enemy for several days and during much of the previous night, was placed in advance, followed by the First Brigade, while the Third Brigade was in the rear. Upon arrival of the advance of the Second Brigade at Okolona, the enemy was promptly driven out of the place, under my direct supervision, and efforts [were] made to bring on an engagement, without avail, the enemy having been discovered in considerable force east of the town and beyond the Mobile and Ohio Railroad. After the Second Brigade was withdrawn, the rebels made their appearance again and were gallantly charged and routed by the 4th U.S. Cavalry. When the First Brigade had moved forward on the road towards Pontotoc and the Third Brigade taken position in the rear, seeing nothing more of the enemy and having directed that the 4th

Regulars, Captain [Charles S.] Bowman commanding, should report to Colonel McCrillis to protect his rear, I left with my staff to rejoin the Second Brigade.

When a few miles from the town, information was received that the Tennessee regiments had been stampeded. I at once sent forward to General Smith to have the First and Second brigades halted and some of the older and disciplined regiments placed in position, while with my staff I returned towards the rear to endeavor to quell the disorder. We soon met the Tennessee cavalry as they were running away from nothing more dangerous than their own shadows. The confusion and disorder could not, with all our efforts and those of Colonel McCrillis and his staff, be effectually quelled until the disorganized troops had passed and those which had been halted brought back and placed in well-chosen positions, after which by well-directed and deliberate volleys all attacks of the enemy were gallantly repulsed with severe loss to them.

At a point about four miles from Okolona, Colonel Forrest was killed while trying to rally his brigade, and soon after [Lieutenant] Colonel [James A.] Barksdale of the rebel forces [was] mortally wounded. Forrest's report shows clearly the obstinate and determined resistance he met with when he came upon our well-organized troops, and especially those of the old Second Brigade. About ten miles from Okolona, at Ivy farm, we overtook General Smith, who had then placed several regiments in position. After a short but sharp engagement the enemy was again repulsed, with about equal loss to both sides. It was there that my aide-de-camp, the efficient and gallant Lieutenant James K. Catlin of the 2nd Illinois Cavalry, was killed. Observing, as he thought, some hesitation on the part of the 4th U.S. Cavalry to charge as ordered, on the spur of the moment he voluntarily and without orders drew his saber and dashed to the front. In a moment, I heard the clear ring of his voice as he charged entirely through the rebel lines. In attempting to return, [he] was surrounded, and refusing to surrender, [was] shot and instantly killed. I was warmly attached to him, and his death was keenly felt by myself and all who knew him. The attack of the enemy was continued during a part of that night, and until after we had passed some distance north of Pontotoc the next day.

On the 23rd we re-crossed the Tallahatchie at New Albany. It was there that a most ludicrous scene occurred, which for a short time placed me in rather a remarkable position for an officer of my rank. As the enemy had, previous to our return to the Tallahatchie River, disappeared entirely, General Smith seemed doubtful as to the propriety of crossing that stream at New Albany. Thinking we might find the rebels there in force, [he] suggested, in view of the large encumbrance in the way of Negroes, horses, mules, etc., another crossing further west. But I felt sure that no force could then be in our front. A regiment had already been pushed forward to secure the bridge and ford at the crossing over the river at that place. It was there, after the command had reached the north side of the river, that the incident occurred.

The immense train of contrabands, horses, and mules which encumbered the command, and was in part the excuse for retreating—though the command never ought to have been so encumbered, as that was not the purpose for which it was sent out—entirely blocked the retreat. They were an enormous undisciplined herd of men, women, children, and beasts. And, like beasts, they huddled together and would not budge. In vain was order after [order] sent to "clear the way" and get them out of the road. Only the outskirts of the large crowd could be reached, and if a few of them were headed in the right direction, they soon turned back and were absorbed in the general confusion. My own staff officers reported that it was impossible to stir them.

I really wish now that the scene could have been photographed. The surging mass contained everything conceivable of the grotesque in feature, figure, headdress, and caparison of all that goes on two feet or on four. The patchwork and the tatters of the garments and no-garments; the rope work and leather work and sheepskin work of the harnesses and saddles; the variety of vehicles and the indiscriminate plunder stored in them; the turbans on the women's heads and the sort of parcels on top of the turbans, all shifting hither and thither, without aim or instinct, was simply wonderful to behold.

After one good look and exclamation of surprise, I set two or three orderlies at work on each side of the crowd, spurred rapidly to the front myself, and shouted: "Follow me. I'll show you the way to Jerusalem, and where to go." They all flocked like sheep, everyone trying to get foremost, shouting as they advanced: "Dar, don't you see? Dar goes de Gineral"; "dar, dar's de way"; "dar's where we wants to go," with a hundred similar expressions, bawled out of the wide-opened mouths and through the grinning teeth that seemed to fill the whole heads of the singular creatures who in part formed that moving, motley mass of human beings and animals.

The rush was then to see who could keep closest to my heels. Those who could not stretch their heads high enough in the air to see and straggled from the way were "showed" by the orderlies into the throng again, and pell-mell, helter-skelter went such an extraordinary escort as never brigadier general on the field had before or since. The aides, staff officers, and other spectators shouted with laughter. But, nevertheless, I succeeded in clearing the track. When I felt sure that I had them a sufficient distance under way, I said: "Now, there's the road I want you to travel. It will lead you all to 'Glory Hallelujah,' and don't let me catch one of you out of it again."

From the Tallahatchie, the brigades marched in separate columns, arriving in the vicinity of Memphis on February 26. The result of the expedition may be briefly summed up as follows: the killed, wounded, and missing from General Smith's command amounted to less than 400 and that of the enemy about the same, although reported to be more. The captures consisted of about 260 prisoners, 1,500 Negroes, and 3,000 horses and mules. The destruction of property was immense, consisting of over 1 million bushels of corn, several thousand bales of cotton, a large tannery with 2,000 hides of Confederate leather, besides the Mobile and Ohio Railroad for thirty miles.

General Smith, in his statements and reports, spoke in the highest terms of the services of myself and the Second Brigade, which I accompanied. He could not do otherwise, for it was true and well known that where danger was most imminent, there was the Second Brigade and myself. Without us, General Smith would not have come so safely off. Viewed as to the extent of rebel property destroyed, it might well be considered a success, but in not carrying out the object as designed, the expedition was a failure.[7]

General Sherman did not meet with much opposition in his march to and return from Meridian, General Stephen D. Lee's cavalry being the largest organized force he encountered. General Sherman expressed great dissatisfaction at the result of General Smith's expedition, and was not entirely satisfied with the success of his own. He felt confident that, had General Smith not waited for Waring's brigade, and left Collierville on February 1, as directed, the expedition would have been successful. Forrest could not have concentrated then in Smith's front, and Lee's cavalry was occupied by Sherman's advance. General Smith's column could thus no doubt have reached Meridian on time and without any serious opposition from the enemy. General Smith left on February 28 for Nashville, turning over the command of the cavalry at Memphis to me before his departure.

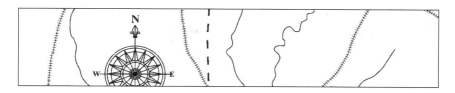

10. Operations against Forrest

Leaving his army at Canton, Mississippi, General Sherman reached Vicksburg on February 27. The rebels were surprised that the Meridian campaign ended as it did. They expected that Mobile would be attacked, or that Sherman's army would at least make a movement into the interior of Alabama. General [Leonidas] Polk[1] issued an order congratulating his army on the successful termination of the campaign, and referring to General Sherman's withdrawal to the Mississippi River, stated "that never did a grand campaign inaugurated with such pretensions, terminate more ingloriously." Although the damage done to the railroads in the vicinity of Meridian by General Sherman's army was very serious, yet the rebels soon had them in running order again, and soon recovered all the territory they had abandoned.

After the return of the Meridian expedition, the entire state of Mississippi and West Tennessee were voluntarily given up to the enemy. Although the exigency for troops elsewhere may have made it necessary, it was unfortunate that, after all the hard work and fighting undergone by our troops, such a course had to be adopted. The Red River campaign, which Banks had been ordered to make, absorbed nearly 40,000 men for a long time and ended ingloriously. Altogether, the spring campaign opened rather discouragingly for the Union cause.

About the same time, too, in the spring of 1864, while yet in the fiercest struggle of the rebellion, the three-years term of enlistment of a large number of the men of our regiments expired. Of course, the army was greatly weakened thereby. The rebels, knowing it, sought their own advantage in the occasion.

The retention of the veteran troops was a matter of vital importance to our cause, and great efforts were made to re-enlist them. I certainly never considered myself a speechmaker. I always, as a rule, avoided placing myself where there would be any probability of being called upon for such a purpose, having a natural dread of attempting to speak in public. Nevertheless, I did the state some service when I went out one March day to a sort of mass meeting of my brigade, to induce the officers and soldiers to continue their service until the war was over. I had used considerable exertion to get the most eloquent and competent speakers in the command for the occasion, and did not suppose it would be necessary to say anything myself, beyond mingling in a social way with the troops, and thus endeavor to bring about the desired result.

Upon my arrival at the camp, addresses had already been made by a number of the regimental commanders, among others Colonels McCrillis and Prince, and Captain [Morland L.?] Perkins, the last two being lawyers and professional orators. But it appeared that no one had touched the right chord to reach or stir up the enlisted men. Even some of the officers seemed to be rather lukewarm in their efforts. The men, who appeared not unwilling to continue a soldier's life, thought they might as well go home first and see what would turn up, stating that perhaps some other regiment would suit them best. And so, the enlisting dragged heavily.

The command had cheered loudly at my first appearance in camp. After mingling with and talking to the officers and men as contemplated, I saw that still greater effort would be required. To the repeated calls of the soldiers, feeling that it was my duty to exert myself to the utmost, I finally responded to the oft-repeated cheers and desires of the officers and men by jumping up into a wagon and giving utterance to my earnest feelings.

Without one moment's thought as to what I would say, the words came to my mind. Being honestly proud of such a command, and knowing that the officers and soldiers entertained warm regard for me in return, I referred briefly but vividly to their services for the past three years. Giving them the credit justly due, [I] appealed to their patriotism and love of country, which I knew to be genuine. Above all else, [I] touchingly pictured their return to the midst of their homes, their families, sweethearts, and friends. Not that they were going there to stay when the life of the nation was still in danger and the country needed their services. But they were going back home to greet warmly their friends and those they loved truly, and to assure them that they had already decided to "see it out"; that they would return to their regiments, brigades, and division, and there to remain until the Union was gloriously victorious and the rebellion and unholy war brought to an end.

All their love of organization—the company, regiment, and the "old brigade"—was aroused; all their "esprit de corps" was kindled at once. As I jumped down among them, they rushed up in crowds to set down their names, vying with each other as to who should be first. They called upon me for another speech. Pushing Major Coon up into the wagon, standing side-by-side, we talked to them as soldiers could not help talking to those in whom they felt the deepest interest. They remembered my words, and when the war was over were fain to recall them to my memory. When the speech was over Colonel McCrillis, Captain Perkins, and other officers sprang forward and warmly congratulated me, perfectly astonished to find that I could talk, exclaiming: "When did you study eloquence?" "When did you become an orator?" "We never knew that was in your line before."

When we left Memphis on the W. Sooy Smith expedition, we expected to be gone at least a month. Mrs. Grierson improved the occasion of my anticipated absence to visit her father's family and other relatives and friends in Ohio and Pennsylvania. She was gone several months, and thus the correspondence between us again opened. About this time, in writing to Mrs. Grierson, I stated: "Yesterday I went to Germantown to talk to the Second Brigade in regard to re-enlisting as veterans. The result was most favorable. The whole brigade is re-enlisting and will soon be on their way home."

The brigade of cavalry brought over from Middle Tennessee all left Memphis early in March for Nashville, the 4th U.S. Cavalry also starting on their return to that point. I did all I could to refit the regiments and get them in condition for the march. This, and the departure of the veterans for the north, depleted the cavalry force in vicinity of Memphis to such an extent as to render it of little service for any extended movements. The 3rd Michigan and 7th Kansas Cavalry had been north for some time. Besides Waring's brigade, there was nothing left but remnants. The larger part of the 3rd Illinois (McCrillis' regiment) had also re-enlisted, in addition to the Second Brigade.

On March 13, I wrote to Mrs. Grierson that: "General Sherman, who is now here, is very severe in his comments on the result of the late cavalry expedition. He showed me his orders to Gen. Smith, which I saw for the first time. I was very glad to be able to assure Gen. Sherman that the return from West Point was against my earnest protest. The General feels all right towards me, and his only regret is that he did not give me command of the expedition. He assures me that I shall have command of his cavalry hereafter, and indicates that there will be active work for us about the middle or last of April, when the veterans return. I will try to be ready as I will also endeavor to discharge the trust successfully."

These promises were, I am confident, made in good faith by General Sherman, and made subsequent events so much the harder to bear. Many changes were occurring in commanders. General Grant had been promoted to the grade of lieutenant general and placed in command of the armies of the United States. General Sherman had been advanced to the command of the Military Division of the Mississippi, Grant's former command; McPherson to the Army of the Tennessee; and General John A. Logan to the XV Army Corps.

Being alone at the old homestead at Jacksonville, my father found it so dreary and desolate for him that he accepted the invitation of myself, my brother and his wife to visit us at Memphis. From a letter written to Mrs. Grierson about this time, it will be seen that a cloud, "when it was no bigger than a man's hand," was rising up to my vision and clearly discernable to me before it was recognized by others. If the stay-at-homes, who a little later yelped so loudly "where's Grierson," when Forrest made his shameful raid into Tennessee and Kentucky, had previously seen what I saw perhaps they would have understood matters better than they did. But to average newspaper readers, a general is a general, whether he have at hand a division or battalion; and a regiment is a regiment, whether it mean a thousand able-bodied men, well mounted and equipped, or a hundred men all told, the fragments of broken companies on worn out horses. As well might they have looked for soldiers' full work from the wasted skeletons of our returned Libby prisoners.[2]

On March 23, I wrote:

> I have been very busy for a few days getting the veteran cavalry volunteers in readiness to go to their homes on furlough. They will be off probably this week. Gen. Hurlbut, who went north to Illinois on short leave after his family, has not yet returned. The rebels are preparing for a movement into Tennessee. All the rebel cavalry in Mississippi is to move north, and I think it is the design to endeavor to cross the Tennessee River and to get in the rear of Chattanooga, and probably form a junction with the cavalry under [John Hunt] Morgan[3] and [Joseph] Wheeler.[4] The plans will be to destroy the railroads in Tennessee and perhaps Kentucky. One of my scouts obtained this information, which I deem reliable. All my old regiments have re-enlisted and are going home. I am sending Col. [Fielding] Hurst with the most effective portion of his regiment [6th Tennessee Cavalry] to watch, hang upon, and harass the enemy under Forrest—now supposed to be moving towards Jackson, Tenn. What cavalry is left here will be held in readiness to move as may be hereafter deemed best. I can do but little good here with the odds and ends left and veterans all gone.

General Hurlbut returned to Memphis on March 27 and found extensive work blocked out for him, with no suitable force left subject to his order to perform the service. I expected the order for me to proceed north with the veteran volunteers tomorrow, but "tomorrow" brought me other things to do than the visiting of friends by means of the veteran's leave or furlough, to which I was so justly entitled. Information received by General Hurlbut prevented him from issuing the contemplated order for my departure for Springfield, Illinois, and the veterans reluctantly left for their homes without me.

Information had been received that Forrest had moved north and had attacked and captured Union City, with its small garrison of a few hundred men, and had gone on into Kentucky to attack Paducah. Reinforcements had been sent on steamboats from Nashville for Fort Donelson. If it was found that Forrest could not cross the Tennessee or Cumberland rivers, the troops were to be pushed rapidly for Savannah and thence to Purdy. I was to be directed to follow Forrest as closely as possible, although 200 miles away. But it seemed that Forrest succeeded in tapping the wires at Paducah and obtaining General Sherman's orders to General Veatch. Forrest was therefore made aware of Veatch's orders to land at Savannah and to move towards the Hatchie via Purdy.

On March 30, I was ordered by General Hurlbut, in compliance with instructions from General Sherman, to proceed with all the cavalry available and push rapidly towards La Grange and Saulsbury; to attack and pursue the enemy and open communication, if possible, with General Veatch at Purdy. I at once prepared for the movement. A letter written to Mrs. Grierson the same day, immediately upon receipt of the order, will show how the matter appeared to me at that time:

> I hoped to be able to inform you that I would this week go north, and to see you, but instead of that I am ordered out with the cavalry. I have left to hunt and attack the enemy wherever found. I will only have about 2,200 men, the remnant of my division, much the less effective portion of it, and not reliable. Of course I cannot expect to accomplish much under the circumstances fighting, as I will probably have to, against a force reported to be three times that number, but I will endeavor to do the best I can, trusting in God and the justice of our cause to take me safely and successfully through all danger. I do not like to start out with such a command, and that too at a time when I expected to be on my way to see you, but I must obey orders and hope for the best. I will go east from here to La Grange and perhaps as far as Purdy near the Tennessee River. I will march at once and endeavor to fight any force with which I may come in contact to the best of my ability. You have doubtless seen by the papers that Forrest attacked Union City and Paducah, and is now reported to have crossed the Tennessee. Other rebel forces have moved up from Mississippi and are said to be at or near La Grange, either with a view to join Forrest or aid him on his return. It is to operate against these forces and those under Forrest that I am sent out.

The next day, April 1, my orders were modified by General Hurlbut in a note stating that "Forrest was in Jackson in person on the 29th ult. Whether his force was with him or not I cannot say. You must be careful that they do not get a force between you and Memphis." I, therefore, moved out in the direction of Jackson on the Somerville road, when between the latter point and Raleigh I received another note from General Hurlbut, stating that he thought the movement was south and that efforts should be made to reach General Veatch. I, therefore, moved in the direction of Hudsonville, via Germantown and Mt. Pleasant, and arranged for the necessary supplies to be in readiness for a rapid march to Purdy, making such demonstrations as would be best calculated to mislead the enemy.

Enclosed with General Hurlbut's note was a copy of [a] dispatch from General Sherman, dated Nashville, April 2, as follows: "Forrest is reported still up about Jackson, Tenn. He will attempt to escape south. With infantry and cavalry, no matter for strength, you should move towards the Hatchie and prevent his escape, more especially with any train or plunder. Communicate if possible with Veatch at or near Purdy. The line of Hatchie should be watched; it must now be impassable save above Bolivar. Forrest has all the means of attacking several places and the more he attempts it the better we should be satisfied." It will be seen that this ordered General Hurlbut to proceed with both infantry and cavalry, and I presumed the movement would be made immediately upon my return to Memphis.

I got back the night of the 6th and had everything in readiness to start with my command, well supplied and freed from all encumbrances, when I received a note from General Hurlbut's headquarters stating that the general had just been informed that the rebels were "laying a pontoon bridge over Wolf River on the New Raleigh railroad," and directing me to "send a force out immediately to reconnoiter."

On the morning of the 8th, I wrote to Mrs. Grierson:

> Everything is so unsettled and orders so conflicting that I hardly know what to write to you. It is reported that the rebels are concentrating a large force in the vicinity of Bolivar and Jackson. They were also reported north of Wolf River near Somerville. An attack has been expected on Memphis, but I hardly think it will be made. Yesterday I was ordered to again move out with all my force towards Purdy to open communication with Gen. Veatch, supposed to be at or near that point, but soon after was ordered to send a force to the vicinity of Wolf River, as it was reported that the rebels were building a bridge in the direction of Raleigh. Have a considerable force now out and suppose if the information is found to be incorrect I will still march towards Purdy. Although the country in that direction is almost destitute of forage and the

rebel forces as reported much larger than the small force at my disposal. I send "Old Barber" by Col. Starr to Jacksonville.

"Old Barber" was my old black war horse, which I had ridden for a long time. In the numerous engagements in the vicinity of Memphis and in West Tennessee and northern Mississippi, he had received a number of rebel bullets in his body, and was really crippled and worn out in the service. Having a good opportunity, I sent him to my father at Jacksonville to rest for the balance of his days and die in peace. He arrived alright and was well taken care of and petted. But, it was not long before he died. My father had him buried with the honors of war in the grove near our old home, firing a few shots over his grave with the carbine which had been presented to me by General Sherman after the fight at Olive Branch, Mississippi.

General Hurlbut did not deem it advisable under the circumstances to comply with General Sherman's orders to move in the direction of Purdy with the small force of infantry and cavalry he then had, and leave Memphis open to attack. To do so would, in his judgment, virtually abandon that important point on the Mississippi River to the enemy. He, therefore, directed me to keep heavy patrols out on all the approaches to Memphis. I did not leave for Purdy as contemplated, but instead remained with my command at Memphis to resist the then-threatened advance of the rebels under Forrest. Over three-fourths of my division had re-enlisted, and it was only just that I should receive the promised leave to go north. But, of course, I would not accept it so long as an attack on Memphis seemed imminent. I, therefore, kept patrols moving night and day as directed.

On April 9, I wrote to Mrs. Grierson:

> I did not leave here this morning and am, in compliance with instructions, looking in all directions for the approach of the enemy. Gen. Hurlbut, from the information he has received, deems the enemy in too large force to be attacked at Jackson or Purdy by the small force available for such a purpose; therefore, he has decided to hold what troops he has here in the vicinity of Memphis until the plans of the rebels are more fully developed. Our pickets had some fighting last night and this morning on the north side of Wolf River, and I have stronger patrols out today in all directions. If the rebels conclude to come here to take Memphis, I think there is sufficient force to repel their attack and give them a very hot reception.

Instead of attacking Memphis as expected, Forrest attacked Fort Pillow on the morning of April 12. After meeting with a stubborn resistance from its small garrison of about 500 enlisted men and officers, with overwhelming numbers he overpowered and compelled its surrender, barbarously murdering the colored troops, of which the garrison was largely composed. He further manifested his inhumanity by boasting in his official report that the Mississippi River was dyed for 200 yards with the blood of the victims. While the South applauded, the people of the North and civilized nations everywhere were appalled and viewed with repugnant horror the vile and inhuman atrocity. The action was denounced to such an extent that even Forrest deemed it advisable to modify his statements in a subsequent report. The offense was not only condoned, but an attempt [was] made to illuminate the heinous act by the prompt tender of thanks to General Forrest from the highly elated rebel Congress, thus clearly indicat[ing] the policy of the so-called Confederate government.[5]

Some contemptible correspondent, who managed to keep his precious body in a distant and safe place from the seat of war, made a scurrilous attack upon me on account of the massacre at Fort Pillow, for which calamity I was in no way responsible and no more to blame than the "man in the moon." I did not answer the article, but treated it and the writer with that silent contempt so well merited. The *Daily Illinois State Journal* of April 23, 1864, fully answered the unwarranted assault in a leading editorial.

[On April 18, 1864,] I wrote to Mrs. Grierson: "Have delayed writing for a day or two thinking I would be permitted to start North this evening, but I cannot go now and it is more doubtful than ever whether I can go at all. Gen. Hurlbut has been relieved from command here by Gen. Sherman, or rather he has been ordered to proceed to Cairo, and although he had consented to let me go North he thinks that he has not really the authority to do so now under the circumstances." At a later hour on the same day, I wrote: "I have just this moment received orders from Gen. Hurlbut to get my available force of cavalry together at once and move out east to attack Forrest, who is reported to be retreating south via La Grange. I have ordered the command to be in readiness tomorrow at daylight in the morning. If it prove true that Forrest's whole force is moving southeast towards Alabama to meet the advance of the Federals into that state, I may yet get permission to go North after my return."

I left Memphis at daylight the next morning and scouted east as far as La Grange and Holly Springs, [and] had some brisk skirmishes with the enemy whose forces were scattered, part retreating northward towards Jackson, Tennessee, and the balance southward towards the Coldwater and Tallahatchie rivers. I pursued a force through Olive Branch towards Hernando, Mississippi, and after several days active scouting, returned to Memphis. On this scout, among other prisoners captured, was a lot of smugglers with wagons loaded with contraband goods, ammunition, clothing, boots and shoes, pistols, etc.

Upon return, I found that General C. C. Washburn, U.S. Volunteers, had arrived at Memphis and assumed command of what was designated the District of West Tennessee. The 4th Iowa Cavalry had been ordered from Vicksburg to Memphis, and troops from other points, on the general principle of "locking the door after the horse has been stolen," the powers that be only finding out it would be well to have a larger force in that vicinity after Forrest had made his shameful raid through West Tennessee and Kentucky, and had gotten off "scot-free," notwithstanding the exertion made by General Sherman to have troops returned from other points to operate against him. Forrest well knew our troops had been withdrawn elsewhere and that our veterans were absent, and of course took advantage of the circumstances.

There was not a northern heart that did not feel indignant at the foul massacre of Fort Pillow, and also humiliated that such a thing could have been possible. General Sherman, whose division had been thus invaded by the marauders, and whose earlier expedition to Meridian had, as he thought, come short of his expectations on account of General Smith's failure to join him, naturally felt sore enough over the late operations. But he was doomed to make another mistake in his efforts to "punish" Forrest, as the following letter received from him about this time foreshadows:

Headquarters Military Division of the Mississippi, Nashville, Tenn.
April 17, 1864

. . . I know that you have been embarrassed by the number of furloughed men, but I did think you would catch in flank some of the detachments in which Forrest had divided his command. If Veatch had remained at Purdy, I believe you would have prevented Forrest from moving out the plunder for which he went. The only question now is which party shall have the animals of that poor country. I will send some infantry to operate about the Hatchie and now send down [Brig. Gen. Samuel] Sturgis,[6] who is an old and experienced officer to command. I mean no reflection on you, but it is necessary to punish Forrest at all costs, and you will find Sturgis a clever and excellent officer. He will explain to you the necessity. I have good evidence that Loring's infantry has passed eastward through Montgomery, and this raid of Forrest's was made in braggadocio and he must be punished. You can take out as far as the Hatchie, say near Somerville, a brigade of infantry, and then with your cavalry can whip Forrest in a fair fight. He has expended most of his ammunition, and cannot get a supply. Seize horses anywhere and everywhere and mount about 4,000 of your best men and pitch into him at all hazards. If you do this you may trust me for proper notice and reward.

Had the command of the brigade of infantry, in addition to the cavalry, increased as it soon was, been given to me as the above letter indicated, General Sherman no doubt would have been better satisfied with the result of the expeditions so soon to be sent out from Memphis.

The following extract from a letter written to Mrs. Grierson, dated Memphis, April 26, 1864, shows how I viewed the occurrences then transpiring, and plainly foreshadows what would be the result. I stated that

> more cavalry and infantry have been ordered here. Gen. Sturgis has arrived to take command of an expedition in the field. He says he wants me to retain command of the cavalry, but of course to operate and be under his control. The thing will be mixed up as it was when W. Sooy Smith came here, and the result will be just about as beneficial to the Government. It appears that Gen. Washburn has been directed to fit out a force of about 6,000 troops—infantry, cavalry, and artillery—to be sent out under the command of Gen. Sturgis to punish Forrest and his marauders. As a matter of course I shall, as heretofore under similar circumstances, obey orders and faithfully perform my duty wherever placed. But this whole business simply means that if everything goes well and proves successful Sturgis is to get the credit and if the expedition fails myself and others are to become scapegoats to place the blame upon. I have today written to Gen. Sherman in answer to a letter received from him and requested that I be relieved from duty here, and ordered to Illinois and Iowa to reorganize, arm, mount, and equip the regiments of my old division now home on furlough. He may or may not grant the request, but my letter will let him know that I understand and fully realize the position in which he has again placed me. Gen. Hurlbut has in my judgment been most harshly and unjustly treated, and time will show it and fully vindicate him. Piecemeal and systematically his corps has virtually been broken up, nearly all his troops thus taken from him and scattered to the four winds, and now because he did not move out and whip Forrest and reinforce Fort Pillow, or prevent its capture, with no sufficient available force to do either with safety to Memphis, which place has been threatened from the first advance of the enemy, his head has been cut off to give place to another not so able or competent to command as he.

General Hurlbut's farewell order to his corps [was] dignified and manly in tone and fully corroborate[d] what has been said heretofore in regard to the condition of the cavalry. Major General Hurlbut was a man of marked ability and generous impulses. The government had few more deserving officers, and no more earnest and devoted servant.

The latter part of April 1864, Brigadier General S. D. Sturgis arrived at Memphis, reporting for duty to Major General C. C. Washburn, in compliance with orders from General W. T. Sherman to command an expedition composed of infantry, cavalry, and artillery against the rebel forces under General Forrest at Jackson, Tennessee.

The advent of General Sturgis at Memphis was not creditable to himself, nor reassuring to those who must be his subordinates—but, on the contrary, extremely discouraging. He was a stranger to them, entirely unknown to the troops assigned to his command, and had no knowledge whatever of the country through which he was to operate. Upon his arrival at Memphis, he put up at the Gayoso House, where, being dissipated in habits, he had a protracted drunken spree for nearly two weeks, during which he smashed looking glasses, crockery, and furniture to his heart's content, kicking up "high jinks" generally, until his condition became notorious. About this time I was taken sick with intermittent fever. Although not dangerously ill, I was for some time incapacitated for field service. Mrs. Grierson, hearing of my condition, gave up a contemplated visit with friends in the north, left her home at Jacksonville, and proceeded with the children to join me at Memphis.

On April 30—the necessary preparations having been made—General Sturgis left Memphis with 6,000 troops and marched eastward, via Somerville, to Bolivar, Tennessee. In the meantime, General Forrest moved from Jackson, Tennessee, with an equal force, for Tupelo, Mississippi, throwing out detachments en route to Purdy and Bolivar to cover the march of his troops southward to their destination. The illness referred to had prevented me from accompanying this expedition, and the depleted division was commanded by Colonel George E. Waring, 4th Missouri Cavalry.

On May 2, Colonel Joseph Kargé,[7] with a force of 600 enlisted men and officers of the 10th Missouri and 2nd New Jersey Cavalry, encountered about an equal force of the enemy near Bolivar, where a brisk skirmish ensued, in which engagement the rebels were repulsed and withdrew with a reported loss of seven killed and twenty wounded, including four officers. The loss of our cavalry [was] two killed and five wounded, a few horses killed and some disabled. The conduct of the troops in this engagement, which lasted about two hours, as reported to me, was excellent. Colonel Kargé and Major P. Jones Yorke of the 2nd New Jersey Cavalry displayed distinguished gallantry.

From that point, Forrest continued his movement southward unmolested. Although General Sturgis followed him as far as Ripley, Mississippi, finding that the rebels had passed that point two days previously, he abandoned the pursuit and returned with his command to Memphis. The reasons for his action are given in his report as follows:

Knowing that a further pursuit in a country entirely destitute of forage, would compel me to abandon much of my artillery in another day, from the fact that many horses had already given out and had been abandoned along the road, and it being reported to me that the condition of the 4th Iowa Cavalry in particular was such that it would necessitate the abandoning of one half of them unless they could have ample rest and forage. I therefore held a consultation with commanding officers of Divisions and Brigades, who unanimously agreed with me to move back to the railroad terminus, and were of the opinion that to continue the pursuit to Tupelo, or Okolona would be certain disaster to ourselves, unless amply provided with rations and forage necessary for such a campaign.

Had he exercised as good judgment and discretion upon his arrival at the same point in a subsequent expedition, it would have been better for his reputation as an officer.

Not wishing to do him any injustice, I quote again from his report the summing up of the result of his first expedition as he himself viewed it. After referring to [a] dispatch from General Washburn, he states: "Though it is desirable to have chronicled a defeat and rout of the enemy, the results of the expedition are the same, his forces were divided and compelled to abandon a section of the country he had so long occupied. His thorough knowledge of the country and the advantage in having good horses, together with the sympathies of the people in giving him information of our movements, enabled him to beat a rapid retreat to Mississippi, into which state he was pursued for thirty miles, and the chase only then given up when the poverty and barrenness of the country to subsist an army unprovided for a regular campaign made it necessary." The facts in the case are that General Forrest had been ordered south and would have gone as he did to Mississippi had General Sturgis and the troops engaged in his expedition remained quietly at Memphis. The general, soon after his return, relinquished command and departed whence he came.

In the meantime, additional troops had reached Memphis, and with as little delay as practicable, were refitted with those already there for a campaign against Corinth and the Mobile and Ohio Railroad, then in the undisputed possession of the enemy. In due time, General Sturgis was ordered back to command this second expedition, which had been gotten up by General Washburn under his general instructions from Generals McPherson and Sherman. Accordingly, on June 1, 1864, having recovered from my recent illness, I in obedience to orders from Major General C. C. Washburn concentrated the effective portion of my division, about 3,000 enlisted men and officers, near La Fayette Station on the line of the Memphis and Charleston Railroad, thirty miles distant from Memphis.

On June 2, General Sturgis arrived by rail with 5,000 infantry and artillery, and assumed command of the whole force, amounting in all to 8,000 troops. On the afternoon of the same day, in compliance with the general's instructions, I moved my division, consisting of two brigades, commanded respectively by Colonels Waring and [Edward F.] Winslow, southward, passing en route through Early Grove, Lamar, and Salem, Mississippi. On June 3, General Sturgis left the line of the railroad with his infantry and artillery, supply train of 250 wagons, and a ten-gallon keg of whiskey.

Before my departure from La Fayette, I had suggested to General Sturgis the propriety of sending a strong detachment of cavalry rapidly to Rienzi, on the Mobile and Ohio Railroad, to destroy the road and supplies thereat, with a view of misleading the enemy, scattering his forces, and covering up so far as possible our own movements and designs. In accordance with orders received, I detached a force consisting of 200 men from each brigade, 400 enlisted men and officers in all, under command of Colonel Kargé of the 2nd New Jersey Cavalry, to proceed via Ripley by a rapid march to the point indicated; to destroy the railroad so far as practicable and any rebel property that might be found in the vicinity, and with instructions to communicate with me at the earliest opportunity on the Danville and Ruckersville wagon road. At the same time, I marched my main force from Salem to Ruckersville, where I halted twenty-four hours to await the nearer approach of the infantry and [the] wagon train.

In the meantime, I sent patrols eastward beyond the Hatchie River to obtain all possible information in regard to the movements of the enemy [and] to endeavor to communicate with Colonel Kargé. Having thus learned that the enemy had left Corinth and passed south, I at once communicated the fact to the general commanding, who was then at the intersection of the Salem and Ruckersville and the Saulsbury and Ripley wagon roads. After due consideration of the subject, [Sturgis] decided to change the direction of his column southward instead of marching on Corinth, which up to that time had been his intention under the orders and instructions received from General Washburn.

Accordingly, on the afternoon of June 7, in compliance with orders from General Sturgis, I marched my division southward to Ripley, where my advance came upon a small party of rebels who were driven through the town and out on the New Albany road. They hurriedly [fell] back about three miles to their reserve, which proved to be a brigade strongly posted. I at once pushed forward part of Winslow's brigade and the 7th Indiana Cavalry of Waring's brigade. After a sharp engagement, [they] succeeded in driving the enemy from his position, inflicting a loss upon him of six killed and fifteen wounded, most of whom were left on the field. He withdrew in a southerly direction, and I fell back a short distance and encamped for the night, our entire loss being only one killed and three wounded.

Information as to the result of this affair was promptly sent the same evening to General Sturgis. The next morning, finding no enemy in our immediate front, and fearing that Colonel Kargé, who had not then been heard from, might be in a hazardous position, I by authority of the commanding general sent an additional force to his assistance. [It] had not proceeded far before the colonel was met safely returning, having successfully accomplished the object of that rather hazardous expedition. By [Kargé's] judicious movement, a large part of [Brig. Gen. Abraham] Buford's[8] division of Forrest's command was drawn to Rienzi, Forrest being deceived and led to believe that our whole force would move against the Mobile and Ohio Railroad at that place.

After directing the balance of Waring's brigade to take suitable position near Ripley to await the arrival of Colonel Kargé and his detachment of cavalry and General Sturgis with the infantry and supply train, I broke camp about noon the same day and marched with Winslow's brigade from the New Albany road across by a by-road to the Ripley and Fulton road, striking it six miles southeast of Ripley, where we halted and occupied a good position. After causing suitable patrols to be sent to watch and report upon the movements of the enemy, we encamped the evening of the 8th. Advising the commanding general in regard to the positions occupied by the two brigades of my division, I awaited instructions.

From the time the expedition left the line of the Memphis and Charleston Railroad, the weather had been very unfavorable for the movement of troops. It had rained almost continually for five days. The roads were very muddy and extremely bad, and the streams were swollen and still rapidly rising. Although Forrest had been ordered to join with [Brig. Gen. Philip D.] Roddey[9] and move to Middle Tennessee to operate against Sherman's communications, and had arranged to cross the Tennessee River, Major General Stephen D. Lee, commanding the rebel forces in Mississippi and Alabama, upon learning that a large force of Federal troops had left Memphis and were moving towards Tupelo on the Mobile and Ohio Railroad, had ordered Forrest to return and had also directed Roddey to join Forrest with the larger part of his command.

At this time, it was well known that the enemy was concentrating a large force to oppose our advance. The cavalry under my command had been actively engaged on the front and flanks of General Sturgis' column. Brisk skirmishes had taken place on June 7. The presence of the enemy clearly demonstrated that the cavalry had been well handled and had accomplished its work in an admirable manner. But, on account of scanty forage, many of the horses were becoming unserviceable. The march of the infantry with General Sturgis, encumbered as it was with a large supply train, however, had been very slow and unsatisfactory. Our advance being made towards the enemy's lines of communication gave him [Lee] ample time to watch our movements, estimate our strength, and concentrate his forces in our front.

General Sturgis, being undecided and apprehensive as to a further advance, or the best course to pursue, called a meeting of his division commanders at Ripley to advise him as to what had best be done. Upon the receipt of his summons, I at once proceeded to his headquarters, where I met the general and Colonel [William L.] McMillen. Casually present at the conference [were] Colonel George B. Hoge, 113th Illinois Infantry, also an officer of General Sturgis' staff, and Captain S. L. Woodward, assistant adjutant general of my division.

After hearing the commanding general's statements on the subject, [and] being asked for my views in regard to the matter, I gave them substantially as follows: That, although I did not know what the orders of General Sturgis required, nor what discretion had been given to him, yet under all the circumstances bearing upon the case—considering the unfavorable weather, the bad roads, the destitution of the country, [the] difficulty of obtaining forage, the proximity of the enemy and his knowledge of our condition—to make a further advance would be hazardous. If the general felt that he must go forward, rations and other supplies should be issued to the command and the supply train left there or sent back. Thus relieved of such a great encumbrance, our movements would be greatly facilitated and our chances for success in our advance and attack upon the enemy, with our whole force available for action, much improved, if not assured. I believed the enemy would attack us in any position we might select, either where we then were or elsewhere, before we got back to Memphis, to which point, in any event, our troops must soon return, as our supplies were being rapidly exhausted. The main object of the expedition would be more certain of attainment by such a course, as the enemy had already been drawn back from other contemplated operations, and [was] then engaged in concentrating his forces to oppose our advance and to attack us whenever found.

At that time, General Sturgis coincided with me in my views and so expressed himself. But later on he called upon Colonel McMillen for an expression of his opinions on the subject matter. The colonel, although admitting that to advance any further would be hazardous, spoke in an excited and rather contemptuous manner of the idea of turning back. He referred to the recent expedition to that point, from which they had returned to Memphis without any satisfactory results. Although he had advocated a return on the first occasion, he was decidedly in favor of going on with the second expedition, "with the whole outfit, transportation and all, until the enemy was found and attacked." "If we went back without a fight, we would be disgraced." He would rather "go on and be whipped than to return from Ripley." He did not seem to relish the idea of being separated from the train, or being deprived of the comforts and conveniences of his camp equipage.

While I did not agree with the colonel in his view of the case, and believed he was more sensitive than discreet, yet I reiterated my statements, some of which Colonel McMillen may not have heard, and further remarked "that I merely did my duty when I thus frankly gave expression to my views on the subject; that I was then and ever would be found ready to promptly and cheerfully obey any orders from proper authority; that, if required, I should go on and fight the foe wherever found, but that my best judgment still led me to believe that if General Sturgis advanced his column beyond Ripley, through the mud and rain, encumbered by transportation and camp equipage, it would result in disaster to our troops, and that the colonel would be apt to have all the fighting he desired before he got back to Memphis." The interview broke up, and General Sturgis, in the face of his better judgment and still foreboding the disastrous consequences, decided to continue the advance and gave his orders accordingly.

On the morning of June 9, I detached my sick men and worn out horses, and sent them back to Memphis in company with the sick of the infantry and empty wagons. [I] took the opportunity afforded to write a hasty note to Mrs. Grierson, in which I stated that: "The continuous rains had made the roads almost impassable and that the command was then only about eighty miles from Memphis; that, the cavalry alone could have marched three times that distance, but that the Infantry, encumbered with a large supply train, had greatly impeded the march of the cavalry."

Thereafter, referring to our fight of June 7, and stating that the rebels were concentrating six or seven thousand men in our front, and that we would soon have more fighting, and indicating the probable date of our return, I jestingly alluded to two of the officers of my staff who accompanied me as follows: "[Lieutenant Alexander?] McClure and Woodward are still very gay and festive, and join me in regards to yourself and the master of the house, Lieutenant [Ruthven W.] Pike." On account of his jovial disposition—being a good lawyer and capable officer—Lieutenant Pike had been detached from his regiment, the 4th Illinois Cavalry, and assigned to duty as judge advocate of the cavalry division. He had, by common consent of all, in view of his recognized fitness, been for some time in charge of our mess arrangement at Memphis, and had proved himself an excellent caterer. Captain Woodward and Lieutenant McClure were also young genial officers, who merrily took things as they came.

They can tell more ludicrously than can be set down with pen how, that very night when we were encamped at Stubbs' plantation, we had gone into the house on a sort of frolic, where we found a feeble old piano, a dilapidated violin with three strings, and a bow with about as many hairs. How, also, the young lady of the family, when politely asked for music, graciously complied; and how she, with a voice as tuneless and twanging as the instrument, but much more powerful, sang: "Weeping sad and lonely," emphasizing and prolonging the words, spitting between the lines, and looking languishingly over her shoulder for our approval and admiration. How I was finally persuaded to perform on the old cracked fiddle, while the company joined hands in a merry dance. It is well to make the most of life as it comes to us, and to be merry even under the most unfavorable circumstances. There was serious work ahead for us, and the comedy of that evening was followed by a tragedy the next day.

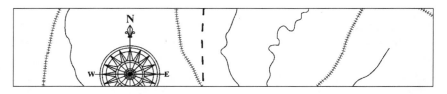

11. Brice's Cross Roads

I had inferred from what General Sturgis had said to me at our interview near Ripley that we were to move forward on the Ellistown road, more to the right and southward. But he afterwards sent me word that he had concluded to advance on the Fulton road, which we were then on, seemingly without making any further effort to deceive the enemy as to our intentions or movements. In accordance, therefore, with the general's instructions, I took up the line of march indicated and proceeded slowly about eight miles and encamped my division at Stubbs' plantation, about fourteen miles southeast of Ripley. It was by such tedious movements the cavalry was obliged to continue the advance, while in our rear, plodding along through the rain and mud, the infantry and doomed train came slowly on, eight miles a day, to "punish Forrest" and the dare-devil rebels under his command; while they were watching our tardy movements, concentrating their forces, and choosing their position to attack us. It should be remembered, too, that on the evening of June 7, we had found a brigade of rebels on the New Albany road south of Ripley, and that the same day Kargé had entered Rienzi on the Mobile and Ohio Railroad, and had drawn a large part of Buford's division of Forrest's command in that direction.

All subsequent information went to show that the rebels were massing troops to attack us and oppose our advance, and these facts were repeatedly made known to General Sturgis. At Stubbs' plantation, where we had found some forage, I again informed the general that I was confident from what I had learned then and the day previous that the enemy was in large force and not far off. Learning that the mules of the train were exhausted and in bad condition after their great exertion in pulling the heavily loaded wagons through the deep mud in which they were frequently mired thus far, I advised the general to remain where he then was, as the position was a good one, and that in my judgment the enemy would attack us there if no further advance was made. Our chances for victory would be greatly strengthened if the infantry and artillery could be quietly put into position for battle, while the cavalry, unencumbered, continued to operate in such manner as to fully develop the enemy's strength and draw him forward to a general engagement.

The general, however, could not believe that the enemy in any large force was anywhere near us, or that we would be attacked where we then were. He seemed inclined to rely on the information given him nearly two weeks previously by General Washburn to the effect that "the enemy would not be found in force nearer than Tupelo or Okolona," although later reports and developments had proven the contrary. In the face of all this evidence repeatedly placed before him to guide his action, and which should have been duly heeded, he still decided to continue the advance, with his troops scattered out in one column on the same road.

The general seemed gloomy and irritable, and in a very decided manner ordered me to proceed early on the morning of June 10, with my division, and "to keep it well in advance of, and out of the way of the infantry and train," directing me to march on to Baldwyn. [He] peremptorily ordered me to attack the enemy wherever he might be found, stating that he would follow promptly with the infantry, well closed up, and proceed to Guntown. His orders to me were imperative, and gave me no discretion whatever but to go on and attack the enemy on sight.

General Sturgis had taken the 19th Pennsylvania Cavalry from my command at La Fayette for his escort. Deducting the number of sick men and worn-out horses sent back from Ripley, I did not have left in my two brigades over 2,400 enlisted men and officers, mounted and effective for duty, when I took the advance with them on the Baldwyn and Guntown road from Stubbs' plantation as ordered. After marching in a cautious manner three or four miles, I halted, as usual, for over one hour to give time for the infantry and train to close up. Presuming that the general with the main column would follow closely in rear as indicated, I continued to advance with the cavalry.

Here it is proper to state that it is evident General Sturgis did not march with the infantry as early as contemplated. In [his] official report, Colonel McMillen states that he "marched from Stubbs' on the morning of the 10th," but does not give the hour. However, Colonel Hoge, commanding the advance brigade of infantry, reports that he moved out his command at 10 o'clock A.M. Even then, instead of moving the brigades of [Colonel Alexander W.] Wilkin and [Colonel Edward] Bouton[1] promptly forward, both were left by order of General Sturgis, so Colonel McMillen states in his report, with the wagon train stuck in the mud, on a road almost impassable from recent heavy rains and badly cut up by the march of the cavalry.

At 9 o'clock A.M. on June 10, while cautiously advancing, we came upon a picket of the enemy in the act of destroying a bridge over a small stream, who fled on our approach. After halting a sufficient time to repair the bridge so as to cross, we moved on over rising ground to a strong position, where we found that the enemy had torn down fences and evidently prepared for, and intended to give, battle. Soon afterward, [at] about 10 o'clock, we reached the forks of the Baldwyn, Guntown, and Pontotoc roads, known as Brice's Cross Roads, where we came upon a wide, deeply marked trail. From reports, [we] learned that Forrest's and Lee's troops had been passing that point for several days in the direction of Baldwyn, a station five miles distant on the Mobile and Ohio Railroad, where trains of cars had been frequently arriving, and where it was reported that a large force of rebels had been concentrated to oppose our advance. This information was at once sent by courier to General Sturgis, patrols sent out on all the roads, and Waring's brigade brought forward and dismounted at the crossroads to await further developments.

The patrol on the Baldwyn road, under command of Captain [Robert N.] Hanson, had not proceeded over a mile and a half before it met and engaged a strong picket of the enemy. Leaving pickets on the Guntown and Pontotoc roads, I at once proceeded with the balance of Waring's brigade to the support of Captain Hanson. With my staff, I thoroughly examined the ground, and finding that our troops were slowly falling back under the increased force and heavy fire of the enemy, I directed Colonel Waring to fall back and get his cavalry into line of battle in the open timber on the right and left of the road, leaving the open fields in his front over which the enemy must pass to attack us. Seeing this order in the course of speedy execution, I returned to the crossroads to hasten forward Winslow's brigade and to communicate again the condition of affairs to General Sturgis.

Colonel Winslow had found the bridge over Tishomingo Creek in such bad condition that he had halted his command and caused it to be thoroughly reconstructed, which proved to be a thoughtful precaution, subsequently of much importance to the command. The colonel arrived at the crossroads with his brigade about 11 o'clock, when I explained to him the position in which Waring's brigade had been placed and then warmly engaged with the enemy. Knowing it to be entirely impracticable to further try to force my way to Baldwyn, as required by my orders from General Sturgis, the road being in the possession of the enemy, and being further instructed to fight him wherever found, I decided to obstinately obstruct his advance and to hold the position, which I deemed an advantageous one, until reinforced by the infantry, which I had been led to believe by General Sturgis was then near at hand.[2]

I, therefore, ordered Colonel Winslow to advance on the Guntown road and to take position with his brigade, connecting with the right of Waring's line and extending it to and as far as possible beyond the Guntown road, obtaining the most advantageous position possible, holding a suitable reserve to strengthen his line and support his artillery, one section of which was advanced to the front and one placed in battery on the right of the Guntown road, in advance of the crossroads. Colonel Winslow carried this order into execution with alacrity, under my personal observation. After these dispositions had been successfully accomplished, my couriers returned with a message from General Sturgis to the effect that "the general thought I must be mistaken in regard to the strength of the enemy; that there could not be more than one brigade in my front; and that he wished me to push on to Baldwyn, leaving a detachment at the crossroads until his arrival, after which he would move on to Guntown."

I again immediately dispatched to General Sturgis in writing, reiterating my statements and informing him that the rebels—6,000 to 7,000 strong—were in my front; that I had only 2,400 men and was fighting against great odds; and that my reserves were being rapidly absorbed in order to prevent the enemy from outflanking us.[3] We could hold our position if promptly reinforced, but [I] suggested to the general that it might be well to get his infantry and artillery into the best position he could find. Upon notification that his line of battle had been formed, I would fall back to him, fighting and facing the foe.

Inexplicable as it may appear, it seems the general still discredited my reports, and sent Captain [William C.] Rawolle, his aide-de-camp, to investigate the matter. By that time it was after 12 o'clock. The enemy had advanced in large force across the open field in his front, and had vigorously attacked our whole line. But their assaults were repulsed. I took Captain Rawolle out to a point near the center of our line where the troops were still engaged, the fire being heavy from both sides. The captain was almost immediately made aware of the close proximity of the enemy by having the heel shot off his boot. He wheeled his horse and rapidly returned to the general, impressed with the idea, I presume, that it was a difficult matter to travel out from there on the road to Baldwyn.

The fight went on. Our artillery had been for some time engaged with that of the enemy. [The guns] near the crossroads had been firing over the heads of our men [and] into the rebel ranks with good effect, and several desperate charges had been gallantly repulsed by the cavalry under Waring and Winslow. With our whole force thus engaged fighting against superior numbers, still no infantry came to our relief. Waring was being strongly pressed and had repeatedly asked for support, but I had none to send to his aid, our small reserves having been all absorbed.

It was not much after that, 1 o'clock P.M., that General Sturgis arrived with his staff and the 19th Pennsylvania Cavalry. I at once advised him as to the position of our troops and the necessity of immediate assistance, and suggested that his escort, the 19th Pennsylvania, be sent forward to the right of Waring's brigade, which was carried into effect by the order of the general. The infantry being reported near at hand, I asked that a brigade be sent forward to Waring's assistance. The general said the infantry would soon be there and that he would attend to the matter. From his manner I judged that he did not, even then, realize the fact that the rebels were in large force in our front—although we had been fighting them since 10 o'clock A.M.

The general moved off excitedly towards the Ripley road, as I supposed to order forward the infantry. I heard him remark in a petulant manner that, "if the damned cavalry could only be gotten out of the way," he could "soon whip the enemy with his infantry." This was unjust and unreasonable, for he knew from my frequent reports, and from the heavy firing which was heard even at the rear of his column, that the cavalry had been gallantly fighting against superior numbers for several hours. The thought of withdrawing the cavalry had not then entered my mind. I could not go on to Baldwyn, as the enemy had possession of the road. But we had opposed his advance, had successfully fought a largely superior force, and had inflicted severe loss upon the foe. I had only asked that a brigade of infantry be sent to my assistance, and wondered at its non-appearance.

I then urgently asked that the brigade I had repeatedly asked for be brought forward, again stating the necessity, as Colonel Waring had reported his ammunition getting short and had applied again to me for assistance, he presuming, like myself, that the whole division of infantry was close by and ready for action. Colonel Waring, not getting the assistance required and so long expected, had finally been obliged to fall back 200 feet, where he formed a new line. This made it necessary for Colonel Winslow's brigade to retire so as to connect with Waring's right. The enemy at the same time also withdrew to a more sheltered position in the timber to await reinforcements. Although the attack was soon after renewed, the new line was firmly held by the cavalry until the infantry arrived and was put into action.

It was 2 o'clock before the advance of Colonel Hoge's brigade arrived at the crossroads, and fully half an hour before it was advanced to the line of battle occupied by the cavalry. I saw Colonel McMillen talking with General Sturgis and apparently receiving and giving orders as the infantry troops were being marched forward, but mostly in the wrong direction to assist Colonel Waring in maintaining his position against the enemy.

I again spoke to General Sturgis in regard to the matter. He was excited and irritable in his manner, and rather briskly informed me that he had ordered Colonel McMillen to relieve Waring's brigade and directed me to withdraw the cavalry. I, therefore, directed Colonel Waring to maintain his ground until relieved by the infantry and then to quietly withdraw, mount and reform his brigade, and take position on our left flank, where the enemy had been observed, and to repel any attack from that direction. Although authorized to do so, I did not withdraw Winslow's brigade. He remained in line of battle for fully one hour after Waring's brigade was withdrawn, for a fierce attack had been made on the right of our line and the infantry was a long time in getting into position. I told General Sturgis that, in my judgment, it would not be judicious to withdraw Winslow's brigade until a larger force of infantry could be brought up and placed in line of battle. Sometime after this, someone reported to General Sturgis that the cavalry horses were in the way, when the general at once sent an order direct to Colonel Winslow to withdraw, or fall back, and get his horses out of the way of the infantry.

At this time the detachments of the 10th Missouri and 7th Illinois Cavalry, which were on the extreme right on the Pontotoc road, had been attacked. [They] had dismounted and sent their horses back, while they moved forward and drove the enemy back and maintained their position. Those detachments remained dismounted and acted for some time under the control of Colonel McMillen, after Colonel Winslow had, under orders received direct from General Sturgis [, withdrawn his brigade]. The general, seeing the horses of the detachments of the 10th Missouri and 7th Illinois, and probably supposing them to be those of the 3rd and 4th Iowa Cavalry, excitedly sent the second order to Winslow to withdraw, or fall back, and get his horses out of the way. The enemy having been again repulsed, Colonel Winslow, after being thus twice ordered by General Sturgis to withdraw, sent me word to look after his artillery, which I did, as he withdrew his brigade in good order.

It was a great mistake to withdraw the cavalry. It should have been continued in action and more infantry brought to its support, and particularly Winslow's brigade, which had so long successfully fought the enemy. Had it been retained, and Bouton's brigade and the balance of Wilkin's [brigade] brought forward and put into action, we could have gained the victory, or at least held our ground and position at the crossroads until night, and either strengthened our lines then or gotten into shape for a battle the next day.

As Winslow withdrew and was mounting, I had his artillery sent back across the creek, to which point also the horses of the detachments of the 10th Missouri and 7th Illinois had previously been sent. I was about to remove a section of the Indiana battery from the crossroads, when General Sturgis, in an excited manner, asked me what I was doing. When I informed him that "I was removing and preparing for the safety of a section of artillery that had been assigned to my command," he peremptorily ordered me to leave the artillery where it was; that he would be responsible for its safety. Therefore, it was continued in action, and was soon thereafter captured by the enemy and turned against our own troops, when the infantry was repulsed and driven in confusion from the field.

The Second Brigade of cavalry under Colonel Winslow had been withdrawn in good order, excepting the dismounted detachments left in action on the Pontotoc road. But scarcely had he and Colonel Waring succeeded in mounting and reforming their brigades—that of Waring in the rear of the left flank and that of Winslow in the rear of the right, after their determined and successful fight of nearly five hours with a largely superior force of the enemy—when he [Forrest] made another fierce charge on the right of the line, which was then formed some distance back of the line of battle so long held by the cavalry, and pressing forward in overwhelming numbers compelled the infantry to fall back in great confusion.

I then observed with surprise that the larger part of Colonel Wilkin's brigade of infantry had never reached Brice's Cross Roads, but had been halted and formed facing east a considerable distance back of Brice's house, in the open field, with a regiment and battery still farther to the rear, 800 or 1,000 yards; and that Colonel Bouton's brigade was still further to the rear and on the rising ground on the west side of Tishomingo Creek, all of the infantry being left entirely too far away to be of any assistance whatever in reinforcing the troops which had been left in line of battle in advance of the crossroads.

I here observed that the ammunition wagons, which had been brought forward to the vicinity of the battleground, were scattered about, mixed up with artillery and caissons and ambulances, and some of them stuck in the mud. Still back of these, the entire supply train was still advancing, by whose order I knew not, with the head of the train near the bridge over Tishomingo Creek. This was very unfortunate, as the train occupied the road and extended back over a rising slope up to the high ground in the timber beyond, over half a mile distant. It was soon after turned back and parked not over a mile from Brice's Cross Roads, by order of the commanding general.

Every effort of the infantry to form new lines on the east side of Tishomingo Creek, to oppose the advance of the foe, proved ineffectual, and the retreat became an utter rout. I then directed Colonel Waring to place his brigade in line on the high ground between the enemy and train, to protect it and [to] check the flying infantry troops who were spreading out on either side of the road, without any apparent order or organization. Colonel Waring states in his report that he endeavored to do this, but owing to the hurried manner in which the disorganized troops were retreating, he was obliged to re-form his brigade in an open field on the opposite side of the train, where he remained until ordered by General Sturgis to proceed to Ripley.

Colonel Winslow's brigade was still operating on the left flank, formerly our right. Although under the fire of the enemy's artillery, his command maintained their position while he withdrew and mounted the detachments of the 10th Missouri and 7th Illinois Cavalry. By judiciously occupying and firmly holding a knoll near the bridge, the cavalry succeeded, with his determined bravery, in rendering timely assistance to the retreating infantry. I directed Colonel Winslow to continue on the flank and rear, falling back slowly so as to protect, as far as in his power, the disorganized infantry troops and the train, which in the meantime was moving back on the Ripley road, and to retard to the best of his ability the advance of the enemy.

I then, with my staff officers and orderlies, did everything possible to get the infantry into line to resist the foe. Myself and Captain Woodward got [Capt. Henry S.] Lee's and Jones' [Capt. Peter Joyce's] artillery into position on a knoll in an orchard near the creek, from which point they opened fire on the rebels, who were screened behind fences on the opposite side of the road, so that the guns also covered the road and open ground by their rapid fire. The rebels were also at this time throwing shells among the fleeing infantry, and I could find no organized force to protect the batteries in that position. The wagons, too, that were still wheeling, got in front and so close to the pieces that the guns could not be fired without endangering our own men.

Soon after this, I got [Lieutenant] Colonel [Charles G.] Eaton to place his regiment [72nd Ohio Infantry], which seemed to be in fair condition, although depleted, into line behind a fence on the left of the road, and with other parts of regiments extended the line to the right, beyond which, in the meantime, Colonel Bouton, with the available force of his brigade, had pushed forward without waiting for orders. On noticing the repulse of the advance infantry brigades, [he] was still seizing upon and reforming at every available place to repel the advance of the enemy, and had thus rendered gallant and timely service.

I had ordered ammunition to be obtained and issued to both the cavalry and infantry, and I knew that Captain Woodward saw the order executed, so far as possible. Infantry soldiers who still retained their arms cheerfully wheeled and helped to strengthen the line. Our troops were already firing over the heads of our soldiers as they made their way to the rear, following rapidly in the wake of General Sturgis and his escort and Colonel McMillen, who had previously gone to the rear, with confused masses of disheartened and disorganized infantry wandering in and out through the woods on either side of the road, hastily making their flight and left to shift for themselves. The enemy were throwing shells from cannon abandoned by General Sturgis, which were turned upon our own men. When they saw myself and staff forming this line from troops over which I had no direct authority, [Sturgis and McMillen stated] that they thought a better place could be found further to the rear. When General Sturgis came up to Waring's brigade in a second line a little further back, [he] ordered it rapidly on to Ripley. Near two or three miles further back, where Colonel Wilkin was found with some of his depleted regiments in readiness to face the foe, General Sturgis and Colonel McMillen left him there while they continued on their way, instead of remaining to encourage and support these troops. The line into which Colonel Eaton had with cheerfulness and alacrity formed at my suggestion, and extended by the efforts of myself and staff, was held for fully one hour—until the train not burned and artillery not abandoned already by General Sturgis had been moved out and [was] well under way towards Stubbs' plantation.

As night was approaching, Colonel Eaton with his regiment took up the line of march with other detachments of infantry troops. Myself, staff, and orderlies proceeded to Stubbs' plantation, where we found Colonel Winslow's brigade, arriving at that place about 11 o'clock P.M. the night [of] June 10. I then found that Colonel Winslow, while engaged in forming his command to continue checking the advance of the enemy, was also ordered direct by General Sturgis to proceed to Ripley. But at the suggestion of the colonel, he was permitted to stop at Stubbs' plantation, where we had encamped the previous night, the general stating to Colonel Winslow that his artillery and train "had already gone to Hell."

———

It was thus by the direct order of General Sturgis that the cavalry division was taken away from me and placed entirely beyond my control at the most critical time after the retreat began, on the evening of June 10, 1864. Had the cavalry been left subject to my orders, I would have held it in the rear and on the flanks, and would have continued to fight the enemy at every available place or opportunity. The last lines formed by the infantry on the evening of June 10 were those where Colonels Eaton and Bouton and Colonel Wilkin took position. Had General Sturgis remained with his troops and the cavalry been left subject to my orders, I believe the artillery and train could have been retained instead of abandoned, and many officers and enlisted men saved from capture or death. I presumed when I last saw General Sturgis, near Tishomingo Creek, from what he then gave me to understand, that he would remain with such infantry organizations as could be gotten together, and that with them and the cavalry, they were to vigorously dispute the advance of the foe. But I never saw the general again until he got ten miles northeast of Ripley in his hasty and disastrous retreat. After repeated messages sent to him for assistance, he was finally induced to halt long enough to have part of Waring's brigade returned to me for duty in repelling the attacks of the rebels—flushed with their victory of June 10.

At 3 o'clock A.M. on the 11th, we resumed the march, it having been reported to Colonel Winslow that all the disarmed and disorganized troops had passed on towards Ripley. I again took up the line of march from Stubbs' plantation with Colonel Winslow, after which the fighting was continued with little intermission to Ripley, where we hoped to find help, but where we looked in vain for General Sturgis. At a bridge some miles out, and before we got to Ripley, myself and staff being with the rear guard then commanded by Lieutenant Colonel [John W.] Noble of the 3rd Iowa Cavalry, we were fiercely assailed by the enemy, but his daring assaults were repulsed by the colonel and his brave cavalrymen. I had learned to know Colonel Noble's worth; he was brave, cool, and determined in battle and handled his men with great skill, always rendering efficient service wherever placed, both in the advance and retreat, throughout the entire expedition. Although outnumbered by the foe, he held his position at the bridge until the enemy withdrew, after severe loss had been inflicted upon him, and [until] the rearguard [was] relieved by the 4th Iowa Cavalry.

As the force of the enemy was evidently increasing and would soon be upon us again, I proceeded to Ripley with the 3rd Iowa Cavalry to see what assistance could be obtained. To our great surprise, we found that General Sturgis, surrounded by his escort and Waring's whole brigade of cavalry and such infantry regiments as Colonel McMillen had gotten together, had hurriedly left the town and gone onward in their flight towards Memphis. Although he must have heard the heavy firing in the rear, [Sturgis made] no attempt whatever to render any assistance to help check the pursuit of the enemy. At the time of my arrival at Ripley, there were a good many unarmed infantrymen loitering about the streets, whom I directed to be sent on. With our reduced force, wearied and worn, and with ammunition almost exhausted, we were obliged to face and fight the foe again, under most unfavorable circumstances, being almost simultaneously attacked in front and [on] both flanks.

Before reaching Ripley, several troops of the 4th Iowa regiment under command of Major [Abial R.] Pierce had, by some mistake, taken a road leading towards the Saulsbury road, following a part of Wilkin's brigade which had there turned north. Thus our force was still further reduced. However, the balance of Winslow's brigade was soon hotly engaged. The only infantry I could find with any organization was scattered detachments of Bouton's brigade, which the colonel was endeavoring to get together.

Coming upon one of these detachments, 100 men or more, I threw them forward to the right of the New Albany road, on which the rebels were charging in. The men obeyed promptly and, screening themselves by a fence, poured rapid volleys into the rebels and checked their advance. Colonel Bouton soon got other detachments into line and persistently held his ground, and rendered valuable aid at this juncture. Here it is only just to state that Colonel Bouton had, from the time he threw his brigade into action in front of the train near Tishomingo Creek, displayed marked energy and ability, bravely resisting the advance of the foe at every favorable opportunity, until the pursuit was abandoned.

In the meantime, Colonel Winslow, with his depleted force, was gallantly fighting the enemy at every point of his advance. Colonel Noble of the 3rd Iowa and Major Pierce of the 4th Iowa [were also] conspicuous for their bravery in their efforts to repulse the foe. But, seeing that we would soon be outflanked on both the right and the left, I directed that the infantry detachments of Bouton's brigade fall back on the Salem road. After the unarmed infantrymen had gone on, the cavalry was withdrawn in good order, facing about and holding the enemy in check at every available point. I know that General Sturgis heard the firing in this engagement, which was very heavy and given by volleys from both sides. Yet he sent no relief. On the contrary, [he] took no notice of the engagement except to accelerate his flight in the opposite direction. I sent [messages] repeatedly during the retreat to General Sturgis, urging that Waring's brigade be sent to my assistance in the rear, or that it be placed in position to relieve Winslow's. But it was long before I succeeded in getting the general to stop long enough to have detachments of the 4th Missouri, 2nd New Jersey, [and] 9th and 3rd Illinois Cavalry sent to my support. Even this tardy aid resulted in saving many men from death or capture.

Colonel Wilkin, on reaching the Saulsbury road, halted. Hearing the heavy firing, and learning that a fierce attack was being made upon us at Ripley and on the Salem road, [he] was about to return to our support. But, finding his troops almost out of ammunition, he continued his march towards Saulsbury, being joined later in the day by Captain [James C.] Foster, 59th [U.S. Infantry] regiment, with about 500 men of Bouton's brigade. The entire force of the enemy having been drawn upon us on the

Salem road, the troops moving by the Saulsbury road were not molested, [and] bivouacked the night of the 11th. [They] proceeded the next day via Davis' Mills, where they encountered a small force. Slight skirmishing ensued soon after resuming the march, but they reached the vicinity of Collierville the night of June 12, in safety.

The fight continued for five miles west of Ripley on the Salem road. At one place, when our men were nearly out of ammunition, the rebels charged through the rearguard, causing some confusion. But two companies of the 4th Iowa, under Captain [Lot] Abraham, and part of the 3rd Iowa, under Lieutenant Colonel Noble, soon succeeded in checking and repulsing the advancing rebels, with a loss to them fully equal to our own, notwithstanding our troops were greatly outnumbered.

At a bridge five miles from Ripley, they were again repulsed. It was there that detachments of Waring's brigade, under command of Colonel Kargé of the 2nd New Jersey Cavalry, were placed in the rear. Thenceforth, there was little trouble in holding the enemy in check, although the pursuit was kept up beyond Salem and well on towards Collierville, where I arrived with the cavalry at about 10 o'clock A.M. on June 12, after fighting and marching almost continuously for two days, without food for men or forage for animals.[4] Had the troops from Waring's brigade been left in the rear, or sent sooner to my assistance, the lives of many soldiers might have been saved, and many officers and enlisted men kept from capture. Had General Sturgis displayed any generalship whatever, or manifested any disposition to fight during the retreat, and had he not been so active in his efforts to save himself, the victory of the foe would have been less complete, and the result would have proved far less disastrous to General Sturgis and his command.

At Collierville, we found 2,000 fresh troops with supplies sent out to meet us there by General Washburn. I presumed that we would be permitted to remain for at least a few days to rest and recuperate. But General Sturgis, still fearing that the rebels would get in between us and Memphis, and stating that he heard they were again advancing to the attack—although they were not, and no one else had heard anything whatever of such a report—he ordered the worn-out and exhausted troops, so much in need of sleep and rest, to continue the march. Thus it was, by the last order given by the commanding general of the expedition, that the wearied and disheartened command were required to proceed to White's Station and Memphis. The general, soon after their departure, [left] by railroad train at lightning speed for the city.

So soon as I learned that he had left Collierville, I sent orders for 200 of the most effective mounted portion of each brigade of cavalry to be sent back to report to me at Collierville, where myself and staff remained for two days, rendering all the assistance possible in bringing in the foot-worn and wounded soldiers who had been left by General Sturgis to save themselves as best they could—many being almost destitute of clothing and without arms or ammunition, having thrown away everything calculated to impede their movements in their hasty flight.

I arrived with my staff at Memphis on June 15, where I learned that General Sturgis had been relieved. Being subjected to the fierce maledictions of the soldiers who had reached the city, [and] possibly fearing bodily injury, he had suddenly left Memphis in search of a safer and more congenial atmosphere. The loss of the cavalry during the expedition was about 300 in killed, wounded, and missing, which was small considering the severity and length of the battle at Brice's Cross Roads, and the almost constant fighting in the rear during the entire retreat, especially the brisk engagements at and in the vicinity of Ripley. The loss of the infantry was nearly 2,000 in killed, wounded, and missing, the most of whom were abandoned, and like the artillery and train, fell into the hands of the enemy during General Sturgis' rapid, disastrous, and disgraceful retreat from the battlefield at Brice's Cross Roads to Memphis.[5]

My brother was at that time living on Third Street in Memphis, which was still a strong "secesh" place. The first his wife, Elizabeth, knew of the disaster was at about 10 o'clock on the morning of June 13, when an army wagon filled with soiled, disfigured men—hatless and stripped to their shirts and pants—rolled by. The little urchins in the street shouted gleefully, "Oh, the Yankees is licked. The Yankees is licked. Here they are." Then came men on foot, bareheaded, coatless, barefoot, weaponless, and with the scant clothing left on their bodies torn to ribbons by their hurried night-scramble through the woods. Their feet were bleeding as they walked, and raw ghastly wounds were open to every gaze. All day long, Mrs. Grierson stood in her door and gave them water as they passed, while her savage rebel neighbors looked on and laughed—and still the childish voices yelled out: "Goodie, there's another Yankee shot." Silent, sullen, with downcast eyes, the dejected soldiers passed on. But it was wonderful to see how quickly they recognized, amid the taunting crowd, the one sympathetic face of the woman of whom they might ask a glass of water.

They had been strong men, and were brave and patriotic still. But then they were weak and spiritless, by no fault of their own—they had been deserted and left to shift for themselves by their chief commander. They were worn-out, and weary from fatigue and want of rest, and felt that they had been wronged by the indifference and incompetency of the general officer who had been placed over them. It was no wonder that they were led to heap maledictions on his head.

I was proud of the officers and enlisted men of the cavalry division, knowing the splendid manner in which they behaved throughout the unfortunate Sturgis expedition. Although their success in repelling the attacks of the enemy would have been still more successful had the entire cavalry force been left subject to my control, [I] yet believ[ed] that by their bravery and efficiency they had, under the most trying circumstances, inflicted a greater loss upon the rebels than they had sustained themselves. Feeling that justice [demanded] that a public recognition be given them for their splendid service, I immediately issued [a] congratulatory address. Never did troops better deserve praise.

Immediately upon the return of General Sturgis to Memphis, some days previous to my arrival, he was relieved from command, and the heaviest maledictions of the loyal people and press were heaped upon him. The soldiers were loud in their denunciations, under which spur the general wrote the following letter [June 22, 1864] to me:

General:

—Soon after reaching this place, after the battle of Brice's Crossroads, I made application to Gen. Washburn for a Court of Inquiry, to investigate the circumstances of our reverse. On last Saturday, (18th inst.), a commission was ordered to convene "immediately." Since that I have heard nothing of it. In the meantime the country is flooded with the stories of skulkers from the battle-field, and other evil disposed persons, and I am anxious to have the real facts set before the country. Will you be kind enough to give me a statement in writing, setting forth your views of the cause of our defeat. Your knowledge of my general management of the campaign, and whether or not, in your opinion, I was to blame for the failure of the expedition, and if so to what extent.

I replied as follows [June 23, 1864]:

In reply to your communication yesterday, I repeat what I expressed to you at Ripley, in presence of Cols. McMillen and Hoge; that, to advance beyond that point, under the circumstances would, in my opinion, lead to disaster. The Command was encumbered with a large train, the roads were in very bad condition, and the movement towards the enemy's line of communication had been so slow, as to give him ample time to learn our strength and to concentrate his forces. Not having seen your instructions, I do not know, except from conversation with yourself, what disposition you were compelled to make in accordance therewith. I cannot form an opinion upon all the points in relation to which you ask it sufficiently decided and satisfactory to admit of its publication.

Since returning from the expedition I have heard reports to the effect that you were drunk on the field of battle, and I take pleasure in saying that I know them to be false. Neither then, nor during the expedition, did I see in you the least sign of an undue use of intoxicating liquor. No other charges of personal misconduct against yourself have come to my knowledge, and I believe that you used your best endeavors to obey the orders of your superiors and to accomplish the objects of the expedition.

It would seem that my answer should have been more severe. But it must be remembered that it is a recognized point of etiquette among military officers not to give, officially, hearsay evidence and to shield each other from censure, unless compelled to do otherwise. There was no danger that Sturgis would again be placed in command. To make known publicly all the circumstances would reflect upon the officer who sent him there, and would weaken the confidence in the government when it was most needed. But now it is different. Simple justice to the living and dead demand that all the facts should be clearly stated and made known, [so] that the responsibility for the disaster may rest where it properly belongs. In talking with General Sherman since the war, he repeatedly acknowledged that he made a great mistake when he sent General Sturgis to Memphis to command so important an expedition or division, as Sturgis' habits were not unknown to General Sherman. Yet by his direct orders or authority, Sturgis was brought from a distance, placed over soldiers he did not know, and required to operate in a country in regard to which he had no knowledge whatever. The court of inquiry made its investigation, but the proceedings did not become known at the time.[6] Soon after, Sturgis went north from Memphis. Persons who were by accident on the same steamer and train could have been witnesses to the fact that beastly drunkenness in man and shamelessness in woman were lessened by two when he disappeared from sight. So far as I know, General Sturgis was not thereafter placed in any important command during the remainder of the war.[7] May God for the future keep such men from our army.

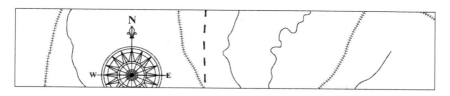

12. A. J. Smith's Operations in Mississippi

The return of the cavalry from Brice's Cross Roads was for no long rest. Even Sturgis' inglorious defeat had kept Forrest, with an efficient force, away from the flank of General Sherman's army and the main line of his communications, and the diversion was required for a yet longer period. For the balance of the year the cavalry was almost constantly on the move, and I was seldom at my headquarters at Memphis, or with my family, for more than ten days at one time altogether. The whole scope of these army operations, and their own consequent usefulness, was not known or appreciated at the time by the troops or the public.

It was, however, terribly discouraging work. Their business was to harass or distract the enemy and cover and aid the movements of larger and distant forces. But the going out without any objective point, and coming back without any tangible results, was extremely dreary occupation for the troops thus engaged. Then, too, as to myself, having had the satisfaction of constant success in independent commands, to have to drink of the dregs of restraint and incompetency from above, was bitter indeed. But I kept on in the even tenor of my way, taking matters as they came, supporting to the utmost and treating with all due consideration all those under whom I was called upon to serve. For I had examples to warn, if not to guide, me.

In the halcyon days after the great raid, when on crutches at Memphis, everybody's hero and favorite, one morning walked into my room and seized me in his hearty embrace my old chief and commander, General Prentiss. Pointing to the star on my shoulder and the two which adorned his own, he said: "We did not think of these in the old days at Cairo." Yet Major General B. M. Prentiss, with his high rank and position, was discouraged and discontented. Feeling that he did not have the command due or adequate to his rank and services, or the field of action equal to his abilities, he had determined to resign, and had really at that time tendered his resignation.

I tried every way in my power to dissuade him from the consequences of such a course, and urged him to withdraw the paper before it was too late, citing instances and showing that it was no unusual thing for officers for a time to be left without a suitable position or command; but that in his case all would be sure to come out all right in the end, and that his excellent record and services would soon be recognized and rewarded, that he had best hold on in any place where fortune put him, and see the war over before he quit the service. But General Grant reluctantly approved or recommended the acceptance of the resignation, at a time, too, when he contemplated placing General Prentiss in an important command. I think the general regretted his action, for I have been told by those in position to know that he subsequently, before the close of the war, sought to obtain a colonelcy of volunteers. Fortunately for me that I could not only recommend to others what were good to be done, but have proven myself to be that "rare one in twenty" who would follow my own teaching or advice, under circumstances, too, which tested to the utmost my power of self-control and endurance.

Major General A. J. Smith was the next officer to make an expedition against the rebels under Generals Lee and Forrest, and I am gratified to be able to record the fact that it was highly successful. Soon after our return from the Sturgis disaster, I got my division into the best possible condition for active and efficient field service. In pursuance of the orders of Major General C. C. Washburn, commanding District of West Tennessee, dated June 18, 1864, [I] directed the movements of the Second and Third brigades of the division in such manner as to concentrate the effective force of my command, amounting to about 3,200 enlisted men and officers, at La Grange, Tennessee, by June 20, where I reported for duty to General Smith, commanding Right Wing, XVI Army Corps. The First Brigade, or part thereof under Colonel Kargé, had been sent on boats to Vicksburg and thence on an expedition, and did not return in time to join in General Smith's first expedition.

I had previously met the general, but had no intimate personal acquaintance with him at this time. I learned to know him well and to recognize his ability as a brave, cautious, and skillful commander. His troops had rendered excellent service in General Banks' Red River campaign. Although the expedition was a failure, it was no fault of General Smith or those under his command. The brunt of the hard fighting in Banks' disastrous retreat had fallen upon Smith's two divisions of the XVI Corps, which had been temporarily detached from the Army of the Gulf. Brigadier General Joseph H. Mower, commanding the First Division, became particularly conspicuous for his gallantry in those operations—for the admirable manner in which he handled his troops and repulsed the enemy.

General Smith had but a short time previously returned to the Department of the Tennessee with his division, and presumed that, upon his arrival at Memphis, he would be ordered on to join General Sherman at Atlanta. But, under the previous instructions of the general, [he] was stopped on the line of the Memphis and Charleston Railroad for operations against the enemy in northern Mississippi, and was getting his troops in readiness for the movement southward from La Grange, under the immediate orders of General Washburn. The aggregate force placed under the command of General Smith was, including my cavalry, about 14,000 men, 11,000 of which consisted of infantry and artillery. This was really the first effective army that had been assembled in West Tennessee since long before General Stephen A. Hurlbut had been relieved from command of the XVI Army Corps. The furloughed men of both infantry and cavalry had returned to their regiments, and the entire force was made up of thoroughly disciplined officers and men, composed as follows:

First Division, XVI Army Corps, Brigadier General Joseph A. Mower, commanding.

Second [Third] Division, XVI Army Corps, Colonel David Moore, 21st Missouri Infantry, commanding; and the cavalry commanded by myself; besides a brigade of colored troops commanded by Colonel Edward E. Bouton, 59th U.S. [Colored] Infantry.

As I, and also the officers and enlisted men of my division, had a thorough knowledge of the country, General Smith consulted me freely. As I considered it absolute folly to move such a large force through such a country on one road, I was authorized to march my division in advance, but mostly on the left flank of the army, by separate roads, so far as practicable, at my own discretion, reporting promptly my position every night to the general commanding, with such information as I had obtained in regard to the movements, whereabouts, force, and intentions of the enemy, then mainly in the vicinity of Tupelo and Okolona, consisting of two divisions, Buford's and Chalmers', under General Forrest, and troops drawn from other points under General Roddey, the whole commanded by Lieutenant General [Major General] Stephen D. Lee, and in all numbering about 10,000 men.

My cavalry consisted of two brigades—the Second, commanded by Colonel E. F. Winslow of the 4th Iowa; [and] the Third, [commanded] by Colonel Datus E. Coon of the 2nd Iowa Cavalry—the detachments of the unfurloughed First Brigade having been left to guard the Memphis and Charleston Railroad, with the dismounted men from the other brigades. Colonel Winslow's brigade, which had been for some time occupied in guarding supply trains sent out from Memphis to La Grange, had been moved on east nine miles to Saulsbury, and Colonel Coon's brigade encamped in the vicinity of La Grange.

Colonel Winslow had been directed to place a strong picket on the road leading to or near Ripley. The outpost, which consisted of two companies of the 3rd Iowa, Lieutenant Colonel Noble's regiment, had not been in position long, when it was attacked by the enemy. After a sharp skirmish he was repulsed, leaving five killed and wounded in possession of our troops. On the morning of July 5, the army moved southward—the infantry, artillery, and train via Davis' Mills, and the cavalry via Grand Junction and Saulsbury—to Ripley. The infantry encamp[ed] the night of the 5th at Davis' Mills; one brigade of the cavalry—Winslow's—seven miles south of Saulsbury; and the brigade of Colonel Coon about fifteen miles north of Ripley, after skirmishing most of the day with the rebel cavalry encountered during his advance.

On the morning of the 7th, Colonel Coon's brigade continued the advance, constantly skirmishing with an increasing force, to a point within three or four miles of Ripley, at which point a considerable force of the enemy—the 16th Tennessee Cavalry—was found in a strong position at the base of a hill, with men dismounted and screened by trees and underbrush. The rebels were promptly attacked by the 2nd Iowa Cavalry, and after an engagement of one hour, driven away, leaving four dead in our hands—their reported loss being eleven killed and twenty-five wounded. Our loss [was] none.

On the 8th, the march was resumed with Winslow's brigade in front, the larger part of the cavalry, as far as possible, being kept on the flanks of the infantry. Much of the time skirmishing as we advanced upon the enemy, [we] encamp[ed] on the night of the 6th, eight miles south of Ripley.

During this day I ordered that Lieutenant Colonel Noble, of Winslow's brigade, be sent on a reconnaissance towards Kelly's Mill, while the main column was marching to Orizaba. Colonel Noble conducted this expedition in a most satisfactory manner, developing a considerable force of the enemy at Kelly's Ford and driving his advance pickets from breastworks on the brow of a hill, without loss—killing one and wounding and capturing two of the rebels. All information as to the constantly increasing force of the enemy in our front was at once communicated to General Smith. I advised him at Ripley that I would keep as far out as possible suitable detachments to the right and left of our line of march, move my main force southward, [and] cross the Tallahatchie at New Albany and in the direction of Pontotoc, unless otherwise ordered.

The weather was hot. The roads [were] dry and dusty, excepting in the bottoms near the river and creeks, where there was occasionally some stiff mud through which it was difficult to pull the heavily loaded teams and the artillery. The higher and ridge roads were much the better, those along the creeks being, even when dry, rough and badly cut up. Our advance on Pontotoc being satisfactory to the general commanding, we crossed the Tallahatchie at New Albany and Williamson's Mills, the Third Brigade in advance. [We] encamp[ed] the night of the 9th at New Albany, the infantry having crossed at that point also, without opposition, the enemy being led to believe the army would advance by the way of Kelly's Ford and Ellistown road.

On the 10th we advanced slowly and cautiously, the enemy withdrawing from our left flank and rapidly concentrating in our front. Winslow's brigade in front occasionally skirmish[ed] through the day with the rebels, driving them before him without halting or checking the march of the column, killing one and capturing horse and equipments and ten guns. The 4th Iowa, however, had to dismount to drive the enemy from a hill. While that regiment was marching, the 3rd [Iowa] was pushed forward to the advance, following up the pursuit of the enemy, the entire command concentrating at the intersection of several roads—in good position—about eight miles north of Pontotoc.

This change of direction from Ripley caused the rebels a good deal of extra marching, two brigades of Buford's division being drawn to Ellistown, and which were, in consequence, obliged to march two days and one whole night to get again in our front. A detachment—16th Tennessee Cavalry of [Colonel Tyree H.] Bell's brigade—was also sent toward our rear, but upon putting in an appearance, was quickly driven away. Moving forward and reaching Pontotoc on the 11th, we found [Colonel Robert] McCulloch's rebel brigade occupying the town with at least another brigade in the rear, in reserve and strongly posted on a hill south of the town. While the enemy were engaging the 7th Kansas Cavalry, which formed the advance guard of the infantry, I moved on rapidly, with Colonel Coon's brigade in front, from the east side of the town, and compelled the enemy to evacuate precipitately, and in some confusion, leaving several dead and wounded in our hands.

Encamping the night of the 11th at Pontotoc, after driving the rebels about five miles south of the town, I sent patrols in all directions. By direction of the commanding general, I remained with the larger part of my division in Pontotoc during July 12. From there I sent the 3rd Iowa Cavalry, Colonel Noble commanding, and the 9th Illinois Cavalry, Lieutenant Colonel Burgh commanding, upon reconnaissances—the 3rd upon the Houston road and the 9th on the Okolona road. Soon after passing the pickets, the 9th became briskly engaged with [Brig. Gen. Hylan B.] Lyon's rebel brigade,[1] and drove it about three miles, when it was largely reinforced. Colonel Burgh, however, tenaciously held his position until he fully developed the force of the enemy, and then fell back to our picket lines, his loss in the engagement, which lasted several hours, being one man killed and seven wounded. The enemy's loss [is] not known, but believed to be greater than ours.

Colonel Noble's regiment was fired upon, almost immediately after passing the picket line, by a force of the enemy posted on a high hill beyond a creek, which was near its base. Having seen Colonel Burgh's regiment well under way and driving the enemy on the Okolona and Pontotoc road, I joined Colonel Noble on the Houston road just after his advance was fired upon, and found the colonel dismounting a portion of his regiment. Soon after, he pushed forward and drove the enemy, getting possession of the hill, without loss to his command, but with his dismounted men much exhausted by the exertion of the rapid advance, mainly on account of the great heat of the weather and roughness of the ground over which they charged.

[I] direct[ed] a strong picket to be placed on the hill in the position gained. After an hour's rest, the firing in the direction of the Okolona road on which Colonel Burgh had advanced becoming quite heavy, I ordered Colonel Noble to proceed as rapidly as possible, by a crossroad, to the Okolona road. Upon our advance in that direction, it was found that the enemy, although driven back from his first position by Colonel Burgh, still held the point where the road joined the one he was on at its intersection with the Okolona road, where his entrenchments could be plainly observed, and from which heavy volleys were fired upon Colonel Burgh's right and also [upon] the advance of Colonel Noble's right. The appearance of Colonel Noble's regiment caused some confusion among the rebels, and he was about to charge the enemy when, seeing that the enemy's force far outnumbered both Burgh's and Noble's, regiments, I directed Colonel Noble to move across to the Okolona road to support Colonel Burgh, should it become necessary.

Having developed the enemy's force and observed their strong position, thus accomplishing the object of the reconnaissance and not wishing to jeopardize the lives of the soldiers unnecessarily, I ordered Colonel Burgh to withdraw slowly from his engagement and directed Colonel Noble to return to his camp, the pickets on all roads being at once strengthened. Strong patrols had also been sent out on other roads. [After] a considerable force of the enemy [was] encountered on the Tupelo road, I reported the facts to the general commanding and returned to camp to await further orders.

In view of the information thus gained as to the strength of the position of the enemy, and learning that the entire combined forces of Lee and

Forrest were being concentrated on the Okolona road, in a strong position [in] back of low swampy ground over which we must pass to dislodge them—believing that it would be hazardous to attack the enemy there, if he could be drawn out and obliged to attack us in our own chosen position—I talked fully with General Smith on the subject, and advised a rapid movement of the command to Tupelo in order that we might be able to select our chosen field of battle, where we could strengthen our position and await the approach and attack of the enemy. [I pointed out] that the movement we had already made to the right flank had disconcerted the enemy and given him long and fatiguing marches; that he could again be placed at a disadvantage by a movement by our left flank, as all his troops had been withdrawn from Tupelo and [moved] almost entirely to distant points from that road, which was thus left open to us for the march, which could be readily made; that I could take the advance at an early hour [and] gain, occupy, and hold Tupelo and the high ground west, near Harrisburg, until the infantry arrived and took position.

The general was at first in favor of attacking the enemy at all hazards, where he then was, as he feared that he might not attack us if we moved to Tupelo. I told the general that he certainly would be attacked, in any position he might select, before our return to Memphis. The general sent for General Mower, and I sent for Colonel Coon of the 2nd Iowa Cavalry, who like myself was well acquainted with the country. I had already talked with Mower on the subject, and when he heard Colonel Coon's statements strongly verifying the reports made by me as to the excellent roads to and the strong position we could gain near Tupelo, the general [Mower] coincided with me and also recommended to General Smith the change of direction as proposed. Small detachments of rebels had been observed on our right flank and rear, and the enemy was led to believe that we would flank off again to the right and return to Memphis. The order for the next day's march was given accordingly by General Smith.

By an early start, the cavalry had advanced and gotten over ten miles on the road before the movement was discovered by the enemy. I presumed that we would probably be attacked on the flank, but believed that no sufficient force of the enemy could be gotten together in time to seriously impede our march, he being worn out and exhausted by his long marches, while General Smith's troops had virtually gained a full day's rest at Pontotoc. The main body of the enemy, therefore, was necessarily obliged to follow in rear, where but little damage could be done.

To screen our movements as long as possible, I had directed that a strong picket from Colonel Noble's regiment be held back until the troops had been withdrawn from the Okolona road and were falling back on Pontotoc, when it was directed to fall back and proceed to the front—Colonel Noble's regiment having been designated for the advance that day. By some mistake, Captain [John D.] Brown, the officer in command of the detachment composed of Companies A, I, K, and L, was not apprised of the withdrawal of the picket from the Okolona road at the proper time. Remaining too long, a force of about 300 rebels got in his rear. Without any hesitation, and with audacious bravery rarely excelled, the captain promptly mounted and charged with his command through the rebels, without the loss of a man; they in astonishment fleeing in dismay, with a rapidity and confusion rarely equaled, while Captain Brown with his brave troopers, in the meantime, joined his regiment in safety. The advance of the cavalry arrived at and occupied Tupelo before noon. Some skirmishing had occurred, but although the rebels left seven dead in our hands, the march was not impeded seriously; the object—the occupation of Tupelo and the high ground near Harrisburg—being promptly attained.

The infantry also marched at an early hour. General Smith, at the head of the column, had gotten well forward when I sent him word that the road was clear and our chosen position occupied by my command. It was not long until the general arrived with his staff. Upon examination of the position near Harrisburg and the surrounding country in all directions, he expressed himself as highly gratified, his only fear being that the rebels never would attack us in such a strong position. I laughingly remarked that if we were not attacked, he might take my head for a football; that the rebels had only recently defeated General Sturgis, and flushed with that victory, they thought that all that would be needed would be to "charge pell-mell, and yell like demons"; and that their attack upon us was as certain as the light of the coming day. The rear of the column was guarded by the 7th Kansas Cavalry and detachments from Colonel Bouton's brigade of infantry.

The enemy, under immediate command of Forrest, made his appearance soon after the column had been withdrawn from Pontotoc. Although repeated charges and almost continuous attacks were made with largely superior forces, the march of the column was not delayed in any manner until within about eight miles of Tupelo, when an attack was made upon the train by [Colonel Edmund W.] Rucker's rebel brigade. Although a few mules were killed and some confusion created, the enemy was severely punished and promptly repulsed. At that time, the 9th Illinois Cavalry was sent back to the rear to the assistance of the 7th Kansas. Thereafter, all attacks made by the rebels upon the rear or flank of the column [were] vigorously met and successfully repulsed. Later, a feeble attack was made by part of Buford's rebel division. In like manner it was quickly driven away, after which no advantage was gained, and the march was successfully accomplished.[2]

The troops composing General Smith's command had all arrived by the evening of the 13th, and had been carefully placed on most advantageous ground—the infantry and artillery occupying a high ridge just west of Harrisburg; the cavalry disposed on the flanks and securely holding the line of the railroad beyond Tupelo, the fords of the streams in the vicinity, and the town; dismounted skirmishers from the cavalry being also placed some distance out in front of the infantry.

In front of the position occupied by General Smith's army was sloping ground and open fields for nearly half a mile over which the enemy must advance, through plowed ground and uphill, to make his attack. Our troops were formed in a prolonged semicircle, turning a little abruptly on our right flank, with the left flank extending in a more direct line, the highest point on the hill of Harrisburg being occupied by our artillery, a battery of six guns near each flank, with sections of artillery advantageously located at intervals along the entire front or line of battle. There was open ground extending for over 1,000 to 2,000 yards all around, with timber in rear towards Tupelo and to the west and south in front of the army, in which the rebels took up their position during the night of July 13.

During the afternoon of the 13th, the enemy made an attack on the northeast side of Tupelo, beyond the Mobile and Ohio Railroad, but were promptly driven away by the cavalry. The army remained bivouacked on the lines of battle during the night. The troops of both sides rested without molestation, with no noise to disturb the stillness other than that occasioned by relieving of the pickets of both armies, neither of which fired upon or interfered with the other.

On the morning of July 14, the entire line of battle, which had been so advantageously chosen, was strengthened in every possible way by such materials as were available, such as rails, logs, and entrenchments hastily constructed by the infantry. The approach of the enemy was awaited with an absolute feeling of security prevailing throughout the entire command, with no apprehension whatever, from the general commanding to the privates, secured as they were, lying down with muskets clasped in their hands, the artillerymen at their guns, and the cavalry disposed on the flanks and rear, with a brigade of dismounted skirmishers some distance in front of the infantry. The sky was clear and the sun shone gorgeously, shining alike upon friend and foe, and inspiriting all the combatants. Not a shot was fired as the enemy could be seen advancing from the timber and taking position for the attack. Ample time had been afforded the contestants for breakfast, and a spirit of serenity prevailed throughout, both sides feeling confident of success.

Our troops did not have long to wait before a large force from the rebel front was seen advancing upon our left, evidently with the intention of capturing the artillery, which General Smith had placed upon a prominent knoll and in full view of the audacious foe, and gain[ing] the high ground. It was not expected that the cavalry skirmishers would resist the attack. [They] were directed to fall back, after discharging their carbines, to their horses—some distance back of the line of battle.

Some confusion could be noticed in the ranks of the enemy, probably caused by conflicting orders. But on they soon came courageously. When the rebel battery opened fire some distance out from the scattered or open timber, they raised the rebel yell and charged impetuously forward, firing as they advanced. Our troops withheld their fire until the enemy was in close range, and then rose and opened upon the foe a most terrific fire of musketry, the artillery firing with great precision and rapidity into the advancing columns of the foe, quickly silencing their shouts [and] decimating and thinning out their ranks. But on they came after a moment's check, with a gallantry worthy of a better cause, but were soon driven back in confusion. All efforts to rally the advance failed, and they fell back to the timber, from which they kept up a desultory fire of artillery and musketry for some half hour or more.

In the meantime, preparations were made for an advance upon the center, or to the right of the Second [Third] Division and left of the First Division commanded by General Mower. Again the rebels came on with a yell, but without organization and more like a mob than disciplined troops. [They] were allowed to come within 100 yards of Mower's troops, when suddenly they arose and poured into the enemy a most galling and terrific fire of musketry. As the rebels gave way, Mower's infantry charged and drove them in great confusion, leaving their dead and wounded on the field.

The battle lasted about four hours. No organized attack of any magnitude was made subsequently during the day, although skirmishing on the flanks continued. Another attempt was made to force a crossing over King's Creek in our rear on the Verona road, but the rebels were promptly driven away by the 4th Iowa Cavalry which, after being withdrawn from the front of the infantry, were sent to hold the roads leading out of Tupelo.

During the second advance of the enemy, Winslow's brigade, being disposed on the right flank with the largest portion dismounted as skirmishers, stubbornly resisted the advance of the enemy. [They] were for a time briskly engaged, and fell back only on receipt of orders to do so, after inflicting considerable loss on the enemy, with slight loss to the cavalry.

About 10 o'clock on the night of the 14th, the infantry lines having been withdrawn some distance from the line of battle occupied that day, the enemy attempted a night attack on the left. The Colored Brigade under command of Colonel Bouton, which had rendered excellent service in repulsing the enemy in their first attack that morning, were promptly thrown forward with a part of the Third Division of infantry, and opened a most terrific fire upon the enemy, driving him away—after which the advanced position was held and strengthened by additional patrols, and nothing more was heard from the enemy until the next day. General Mower again distinguished himself in the battle of the 14th by the skillful manner in which he handled his division and repulsed the enemy. The Second [Third] Division, XVI Army Corps, under Colonel Wood [Moore], and Colonel Bouton's brigade displayed conspicuous gallantry in the engagement of the early morning.[3]

The great credit of the victory was due to the infantry and artillery, although the services of the cavalry were important and helped materially to bring about the desired result. The loss of the enemy in the engagements of July 14, known as the battle of Harrisburg, could not have been less than 1,500 in killed and wounded. The loss in Buford's division, alone, is officially reported at nearly 1,000; and our loss was not more than one-third of that number, footing up during the entire expedition at less than 700 in killed, wounded, and missing.

It was presumed by all that, in view of the crippled condition of the enemy, General Smith would order a vigorous pursuit and attack the next day. But, unfortunately, the want of supplies made him deem a return to Memphis necessary. With this exception, the army was in splendid condition, and never was there a better opportunity to destroy Lee and Forrest's army than at that time—before the rebels could obtain needed rest and recuperation. In my judgment, it would have been better to have gone on and taken the chances of obtaining supplies from the enemy, or to have lived on corn and other products, or even sent back for supplies to be forwarded from La Grange, than to have at that time returned there without a forward movement. The enemy had fallen back a few miles on the Pontotoc road, and taken up a strong position and constructed fortifications, where he reorganized his forces and awaited for a time for our advance.[4]

On the morning of the 15th, General Smith, upon a further reexamination of his supply department, found that owing to the fact that much of the bread which had been issued to the command was spoiled and little over one day's rations of that important article left, [and] having not over 100 rounds per gun for his artillery, he deemed it an absolute necessity to withdraw his command to the line of the Memphis and Charleston Railroad. After disposing of the dead and looking after the wants of the wounded—those of the rebels as well as his own—he made his preparations to march back via the Ellistown road leading northward from Tupelo and Harrisburg. I was ordered to destroy the Mobile and Ohio Railroad each way from Tupelo, which was effectually accomplished for a distance of fully ten miles. The wounded of the enemy—several hundred—with about forty of our own, were removed into comfortable quarters at Tupelo and U.S. surgeons left to look to their wants. The movement of the army began about noon.

The rebels remained in their position at the plantation of Mrs. Sample where, among other materials such as rails and logs, cotton bales were used in constructing fortifications. About 11 A.M., they commenced to advance upon our position, throwing the larger part of their troops around to our left. Soon after General Smith withdrew his troops from their position on the high ground south of Harrisburg, the rebels advanced and took up the ground vacated. A regiment or two of cavalry had been advanced on the Pontotoc road, to cover the movement of the infantry from that direction, and brought away a gun the enemy had abandoned. The remainder of the cavalry covered the withdrawal of our troops from the south and [the] direction of the Verona and Tupelo roads. Colonel Wood's [Moore's] division was being passed to the new front on the Ellistown road, the train following. General Mower's division was ordered to follow with the cavalry not disposed in the advance, on the flanks, in rear of the army. (Colonel Bouton's brigade being directed to follow in rear of train.)

Before the infantry had completed the withdrawal, the enemy, who had occupied the high ridge to the south, began to advance and endeavored to place a battery in the position where ours was placed the day before. [The rebels were] forcing the cavalry back, when Colonel Bouton came to its support with infantry. [He] charged forward gallantly with his command, opening a vigorous fire of musketry, until the enemy was driven back and our troops occupied again the position of the day previous. About the same time, Colonel Winslow's brigade had made a reconnaissance on the Pontotoc road and had developed a large force of the enemy, by his maneuvers evidently desiring to draw the cavalry into an engagement. General Mower, noticing the approach of the rebels, promptly wheeled about with a brigade of his division and advanced rapidly in support of the cavalry, driving the rebels back for two miles, when four companies of the 9th Illinois charged upon the retreating rebels, driving them back to their entrenchments, losing one officer, 1st Lieutenant [John H.] McMahan, [along with] one enlisted man killed and six men wounded.

The march was then resumed. The cavalry, besides furnishing the rearguard, were also on both flanks and in the advance. The column had scarcely moved out and gotten under way on the Ellistown road, when the enemy attacked the rearguard. It was not long until Buford's and Chalmers' divisions were following and taking advantage of every opportunity to charge upon our troops. But [they] were stubbornly resisted at every point and repulsed at every charge. The fight continued with but little interruption to Oldtown Creek, ten miles south of Ellistown.

Never did a small force of our cavalry repel a largely superior force of the enemy more successfully than during the retreat that day. We had repeatedly selected positions where the battalions were well-screened from view, and successfully ambushed the enemy, with heavy loss to him. We had some men wounded but none killed. [Still, we] had a good many horses shot while repulsing the enemy's attacks. The rearguard was composed mostly of Winslow's brigade, and never did cavalry perform their duty more satisfactorily. I was present at the rear and clearly observed their movements. Although assaulted by so large a force, no confusion was caused.

When thus engaged following the main column, falling back from one position to another, I suddenly discovered at 5 P.M. that we had closed up on the wagon train, which was in park with the encamped infantry and artillery—all except Mower's division, which was moving to the advance, directly in the front. As I received no notice of this halt, the enemy was unfortunately allowed to approach to a good position on a hill south of the creek, within easy range of the train. Soon, our rear was attacked by Buford's and Chalmers' divisions, two brigades having been pushed forward through the woods in the creek bottom. We were obliged to fight without room to maneuver. The enemy having opened with artillery from the hill, a number of shot and shell were thrown directly into the wagon park, causing some confusion. To add to the difficulties of the situation, the cavalry then in the rear had previously expended most of their ammunition during the constant skirmishing of that day. I applied to General Smith for the Third Brigade of cavalry to be sent to me, or an infantry support.

After nearly half an hour's delay, during which the cavalry held its position at the creek, we were reinforced by General Mower with part of his division of infantry. When the two arms of the service united, the cavalry dismounted, charged upon the enemy, and drove him through the woods; [and] also from his position on the hill and back for some distance beyond. General Forrest joined Buford and Chalmers with an additional force during this engagement, which lasted about one hour. He was soon after wounded and had to leave the field. Our loss in this affair was light, as the impetuosity of our advance, when reinforced, disconcerted the enemy and caused him to fall back in dismay. The rebels were completely demoralized by their repeated defeats. Had they been attacked and vigorously pursued after the fight of the 14th, they could have been entirely broken up and driven out of Mississippi.

On the 16th the column took up the march to Ellistown, where it encamped. The 7th Kansas Cavalry being placed in rear to relieve Waring's brigade, and having learned from my scouts that the enemy was in considerable force at Kelly's Mill and ford, that being a difficult place to cross the troops and train, I recommended to General Smith a return via New Albany, the road being better and the crossing of the Tallahatchie at that point more desirable. Roddey's rebel brigade had been sent to Kelly's Ford, and McCulloch's brigade kept up the pursuit in rather a feeble manner to a point beyond Ellistown, after which the command was not molested. The column took up the march on the 17th, encamping that night at New Albany, the cavalry having been sent forward to secure the bridge over the Tallahatchie, from which point to La Grange, Tennessee, the march was without any remarkable incident.

During the entire expedition, the loss inflicted upon the enemy must have been over 2,000 in killed, wounded, and prisoners; while that of General Smith's command was less than 700.[5] The loss in the cavalry division, in officers, was one killed and two wounded; enlisted men—seven killed, fifty-five wounded, and two missing, the largest percentage of loss being in the 9th Illinois Cavalry. The troops reached La Grange on July 17, after an absence of seventeen days. Everything considered, the expedition to Tupelo and return was well managed throughout. Although our movements were slow, the rebels were repeatedly deceived as to our intentions; wearied and worn out by the extra marching they were obliged to do; and beaten in every skirmish or engagement. They were taught a lesson they did not soon forget.

Although the cavalry was not in position to do the hard fighting during the battle of July 14 at Harrisburg, yet it rendered valuable service during that day and every other day during the entire time the troops were absent. But, being fastened to an infantry command, and being obliged to cover the movements of such a column of troops, was very onerous and tedious work that, however important, [was] rarely fully appreciated. The very day we reached La Grange, I learned that the Pioneer Corps of mounted colored men, that I had carefully selected and organized [and] which had accompanied the cavalry division, to repair roads, bridges etc., and had been of invaluable assistance in many expeditions, had by orders of the

Adjutant General of the Army been turned over to an artillery company or command in want of recruits.

———

On July 25, 1864, I was by order of Major General C. C. Washburn placed in command of all the cavalry of the Military District of West Tennessee, and directed by him to reorganize it into two divisions or cavalry corps. This cavalry was really at the time all under my command and designated the Cavalry Division, XVI Army Corps. But Colonel Hatch, who had been absent for several months on account of a wound received in the fall of 1863, had received the promotion to which I had recommended him—to brigadier general of volunteers—and had rejoined the command. And there were subordinate officers: Colonel Winslow, who had commanded a brigade for quite a length of time, and to whom it was desirable to advance to a higher command; and also Colonels [T. P.] Hendrick, Kargé, Coon, and Noble, who had really earned the command. As more cavalry regiments were expected, it was deemed best at the time to reorganize the command into a corps.

It was at this time expected that more cavalry would be sent to report to General Washburn, and that another division could soon be added to the Cavalry Corps. The additional cavalry did not come, and the arrangement, although complimentary and indicating an advance in my position, proved an unfortunate thing, as it was calculated to remove the organizations from my more direct control and gave excuse for sending the troops away to distant points and entirely beyond my jurisdiction.

As reports reached us again to the effect that Forrest was reorganizing and getting his troops into shape for another advance on General Sherman's communications, I was directed to arrange for the concentration of the Cavalry Corps on the Memphis and Charleston Railroad, with a view of opening the railroad leading from Grand Junction, Tennessee, through Central Mississippi, southward towards the Tallahatchie, in order to more readily accumulate supplies for another expedition into Mississippi to be commanded by Major General A. J. Smith.

The Mississippi Central Railroad had been effectually destroyed at times by both our own troops and the rebels, and to repair it again would necessitate much labor and expense. Accordingly, in compliance with Special Orders No. 97, Headquarters District of West Tennessee, dated July 30, 1864, I reported with my command for duty again to Major General A. J. Smith, commanding Right Wing, XVI Army Corps. In obedience to his instructions, on August 1, I ordered Brigadier General Edward Hatch, commanding First Division, Cavalry Corps, to move southward, concentrate his command at or near Holly Springs, and in conjunction with the infantry, push the repair of the Mississippi Central Railroad towards the Tallahatchie River. The Second Division, Colonel E. F. Winslow, commanding, was sent in detachments from Memphis and White's Station on the Memphis and Charleston Railroad, as guard to wagon trains and artillery, direct to Holly Springs, on the Mississippi Central Railroad. On the 7th, the 12th Missouri Cavalry and 35th Iowa Infantry were ordered southward to the Tallahatchie River, had a skirmish with the enemy there, secured a ferryboat, and crossed to the south bank.

On August 8, communication by railroad having been opened to Holly Springs, in obedience to instructions from General Smith, the First Division, Colonel Noble's brigade of the Second Division, and two brigades of General Mower's [division]—Col. Noble's brigade in advance, freed from transportation and unencumbered—all under the command of General Hatch, moved southward, skirmishing with the enemy's pickets [and] driving them to the Tallahatchie bottom, where an increased force was encountered, screened by the debris of fallen timber, underbrush, and weeds, on ground broken by small creeks and bayous. After a brisk engagement, the enemy was forced to retreat. Colonel Noble pressed forward his troops, opened with one section of artillery on the retreating foe, and dismounting the 3rd Iowa Cavalry, crossed that regiment on the railroad bridge to the south side of the Tallahatchie, the enemy having fallen back to their entrenchments on the high ground bordering the river bottom, about two miles distant. Colonel Noble withdrew all but a picket of his brigade. The First Division of cavalry and infantry having arrived, General Hatch encamped with his command on the north side of the stream for the night, having marched, notwithstanding the extreme heat of the day, a distance of seventeen miles.

During the evening and night, the Engineer Corps attached to the infantry constructed a bridge over the Tallahatchie. At 2 A.M. on the morning of August 9, Colonel Noble crossed his brigade and thus gained the advance of the army. Being reinforced by the 7th Indiana Cavalry at daylight, another movement was made against the enemy—the 4th Iowa, dismounted and placed in line on the left; the 10th Missouri, dismounted, on the center in front of a section of artillery; the 7th Indiana, dismounted, on the right; and the 3rd Iowa remain[ing] mounted and formed in line in rear of the artillery. With these dispositions made and troops held well in hand, an advance was ordered. The whole line moved cautiously forward, under cover of the woods, towards the enemy's position, a distance of about two miles, skirmishing with the enemy's pickets as the command emerged from the heavy timber of the bottom, when suddenly the enemy opened with a battery of artillery. The fight began and continued until the position was gained, the enemy falling back, pursued by our troops to Hurricane Creek, a distance of six miles, where he took position and again opened fire with a battery. Upon our troops advancing to the attack, the enemy fled precipitately southward, showing evident signs of demoralization.

The First Division, under the immediate command of General Hatch, took up the pursuit, relieving Colonel Noble's brigade in rear of the cavalry column, which followed the enemy to Oxford, where getting his artillery again into position, another ineffectual attempt was made to resist the advance of our troops. But, being attacked on all sides, he broke and fled in confusion, leaving his camp equipage. General Hatch encamped with his command at Oxford. On the morning of the 10th, finding no enemy in his front, he returned to Abbeville, three miles south of the Tallahatchie River, where he soon after was joined by General Mower with his division of infantry.

On the evening of August 11, by direction of General Smith, I ordered Colonel Winslow with his Second Brigade (his First Brigade having remained during this interval at Holly Springs) to proceed to Waterford, reporting on arrival there to General Smith at Holly Springs for further instructions. From Waterford, Colonel Winslow moved to Holly Springs, where he concentrated his available force and remained until the trains and infantry had all left that point for the south. Colonel Winslow, suffering from a disordered limb, was relieved from duty with the expedition by the general commanding, and ordered to take charge of the railroad train guards and conduct them safely back to Memphis. Colonel Joseph Kargé was then placed in command of the Second Division. In the meantime, the First Division was engaged in almost daily skirmishes with the enemy.

On the 13th I accompanied General Mower and General Hatch on a reconnaissance to Hurricane Creek, where a brisk engagement ensued in which the enemy was driven from his works, with considerable loss, by the cavalry (the infantry ordered on this reconnaissance by General Mower not being engaged) and where the 6th and 9th Illinois Cavalry, under command of Colonel M. H. Starr, displayed intrepid bravery by their bold attack on the left flank of the enemy. Colonel Hendrick, at the same time, was ordered to attack the right flank, while the 2nd Iowa Cavalry moved in advance of the infantry and artillery on the main road and directly in front of the enemy's position. The enemy's skirmishers were met and driven back across the creek in front, while Colonel Starr crossed his command two miles below and made a vigorous attack on the enemy's left flank, and Colonel Hendrick crossed two miles above and attacked the enemy's right flank. These movements were all successfully carried out. Our troops in the front and on the right flank held the enemy in check while Colonel Starr with his two regiments, after a severe engagement, drove the enemy back a mile or more and captured his earthworks. Pressing forward again, the enemy was obliged to fall back, and soon after retreated in a disorderly manner.

In the meantime, a battery of artillery of General Mower's division had opened, and was quickly replied to by the enemy. The artillery fire continued for an hour or more, without injury to either side. When the infantry advanced over the creek, no enemy being found and it being nearly night or dark, the troops returned under the orders of General Mower to their camps at Abbeville. The Second Division of cavalry being back near Holly Springs at this time, I was merely a spectator of the fight on the 13th, and I would not assume command of the cavalry, over General Hatch, during the engagement. The gallantry of the troops engaged was conspicuous, and reflected great credit on the command. General Mower expressed himself as highly gratified at the result.

During the time the two divisions of the cavalry were so widely separated, the troops of both were actively occupied picketing all roads and scouting throughout the adjacent country as the infantry was being withdrawn from the line of the railroad, detachments of which were sent out along the road as far north as Hudson and Lamar. On the 15th, four companies [of the] 7th Iowa Cavalry, under Captain H. F. Wright, had been sent as far north as Hudsonville. One of these companies, under command of Lieutenant J. W. Skelton, was sent out to Lamar, supposing that station was still occupied by 300 of our infantry. Not finding any infantry, Lieutenant Skelton had gone into camp there.

About 9 o'clock that night, he observed four wagons crossing the railroad track. Approaching them with the picket, [he] saw about a dozen men in their shirtsleeves following the wagons. Supposing them to be guerillas attempting to capture the wagons, he ordered his picket to fire, sent a corporal and three men to get in their rear to cut them off, and then went back to camp. He got a part of his company and started out. Not hearing anything from his corporal and his three men, he still supposed the men in shirtsleeves with the wagons were guerillas. He soon after came in sight of a force partly in line and partly in column. Presuming them to be our own troops, [he] rode down within a few feet. They opened to let him pass through when, discovering that the soldiers were also in their shirtsleeves, [he] concluded they were rebels and promptly ordered a charge, by which he broke up and scattered the left of the line. The right swung around in his rear, when with supreme audacity, he charged again and cut his way back. Some of the men got separated from him and, with those left in camp, proceeded to La Grange. Lieutenant Skelton reach[ed] Hudsonville, with only six men, before daylight.

Colonel Samuel R. Baker, 47th Illinois Infantry, commanding that station, sent Skelton, at his own request, with another detachment to the point where the affair occurred. He found, to his great surprise, that he had attacked a whole regiment of rebels that had been ordered to Lamar to destroy the railroad. His sudden and unexpected appearance had so alarmed and disconcerted the rebels that they dropped their crowbars, axes, picks, and shovels and fled rapidly, passing through Salem and abandoning the designs of tearing up and destroying the railroad and telegraph line. In their hurried flight, supposing that the country surrounding Lamar was literally alive with "Yankee soldiers," they left some of their dead and wounded on the field, and also a good many guns and muskets. A citizen of the neighborhood, who had been awakened by the firing, got out in time to see the rebels hastily disappearing. [He] told Skelton that when last heard from the next morning, they were still running hastily through Salem, ten miles distant from there. Captain Skelton had but one man wounded, the orderly sergeant of his company. All others regained his command in safety.

Much credit is due the captain and his brave troopers for their gallant and successful charges, so opportunely made, which resulted in forcing the rebels to abandon their designs, and thus saved a large amount of government property and prevented the interruption of railroad communications. Skelton was a perfect daredevil, who was well known to be always ready for any expedition, however hazardous, and quick as lightning in his resources to meet any emergency. The force he had attacked turned out to be the 7th and 26th Tennessee Cavalry of Forrest's command, numbering over 700 officers and men, who had been directed to destroy the railroads between Grand Junction and Holly Springs, and between Memphis and Grand Junction.

Having the opportunity of communicating with Mrs. Grierson by hand of Colonel Winslow, who was ordered back to Memphis, I hastily wrote to her on August 17: "We are moving south again without objective point, merely striking out in a haphazard sort of fashion, and as likely to hit the air as the enemy. We can do but little good by such movements beyond occupying the attention of the rebels and keeping Forrest's troops from interfering with Sherman's movements further east. One division of my command is below the Tallahatchie, and the other here and along the railroad. I will remain here tonight to push forward troops, ammunition, and other supplies, and return to Abbeville tomorrow."

On August 18, all government supplies having been removed from Holly Springs, Colonel Joseph Kargé, commanding Second Division, Cavalry Corps, proceeded with his command to the Tallahatchie, and arrived at Abbeville, south of the river, on the 19th. I therefore ordered General Hatch to move forward with his division towards Oxford. Again, he found the enemy in force on Hurricane Creek, and after a short engagement, drove him away. General Smith having concentrated his army at Abbeville and made his arrangements for his advance on Oxford, I in obedience to his orders moved forward with my Second Division and joined General Hatch south of Hurricane Creek.

On the 21st patrols were sent out in all directions; and on the 22nd the advance of the army towards Oxford was continued. General Hatch's division was placed on the right flank, and Colonel Kargé's division, excepting one regiment, on the left. With that regiment, I took the advance of the center column of infantry. The whole army moved forward at daylight, and the cavalry entered Oxford about 8 o'clock A.M., simultaneously from the north, east, and west. The enemy had constructed earthworks in various parts of the town, but had evacuated them the day before our arrival. The rebels had quickly disappeared from our front. Hearing from rebel sources that General Forrest had, with a portion of his force, made a circuit and rapid march to Memphis and had attacked that place, I by authority of the general commanding ordered General Hatch to proceed at once with his division to Panola to intercept the rebels in their retreat. In compliance with instructions, I returned to the Tallahatchie at Abbeville with the Second Division of cavalry, to watch the line of the river between the railroad and Panola and to attack the rebels under Forrest at any point they might make their appearance in their retreat southward.

General Smith was greatly disappointed at not being able to get a fight from the rebels at Oxford. Finding that Jake [Jacob] Thompson, formerly President Buchanan's secretary of the interior, resided in the place, he ordered the immediate destruction of his residence, then occupied by Mrs. [Kate] Thompson and family. It was a fine house and elegantly furnished. Mrs. Thompson, being at home, was notified by one of General Smith's staff officers in regard to the order of the general. She did not seem to be disturbed at the information, and took the matter very philosophically and loftily. She asked permission to remove some family portraits. That being accomplished, she then pointed out to the soldiers a closet under the staircase filled with papers and other combustibles, which she coolly observed would be a good place "to kindle a fire." Hearing that the Thompson house was to be burned, I rode up to the place, where I met General Smith, looking grim and determined. He seemed anxious to see the order executed, and there can be no doubt but he deemed the act justifiable. I saw the portraits carried out of the house; met and spoke to Mrs. Thompson, who was calm and ladylike; and noticed the occurrences as herein related. It is only just to the cavalry organizations to state that no private property was destroyed or disturbed by them, nor were non-combatants treated with harshness or discourtesy by the officers or soldiers of my command.[6]

When our troops entered Oxford, they found placarded on the walls in the courthouse, and on some other buildings, in large rough letters: "Gen. Forrest in Memphis." The information thus conveyed was not credited at first, but it was verified by the statements of residents of the town. General Smith seemed perplexed and undecided as to what had best be done, and was unwilling to act without orders from his superiors. I urged very strongly that the cavalry be cut loose, and while Forrest was engaged with his raid on Memphis, that I be permitted to make a dash through Mississippi, Alabama, and Georgia. The cavalry was in fair condition, strong enough, and invaluable results might have thus been attained. General Smith seemed to agree with me, but did not feel that he had the authority to give the order. I suggested that we at least be allowed to make an effort to intercept Forrest. Had we at once followed the trail of the raiders, we would have met them returning, encumbered with prisoners and plunder. With the force pursuing them from Memphis, I had no doubt of being able to have turned the tables on them, badly crippled as they were from the punishment received by Smith's former expedition and [by] their later encounters and rapid movements. The general finally assented to the last proposition. On that I had ordered Hatch to Panola, and had gone myself to the Tallahatchie with Kargé's division. But General Smith soon after sent an order to General Hatch to return, and directed me to proceed to Holly Springs. The same day he entered Oxford, he retraced his steps with his troops and fell back to Abbeville.

As we found the bridge at the Tallahatchie partly washed away, I again proposed to have one division moved west on the south side of the river, while the other repaired the bridge and moved down the north side, keeping up communication with each other so that if one division should intercept the rebels, the other could be thrown upon them with an excellent prospect of success. But General Smith, upon receiving some communication from General Washburn, ordered me to move rapidly on to Holly Springs, while General Hatch moved upon the left flank of the army, presuming that Forrest might retreat via Holly Springs.

While encamped at the Tallahatchie waiting for General Smith to bring up his supplies and concentrate his army, the principal event of almost every day was a fight with the rebels at Hurricane Creek. At my headquarters in an abandoned and dilapidated old building, the officers of my staff made a life-size sketch of a man on the wall, with charcoal, and employed their leisure moments in practicing a new saber exercise under the direction of Lieutenant Sheiver [Anton Scherer] of the 2nd Iowa Cavalry, an old Prussian soldier who commanded our escort.

On the morning August 24, by direction of the major general commanding, I ordered General Hatch to make a circuit to the west with his command and encamp at night near Waterford, nine miles north of the Tallahatchie, while with Colonel Kargé's division I proceeded direct to Holly Springs, with instructions to occupy the town until arrival of the infantry, and if possible, open railroad and telegraph communication with La Grange. On reaching Holly Springs, some lively scenes and spicy conversations occurred at headquarters with the people of the town, mostly ladies, who came to recover their cows, which we had gathered en route from the south and corralled in [a] lot near[by] for beef for the troops. The young officers of the staff were as jolly as any of Charles Lever's Irishmen.[7] They particularly enjoyed a little sharp sparring with the young ladies who came to headquarters to complain of raids upon their stock, or to plead for its return.

It was at this place that two such, asking for me, met Lieutenant [Alexander W.] McClure, who on the whim of the moment affected an Irish brogue. Soon some spirited chaffing occurred. McClure was suddenly asked what part of Ireland he was from. He, in a vague remembrance of something about cats, could in his dilemma think of nothing but "Kilkenny." He finally gave them an order for their cow, and subsequently took them by surprise by calling to see them. A very sweet-looking, delicate little woman coaxed her cow from Captain Woodward, and the next morning sent to us for breakfast a nice roll of fresh butter.

At this same place, at a house near by my office which I accidentally entered, I met to my surprise two prim and formal English maiden ladies, of mature age, who proved to be sisters of a resident of Jacksonville, whom I knew, by the name of Mathew Stewart. They had not heard from their brother since the war began. So our interview was quite lively and agreeable, and they surely looked upon that invasion of the Yankee foe as in every way an interesting and welcome one.

Upon arrival of General Smith at Holly Springs, I was instructed to communicate with General Washburn for orders. Upon their receipt, [I] ordered General Hatch to proceed by easy marches with his division to La Grange. Taking up the line of march with the Second Division, the cavalry all reached the Memphis and Charleston Railroad, near La Grange, on August 28, having been absent in the field for nearly a month, without baggage transportation or camp equipage. So that the return to the limited comforts and luxuries of our army home and mess at Memphis, soon afterwards, was very refreshing and duly appreciated by myself and staff officers.

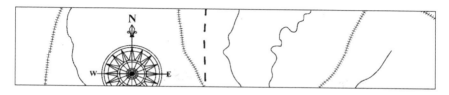

13. Reorganization and Controversy

After the fight of the cavalry at Hurricane Creek, Mississippi, on August 13, in which Colonel M. H. Starr distinguished himself by driving the rebels out of their fortifications, he was permitted to return to Memphis to hasten the equipment of his regiment, which had not been fully mounted and armed after re-enlistment. It was thus that he happened to be in the city at the time it was attacked.

General Forrest, finding that he had not sufficient force to prevent the advance of General Smith's army, or give him battle at the Tallahatchie or Oxford, conceived the idea of making a raid on Memphis, with the hope that he could thus cause the withdrawal of the Federal army from its expedition southward. He was fully advised of the condition of affairs at Memphis by rebel sympathizers in the city, and the weakness of our force there, and took advantage of the occasion. Leaving General Chalmers to occupy the attention of General Smith's command, he made a forced march with the effective force of three brigades. Starting from Oxford on August 19, [he] entered Memphis from the Hernando road at 4 o'clock A.M. [on] the 21st, scattering his troops throughout the city with a view of hastily gathering up such plunder as he could, his main object being to capture General Washburn and other officers in the city, with such property as he could gobble up in his hurried movements.

Colonel Starr, being in camp near the Hernando road with a small detachment of his regiment, on the approach of the rebels threw his men in Forrest's front, retarding as much as possible his advance. [He] then galloped rapidly to General Washburn's headquarters, where he rushed in without the usual ceremony of announcing his arrival to the general. Knowing the location of his room, [he] burst open the door and succeeded in awakening and hustling him out of bed, and without giving him time to arrange his toilet, got him safely within Fort Pickering. Colonel Starr then galloped off and stirred up the provost guard, notifying officers here and there of the attack, and then returned with the utmost speed to his small command. Getting together such other detachments as he could arouse,

[he] continued to fight the rebels so long as any could be found, until he was severely wounded by a ball which passed through his hip and abdomen. The wound was severe and dangerous, and disabled him for further duty. But he managed to make his escape, although he and his little command were at one time almost surrounded by the enemy. He recovered sufficiently to be removed to his home at Jacksonville, Illinois, but died soon after from the effects of the injuries received in this engagement.

Sometime previous to this occurrence, Colonel Starr had expressed a desire to write a history of the 6th Illinois Cavalry, formerly my regiment. To aid in this purpose, I furnished him with many valuable documents, which in some manner were mislaid or lost, and never afterward recovered. Colonel Starr was a brave, zealous, and capable officer. His death was a loss which was deeply felt by the regiment and other army associates.

The rebels did not do as much damage in Memphis as was expected. They attacked the provost guardhouse, with a view of liberating the prisoners there confined, but were handsomely repulsed. They then intended an attack on General [Ralph P.] Buckland's headquarters, but made a mistake in the street, while the general quietly made his escape.[1] Another party surrounded the Gayosa House, with a view to capture [General] S. A. Hurlbut, who happened to be in the city en route to the Department of the Gulf, but who that night stopped with Colonel A. R. Eddy. By that time the remnants of troops, infantry and cavalry, were thoroughly aroused, and with or without officers, were resisting the rebels. Firing could be heard in all directions, but mostly on the outskirts of the city near where the camps were located. The fort was, as the rebels well knew, impregnable to their forces. The time they could afford to stay was short. Probably, too, they wished to spare the city, where they had many friends and sympathizers. So, after hurriedly riding about the streets, whooping and yelling and playing pranks when the whim seized them, they with such prisoners and plunder as could be hastily captured vanished like the wind, retreating whence they came. Then all became quiet and serene, and the citizens and soldiers in the city soon recovered from their astonishment.

Owing to the hasty manner in which General Washburn had issued his dispatches to General Smith, or their being misinterpreted by the latter, the troops were not thrown against Forrest to intercept his retreat at Panola, but were moved towards Holly Springs instead of the direction of the enemy. Thus Forrest's command, instead of being seriously crippled or destroyed as it might have been, was allowed to go scot-free, returning south the way it came, unmolested and unharmed; and the Federal expedition, gotten up at such trouble and expense, returned when it should have gone on with the invasion of the enemy's country. By the unfortunate course pursued, nothing beyond keeping Forrest engaged and away from Sherman's communication was gained by all the long fatiguing marches endured by the troops during the last expedition sent out by General Washburn and commanded by General A. J. Smith.

Soon after this, General Smith's troops were withdrawn and sent in boats to Cairo en route to Nashville. General Mower's division [was sent] into Arkansas to operate against the rebels under Price, my one division of rear cavalry (Winslow's) also going to Arkansas and thence to Missouri. Soon after the other division (Hatch's) proceeded to Middle Tennessee, where Washburn was also ordered for temporary duty in the field. Had General Hurlbut been retained permanently at Memphis, with his thorough knowledge of the country and greater experience with the usual methods and operations of the enemy, it would have gone far to have prevented the unfortunate occurrences that resulted from placing less capable officers in such an important command.

During the summer and fall of 1864, many changes of officers of high rank from one command to another were made throughout the army, especially in the West. Troops were hurriedly sent away from one department to another without proper preparation or transfer, and much confusion and conflict of authority [was] thereby occasioned. General E. R. S. Canby,[2] commanding the Division of West Mississippi, exercised for a time control over all the troops on either side and adjacent to the Mississippi River, among others the remnants of the XVI and XVII Army Corps, really belonging to General Sherman's division.

At the death of General McPherson, it was thought that Major General John A. Logan, whose distinguished services were so well known, and whose fitness to command was recognized by General Grant, by the army, and by the people of the entire country, would be assigned to the command of the Army and Department of the Tennessee, a promotion which, it would seem, properly fell to him in the midst of battle as the senior officer present. Logan had persistently maintained his position against the repeated assaults of the enemy where the battle fiercely raged. He and his brave corps bore the brunt, and with intrepid gallantry, did much to gain the victory which saved Sherman and his army from defeat. General Logan, however, was an officer of volunteers. Although he had gained his knowledge of the art of war in the face of the enemy—was capable, worthy, and efficient, and always successful wherever placed (which is more than can be truly said of some officers who held higher positions)—yet he was passed over, or pushed aside, [so] that an officer of another army, lately brought from the East, might be given the place. Under all the circumstances, it still seems to many that General Logan had fairly earned, and was justly entitled to, the position for long and faithful service in the field, in the army with which he had so long been identified. I recognize General [O. O.] Howard's[3] ability as an officer and sterling worth as a man—and also General Sherman's right to choose his army commanders—but, nevertheless, he may have erred in his judgment on that occasion.

It should be remembered, however, that General Sherman at that time, with consummate skill and persistent effort, by a series of brilliant strategic maneuvers, rarely if ever excelled, had pushed his armies forward into the interior of the enemy's country, forcing the rebel army under [Joseph E.] Johnston and [John Bell] Hood[4] to withdraw from Atlanta, which was occupied by the Union troops on September 2 [1864]. For the victories gained, how much is due to General Logan, who fell into command of the Army of the Tennessee during the hardest fight of the campaign, is a matter for the future historian to determine.

In the meantime, General Grant had, with the Army of the Potomac, crossed the Rapidan and fought through the Wilderness to the vicinity of Richmond, after desperate fighting and immense loss to his army, as well as to that of the rebel army under the greatest general the South produced—Robert E. Lee. While Sherman was preparing for his march through Georgia, Grant was arranging to drive [Jubal] Early out of the Shenandoah Valley.[5]

General Canby's military division included the Department of Arkansas and the Gulf, and for a time, a part of the Department of the Tennessee. In conjunction with the navy, the general had sent an expedition to threaten Mobile. Forts Gaines and Morgan had been captured, and the enemy practically cut off from the waters of the Gulf of Mexico. Up to about this time it had been the intention for General Sherman's army to swing through Alabama against Mobile. But this was given up after its arrival at Atlanta, of which place possession was only gained by fatiguing marches, hard fighting, and immense loss of life.

It had been General Sherman's wish that General Smith, after arriving at Oxford, should swing over to Columbus, Mississippi, and thence to Decatur, Alabama. But Forrest's raid on Memphis resulted in causing Smith's return to Memphis. It was under orders from General Canby that General Mower's division of infantry and my Second Division of cavalry (Colonel Winslow's) were ordered into Arkansas, to Duval's Bluff, to operate under General Steele against Price's rebel forces, reported to be making their way northward into Missouri, while under General Sherman's orders, General A. J. Smith's division was ordered on transports to Cairo, with the intention of proceeding thence to Nashville. But from Cairo, by order of [the] War Department, it was sent up into Missouri for temporary service in Rosecrans' department, to assist in expelling Price's rebels from that state.

Thus, the force at Memphis was so much reduced that no further offensive demonstrations could be made from there at that time into northern Mississippi. The rebels, after retreating from Memphis, fell back to Granada, Mississippi. Forrest was at once advised of the departure of the troops into Arkansas and Missouri, and promptly took advantage of the opportunity to extend his operations. The state of Mississippi was re-districted and Chalmers placed in command of the northern district. Forrest was soon after ordered on an expedition against Sherman's communications in Middle Tennessee. Notwithstanding nearly 20,000 troops were sent out against him, he succeeded in thoroughly destroying the railroad west [south] of Pulaski, but was finally repulsed and driven off by the troops under General [Lovell S.] Rousseau.[6]

General Napoleon J. Dana[7] had been assigned to command at Vicksburg, with jurisdiction over Washburn's command at Memphis and the District of West Tennessee. On September 14, the 7th Kansas was sent to Cairo to join Smith's division. Thus it was that after untiring and incessant work I had recruited, reorganized, and brought to a high state of efficiency the cavalry with which I had been so long identified, it seemed only to have become a treasure for every major general near to snatch at and appropriate for operations at distant points. By piecemeal it was cut and carved up and taken from me, and left subject to the whims of military cormorants who were insatiable and perfectly indifferent to the claims of others.

While the Second Division (Winslow's) was following Price into Missouri and soon came under the control of Rosecrans, the First Division (Hatch's) was marching into Middle Tennessee, presumably for temporary duty, but was thereafter lost entirely from my command. To add to the perplexity of my situation, about this juncture, General [Joseph F.] Knipe,[8] General Howard's chief of cavalry, came to Memphis and assumed control over me and the cavalry with which I had hoped to make important expeditions in the field.

This was a little more than I could bear without making an appeal to someone. General Howard had only recently been assigned to the command of the Army of the Tennessee, and was a total stranger to me. With General Sherman I had been long and pleasantly associated. I had known him well since the first year of the war. We had frequently corresponded with each other, and he had told me when I last met him to write to him whenever I had anything to communicate, or when anything went wrong to let him know and he would assist me in any way possible, consistent with his duty and the interests of the service. Therefore, I addressed a letter to the general, without any thought of being insubordinate, or in any manner disrespectful to General Howard. If not strictly according to military etiquette, it certainly seemed justifiable, considering the trying situation in which I was placed:

> Headquarters Cavalry Corps,
> Dist. of West Tenn.
> Memphis Tenn. Oct. 5th 1864.
> General:—
>
> I take the liberty of addressing you personally upon a subject which is certainly of considerable importance to me if not to the service.
>
> About fifteen months ago, immediately after my return from Port Hudson, I was placed by Gen. Hurlbut's order in command of the Cavalry Division, 16th Army Corps, and remained in command thereof until last February, when I was virtually superseded by Gen. Wm. Sooy Smith, who assumed command of my Division during the expedition, with the object and result of which, you are well acquainted. That it was not successful, God knows was no fault of mine. Immediately after its return, by dint of much labor, I succeeded in reenlisting as veterans, over three-fourths of the entire command which were eligible. By virtue of this reenlistment, I might have obtained a leave of absence, but steadily remained with the disorganized remnant, which could certainly perform nothing to reflect credit upon its commander.
>
> In this condition, with a mounted force of about 1,500 men I was found when Forrest made his raid into West Tennessee and Kentucky, resulting in the capture of Fort Pillow and Union City. When my veteran troops had returned, and I had succeeded in reorganizing and re-mounting a portion of them, Gen. Sturgis appeared and assumed command of the whole, and I took part in an expedition, with the result of which you are also acquainted. I again reiterate what I have stated in my official report, that the movements which resulted in disaster were made against my earnest advice and protest, and it would be unjust to the brave men under my command to speak of their conduct under those trying circumstances in other than the highest praise. Since the return of that expedition I have taken part in two others under Gen. A. J. Smith, each of which occupied over twenty days. In connection with these I should be sorry to claim credit for anything which was not justly due me, but I do assert that, on the first of those expeditions, when Gen. A. J. Smith had determined to move from Pontotoc upon the enemy who was entrenched in a strong

position, one with which I was well acquainted at Prairie Mount, which, if we had been successful in taking, could not have been with a loss of less than 1,500 men; by my earnest advice Gen. Smith changed his plan and marched to Tupelo. The movement was a strategic one which drew the enemy from his entrenchments and resulted in the battle of Harrisburg, with the eminent success of which you are well advised. In the second expedition, after Gen. Forrest had left our front below the Tallahatchie, and made his raid upon Memphis, I requested permission from Gen. Smith to pursue him with my entire force, as in his jaded condition satisfactory results would certainly have been accomplished. I was not, however, permitted to do so, but was tied hand and foot to an infantry command with a train of 300 wagons, and my command was used entirely in guarding the front, flanks and rear of the infantry and train. Notwithstanding all this, by dint of work and perseverance I have succeeded in almost entirely re-mounting and arming (in a great measure with Spencer carbines) my corps, and venture to state that I have now the finest Cavalry Command in the service. By referring to the report of the Inspector General, District West Tennessee, of Sept. 30th 1864 you will find the following remark:

"I am happy to say that, at this time the Cavalry Corps, Dist. West Tennessee is in better condition as to mounts, arms, discipline and drill, than any body of cavalry I have seen during three years in the West."

Just when my Cavalry is in shape when I can use it with advantage to the Government, and honor to myself, Brig. Gen. Joseph F. Knipe, of whom I have never heard in connection with cavalry, and who (after having conversed with him) I am satisfied is almost wholly unacquainted with that arm of the service, appears upon the scene and assumes control of my command. Some time since, however, it having been considerably strengthened by recruits, by direction of Gen. Washburn, I organized it into two Divisions, placing Gen. Hatch in command of one, and Col. Winslow of the other. With the records of those two officers you are well acquainted; suffice it to say that they both suit me well as Division Commanders. Col. Winslow is at present absent with 3,200 of his division in Arkansas or Missouri and Gen. Hatch is on an expedition eastward towards the Tennessee River, but I look anxiously for their return at an early day.

I beg leave General, to refer you to our past intercourse, and express the hope that when I have acted under your immediate direction, both as a regimental and brigade commander, that my services thus rendered met your approval. That I have always been successful when my actions were untrammeled by others of less experience in cavalry service, cannot, I think, be denied. If I have lost aught of your confidence as a cavalry officer, I but simply ask an opportunity to redeem it. If this command, with which I have been identified for the past fifteen months, and which I have striven hard to place in condition for active service, is to be sent to the front I but ask the liberty of leading it there, and not to be placed second to a man in whom I can possibly feel no confidence as a cavalry officer. Brig. Gen. Knipe proposes to cut my command in two, sending one half away under another officer, leaving me here with the remainder. As I have told you before both verbally and by letter; *block out the road you wish me to travel, and I stake my life upon my ability to make the trip.*

What I then ask, General, is your support. I request the necessary orders from you to select from my command a force of five or six thousand men (which I can readily do, and leave sufficient cavalry here for all practical purposes) and to join you in the front when the proper time arrives. I wish sufficient authority to organize and to proceed with such command free from the orders of your subordinate commanders. I had, some time since, selected a route, in case I should be called upon to make such an expedition, viz.: via Aberdeen, Tuscaloosa, Selma and Montgomery. That I could travel that route with immense advantage to the service, I feel confident, and earnestly trust that my wishes in the matter may meet your approval. Permit me General, to lead into the field *untrammeled*, the troops which I now command, and if the result does not reflect credit upon my superior officers, I shall certainly be at fault. As I have but seldom troubled you with correspondence, I ask to this your earnest attention.

Very Respectfully and Truly,
B. H. Grierson

The letter was sent by the hand of Captain S. L. Woodward of my staff as special messenger, with the hope that he would see General Sherman and thus have an opportunity to supplement by word of mouth what pen could not write. But the general was south [northwest] of Atlanta busily occupied watching Hood's movements, and it was impracticable for Woodward to go through to the general's headquarters while the rebels under Forrest and Wheeler were threatening his communications. The letter was mailed and reached its destination, but the general was so engrossed with his own affairs that he referred it to General Howard, undoubtedly with words of commendation for the writer. General Howard, being unacquainted with me personally and knowing but little of my former friendly relations with

General Sherman, could not be expected to thoroughly understand all the circumstances bearing upon the case.

———

Gen. Sherman's answer to my letter, written in the midst of his more immediate and overwhelming engagements, at least clearly manifests his personal regard and appreciation of my services:

Headquarters Mil. Div. Miss.
In the field, Gaylesville, Ala.
Oct. 21st 1864.
Dear General:—

I have received your long letter and have shown it to Gen. Howard, who says that Gen. Knipe is not designed to command the cavalry, but as Chief of Cavalry or Inspector. I understand you to have the Division at Memphis, with two brigades, Hatch and Winslow, but for a time Gen. Canby exercised a command on the river, pursuant to some order of the War Department, which threw matters into some confusion and led to the detachment of the troops to Arkansas and Missouri, which will never get back unless Rosecrans can manage to overwhelm and destroy Price. Howard has always wanted to bring some of his Cavalry over here, but the distance was so great, and the uncertainties of Forrest's positions and movements prevented my making distinct orders. Even now I am satisfied the best work Cavalry can do is to operate from Memphis against the railroad from Corinth south, to prevent Forrest and Hood getting over to Tuscumbia and operating in Tennessee. I have driven him from Georgia and he is now at Pine Mountain, the end of the Selma road, with the object of hanging near my flank and preventing me advancing into Georgia. He can not do this, but if he moves over to Tuscumbia, it will force me to change somewhat the position of my forces.

I hardly think the long march from Memphis to me is practicable. Indeed nearly all the attempts of that kind have been fruitless; but if you can hover about Ripley and dash against that railroad from Corinth to Meridian, you can force Forrest to detach from Tuscumbia, or actually to give up that road, which is now the only one that can supply an army in threatening distance of Tennessee. It will at all events be impossible for you to reach me in time for contemplated movements.

I assure you of my good will and friendship, and I will so express myself to Gen. Howard. It was Gen. Grant that sent Gen. Wm. Sooy Smith to Memphis with the Cavalry last winter, which gave him command that time, and I sent Gen. Sturgis down, as I thought him familiar with both Cavalry and Infantry, to manage that trip. Accidents will happen, and I want you if you are ambitious of a lasting military fame to persevere. Do your best. Keep your command in as good shape as possible, and an opportunity of distinction will arrive when you least expect it. The war is not yet over; is hardly begun for the Cavalry arm of the service, and I will promise you as brilliant chances for distinction as you could ask. We must break up the big armies, and when they disintegrate, then will be your time. All the Memphis Cavalry should be well out towards Tupelo, all the time; not in position but moving and living on the country. Keep active, and I promise you all the honor and credit you covet.

Your Sincere Friend
W. T. Sherman
Major General

At this time Hatch's division had started eastward to the Tennessee River, Winslow's division was following Price into Missouri, and there was nothing at Memphis but small detachments of cavalry from the different regiments of the two divisions left back with unserviceable horses and dismounted men. Altogether there was hardly sufficient cavalry for picket and patrol duty, and nothing whatever effective for a movement into Mississippi as then desired by General Sherman.

To anyone who knew all the circumstances, it would seem that General Howard need not have taken any exception to my letter to General Sherman, considering the terms upon which I stood with the general previously. But, if it is remembered that General Howard did not know, he having been recently assigned to the command, perhaps his reply may not seem strange nor unwarranted:

Headquarters Dep't. Army of the Tenn.
Near Gaylesville, Ala. Oct. 22nd 1864.
General:—

Your Letter of Oct. 5th 1864 to Major Gen. Sherman has been referred to me. Your complaint seems to be in substance that Gen. Knipe has been assigned to the command of your Division, and your request is to hold your command subject to no orders of subordinate commanders, i.e., subordinate to Gen. Sherman. Now, first, your Division has not been given to Gen. Knipe, nor is there any such intention. Gen. Knipe is simply placed on my staff as Chief of Cavalry, and will be with me in the field. The interests of the service demanded a small division of Cavalry with the army, but the greater portion under an able officer on the Mississippi. Such, I took you to be and am therefore the more surprised at your letter. As to your request, I think you ought to have referred it to me. I can hardly be held responsible for the Army and Department of the Tennessee without Cavalry, and be assured, General, that Gen. Sherman and myself cooperate in every movement. Surely you do not wish to leave the field and go upon staff duty, or if you do so wish, we can not well spare you from your troops. I want all the Cavalry well mounted and well in hand to assist the Corps or District Commanders in watching the enemy, and in going upon important expeditions when ordered. A very small force, not to exceed three thousand Cavalry, will answer my purpose here. I do not even insist upon having Gen. Hatch if you need him. Unless the small division is on the way here, I suspect I shall have to do without it altogether. In that case you will command all the Cavalry as heretofore, but dispel from your mind any apprehension that your services are not appreciated, and write to me or the Cavalry Officer on my staff fully, with regard to your command, and all your complaints or requests will be carefully attended to. An appeal over my head is improper unless I have the opportunity of endorsing. If you are not satisfied to serve under my command, please so inform me frankly.

> Very Respectfully
> Your Ob't. Serv't.
> O. O. Howard
> Major General

General Howard evidently did not fully realize the situation, for General Knipe plainly indicated that he was authorized to take command as chief of cavalry, just as General W. Sooy Smith had done, without direct orders. It was only a natural inference that a similar result would follow General Knipe's arrival on the return of the cavalry, which at that time was contemplated, as it was distinctly understood that it was sent away only for temporary duty. Nothing could be further from my wish than to leave my command for staff duty. My complaint to Sherman was that my troops had been taken from me, and that I wanted to get them back under my control and to retain command of the Memphis cavalry as then organized.

Although it was plain to be seen that, during the summer and fall of 1864, the daring rebels of the South, aided in every possible manner by their copperhead allies of the North, were putting forth tremendous efforts to regain the territory they had lost in the three past years of relentless warfare. Still, it was observable by those in position to know and watch the events transpiring that the Confederacy had become greatly weakened and that the long, fierce, gigantic struggle was gradually but surely drawing to a close, when final victory would rest in triumph with the cause of the Union. Therefore, those who held life positions in the regular army, temporarily vacated for higher ones in the volunteer service, naturally began to look about them in concerted wonderment as to what would be done when the great volunteer army of the Union, that grand bulwark of national strength and life, was mustered out and the new army organized, enlarged as it necessarily must be for a considerable time, on a peace footing, by the government. Already there was a perceptible, though hidden, movement among the West Point graduates to push their way to the front with intent, so far as possible, to bring the army under the control of their own class, with the hope of eventually appropriating to themselves whatever distinction might be thus gained from the closing operations of the War of the Rebellion.

Brigadier General Morgan L. Smith, who fell temporarily into the command at Memphis on the departure of General Washburn, felt the crowding tendency of the influence referred to. He had served with great honor and distinction, and felt that he, like many other gallant and successful officers of volunteers, had been pushed aside and not advanced or promoted in accordance with his just desserts, simply that place might be given to those really less deserving. Without attaching any blame to any particular individual, he plainly indicated that facts well known to him fully justified his assertions. General Smith quickly saw the necessity for active measures and would have gladly organized and sent out an expedition to meet and thwart the rebels, who were at the time he assumed command almost nightly attacking our picket lines and threatening another attack on Memphis. But upon examination, the general found that there were no troops at or in the vicinity to make any aggressive movement against the enemy.

He sent for me with a view of getting a clearer understanding as to the whereabouts of my command and to see what could be done to hasten the return of the cavalry. I at once informed the general as to the disposition which had been made by others of the cavalry properly belonging at Memphis, and the uncertainty of its return within any reasonable time; that all I had left were detachments of the different regiments, with the unserviceable horses [and the] sick and dismounted men, out of which no effective force could be gotten beyond what was constantly needed for picket and patrol duty. Colonel Winslow had written that his division would be retained in Canby's command—probably—if something was not done at once to get it back to Memphis. General Smith, feeling the great necessity for the quick return of the absent cavalry, decided it was best that I be sent to St. Louis forthwith, thinking that I might by my personal exertions be able to have the troops returned at an earlier date than then seemed probable.

In accordance with the orders and instructions of the general, I started at once for St. Louis. Upon arrival there, [I] proceeded to General Rosecrans' headquarters, where I met the general, who received me in a very cordial manner and at once explained the condition of affairs within his department, the whereabouts of Price, [and] the disposition that had been made. [He] expressed the hope that the rebels would soon be drawn into a place where they would be overpowered and destroyed. [He] said he would cause my cavalry to be returned at the earliest possible moment; that he could not get at the troops at once, but hoped that he would have his own cavalry concentrated for operations and that then mine would be ordered back and returned to me. The general told me about the great conspiracy which existed throughout Missouri to aid Price and his rebels; that if he had his way he would shoot or hang the ringleaders when caught, and that he hoped to get them into his clutches at an early date. The general was very vivacious in his manner, and as I had never met him before and knew him only from his military services, he seemed pleased to give some details of his services as commander of the Army of the Cumberland. All of which afforded me much pleasure.

We were still thus engaged when General [John A.] Rawlins was announced. I had not met the latter since I saw him after the fall of Vicksburg, and was very glad to see him again. As General Rosecrans had stepped out of the room for a moment, I seized the opportunity to advise General Rawlins as to my business there, and asked him to give such orders as would insure as speedy return of my cavalry as possible. All of which he promised to do. Meeting the general at the Planters House subsequently, I learned that the orders had been given.

The latter part of October, Brigadier General J. H. Wilson,[9] whom I out-ranked [by] several months, was assigned to duty with the brevet of major general and sent to report to General Sherman, and [was] placed in command of the cavalry of the Military Division of the Mississippi and was thus enabled to assume command over a number of officers really senior in rank to him. He at once set about the reorganization of the cavalry, which was widely scattered. Early in November, I received the following telegram:

Nashville Tenn. Nov. [illegible] 1864,
To Gen. Grierson:

Winslow's troops are ordered here; meet them at St. Louis and direct them to Louisville. I will send Col. [Albert] Brackett[10] to confer with you in regard to the movement. Capt. Woodward of your staff is here, I will send detailed instructions by him.

J. H. Wilson B'v't. Maj. Gen.

Captain Woodward rejoined me on November 9, and the detailed instructions which he brought were as follows:

Hd'qrs. Cav. Corps, M.D.M.

Nashville Nov. 6th 1864

Special Orders

No. 7

I. Brig. Gen'l. B. H. Grierson will assume command of the 4th Div. Cav. Corps. M.D.M. consisting of the Division now under command of E. F. Winslow, and such other troops as may be assigned to him.

II. In pursuance of instructions from Maj. Gen. Thomas, Brig. Gen. Grierson will collect the various detachments of his Division, now in West Tenn. and Missouri and with them join the Cavalry Corps at this place, via Louisville Ky. or such other route as may be found more convenient. All men on detached duty mounted or dismounted, of this Division, will be immediately returned to their regiments. The command will be remounted and equipped for the field at St. Louis Mo. and Louisville Ky. with the least possible delay.

III. Gen. Grierson will also send the dismounted men of Hatch's Division under proper officers to Louisville Ky. with the least possible delay.

By Command of
Maj. Gen'l. Wilson

The foregoing order assigned me to the command of half my own corps, and that half at the time out of my reach, being near the state line between Missouri and Kansas under control of Generals Canby and Rosecrans, both fighting for its possession.

Upon investigation, finding that nothing more could be done then and that my presence at St. Louis would be for some days unnecessary, I made a short visit to relatives in Illinois, having business in connection with my command at Springfield under instructions received from General Smith. Before leaving St. Louis, I again saw General Rosecrans. Although the general wished very much to keep the cavalry in his own department, he promised to do all in his power to hasten its return to Memphis, to which point it was understood [Lieut. Col. Frederick W.] Benteen,[11] with part of the Fourth Division, was marching through Arkansas. The troops had been marching and fighting their way through Arkansas and Missouri; had traveled over 1,000 miles; and by their fighting and good soldiership had won battles—praise from and for every successive commander, and were detained by each as long as possible. General A. J. Smith, who with his division had been stopped at Cairo when en route to Nashville and sent into Missouri, was directed to proceed, with his force and the division which had crossed into Arkansas, to Nashville.

Leaving matters in the special charge of Captain S. L. Woodward, and learning that the scattered troops had been ordered to St. Louis, I left on the 10th for Illinois. Within a few days, some of the detachments came in, as they could escape the clutches of the officers who wished to retain them. On November 15, Captain Woodward advised me by telegraph that a detachment from Benteen's command, amounting in all to about 300 men, had reached St. Louis and that Benteen was, in accordance with orders from General [Samuel] Curtis,[12] so it was reported, marching from Kansas through Missouri and Arkansas to Memphis. General Mower had previously been relieved and assigned to a division in General Frank Blair's corps.[13] His old division and that of Smith's had been assigned, one to the XV Corps and one to the XVII Corps, and the XVI Army Corps, as an organization, abolished.

Captain Woodward, therefore, obtained the necessary orders for those detachments to be sent to Memphis, and left St. Louis the next day, via Cairo, for Memphis on the *Marble City,* with about 400 men. The river was low, and the boat got aground and did not reach Cairo until November 19. There he met the remnants of Hatch's division, with Colonel Lynch in charge, en route to Nashville, having been ordered there by General Washburn, who had returned to that place after his expedition over to the Tennessee River. Woodward had about 200 men of the 2nd New Jersey Cavalry with him on the *Marble City.* Orders had been given for the other detachments to follow, and [I] presumed all would have reached and left St. Louis by November 20.

It was, therefore, unnecessary for me to return to St. Louis. [So] I arranged to return direct to Memphis, with a view of getting the divisions together and to march across from there to Nashville, which would have been much the best route had Benteen returned through Arkansas to Memphis, as was then expected. General Wilson, however, became impatient at the delay occasioned by the detention of the cavalry in Missouri, and relieved his anxious mind by a letter addressed to me under date of November 20, 1864, from Nashville:

> This will be handed you by 1st Lieut. Henry E. Noyes of my staff. He is authorized to bring your Division to this place. In spite of instructions sent you by Capt. Woodward of your staff, it seems that you have misunderstood the instructions of Gen. Thomas, now vested with ample authority over all the troops left in the Military Division of the Mississippi. When I wrote you from Gaylesville it was expected that the operations alluded to in my

communication, would be successfully carried out; but since then, owing to the threatening attitude of Hood's Army, Gen. Thomas has decided upon a different policy—essential to the execution of which is the concentration of a large force of Cavalry in Middle Tennessee. It was to this end that instructions were sent to you by Capt. Woodward, to bring your command to this place by the most direct and practicable route, ample authority having been given for your reorganization at St. Louis. Maj. Gen. Rosecrans informs Gen. Thomas that, through the representations of Capt. Woodward, he had been induced to send your dismounted men direct to Memphis, in compliance with my request. Capt. Wood-ward, in using such authority, has transcended his instructions. My letter of instructions to you was plain and unmistakable, and neither yourself nor your Adjutant General could reasonably affect to misconstrue it into a consent for ordering your Divi-sion to Memphis. Gen. Knipe has been sent to that place for the purpose of bringing your detachments and trains, as well as those of Gen. Hatch to this place at once. It is also understood here that Winslow has been ordered by Gen. Curtis across the country to Memphis. Lieut. Noyes, you will perceive, has been armed with ample authority to bring him from there, or wherever else he may be without delay. I am also informed that, instead of being at St. Louis, attending to the orders sent you through Capt. Woodward, you are now, or have been at Chicago Ills. There being no record at Army Headquarters of a leave of absence to you, you will report without delay by what authority you are absent from St. Louis or Memphis, your original post.

To which lofty and imposing communication I answered as follows [December 1, 1864]:

Yours of Nov. 20th by Lt. Noyes has just been received by mail at this place. Since Capt. Woodward reached me with your orders I have twice written you, neither of which letters you appear to have received. I shall send this by special messenger, that you may be more sure of receiving it.

That your orders and those of Maj. Gen. Thomas concerning the Cavalry, have not been carried out, is certainly no fault of mine. Half the command was in Missouri and Arkansas, where it could not be reached, and was acting under the orders of officers above me in authority. The other half was at Memphis and could not be taken away from there, because Maj. Gen'l. Washburn would not permit it, nor will he now, until Gen. Dana arrives. He is expected here next Saturday. The Cavalry which first arrived at St. Louis, and which was ordered to Memphis by Gen. Rosecrans upon Capt. Woodward's suggestion, was a detachment of 400 men consisting of detachments of from one to ten men of every company in seven regiments; these men had been absent from their companies seventy-five days without clothing etc., and had not been paid for six months; nor could they receive pay until the description rolls of each one were sent to the officers commanding them; besides this they all belonged to the regiments which Lt. Noyes and Gen. Washburn arranged to leave here. When Capt. Woodward arrived at St. Louis, after leaving you, he found that, with the exception of this mixed detachment, all the rest of Winslow's Division had proceeded back through Missouri and Arkansas, and he received intelligence from officers of that command that they had already been detached from Gen. Curtis' command and sent overland to Memphis. Woodward, therefore, told Gen. Rosecrans that it was your wish to have the Cavalry concentrated at some convenient point as quickly as possible, and sent to Nashville. Gen. Rosecrans stated that it was contrary to his orders to [do] so, but agreed with Capt. Woodward that as at that time it was more than probable that the majority of Col. Winslow's troops would come out at Memphis, it would be best for that detachment to go there to re-fit. In doing this Capt. Woodward also acted in obedience to my directions; as Memphis would certainly have been the best point to have concentrated, had Winslow's command arrived there as was expected at that time. Besides, could I have concentrated Winslow's and the Vicksburg Cavalry at Memphis, immediately upon the receipt of your orders, as was undoubtedly your intention, I would have had force sufficient to have marched overland via Fort Henry to Nashville, which would have been the most expeditious route; but as you will see I was powerless; my command being scattered, by orders from superior authority, from Kansas to Middle Tennessee. I certainly understood your instructions; as every move which I have made, was with the intention of carrying them out with the least possible delay.

In answer to your query as to why I was absent from St. Louis or Memphis, I have to state, that it was by virtue of "special orders No. 183, extract 7, from Headquarters Dist. of West Tennessee," by which I was sent to "Missouri and Illinois on military business connected with my command." While in St. Louis, I made application to Washington through Capt. Coryell of the Cavalry Bureau, for an entire re-mount for Col. Winslow's command, which I obtained, and had the horses—two thousand in number—"shod in readiness for the field." My being here in the first place, was for the purpose of getting together all the troops I possibly could in pursuance of instructions from Maj. Gen. Howard and yourself, in order that I might make the expedition referred to by you, and which was afterwards abandoned.

I never reported in person to General Wilson for duty, and the instructions he gave to me could not be carried into effect at the time they were received, and they became entirely inoperative. It should also here be remembered that previously, when my cavalry corps was well in hand and in good condition, soon after the return of General A. J. Smith's expedition the last of August 1864, I had hoped to make an effective demonstration to the eastward through Mississippi and Alabama, as indicated in my letters to General Sherman. It had been the general's wish that General Smith, instead of returning to Memphis, should move on eastward with his infantry divisions, via Columbus, to Decatur, Alabama, and I had then wished to make a raid with the cavalry to join General Sherman in Georgia, or anywhere else he desired.

I was desirous to undertake the march by the general's expressed wish to have me and my command again with him in the field. I had given the subject much thought, had gained a thorough knowledge of the country through which I should pass en route, and felt confident of my ability to make such an expedition every way successful. It was a movement which General Sherman had desired to have me make, which General Howard alluded to, and which General Thomas subsequently abandoned on account of General Hood's threatened movement of his army northward into Middle Tennessee. It was similar to the movement which General Wilson made with cavalry the following year, near the close of the war, when the necessity for such an expedition had passed by, making it then, as General Grant states in his *Memoirs*, "of little or no importance."[14] But my well-trained, disciplined troops were drawn away to distant points, far beyond my reach, leaving me virtually without any effective force at a time when most needed.

At the close of Price's raid through Arkansas and Missouri, General Rosecrans, needing cavalry, had applied to General Sherman for Winslow's division to remain in Missouri. But Sherman, on November 1, 1864, telegraphed that it must be sent back to Memphis. Soon after, General Canby gave similar instructions to General Rosecrans. General Morgan L. Smith, recognizing the importance of my contemplated expedition through Mississippi and Alabama, ordered me to Missouri and Illinois with the hope that by my personal exertion I might be able to get together enough cavalry in time to execute the desired movement, the plans for which had met his heartiest approval. Nevertheless, upon my return to Memphis, when those plans had to be abandoned and my hopes deferred, I in good faith set to work to carry out the instructions received, which would take me, with less than half my former command, to Nashville. I felt then, and believe now, that it would have been better to have marched the cavalry directly across the country than to have it shipped around by boats via Louisville, as there was ample time for the movement, which was certainly practicable and fully warranted by the instructions received. In endeavoring to concentrate the division at Memphis, I was not unmindful of the needs of the enlisted men away from camps, [and] deprived of their description rolls and the pay so long due them.

The change in commanders at Memphis continued. Upon return of General Washburn, General Morgan L. Smith was assigned to command the post and defenses of Vicksburg. The cavalry in that vicinity had been ordered to Memphis, where General Dana soon after arrived and established his headquarters, his command being designated as the Department of the Mississippi; he being subject to the orders of General Canby, commanding the Military Division of West Mississippi with headquarters at New Orleans. In the meantime, the small force of cavalry at Memphis had been kept actively employed under the supervision of Colonels Kargé and Noble, scouting and patrolling the surrounding country as far as practicable, and also performing the regular picket duty. An attack on Memphis was at that time expected, and the utmost vigilance was required in order to gain information as to the movements of the enemy and prevent the disasters that might otherwise arise from any surprise. Great credit is due Colonels Kargé and Noble for the judicious manner in which they discharged the difficult duties devolving upon them at that period.

By the middle of November 1864—after active operations had been suspended in the vicinity of Richmond, Virginia, and quiet had settled down upon the Armies of the Potomac for the winter—General Sherman, having perfected his arrangements, destroyed Atlanta, burned the bridges behind him, [and] started on his memorable march through Georgia. The rebel General Hood, instead of pursuing or following in Sherman's wake, marched his army northward, possibly with the hope of forcing Sherman to retreat. The two armies, so long opposed and in close proximity, were soon too far apart to again come into contact. Therefore, while General Sherman, with an army of 60,000 men, marched unmolested towards the sea, the defeat of the rebels under General Hood devolved upon the troops left with, and those to be assembled by, General George H. Thomas. In time, the much-desired result was attained by that distinguished and most deserving general and the gallant officers and soldiers under his command, who proved everyway equal to the great emergency. General Hatch's division rendered important service in retarding the advance of the enemy and in gaining information as to his movements. The manifest bravery and efficiency of that cavalry, previously so long under my command, was particularly observable at the battles of Franklin and Nashville, Tennessee.

The orders from the War Department for the troops on the east side of the Mississippi River to report to General Canby continued to trouble General Wilson. Hence his anxiety to have me hurry the cavalry away from Memphis, although he well knew then that it was subject to the orders of those superior to me in rank. Even Hatch's division, formerly a part of my old command, had gotten far beyond General Wilson's control and had rendered excellent service under the direct orders of General [David S.] Stanley[15] and other officers. No doubt like myself, General Wilson was greatly annoyed on account of the scattered condition of cavalry, but neither General Hatch nor myself were to blame for that which was beyond our power to avoid. At a future time Hatch's division was pushed aside and left dismounted and without proper equipments by General Wilson, but for the time being he manifested his spleen towards myself, and gave vent to his venom and vexation by issuing the following orders [December 13, 1864]: "Brig. Gen. B. H. Grierson U.S. Vols. is relieved from command of the 4th Division Cav. Corps, Mil. Div. of the Mississippi."[16] Another paragraph of the same orders assigned General E[mory]. Upton[17] to the command of the division of which I was so unceremoniously relieved.

At this juncture, however, there was fortunately a higher power that knew nothing of these smaller embroilments. The day after the foregoing orders reached me at Memphis, a telegram sent by General Halleck from the War Department to General Dana caused those same troops, and all other cavalry then at Memphis, to be placed at once under my command for the purpose of making an important expedition against the Mobile and Ohio Railroad, then the main line of communication for the rebels with the South.

It was while these events were transpiring that the rebel army under General Hood, numbering about 45,000 men, had forced its way northward without meeting with any serious opposition until it reached Franklin, Tennessee, where after a hard-fought battle, it was repulsed by General [John M.] Schofield's army.[18] It was there that General Stanley displayed such conspicuous gallantry and, with less than his corps, "bore the brunt of the battle." Although severely wounded, [he] tenaciously held the field against the enemy until ordered to withdraw his troops and continue the retreat. General Thomas finally succeeded in concentrating all his available force at Nashville, to which point the rebels promptly advanced and invested, and where the Union Army was for a time virtually besieged.[19]

The threatening position of the enemy created great excitement at Washington and throughout the North for fear an invasion of Kentucky and Ohio would be made. General Grant had become impatient and much dissatisfied on account of what seemed to be an unnecessary delay in the attack on the enemy, and had ordered General Logan to relieve General Thomas of command. But the latter, having perfected his arrangements for battle, did on December 15 and 16, 1864, assault the enemy in his entrenched position, and continued the attack until Hood's army was utterly defeated and obliged to retreat southward in great confusion and disorder, leaving their dead and wounded on the field. The enemy also suffered seriously in loss of artillery, small arms, and other war materials, besides the prisoners which were taken by the Union Army.

On the presumption that a vigorous pursuit of the enemy would be made on his retreat from Nashville, the destruction of the Mobile and Ohio Railroad, which seemed to be the only route by which the demoralized rebels could make their escape, became a matter of great importance. Hence, I was suddenly ordered out with all the cavalry at Memphis to accomplish that desirable object. Before my departure on the expedition, General Upton arrived at Memphis for the purpose of conducting the Fourth Division of cavalry to Louisville. But upon reporting at department headquarters, he learned that the orders and instructions he had received were, for the time being, of no force or avail. He was surprised and considerably disappointed, but under the circumstances seemed to take the matter in a philosophical manner.

I was then busily engaged in preparing the troops for the field, but managed to gain the time to call upon General Upton and to render him every possible attention. He was a very courteous gentleman, and his record as an officer was not unknown to me, I being aware of his promotion for gallantry in the field during the campaign in Virginia. Our interview was most pleasant and satisfactory. He accepted my invitation to accompany me to the various camps to have a look at the cavalry. [He] quickly noticed the many small detachments and few full regiments of which the command was composed, and saw that the force available was neither well organized nor equipped, and necessarily not very effective. Yet he was pleased to observe the determination on my part to accomplish my orders with the troops assigned me, notwithstanding that even the elements were against me, the weather then being very unfavorable for such a hazardous undertaking. In parting, the general extended his hand to me and warmly expressed his best wishes for the success of my enterprise. Soon after, [he] left on his return to Kentucky, without the cavalry to which he had been so near but unable to obtain.

Before entering upon the story of the expedition and its success, it is proper here to state that General Dana, who had been only a short time in command at Memphis, was entirely unacquainted with me and had but little knowledge of the surrounding country. He, therefore, upon receipt of the telegram from General Halleck, sent for me to ascertain my views as to how the movement then pending should be arranged and conducted. We talked on the subject for some time in his office, with the map before us. In accordance with his wish, I furnished him a written statement on the subject as to the plan of operations which should, in my judgment, be adopted. He was well pleased, and promptly did me the honor to embody it in his letter of instructions to me, adding thereto as he saw fit, and personally giving me such discretionary power as he deemed important under the circumstances.

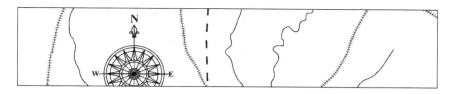

14. Raid on the Mobile and Ohio Railroad

Throughout the southwestern states, the month of December 1864 was unusually stormy and disagreeable. The rains were frequent, and of long duration and severity. From the 15th of the month, in the vicinity of Memphis the downpour was almost constant, day and night, until the mud became so deep that the roads were absolutely impassable for all kinds of vehicles, many wagons and carriages being stuck and sunken down so far in the mire on the roads leading out from the city that abandonment for the time being became a necessity. It was during such great discouragements that I was obliged to prepare my command for the field.

In obedience to orders received from General Dana, and in accordance with the plan of operations as adopted, I ordered Colonel Kargé, commanding First Brigade, Cavalry Division, to proceed on December 19 northwest [northeast] from Memphis, to cross Wolf River at Raleigh, to demonstrate and strongly threaten the crossings of the Hatchie at Bolivar and Estenaula, Tennessee, and from thence swing southward to destroy the telegraph between Grand Junction and Corinth, and to join the main column, which was to start the next day, at or near Ripley, Mississippi. Owing to the continued heavy rains which had so long prevailed, the roads in that direction were found to be so flooded and overflown by the swollen streams that a crossing of Wolf River could not be effected without too much delay. Therefore, Colonel Kargé, after floundering about the whole day with his troops, was obliged reluctantly to return to Memphis in the evening to report the impracticability of carrying out his orders.

The next day, December 20, the weather became cold, [and] the rain changed to sleet and snow. As there seemed to be a good prospect for the mud to soon become frozen, the movement was deferred for twenty-four hours. Up to that time General Dana had desired me to take a battery or section of artillery and a few wagons. But, upon return of Colonel Kargé, it was found to be entirely impracticable. The general, in view of the many obstacles which were presented to his mind, was much inclined to abandon the expedition, but I assured him of my determination and ability to accomplish the task in the face of all the difficulties that could possibly arise.

Accordingly, on the morning of December 21, I moved with the entire available force of my command, consisting of detachments of the 2nd New Jersey, 7th Indiana, 1st Mississippi Rifles, 4th and 10th Missouri, 3rd and 4th Iowa, 2nd Wisconsin, 4th and 11th Illinois, and 3rd U.S. Colored Cavalry—in all about 3,500 men, organized into three brigades and commanded respectively by Colonels Kargé, Winslow, and [Embury D.] Osband; also Company E, 2nd Iowa Cavalry, numbering forty men, Lieutenant A. Scherer commanding, as provost guard and escort, and a pioneer corps of fifty Negroes commanded by Lieutenant [Sylvester L.] Lewis of the 7th Indiana Cavalry—without artillery or wagons and with twenty days' light rations carried on pack mules.

The whole force moved eastward along the line of the Memphis and Charleston Railroad to a point west of Moscow Station, threatening Corinth, and thence southeast through Early Grove, Lamar, and Salem to Ripley. From Early Grove, the 10th Missouri Cavalry under Captain F. R. Neet was sent to La Grange and Grand Junction, Tennessee, to destroy the telegraph and stations at those points. After accomplishing the important work as assigned, which continued the threatened advance on Corinth, the detachment rejoined the column near Salem, Mississippi. From Ripley, a detachment of 150 men of the 2nd New Jersey Cavalry, under Major [Philip L.] Van Rensselaer, was sent to destroy the Mobile and Ohio Railroad and the telegraph at or near Booneville. At the same time the 4th Illinois, under Captain A. T. Search, was sent to destroy the railroad and telegraph further south and near Guntown or Baldwyn, Mississippi. Those detachments rejoined the main column, one at Ellistown and the other at Shannon's Station, having satisfactorily accomplished the duties assigned them by destroying four railroad bridges and ten culverts, several miles of track and telegraph, and two storehouses filled with quartermaster and commissary stores, clothing, and other army supplies; killing several of the enemy, capturing seven prisoners, and destroying a caboose on [the] railroad, containing arms, ammunition, and railroad implements.

For several days after leaving Memphis the ground was frozen enough to form a crust to the deep mud, but not sufficient in strength to bear up the horses and pack-mules. The march was therefore tiresome, and much impeded near the streams and bottom lands. Many shoes were pulled from the feet of the horses and mules by frozen mud and the ice. The legs of animals were frequently cut, sprained, and otherwise injured. Some gave out and were abandoned, but were replaced by captured stock. After arrival of the command at Ripley, the rains were not so heavy or continuous, the mud was not so deep, the sun occasionally shone out, and the clouds were not so thick and dark. From that place I marched the main column on Tupelo.

On arriving at Oldtown Creek, about five miles from the railroad, I learned from my scouts of the existence of a rebel camp and large depot of supplies at Verona Station south of Tupelo. I halted and dismounted the command. As Colonel Kargé's brigade was then with me in the advance, I directed him to leave his pack mules and the least serviceable animals and men, and to then proceed rapidly to Verona, to keep his scouts and advance well out, and if deemed advisable, upon nearing the position of the enemy, to make a night attack on the place. Any support required would be promptly sent forward. The order was given about 11 P.M. Christmas night. It was dark, cloudy, and raining, but the colonel obeyed the order with alacrity and was soon under way with his troops. Our movements thus far, considering the bad roads and weather, had been rapid. The indications were that the enemy had no knowledge of our presence, as our appearance everywhere had been a complete surprise to the citizens on our line of march.

Guided by the lightning as it flashed through the storm, Kargé proceeded and suddenly struck the enemy's pickets about one mile from Verona. Notwithstanding the darkness of the night, his advance regiment, the 7th Indiana Cavalry, with Captain Skelton in the front, charged impetuously into the rebel camp, dispersing the garrison there and in the town, capturing and destroying two trains of thirty-two cars loaded with supplies and eight warehouses filled with ordnance, quartermaster, and commissary stores, besides 300 army wagons, most of which were marked "U.S.A.," having been captured from General Sturgis at the time of his defeat by General Forrest near Brice's Cross Roads and Tishomingo Creek in June 1864. The wagon trains were about to be sent loaded with provisions, clothing, and other supplies to Hood's defeated and demoralized army. The bursting of cartridges and shells that were stored in that immense depot of army supplies at Verona continued until the afternoon of December 26.

Upon receiving information of Colonel Kargé's success and that he was going into camp with his command, I moved on with the balance of the command and encamped on the high ground near Harrisburg, between Oldtown Creek and Tupelo. On the same night, before going into camp at that point, the 11th Illinois Cavalry, Lieutenant Colonel [Otto] Funke commanding, with the pioneer corps, was sent to destroy the extensive railroad bridge, nearly 1,000 feet long, over Oldtown Creek, and the track between that point and Tupelo. Although still very dark and rainy, the order was promptly obeyed. Before morning, by great exertion, the work was accomplished in a most complete and satisfactory manner.

From Tupelo, I moved my entire force south along the Mobile and Ohio Railroad, thoroughly destroying it to a point between Egypt and Prairie stations, fifty-six miles from Booneville, where it was first struck. The destruction of the railroad between Tupelo and Okolona was specially assigned to Colonel Osband's brigade. Nearly two days were occupied in accomplishing that important work, besides which two trains of twenty-three cars, one wagon train of twenty wagons all loaded with army supplies, and two storehouses filled with quartermaster, commissary, and ordnance stores were captured and destroyed at or between those stations.

The rebels had concentrated a considerable force at Okolona, which fell back on our approach. After entering the place and halting long enough to destroy all the rebel government property contained in six buildings, including the railroad depot at that station, which were filled with corn, meat, meal, clothing, hospital, commissary, and quartermaster stores, I moved on southward with my command, encamping the night of December 27 about three miles north of Egypt Station. Before destroying the telegraph line, having tapped the wire near Okolona and intercepted dispatches from General [Franklin] Gardner, Lieutenant General [Richard] Taylor,[1] and others indicating that reinforcements would be sent from Mobile and other points, and learning from deserters who came into our camp on the night of the 27th that the reinforcements would not be likely to arrive before 10 or 11 o'clock the next day, I accordingly on the morning of December 28 attacked the enemy, variously estimated at from 1,200 to 2,000 strong, consisting of cavalry, infantry, and one battery of artillery on platform cars at Egypt Station.

The First Brigade, Colonel Kargé commanding, was in advance. After encountering the enemy's cavalry pickets, his line of battle was discovered with its center secured by large stockades and flanked by railroad earth embankments. The advance companies of the 2nd New Jersey Cavalry promptly charged and drove in the second line of pickets. While this was being done, I directed Colonel Kargé to form his line of battle and advance to the attack of the enemy in his strong and well-chosen position. The commanding officer of the Second Brigade, Colonel Osband, was ordered to move forward to the support of Colonel Kargé's brigade, and the Third Brigade, Colonel Winslow commanding, was held in reserve. The enemy made a stubborn resistance, but was steadily driven back on both flanks. The gallant Captain [Michael] Gallagher had been killed in the first charge.

At this juncture, the enemy's artillery opened with rapid firing on our right, and caused some confusion in our advancing line by the bursting of shells. Two trains of cars with reinforcements, said to be under the command of the rebel General Gardner, having come in sight, [and] seeing the importance of prompt action to prevent the enemy from forming a junction of his forces, I directed Colonel Kargé to steadily persist in his attack and to advance his troops at all hazards on the left flank with a view to surround the enemy, while with a small detachment of the 7th Indiana, 4th Missouri, and my escort of cavalry, I accompanied by Captain S. L. Woodward of my staff charged the enemy's battery of artillery and the reinforcements then advancing from the south, driving them back [and] preventing them from re-forming any effective line of battle. [I] soon succeed[ed] in capturing a train of cars and in tearing up the railroad track between two and three miles south of the station. We continued to engage the rebel reinforcements and effectually prevented them from joining the rebel garrison at Egypt Station, where the fight was still in progress.

Placing the small force then with me in line facing south, with instructions to the commanding officer, Captain [Joel] Elliott,[2] to resist any advance of the enemy from that direction, I with Captain Woodward and a few orderlies rapidly returned to Egypt Station, and arrived there in time to direct and take part in the closing scenes of the battle. Colonel Osband's brigade had advanced opportunely to support and extend our line on the right, which had been weakened to some extent by the withdrawal of the detachment to intercept and drive away the rebel forces arriving from the south. The two advance regiments of the Second Brigade, the 4th and 11th Illinois Cavalry, promptly charged and drove back the enemy on the left of his line, some distance beyond the railroad. As the firing was still continuous and heavy on our extreme left, I ordered Colonel Osband to send two companies of the 2nd Wisconsin and two companies of the 3rd U.S. Cavalry to report to Colonel Kargé, and to dispose of the balance of his brigade in such manner as to connect with Colonel Kargé's command on the east side of the railroad as soon as possible, so as to complete the circumvention of the rebels and prevent their escape. The movements were well executed with promptitude under the immediate direction of Colonel Osband, who in getting his troops into the desired position, lost only one man killed, two officers and thirteen men wounded, and a few horses shot.

Thus far our troops had been obliged to advance over open ground, without any shelter whatever, in the face of the enemy's well-directed fire from their sheltered position. Several charges had been made and considerable loss had been suffered by Colonel Kargé's command, especially in horses disabled or killed. Lieutenant Colonel [P. Jones] Yorke, commanding the 2nd New Jersey Cavalry, had persistently held the most advanced position in our line and, by a well-executed maneuver, had gained the shelter of some huts and buildings, from which his men kept up a galling fire into the enemy at short range. In the meantime, Colonel Osband was preparing his troops for a charge on foot when Colonel Yorke, seizing the opportunity of a lull in the enemy's fire, with the inspiration and enthusiasm of a true soldier, intrepidly placed himself in front of his men and impetuously charged the enemy's works [and] reached the stockade, over the timbers of which his brave troopers fired a volley into the rebels, creating such confusion and consternation as to quickly oblige the garrison to surrender.

The engagement lasted nearly three hours, during which the enemy's reinforcements were driven back and defeated; his cavalry attacked, routed and dispersed. Some were killed [and] others wounded, taken prisoners, and paroled. Among the badly wounded of the enemy were General [Samuel J.] Gholson[3] and a number of other officers. Besides the loss inflicted upon the enemy in killed and wounded during the fight, over 500 were captured, with their arms and equipments, within the stockades alone at the time of the surrender. Our loss was three officers and nineteen enlisted men killed, four officers and ninety-seven enlisted men wounded, and about 100 horses disabled or killed in action, which however were replaced by those captured from the enemy.

Under all the circumstances, considering the strength and security of the enemy's fortified and sheltered position, our success and signal victory was the more remarkable. But it was only attained by decision, dashing celerity of movements, and the conspicuous gallantry of officers and irresistible intrepidity of the enlisted men, which enabled our immediate available force to overcome the obstacles encountered. The greater part of our loss was sustained by the First Brigade, which happened to be in front when the attack was made and therefore had to bear the brunt of the battle. The Second Brigade, however, had rendered timely and important service, and the Third Brigade, Colonel Winslow commanding, arrived on the field just after the surrender and was held in readiness to move against the rebel forces under General Gardner, should they again put in an appearance or attempt another advance.

After resting the command and learning from my scouts that the enemy was retreating south, the detachment previously sent in that direction was ordered to discontinue the pursuit and rejoin the main column. Having taken the necessary measures to properly care for the dead, leaving a surgeon with attendants in charge of the wounded who could not be moved, including those of the enemy, and seeing that the orders for the destruction of all rebel government property at Egypt Station had been carried into effect, I proceeded with my entire force due west to Houston, crossing en route to that place the Sooukatonchie and Houlka rivers, to both of which streams I had previously sent detachments to secure the bridges. The 2nd Wisconsin Cavalry, Major [William] Woods commanding, was specially detailed to take charge of and guard the prisoners, who were mounted on captured stock. The officers and men of the regiment deserve much credit for the cheerful and successful manner in which they performed the arduous duty assigned them during the continuation of the march. From Houston, demonstrations were made to the north toward Pontotoc and southeast toward West Point, while the column moved southwest via Bellefontaine to the Mississippi Central Railroad, striking it at Winona Station. From Bellefontaine, Captain [George] Curkendall, with a detachment of 150 men from the 3rd Iowa Cavalry, made a demonstration to the southeast toward Starkville to threaten again the Mobile and Ohio Railroad, and mislead the enemy. The detachment destroyed a large lot of arms and accoutrements, and rejoined the column after a continuous march of sixty hours.

At the same time, from the same place a detachment of 120 men from the 4th Iowa Cavalry, under Captain [Warren] Beckwith, was sent south via Greensborough to Bankston to destroy large cloth and leather factories at that place, where over 500 persons were employed and actively at work in the manufacture of cloth, leather, clothing, boots, and shoes, those articles then being of prime necessity and great value to the rebel army under General Hood then on its retreat in a destitute condition. In carrying out the instructions received, Captain Beckwith and his men were obliged to be in the saddle nearly two days and one whole night without rest or sleep. But the orders were obeyed with cheerfulness and promptitude, and the object in view accomplished in a thorough manner. The detachment suffered no loss, and rejoined the main column when on its march southward some distance north of Middleton.

Colonel Kargé's brigade was in advance on arrival of the command at Winona Station on the Mississippi Central Railroad, and there destroyed a large amount of quartermaster and commissary stores accumulated in the depot and other buildings, besides two locomotives [and] a train of cars. [It] also tore up the railroad track and cut down the telegraph line. The brigade then moved on and encamped on the night of December 31 on the road to Middleton.

From Winona Station, Colonel John W. Noble, with a detachment of 300 men from the 3rd and 4th Iowa Cavalry of Winslow's brigade, was ordered on the night of December 31 to proceed early the next morning to destroy all public property to be found between that point and Grenada, Mississippi, and after accomplishing the necessary work, to return and rejoin the column as expeditiously as practicable. At the same time, I ordered Colonel Osband to proceed with his brigade south along the line of the Mississippi Central Railroad [and] destroy it as far as possible; to attack the enemy wherever found, and rejoin the main column at or near Benton. Both of these officers left our camp at Winona early on the morning of January 1, 1865, to execute the orders they had received.

When the detachments were well under way, I with the main column, Colonel Winslow's brigade in advance, continued the march towards Vicksburg, encamping for the night near Lexington, where we had a slight skirmish with the enemy and communicated with Colonel Osband. The next morning, the guard for the prisoners and captured stock was strengthened, and the command moved on through Lexington, unmolested, and went into camp for the night at Benton, the Third Brigade being then in camp to our left near Ebenezer. At 8 o'clock that night, Colonel Noble with his detachment arrived at Osband's camp (at Ebenezer). After an hour's rest, they both moved forward the same night with their troops to Benton, reporting their safe arrival, rejoining and going into camp with us at 3 o'clock A.M. on January 3, having been remarkably successful in accomplishing the important and arduous duty assigned to them.

Colonel Noble, while en route to and returning from Grenada with his detachment, had several skirmishes, inflicting loss and great damage on the enemy, having destroyed several railroad depots and a number of other buildings filled with army supplies; a machine shop with all necessary fixtures for the repair of locomotives and cars; a pile-driver with steam engine and tackle; four locomotives with tenders; two trains of over thirty cars, some of them loaded with seasoned lumber and other materials of war; also, the press of the rebel sheet called *The Grenada Picket*. In addition to the labor performed in the destruction of public property, Colonel Noble and his detachment marched over 100 miles in forty-eight hours. Colonel Osband, by suitable details from his brigade, succeeded in destroying the railroad for a distance of twenty miles, burning over twenty bridges and culverts, station houses, and water tanks.

After the destruction of the railroad was effected, General Wirt Adams' brigade, variously estimated at from 500 to 1,500 strong, was encountered near Franklin. After a brisk fight of about two hours, the enemy was defeated and driven away, leaving two officers and over thirty enlisted men dead or wounded on the field, and seven more captured during the engagement.

On the morning of January 3, all detachments having returned and rejoined their respective commands, I with my entire force, united and held well in hand, ready for any emergency, continued the march southwest toward Vicksburg, Colonel Winslow's brigade in the advance. During the day, we had some skirmishing in front and on the left flank, which however did not impede the march of the column. The command reached Mechanicsburg in the evening, where it encamped for the night. Moving onward on the morning of January 4, skirmishing occurred at intervals during the day. In the afternoon, an attack was made on the rear of the column at a place known as the "Ponds," but was promptly repulsed by Colonel Noble's regiment of Winslow's brigade, with some loss to the enemy. One man of Company B, 3rd Iowa, [was] mortally wounded. The command went into camp at Mill Creek, twelve miles northeast of Vicksburg, where we found forage and rations, which on my application had been sent out to us by Major General C. C. Washburn. During the night the pickets were fired upon, but the enemy was quickly driven away and did not again put in an appearance.

We arrived at Vicksburg, with the entire command in good condition, at 3 o'clock P.M. on January 5, 1865. The distance marched was 450 miles. Making proper allowance for the time occupied in destroying railroads and public property, the average daily march of the troops was over forty miles, which affords a striking example as to the power of endurance and efficiency of cavalry when operating alone, separated from infantry and artillery, and freed from the encumbrance of wagon transportation. It also demonstrates the fact that the rapidity of movement of cavalry on the march and in face of the enemy is an important element in the attainment of success, especially when guided by sound discretion and good judgment.

The loss in killed and wounded of the enemy was severe, but not so large as our own. By capture it was far greater, being thirty field and line officers, about 600 enlisted men, [and] 800 head of horses and mules. Over 1,000 Negroes joined the column during the march. The destruction of railroads and materials of war was so immense that it can hardly be overestimated. Briefly summed up, it was as follows: 20,000 feet of bridges and trestle-work (cut down and burned); ten miles of track (rails bent and ties burned); twenty miles of telegraph (poles cut down and wire destroyed); six serviceable locomotives and tenders, and ten in process of repair; 100 cars; over 300 army wagons loaded with supplies; two caissons; thirty warehouses filled with quartermaster, commissary, and ordnance stores; large cloth and shoe factories (employing 500 hands); several tanneries and machine shops; a steam pile-driver; twelve new forges; seven depot buildings; 5,000 stands of new muskets; 700 head of fat hogs; 500 bales of cotton (marked C.S.A.); and a large amount of grain, leather, wool, and other public property, the value and quantity of which could not be fully ascertained. Over 100 of the prisoners captured at Egypt Station formerly belonged to the Union Army, and were recruited from Southern prisons into the rebel service. Many of them, no doubt, were induced to join their ranks from a desire to escape a loathsome confinement. In my official report, I commended them to the leniency of our government.[4]

The entire loss in my command during the expedition was four officers and twenty-three enlisted men killed, four officers and eighty-nine enlisted men wounded, and seven enlisted men missing, besides about 200 horses and mules killed or wounded in action and abandoned on the march. The loss in animals, however, was promptly made good by stock captured from the enemy. About forty of the badly wounded soldiers were left at Egypt Station and other places; those less severely or slightly wounded accompanied the command to Vicksburg.

Colonels Kargé, Winslow, and Osband displayed skill and ability in handling their troops, and their valuable assistance did much towards securing the desired result. Major M. H. Williams and Captain S. L. Woodward of my staff were untiring in their efforts during the march, and deserve great credit for the energetic efficiency manifested in the discharge of the important duties assigned them. Captain Woodward's gallantry was especially conspicuous in the fight at Egypt Station, and he afforded invaluable aid not only in preparing the troops for the field, but also in conveying my orders to the various commands and insuring their prompt execution throughout the entire time, day and night, while on the expedition. For the services thus rendered, he was promoted to the position of major and assistant adjutant general, U.S. volunteers.

We reached Vicksburg in the midst of a cold and pelting rain, so travel-stained and begrimed with mud as to hardly be recognizable one from the other. It was almost impossible to distinguish the officers from the enlisted men, or the Union soldiers from the rebel prisoners who were mounted and under guard. The 1,000 or more Negroes in rear of the column, some mounted on bare-backed bridleless mules, two to four on one animal, others on foot, many with open mouths and grinning teeth, shouting and singing plantation melodies varied to suit their whims, all joyously marching onward en mass to freedom and glory through mud and mire despite the storm, presented a picturesque appearance and a remarkable ending to our grand cavalcade. Soldiers from camps and people from houses flocked to the roadside to see and cheer us as we passed into the city. Upon reporting to General Washburn at his headquarters, we were warmly greeted by the general, and vociferously cheered by the officers and soldiers there assembled to welcome us.

The reports of rebel officers, from first to last, show that they were misled in regard to our movements and intentions. It was four days before they received information of our departure from Memphis. When a detachment from my command struck the Mobile and Ohio Railroad at Booneville, it was thought to have come from another direction. For days thereafter they believed that our objective point of attack was Corinth, and their reinforcements were therefore ordered to that place. The night attack on Forrest's camp at Verona was a complete surprise. It was not long after the sudden advent of Skelton and his raiders until the light of burning trains and storehouses illuminated the surrounding country for many miles, and the rapid bursting of shells and other ammunition there stored added terror and confusion to the midnight scene of havoc.

The rebels were ordered by General Gardner to make a stand and resist our advance at Okolona. The place being in the midst of an open plain, for once the cavalry had a chance for display while doing actual service in the field. [We] entered the town as if prepared for review or dress parade, with banners flying and guidons unfurled to the breeze. But the rebels retreated to Egypt Station, where they were in due time suddenly attacked and utterly defeated, much to the astonishment of Generals Gardner and Taylor, who were not prepared to believe that mounted cavalry, without infantry or artillery, could successfully charge troops sheltered and protected by fortifications. When General Gardner arrived at West Point and found that his reinforcements had been intercepted and driven back, he was no doubt perplexed.

Our movement due west from Egypt Station was another surprise, as the rebels thought we were merely flanking out to head or cross the swollen streams in our front, and then to continue the march southward along the line of the Mobile and Ohio Railroad. Again, the detachment sent north towards Pontotoc gave the rebels the impression that we had gone north and were returning to Memphis. Then the sudden night attack on the rebel factories at Bankston, over fifty miles south of the line of march of our column, was so unexpected that the superintendent rushed out of his house swearing at his guard and watchmen for not putting out the fires, never even dreaming that Yankee soldiers were in possession of the burning premises. He was no doubt still more astonished when, without much ceremony, he was required by Captain Beckwith to hastily dress, to be turned over to the provost guard with other prisoners. It was then the rebel commanders concluded that we were surely moving south through the center of the state, and ordered troops in that direction to intercept us.

Our sudden appearance at Winona on the Mississippi Central Railroad was, therefore, the more astonishing and Colonel Noble's rapid march into Grenada with his detachment again fooled the enemy, and led him to believe that we were certainly going north on our way back to Memphis. General Forrest ordered out cavalry from Corinth to get into our front and prevent our return. Then Colonel Osband's movement with his brigade south along the line of the Mississippi Central Railroad satisfied the rebels, in the midst of their bewilderment, that we were really ubiquitous, as we were reported everywhere at the same time and going in all directions.

About that time, however, General Wirt Adams was amazed to find his command suddenly attacked and whipped by Colonel Osband's colored cavalry. While Adams withdrew and endeavored to concentrate his forces and await further developments, to the still greater astonishment of all the rebels, my numerous detachments rejoined our column in safety. And we, after so successfully accomplishing the important work which had been assigned to us, marched on unmolested into Vicksburg.

In the meantime, General Hood's army, after its disastrous defeat at Nashville, had hastily retreated southward in a demoralized and destitute condition. Upon re-crossing to the south side of the Tennessee River on December 27, that unfortunate general and all the rebels left under his command, from the highest officers down to the barefooted, unclothed, and hungry privates, were most disagreeably surprised and chagrined to find their railroad communications with the south interrupted, and their much needed food, clothing, and other supplies destroyed by our audacious raiders.

———

During the time occupied by myself and command in attaining such important results, the officers and enlisted men, as well as our animals, were obliged to undergo great exertion and were subjected to many hardships. But their power of endurance proved equal to all demands and emergencies. Occasionally, however, amusing incidents occurred to enliven and cheer us on our otherwise laborious expedition.

I remember that on Christmas day, after we had been plodding on for several hours through the mud and mire, we halted for the column to close up, and for the readjustment of saddles, etc. Before moving on, word reached me to the effect that our flankers reported that great preparations were being made by the people of the country for the holiday feast, that considerable food had already been brought in by our foragers, and that enough additional could readily be obtained to supply the whole command with at least one good meal. I, therefore, directed that larger details be sent out from the various organizations to gather provisions such as could be obtained in the vicinity of our line of march. Then we marched on slowly for a time, but more cheerfully in the anticipation of the result.

About 1 o'clock P.M., it was found that the detachments were returning, laden down with roast pigs, turkeys, chickens, boiled hams, and other kinds of cooked meats, besides many delicacies suitable to the occasion. I accordingly halted the command and gave orders for all to eat. I never knew of an order that was more generally satisfactory. It was received with smiles and obeyed with alacrity. Myself and staff had a fine roast turkey and such other good things as fell to our share, placed on a large flat-surfaced stump which happened to be near at hand. The meal was greatly relished by everyone, so far as I was able to observe. When informed that all had partaken abundantly of that Christmas dinner, we resumed the march feeling greatly refreshed, while singularly cheerful countenances were noticeable throughout the command. Those who were present and participated on that delectable occasion will doubtless remember the welcome occurrence with much satisfaction. If the surrounding families mourned over their interrupted festivities, possibly they were better prepared to ponder on the things that would lead to peace.

Colonel Noble, when at Grenada, Mississippi, with his detachment of the 3rd and 4th Iowa Cavalry, after destroying all public property at the place, learning that there was a rebel newspaper published there, he entered the establishment in order to ascertain the latest news of the enemy. He asked the editor and proprietor for a copy of the last paper issued, and upon examining the rebel sheet, the colonel's attention was soon attracted to an article on our raid, the heading to which was printed in large type, as follows: "GLORIOUS NEWS!!! The Yankee raid played out! Grierson and his vandals repulsed! Fleeing in great haste through Pontotoc toward Memphis!!!"

The colonel smiled and advised the editor that the statements were not correct and might mislead his own people. The editor was at first rather lofty and pompous in his bearing. He manifested his indignation by impatiently walking about and apparently debating in his own mind the propriety of ordering the colonel out of the office. He suddenly grew pale with terror when he heard the order given for the destruction of the rebel press, type, and other materials pertaining thereto, together with the building in which they were contained, so there would be nothing whatever left with which to print and publish lies on the morrow.

Late one evening, a rebel provost marshal or conscripting officer was captured. [He] had been engaged in hunting throughout the country, with a pack of bloodhounds, for deserters and Union men, with a view to force them into the rebel army. A number of men who had been hunted down, captured, and chained together were found in that condition and the fact reported to me. I at once gave orders to have them unshackled, provided with food, and set at liberty. The bloody dogs of war were shot. But, unfortunately, the rebel official culprit was either spirited away in some mysterious manner or adroitly made his escape from our special guard during the night.

A few days after, when the command was well down toward the center of the state, we encamped for the night on a large, well-supplied plantation where the proprietor kindly invited myself and staff into his mansion. Upon entering the parlor, we quite astonished the family by our resemblance to "their folks," and by having some knowledge of Longfellow as a poet, music as an art, and the piano as an instrument (we being previously presumed to be outside barbarians with hoofs and horns, and adorned inwardly and outwardly as absolute savages). We were hospitably entertained, but in the morning I jokingly complained to the proprietor for permitting my saddle blanket to be stolen from the premises, when I had taken so much pains to guard and protect his property. He smiled and expressed his regrets at the occurrence, but I judge he did not view the matter in that light, as I had entirely ignored the fact that my raiders had not left a chicken or turkey or pig or mule or horse or forage on the plantation. It was the first visit ever made there by the "Yankees," and no doubt the planter hoped it might be the last. I left a suitable guard at his house to remain a few hours for the protection of himself and family. With friendly salutations for all, we mounted and took our departure.

Near Lodi, Mississippi, we captured a large drove of fat hogs that had been gathered up as supplies for Hood's army. The hogs were required to change front and move in the opposite direction. A special detail was made to take charge of them. All went well for a while. The hogs were driven along amid much merriment until, finding them too slow as a supply train, they necessarily had to be gotten rid of in some way so as to prevent them from falling into the hands of the enemy. Colonel Winslow suggested that they be killed and burned. I thought it was a capital idea, and gave orders accordingly. They were soon after driven into a pen near at hand, shot and sabered to death, thrown into piles with the materials and debris of log buildings, then set on fire and consumed. Possibly the fragrance of the roast pork ascended to regale Charles Lamb in Heaven,[5] and the well-tried lard descended to reservoirs that may some day make the state of Mississippi rival Pennsylvania.

While destroying rebel government property by wholesale, we allowed the miserably poor families along the line of our march to freely help themselves to salt, sugar, meal, flour, bacon, pork, and molasses. Therefore, while the rich feared and deplored our presence, our kind actions gladdened the hearts of the poor—although previously all may have looked upon us as foes.

As those events were transpiring in Tennessee and Mississippi, General Sherman's army had, without meeting with any serious opposition, marched onward through Georgia to the sea, and was preparing for a movement northward through the Carolinas, having occupied Savannah, Georgia, on December 24, 1864—the same day I left Memphis with the cavalry to destroy the rebel railroad communications and army supplies.

It is obvious that the winter of 1864–65 was made the more memorable by the many important successes gained by the Union forces throughout the South, which clearly pointed to the hour as near at hand for the close of the war and downfall of the great rebellion.

After a few days' rest at Vicksburg, and as soon as river transportation could be furnished, I returned with my command to Memphis, where, after making my official report to General Dana, I relinquished command and received orders to report to General [George H.] Thomas at Nashville. I at once arranged for my departure. In view of the uncertain condition of military affairs—army operations having terminated for the winter; troops being in quarters for rest and recuperation; and not knowing when I would be ordered to duty in the Spring, or what would then be my chances for quarters in the South—it was deemed best that Mrs. Grierson and the children return to Jacksonville, there to remain until more definite and satisfactory arrangements could be perfected. Therefore, the latter part of January, I left Memphis with my family on steamboat for Cairo. Upon arrival at the latter place, I and Captain Woodward continued on our way towards Nashville, stopping for a short visit at Paducah, Kentucky, with the captain's father and mother, while Mrs. Grierson and the children proceeded northward by railroad, via Decatur, to Jacksonville.

Although delayed for a time, we succeeded in getting away from Cairo about 5 o'clock the same day Mrs. Grierson left there. But the boat on which we embarked, the *Cottage*, was too small or over-crowded to take our horses and baggage, which at the last moment, we had to leave in charge of our servants to be shipped to us the next day. Upon arrival at Paducah, we found a portion of Colonel Winslow's brigade and my old escort company from the 2nd Iowa Cavalry. They had been disembarked, and the boats on which they had been thus far transported on their way to Louisville were taken by the quartermaster's department for the purpose of shipping supplies to General Thomas' army at Eastport, which was then reported entirely out of provisions. A number of boats loaded with commissary stores for Thomas' army were frozen in between Cairo and St. Louis, and others [were] stopped by floating ice on the Ohio River between Paducah and Evansville, Indiana.

After receipt of orders to report to General Thomas, I had written to him, stating in substance that since General Wilson had seen fit to relieve me from command, entirely without cause when I was endeavoring by every means in my power, under the most adverse circumstances, to comply with the many conflicting orders I had received, that I would prefer if consistent with the good of the service to have no further relation with him, but to be permitted to go on duty elsewhere. The letter had the desired effect, and I soon received a favorable response [ordering Grierson to report to Grant at Annapolis, Md.].

Before receiving the answer from General Thomas, I had applied to the War Department for a thirty-days' leave of absence, intending, should General Thomas' reply be unfavorable, to go to Washington, and by personal application at headquarters of the army procure, if leave was granted, some command that would effectually separate me from General Wilson. On receipt of the order to proceed to Annapolis, I and Captain Woodward immediately started for that city, sending our baggage forward by the quartermaster's department. Circumstances afterwards changed our route, and the baggage, which had been imperfectly marked and hastily shipped, was unfortunately lost and never recovered. It was sent to Annapolis and then to Washington, where despite all our efforts no further trace could be found. It consisted of a number of chests filled with our bed clothes and camp outfit, besides many things of peculiar value to us, among which were a fine pair of panniers, conveniently arranged with compartments, and also the beautiful saddle and equipments presented to me at New Orleans after the raid of 1863.

Mr. and Mrs. Woodward did everything possible to make our visit in every way agreeable during our short stay at Paducah. They lived in a large, fine house of many rooms, conveniently arranged, nicely furnished, and in excellent order. The hearty welcome so cheerfully extended made me feel at home. The generous hospitality of the family was greatly appreciated and will not be forgotten. Captain Woodward and I had two servants. While one attended to our horses and other outdoor work, the other looked to our wants indoors and was otherwise made useful. On our departure, we left our horses and servants at the Woodwards' until we could learn further as to our destination. As it turned out, it would have proved much to our advantage had we also left our baggage there.

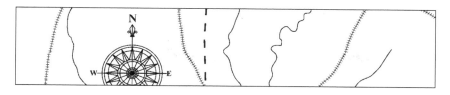

15. A Visit to Washington

We took our departure for the East on the morning of February 3, [1865,] and reached Pittsburgh at 3 o'clock A.M. on the 5th. The captain and I being on the sleeping car were dropped off, or run back, two miles from the station where we slept until morning, and did not get to the hotel until 9 o'clock A.M. I retained a warm feeling in my heart for the old smoky city. The loyalty of the people I knew to be as firm as the iron hills by which they were surrounded. It gave me satisfaction to remember it as my birthplace, and recalling the fact made me wonder if that occurrence there did not have something to do with establishing my own loyalty to my country.

If there had been any direct communication by rail with Youngstown, Ohio, I should have gone to that place, if only to shake hands with some of my old friends there, but I found it would have been necessary to have gone via Cleveland. As the detention would have been too great, although sorely tempted to undertake the additional journey I decided to undergo the disappointment and deprive myself of the pleasure until a more favorable opportunity could be afforded.

We left Pittsburgh at 4 o'clock P.M. on the 5th, and arrived at Philadelphia at 10 o'clock A.M. on February 6, where we put up at the Continental Hotel. I at once reported by letter to General Grant and requested an order to report to him in person before my assignment to duty. While Captain Woodward was out calling on relatives and friends, I strolled through the streets and was wonderfully well pleased with the quiet, home-like appearance of the Quaker City. I saw around me everywhere the unmistakable evidence of culture, refinement, and prosperity, and felt a great desire then to make that prosperous city my residence after the war was over.

Mr. Richard Campion, a cousin of Captain Woodward, called in the afternoon and took me out for a drive. In the evening we visited the skating park, which was filled with gentlemen and ladies. I tried skating the first time for many years. Strange to say, I did not tumble but managed to get along over the ice quite lively, as I had been at one time an expert, well-practiced in that amusement or art. After that sport was over, I called with Mr. Campion upon his father and mother, and later in the evening attended the theatre, which added still greater variety to the scenes which had occupied my attention for the day.

On the morning of the 7th, when continuing my efforts at sightseeing, I received complimentary cards of invitation and tickets to attend a grand masked-ball at the opera house that evening. I accepted with pleasure, as I had a desire to observe the fashions and ascertain whether or not I had forgotten how to dance. I enjoyed the entertainment exceedingly and passed most of the night there. February 8 was spent by myself and Woodward in making calls and a general round of festivities.

On the 9th, I received a telegram from General John A. Rawlins, directing me to proceed to Washington, where I would meet General Grant and receive orders. I had obtained the thirty-days' leave of absence from the War Department, but without hesitation decided that if General Grant wanted me for an important duty I would not make use of the leave at that time. The same day, I attended the wedding of a Miss Souder, the beautiful daughter of a wealthy resident of the city. It was a very grand affair. Woodward was one of the groomsmen. Everything was arranged in magnificent style and the presents to the bride were numerous and costly.

Altogether, I had a most agreeable time at Philadelphia during my short stay; the recreation was really beneficial as well as enjoyable. In a short time I had made the acquaintance of many pleasant people. I would have gladly remained longer in the city, but the orders received made my departure a necessity. Accordingly, I and Captain Woodward left the same night for Washington, where we arrived on February 10 and stopped at Willard's Hotel. When at supper late in the evening, General Grant, who had reached Washington the same day, entered the dining room, and seeing me as I arose to salute him, greeted me very warmly, remarking, as he took a seat at the same table, that he had already recommended my promotion and would issue orders directing me to report at New Orleans to Major General Canby to command his cavalry.

The same evening I called with General Grant at the White House to see President Lincoln, and had a delightful interview of over an hour's duration. Mr. Lincoln remembered me very well, we having frequently met during the Douglas-Lincoln campaign in Illinois and subsequently, up to the time he left Springfield on his way to Washington after his first election to the Presidency. But I did not see him again until my good fortune afforded me the opportunity the day after my first arrival at Washington, February 11, 1865. He gave me a most cordial reception, and complimented me highly on my successful service in the war. Our greeting over, the president was informed by General Grant that he had recommended my promotion. As there was no vacancy of full major general, I would be given the brevet of that grade and assigned to duty with my brevet rank. [Grant] add[ed] that he would subsequently recommend my advancement to a full major generalcy. To all of which Mr. Lincoln gave his hearty assent and approval.

He was in excellent spirits in view of the prospect of approaching peace and restoration of the Union. He referred to his interview with the so-called peace commissioners from the South,[1] and viewed their coming North as a strong indication that the rebel confederacy was nearing its death struggle. He also spoke of reconstruction, a subject to which he was evidently giving much thought at that time. He was particularly well pleased with my statements in regard to the condition of affairs in Tennessee. He told an anecdote that amused General Grant as much as myself.

The general had been quietly looking over the military map, which was spread out on a table in the room. As he walked over to where we were seated, he suggested to the president that it might be well for them to look it over again together. Mr. Lincoln and I arose. Thinking they might prefer to be alone at such a time, I was about to bid them good night, when they both expressed a wish for me to remain. Of course it was a great pleasure for me to do so, being really delighted with that additional mark of their regard and confidence. Our eyes were soon riveted on the war map, and General Grant, without a moment's hesitation, pointed out the position of the contending armies. Then, in more detail he showed the location of the troops under his own immediate command; those under Generals Sherman and Thomas; and indicated the movements that Generals Canby and Thomas would be ordered to make. All those movements of our forces, from widely separated points, were contemplated to be made simultaneously, and were the result of General Grant's well-matured plans to effectually end the war in the coming Spring campaign. There was not a particle of doubt in General Grant's mind at that time as to the result of the movements of our armies to be effected as then planned; the only apprehension in the general's mind was the fear that General Lee might make his escape with his army before the plans for the concerted operations of our forces could be executed. He pointed to Columbia, South Carolina, on the map and stated that General Sherman would be there with his army between February 15 and 20. Then the attention of the president was drawn to the sea coast by the general. They both recognized the great importance of the capture of Fort Fisher by General [Alfred] Terry's forces, assisted by the navy,[2] and felt sure that Wilmington and Charleston would soon fall into our possession.

The visit and interview soon after terminated, and the general and I bid Mr. Lincoln good night. Just then, not being able to resist the impulse at the moment of parting, I turned and grasped the president's hand again and in a few earnest words expressed the hope that many years of life were still in store for him; that I trusted he would not only live to see the Rebellion put down, but to also behold the Union restored with a thoroughly united country. A sudden thought seemed to flash over the countenance of Mr. Lincoln, who seemed to be looking far beyond into the future. In a moment, however, the former look returned to his remarkably kind and expressive face. He smiled and politely asked me to call upon him again if I had the time before my departure. In response, I stated that I would be most happy to do so; but if I did not, I certainly would endeavor to visit him again after the war was over. I little thought then that I would never see him again, and have often since wondered if behind the singular look I had observed upon his face, there could have been a premonition of his approaching death. I now look back upon that interview with Mr. Lincoln, in the presence of General Grant, so vividly impressed on my memory, as one of the brightest spots in my military experience.

My appointment was confirmed by the Senate without reference to the Military Committee, and on February 12 I received the following order: "By direction of the President, Brevet Major General B. H. Grierson, U.S. Vol's., is hereby assigned to duty according to his brevet rank, in the Military Division of West Mississippi. He will proceed without delay to New Orleans, La., and report in person to Major General Canby commanding, for assignment to the Cavalry in the Military Division of West Mississippi, organized for operations in the field."

I was also the bearer of the following letter from General Grant, written before the general left City Point, in anticipation of our interview in Washington:

Headquarters Army of the United States,
City Point Va. February 9th 1865,
Major General Canby, commanding Military Division West Mississippi
General:

I have ordered Gen. Grierson to report to you, to take the chief command of your Cavalry operating from Mobile Bay. I do not mean to fasten on you, commanders against your judgment or wishes, but you applied for [William W.] Averill,[3] I suppose for that service. I have no faith in him, and cannot point to a single success of his, except in his reports. Grierson, on the contrary, has been a most successful commander. He set the first example in making long raids by going through from Memphis to Baton Rouge. His raid this winter on the Mobile and Ohio Railroad was most important in its results and most successfully executed. I do not think I could have sent you a better man than Grierson to command your cavalry on an expedition to the interior of Alabama. Unless you go yourself I fear your other troops will not be so well commanded. What is wanted is a commander who will not be afraid to cut loose from his base of supplies, and who will make the best use of the resources of the country. An army the size of the one you will have can always get to some place where they can be supplied, if they fail to reach the point started for.

I had never been in Washington before. The announcement of that fact was very surprising to the heads of departments and men in high civil and military positions. When I called upon Secretary [of War Edwin M.] Stanton,[4] General [Winfield Scott] Hancock[5] was already in waiting at the door of the secretary's office. I was received first by Mr. Stanton. After our interview, he half apologized as he accompanied me out and introduced me to the general, good-humoredly remarking, "I can see you often Hancock, but this is Grierson's first call." Then, looking at me with a pleasant smile lightening up his remarkable face, Mr. Stanton continued, "Never in Washington before! Why you are a natural curiosity. We are besieged by officers. Many are here when they ought to be in the field or in camp." That was in substance a frequent greeting extended to me while in the capital.

Secretary Seward and other members of the Cabinet were equally glad to meet me and were free in their expressions of approbations as to my services. General Halleck, with whom I had frequently corresponded, but whom I had not met since 1861 at St. Louis, was delighted to see me again. He was especially elated over the success of my last expedition through Mississippi, as he had given the order to General Dana, and expressed great satisfaction in view of the fact that I had been selected to command and to carry the orders into execution. He hastily reviewed the situation of affairs, especially in the Military Division of West Mississippi, with which he was fully acquainted, and promised to assist me all in his power towards getting the cavalry of General Canby's command equipped for the field. He warmly shook my hand at parting, wishing me continued success.

The short time spent in Washington had passed pleasantly, and I had arranged to leave for New Orleans on the 13th. But there is yet another circumstance connected with that visit to the capital of the country yet to be related. As I was about to step on board the train with satchel in hand and all ready to start away, a card was handed to me by Senator [John P.] Hale,[6] who upon introducing himself requested me to please read it at once, as he had a message to me from the president. I glanced at the card and saw written on one side: "If it would be no detriment to the service

I would be glad for Gen. Grierson to remain at Washington two days longer.—A. Lincoln." On the other side of the card I found the following: "Gen. Grierson has permission to remain at Washington two days.—E. M. Stanton, Secretary of War." I still have the card, which I highly value.

Of course, I did not go off on the train that day. The president's request was really good authority for my delay, but I was glad to have the permission of the secretary of war. The card as written upon is strikingly characteristic of the two men. While Mr. Lincoln, although commander in chief of the army and navy, was careful and diffident about interfering directly in military matters; on the contrary, Mr. Stanton never hesitated about assuming any amount of responsibility.

The message I received from the president was simply that he had been so much interested in the conversation he had with me when I called with General Grant to see him that he wished me to say to the members of Congress the same things I had said to him, in the same earnest manner. The subject was the reconstruction of the conquered Southern states. Mr. Lincoln was then in favor of allowing Tennessee to elect her own state officers and form her own government as one of the states of the Union. I being fresh from the state of Tennessee, with my extended opportunities for observation in view of my long service there during the war, could bear witness as to the true condition of the people. Although the state had occupied a central position since the so-called Confederacy, East Tennessee had from the first manifested its devotion to the Union and maintained that feeling throughout the years of the Rebellion. The rebels of the central and western part of the state were still away in the rebel army or elsewhere giving their support to the rebel government. The few that were left back were tired of the war and really as loyal as they dare be, considering their associations and former proclivities, and could then have been trusted to act with the preponderating loyal element at the polls.

The most of the time during the two days that I remained at Washington was spent within the Senate Chamber and Hall of Representatives, both of which were open to me, where I met and conversed freely with all of the most prominent members of Congress on the subject as desired by the president. Many of the senators and representatives were strongly in favor of adopting Mr. Lincoln's proposition, but others were still afraid to trust the Tennesseans at that time. The failure of Congress to seize the opportune moment to carry that feasible project into effect caused much subsequent embarrassment. By waiting until peace was proclaimed, the turbulent element returned to oppose the administration in every possible manner, and thus greatly retarded the enforcement of the reconstruction measures finally adopted by the government.[7]

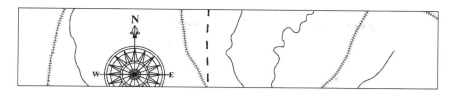

16. Final Operations

Being advised to go by the ocean route to New Orleans, and thinking it might be the most expeditious, we left Washington on the evening of February 15 with that purpose in view. But upon arrival at New York City the next day, [we] found that in order to embark on a through or fast ocean steamer there would be several days' delay. Therefore, I decided to proceed via Cairo and the Mississippi River to the Crescent City.

We left New York via the Pennsylvania Central Railroad on February 17. Upon arrival at Pittsburgh, I instructed Captain Woodward to go direct to Paducah to arrange for the shipment of our horses; also to trace up and have our baggage shipped to New Orleans and to procure transportation for our servants. While he was performing that duty, I in the meantime snatched one day to visit my family at Jacksonville. From thence I proceeded via Tolono on the Wabash and Illinois Central Railroad and thus managed to rejoin Woodward at Cairo on the 22nd. We then continued our journey together by steamboat to our destination.

Early on the morning of the 24th we reached Memphis. While the boat remained at the landing putting off and receiving freight, we called upon the officers of our acquaintance in the city and made a short visit with my brother and family. His wife had been dangerously ill, but was then convalescing and felt sure of a speedy recovery.

We left Memphis the same day but were delayed by fog and violent winds, and did not get to Vicksburg until sometime before daylight on the 27th. While the boat stopped, we made our way in the dark into the post to call upon Generals Washburn and Morgan L. Smith, both of whom we found in bed, but who cheerfully got up to receive and have a talk with us in regard to army matters.

We passed Natchez, Mississippi, on the evening of the 27th and made tolerably good time thereafter until arrival at Baton Rouge, where the boat remained for several hours discharging freight. The place seemed remarkably familiar to us and brought fresh to our minds the scenes connected with the raid of 1863. From that point our progress was slow, as numerous delays occurred on account of the continued stormy weather. Within six miles of New Orleans, the boat had to lay up for one whole night owing to an unusually dense fog then prevailing, and we did not reach New Orleans until March 1, 1865.

Upon arrival, I at once reported to General Canby and soon after received the following orders [March 1, 1865]: "Brevet Major General B. H. Grierson, U.S. Vol's., is hereby assigned to the general command of all the Cavalry in this Military Division, and to the special command of all the Cavalry forces designated for service in the field."

I accepted General Canby's kind invitation to dine with himself and family at 4 P.M. that day, and remained at his house until 7 P.M., where I had the pleasure of meeting Mrs. Canby, her niece, and another lady. I was delighted with Mrs. Canby's quiet, unassuming manner, and judged her to be much like the general in temperament. She possessed a fund of information well stored in memory, with a rare faculty of imparting it, and she related many amusing reminiscences of army life, much to the enjoyment of all who were present.

Captain Woodward and I passed the evening from 7 to 9 o'clock at General Hurlbut's quarters, situated on the same street only a few doors from General Canby's. Besides the genial general, we met Mrs. Hurlbut and were most agreeably entertained. Upon return to the St. Charles, to give still greater variety to the day's operations, we went to the theatre. After the performance, [we] returned to the hotel, where before going to bed I wrote my daily letter to Mrs. Grierson giving a detailed account of those occurrences.

In accordance with the wish of General Canby, I called at his office at 10 A.M. on March 2 to confer with him in regard to the selection and concentration of the cavalry for field operations. From a list prepared by Colonel [T. C.] Christensen I found that there were about 36,000 cavalry and mounted infantry in the Military Division of West Mississippi, widely scattered throughout the departments of the Gulf, Arkansas, and Mississippi, all in bad condition for want of horses and proper arms and equipments. General Canby desired me to get together, with the least possible delay, a corps of cavalry consisting of three divisions, numbering in all 10,000 or 12,000 men. I found from an examination of the rolls, inspection reports, and other papers bearing on the subject that it would require a month, and perhaps more, to carry the instructions of the general into effect, but at once set to work with the determination that there should be no delay by any fault of mine in accomplishing the desired result.

I had never met General Canby until my arrival at New Orleans, although I had previously been under his command. I was greatly pleased with his appearance. He was affable and courteous in his manner, tall and fine looking, soldierly in his bearing, and I soon became much attached to him. His office was open to me at all hours and I never found him too busy to promptly respond to my inquiries. He was very entertaining in conversation; had a thorough knowledge of the details of the service; and [was] especially well versed in regard to the duties of the various staff departments of the army, in which he had spent the most of his time during his long service as an officer. The members of his staff were obliging, and cheerfully rendered me every assistance in their power in obtaining supplies for the troops designated for service in the field.

The infantry and artillery were being pushed forward to the vicinity of Mobile as rapidly as transportation was available, and General Canby and his staff, excepting such officers as had to be left to take charge of the division headquarters at New Orleans, arranged to leave for the front on March 6. One division of cavalry, under command of General [Thomas J.] Lucas,[1] was shipped to Pensacola, Florida, and another, under General Knipe, was being organized as the regiments arrived, and held in readiness for shipment to the vicinity of Fort Gaines, Alabama, as transportation could be provided by the quartermaster's department.

Instead of the veteran regiments promised me, and which General Grant had directed to be sent to General Canby, I found that Knipe's division was mostly composed of new Indiana and Tennessee troops. I sent the 19th Pennsylvania Cavalry, which was not in condition for the field, back to Baton Rouge; the 10th Tennessee to Natchez; the 2nd Tennessee and 9th Indiana Cavalry to Vicksburg, and substituted in their stead the 2nd New Jersey and 4th Wisconsin Cavalry. Colonels Kargé and [Gilbert M. L.] Johnson were assigned to the command of brigades in Knipe's division, both being active and competent officers. Eleven regiments of cavalry, in addition to those enumerated, were ordered to New Orleans—seven from Memphis, two from Little Rock, and two from Baton Rouge—with which I hoped to form another division under command of General [Joseph R.] West, who was subsequently, during the days of Reconstruction, United States senator from Louisiana.[2]

For ten days after our arrival at New Orleans, we had been rooming at the St. Charles Hotel and getting meals at restaurants. But, finding it expensive and inconvenient to continue living in that manner, we had a building assigned to us on Carondelet Street as private quarters, and soon after rooms for office purposes on another street near Generals Canby's and Hurlbut's headquarters.

Before leaving the hotel, the clerk handed me a package which he found in the hotel storeroom, where it had been packed away for nearly two years.

It was securely done up and plainly addressed to "Col. B. H. Grierson, 6th Ills. Cavalry." Upon opening it, I was surprised and much pleased to find therein a fine pair of gold-plated spurs. There was also a note from the donor, apologizing for not giving his name; stating that he was strongly identified with Southern interests, but presented the gift to simply indicate his ability, notwithstanding his prejudices, to thus recognize the valor displayed on my daring and successful raid through the Confederacy. The spurs fit me admirably, and I wore them during my subsequent service in the war.

Much of southern Louisiana and Alabama being low flatlands and frequently impassable during the spring of the year, it was thought by General Canby and others that the wet weather would greatly delay military operations against Mobile. The South was not always sunny, but brighter days were soon coming to enable "Uncle Sam's" bodyguard to march onward to victory.

Upon arrival at New Orleans, I had applied for a quartermaster and commissary of subsistence to be ordered to report to me, but I found it difficult to obtain suitable officers for those positions. There had been a board of officers in session for several weeks, jokingly called the "Inquisition," which assembled for the purpose of examining officers of the staff departments as to their qualifications and general fitness for the service. Several officers, on an adverse report of the board, had been dismissed for alleged incompetency. Learning from the *Army and Navy Journal* of the confirmation of my brother's appointment as captain and a.q.m. [assistant quartermaster], U.S. volunteers, I hoped to have him ordered to duty with the cavalry corps. But illness prevented his joining us in the field.

The 3rd Michigan Cavalry, from Little Rock, arrived at New Orleans on March 23. With it and the regiments expected from Memphis, I hoped to organize another division of cavalry. I had been authorized by General Canby to proceed to Memphis and, if necessary, to General Thomas' headquarters to hasten the shipment of the cavalry to New Orleans. Not deeming it best to go myself, I ordered Captain [Charles J.] Walker on that duty. But, in the face of orders from Generals Grant, Canby, and Halleck, General Washburn persisted in holding the cavalry on a report that the rebels were advancing from the direction of Eastport to attack the city. The infantry and artillery then at Memphis were sufficient for the defense of the place, even had the report been true. Yet eleven regiments of cavalry, mostly veteran troops, were kept there on picket duty.

Previous to the inauguration of General Grant's last campaign in Virginia, orders had been issued by the War Department transferring the Department of the Arkansas to General [John] Pope's command, thus reducing by one-third the dimensions of General Canby's military division, and removing from his control a large force of cavalry and other troops.

During our stay at New Orleans, through the kindness of General and Mrs. Hurlbut, we frequently spent an evening at their quarters, where we occasionally met friends from Illinois. Our visits were always homelike and enjoyable. While there one evening, I remember the general alluding in an amusing manner to the controversy which had for some time been going on between the churches and theatres on account of Sunday theatrical performances. Several prominent ministers of the city were holding services in the streets, in close proximity to the theatres, and some disturbances had occurred. The general decided to restrict the preaching to the inside of church buildings, and close all the theatres on Sundays. The next day orders were issued accordingly, on the general principle that the Seventh-day rest, distinctive of Christendom, should be maintained in every Christian community. The ministers who had been preaching in the streets, although endowed with stupendous lungs and stentorian voices, probably did not offer attractions equivalent to the theatres. But their whole souls were enlisted in the cause they were advocating in their earnest attempt to unfold what they believed to be the highest treasures for humanity. The result of General Hurlbut's timely action was viewed as a decided victory for those who valued Christian observances.

Although the time fixed upon for the further concentration of the cavalry had come, the six regiments of cavalry ordered from Memphis were still held there by General Washburn in violation of orders. It was therefore impossible for me to organize the cavalry corps as required for field service by General Canby's instructions. I wrote to him in regard to the matter and asked that I be permitted to go into the field with the force then available—6,000 men instead of 12,000 as previously directed. The following answer was soon received [April 6, 1865]: "Be pleased to perfect the organization of the 6,000 cavalry with the utmost dispatch, and let that number suffice for the present. The General commanding desires you to report to him at once, and to take measures to see that everything will work well after you leave New Orleans. We have received no plans of organization and [I] am therefore compelled to order all detachments to report temporarily to Gen. Knipe, that is, those that do not belong to his Division, as, for instance, the 4th Wisconsin Cavalry."

The advance of General Grant's army on Petersburg and Richmond had caused the evacuation of those strongholds, and the rebels under General Lee were fleeing southward in great disorder. The Confederacy had already become a skeleton almost as pitiable as some of our martyred heroes in their Southern prison hells. The sufferings and wrongs inflicted upon our soldiers when taken prisoners by the enemy justly called for punishment to our country's inhuman foes in the last struggles of the rebellion. The war was rapidly nearing its close, but it was still necessary to fight on until such a peace could be obtained as would secure the respect and confidence of the world, and silence forever the incredulous taunts of our European enemies.

I made arrangements at once to promptly carry into effect the instructions received from General Canby. An officer was detailed to take charge of our office at New Orleans, to remain during our absence, to receive and forward mail, and with a view to relieve Major Woodward so far as possible from the extra work which had been devolving upon him. An acting quartermaster and commissary was selected and detailed, and instructions given to prepare for our departure on April 10. As our baggage had not been received from Annapolis, we were obliged to purchase saddles and equipments, mess chest, and outfit sufficient for our immediate wants. Before leaving the city for Mobile, I wrote to Gen. Halleck [April 7, 1865]:

> Before leaving for the field, permit me to state for your information the condition of the cavalry of this Command. The eight regiments sent from Tennessee under Brigadier General Knipe, consisted of four new Indiana regiments, three Tennessee regiments and the 10th Pennsylvania, and arrived here about half mounted and poorly armed. Four of the poorest of those regiments are now at points on the Mississippi River above this place; dismounted, having been sent to take the place of Cavalry now at the front, and that which was temporarily sent to Memphis, Tenn., which is being detained by Gen. Washburn, and in regard to which, I telegraphed you on the 28th of March. The want of transportation has very much delayed the shipment of the Cavalry to Mobile Bay. I have organized it as effectively as possible with the material at hand; but we are very much in need of arms. I hope the Spencer Carbines and accoutrements for which I applied on arrival here have been forwarded. Very few horses have been received since my arrival and nearly all the Cavalry left in the Departments of the Mississippi and the Gulf is entirely dismounted. There are now at Memphis eleven regiments of Cavalry, mostly veteran troops; if it is deemed best to keep a force of Cavalry there, and if all the Cavalry applied for by Gen. Canby cannot be spared, I hope the following at least may be ordered to join us in the field, viz.: 1st Iowa, 12th Ills. and 11th New York Cavalry, and if consistent with your views, I would request that the 8th Missouri be ordered here also from the Department of Arkansas; relying upon your assistance and necessary orders for the material to fully equip and render effective the Cavalry of this Military Division.

I deemed it important that the foregoing letter be written and placed on file at the War Department, [so] that the authorities and others properly concerned might fully understand the true condition of affairs within the Military Division of West Mississippi at that time, and the impossibility for me, under the circumstances, to take into the field the three divisions which were required by my orders and instructions to constitute the cavalry corps it was intended that I should command on the expedition made through Alabama by me near the close of the war.

———

Quickly following the fall of Richmond and flight of Lee's army, information reached me of the capture of Spanish Fort and Fort Blakely, Alabama. It became evident that Mobile would soon be in possession of General Canby's troops. It really seemed to me then that the war might end before I could even start on my last march through the shaky Confederacy.

For some unaccountable reason, Woodward's commission as major and assistant adjutant general had been long delayed. Naturally enough it was looked for with a feeling of anxiety by Woodward and myself. Fortunately, the gloom vanished from our minds and gave place to satisfaction when we saw the long expected parchment, which luckily was received on April 10, the day fixed upon for our departure. With his commission in hand the major hastened off to find a notary in order to take the oath required by law from every officer advanced to a higher grade in the army. The commission then obtained by Woodward was gained by energetic and successful field service during the war, then so near its close, and I was as much pleased as he at his well-deserved advancement.

We were in readiness to leave New Orleans on the morning of April 9, and expected to get away the next day. But the steamer on which we were to cross the Gulf of Mexico failed to reach Lakeport on the 10th, when due, and did not get into the harbor until late the following day, so that we were unavoidably detained twenty-four hours, when anxiously desiring to get underway. We finally started from the city at 4 o'clock P.M., April 11, on a special railroad train for Lakeport, and left the latter place at eight the same evening on board the steamer bound for Mobile Bay.

The weather was clear and really delightful. There was a gentle invigorating breeze from the ocean, but it was not cold enough to be disagreeable. A few light fleecy clouds were flitting over the face of the full moon that seemed only to add to its brilliancy. With such apparently auspicious surroundings, the change for us from land to water leading out into the open sea was, for a time at least, particularly enjoyable. But the steamship, in its usual course, rapidly bore us away from land. The breeze, at first so mild and pleasant, increased in force and soon became almost a gale. Dark clouds could be seen gathering near the horizon, and there were other indications of an approaching storm. It was not long before it burst upon us in earnest and we realized the fact that we were in the midst of a rough and boisterous sea. The waves rolled high and at times dashed furiously against the vessel, tossing it about like a leaf in the air. It became difficult for us to keep step together. Yet manfully, like two old tars, we continued to brave the storm and pace the deck.

I soon perceived that my adjutant general, usually so vivacious and buoyant in spirits, was becoming singularly dull and quiet. Upon closer observation, I noticed that he became pale and ghost-like in appearance. Suddenly, I missed him from my side, which caused me some alarm. But upon investigation, being made aware of his safety and whereabouts, I resumed the march alone on the deck until the sky became entirely obscured by clouds accumulated during the storm which continued to rage throughout the night. It is said that a person who remains absolutely well at such a time is apt to have an uncontrollable desire to laugh at a companion who may have a less fortunate experience. Be that as it may, to the best of my recollection I retained my self-control and composure. Possibly, although feeling splendidly myself during the entire voyage, I could not know at the time of Woodward's indisposition, when things looked so awfully squally, or be at all sure that I would not be seasick before reaching land. It may be true, as generally considered, that illness of such a nature is frequently more beneficial than dangerous, despite its many discomforts. But I can here bear testimony to the fact that Major Woodward was a very sick man indeed, and I doubt if he would care to have another such lively whirl on the ocean. Even after he got safely on shore, he looked like a thunder cloud and it required a day or two for him to regain his usual serenity

We arrived safely at Fort Gaines on April 12, where we were freshly reminded of the brilliant achievements of the navy under the command of the renowned hero Admiral Farragut. Although the steamer stopped only a few minutes, I seized the opportunity to write to Mrs. Grierson a short account of the voyage thus far. We were soon under way for Stark's Landing, a point about eight miles south of Fort Blakely, where we arrived in the night. [We] reached the fort the next morning, when we learned that Mobile—having been evacuated by the enemy—was occupied by the United States troops the day before our arrival.

Fortunately, it so happened that I met General Canby at Fort Blakely, just as he was about to start with his staff for Mobile. The general kindly asked me to accompany him to the city, and I cheerfully accepted the invitation. It was my first visit there, and I was much pleased with the appearance of the place. All approaches to the city were strongly fortified. The bay was said to be literally filled with torpedoes and other obstructions. It seemed, however, that there never was anything constructed, either on land or water, so strong or impregnable that the "Yankees" could not manage to get under or over. General Canby was in excellent spirits and much elated over his success. The troops under his command had captured in and around Mobile about 4,000 prisoners and 210 cannon, besides a large amount of other war material and rebel government property.[3] The general at once established his headquarters in the Custom House at Mobile, which seemed to be the most suitable building available for the purpose.

Upon my return to Blakely, I found the cavalry there, excepting two regiments daily expected from New Orleans. The command was not such as I desired to have for the movement I was about to make, but I was determined to do the best I could with it; and, in any event, to endeavor to be successful. I therefore reorganized the cavalry into brigades, which made a division, instead of the corps I had previously hoped to command.

While passing over the bay with General Canby, he confidentially informed me in regard to his plans for further operations. He desired that I should move out with my available force in the direction of Montgomery, Alabama, in conjunction with General A. J. Smith's corps; to cooperate with and support it in case of necessity. I was, however, to have an independent command with discretionary power, and to be guided by my own judgment as to movements after reaching the central portion of the state. General Smith's command was already on the march northward, and it was expected that I would overtake and pass his corps at or near Greenville, Alabama. In compliance with orders, I again crossed the bay on a steamer to Mobile in the afternoon of April 15 for the purpose of receiving my final instructions. I was then accompanied by Major Woodward, assistant adjutant general of my staff. We remained in the city until the evening of April 16, when the following communication was received:

> . . . You will start with your command to-morrow, following Gen. Smith's column on the Stockton and Montgomery stage road, and marching with the greatest possible rapidity—without injuring your horses—in order to overtake Gen. Smith; as soon as you have reached his column, you will leave the Montgomery road to your left, pushing to the front and right of the Infantry Column. The objective point of the main column is Montgomery. While operations against that place are going on, you will secure with such portion of your command as are not needed in Montgomery, the country between Tallaposa and Chattahoochie [sic] rivers as far

north as Danville and West Point. Opelika must be broken and destroyed at once, and the attention of the rebels drawn in a northward direction. You will however keep the best mounted portion
of your command in reserve behind your extreme right and ready
to cross the Chattahoochie River at any point below Columbus,
surprising and capturing it and breaking and burning the railroad
bridges and trestle-work east of Columbus as far as possible, in
and around Columbus. Everything that can be made useful to the
enemy will be destroyed. If you consider it prudent and advisable,
you may after the successful capture of Columbus, remain and
advance on the east bank of the river to West Point, treating that
place in the same manner as Columbus; this however, ought not to
be done without a cooperating force on the west bank; it will not
be desirable to meet with any opposition of the enemy until West
Point and the rail-road bridge across the Chattahoochie River
are in our hands, and if you should anticipate a serious collision,
not easily overcome before attaining the above results, you had
better recross the Chattahoochie at Columbus and descend on
West Point on the west bank. Returning from these expeditions
you will destroy the railroad track from Columbus to Opelika,
and await the development of the result of the movements of the
cooperating columns of Generals Steele and Smith. The task assigned you is very great. A successful result is dependent on the
most rigid discipline, and the heartiest cooperation of every officer
and man; the work can only be achieved by energy, vigilance, valor
and intrepidity. The command must be kept well in hand, and the
Commanding Officers are to be held personally responsible for
the maintenance of the strictest order, while the destruction of the
enemy's lines of communication and his sources of supply is going
on. It is most essential to capture and destroy the greatest number
of locomotives and rolling stock, as they are of greater value to the
enemy than the track itself; the latter can be repaired, the former
never replaced.

The foregoing instructions were carried out so far as practicable. They
were given under the impression that resistance would be met with on the
line of march designated, but events then transpiring and soon to take place
made it impracticable to destroy property in a country already destitute
from the effects of a prolonged war, when it was evident that the states in rebellion would soon fall back under the control of the federal government.

In view of the condition of affairs at that time, it is proper here to state
that previous to our departure from Blakely, on the march through Alabama
to Georgetown, Georgia, official information had been received at Mobile
of the surrender of Lee's army to General Grant. It was also rumored that

Johnston's army had surrendered to General Sherman. I hoped, however, that the two regiments from New Orleans would arrive in time to join us, so as to increase my force to at least 5,000 men. But, under all the circumstances, I judged the regiments then immediately available a sufficient force to accomplish the main object of the expedition—even if we met with resistance. A still further reduction in the strength of my command—although unexpected—being unavoidable, it was viewed by me as a matter of indifference.

Therefore, with cheerfulness and alacrity, I moved out from Blakely on April 17, 1865, with the brigades of Generals T. J. Lucas and Joseph Kargé, a force amounting in all to 4,000 men. We marched, when practicable, in two columns and proceeded northeastward towards Montgomery. It was the same date of the month and just two years from the time I had started on the raid from La Grange to Baton Rouge. The weather was favorable for military movements. Having heard the good news of Lee's surrender, the troops were in excellent spirits and the officers and enlisted men looked forward to a speedy termination of hostilities, feeling assured that they would soon be permitted to return to their homes in the North after the fatiguing marches and many hardships endured during the war.

Our route from Mobile Bay was mostly through pine forests, which were lighted up here and there by openings and settlements, where we found the inhabitants much surprised at our sudden appearance, they at that time not being aware of the collapse of the rebellion and still imbued with the belief that the "Yankees" would never be allowed to enter that section of the so-called Confederacy. After continuing the march for a day or two, although pine woods were still the prevailing feature of the country, the undergrowth was less dense [and] the timber was more open.

At one time, while approaching a gentle rise near which the road wound about in a singular manner over undulating ground, I noticed from the head of the column that nearly the entire command could be seen apparently marching in all directions, with arms and equipments one moment flashing and the next obscured by alternating sunlight and shadow, while tall pines seemed to mingle with and surround the moving troopers like stately living sentinels. The view as then observed was remarkably attractive to the eyes and senses of the beholders, and will probably be remembered by others whose presence there that day helped to give life, strength, and motion to the picturesque scene. To soldiers, however, presumably marching through an enemy's country fully prepared to fight on a moment's notice, not meeting with any opposition whatever and not required to fire a shot, being deprived of everything in the way of excitement to which they were so well accustomed, even the grateful shade of lofty pines and beauty of the varied landscape became wearisome in time. Therefore, the opportunity which was offered for an exchange of friendly greetings between old comrades when we overtook and passed General A. J. Smith's corps, some distance south of Greenville, proved decidedly exhilarating and a welcome break in our hitherto quiet and rather monotonous march.

After a short halt, we moved forward and encamped for the night of April 22 at the town of Greenville, where we found the people filled with apprehension and hurriedly fleeing from their houses in amazement. The prompt placing of pickets and other guards throughout the town, to preserve order and prevent depredations, soon had a quieting effect, and the anxiety at first so manifest gradually gave way to a general feeling of security.

In the evening, a note was received from General Smith, stating that he would be at my camp at 8 o'clock the next morning, as he had important information to communicate in regard to future movements and desired to know at what time I intended to resume the march. I answered accordingly and awaited his arrival. He reached my camp at the hour specified. I soon learned that he, like myself, was much disappointed at not meeting with any opposition from the rebels, and also disgusted at the poor prospect for any fighting further north, as it was evident from the latest information we had received from our scouts and other sources that there was really no effective force of the enemy in the state of Alabama. As General Smith's orders required him to move on at once to Montgomery, I sent with his command my wagon train, sick men, and convalescents to that place, it being then understood that transports would soon arrive there with troops and supplies from Mobile.

My command having been placed in light marching order, supplied with ten-days' rations and such forage as could be carried on our limited transportation, I ordered General Lucas to proceed with his brigade northeastward to Union Springs, Bullock County, while with Colonel Kargé's brigade I moved east through Butler, Crenshaw, Pike, and Barbour counties, via Rutledge, Troy, Louisville, and Clayton, to Eufaula, Alabama, and Georgetown, Georgia. The excitement and alarm among the inhabitants of that section of the state, which hitherto had not been occupied by United States troops, was universal and intense. Delegates of prominent residents of the towns through which we passed met us at the outskirts, trembling with fear for the safety of their families and property. They were in every instance kindly received and promptly assured that it was not our intention to interfere in any manner with non-combatants; that to avoid molestation they should remain quietly at their homes and pursue their usual peaceful occupations and not attempt to interfere with [the] duties devolving upon us.

Although we did not expect to meet with resistance, yet we realized the fact that we were passing through a region that had been in the undisturbed possession of the rebels for several years. Therefore, the usual precautions were at all times taken. Suitable details under discreet officers, well-instructed in their duties, were sent from time to time well out upon our flanks to gain information and to rapidly advance to occupy towns, picket roads, guard bridges, and take possession of all the public property that could be found.

While those duties were being performed, the main column halted at proper intervals and positions to await the result and receive reports from the officers in charge of such details. It was generally at such times that the delegations above referred to would meet us, under a small guard from our advance. After the interviews terminated, they were allowed to return under suitable escort to their homes in order that the people might be better prepared for our entrance. Those who came or were sent to meet us were men of recognized standing in the community where they resided, quick to perceive the true situation of affairs and capable of appreciating our lenience and courtesy. Upon return to their homes, they were able to allay all misapprehensions in the minds of the people. It was seldom, therefore, that any serious disturbances arose.

It was at Clayton, Alabama, when entirely cut off from all communication from other Federal troops, that the first report of the assassination of President Lincoln was received through captured rebel mail. We were, of course, filled with amazement but placed little reliance in the rumor, as it seemed incredible and really too horrible to be true. Subsequent information, however, from reliable sources, confirmed the first report. With profound sorrow, we were reluctantly obliged to realize the fact that the heinous crime had been perpetrated. The inhuman act was universally deplored, and viewed by the soldiers then under my command as a despicable and savage thrust at the heart of the nation. The excitement for a time was extremely alarming, and tested to the utmost our power of forbearance and self-control. The least expression of a revengeful spirit upon my part, or indication that retaliation would be tolerated, would have gone throughout the command like a flash of lightning and resulted, no doubt, in the complete desolation of the surrounding country and death of many comparatively innocent people. To me it is now exceedingly gratifying to be able to look back on that trying scene in my experience [and know] that, notwithstanding the aggravating circumstances by which we were confronted, impelling us to take a different course of action, our supreme sense of right and adherence to the demands of duty as soldiers of the Republic enabled us to rise above the trying emergency by remaining passive observers of that deplorable event in the history of our country.

It had been my intention on crossing the Chattahoochee River to make a dash to Andersonville, Georgia, to liberate the Union soldiers there held in loathsome prisons,[4] and with my force thus augmented to proceed to some place on the Atlantic Coast, or northward through the Carolinas and Virginia to Washington, D.C. Upon reaching Eufaula, Alabama, however, information was received of the armistice between General Sherman and General Johnston, in view of which it was of course impracticable to make the contemplated movements. Therefore, the command was quietly held in camps in the vicinity of Georgetown and Eufaula until the terms of the surrender of Johnston's army were adjusted in such manner as to meet the approval of the authorities at Washington. In the meantime, however, I had instructed General Lucas to join me with his brigade in order that my entire force would be well in hand for active operations in the event of a renewal of hostilities.

At the date of my interview with President Lincoln and General Grant at Washington, D.C., in February, General Sherman's troops were approaching Columbia, South Carolina. From thence, the general marched his army northward without encountering any serious opposition until engaged by General Johnston's rebel forces near Bentonville, North Carolina, between March 15 [19] and 20 [21]. A few days after, by forming a junction with General Terry's and General Schofield's commands, General Sherman's force was increased to nearly 80,000 men. With his army thus strengthened, he was again preparing to advance when official notice reached him of the surrender of General Lee's army to General Grant. Soon after, the armistice was arranged between General Sherman and General Johnston, information in regard to which, however, did not reach us until our arrival at Eufaula on April 29, my command then being one of the most isolated in the service. General Wilson had crossed the Chattahoochee, north of us, with a large force of cavalry and was moving eastward when his further advance was stopped by instructions from General Sherman.

We were much pleased with Eufaula, which is beautifully situated on the west bank of the Chattahoochee River. Our entrance into the town was made by a road located on high ground from which an extended view could be obtained, presenting remarkably picturesque scenery that might well fill with emotion the heart of an artist. The streets were entirely deserted, the guards and pickets from my command then being the only moving objects to be seen. The column had been well closed up and the cavalry advanced in excellent order. To the best of my recollection, on every house we passed provided with shutters or blinds, they were securely fastened. In those which had none, the curtains were down, as if the occupants were determined not even to look upon the so-called "barbarous Yankee soldiers." It seemed as if the people must have departed to some other region, or suddenly died, so quietly were they housed within doors.

The bridge over the Chattahoochee had previously been secured and properly guarded. When it was learned that the people were not to be molested, a change gradually "stole over the spirit of their dreams," and in a few days they were pursuing their usual occupations. The first to call to see me were the gentlemen who had met us at the outskirts of the town, the leading spirit among whom was a Mr. Hughs [James L. Pugh], who since the war has been United States senator.[5] He was very affable in his bearing, and the second greeting with the delegation was cordial and satisfactory to all. I suggested that it might be well for someone to give me a full account of all public property at or in the vicinity of the town, which was done without hesitation. Some of the party accompanied me to the buildings where the Confederate government cotton was stored, expecting no doubt to witness its destruction. They were agreeably surprised when they heard me give instructions for an increase of the guard for its greater security, although under my orders I might have caused it to be burned at once. We remained at Eufaula and vicinity for about one week.

As an evidence of the marked change in the sentiment of the people in regard to us, it is only necessary to state that it was not long before I was kindly invited to the houses of some of the most prominent citizens of the place. But I excused myself from accepting their hospitality on account of my time being so much occupied with the official duties then devolving upon me. It so happened, however, that one of the leading society women there, who felt herself in some manner indebted to us for some favor or courtesy, showed her appreciation of our action by giving myself and staff a written invitation to spend the evening at her house to meet in an informal manner a few of her friends who desired to make our acquaintance. The lady was so fortunate [gracious?] in giving expression to her request that I could not well refuse compliance.

Therefore, at the appointed time leaving my quartermaster and commissary in charge of headquarters and directing Colonel Kargé to look after such matters as might require attention, I accompanied by Major Woodward proceeded to the residence designated, where we were gracefully received and agreeable entertained by the lady of the house. The mansion was one of the finest in the place and comfortably, if not gorgeously, furnished. The lady's husband was absent, having had some position in the doomed Confederacy, whether in the military or civil service I was not informed. Two of their children—bright, neatly clad youngsters—were present. Among the invited guests, besides ourselves, there were six or eight tastefully, if not over-fashionably, attired women. I must state that they gave evidence of refinement and culture that rather surprised me, two at least being musicians of superior attainments.

A most cordial feeling prevailed during our visit. After refreshments were served, noticing a fine piano in the parlor I requested the hostess to favor us with a song, seeing on the instrument with other music several songs with which I was familiar. She, without hesitation or excuse, nodded to another lady present to play the accompaniment, while she sang the piece selected in an exquisite manner, showing that she possessed a cultivated voice of much sweetness, power, and compass. The piece being concluded, I was reminded of the fact that a young lady then there was considered one of the most skillful performers on the piano in the place. Woodward's eyes flashed out in the direction of the handsome young woman. Both he and myself expressed the wish that we might have the pleasure of listening to her performance. The exercise of our powers of persuasion was not long required, as the musician at once said she had come expressly to meet and entertain us to the best of her ability. She proved to be a very skillful performer who with ease executed the most difficult music with rapidity and precision, the most of which was well known to me.

I had cautioned Woodward not to give me away by indicating that I knew anything about music. But seeing a look on his face that warned me that he would not heed my admonition, I in an effort to get the start of him announced that my adjutant general had a fine voice, was a fine singer as I could testify, and that he frequently sang for me in an admirable manner. That was simply a statement of fact. But Woodward winced under it and remarked good-humoredly that he only sang for me when we were alone. That, too, was about the fact in the case. Nevertheless, I have often been amused and entertained by listening to his comic songs.

It was not long until he managed to make known to the company that I was a musician, and although at that time out of practice, I did and could play on all instruments from a jew's harp to an organ. Not being able to deny the assertion, and having enjoyed the music furnished by others, I played some waltzes of my own composition, so that my stumbling might not be so noticeable. Being further importuned, [I] sang one song, a "Farewell Serenade," which was somewhat appropriate to the occasion. The music, not having been published, was unknown to all present excepting Woodward and myself, and I had to finally acknowledge that it was of my own production.

The evening passed in a most delightful manner and it was with feeling of reluctance, on our part at least, that we bid our new acquaintances good-bye. We bore away with us a pleasant remembrance of that entertainment and of the genial people we met far down in the South who, if still living, will recollect the occurrences with a feeling not devoid of satisfaction.

A large amount of grain and provisions that had been gathered from the surrounding country as supplies for the rebel army were found hid away in cellars of private houses. Of these stores, such as were needed by my command were regularly issued to the troops, and whatever was left gratuitously divided among the inhabitants of the town and adjacent country. Many poor people, hearing that provisions were being thus distributed, came from a long distance and gladly availed themselves of the opportunity to obtain in that manner food for their suffering families. Those who had no means of transportation were given broken-down captured stock to enable them to return to their homes, while smiles of satisfaction would momentarily appear to enliven the habitually sad expression of their wan and disconsolate faces.

On May 5, being notified of the surrender of all the rebel troops east of the Chattahoochee River, I gave the necessary orders for the movement of my command and proceeded with the least practicable delay from Eufaula and Georgetown to Montgomery, arriving there on the 10th of that month, where we learned of the surrender [by] General Dick Taylor to General Canby of all the rebel troops and material of war pertaining to the Confederate government within the department east of the Mississippi River. During our short stay at Montgomery, I fell under the command of General A. J. Smith. On the evening of May 10, in obedience to his instructions, I ordered the 2nd New Jersey Cavalry to proceed at once to Talladega, Alabama. On the 11th I marched with the balance of my command northwest via Kingston, Centerville, Marion, Greensboro, Eutaw, and Pickensville to Columbus, Mississippi, reporting my arrival at the latter place on May 20, by telegraph, to General Canby.

At a point near Marion while en route from Montgomery, I sent the 2nd Illinois Cavalry to Tuscaloosa and with numerous detachments scoured the country in all directions; watched the crossings of the Black Warrior and Tombigbee rivers with a view of intercepting and capturing Jeff Davis, who was reported to be trying to reach the Trans-Mississippi Department through Alabama.[6] Upon reaching Columbus, I sent the 13th Indiana Cavalry south along the line of the Mobile and Ohio Railroad to Macon for the purpose of collecting and guarding all public property at or near that place.

The expedition terminated at Columbus; the distance traveled was about 700 miles. While en route, over 10,000 Confederate officers and soldiers were paroled under my supervision. Although we passed directly on the line of march over 3,000 bales of cotton, much of it public property, and also large quantities of grain and other supplies, not deeming it good policy to destroy property when the war was so near its end, I did not permit the cotton to be burned, believing it would all find its way to market under the control of the United States government. The unserviceable animals, and such supplies as could not be made use of by the command, were by my direction distributed to the poor, many of whom were entirely destitute. My action was heartily approved by General Canby and those in higher authority.

We found the country filled with small bands of marauders, composed mostly of deserters from the late rebel armies who had returned to their homes and there [discovered] their families suffering from neglect and persecution of the wealthier classes and leaders at whose instigation they had joined the rebel ranks. Naturally enough, they were helping themselves to such provisions as the country afforded to satisfy their wants. As a rule, we found the poor people and the returned Confederate private soldiers heartily tired of the war and inclined to be loyal to the government. But the far greater portion of the wealthy classes were very bitter in their sentiments and seemed to still clutch onto slavery with a lingering hope of saving at least a relic of that barbarous institution for the future. The Negroes, however, who were well aware that a great change was about to take place in their status, began to follow the column with no definite idea in their minds beyond the belief that freedom was in store for them somewhere, and that their former masters had neither the right nor the power to retain them in slavery. Immediately on our arrival at Columbus, large numbers of the colored people flocked into the place from all directions, despite the efforts of their late owners to detain them on the surrounding plantations. In the absence of any definite instructions, I allowed the Negroes to remain at Columbus undisturbed, and caused food to be issued to them pending the action of higher authority as to their further protection, sustenance, and control by the "Freedmen's Bureau," then being established throughout the South by [the] government, and under the supervision of General O. O. Howard, whose well-known anti-slavery sentiments, Christian character, and philanthropy well fitted him for that important position.

During the expedition, Major Peter D. Vroom of the 2nd New Jersey Cavalry, who had previously served as inspector on my staff, again acted as division inspector. He, Woodward, and myself were warm friends and genial companions. After his muster-out of the volunteer service, Vroom was appointed to a lieutenancy in the 3rd U.S. Cavalry, and ten years later promoted to a captaincy in that regiment. Subsequently, he was appointed major in the Inspector General's Department, and since advanced therein to a colonelcy. The experience and knowledge gained in the service, during and since the war, admirably fit him for any position in the army to which he may aspire. Colonel Joseph Kargé of the 2nd New Jersey Cavalry was an excellent officer, brusque and impatient under restraint, but soldierly in bearing, energetic and efficient in the performance of duty. He was always successful in accomplishing orders in any task assigned him while serving under my command. Some years after the close of the war, he became a member of the faculty in Princeton College as professor of languages, a position he continued to fill up to the time of his death.

On May 27, I received information of the surrender of General E. Kirby Smith's army to General Canby, which included all the rebel forces and material of war west of the Mississippi River.[7] On the same day, in compliance with telegraphic instructions, I ordered General Lucas to proceed with his brigade by the most practicable route to Vicksburg, and leaving Colonel Kargé in command at Columbus, with such instructions as were necessary for his guidance, I and my staff proceeded without delay by railroad via Mobile to New Orleans, reporting on my arrival there, May 29, to General Canby for further orders.

———

Upon my return to New Orleans, I learned that General [Philip] Sheridan[8] had been assigned to a new district or division embracing the state of Texas and that part of Louisiana west of the Mississippi River, and the special command of an army to operate on the frontier, along the line of the Rio Grande, in view of apprehended trouble on account of the occupation of Mexico by the French and Austrians under Maximilian.[9] General Sheridan arrived at New Orleans on June 2, and about the same time General Banks was relieved and ordered to report to the adjutant general at Washington, D.C. General Canby [was] assigned to command the Department of the Gulf, with the state of Texas and part of Louisiana withdrawn, and Alabama and Florida added hereto. The headquarters of Generals Sheridan and Canby were established at New Orleans.

As the war was over, it was evident that the army would soon be greatly reduced. Orders had already been issued by the War Department directing that all of the cavalry regiments whose term of enlistment would expire before October 1, 1865, be at once mustered out of the service, and those which were to be temporarily retained consolidated into full regiments. From the date of my arrival in the city, I had been engaged in organizing a force of cavalry for service in Texas; but I felt that, in the midst of all the military changes then occurring and foreshadowed, it was uncertain as to what disposition would be made of me. A notice that I, too, had been mustered out of service would not have caused me much surprise or annoyance.

In May 1863, on my first visit to New Orleans, some admiring gentleman had been kind enough to send to the St. Charles Hotel a fine pair of
spurs for me. On entering my room on the night of May 31, 1865, at the
same hotel, after my last expedition of the war, I found enclosed in a box
another fine pair of spurs. The clerk of the hotel in again looking over the
articles in the baggage room found a second package addressed to me,
and had sent it to my room. Nothing in or about the box indicated from
whom the gift came.

On June 2, I was informed by General Canby that I was to remain with
him to command the cavalry of the department; that his command, though
changed in name, would be virtually the same as previously, although
somewhat reduced; that he did not think General Sheridan would require
the division of cavalry I had prepared for service in Texas, as he had contemplated drawing such additional troops as might be needed from Arkansas
and elsewhere; and that the necessary orders for the coming changes would
be issued in a few days, on receipt of further information from Washington
in answer to communications of Generals Sheridan and Canby.

The same day, while in conversation with Colonel [C. T.] Christensen,
I learned that he decided to resign at once and return to his home and
to civil pursuits. He was very anxious to rejoin his family, deeming it his
imperative duty to devote the remainder of his life to his wife and children. I was in position to fully realize his sentiments and feelings, and
although I much regretted his departure, I could not advise him to delay
it, as I felt much like following his example that I, too, might soon proceed
northward en route to my home

I am more than willing to leave on record the very high opinion I entertained for Colonel Christensen as an officer and gentleman. His position at
the time of his resignation was that of adjutant general at General Canby's
headquarters. In all the annoyances, great and small, which attend such
a place, he was uniformly and exceptionally patient, courteous, efficient,
and faithful to duty; and in private as in public life demeaned himself as
an honorable and trustworthy man.

On June 5, I was, by orders of Gen. Canby, placed in command of the
cavalry of the Department of the Gulf. After the transfer of about 5,000
cavalry to General Sheridan, there remained in the department an aggregate force of about 10,000 men scattered throughout the different districts
comprising the Department of the Gulf. I judged it would take about two
months' work to properly refit and prepare it for the field. It was evident,
however, that if no war should arise in regard to the Mexican Maximilian
question, it would not be long before another order would be issued still
further reducing the army. But, as a matter of course, a considerable time

would necessarily elapse before it would be prudent to withdraw the government troops from the South, as a sufficient force to hold the rebellious people of that section of the country at bay; or, in other words, to remind them, without any further manifestation of hostility than the mere presence of United States soldiers, as to what might be expected in case of a too violent exhibition or superabundance of that peculiar loyalty apparently so ready to be manifested throughout most, if not all, the Southern states. Already, under the extraordinary leniency of the government, the rebels, or those lately in rebellion, were becoming more exacting. From unmistakable manifestations, it was evident that they would be glad to take part in another war, if any chance for their success could be afforded.

In the afternoon of June 6, I called with General Canby and staff upon Chief Justice [Salmon P.] Chase and daughter,[10] who were at that time on a brief visit to the city. The young lady, whom I judged to be about eighteen years of age, was remarkably bright, sprightly, and vivacious. Both she and her father were apparently in excellent health and spirits. Mr. Chase expressed himself as highly gratified over the close of the war [and] the prospect for permanent peace and restoration of the Union. After a pleasant interview of a half an hour, we withdrew to give place to other callers.

Soon after arrival at New Orleans, in accordance with General Canby's approval, I made application for quarters. The quartermaster's department assigned to me the house known as No. 145 St. Charles Street, in which Colonel J. Schuyler Crosby and another officer were rooming, who on my invitation remained there with myself and staff. The building was suitable and centrally located. About a week later, the same quarters were assigned to General Sheridan and staff by the obliging quartermaster's department, on the presumption that they would just suit their purposes. The general did not know that I was in the house, and came there to take possession before other quarters had been assigned to me. He expressed great regret at finding that I was to be turned out, and kindly asked me to remain as long as I felt inclined, as he expected to leave the city on a trip into Texas. But knowing that he would really need the whole house for himself and staff, let his stay be long or short, I declined his invitation and vacated the premises on the afternoon of June 8 to occupy a much larger and finer house assigned to me, but which was situated at a greater distance from my office.

In view of the action of the quartermaster's department, I immediately on being notified that I was to be dispossessed made written application for the quarters occupied by the chief quartermaster himself, Colonel [Samuel B.] Holabird, U.S. Army, merely to let him know how delightful it was to be so unceremoniously dispossessed. I forthwith rode out to the outskirts of the city to take a look at the house. The place was pleasantly situated and superb in all its appointments and surroundings, made the more so, no doubt, by the tasteful care and attention of Mrs. Holabird, the house being literally encompassed with roses and numerous other beautiful flowers. I found Mrs. H. and the colonel both at home, the latter apparently quite ill, possibly made the more so by a knowledge of my action. Altogether, however, I was most pleasantly received and entertained during my short call. I could not do otherwise than to give expression to my delight on beholding the place, so luxuriously furnished; apparently so suitable in every way for an officer of even higher rank than myself. In my own mind, however, I resolved not to take the place. But, without indicating my determination to the colonel, I before leaving gave Mrs. Holabird clearly to understand that I would not turn them out of their beautiful home, and instead at once made application for the quarters then occupied by Major [Amos] Beckwith, chief commissary of the department, who was living all alone in an enormous house, finely furnished, in the suburbs of the city, situated on the corner of "Coliseum and Felicity Streets," which seemed not to be too high sounding or inappropriate names, considering the mansion and its appointments.

Upon examination of the cellar, I found hundreds of wine bottles. Unfortunately for myself and staff, they were all empty. Everything considered, however, we were well pleased with the change. Subsequently, and before my departure from New Orleans for duty elsewhere, I suggested to General Sheridan that he had best obtain for his private quarters the beautiful place I was about to vacate, and retain the house he then had on St. Charles Street for office purposes. He was at once driven out, and upon inspection of the house, was so well pleased that he had it assigned to him. I think he retained those quarters during his long stay in the city, until relieved of command of the Fifth Military District by General Hancock.

Under date of June 12, my brother advised me of the receipt and acceptance of his commission as captain and a.q.m., U.S. Volunteers. It was then expected that he would soon be ordered to report to me for duty, on the application previously made, as my acting assistant quartermaster had been relieved and ordered to join his regiment. But my brother was retained at Memphis and at Alexandria, Louisiana, in connection with the equipment and shipment of the cavalry being transferred to General Sheridan's command.

On account of the confusion of affairs at that time in General Canby's department, he directed me to proceed to Memphis to facilitate the movement of troops and gain desired information as to the real extent or jurisdiction of the command to which he had some days previously been assigned. Upon arrival at Memphis, I learned that five regiments ordered transferred to Sheridan—the 1st Iowa, 2nd Wisconsin, 5th and 7th Indiana, and 7th Illinois—had already been ordered south in accordance with instructions from General [James W.] Forsyth,[11] General Sheridan's chief of staff. As transportation had not then been furnished for the 5th Iowa and 2nd Wisconsin, and there being 1,800 serviceable horses still reported with the cavalry to be left at Memphis, I gave such instructions as were required to place the cavalry regiments still left at Memphis, and designated for field service in Texas, to be thoroughly equipped before leaving the city, as the cavalry previously shipped had not been put in effective condition before embarking. On the 18th, I telegraphed to General Canby my observations and action. On June 19, I was ordered to proceed to Nashville to confer with General Thomas in regard to the cavalry then in northern Mississippi, Alabama, and Florida, which it was understood had been transferred to General Canby's command and which included Hatch's division of my old corps.

I left Memphis on the 21st, and upon arrival at Cairo could not resist the temptation to visit home. Finding a train in readiness, I flanked off to Jacksonville to pass a few hours with Mrs. Grierson and the children. From there, I proceeded by the most direct route to Nashville, where I met General Thomas and learned that the states of Mississippi, Alabama, and Florida had, by orders of [the] War Department, been transferred back to General Thomas' command. I found the general looking healthy and vigorous, and like all other officers who had taken an active part in the war, greatly rejoiced at its close. He kindly invited me to dine with him, and our interview was extremely agreeable.

I regretted to learn, however, that General Canby's department had been so much reduced. After one-day's stop at Nashville, I returned via Cairo and thence by steamboat via Memphis to New Orleans, where I found General Canby ready to submit to all orders given him, yet rather depressed at the late restriction in his sphere of action, as the last order then received confined the limit of his department to the state of ~~Georgia~~. Of course, my command was correspondingly reduced. I reached New Orleans on my return about July 1, and found little to do but to await further developments.

In the meantime, we found our quarters in the suburbs of the city so cool and pleasant that we preferred remaining there in the evenings to tramping about the streets as hitherto we had frequently done in search of amusement. [We] thereby saved some money that would have otherwise slipped out of our pockets for ice-cream, cool drinks, cigars, etc. By a notice in the newspapers of July 6, it was stated that Florida had been again transferred to General Canby's command. If true, the orders would increase the force of cavalry. Besides the 1st Florida Cavalry, a brigade was reported to be in the vicinity of Tallahassee, which of course would be thereby transferred to the Department of the Gulf. On the 10th, I learned from General Sheridan that he had been notified of the enlargement of his command, but he preferred to await the receipt of the orders of the War Department before making any further changes. On the 14th, in the dispatches from Washington published in the papers it was stated that General Canby was to command the Department of Louisiana and Texas in General Sheridan's division. A few days thereafter, General Sheridan assumed command of his division, which was designated as the Military Division of the South, within which General Canby was assigned to the Department of Louisiana and Texas.

Such change, in the event I remained on duty with General Canby, would require the issuing of an order from me assuming command of the cavalry forces, Department of Louisiana and Texas. That would complicate matters, unless the cavalry designated for field service reported direct to General Sheridan or General [Wesley] Merritt,[12] who had been assigned to command that cavalry but ranked me, he having been appointed a full major general. Soon afterwards, orders were received assigning General [Horatio G.] Wright[13] to the department, leaving General Canby in command of the Department of Louisiana, consisting of that state alone and one of the departments within General Sheridan's division. Thus, General Canby's previously large command of the Division of West Mississippi had been gradually reduced and finally absorbed by Generals Sheridan and Thomas. General Canby good-humoredly remarked in a felicitous manner to me that his command had not only been whittled down to a point, but the point cut off. He seemed contented, however, with any arrangements the authorities might see fit to make. As the war was over, there could be but little for anyone to do in the army, compared to that which had to be done while the balls were in motion, except to attend to the muster out of troops, pending the enlargement and reorganization of the United States Army.

It was, however, becoming a matter of some concern to me to know what kind of business I should undertake or find myself employed in after my occupation as an officer had been brought to a close. Except in the way of experience gained during the exciting period of the war, I was like at its beginning, without means to warrant entering upon any pursuit with any certainty of success, and could really not see or determine what would be best for me to undertake to do.

From what Generals Grant, Rawlins, and others told me, it seemed probable that the government would need my services in the regular army, which no doubt would be considerably enlarged. I was advised by some of my political friends in Washington that if not appointed in the army, if I desired such a position I could no doubt obtain the appointment of governor of one of the territories. I answered that I would be as likely to apply for an appointment to the "kingdom of the moon" in order to ascertain if it was really made "of green cheese." Although the future did not look to me then as particularly bright or promising, I resolved to be philosopher enough to be content with my lot, whatever it might be.

In such mood, in the midst of the uncertain condition of military affairs [and] realizing the fact that I could not be of any real benefit by remaining longer on duty at New Orleans, I on August 6 called to see General Canby for advice as to what I had better do under the circumstances. The general was affable and courteous as usual, but feeling that his own movements and position were so indefinite and uncertain, that he did not know what further action would be taken by the War Department in his own case and therefore could not well give advice to any one. He freely proffered his assistance to the extent of his power or ability in furthering my wishes, and suggested that it would be well to call upon and consult General Sheridan in regard to the matter.

Having decided upon taking some further action at once, I called the same day on General Sheridan with a view to obtain either a leave of absence or an order to enable me to proceed to my home, and from there to report to the War Department at Washington for further orders. The general received me very kindly and quickly advised me by all means to be ordered to my home to report to the secretary of war or the adjutant of the army for assignment to duty, in preference to taking a leave of absence. That I would then be entitled to mileage home and could then apply for leave of absence, if desired. If assigned to duty, as I probably would be, the orders would cover my mileage to my destination. He said he would be glad to give me a letter to General Grant and the secretary of war recommending my assignment to command a department or district in the South, or wherever my services might be required. He said he did not think I would be mustered out, even if not immediately assigned to command, as there would not be much further mustering out until after the meeting of Congress and consolidation of the army.

I, therefore, requested an order directing me to proceed to my home to report to the War Department for further orders or assignment to duty. I also arranged to have Major Woodward ordered to accompany me, or leave granted to him with orders to report to me for duty at its expiration, which would enable him to go home at once and there await further developments. The major was very anxious to get away from New Orleans [as] soon as possible, and I think he left there before I did, as I remember that Major Frank Eno,[14] assistant adjutant [of] volunteers, who had been previously on duty with General Rosecrans, and afterwards with General [Alexander] Asboth,[15] I think in Florida, was ordered to report to me temporarily in place of Major Woodward.

On August 9 or 10, just after receipt of orders from headquarters Division of the Gulf ordering me to my home as had been requested, I saw a notice in the morning papers stating that I had been assigned to duty and ordered to report to General [Charles R.] Woods[16] at Mobile, Alabama, to command a district in that state. I delayed a few days in New Orleans. But as the order had not reached me then, I concluded to obey the official order already received, which would, if the good Lord was willing, take me home once more at all events. I reached Jacksonville about August 20, 1865, reporting upon arrival to the adjutant general of the army for orders and requesting that, if practicable, a leave of absence previously granted to me for thirty days, of which I had not availed myself, be extended to me before assignment to duty.

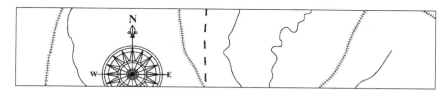

17. Reconstruction Duty

My arrival at Jacksonville was opportune and highly gratifying to Mrs. Grierson as well as myself, for on August 27, 1865, a daughter, Edith Clare,[1] was born to us. She at once became the light and life of our home. A few days after that important event, I went to Chicago to meet General Grant, who had arrived there on his way to Galena, where he anticipated a pleasant reunion with his old friends and neighbors.

On September 4, I received a telegram from Washington directing me to proceed to Mobile to report to General Woods for duty. Leaving my family comfortably provided for at the old home in Jacksonville, I started on September 9 and proceeded by railroad via Springfield to St. Louis, where I embarked on the steamer *Alton* for Memphis, thence via the Memphis and Charleston and Mobile and Ohio railroads to Mobile.

On account of numerous delays, the journey was tedious and fatiguing. I spent one night at Springfield, where I stopped at the Chenery House. [I] was roused up at 4 o'clock in the morning and found that the Chicago and Alton train for St. Louis was several hours behind time. I returned to the hotel and to bed with my clothes on. Being awakened again at 6 o'clock, [I] hastened to the station—where an engine was switching about, making an unusual amount of noise—and learned that a freight train, only, had arrived. I went back to the hotel, got breakfast, and finally left Springfield at about 8 o'clock A.M., and reached St. Louis at 2 P.M. the same day.

I was warmly received there by General Sherman, who gave me a hearty letter of introduction to General Woods. He also wrote a letter to the adjutant general at Washington, strongly recommending my appointment to the position of colonel of cavalry in the regular army. He gave me a copy of the letter and retained the original for General Grant's endorsement, as the general was expected at St. Louis within a few days. From there, I telegraphed Major Woodward at Paducah, Kentucky, to meet me at Cairo, and left the city at 10 o'clock that night on the steamer *Alton* on my winding way southward.

I found Woodward at Cairo upon my arrival there the next day, but was disappointed to learn that he had not received orders from Washington to report to me again for duty. I communicated with General Grant, who was still at Galena, with a view to have Woodward ordered by telegraph to report to me, but reluctantly had to leave Cairo without him. [I] learned soon afterwards that he had, with many other officers of volunteers in the adjutant general's department, been mustered out of the service. My request to the adjutant general of the army to have the order, so far as it related to Major Woodward, revoked was not favorably considered on the ground that there were then many officers of his grade and department still in the volunteer service without employment. Suddenly to find myself deprived of his services and companionship was a disappointment which caused me the deepest regret.

My trip down the Mississippi River on the *Alton*, I being well acquainted with the officers of the boat, was the most pleasant part of the journey. That made by railroad from Memphis to Mobile, on account of the dilapidated condition of the roads and rolling stock, was extremely slow and tiresome; so much so that I did not get to the city of Mobile until 9 P.M. on the evening of the 16th. The next morning I reported to General Woods for orders. He had been expecting me for some time, but my explanation as to [the] delay was entirely satisfactory. I dined with the general and, after a pleasant interview relative to the condition of affairs in his department, returned to the "Battle House," where I had stopped on arrival. It was the best hotel in the city, but at that time [it was] a dilapidated and dirty institution, where one might come near starving to death even at four dollars a day. I was in due time assigned to the command of the Northern District of Alabama, with headquarters at Huntsville, for which place I left on September 18 via Montgomery, Atlanta, and Chattanooga, with the prospect, as advised by General Woods, that I might have to go as far north as Nashville to reach my destination. The Memphis and Charleston Railroad was not at that time repaired farther east than Iuka, and it would have been still more difficult to get to Huntsville by that route.

I arrived at that city on September 23 and assumed command the same day. I was entirely alone, without any staff officers. Major J. B. Sample, assistant adjutant general, U.S. Volunteers, soon after reported to me for duty. I found the people of the northern part of Alabama more loyal, as a general thing, than those throughout the central and southern portions of the state. I entered upon the performance of my duty, therefore, with more satisfaction than if I had been assigned to duty in either of the other districts into which the state had been divided.

From information gained by close observation while passing through the state, and from all other sources, I learned that there was much rascality going on in the cotton-growing portions of the state. It appeared that a perfect grab-game had been inaugurated. But, as there was comparatively little cotton within my district, I was not so much troubled by cotton thieves and speculators as I probably would have been in either of the other districts. The white troops which had been on duty in the state were being removed or mustered out, and Negro troops were taking their place, which seemingly was very unsatisfactory to most of the white people. It was feared that trouble would result from such an arrangement. Without openly expressing any opinion on the subject, I deemed it the best thing that could have been done under the circumstances for the real mudsills to be raised to the top from the bog and mire in which so long buried, in order that the downtrodden Negro might be in a position where those who still cherished the institution of slavery might behold "Cuffy," with a musket on his shoulder, in the responsible and dignified position of a United States soldier.

Upon my arrival at Huntsville I received a letter, forwarded from department headquarters at Mobile, from a soldier of the 6th Illinois Cavalry, that regiment being then at Demopolis, Marengo County, Alabama. After its active and remarkably successful services in West Tennessee and Northern Mississippi in 1862, the regiment was brigaded with the 2nd Iowa and 7th Illinois Cavalry, and took part in the "great raid of 1863." In all vicissitudes of fortune or subsequent changes, the regiment continued to render distinguished service to the government. The war being over, the officers and men chafed at the changes which placed them beyond my control. I communicated with the War Department relative to the situation and wishes of the officers and men of the regiment, recommending its muster out of the volunteer service. The letter had the desired effect and the soldiers of the old 6th Illinois Cavalry were soon after on their way to their homes.

Upon full investigation I found that there were, besides the 1st Alabama and 7th Illinois Cavalry—the last two regiments awaiting muster out and not in condition for duty—still five or six regiments of colored infantry in my district. The house I selected for quarters and office purposes had, previous to my arrival at Huntsville, been assigned to officers of the Freedmen's Bureau, who were occupying the place with their furniture, which had become a sort of rendezvous for the white and black people of the city. At first I had only one room for office and sleeping apartments. But, finding such arrangement too disagreeable to be endured, I caused the premises to be vacated, the property cleaned and placed in order that it might be in good condition for occupation by Mrs. Grierson and the children, whom I expected to soon join me from Jacksonville.

While at New Orleans, I had drawn pay as major general on my assignment to duty with my brevet rank of that grade, and had subsequently learned that I would probably be required to refund the difference between the pay of brigadier and that of major general. I had written to Washington with a view to ascertain the facts in the case. I was obliged to refund to the government, through the Pay Department, the money I had received, amounting to about $1,100, and therefore had to economize at a time when it was rather difficult to do so. Fortunately, I subsequently received the money by promotion to a full major generalship, on General Grant's recommendation.

———

On October 1, 1865, I proceeded to the camp of the 7th Illinois Cavalry, then located about twelve miles from Huntsville. I enjoyed the ride on horseback and also my visit of several hours' duration among my old comrades. The officers and enlisted men manifested great satisfaction at meeting me again and gave me a most cordial welcome. The regiment was assembled at an earlier hour than usual for "dress-parade," and subsequently massed in close column by companies in my immediate front. I was then called upon by the commanding officer to talk to the troops. As there seemed to be no chance to escape I was obliged to submit to the colonel's request and made a speech. I found the regiment anxiously desiring to be mustered out of the service. Being under my control as district commander, the officers and enlisted men felt sure that the time was then near at hand when, through my influence and efforts, they would be enabled to return to their homes. It was my duty as well as pleasure to do everything possible to obtain the orders for their honorable discharge from the service, wherein they had displayed conspicuous gallantry, and I did not fail to communicate with the War Department on the subject immediately on my return to my headquarters.

My time was fully occupied with the many duties devolving upon me in the new position to which I had been assigned as a district commander over various conflicting elements and interests by which I found myself surrounded. In the midst of Southern men and women of the higher classes blinded by caste prejudices; miserably poor, ignorant, destitute whites and blacks; self-asserting and so-called reconstructed citizens; and Negro soldiers—all at that time, to a greater or less extent, incapable of judging correctly of what properly belonged to their changed condition or position and doubtful or uncertain as to what would be exacted or required of them in their new relations to the government—required of a commanding officer a peculiar mingling of firmness, tact, patience, and forbearance, besides the constant exercise of sound judgment, experience, and discretion, in order to avoid and prevent injustice being done to anyone in the management of the complicated semi-military and civil affairs coming under his supervision.

About the middle of October, Mrs. Grierson and the children arrived at Huntsville. Sunshine prevailed as it generally does at that season of the year in the South and the North. The presence of my family was of itself enough to make a cheerful illumination, and happiness naturally followed in its wake. After a long forced separation and many trying experiences, our reunion was the more enjoyable.

Huntsville, with its many natural attractions in the way of picturesque surroundings, soon became well known to us by means of frequent drives made almost daily in the afternoons and evenings through the streets and suburbs of the quiet city. A favorite resort for us was to the mountain that at a few miles' distance dominated the country for a long distance in all directions. Its summit could be easily approached over a good macadamized roadway, which gradually rose like an inclined plane. When reached, the fresh invigorating breeze [and] pure air, together with the magnificent scenery that suddenly opened to view, all tended to cheer and enliven the spirits, [and] strengthen the inclination and ability for rustic enjoyment. When we were once at the top of the mountain, with clear skies above us and with varied and enchanting landscapes spread out beneath us, we usually called a halt and sojourned there long enough to have a sort of improvised picnic. Our life at Huntsville was thus, and in many other ways, made extremely pleasant during our stay of a few months as I was nearing the end of my military service as an officer of volunteers.

From observations made while in command of the district, which included the counties constituting the northern portion of the state, I became aware of the fact that many of those who just previous to the close of the war, on perceiving the approach of the downfall of the rebellion, had claimed to be loyal to the government of the United States were sailing under false colors. Many of them, within a few months after the surrender of the rebel armies, became insolent and exacting, even overbearing, in their manner. A marked change was manifested and their actions were very different from those observed less than a year previously, when it seemed that the greater the rebel the more effort he made to convince the Federal authorities that he was a veritable *ne plus ultra* Union man.

In the fall of 1865, the same man would openly deny having ever been anything but the rankest rebel, and boast of it publicly. Those who used to curse Andrew Johnson,[2] when he became president were ready to endorse and embrace him when it seemed that the "ship of state" was headed southward with all sails set. The rebellious spirit manifested itself in various ways in the South and created a widespread feeling of apprehension and alarm throughout the Northern states. It was surely a rather bad state of affairs when those so lately in open rebellion against the government were in jubilant spirits, and the Union men, including many who fought to sustain the nation, were at the same time becoming discouraged and despondent for the future welfare and safety of their country.

It was still evident, however, that even under such discouraging circumstances the government should continue to manifest in an unmistakable manner the most generous and trustful policy towards the ex-rebels, in order that they should have no excuse or just cause for complaint. The humiliation of defeat was hard for them to bear and the changed conditions of the Negroes was a matter which was galling to their pride, difficult to be realized or submitted to by the white people of the South. An increasing bitterness of feeling was, therefore, openly manifested towards the Freedmen's Bureau, while everything connected therewith was daily becoming more and more obnoxious to them. That humane institution for the protection of the freedmen was looked upon in a very different light by the people of the North. They could not give consent or for a moment harbor the thought that the redeemed national life after such a desperate struggle for existence should ever be dishonored by any breach of faith towards the freedmen. It was absolutely necessary that the world should see that the government was not only strong enough to maintain itself, but also able to hold over the freedmen, however repulsive or unsightly in appearance, the mighty shield of a just and absolute protection.

The course pursued by many ministers of the Episcopal Church throughout the South was not conducive to harmony. While they freely offered up prayers for the salvation of Jeff Davis—which was all well enough perhaps, in view of the fact that he was in need then, and thereafter, of spiritual comfort and assistance—they invariably failed to make any allusion whatever to the supreme head of the government at Washington, D.C. I therefore took occasion to call the attention of Generals Woods and Thomas to the matter, who promptly directed me to communicate with the said offenders within the limits of my district and require them to no longer omit from the church service the usual prayer for the president of the United States.[3]

The order, therefore, was promulgated accordingly from my headquarters in the most courteous manner. The following Sabbath, however, finding from personal observation that the stubborn divine in charge of the Episcopal church service at Huntsville disregarded the instructions given and adhered to his former obnoxious course, I immediately caused the building to be vacated and directed the officer of the day, who was near at hand with a suitable detail of soldiers, to take possession of the premises, much to the disgust of the irate minister and the astonishment of his congregation, all of whom with manifest indignation departed hurriedly to their homes, evidently submitting only under protest to the military mandate. The church building remained closed at that place until such time as the minister could make up his mind to comply in an apparently proper spirit with the requirements of the order which had been given to him in pursuance of instructions from the division commander.

My brother, who had finally received his commission as captain and assistant quartermaster, U.S. Volunteers, was about the middle of November 1865 relieved from duty at Memphis. [He] expected to be mustered out of the service, but received instead an order from the secretary of war to proceed to Mobile to relieve Captain John Stewart, a.q.m. Captain Grierson reached the city on December 12, and ascertained that Captain Stewart had already been relieved by another officer. Soon after, Captain Grierson was directed to proceed to Huntsville, where he arrived the latter part of December and remained on duty at that place for some time after my departure for the North.[4] In response to my invitation, my father had previously joined the family circle at Huntsville from Jacksonville. So that, after the arrival of my brother with his wife and daughter, the number had been increased to nine members of the tribe, all of whom in the most joyous mood and spirits were thus luckily assembled for the holiday festivities, which proved to be an extremely happy occasion after our long-continued separation. There were but two living members of the family in the direct line absent—my two sisters, Mrs. Fuller and Mrs. Semple, who were still at their homes in Illinois. Fortunately for us, there was in the house which had been assigned to me as quarters at Huntsville an unusually large and really excellent library. Mrs. Grierson and myself, therefore, spent much of our leisure time in reading aloud to each other from the books selected from the library, sometimes sitting up late at night for that purpose.

On January 7, 1866, I received an official copy of General Orders No. 168 of the War Department, Washington, D.C., by which 120 general officers of volunteers, including myself, were honorably mustered out of the military service of the United States to date from January 15. The Freedmen's Bureau was then in full operation throughout the South, and the colored troops so disposed as to be available for active service in case of necessity to meet any emergency that might arise during the enactment and enforcement of the reconstruction measures still pending before Congress.

Many of those who had only a short time previously been engaged in active hostilities against the government of the United States were clamorous for national recognition. They were making strenuous efforts, through their leaders, to have the Freedmen's Bureau abolished and the colored troops removed from the South. They desired to substitute in their stead the militia, ostensibly for the support of the provisional state governments and so-called civil authorities. They viewed the operations of the Freedmen's Bureau and presence of Negro troops in the South as an outrage and insult to the inborn dignity of the white people of that section of the country. They did not seem to realize the great difficulties to be encountered and overcome by the government in properly readjusting the union of all the states. Those who had been in open rebellion were still rebels at heart, and there was no evidence whatever at that time to show that any of them had, or ever would, acknowledge that they did wrong in their attempts to secede and put forth their united and most strenuous efforts to destroy the Union.

The greatest regret they then entertained was that they did not succeed in their nefarious design. Although greatly chagrined at their defeat, and inclined to mourn over their lost cause, they were exceedingly arrogant in their demands and persistently claimed the right to have their senators and representatives admitted to Congress. They also questioned the power of the federal government to interfere in any manner with state legislatures and local affairs in the Southern states.

Notwithstanding the spirit of rebellion still openly manifested by the people of the South and the generally unsatisfactory condition of affairs there, [and] although my service as a district commander was in striking contrast to that rendered while actively in command of troops in the field, still my few months sojourn at Huntsville, everything considered, was peculiarly agreeable, especially after the arrival there of Mrs. Grierson and the children and other members of our little family party.

Although within our little home circle at Huntsville all had been bright and cheerful, and especially hilarious during the holidays for us, still we found, in looking beyond its limits in every direction, much unmistakable evidence of the saddening desolation which ever follows in the wake, tramp, and clash of hostile armies. Notwithstanding that it was mid-winter and we were so comfortably housed and situated, yet being in the midst of so many elements of discord and discontent, we were not at all distressed at the prospect of a change which would take us away from the Sunny South. The order, therefore, mustering me out of the volunteer service was received with a genuine feeling of satisfaction, as it enabled us to arrange for our return to the more congenial region of Illinois, although Jacksonville at that season of the year was not so warm and agreeable as to climate as the milder latitude of northern Alabama.

Accordingly, we took our departure from Huntsville in excellent spirits on January 30, 1866, and proceeded via the Memphis and Charleston Railroad to Memphis, where we remained for a few days to visit relatives and acquaintances. We continued our journey via steamboat to Cairo, thence by the Illinois Central and Wabash railroads to Jacksonville, where we arrived on February 7. We at once found the place much more homelike than it had appeared to us at any time during the preceding five years. I recognized and appreciated the fact that I was once more free from the binding influences and control of army orders.

––––

Before leaving Huntsville, I had received notice from Washington to the effect that my testimony would be required before the Congressional Committee on Reconstruction, which I presumed was in view of certain official reports made by me as district commander, which I was told had been forwarded to the War Department by General Thomas. Mrs. Grierson and the children accompanied me as far as Chicago, where they remained to visit relatives in that city during my absence from home. I reached Washington on the last day of February. On March 1, I reported to the chairman of the committee, who appointed 10 o'clock the next day as the hour for me to give my testimony. I appeared punctually at the hour specified and was relieved between 12 and 1 o'clock the same day.[5]

––––

Having finished my business before the Reconstruction Committee of Congress, [and] finding myself free and at leisure to dispose of my time as seemed most advisable, I determined first to obtain another unobstructed view of the city and its surroundings. Therefore, I started at once, not on a run as on a former occasion, but leisurely on my winding way upward to the dome of the Capitol. I [then] retraced my steps and soon found myself at a suitable distance from the stately structure, engaged in gazing upward with admiration at its faultless symmetry, immense proportions, and superb appearance. The thought flashed through my mind that, surely, of such a grand national object every citizen of the Republic should well be proud. As some passers-by jocosely remarked, "That man is sort of struck on the Capitol Building," I smiled in acknowledgement of the fact, and started off to look at other public buildings and such places as seemed to be of most interest to a non-resident and infrequent visitor like myself of the really beautiful City of Washington.

In response to a kind and cordial invitation, I dined that day at 6 o'clock P.M. with Senator and Mrs. [William] Sprague,[6] and was most agreeably entertained by them at their tasteful and commodious home. By special arrangement I spent the evening at General Grant's house, where I met the general, Mrs. Grant, and other members of the family, and had an exceedingly enjoyable visit. The previous evening, I had called, in company with General Hurlbut, on my esteemed townsman, Senator Yates,[7] who was then occupying rooms in a large block of buildings.

Unfortunately, we found upon taking our departure that during our visit our hats and overcoats had been stolen from the lower hall where we had carelessly left them on our entrance, not knowing that it was a common passageway. We were obliged to return to Willard's Hotel in borrowed apparel, and the next morning purchased other garments in place of those stolen from us. Efforts were made through policemen and detectives to recover our hats and overcoats, but after the useless expenditure of some money in that manner, the matter was given up, as no trace of the articles could be obtained. General Hurlbut, I remember, congratulated himself on the fact, as he smilingly remarked, that his hat and coat were both worn out. On the contrary, my hat was new, and the overcoat had been made to order for me only a short time before by an army tailor. [It] was a fine one, besides being the regulation pattern for a general officer, and cost me $120. I never had so expensive an overcoat before or since, and probably never will again, as such a costly article of dress is seldom required by a retired officer of the army.

As during my visit to Washington in 1865, I was again received in a cordial manner by the president, members of the Cabinet, members of Congress, General Grant, and other officials of the military and civil branches of the government. On March 3, at 10 o'clock A.M., I called at the War Department to pay my respects to the Honorable Secretary of War, E. M. Stanton, and also for the same purpose called to see the general officers of the various staff departments of the army

That customary duty performed, which was strictly proper and within the province of military etiquette, I proceeded to General Grant's headquarters with a feeling akin to that of a person on entering his own home or apartments. The general was not in his office when I entered, but soon after came in with his chief of staff, General Rawlins, whom I had not seen since my former visit to Washington. We were very glad indeed to meet each other again. I regretted to observe that he did not look so robust as formerly, and I judged that the climate of the East did not agree with him. He was in excellent spirits, however, and after a few minutes' conversation in which General Grant took part, I sat down near Rawlins' desk and we there had a long friendly talk together. I was very fond of Rawlins; had learned to know him well and to appreciate his many noble qualities. I liked him for his frank, manly, unmistakably earnest manner and sterling integrity. I admired him, too, for his warm-hearted friendship and loyalty to his chief, as I did also for his thorough devotion to the cause of the Union. Few officers came to the front during the War of the Rebellion with greater vim or a clearer understanding of the great struggle. Few gained distinction who were more worthy, or who better deserved the lasting gratitude of their countrymen. General Rawlins was remarkably well informed in regard to the condition of the national affairs at that time, and few matters of moment transpired at the Capitol that did not come under his keen scrutiny and observation. Important events soon thereafter to take place were plainly foreshadowed to his clear and comprehensive mind, and he did not hesitate about giving free expression to his views when in conversation with those he knew or had confidence [in].

Although the military bill for the reorganization and enlargement of the regular army had not been passed by Congress, it was evident that such a measure would be enacted. There had already been much speculation in regard to the appointment of officers for the new regiments to be added to the army. A large number of officers of the regular army who had held high positions in the volunteer service during the war were making strenuous efforts for advancement to colonelcies and other desirable field and staff positions. Although General Rawlins seemed to have little if any doubt that I would, on the strong recommendations of Generals Sherman and Grant, approved by the secretary of war and already on file in the War Department, receive the appointment of colonel of cavalry in the regular army, yet in view of the clamor that had been and would continue to be made for such appointments, he advised me to obtain and file with the adjutant general of the army a similar recommendation for my appointment from the delegation in Congress from Illinois. I quickly obtained and forwarded the desired communication, which was chiefly valued by me for the readiness with which it was signed by every member of the delegation from Illinois, without regard to party.

In consultation with Mr. Stanton during my second call upon him, I referred to the fact that President Lincoln and General Grant had in February 1865 expressed the wish to have me promoted to a full major generalcy. But, as there was no vacancy at that time, I was given the appointment of brevet major general and assigned to duty accordingly. That it was then understood that I would be promoted a major general of volunteers. That probably the matter had been overlooked on account of the untimely death of Mr. Lincoln, but that I thought General Grant would still remember the occurrence. That, as I had served as a major general, and drew pay on my brevet assignment and had to refund the money, I thought that some action should be taken for my relief. Mr. Stanton expressed regret that the appointment had not been made, and remarked that if he had known all the facts in the case, he would have taken great pleasure in promoting me to a full major generalcy, and that he would at once see if it could not still be done. He turned to his desk and there made a memorandum and kindly asked me to call on him again in a few days; that, in the meantime, he would see the adjutant general on the subject. In fact, Mr. Stanton sent for that officer as I left the War Office.

Soon after the interview, I called again to see General Grant, who with much satisfaction and without hesitation informed me that the recommendation filed on the suggestion of General Rawlins from the Illinois delegation in Congress would undoubtedly make my appointment to a colonelcy in the regular army a certainty in due time, and that I could safely make my arrangements accordingly. The new army bill would soon become a law, and he would give the matter his personal attention when the new appointments were made by the War Department. I put implicit reliance on the general's statements, and subsequently made no further effort whatever to obtain said appointment in the regular army.

The general then referred to my former visit to Washington and to the remarkable changes that had occurred. He spoke in the most feeling manner of Mr. Lincoln, of his sad death, [and] the great loss the country had thereby sustained, and expressed deep regret that the nation had been deprived of the invaluable services of such a noble man, particularly at such a critical period in the affairs of the nation. I listened with intense interest to the general's eloquent remarks. The conversation then turned to the general topics of the day: President Johnson and his avowed policy for readjustment; the wide differences in views entertained by the president and Congress and [the] prospect of still further controversy.[8]

The call we had made together on President Lincoln in February 1865 was then alluded to and the incidents of the pleasant interview recalled to our minds. I asked the general if he remembered the wish expressed by himself and Mr. Lincoln to have me appointed a full major general of volunteers, when I had received only a brevet appointment to said grade. "Yes," replied the general, "I well remember the occurrence. I believed then and do still, that you richly deserved promotion to a major generalcy for services rendered the government, and regret that the appointment was not subsequently made." I then referred to my conversation with the secretary of war on the subject and the wish expressed by Mr. Stanton to make the appointment, if it could still be done. The general said that he would see Mr. Stanton in regard to the matter at the earliest moment. All that would be necessary would be to have the general order of muster out, so far as it related to me, revoked from its date. Then, by direction of the president, appoint me a full major general of volunteers to the first vacancy that occurred, which would entitle me to the rank and pay of said higher grade. Feeling elated by the general's remembrance of the occurrence and the intention of President Lincoln and himself to have me promoted, I thanked the general for his kindness and contemplated action in my behalf and bid him good day.

My earnest desire to have the appointment of full major general of volunteers can be readily understood. The main reasons were as follows: When I went to Washington in 1865, soon after my successful expedition against Hood's communications with the South, there was no vacancy in the number of general officers as limited or prescribed by law. Therefore, all that could then be done was to give me the brevet of major general and assign me to duty accordingly. By the law existing February 10, 1865, my assignment to duty entitled me to major general's pay. But, by subsequent act of Congress passed March 4, 1865, pay according to brevet rank was prohibited. Although I had for a time drawn the full pay of major general, I was obliged to refund it to the government. The favorable action of the War Department in my case, as then pending, had become a matter of deep concern to me and was looked forward to with pardonable pride, and no small amount of interest, on the part of myself and friends.

On March 13, I called with General Grant to see the secretary of war in regard to my promotion and was immediately appointed a full major general of volunteers, to rank from March 13, 1865, from which date I had received and returned pay of major general on my previous assignment to duty with my brevet rank. Mr. Stanton had already given instructions to have the order mustering me out as brigadier general revoked from its date, in order to cover all the time up to the date of my final muster out of the volunteer service as major general, which it was understood would make a difference of over $1,500 in my pay that, to a poor man like myself, was much better than a *lick on the head with a sharp stone*. The most gratifying thing, however, was that Secretary Stanton, on his own volition and without hesitation, made the appointment to show that it was given "for gallant and meritorious services during the war," which was received by myself and friends—like that in my commission as brigadier general "for distinguished service in the great raid through Mississippi in 1863"—as something truly substantial to leave to my children. The appointment, too, was sent the same day it was made into the United States Senate and promptly confirmed at the next executive session. My commission as major general of volunteers was signed by the president and [the] secretary of war on March 19, and received by me on the 22nd.

It was evident that the "red tape" of the Adjutant General's Office would have opposed and delayed all these arrangements. While the adjutant general had been fumbling for precedents and talking of irregularities, the decisive action of General Grant, Mr. Stanton, and myself had proved effective, and pushed through the appointment in the face of all opposition. In like manner, after the receipt of my commission, I presented my application for pay to the secretary of war for his approval. Mr. Stanton was about to append his signature when General [James A.] Hardie[9] of the

Inspector General's Department, then at the secretary's elbow, suggested that the papers be referred to the Adjutant General's Office.

As I realized the fact that they would, if thus referred, be there pigeon-holed for an indefinite period, I instantly answered that, if there was to be any delay or doubt about the matter, I would prefer to withdraw the papers. [I] did so and went directly with them to General Grant who, without hesitation, at once wrote the required certificate. General Grant also directed the adjutant general to issue the necessary order to adjust my record without further delay. My appointment had been made to date from May 27, 1865, instead of March 13 as ordered by Mr. Stanton. Whether the change was made by some manipulation in the Adjutant General's Department or for the reason that no vacancy existed at the former date, I have not as yet ascertained, but have presumed that the intention of Mr. Stanton to give me rank from the earliest day practicable was carried into effect.

It was not until March 28 that the necessary orders in my case were issued from the Adjutant General's Office. Official copies were furnished to me and the Pay Department, by means of which, with General Grant's certificate, I was enabled to obtain the pay due me as major general of volunteers.

Soon after my arrival at Washington, I called to pay my respects to President Johnson, and was promptly and kindly received. I had no previous acquaintance with him, but his political history was not unknown to me, and I was pleased to learn that my name had become familiar to him. He complimented me highly on my successful service during the war, was affable and courteous in his manner, and expressed his views freely in regard to the general condition of affairs in the South. While I judged from all he said on the subject of Reconstruction that he was not in accord with Congress or in touch with the sentiment of the people of the North, he really seemed to be honest in his convictions and desirous of such an adjustment of differences then pending as would tend to effectually restore the Union on a basis that would insure stability and a thorough reconstruction with the states which had been in rebellion against the government.

—————

Much of the time during my stay in Washington was spent within the Capitol building in hearing the debates on the Reconstruction measures and in conversation with congressmen, I having, through their kindness, free access to the floor of the Senate Chamber and that of the House of Representatives. My testimony given before the Committee on Reconstruction, which was fully in accord with that of General Thomas, had, with it, been published and commented on in the newspapers through the East and North. It had thus been brought to the notice of the people and members of Congress, and I was frequently told by those in high positions that it was having a good effect. All those who knew me believed implicitly in its sincerity, and even those who were considered rather conservative, or "copperheadish," by the majority of congressmen, conversed with me in a friendly manner on the subject. Although they expressed surprise that I could see things in such a light, yet they were influenced to a certain extent and were for a time at least less demonstrative in their opposition to the measures then pending, and were inclined to call a halt in order to more clearly ascertain the views and will of their constituents.

None could well doubt that I had opportunities for obtaining correct information during my long service in the South. While there I had merely used my eyes and understanding to the best of my ability to gain as thorough knowledge of the condition of affairs in the midst of those who had taken part and openly sustained the rebellion. When called upon to state my views, I did so at all times without hesitation, simply speaking the truth as I saw it, without thought as to the people of any particular section of the country, or to those whom it might please or displease.

Among congressmen, I found some "weak kneed" Republicans who needed propping up. I was determined in my efforts to encourage them in standing in their support of what was known as the "Civil Rights Bill," so they might face the music during the continuance of the great fight for human liberty.[10] There were many men at that time in Washington from various parts of the North who were in sympathy with the South, and who were doing all in their power to obstruct legislation and to widen the breach between the president and Congress. It was plain to my mind at that time that President Johnson's policy, as generally understood, would if strictly adhered to sooner or later involve the country in another rebellion—one that, if another war did come, the president with all the power he could wield would be found among the enemies of the nation [and] fighting against the liberties of the truly loyal people of the Union.

Wily representative men of the South were also in the city, watching for the opportunity to attempt to regain by artifice all possible advantages for their section of the country and its so-called "cause," lost by open warfare against the government. They never had any love or admiration for the "rail splitter" of Illinois, Mr. Lincoln, while alive, or for his memory after his death, by whose skillful maneuvering they were at all times out-generaled and defeated. They had a supreme contempt for the "mechanic," known as the "Tailor of Tennessee" [President Johnson], who had been separated by too wide a gulf to ever be permitted to enter the so-called elevated circle of Southern society. But the people of the South, through their sharp leaders, were ready to fawn on Mr. Johnson while president, and were so persistent in their efforts to win him over to the support of the "lost cause" that it resulted, not only in causing him to lean in that direction, but to apparently fall over body and soul into their outstretched arms, where they could *ad libitum* hug him to their hearts' content until ready to drop him like a hot potato. So, instead of making treason odious as he first proposed when he became president, he so conducted himself in that high position of trust as to seemingly cause his apparently treasonable acts to culminate in an effort by Congress to impeach and depose him from the high place he held as chief magistrate of the United States, which was made possible for his occupation by the unfortunate and certainly untimely death of the martyred Lincoln.[11] Thus it was that, even so soon after the close of the war, the sharp practice and deep-laid schemes of designing men were systematically at work to delay and by every possible means obstruct legislation designed to amend the constitution, and so surround it with safeguards as to insure the maintenance of a free government, in fact as well as name, so reconstructed as to afford absolute protection for and equal rights to all, without regard to race or color.

During my stay in Washington I kept my eyes and ears open, I trust, to some purpose. I attended suppers and other social entertainments where the conservatives and "copperheads" were decidedly in the ascendant, [and] where political matters were quietly but carefully considered and discussed. Although it so happened that I then got into the wrong pew, so to speak, still by discreet conduct and self-restraint I managed to obtain an inside view of affairs, and was thereby enabled to see how the wires were being set and helped prevent them from being effectually pulled by the designing manipulators, much to their disgust and disappointment.

Great efforts were, about that time, being put forth by the recognized managers of the Democratic party to induce General Grant to commit himself in some manner, so that the conservative (really copperhead) element which dominated that party could publicly identify him with their interests; so that he might be made available as their candidate for the presidency at the close of Johnson's term of office. Although Grant had not hitherto taken any active part in politics, he had voted for Buchanan. It was claimed by some that he had not gotten so far outside the limits of the party lines but what by judicious management he might be pulled back within the fold for political purposes. I had become devotedly attached to General Grant. He was well aware of my warm feelings towards him, and fully realized the fact that my personal friendship for him was of such a nature as to prove enduring to the end.

In any event, I determined in my own mind not to leave Washington without first advising General Grant fully as to the result of my observations. I had frequent conversations with him for that purpose. I knew that the general was inclined to avoid, so far as possible, attending suppers or social gatherings where political matters were likely to be discussed. But I also believed that he could not avoid going to some of them, and I felt that to be forewarned was to be forearmed against the influences which would be brought to bear upon him. In fact, the suppers were really given for General Grant, and those to which I especially refer, with the sole object in view as already indicated. I, being presumed to be on terms of intimacy with the general, was invited, and was present with him on several such occasions.

Besides the delicacies with which the tables abounded, champagne, wines, and liquors in great variety were not wanting, being well calculated to loosen the tongue and give freedom to speech. I had gone through the war without indulging in intoxicating liquors of any kind, and it is hardly necessary to state that I did not partake of those stimulants on such occasions. It was also gratifying to observe that General Grant could not be induced to even taste wines or liquors at any supper he attended where I was present. He talked freely on all subjects except political affairs, and when they were broached he invariably maintained an admirable silence. His shoulders seemed broad enough to bear the weight of all the compliments which were lavished upon him in profuse terms. The general, too, was fortunate in always seizing upon the proper moment to arise from the table to withdraw, and could not be induced to sit down again, or remain, after once getting up from his chair to depart. When he thus walked away with his soft-felt black hat carelessly pulled down over his brow, I have no doubt he felt that another victory had been added to those already attained.

After such entertainments, I invariably made it a point to call upon the general the following morning to congratulate him on the result. While I firmly believed that, in spite of all dissentions in the Republican party, the true sentiment of the loyal people of the country would eventually be fully sustained, I was not unmindful of the fact that strenuous efforts were being made to bring about a different result. It needed not the wisdom of a seer or prophet to foresee that the nation would, in due time, be in readiness to bestow still higher honors upon General Grant, in view of his invaluable services and the exalted position he had already attained. He, however, was disinclined to take part in political matters and was not ambitious to become a candidate of any party for the presidency. He was already known as "the silent man," a veritable *sphinx*, or unknown quantity. He did not, even at that time, hesitate to express his views fully on all subjects in the presence of those in whom he had faith and in whose judgment and discretion he had absolute confidence. His sentiments were in accord with the principles maintained by the great Republican party, based on the supreme voice of the loyal people of the country, on which he would implicitly rely for guidance of his actions in the future, as he had in the past.

Before leaving Washington, I was well assured in my own mind, from statements made to me during our frequent conversations, that no power or influence could possibly be brought to bear upon General Grant to make him swerve from the right, as he saw it, [and] which he would steadfastly pursue to the end; that, in any event, when the proper time came, as it surely would, he would be found leading the Republican hosts onward to greater victories. Events then transpiring made it quite evident to me that no man, however great or famous, who failed to come fully up to the great principles of human liberty or progress of the age could be elected to the position of president of the United States to succeed Andrew Johnson, in whom the people were manifestly rapidly losing confidence, which necessarily must be fully restored by the nation's faith in any new incumbent of the presidency.

Being again in the volunteer service, I had endeavored to learn from Adjutant General [E. D.] Townsend[12] when the order would probably be issued mustering me out of the service. But he did not seem to be able to give me any information on the subject. I, therefore, called to see General Grant in regard to the matter. Some changes were about to be made in commanders of districts in the South, and the general asked me if I would not prefer to be assigned to duty. And, if so, where I would like to be ordered.

It was then that I made a great mistake. The thought of being separated from my family, or sent away from my home to any point of the South, was so repugnant to my feelings that I answered hastily and without proper consideration of the subject. I told the general that I would rather be mustered out at once than be assigned to duty again anywhere in the South. Therefore, by my own request, my name was entered on the list of officers to be discharged by the next order to be issued by the War Department. Had I remained on duty until after the passage of the Act for the Reorganization of the Army,[13] it would have given me an increase in rank in my new appointment as colonel of cavalry in the regular army, on account of my greater length of service, and greatly strengthened my chances for promotion to the higher grade of general officer. I subsequently regretted that I declined the kind offer of General Grant to retain me in the volunteer service and assign me to duty as indicated.

I spent the latter part of April visiting among friends old and new in Philadelphia, New York, Boston, and other places in New England, and returned again to Washington to settle my accounts with the government after my formal muster out of the volunteer service April 30, 1866. It did not take me over half an hour to obtain the necessary receipts from the various staff departments. I had kept a careful account of all government property that had come into my hands during the war, and had made my returns as required by law and army regulations. I found many officers, however, then at Washington who had not been so fortunate; some of whom had been detained there for months endeavoring to settle their accounts, on account of carelessness or failure to make returns at the proper time. As Grant, Sherman, and other general officers of high rank and command had been somewhat negligent with reference to those duties or requirements, it was thought all such accounts in time would be satisfactorily adjusted.

I remember when calling at the Ordnance Department to examine my account and to ascertain if it was properly balanced that the officer in charge of the books, in answer to my inquiry, stated that he thought it was all right, but in my presence turned to the account in the books to verify the statement. Standing by, I saw that the account was squared off complete and properly settled. As the officer was making a certificate to that effect, he smiled and invited my attention to an account opposite to that of my own. To the best of my recollection, the account stood open with numerous entries on the debtor side but none whatever on the credit side—the charges dating back to 1861. I did not stop to examine closely or foot up the account of indebtedness. At the top of the page, I saw a name which I never looked upon without emotion. It was simply "U. S. Grant." The account against him on those books was much too large for me to settle, however willing I would have done so had my ability been equal to my desire. In answer to the ordnance officer, I smiled in return, remarking that my own accounts were all that I was able to adjust at that time, but that I judged if General Grant did not see fit to give the matter his attention, and it could not be adjusted by the proper accounting officer in some manner, that if it had to remain on there, an open question, in the end it would be found in any event that in the public opinion the nation was really indebted to General Grant far beyond its ability to pay.

I subsequently, on visiting General Grant, referred to my interview with the ordnance officer and the manner in which my attention was called to the fact of open accounts in the Ordnance Department; that my name, beginning with a "G" like his own, and our accounts being close together on the books had led to the discovery by myself that his account remained open and unsettled. The general stated that his attention had been called to the matter, but that he did not then see and was still unable to understand just how the books could be adjusted to the satisfaction of the Ordnance Department. Whether or not the account still stands open, or was subsequently settled, I am unable to state. In any event, the claim was then good, and the account an object of interest to many others, no doubt, besides myself. As time rolls on it will not, if left open permanently, be likely to become less valuable as an incident in the record of one whose deeds during the War of the Rebellion will ever adorn the brightest pages of his country's history.

Conclusion

I left Washington early in May 1866 for my old home in Youngstown, Ohio, where, after visiting friends [and] recalling to mind familiar scenes and associations of bygone days, I again rejoined my family at Jacksonville, Illinois. Without making any arrangements in the way of business, I quietly awaited the passage of the bill for the reorganization of the army and action of the War Department as to my expected appointment as colonel of cavalry in the regular army. My commission as colonel of the 10th U.S. Cavalry was duly received and accepted, to take rank from July 28, 1866. Upon its receipt, I reported for duty to Major General Hancock at St. Louis and was ordered thence to Fort Leavenworth, Kansas, and there organized my regiment.

After nearly a quarter of a century of active duty on the frontier, where I was constantly coming in contact with the most warlike and savage Indians of the plains, I was, in accordance with law, retired from active service, July 8, 1890, while in command of the Department of Arizona, with my headquarters at Los Angeles, California. I then [held] the rank and grade of brigadier and brevet major general, U.S. Army.

Upon my retirement, Major General Nelson A. Miles,[1] then commanding the Military Division of the Pacific, and at this writing in command of the United States Army with headquarters at Washington, D.C., assumed the command of the Department of Arizona, in addition to his other duties. Immediately upon his arrival at Los Angeles, the general took occasion, unsolicited, to hand me a communication which is retained among my papers and highly prized [July 8, 1890]:

> In accordance with the Act of Congress in which officers of the Army are retired from active service at a given age, and the orders of the President thereon, it becomes my duty to relieve you of the command of the Department of Arizona and temporarily assume the duties of that department. In doing so I desire to express to you the regret that the service loses one of the most distinguished and zealous officers, and at the same time to convey to you my

expression of good will and appreciation of your long, faithful and
valuable services to the Republic.

At a time when the existence of the Government was in serious
peril your gallant and meritorious services were of immeasurable
value to the country. To a remarkable and distinguished war record
you have added twenty-five years of service on a remote frontier in
command of one of the cavalry regiments and the most important
military departments of the country; you have rounded out your
military career and completed a term of service of honor and one
that is pleasing to all patriots, and must be gratifying to you and
yours, and that will be a credit of honor to your name for all time.

It is possible that a history of my experiences in connection with important events occurring during the period of my long service in the army
on the extreme western frontier may hereafter be written for publication—provided the foregoing record of my services, experiences, and recollection of events connected with the War of the Rebellion are published
and favorably and kindly received by an indulgent public.

In conclusion, I shall merely quote the final paragraph of my last official
report, made to Major General Nelson A. Miles under date of July 1, 1890,
while I was in command of the Department of Arizona at Los Angeles:

In closing this report past associations and vague conceptions of
the future are strangely intermingled with emotions of pleasure
and pain, for while looking forward with satisfaction at being
freed from the cares and responsibilities of active service, I am
impressed with the deepest regret at being separated from those
to whom I have become so greatly attached. It is a satisfaction,
however, to believe that our social and official relations have been
so friendly, that it will be pleasant to recall them and that the
sentiments of mutual regard which bind us together are strong
enough to prove enduring in the face of separation. While cheerfully submitting to the law, which is alike applicable to all officers
of the Army, it is well to know that my health remains unim-
paired, and that vigor will give zest to the enjoyments which may
yet fall to my lot. Conscious of having performed my duty at all
times, and possessing the warmest feelings towards those with
whom I have been associated—my seniors and juniors alike—gives
assurance that neither time nor distance can efface from my mind
those pleasurable recollections. Whatever the future may bring
forth, I shall endeavor to accept its joys and sorrows with a brave
heart and clear conscience which should, in any event, be sufficient to carry an old soldier through the remainder of a life, the
best of which has been devoted to his country.

Notes
Bibliography
Index

Notes

Editors' Introduction

1. In addition, the Fort Davis National Historic Site in Fort Davis, Texas, has duplicates of the Grierson Papers from the Southwest Collection at Texas Tech University and many excellent photographs of the Grierson family. Other Benjamin and Alice Grierson Papers are on extended loan from the Tom Green County Historical Society to the Fort Concho Museum in San Angelo, Texas. This collection deals largely with Ben Grierson's career after 1875 as colonel of the 10th Cavalry in the Trans-Pecos region of West Texas. For Grierson's family life and military career, see Leckie and Leckie, *Unlikely Warriors*; Leckie, *Colonel's Lady*; Dinges, "Making of a Cavalryman"; and Bruce Dinges, "Benjamin H. Grierson," in Hutton, *Soldiers West*, 157–76.

2. *Jacksonville Journal*, September 2, 1911; Leckie and Leckie, *Unlikely Warriors*, 306.

3. Halleck quote in Benjamin H. Grierson, "The Lights and Shadows of Life: Including Experiences and Remembrances of the War of the Rebellion" (1892), 121, Grierson Papers, Illinois State Historical Library, Springfield; William T. Sherman to U. S. Grant, December 8, 1862, Grierson Papers, Newberry Library, Chicago; Dinges, "Running Down Rebels."

4. Grant to J. C. Kelton, July 8, 1863, *War of the Rebellion* (hereafter cited as *O.R.*), Series 1, 24, part 1: 58. For the 1863 Mississippi raid, see Brown, *Grierson's Raid*; Surby, *Grierson Raids*; Dinges, "Making of a Cavalryman," 247–393; Dinges, "Grierson's Raid"; York, *Fiction as Fact*; Underwood, *Butternut Guerillas*.

5. For Union cavalry operations in the West, see Starr, *Union Cavalry*.

6. Grant to E. R. S. Canby, February 27, 1865, *O.R.*, Series 1, part 1: 780–81.

7. Leckie and Leckie, *Buffalo Soldiers*.

8. At the time of his death, Grierson was one of only six surviving Union major generals of the Civil War. The others were Nelson A. Miles, Daniel E. Sickles, James H. Wilson, Peter J. Osterhaus, and Grenville M. Dodge. *Official Army Register, 1912*.

9. James M. McPherson has reopened the question of why men fought. Bell Wiley, in *The Life of Johnny Reb and the Life of Billy Yank*, published more than six decades ago, concluded that ideological commitments played only a small role in motivating men to join either army. More recently, McPherson, in *For Cause and Comrades* (a study that again focuses on enlisted men), finds evidence that ideology not only inspired men to enlist and serve their country but often prompted them to reenlist. Grierson, who served as an officer from the beginning of his Civil War career, was similarly motivated by his attachment to the Union cause, as his months of unpaid and officially unrecognized early service so clearly demonstrate.

10. For Scots-Irish emigration, see Leyburn, *Scots-Irish*, xv, 186–88; Chepesiuk, *Scotch-Irish*, 33–50; and Fisk, "Scotch-Irish in Central Ohio."

11. Doyle, *Social Order of a Frontier Community*, 68–79.

12. See Alice to Ben, January 5 and 11, 1855, in Grierson Papers, Illinois State Historical Library, Springfield; Leckie and Leckie, *Unlikely Warriors*, 239–40, 253, 276–80, 303, 305–8. Eight of Alice's eleven siblings survived to adolescence and only five to adulthood. Although Grierson fails to mention it, mental illness also afflicted Alice's family. Both her brother Henry and sister Maria were committed to the Columbus, Ohio, asylum. Alice's brother Tom committed suicide in 1881. Ibid., 24, 269.

13. Foner, *Free Soil, Free Labor*; Kraditor, *Means and Ends*; Lott, "Blackface and Blackness," 17–19; Ben to Alice, May 27, 1863, Grierson Papers, Southwest Collection/Special Collections Library, Texas Tech University (hereafter cited as TTU).

14. For examples of similarly titled nineteenth- and early twentieth-century autobiographies, see W. W. Lyle, *Lights and Shadows of Army Life; or, Pen Pictures from the Battlefield, the Camp, and the Hospital* (Cincinnati: R. W. Carroll, 1865); Samuel D. Woods, *Lights and Shadows of Life on the Pacific Coast* (London: Funk and Wagnalls, 1910); and Joseph G. Clark, *Lights and Shadows of Sailor Life* (Boston: Benjamin M. Mussey, 1848). Ben's cousin, musician and spiritualist Francis Grierson (Benjamin Henry Jesse Francis Shepard), entitled his impressionistic memoir of the coming of the Civil War in the Midwest *The Valley of Shadows* (London: Archibald Constable, 1909).

1. An American Boyhood

1. There is no evidence to support the often-repeated claim that Grierson, who suffered at least three serious horse-related injuries during his long life, was afraid of horses. After fracturing a rib and rupturing his abdomen while mounting a skittish horse at his Fort Davis, Texas, ranch in March of 1897, the almost seventy-one-year-old ex-cavalryman wrote to a San Antonio doctor for a truss, explaining that "if this rupture should prevent me from hereafter riding on horse-back, it would take from me one of the greatest pleasures of my life, and I feel that nothing could compensate me for such a loss, or enable me to be reconciled thereto. Knowing how active I have always been, you can readily understand how irksome it is for me to be forced to be quiet." Grierson to D. F. Kingsley, March [12], 1897, Box 3, Grierson Papers, Fort Davis National Historical Site.

2. For background and an assessment of Grierson as a musician and band leader, see Wagner, *Band Music from the Grierson Collection*, xii–xiv.

3. A prominent Youngstown businessman and railroad promoter, Democrat David Tod (1805–68) was elected Ohio governor on a Unionist ticket in 1861. Tod threw himself into the war effort, raising troops, quelling draft resistance, and repelling Confederate raiders. Nonetheless, he was denied renomination in 1863. Hubbell and Geary, *Biographical Dictionary of the Union*, 535–36.

4. The "Log Cabin and Hard Cider" presidential campaign of 1840 pitted Whig presidential candidate William Henry Harrison, victor over the Shawnee leader Tecumseh and his brother Tenskwatawa at the battle of Tippecanoe in 1811, and vice presidential candidate John Tyler against Democrat Martin Van Buren. In the raucous campaign that catapulted Harrison into the White House, the Whigs utilized portable log cabins and barrels of cider to burnish Harrison's image as a man of the people. Morris, *Encyclopedia of American History*, 217–19. Sheet music for Henry

Schmidt, "The Tippecanoe or Log Cabin Quickstep," is in Wagner, *Band Music from the Grierson Collection,* 19–34.

5. In the late 1850s, George King organized the Brodhead, Wisconsin, band that earned Civil War fame as the 3rd Wisconsin Volunteers band and, eventually, the band of the First Brigade, Third Division, XV Army Corps. Wagner, *Band Music from the Grierson Collection,* xiv n.6.

6. Ben's sisters, as the daughters of an immigrant family, were the beneficiaries of improved educational opportunities for women through the expansion of primary schools in the North. By 1860, American white women had attained literacy rates of over 90 percent, virtually the same as their male counterparts. See Degler, *At Odds,* 308–9.

7. A powerful orator, Wendell Phillips (1811–84) crusaded for the immediate emancipation of slaves, racial equality, women's rights, and labor reform. He was closely associated with William Lloyd Garrison, with whom he sometimes clashed. Phillips assumed leadership of the American Antislavery Society upon Garrison's retirement in 1865. Stewart, *Wendell Phillips*; Mayer, *All on Fire.*

8. William Lloyd Garrison (1805–79), editor of the antislavery newspaper *The Liberator,* visited Youngstown, Ohio, in the summer of 1847 at the beginning of a galvanizing tour of northeastern Ohio, where he spoke to some 20,000 people. Ohio, the gateway to the Midwest and home of Oberlin College, became a focus of the abolitionist crusade. Mayer, *All on Fire,* 365–71.

9. Band member Henry Holcomb recalled in 1910 that Grierson formed his own band on December 6, 1846, and that he later organized various combinations of band members into an orchestra and a minstrel troupe. After the passage of a half century, there apparently was some confusion about when the minstrel troupe was organized and its composition. Wagner, *Band Music from the Grierson Collection,* x, xix n.7, xx n.36.

10. The response of Alice Kirk's father seems extreme by modern standards, but during the antebellum period, upwardly mobile middle-class families sought to inculcate the virtues of "true womanhood." These were "piety, purity, submissiveness, and domesticity." Young women were closely guarded so that not even the slightest whiff of inappropriate behavior would tarnish their reputation. In this context, John Kirk's response is less unreasonable than Grierson is willing to acknowledge. See Welter, "Cult of True Womanhood."

11. John Kirk was an elder in the Disciples of Christ Congregation. A self-made man who parlayed a schoolteacher's salary into a comfortable merchandizing fortune, he was a hard-nosed businessman who supported antislavery and woman suffrage while exercising autocratic control over his wife, Susan Bingham Kirk, and their children. Although John Kirk loaned Ben $1,000 to help start his partnership with John Walihan in 1855, he feared that the debt sentenced his son-in-law to "the prison house of bondage." He directed Ben to pay the 6 percent interest on the loan to Alice and warned that he would "call for both principal and interest" if payments were less than punctual. In early 1858, John Kirk moved the family to Chicago, where he was a sales representative for Jones and Laughlin's American Iron Works, while continuing to speculate in real estate. Alice's mother died in 1872, and five months later John Kirk married Ann Bayne, a Youngstown widow. John Kirk outlived his daughter, dying in 1891. Ben to Alice, October 23, 1855; John Kirk to Ben and Alice, December 31, 1855, Grierson Papers, Illinois State Historical Library, Springfield. See also Leckie and Leckie, *Unlikely Warriors,* 14–16, 38, 208–9, 305.

12. Wagner, in *Band Music from the Grierson Collection*, ix–xi, xx n. 33, surveys archival repositories of Grierson sheet music. Wagner notes that, although most of this material is band music gathered from other sources, Grierson "did write songs for family entertainments, at least one of which survives. He might also have arranged some dance music for his performing groups." Ibid., xiv.

13. The 1856 presidential campaign revolved around the issue of "Bleeding Kansas." The fledgling Republican Party, asserting Congress's authority to control slavery in the territories, nominated Frémont and Dayton as its first national standard-bearers. The Whigs and Know-Nothings nominated Millard Fillmore of New York and Andrew J. Donelson of Tennessee for president and vice president on a nativist platform. The Democrats advanced James Buchanan of Pennsylvania and John C. Breckinridge of Kentucky as their presidential and vice presidential candidates, supporting the Compromise of 1850 and the Kansas-Nebraska Act. Buchanan polled 1,838,169 votes (174 electoral votes) to 1,335, 264 votes (114 electoral votes) for Frémont and 874,534 votes (8 electoral votes) for Fillmore. Morris, *Encyclopedia of American History*, 263; Foner, *Free Soil, Free Labor*, especially 107–8, 163–64, 198–200. John Charles Frémont (1813–90) was arguably the best-known American of his era. Nicknamed the "Pathfinder" because of his well-publicized explorations of the West, he had a flamboyant if controversial military career and, through his marriage to Jessie Benton, enjoyed the patronage of her father, powerful Missouri senator Thomas Hart Benton. Although Grierson never lost his admiration for the Frémonts, the Pathfinder's fortunes declined rapidly during the Civil War. Appointed governor of Arizona Territory in 1878 in recognition of his service to the Republican Party, Frémont tried, but failed, to revive his ruined finances. Rolle, *John C. Frémont*.

14. John Ludlum McConnel (1826–62) was a Mexican War veteran, author, and Jacksonville attorney. His books included *Talbot and Vernon; Grahame, or Youth and Manhood; The Glenns;* and *Western Characters, or Types of Border Life. Appleton's Encyclopedia.* <http://www.famousamericans.net/johnludlummcconel/>.

15. James Buchanan's (1791–1868) administration would prove to be a failure by almost any standard. His support of the proslavery Lecompton Constitution for Kansas split the Democratic Party and practically ensured Lincoln's election in 1860, while his inability to deal with secessionists left the country teetering on the brink of disunion. Hubbell and Geary, *Biographical Dictionary of the Union*, 65–66.

16. From August to October 1858, Republican senatorial candidate Abraham Lincoln and Democratic incumbent Stephen A. Douglas (1812–61) staged seven debates around Illinois. Although Douglas narrowly won reelection, his apparent willingness to limit the doctrine of "popular sovereignty" and reject Kansas's Lecompton Constitution recognizing slavery cost him Southern backing in his bid for the 1860 Democratic presidential nomination and made Lincoln a rallying point for slavery opponents. Morris, *Encyclopedia of American History*, 267; Holzer, *Lincoln-Douglas Debates*; Johannsen, *Stephen A. Douglas*, 664–77.

2. Rallying around the Flag

1. Seward (1801–72), a seasoned and powerful New York politician, was a commanding force in the Republican Party but lacked the popular appeal of Frémont and Lincoln. As secretary of state in Lincoln's cabinet, Seward deftly kept European powers neutral during the Civil War. J. Taylor, *William Henry Seward*.

2. Like Ulysses S. Grant, William T. Sherman (1820–91) had a lackluster prewar military career marred, in Sherman's case, by rumors of mental instability. Grierson

benefited early in the war from Sherman's high regard and reciprocated the warm feelings. Only Lincoln and Grant surpassed Sherman in Grierson's estimation. Sherman succeeded Grant as general of the army in 1869 and retired in 1884. Marszalek, *Sherman*; Fellman, *Citizen Sherman*.

3. Defeated as the Northern Democracy's candidate for president in the four-way 1860 election, Douglas urged strong military measures against the seceding states and returned to rally support in Illinois for the war. He died at Chicago on June 3, 1861. Johannsen, *Stephen A. Douglas*, especially 840–74.

4. A rough-and-tumble politician, Richard Yates (1815–73) was born in Kentucky, graduated from Illinois College, served in the Illinois General Assembly and the U.S. Congress, and practiced law in Jacksonville prior to his 1860 election as governor on the Republican ticket. A supporter of Radical Reconstruction, his single term in the U.S. Senate (1865–70) was tarnished by alcoholism. Hubbell and Geary, *Biographical Dictionary of the Union*, 609–10; *Biographical Directory of the United States Congress*.

5. An unsuccessful Republican candidate for Congress in 1860, Benjamin M. Prentiss (1819–1901) had served in the Illinois militia during the Mormon expulsion from Nauvoo and as a captain in the 1st Illinois Volunteers during the Mexican War. Appointed colonel of the 10th Illinois Infantry in April 1861, he occupied Cairo and was promoted to brigadier general of volunteers in May. Prentiss distinguished himself by his stubborn defense of the Hornet's Nest at the battle of Shiloh, where he was captured. After his exchange, Prentiss was assigned to command the District of Eastern Arkansas and promoted to major general of volunteers. He repulsed a Confederate assault on Helena but resigned on August 3, 1863, complaining that he was "without an adequate command." Hubbell and Geary, *Biographical Dictionary of the Union*, 415–16; McDonough, *Shiloh*, especially 48, 125, 164–67.

6. An 1842 graduate of West Point, John Pope (1822–92) was a veteran of the Mexican War and captain of topographical engineers at the outbreak of the Civil War. When Fort Sumter was fired upon, he offered his services to Governor Yates, who immediately put him to work mustering Illinois soldiers. Appointed brigadier general of volunteers on June 14, 1861, Pope enjoyed early success along the Mississippi River and was promoted to major general of volunteers. Transferred east, he quickly alienated many with his bombastic pronouncements and suffered a humiliating defeat at Second Manassas (the second battle of Bull Run). Pope quietly served out the remainder of the war in command of the Department of the Northwest, where he effectively dealt with the Sioux uprising in Minnesota. Grierson and Pope developed a postwar friendship based in part on their shared views on humanitarian treatment for subjugated Indian tribes. Warner, *Generals in Blue*, 376–77; Cozzens, *General John Pope*; Ellis, *General Pope and U.S. Indian Policy*.

7. President of the City National Bank, Alfred B. Safford was the wealthiest man in Cairo. In 1858, the Vermont native relocated with his sister, Mary Jane, from Shawneetown, Illinois, where she taught school and he was a merchant. During the Civil War, Mary Jane nursed Union troops and her brother contributed money to soldier hospitals. U. S. Grant established his headquarters on the third floor of Safford's bank during his command of the District of Cairo. Kionka, *Key Command*, 6, 21, 65–66.

8. Although Unionists held a majority in the legislature, Kentuckians were divided in their loyalties. Failing in his efforts to form a coalition of border states to mediate between the North and the South, Governor Magoffin, who harbored Southern sympathies, declared Kentucky's neutrality. While Lincoln agreed to honor Magoffin's

proclamation, Kentucky found itself in an uncomfortable position, with Confederate forces poised in northwestern Tennessee and Union forces keeping a wary eye on southwestern Kentucky from across the river at Cairo. Both sides established recruiting camps for Kentuckians. Overwhelming Unionist victories in a June 20 special congressional election and the August 5 regular election of the state legislature effectively ended the military face-off. R. M. Kelly, "Holding Kentucky for the Union," in Buel and Johnson, *Battles and Leaders*, 1:373–92; McPherson, *Battle Cry of Freedom*, 293–97.

9. Richard J. Oglesby (1824–99) was born in Kentucky but moved as a child with his parents to Decatur, Illinois. He served in the Mexican War and joined the California Gold Rush. An attorney and land developer, he was an unsuccessful Republican candidate for Congress in 1858 and was elected to the Illinois state senate in 1860. Oglesby organized the 8th Illinois Infantry at the beginning of the war and was promoted to brigadier general and major general of volunteers for his performances at Fort Donelson and Corinth, where he was wounded. He resigned in May 1864 to run successfully for the first of three terms as governor (1864, 1872, 1884). Oglesby resigned the governorship shortly after his election in 1872 to serve in the U.S. Senate. With John A. Logan and others, he was one of the founders of the Grand Army of the Republic. Hubbell and Geary, *Biographical Dictionary of the Union*, 380; Heitman, *Historical Register*, 1:757.

10. Nicknamed "The Young Napoleon," McClellan (1826–85) was the Union's most promising military commander in 1861. Graduating second in the West Point class of 1846, he distinguished himself in the Mexican War and was dispatched to observe the Crimean War before resigning his commission in 1857. He became chief engineer of the Illinois Central Railroad and was president of the Ohio and Mississippi Railroad in Cincinnati at the outbreak of the Civil War. Appointed by Governor William Dennison to command Ohio state forces, McClellan was quickly elevated by President Lincoln to major general of volunteers. He rushed to garrison Cairo and other strategic points along the Ohio River, and on June 7, 1861, met with Simon Bolivar Buckner, commander of Kentucky state troops, to ensure that Kentucky would resist Confederate efforts to violate its neutrality. McClellan had a checkered career as commander of the Army of the Potomac until Lincoln finally removed him from command on November 7, 1862. He was the Democratic candidate for president in 1864 and was elected governor of New Jersey, 1878–81. Warner, *Generals in Blue*, 290–92; Sears, *George B. McClellan*, especially 68–78.

11. Quartermaster Hatch was the brother of Illinois secretary of state Ozias Hatch. A congressional committee in the spring of 1862 discovered enough evidence of corruption to suspend Reuben Hatch from his Cairo post. Kionka, *Key Command*, 162–65.

12. Ransom (1834–64) attended Norwich University in Vermont, where his father was president, and then engaged in engineering and real estate in Illinois. He was agent for the Illinois Central Railroad at Vandalia when the war broke out. He rose to colonel of the 11th Illinois Infantry; was wounded in Missouri and at Fort Donelson and Shiloh; served as Gen. John A. McClernand's chief of staff and inspector general of the Army of the Tennessee; and commanded brigades of the XIII and XVII Corps. Appointed brigadier general of volunteers on April 15, 1863, Ransom participated in Gen. N. P. Banks's Red River campaign and the fighting around Atlanta, and eventually commanded the XVII Corps. He succumbed to illness and the effects of his wounds near Rome, Georgia. Warner, *Generals in Blue*, 389–90; Eddy, *Patriotism of Illinois*, 487–94.

13. A native Virginian and flamboyant secessionist, Meriwether "Jeff" Thompson (1826–76) was a successful businessman and former mayor of St. Joseph, Missouri. He earned his nickname "Swamp Fox of the Confederacy" as a brigadier general of state militia in southeastern Missouri and northeastern Arkansas. During the spring and summer of 1862, he conducted guerrilla raids in the vicinity of Memphis and as far south as New Orleans. Captured in August 1863, he spent a year imprisoned at Johnson Island, Ohio. Upon being exchanged, he commanded a brigade in Maj. Gen. Sterling Price's cavalry corps in Arkansas and Missouri. After the war, Thompson engaged in business and politics in Memphis and New Orleans, where he died. Allardice, *More Generals in Gray*, 321–22; Monaghan, *Swamp Fox of the Confederacy*.

14. The beautiful, charming, and ambitious Jessie Benton Frémont (1824–1902) was the daughter of powerful Missouri senator Thomas Hart Benton. As an accomplished writer and skillful lobbyist, she tirelessly promoted her husband's military and political career. "Frémont and Jessie" was the rallying cry of antislavery proponents in the 1856 presidential campaign. Herr, *Jessie Benton Frémont*. On August 5, 1861, Jessie wrote to Postmaster General Montgomery Blair: "The sound of the shouts with which we were welcomed at Cairo stays in my memory. Only a weak & threatened garrison seeing aid coming could make such sounds. Gen'l. Prentiss's voice as he said 'I shall sleep tonight' said volumes. . . . Undisciplined & untrained they are, but the volunteers are knights and crusaders of the best kind and a little loving care such as the first Napoleon gave would make an invincible army of them." Herr and Spence, *Letters of Jessie Benton Frémont*, 261.

15. Born in Oswego, New York, C. Carrol Marsh was a Chicago corn merchant at the outbreak of the war. He was mustered in as colonel of the 20th Illinois Infantry at Joliet on May 11, 1861. Marsh commanded the Second Brigade of John A. McClernand's division at Shiloh and participated in the pursuit of Van Dorn's cavalry following the raid on Holly Springs in December 1862. Grant recommended Marsh's promotion to brigadier general in October 1862, but apparently it was not acted on. Marsh resigned on April 22, 1863. Illinois Civil War Muster and Descriptive Rolls Database; Grant to Halleck, October 21, 1862, *O.R.*, Series 1, 52, part 1: 293; Grant, *Personal Memoirs*, 1:421.

16. Born in Scotland, John McArthur (1826–1906) owned the Excelsior Iron Works and was captain of the Chicago Highland Guards. At the outbreak of the war, he was commissioned colonel of the 12th Illinois Infantry assigned to garrison Cairo. Promoted to brigadier general in March of 1862, McArthur distinguished himself during the fighting at Vicksburg and Nashville. Like Grierson, at the end of the war he was serving under Maj. Gen. E. R. S. Canby in Alabama. Eddy, *Patriotism of Illinois*, 494–95; Warner, *Generals in Blue*, 288–89.

17. An 1841 West Point graduate, Nathaniel P. Lyon (1818–61) commanded the St. Louis Arsenal at the outbreak of the war and was killed at the battle of Wilson's Creek on August 10, 1861. As the first Union general to fall in battle, Lyon was heralded as a martyr and the "Savior in Missouri." In fact, his biographer suggests, Lyon's "violent dogmatic personality" and a blind hatred of secessionists, formed while he was on duty in "Bleeding Kansas," plunged the state into a war it would have preferred to avoid. Phillips, *Damned Yankee*, especially xiv–xvi in the preface to the paperback edition.

18. As the author of *Rifle and Light Infantry Tactics* (1855), used by both Union and Confederate armies, Hardee (1815–73) enjoyed instant name recognition. An 1838 West Point graduate, he fought in the Mexican War and the Second Seminole War, rose to lieutenant colonel of the 1st Cavalry, and served as superintendent of the U.S.

Military Academy. Nicknamed "Old Reliable," Hardee rose quickly to Confederate lieutenant general in October 1862. As a corps commander in the Army of Tennessee, Hardee became a harsh critic of Gen. Braxton Bragg and, with Gen. Leonidas Polk, schemed for Bragg's removal. He surrendered with Gen. Joseph Johnston on April 26, 1865. Hughes, *General William J. Hardee*; Woodworth, *Jefferson Davis and His Generals*, 162–68.

19. Ulysses S. Grant (1822–85), who was living as a civilian in Galena, Illinois, at the outbreak of the war, rose from obscurity to lieutenant general and commander of the Union armies. Although slow to appreciate the role of cavalry, Grant was nonetheless impressed with Grierson's performance in West Tennessee and especially his 1863 raid through Mississippi that diverted Confederate attention while he crossed the Mississippi River to attack Vicksburg. In the 1866 reorganization of the army, Grant recommended Grierson to organize the 10th Cavalry. Simpson, *Ulysses S. Grant*; Starr, *Union Cavalry*, 145; Dinges, "Making of a Cavalryman," 353, 522, 530.

20. Turchin and Hecker commanded the 19th and 24th Illinois Infantry regiments, respectively. Eddy, *Patriotism of Illinois*, 108, 113, 339–40. Hecker was mustered in at Chicago on July 8 and resigned on December 23, 1861. Illinois Civil War Muster and Descriptive Rolls Database. A court-martial board sentenced Turchin (1822–1901), a Russian émigré and Crimean War veteran, to be dismissed from the service after his men pillaged Athens, Alabama, on May 2, 1862. Reinstated as brigadier general of volunteers, Turchin distinguished himself at Chickamauga and earned the nickname "The Russian Thunderbolt" in fighting at Missionary Ridge. He resigned because of ill health on July 15, 1864. After the war, Turchin was solicitor of patents in Chicago and established a Polish settlement at Radom, Illinois. For biographical details and an assessment of Turchin's actions within the context of hardening Union attitudes toward Southern civilians, see Bradley and Dahlen, *From Conciliation to Conquest*. The uproar over the conduct of Turchin's men in Missouri is discussed in ibid., 50–56; and Hecker's stormy relationship with his subordinates and the chaotic state of affairs within the 24th Illinois are described in ibid., 64.

21. Prince Napoleon (1822–91) and his wife, Princess Clotilde of Italy, visited St. Louis on their two-month tour of the United States, July 27 to September 26, 1861. Secretary of State Seward had presented the prince and his entourage to President Lincoln at the White House on August 3 before the party set out for the upper Midwest. They left Chicago on September 4 and spent ten days touring the Western Military Department before returning east. The cousin of Napoleon III, Napoleon Joseph Charles Paul Bonaparte (popularly known as "Plon-Plon") "openly and liberally supported the North" upon his return to France, though his views carried little official weight. In 1852–53, the Frémonts had been present in Paris for Napoleon III's installation as emperor and his subsequent marriage to Eugenie Montijo. Ferri Pisani, *Prince Napoleon in America*; *Columbia Encyclopedia*, 6th ed., s.v., "Bonaparte"; *Harper's Weekly*, August 24, September 7, 1861; Nevins, *Frémont*, 403–4; Jordan and Pratt, *Europe and the American Civil War*, 230–31.

22. Grant expressed similar sentiments, writing in his *Memoirs*, 1:263–64, that "General Prentiss made a great mistake on the above occasion, one that he would not have committed later in the war. When I came to know him better, I regretted it much. In consequence of this occurrence he was off duty in the field when the principal campaign in the West was going on, and his juniors received promotion while he was where none could be obtained. He would have been next to myself in rank in

the district of south-east Missouri, by virtue of his service in the Mexican War. He was a brave and very earnest soldier. No man in the service was more sincere in his devotion to the cause for which we were battling; none more ready to make sacrifices or risk his life in it."

23. Sterling Price (1809–67) had served as a state legislator, U.S. congressman, brigadier general and military governor of New Mexico during the Mexican War, governor of Missouri, and president of the state convention that opposed secession. Beginning the war as commander of the Missouri state guard, in March 1862 he accepted a commission as major general in the Confederate army. "At best a respectable mediocrity," in the estimation of his biographer, Price nonetheless was "the central figure in the Civil War west of the Mississippi." Castel, *General Sterling Price*, quote on 4.

24. Frémont created an uproar with his August 30, 1861, proclamation authorizing military commanders to emancipate secessionist-held slaves. He compounded his difficulties on September 18 by arresting Francis P. Blair Jr., the brother of Postmaster General Montgomery Blair, for insubordination. Frémont was in the field outside Springfield, Missouri, on November 2 when a messenger delivered Lincoln's October 24 letter relieving him from command. Nevins, *Frémont*, 499–549. Grierson goes on to refer to Frémont's comments, in a letter published in the *St. Louis Democrat*, that while he felt competent "to meet the enemy in the field, I am not able at the same time to attend to the enemy [his critics] at home." Quoted in ibid., 532.

25. Described by his biographer as "a respected intellectual, a prolific writer, a brave soldier, a practical statesman, a brilliant attorney and businessman, an efficient organizer, and a no-nonsense man of action," Henry W. "Old Brains" Halleck (1815–72) was considered one of the nation's most experienced and accomplished soldiers at the outbreak of the war. Replacing John C. Frémont in November 1861, he quickly restored order in the Department of the West. Advanced to command the Department of the Mississippi, Halleck's indecisiveness in the Corinth campaign prompted Lincoln to order him to Washington as general-in-chief. He essentially became chief of staff after U. S. Grant assumed command of the Union armies in March of 1864. After the war, Halleck successively commanded the military divisions of the James, the Pacific, and the South. Marszalek, *Commander of All Lincoln's Armies*, quote on 2; Warner, *Generals in Blue*, 195–97.

26. In an effort to placate the powerful slaveholders angered by Frémont's emancipation proclamation, on November 20, 1861—the day after assuming command of the Department of the West—Halleck issued General Orders No. 9 barring fugitive slaves from entering Union lines and instructing military commanders to expel those already under military protection. Ostensibly issued to prevent fugitive slaves from providing information to the enemy, the order generated outrage across the North. Marszalek, *Commander of All Lincoln's Armies*, 111.

27. An engineer by training, Gustav Waagner had served as an artillery officer in the Hungarian Army before fleeing to the United States in 1851. McClellan dispatched Waagner to train troops at Cairo at the outbreak of the war. Appointed chief of artillery at Cairo by Frémont, he participated in the Union expeditions to Belmont, Missouri, and Paducah, Kentucky. Frémont advanced Waagner to chief of artillery of the Department of the West in late September 1861, but his tenure was short-lived, ending when Frémont was relieved of command in November. In March of 1862, he was commissioned colonel of the 2nd New York Heavy Artillery. Beszedits, "Hungarians in Civil War Missouri."

3. Colonel of the 6th Illinois Cavalry

1. The Emancipation Proclamation, issued on September 22, 1862, five days after the battle of Antietam, declared that after January 1, 1863, slaves in the rebellious states "shall be then, thenceforward, and forever free." McPherson, *Battle Cry of Freedom*, 357–58.

2. An 1822 graduate of West Point and veteran of the Mexican War, David Hunter (1802–86) had resigned in 1836 to enter business in Chicago but rejoined the army as a major and paymaster in 1842. He struck up a correspondence with Lincoln from Fort Leavenworth, Kansas, that led to his invitation to accompany the inaugural train to Washington, D.C. Appointed brigadier general of volunteers in May and major general in August 1861, he performed poorly, prematurely abolishing slavery in the Department of the South and burning the Virginia Military Institute. Hunter accompanied Lincoln's body to Springfield and presided over the military tribunal that tried the assassination conspirators. He retired in 1866. Hubbell and Geary, *Biographical Dictionary of the Union*, 268; Warner, *Generals in Blue*, 243–44; Miller, *Lincoln's Abolitionist General*.

3. Grant's inconclusive amphibious assault on the Confederate encampment at Belmont, Missouri, opposite Columbus, Kentucky, on November 7, 1861, bolstered Union confidence and lowered Confederate morale along the Mississippi. Although little more than a bloody diversion that left Confederates in possession of the field, it upset the stalemate along the Kentucky-Tennessee line and set the stage for Grant's descent on Forts Henry and Donelson. Hughes, *Battle of Belmont*.

4. On September 20, 1861, General Sterling Price captured the town and Union garrison at Lexington in central Missouri, along with its arms and supplies. The quantity of weapons and provisions seized, although large, was inadequate to accommodate the flood of recruits, most of whom promptly deserted, forcing Price to withdraw on September 29. James A. Milligan, "The Siege of Lexington, Mo.," in Buel and Johnson, *Battles and Leaders*, 1:307–13: Cutrer, *Ben McCulloch*, 247, 259; Castel, *General Sterling Price*, 50–56.

5. An Ohioan, Eleazer Paine (1815–82) graduated from West Point in 1839 and served briefly on Zachary Taylor's staff during the Second Seminole War. A friend of Abraham Lincoln, he was practicing law in Monmouth, Illinois, when he was appointed colonel of the 9th Illinois Infantry. Commissioned brigadier general of volunteers on September 3, 1861, he commanded a brigade at Paducah, Kentucky, and at Cairo, Illinois. Paine led a division in operations along the Mississippi River, in western Tennessee, and during the advance on Corinth, Mississippi. Thereafter, he was relegated to guarding railroads in western Tennessee and Kentucky. Warner, *Generals in Blue*, 355–56.

6. On April 15, 1861, President Lincoln had called for 75,000 ninety-day militia to suppress the rebellion. In Illinois, 10,000 men rushed to the colors, more than enough to fill the state's six-regiment quota. Reluctant to turn away patriotic citizens, the legislature provided for the organization of ten regiments, holding the excess companies in camp until June when the War Department authorized their enrollment. Union reverses, particularly at First Manassas (first battle of Bull Run), persuaded Congress in July to authorize the enlistment of up to one million three-year volunteers. In the meantime, field operations were disrupted as the original ninety-day enlistments expired. McPherson, *Battle Cry of Freedom*, 322; Eddy, *Patriotism of Illinois*, 102, 106, 112; Hicken, *Illinois in the Civil War*, 2–3.

7. John M. Palmer (1817–1900), a former Democratic Illinois state senator, joined the Republican Party in 1856. He was a delegate to the 1860 Chicago convention that nominated Lincoln for president and to the 1861 Washington Peace Conference. Defeated in his bid for a congressional seat, he was commissioned colonel of the 14th Illinois Infantry in May 1861 and promoted to brigadier general of volunteers in December. Palmer was a brigade and division commander in the major western campaigns from New Madrid through Stones River. Promoted to major general of volunteers in March 1863, he fought at Chickamauga and Chattanooga, and commanded the XIV Corps during the Atlanta campaign until a dispute with William T. Sherman sent him to command the Department of Kentucky. Palmer was elected governor of Illinois as a Republican in 1868 but was defeated as a Democrat in 1888. He was elected to the U.S. Senate in 1891 and was presidential standard-bearer of the Gold Democrats in 1896. Hubbell and Geary, *Biographical Dictionary of the Union*, 391–92.

8. Grierson refers to Garfield's victory over Brig. Gen. Humphrey Marshall at the battle of Middle Creek. A congressman-elect and close friend of Treasury Secretary Salmon P. Chase, Garfield (1831–81) was colonel of the 42nd Ohio Infantry. On February 13, 1863, Maj. Gen. William S. Rosecrans named Garfield chief-of-staff of the Army of the Cumberland. He proved extremely effective, prodding Rosecrans to pursue Braxton Bragg's army after the battle of Stones River, playing an important role in the Tullahoma campaign in which Rosecrans maneuvered Bragg out of Tennessee, and making a heroic ride to Gen. George Thomas's beleaguered position at Chickamauga. A grateful Lincoln promoted Garfield to major general of volunteers. Garfield resigned his commission on October 10, 1863, and took his seat in Congress, still wearing his general's uniform. He was elected president of the United States in 1880 and was assassinated the following year. Like Grierson's in-laws, Garfield was a devout member of the Disciples of Christ Church. Edward O. Guerrant, "Marshall and Garfield in Eastern Kentucky," in Buel and Johnson, *Battles and Leaders*, 1:393–97; Perry, *Touched with Fire*, 105–30; Peskin, *Garfield*; F. D. Williams, *Wild Life of the Army*.

9. An 1841 West Point graduate, Don Carlos Buell (1818–98) served in the Second Seminole War and in the Mexican War, where he was wounded at the battle of Churabusco. Thereafter, he held mainly administrative positions. Commissioned brigadier general of volunteers on May 17, 1861, he assisted in organizing and training the Army of the Potomac. "A self-absorbed, distant, and private man," according to his biographer, Buell enjoyed early success at the head of the Army of the Ohio in Kentucky and Tennessee but was relieved of command for his slow pursuit of Braxton Bragg's army after the battle of Perryville on October 8, 1862. He resigned his commission on June 1, 1864, and operated a Kentucky coal mine and ironworks after the war. Warner, *Generals in Blue*, 51–52; S. Engle, *Don Carlos Buell*, quote on xiii.

10. Brig. Gen. George H. Thomas (1816–70) was leading the advance of Buell's expedition into East Tennessee when he was attacked by George B. Crittenden and Felix Zollicoffer at Mill Springs, or Logan's Cross Roads, Kentucky. Although the Federals routed the enemy, bad weather and lack of supplies forced Buell to recall Thomas and abandon the invasion. Thomas, an 1840 West Point graduate and Mexican War veteran, was a native Virginian who remained loyal to the Union. His heroic stand nine months after the Mill Springs victory earned him the sobriquet "The Rock of Chickamauga" and command of the Army of the Cumberland following William S. Rosecrans's removal. Thomas's attack on Hood at Nashville, December 15–16, 1864, virtually destroyed the Army of Tennessee. R. M. Kelly, "Holding Kentucky for the

Union," in Buel and Johnson, *Battles and Leaders*, 1:387–91; McKinney, *Education in Violence*; Thomas, *General George H. Thomas*.

11. A Tennessee newspaperman and Whig politician, Felix Zollicoffer (1812–62) served three terms in Congress and was a member of the 1861 Washington Peace Conference. Appointed a brigadier general in the Provisional Confederate Army on July 9, 1861, he led an ill-advised movement across the Cumberland River into Kentucky that resulted in the fight at Mill Springs on January 19, 1862, in which he was killed. Kelly, "Holding Kentucky for the Union," 386–92; Warner, *Generals in Gray*, 349–50.

12. A Philadelphian, C. F. Smith (1807–62) was an 1825 graduate of West Point, where he served as an instructor and superintendent from 1829 to 1842. He rose to colonel during the Mexican War and was stationed in Utah at the outbreak of the Civil War. Appointed brigadier general of volunteers, Smith performed admirably under younger officers (including U. S. Grant), who had once been his students at the military academy. After the Fort Donelson victory, Gen. Henry Halleck ordered Smith to relieve Grant in charge of the Tennessee River expedition. Smith seriously injured his leg, and Grant resumed command on the eve of the battle of Shiloh. Smith died on April 25, 1862. Hubbell and Geary, *Biographical Dictionary of the Union*, 484–85; Benjamin Franklin Cooling, "The Reliable First Team: Grant and Charles Ferguson Smith," in Woodworth, *Grant's Lieutenants*, 43–62.

13. Kentucky-born John A. McClernand (1812–1900) had a distinguished prewar career as an Illinois state legislator and U.S. congressman, when Lincoln appointed the War Democrat brigadier general of volunteers in order to hold southern Illinois in the Union. McClernand fought bravely in the Shiloh and Vicksburg campaigns, advancing to major general of volunteers in command of the Army of the Tennessee's XIII Corps. Unfortunately, McClernand was a contentious and outspoken subordinate whose successful scheming to raise an independent Army of the Mississippi and overweening pride in his corps's accomplishments at the expense of others brought him into conflict with Ulysses S. Grant. Ill and increasingly frustrated, McClernand resigned in November 1864 and returned to Illinois. He remained active in state and national politics until his death. Kiper, *Major General McClernand.*

14. The combined army and navy victories at Fort Henry (February 6, 1862) and Fort Donelson (February 16, 1862) punched a huge hole in the 200-mile-long Confederate line between Columbus, Kentucky, and Nashville, Tennessee. By the end of the month, the Confederates had abandoned both positions, leaving all of Kentucky and most of Tennessee under Union control. Grant's demand for the "unconditional surrender" of the Fort Donelson garrison became a Northern rallying cry. McPherson, *Battle Cry of Freedom*, 396–405.

15. The fatal chink in the Fort Donelson defenses resided with the Confederate commanders. Hamilton, in *Battle of Fort Donelson*, attributes the surrender to "indecision, quarreling, and misunderstanding" (8) among the Rebel generals from Albert Sidney Johnston, who failed to appreciate Fort Donelson's strategic importance and adequately defend it, to John B. Floyd and Gideon Pillow, first and second in command of the fort, incompetents of the first order who ultimately slipped out of the post, leaving Forrest's cavalry to break through the Union lines to safety and Brig. Gen. Simon B. Buckner to surrender the garrison to Grant. See also Tucker, *Unconditional Surrender*, 61–104.

16. Prewar attorney and Democratic congressman John A. Logan (1826–86) was arguably the Union's most able political general. Although many observers feared that

Logan would lead a secessionist movement in southern Illinois, he instead became a vociferous defender of the Northern cause and an able battlefield commander, rising quickly to major general of volunteers at the head of the Army of the Tennessee's XV Corps. A Radical Republican after the war, he wielded considerable power as a member of the House Ways and Means Committee, chair of the Senate Military Affairs Committee, national commander of the Grand Army of the Republic, and vice presidential candidate. Logan was author of *The Great Conspiracy* (1886) and *The Volunteer Soldier of America* (1886), and architect of a national Memorial Day. Logan, Grierson, and Grant were honored guests at the 1865 Illinois State Fair. Ecelbarger, *Black Jack Logan*, especially 235.

17. The stress of command in Kentucky during the chaotic early days of the war had triggered anxiety and depression in Sherman so severe that, during the winter of 1861–62, Northern newspapers openly questioned his sanity. The Ewing family and General Halleck rallied to Sherman's defense. The crisis passed after Halleck assigned Sherman to Missouri and eventually gave him command of the District of Cairo, where he worked in concert with Ulysses S. Grant, who commanded the District of West Tennessee. Marszalek, *Sherman*, 154–70; Fellman, *Citizen Sherman*, 71–109.

18. Rawlins (1831–69), a young Galena, Illinois, attorney, served at U. S. Grant's right hand throughout the war, rising from captain to brigadier general and chief of staff in the regular army. As president, Grant appointed his close friend and confidante secretary of war in March 1869. Rawlins, who had contracted tuberculosis, died six months later. Warner, *Generals in Blue*, 391–91; McFeely, *Grant*, 85–87, 298–300.

19. Strong (1805–67) was a wealthy, retired New York City businessman who helped purchase weapons for the Union in France at the outbreak of the war. Commissioned brigadier general of volunteers on September 28, 1861, he commanded Benton Barracks at St. Louis and, in March of 1862, assumed command of the District of Cairo. Strong headed the commission that investigated the evacuation of New Madrid, Missouri, and in June 1863 took command of the District of St. Louis. He resigned on October 20, 1863. Warner, *Generals in Blue*, 484.

20. John Wood (1798–1880) was elected lieutenant governor of Illinois on the Republican ticket with William H. Bissell in 1856 and served ten months as governor after Bissell's death on March 18, 1860. Wood was Illinois quartermaster general throughout the war. *Portrait and Biographical Album.*

21. Henry Emerson Etheridge (1819–1902) was a staunch Tennessee Unionist who served three terms in Congress and was elected clerk of the U.S. House of Representatives (1861–63). He ran unsuccessfully for governor in 1867, as a Conservative Unionist, and was elected to the state senate (1869–71), after which he retired from politics. *Tennessee Encyclopedia of History and Culture*, s.v., "Henry Emerson Etheridge."

22. Although Prentiss's division was eventually surrounded and captured, their desperate defense of the Hornet's Nest at Shiloh, Tennessee, on April 6, 1862, saved the Union army from destruction by delaying the Confederate advance and allowing Grant critical time to re-form his lines to resist the Rebel assault the following day. McDonough, *Shiloh*, 167.

23. Grant was caught off guard at Pittsburg Landing by Confederate forces under Generals Albert Sidney Johnston and P. G. T. Beauregard, who came close to overrunning the Union position on the first day of fighting. Prentiss's stand at the Hornet's Nest and Johnston's death turned the tide of battle, and on April 7 Grant's and Buell's troops forced the Rebel forces, now under Beauregard's command, to retreat. McDonough, *Shiloh*.

24. An Indiana lawyer and politician, Lew Wallace (1827–1905) had served as a lieutenant of Indiana volunteers in the Mexican War and was quickly advanced to major general of volunteers in the Civil War. Ordered by Grant to march his division from Crump's Landing and fall on the Confederate army's left flank, Wallace inexplicably became lost and arrived hours too late to participate effectively in the first day's fighting at Shiloh. Controversy immediately arose over whether Wallace had disobeyed orders, become lost, or was criminally slow. Wallace's defenders suggest that Grant's instructions may have been garbled in transmission. After the war, Wallace served as governor of New Mexico Territory and was much in demand as an author and lecturer. He is best known as the author of *Ben Hur*. Warner, *Generals in Blue*, 535–36; Morsberger and Morsberger, *Lew Wallace*; McDonough, *Shiloh*, 158–61; Stacy D. Allen, "'If He Had Less Rank': Lewis Wallace," in Woodworth, *Grant's Lieutenants*, 63–90.

25. A phrase is missing in the original typescript. However, Ben informed Alice at the time that the Paducah garrison consisted of "one Company of artilery [*sic*] who have 4, 6-pdrs., the bal. of the force here are cavalry, about 600 effective men." Ben to Alice, May 6, 1862, roll 4, Grierson Papers, TTU.

26. Alice's arrival with her son Charlie, surprising Ben in camp in the middle of the night, is an example of the way in which the Civil War was expanding the activities middle-class women undertook. Before the war, Alice often visited her family by train, with her children in tow, but making her way to an army camp, unescorted, would have been unthinkable. In the North, such experiences for women led afterwards to more professionally organized female volunteerism and the opening of nursing as an occupation that over time in the twentieth century would finally become one of the new women's professions. Mary R. Livermore, who was one of the female leaders of the Northwestern Sanitary Commission in Chicago, noted at the end of the Civil War, "We can't be the women we were before." Livermore, *My Story of the War*. Livermore quote from L. C. B., "Woman Suffrage at Worcester, Mass." *National Anti-Slavery Standard* 30 (December 25, 1869): 3–4, cited in N. Engle, "'We Can't Be the Women We Were Before,'" 80. Elizabeth D. Leonard, in *Yankee Women*, explores the Civil War careers of military nurse Sophronia Bucklin, United States Christian Commission national supervising agent Annie Wittenmyer, and army surgeon Mary Walker, M.D., to discern the extent to which women expanded their roles and the barriers they still faced after the war. Although Alice would be occupied bearing and rearing her growing family at western forts once Ben became colonel of the 10th Cavalry, she would also prove a more assertive woman than she had been before the conflict, as she often intervened on behalf of black troopers and took it upon herself to inform her husband of military matters. In effect, she often acted as if she were Ben's informal, but very real, adjutant. See Leckie, *Colonel's Lady*.

4. Scouting after Guerillas in West Tennessee

1. In the fall of 1860, Illinois voters called for a convention to revise the state's 1848 constitution. The document provided by the Democratic-controlled 1862 constitutional convention generated protest from the industrializing, and overwhelmingly Republican, northern counties. Voters rejected the proposed constitution, although they overwhelmingly approved provisions that prohibited blacks from immigrating to Illinois and barred them from voting and holding public office. Cole, *Era of the Civil War*, 267–72; VandeCreek, "State Constitutional Convention of 1862."

2. Grierson refers to the predominantly Democratic counties of southern Illinois. It was widely feared at the outbreak of the rebellion that the region, heavily settled

by immigrants from the Southern and border states, and popularly known as "Little Egypt," might join the Confederacy. Cole, *Era of the Civil War*, 302.

3. Samuel L. "Sandy" Woodward (1840–1924) formed a lifetime association with Grierson. Born in New Jersey, he moved at an early age with his parents to Philadelphia and later to Paducah, Kentucky. Enlisting as a private in the 6th Illinois Cavalry on February 1, 1862, he was detailed as a clerk at Brig. Gen. William T. Sherman's head-quarters. He fought at Shiloh and in engagements during the advance on Corinth, Mississippi. Promoted to lieutenant in November 1862, the following month he was detailed as Grierson's acting assistant adjutant general, serving in that capacity throughout the war and rising to the rank of major. At Grierson's urging, Wood-ward in 1867 was commissioned a second lieutenant in the 10th Cavalry, serving as regimental adjutant in 1867–76 and 1883–87. He retired as lieutenant colonel of the 7th Cavalry in 1903. Woodward performed the ceremonial of the Legion of Honor at Grierson's funeral in 1911. A lifelong bachelor, he died in St. Louis on April 17, 1924. *St. Louis Daily Globe-Democrat*, April 18, 1924; Surby, *Grierson Raids*, 18–19; Heitman, *Historical Register*, 1:1059; Leckie and Leckie, *Unlikely Warriors*, 306.

4. An 1856 graduate of West Point, Jackson (1835–1903) resigned from the Regiment of Mounted Rifles to accept a captaincy in the Confederate artillery. Wounded at the battle of Belmont, he was appointed colonel of the 1st (later the 7th) Tennessee Cavalry and promoted to brigadier general after the December 1862 raid on Holly Springs, Mississippi. He commanded Confederate cavalry during the Meridian expedition, in the Atlanta campaign, and during Hood's invasion of Tennessee. At the end of the war, he commanded Tennessee cavalry under Forrest. Warner, *Generals in Gray*, 152–53.

5. A Holly Springs attorney and member of the Mississippi secession convention, James R. Chalmers (1831–98) was appointed colonel of the 9th Mississippi Infantry and commanded at Pensacola, Florida. Promoted to brigadier general in February 1862, he fought at Shiloh and Murfreesboro. Transferring to the cavalry, Chalmers commanded the District of Mississippi and East Louisiana in 1863. As a division commander under Forrest in 1864, he participated in operations in northern Mississippi, West Tennessee, and Kentucky. After the war, Chalmers served three terms in the U.S. Congress. Warner, *Generals in Gray*, 46.

6. A civil engineer, Joseph D. Webster (1811–76) had served in the Corps of Topo-graphical Engineers during the Mexican War and reentered the army as a paymaster on July 1, 1861. He was dispatched to supervise construction of the defenses at Cairo, Illinois. Webster was Grant's chief of staff from Belmont through Shiloh. Promoted to brigadier general of volunteers on November 29, 1862, he supervised the Union army's railroad supply lines during the Vicksburg campaign. At Nashville, he performed the same function for Sherman's army during the Atlanta campaign and for Gen. George H. Thomas. After the war, Webster was assessor and collector of internal revenue for Chicago. Warner, *Generals in Blue*, 546–47; Kionka, *Key Command*, 71.

7. An 1838 graduate of West Point, Beauregard (1818–93) had seen distinguished service as an engineer officer in the Mexican War and, as a Confederate brigadier general, he ordered the firing of the opening shots of the Civil War at Fort Sumter. Promoted to full general after First Manassas, he was sent west as second in command to Albert Sidney Johnston. After Johnston's death at Shiloh, Beauregard withdrew the Confederate army to Corinth, which in turn he was forced to evacuate. An officer whose grandiose visions invariably exceeded his talents and resources, Beauregard engaged in a bitter feud with President Jefferson Davis. He commanded the coastal defenses

of South Carolina, East Florida, and Georgia in 1863–64, and participated in the final campaigns in Virginia and the Carolinas. Warner, *Generals in Gray*, 22–23; T. H. Williams, *P. G. T. Beauregard;* Woodworth, *Jefferson Davis and His Generals*, 102–7.

8. As the local military commander, Grierson regulated the cotton that passed to market from the Germantown area. Like some other army officers, he saw opportunity for personal gain in his position. In a letter to Alice, Ben speculated that if John Grierson could reach Memphis quickly the two brothers "might make some money, buying cotton." He explained that "the Cotton in many places near here has been, or considerable of it has [been] hid away and was not burned. The men who owns [*sic*] it are affraid [*sic*] to haul it to Memphis and would sell it very cheap or so money could be made on it, and I have the military force at my command, [and] could protect the transportation to Memphis, at the same time I do our trains and not do any injustice to the Government." Grierson was ordered back to the city before he could put his scheme in motion. Ben to Alice, July 14, 1862, roll 4, Grierson Papers, TTU; Dinges, "Making of a Cavalryman," 182.

9. Hovey (1821–91) was an Indiana attorney and unsuccessful Republican congressional candidate who recruited troops at the outbreak of the war and was commissioned colonel of the 24th Indiana Volunteers. He was promoted to brigadier general of volunteers after the battle of Shiloh and commanded a division of the XIII Corps in Arkansas and during the Vicksburg campaign. Hovey ran afoul of Gen. William T. Sherman with complaints of unfair treatment during the Atlanta Campaign. Sherman accepted Hovey's resignation and broke up his command. As commander of the District of Indiana until the end of the war, Hovey raised 10,000 new troops for the Union. After the war, he served as U.S. minister to Peru, congressman, and governor of Indiana. Hubbell and Geary, *Biographical Dictionary of the Union*, 261; Warner, *Generals in Blue*, 235–36; Castel, *Decision in the West*, 265–66.

10. Twenty-four-year-old Matthew H. Starr enlisted as major in the 6th Illinois Cavalry at Paducah, Kentucky, on May 8, 1862. He was promoted to lieutenant colonel on January 20 and to colonel on July 19, 1864. He died of wounds on October 3, 1864, at Jacksonville, Illinois. Illinois Civil War Muster and Descriptive Rolls Database.

11. Born in Charleston, South Carolina, Stephen A. Hurlbut (1815–82) embraced at an early age his transplanted New England father's Whig politics and staunch Unionism. As a young attorney in Belvedere, Illinois, he campaigned unsuccessfully for the state legislature and played a highly visible role in Republican politics that brought him to the attention of Abraham Lincoln, who at the outbreak of the Civil War appointed him brigadier general of volunteers. Although intemperance and incompetence in northern Missouri nearly wrecked his military career, Hurlbut redeemed himself as a courageous fighter and competent tactician at the battles of Shiloh and Hatchie Bridge in 1862. Promoted to major general of volunteers in command of the XVI Corps, Army of the Tennessee, as military commander at Memphis and later at New Orleans, Hurlbut, in the words of his biographer, "masterfully concealed a clear pattern of official misconduct under a façade of strict and efficient administration." He persistently lined his own pockets and those of his loyal subordinates. An energetic, but not especially adroit politician, after the war Hurlbut helped organize and served as first national commander of the Grand Army of the Republic, was elected to the U.S. Congress, and was appointed minister to Columbia and Peru. Lash, *Politician Turned General*, quote on 177.

12. Alice's sister, Mary Kirk Fitch, died in April 1856. Leckie and Leckie, *Unlikely Warriors*, 28–29, 315 n.23.

13. This incident illustrates the ferocity of guerrilla warfare in northwestern Mississippi and southwestern Tennessee. Capt. John Boicourt, Cunningham's company commander, and twenty-five 6th Illinois cavalrymen retaliated by killing a twenty-three-year-old civilian named White and burning his house near the scene of the ambush. On November 12, Lieut. Gen. John C. Pemberton, commanding the Department of the Mississippi, notified Maj. Gen. William T. Sherman at Memphis that, unless White's killers were punished, he would retaliate on four Union prisoners of war, selected by lot, in Confederate hands. Sherman, while acknowledging that White's death was "unfortunate," nonetheless argued that it "was the legitimate and logical sequence of the mode of warfare chosen by the Confederate Government—by means of guerrillas or partisan rangers." He threatened to halt prisoner exchanges if any harm befell the four men singled out by Pemberton. "Of course, I cannot approve the killing of any citizen on mere suspicion," Sherman informed Maj. John A. Rawlins, Grant's assistant adjutant general, "but the firing from ambush near White's house, and the fact that Lieutenant Cunningham was mutilated and stripped of money and clothing, were circumstances calculated to inflame the minds of soldiers. The neighborhood, too, was, and is, infamous, so that I charge the whole on the system of guerrilla warfare adopted, approved, and encouraged by the Confederate authorities. . . . Strange that these partisans hang, kill, and shoot on any and all occasions, and yet we are threatened with retaliation in a case such as White's." Boicourt resigned on October 21, 1862, six weeks after the incident. *O.R.*, Series 1, 17, part 2: 870–73; Illinois Civil War Muster and Descriptive Rolls Database. For Union attitudes toward guerrillas, see Ballard, *Vicksburg*, especially 69–71.

14. An 1842 graduate of West Point, Mexican War veteran, and Indian campaigner, Earl Van Dorn (1820–63) never fulfilled the high hopes the Confederacy held for him. As major general in command of the Army of the West and then the Army of Mississippi, he suffered defeats at Pea Ridge and Corinth. He performed more creditably in charge of cavalry under Gen. John C. Pemberton, who replaced him as army commander, especially in the lightning raid on U. S. Grant's supply base at Holly Springs, Mississippi, in December 1862. Van Dorn was assassinated at Spring Hill, Tennessee, by an aggrieved husband. As one biographer notes, the dashing cavalryman "excelled at swift, small-scale raids" and yet "lacked some vital quality as a man and as a general that kept him from achieving the success that his country expected." Hartje, *Van Dorn*, x–xi. See also Carter, *Tarnished Cavalier*.

15. Braxton Bragg replaced Beauregard as commander of the Western Department on June 20, 1862, and set in motion a grand movement of 34,000 Confederates from Tupelo, Mississippi, to Mobile, Alabama, and then north to Chattanooga, Tennessee. His objective was to unite with Gen. Edmund Kirby Smith's army in eastern Tennessee and then Kentucky and disrupt Buell's advance on Chattanooga by getting between the Union army and its supply base at Nashville. The campaign achieved its high-water mark at the battle of Perryville, Kentucky, on October 8, 1862, after which Bragg withdrew south. McWhiney, *Braxton Bragg*, 260–325; McPherson, *Battle Cry of Freedom*, 515–22.

16. A steamboat operator at the outbreak of the Civil War, Morgan L. Smith (1821–74) had served, under an assumed name, as an army sergeant and drillmaster. As colonel of the 8th Missouri Infantry, he won praise for his performances at Fort Donelson, Shiloh, and Corinth. Promoted to brigadier general on July 26, 1862, he participated in operations in northern Mississippi and was wounded at Chickasaw Bayou during the Vicksburg campaign. Smith was less successful as a division and

temporary corps commander in the fighting around Atlanta. At the end of the war, he commanded the District of Vicksburg. Hubbell and Geary, *Biographical Dictionary of the Union*, 489–90.

17. On August 7, 1862, Capt. George W. Peck and fifty-three men of the 6th Illinois Cavalry attacked W. W. Faulkner's camp at Wood Springs, near Dyersburg, Tennessee, scattering the Confederates and capturing fifty-three horses, along with arms and equipment. Three days later, Brig. Gen. Grenville Dodge sent Capt. Cressa K. Davis of the 6th Illinois Cavalry to join Capt. John Lynch in breaking up a Rebel force reported to be operating in the vicinity of Chestnut Bluffs and then proceed to disarm Southern sympathizers at Dyersburg and arrest anyone known to have assisted Faulkner, who was in the vicinity gathering recruits. On August 18, Captain Lynch dispersed another Rebel band near Dyersburg. Dodge, commanding the Central Division of the Mississippi, informed Grant that "Large numbers of rebels are flocking into this country from Missouri and Kentucky, well armed, and forming bands under leaders from [Red] Jackson's and [John Hunt] Morgan's cavalry. The draft drives them over." *O.R.*, Series 1, 17, part 1: 29–30, part 2: 164.

5. From Iuka to Holly Springs

1. Confederate generals Sterling Price and Earl Van Dorn moved in early September 1862 to prevent Grant from sending reinforcements to counter Braxton Bragg's invasion of Tennessee. Grant, seeing an opportunity to destroy the Confederate Army of the West, dispatched William S. Rosecrans and E. O. C. Ord to launch a pincers attack. Price struck first, attacking Rosecrans at Iuka, Mississippi, on September 19, and escaping before Ord could close the trap. Price then joined Van Dorn for the unsuccessful assault on Corinth. C. S. Hamilton, "The Battle of Iuka," in Buel and Johnson, *Battles and Leaders*, 2:734–36; William S. Rosecrans, "The Battle of Corinth," ibid., 737–60; McPherson, *Battle Cry of Freedom*, 522–23; Ballard, *Vicksburg*, 74–76.

2. Although William S. "Old Rosy" Rosecrans (1819–98) handed the Confederates back-to-back defeats within two weeks of each other at Iuka (September 19) and Corinth (October 3–4) in 1862, Grant refused Rosecrans's request to pursue the fleeing Rebels. As commander of the Army of the Cumberland after October 26, 1862, Rosecrans won a hard-fought victory at Stones River (Murfreesboro) and conducted a slow-but-skillful pursuit of Braxton Bragg's Army of Tennessee. Rosecrans's star plummeted after the disaster at Chickamauga and subsequent siege of Chattanooga. He was relieved of command on October 19, 1863, and assigned to command the Department of the Missouri, January 1863 to December 1864. After the war, Rosecrans was involved in railroading and mining, served as U.S. minister to Mexico, and was elected as a Democrat to the U.S. Congress from California. Lamers, *Edge of Glory*; Ballard, *Vicksburg*, 78.

3. Sherman married his foster sister, Ellen Ewing (1824–88), the daughter of powerful Ohio politician Thomas Ewing, in 1850. Although Ellie rallied to her husband's defense in the dark early days of the Civil War, the thirty-eight-year marriage between the crusty and outgoing soldier and his intensely private, Roman Catholic wife was stormy, characterized by frequent separations and angry correspondence. Fellman, *Citizen Sherman*, especially 35–50.

4. A Pennsylvanian who cast his lot with the Confederacy, John C. Pemberton (1814–81) was sent west to defend Mississippi and eastern Louisiana against advancing Union army and naval forces. Hampered by conflicting orders and committed to holding Vicksburg at all costs, he was forced to capitulate after a stubborn siege on July 4, 1863. Pemberton resigned his commission as lieutenant general in 1864

and served out the remainder of the war as a lieutenant colonel of artillery. Warner, *Generals in Gray*, 232–33; Ballard, *Pemberton*.

5. James B. McPherson (1828–64) graduated at the head of the West Point class of 1853 and was a captain of engineers at the outbreak of the war. Assigned as a lieutenant colonel to U. S. Grant's staff, he rose to major general of volunteers and command of the XVII Corps during the Vicksburg campaign. He commanded the Army of the Tennessee under William T. Sherman during the Atlanta campaign, where he was killed on July 22, 1864. Warner, *Generals in Blue*, 306–8; Hubbell and Geary, *Biographical Dictionary of the Union*, 337; Castel, *Decision in the West*, 79–81, 398–99.

6. A New York native, Hamilton (1822–91) graduated with U. S. Grant in the West Point class of 1843 and served in the Mexican War. He resigned from the army in 1853 and was farming at Fond du Lac, Wisconsin, at the outbreak of the Civil War. He was commissioned colonel of the 3rd Wisconsin Infantry on May 11, 1861, and almost immediately was promoted to brigadier general of volunteers. Hamilton commanded a division in the Army of the Potomac until relieved by McClellan on April 30, 1862. He led a division under Rosecrans at Iuka and Corinth and was promoted to major general of volunteers to rank from September 19, 1862. Hamilton's criticism of Grant and others, combined with his efforts to undermine Gen. James B. McPherson, backfired and forced his resignation on April 13, 1863. Warner, *Generals in Blue*, 198–99; Hubbell and Geary, *Biographical Dictionary of the Union*, 231.

7. A New Yorker, Mizner graduated from West Point in 1852 and was a captain in the 2nd Cavalry at the outbreak of the war. He was commissioned colonel of the 3rd Michigan Cavalry on March 7, 1862. According to one historian, "Colonel Mizner did not have the makings of another Murat, but he more than made up for his shortcomings as a commander of cavalry by the verbose eloquence of his reports." Starr, *Union Cavalry*, 104. Mustered out of the volunteer service on February 12, 1866, he was appointed major of the 4th Cavalry in 1869 and was promoted to lieutenant colonel of the 8th Cavalry in 1886. He succeeded Grierson as colonel of the 10th Cavalry in 1890. Heitman, *Historical Register*, 1:718; Glass, *History of the Tenth Cavalry*, 28–30.

8. T. Lyle Dickey was mustered in as colonel of the 4th Illinois Cavalry at Ottawa, Illinois, on October 12, 1861. On June 11, 1862, Grant appointed him to command a cavalry division. The organization Dickey announced on November 26 consisted of three brigades under Col. A. L. Lee of the 7th Kansas Cavalry, Col. Edward Hatch of the 2nd Iowa Cavalry, and Grierson of the 6th Illinois Cavalry. Described by one historian as "generous, gracious, and popular" and by another as having given "no indication of outstanding abilities as a cavalryman," Dickey failed to distinguish himself during Grant's advance on Oxford, Mississippi, and the pursuit of Van Dorn following the Rebel raid on Holly Springs. Dickey resigned on February 16, 1863. Illinois Civil War Muster and Descriptive Rolls Database; K. Williams, *Lincoln Finds a General*, 190; Starr, *Union Cavalry*, 25, 129–46.

9. Albert L. Lee (1834–1907) stepped down from the Kansas Supreme Court bench to command the 7th Kansas Cavalry ("Jennison's Jayhawkers"). Promoted to brigadier general of volunteers in April of 1863, he performed poorly as cavalry commander during Nathaniel P. Banks's Red River campaign and subsequently ran afoul of Banks's successor, Gen. E. R. S. Canby. Lee resigned his commission on May 4, 1865. After the war, he engaged in business in Europe and New York City. Warner, *Generals in Blue*, 278; Starr, *Jennison's Jayhawkers*; Starr, *Union Cavalry*, 491–502.

10. The garrulous Hatch (1831–89) led a peripatetic early life. Born in Bangor, Maine, he attended Norwich Military Academy and spent time at sea before embark-

ing on a business career that took him to Virginia, Pennsylvania, and Wisconsin. At the outbreak of the Civil War, he owned a lumber operation in Muscatine, Iowa. He rose quickly from captain to colonel of the 2nd Iowa Cavalry. Despite Grierson's recommendation, Hatch was not promoted to brigadier general of volunteers until April 27, 1864. As a division commander under James H. Wilson, Hatch participated in the hard fighting during John Bell Hood's invasion of Tennessee, where he was wounded. After the war, Ulysses S. Grant recommended Hatch to organize and command the 9th Cavalry, with Grierson's 10th Cavalry, one of the army's two black cavalry regiments. Grierson's and Hatch's paths crossed again in April 1880, when the 10th Cavalry assisted the 9th Cavalry in disarming the Mescalero Apaches near Fort Stanton, New Mexico. Hatch died of injuries suffered in a carriage accident at Fort Robinson, Nebraska. Kenner, *Buffalo Soldiers and Officers*, 30–50; Bruce Dinges, "Benjamin H. Grierson," in Hutton, *Soldiers West*, 165–66.

11. Frederick Steele (1819–68) graduated from West Point in 1843 and served in the Mexican War. A captain at the outbreak of the Civil War, he commanded a battalion of regulars in Nathaniel Lyon's Missouri campaign before being commissioned colonel of the 8th Iowa Infantry in January 1862. Promoted to brigadier general of volunteers, he commanded a division of the Army of the Southwest at Helena, Arkansas, during the summer of 1862. Steele returned to Arkansas, as a major general of volunteers, in the fall of 1863, capturing Helena and seizing control of the eastern part of the state. In the spring of 1865, he participated in the Mobile campaign and commanded the District of West Florida. As colonel of the 20th Infantry after the war, he commanded the Department of Columbia until his untimely death from a carriage accident. Warner, *Generals in Blue*, 474–75; Hubbell and Geary, *Biographical Dictionary of the Union*, 503–4.

12. Here and in his official report, Grierson uses a variant of *Yoknapatwpha*, from which the Yocona River apparently derives its name. In the twentieth century, William Faulkner adopted the name for the fictional county that provides the setting for many of his novels and stories. *O.R.*, Series 1, 37, part 1: 516–20; Padgett, "People, Places, and Events."

13. Grierson refers to Thomas Haynes Bayley's (1797–1839) composition, "The Mistletoe Bough," or "The Ballad of the Mistletoe Bride," in which

> The Baron beheld with a father's pride
> His beautiful child, Lord Lovell's bride.
> And she, with her bright eyes seemed to be
> The star of the company.

The bride playfully runs off and hides from her husband and holiday revelers.

> They sought her that night, they sought her next day,
> They sought her in vain when a week passed away.
> In the highest, the lowest, the loneliest spot,
> Young Lovell sought wildly, but found her not.

Years later, her skeleton is discovered in an old chest. Bayley and Bishop, "The Mistletoe Bough," 30–31.

14. Entrepreneur, philanthropist, and Republican congressman Cadwallader C. Washburn (1818–82) was the brother of Elihu Washburne, an intimate adviser to Abraham Lincoln and patron of U. S. Grant. Commissioned colonel of the 2nd Wisconsin Cavalry in February 1862, C. C. Washburn advanced to major general

of volunteers in March 1863 and commanded the District of West Tennessee. After the war, he served two terms in Congress, was governor of Wisconsin, and amassed a fortune as, among other enterprises, a cofounder of today's General Mills. Warner, *Generals in Blue*, 542–43; Hubbell and Geary, *Biographical Dictionary of the Union*, 570.

15. Maj. Gen. John McClernand had spent the fall recruiting troops in Illinois, Indiana, and Iowa and politicking in Washington for command of the Mississippi expedition. Grant sent Sherman to seize Vicksburg before McClernand arrived on the scene and assumed command. The Confederates repulsed the Union forces at the battle of Chickasaw Bayou on December 28, 1862, forcing Sherman to withdraw. Ballard, *Vicksburg*, 101, 128–55; Kiper, *Major General McClernand*, 140–55.

16. Grierson presumably refers to the "watery flatland of northwest Mississippi called the Delta." Ballard, *Vicksburg*, 175.

17. Jacob Thompson (1810–85) resigned as secretary of the interior on January 8, 1861, served as an aide to Gen. P. G. T. Beauregard at Shiloh, and eventually attained the rank of lieutenant colonel. He was elected to the Mississippi legislature after the fall of Vicksburg, but was dispatched by President Jefferson Davis, in March 1864, to conduct covert operations against the Union from Canada. Implicated in the Lincoln assassination conspiracy, Thompson traveled abroad with his wife until emotions cooled, before returning to the United States and taking up residence at Memphis. Cooper, *Jefferson Davis*, 496–98; Kinchen, *Confederate Operations in Canada and the North*.

18. An attorney and newspaper editor, Mason Brayman (1813–95) served as major and colonel of the 29th Illinois Infantry and was commissioned brigadier general of volunteers to rank from September 24, 1862. He participated in the battles of Belmont, Fort Donelson, and Shiloh and commanded the post of Bolivar, Tennessee, until June 1863. Thereafter, he commanded Camp Denison, Ohio, and the post of Natchez, Mississippi. In 1876, he was appointed governor of Idaho Territory. Warner, *Generals in Blue*, 43–44; Eddy, *Patriotism of Illinois*, 270–71; Illinois Civil War Veterans Muster and Descriptive Rolls Database.

19. Van Dorn's destruction of Grant's supply base at Holly Springs had far-ranging military consequences, forcing Grant to reverse his overland advance on Vicksburg, which then allowed Pemberton to shift sufficient troops to repulse Sherman's December 29 assault on the Vicksburg defenses overlooking Chickasaw Bayou. Although Grierson failed to snare the Rebel raiders, his close and aggressive pursuit brought the Illinois cavalryman to Grant's favorable attention. Finally, as evidence that "a well-organized and well-disciplined cavalry force could suddenly swoop down on a poorly defended, relaxed enemy base from the rear and deal it a devastating blow and then vanish like the morning mist," Van Dorn's raid set a clear example for Grierson's dash through Mississippi the following spring. Carter, *Tarnished Cavalier*, 157–59, quote on 158; Dinges, "Running Down Rebels," 18.

20. Variously a lawyer, surveyor, newspaper editor, and schoolteacher, Virginia-born James W. Denver (1817–92) participated in the Mexican War and the California Gold Rush. He was serving as a Democratic congressman when President James Buchanan appointed him commissioner of Indian affairs, territorial secretary, and eventually governor of Kansas. As a brigadier general of volunteers, he participated in the siege of Corinth and commanded a brigade under William T. Sherman. During the winter of 1862–63, he was guarding Union supply lines. Denver resigned his commission on March 5, 1863. Warner, *Generals in Blue*, 120.

6. Grierson's Raid

1. Confederate Gen. Joseph E. Johnston set the stage for Grierson's Raid when, in early January 1863, he dispatched Earl Van Dorn with two thirds of the cavalry in the Department of Mississippi and East Alabama to operate with Nathan Bedford Forrest in disrupting supplies and reinforcements from reaching Gen. William S. Rosecrans's Army of the Cumberland, which was threatening Gen. Braxton Bragg in middle Tennessee. "It seems to me," Grant suggested to Hurlbut on February 13, "that Grierson, with about 500 picked men, might succeed in making his way south, and cut the railroad east of Jackson, Miss. The undertaking would be a hazardous one, but it would pay well if carried out. I do not direct that it should be done, but leave it for a volunteer enterprise." Grant also wanted to use the raid as a diversion while he transferred his army to the east bank of the Mississippi and advanced on Vicksburg by land. By early April, the pieces were all falling into place. While Grierson marched south, simultaneous raids by Gen. Grenville M. Dodge and Col. Abel Streight against Bragg's lines of communication kept Forrest's cavalry occupied in Alabama. Grant to Hurlbut, February 13, 1863, *O.R.*, Series 1, 24, part 3: 50; Dinges, "Making of a Cavalryman," 247–55.

2. Starr, in *Union Cavalry*, 359, maintains that if Grierson's raid played a strong role in his promotion, "his persistence as a promoter" was also a factor. In Starr's estimation, "No other officer of cavalry was so assiduous an inspirer of testimonials to his own merit addressed to higher authority, the language of which (reminiscent in tone of the hair-restorer testimonials of the day) suggests a common source, whoever the actual signers may have been." That said, it should be remembered that officers during the Civil War, and after, routinely vied with one another for accolades and promotions.

3. Sherman was correct. At Lincoln's suggestion, but mostly to keep his soldiers occupied, Grant had set the army to work digging a canal across a loop in the Mississippi River. The labor was backbreaking and, when completed, the channel was too shallow to divert the Mississippi's course. Grant's opportunity came when Adm. David Dixon Porter's gunboats ran the river beneath the Vicksburg defenses on April 16. On May 2, Gen. John A. McClernand captured Port Gibson on the east bank of the Mississippi, giving Grant the toehold he was looking for on dry land below Vicksburg. McFeely, *Grant*, 128–30; Kiper, *Major General McClernand*, 221–26; Ballard, *Vicksburg*, 193, 198–203, 221–40.

4. Starr, in *Union Cavalry*, 189, calls attention to the discrepancies between Grierson's official report on this engagement and Col. Richardson's account. Although Richardson acknowledged being driven from his camp, he claimed to have had only 150 men engaged in the fight, of which 5 were wounded, 7 killed, and 8 taken prisoner. Grierson, on the other hand, reported 22 Confederates killed and more than 70 captured.

5. William Sooy Smith (1830–1914) graduated from West Point in 1853 but left the army the following year to work as a construction engineer on the Illinois Central Railroad, eventually forming his own engineering firm. Commissioned colonel of the 13th Ohio Infantry in 1861 and promoted to brigadier general of volunteers in April of 1862, he fought at Shiloh and Perryville and in the Vicksburg campaign prior to his assignment as chief of cavalry, Department of the Tennessee, in July of 1863, and Military Division of the Mississippi in October. Smith resigned because of ill health on July 15, 1864. After the war, he gained international recognition for his innovations in bridge and skyscraper construction. Warner, *Generals in Blue*, 464–65; Hubbell and Geary, *Biographical Dictionary of the Union*, 492.

6. Edward Prince was born at East Bloomfield, New York, on December 8, 1832, and at age three moved with his parents to Payson, Illinois. After graduation from Jacksonville College in 1852, he practiced law in Quincy. He served as lieutenant colonel and colonel of the 7th Illinois Cavalry and was mustered out at the expiration of his term of service on October 15, 1864. Illinois Civil War Muster and Descriptive Rolls Database; Surby, *Grierson Raids*, 13–15.

7. In October 1862, Lincoln had authorized McClernand to raise troops for an expedition against Vicksburg. McClernand interpreted Lincoln's order as giving him an independent command and briskly set to work. Halleck and Grant protested placing McClernand in command of the Vicksburg expedition, and Lincoln upheld their position. Relations between Grant and McClernand were strained thereafter, with McClernand working behind the scenes with his political contacts in Washington to undermine Grant. Nevertheless, Grant selected McClernand's XIII Corps to spearhead the advance on Grand Gulf. Kiper, *Major General McClernand*, 133–55, 186–211. For Sherman's clash with McClernand, see ibid., 159–60.

8. One of the most prominent of Lincoln's political generals, Nathaniel P. Banks (1816–94) served ten terms in the U.S. Congress, where he was the first Republican Speaker of the House, and was elected to three terms as governor of Massachusetts. Appointed major general of volunteers in May of 1861, Banks suffered disastrous defeats in the Shenandoah Valley, in two rash assaults on Port Hudson, and in the 1864 Red River campaign. "A politician of . . . great ambition but little fixed principle," in Secretary of the Navy Gideon Welles's estimation, Banks's military career was tarnished by his reliance on "expediency," according to Harrington, in *Fighting Politician*, viii, 212. His more recent biographer adds that he suffered from an even more serious flaw, "his inability to learn from his mistakes." Hollandsworth, *Pretense of Glory*, 255.

9. David G. Farragut (1801–70) was a fifty-year veteran of the navy at the outbreak of the Civil War, having gone to sea at age nine. He performed spectacularly in command of the U.S. naval squadron on the Mississippi River, compelling the surrender of New Orleans on May 1 and running the Vicksburg batteries on June 27, 1862. The following March, he launched a spectacular night assault on Port Hudson. On August 5, 1864, he defeated Confederate naval forces in the battle of Mobile Bay. Farragut was promoted to rear admiral in July of 1862, and elevated to vice admiral, a rank Congress created for him, on December 22, 1864. In the summer of 1866, he became the navy's first full admiral. Duffy, *Lincoln's Admiral*.

10. A joint army-navy operation under McClernand and David Porter seized the Confederate defenses at Arkansas Post, north of Vicksburg, on January 11, 1863. As Grant pointed out, the operation had little strategic value in the campaign to capture Vicksburg. Nevertheless, it opened the Mississippi River to Little Rock, boosted Union morale along the river, and dealt a blow to wavering Confederate morale in Arkansas. Ballard, *Vicksburg*, 147–55; Kiper, *Major General McClernand*, 156–85.

11. The battle of Stones River (Murfreesboro), December 31, 1862, to January 2, 1863, pitted Maj. Gen. William S. Rosecrans's 41,000-man Army of the Cumberland against Confederate Gen. Braxton Bragg's 35,000-man Army of Tennessee. Although a tactical draw, the bloody fighting crippled the Confederate army in the West, lost much of Tennessee for the Confederacy, and bolstered anti-Bragg sentiment among the Army of Tennessee's senior commanders. Cozzens, *No Better Place to Die*; McDonough, *Stones River*.

12. While Grierson rode due south, Brig. Gen. William Sooy Smith moved southwest from La Grange with 1,500 infantry and an artillery battery. Simultaneously,

Col. George E. Bryant marched south from Memphis with another 1,300 troops. As Sgt. Stephen A. Forbes of the 7th Illinois Cavalry later described it, "with the thin confederate line in northern Mississippi thus completely pulled apart and piled up at its ends," Grierson's "slender column" of cavalry was "thrust, like a nimble sword through an unguarded point, into the very vitals of the confederate position." Forbes, "Grierson's Cavalry Raid," 102; Dinges, "Making of a Cavalryman," 255–56.

13. Datus Coon succeeded Hatch as colonel of the 2nd Iowa Cavalry on May 5, 1864, and was promoted to brigadier general of volunteers on March 8, 1865. He was mustered out on September 1865. When Grierson encountered Coon again in the late 1880s, Coon was selling real estate in San Diego. Coon died on December 17, 1893. Heitman, *Historical Register*, 1:325; Coon to Grierson, September 12, 1888, Grierson Papers, Fort Davis (Texas) National Historic Site.

14. Deceived by Grierson's ruse, Lt. Col. Clark Barteau's Tennessee and Mississippi cavalrymen attacked Hatch's Iowans at Palo Alto, believing they were the main Yankee column. Grierson may be too sanguine about Hatch's prospects for striking the Mobile and Ohio Railroad, as nightfall found the Confederates dug in and blocking Hatch's movement toward Macon. As Hatch explained it, "Believing it was important to divert the enemy's cavalry from Colonel Grierson, I moved slowly northward, fighting by the rear, crossing the Houlka River, and drawing their forces immediately in my rear." Brown, *Grierson's Raid*, 66–71, quote on 71.

15. Grierson seems to be confusing details of his 1863 and 1864–65 raids. According to Grierson's official report, the tannery Graham's detachment destroyed on the 1863 raid was located four miles off the Starkville and Louisville road. Surby, in *Grierson Raids*, 31, likewise identifies it as "a shoe and saddle manufactory near Starkville." Capt. Warren Beckwith and a contingent of the 4th Iowa Cavalry burned the Bankston tannery and shoe factory during Grierson's 1864–65 raid on the Mobile and Ohio Railroad. *O.R.*, Series 1, 24, part 2: 523; 45, part 1: 846, 852. Brown, *Grierson's Raid*, 77–78; Bearss, "Grierson's Winter Raid," 33. In his 1904 article, "Grierson's Raid," S. L. Woodward also claims that Graham destroyed the Bankston tannery and shoe factory on the morning of April 22, 1863. It is conceivable that Woodward may have had access to Grierson's memoir in preparing his article.

16. Franklin Gardner (1823–73), born in New York City, graduated from West Point in 1843 and served in the Mexican War. Married into a prominent Louisiana family, he entered the Confederate service as a lieutenant colonel, commanded cavalry at Shiloh, and was promoted to brigadier general in April of 1862. He was appointed major general in December of 1862 and given command of Port Hudson shortly thereafter. Exchanged in August 1863, he served out the remainder of the war in Mississippi. Warner, *Generals in Gray*, 97.

17. Surby was born in Kingston, Ontario, on May 23, 1832. He worked for the New York Central Railroad and the Great Western Railroad (Canada) and was visiting in Edgar County, Illinois, when Fort Sumter was fired upon. Surby, *Grierson Raids*, 186–87. Captured during Grierson's Raid and briefly imprisoned at Libby Prison, he rejoined his regiment in October 1863 and was mustered out as a hospital steward on November 4, 1865. Underwood, *Butternut Guerillas*, 161.

18. Brothers Henry and Stephen A. Forbes enlisted in Company B, 7th Illinois Cavalry, at Lightsville on September 5, 1861, and were mustered in at Camp Butler. Henry is described as twenty-eight years old, married, 5 feet 8 inches tall, with brown hair, blue eyes, and light complexion. Stephen was eighteen years old, single, 5 feet 9 inches tall, with brown hair and brown eyes. Both men listed their residence as Ridott,

Stephenson County, and their occupation as "farmer." Henry Forbes was promoted to major on August 25, 1863, and was mustered out as lieutenant colonel at Eastport, Mississippi, on November 4, 1865. Stephen Forbes, who was a sergeant during the raid, was promoted to second lieutenant on February 10, 1864, and to captain on April 17, 1865. After the war, Henry became a newspaper editor and wrote poetry. Stephen was a professor of entomology at the University of Illinois. Illinois Civil War Muster and Descriptive Rolls Database; Colley, *Century of Robert H. Forbes*, 3–4, 120.

19. This incident illustrates the fluidity of Mississippians' loyalties after two years of war, often depending on which army happened to be in the area. Ballard, *Vicksburg*, 107–8.

20. Brookhaven revealed further evidence of civilian disaffection with the Confederate cause. According to Adj. Woodward, "when it was ascertained that the captives were being paroled and released instead of being carried away, it was surprising to see the eagerness with which every man liable for military duty, sought one of the papers which exempted him until exchanged. Many who had escaped and were hiding out were brought in by their friends to obtain one of the valuable documents. The citizens generally expressed great surprise and gratitude at the treatment accorded them." Woodward, "Grierson's Raid" (pt. 2), 101.

21. Pvt. George Reinhold of Company G, 7th Illinois Cavalry, was buried on the spot. The five wounded troopers, including Sgt. Surby and the mortally wounded Blackburn, were removed to the Newman Plantation and left under the care of Dr. Erastus Yule of the 2nd Iowa Cavalry. Sgt. Maj. Augustus Lesieure and Pvt. George W. Douglass of the 7th Illinois Cavalry volunteered to remain behind with the wounded men. Before leaving, Sgt. Surby's fellow scouts removed his butternut disguise and dressed him in his uniform. Col. W. R. Miles's Louisiana Legion took the Illinois troopers into custody around sunset on May 1. Surby, Yule, and Lesieure were incarcerated at Libby Prison in Richmond, Virginia. Quickly paroled, Surby rejoined his regiment in October 1863. Dinges, "Making of a Cavalryman," 334–35, 386–87 n. 144.

22. An 1843 graduate of West Point, Christopher C. Augur (1821–98) served in the Mexican War and on the frontier. Commandant of cadets at West Point at the outbreak of the Civil War, he was posted to the Washington defenses and later, as a brigadier general of volunteers, commanded a division under Maj. Gen. Nathaniel P. Banks. Augur commanded the left wing of Banks's army during the Port Hudson siege. After October 1863, he commanded the XXII Corps and the Department of Washington. Grierson later served under Augur who, as a brigadier general in the regular army, commanded the Department of Texas. Warner, *Generals in Blue*, 12; Dinges, "Benjamin H. Grierson," in Hutton, *Soldiers West*, 163–67.

23. See, for example, *Harper's Weekly* and *Frank Leslie's Illustrated Newspaper*, June 6, 1863. Grierson's Raid inspired Harold Sinclair's 1956 novel *The Horse Soldiers* and John Ford's 1959 film of the same title. For the relationship between history and myth, see York, *Fiction as Fact*.

24. A Maine attorney, George F. Shepley (1819–78) was a close friend of Benjamin Butler, who made him post commander at New Orleans and then military governor of Louisiana. He served again under Butler in Virginia in 1864–65, and became military governor of Richmond after its capture in April 1865. Warner, *Generals in Blue*, 436–37.

25. Starr, *Union Cavalry*, 331, notes that "when Banks laid siege to Port Hudson, Grierson covered the rear of the army, protected its foraging parties, and dispersed the groups of enemy cavalry hovering about behind the lines of investment, work

that in General Banks's opinion 'contributed to a great degree to the reduction of the post.'"

26. William W. Loring (1818–86), who lost an arm during the Mexican War, was colonel of the Regiment of Mounted Rifles at the outbreak of the Civil War. Commissioned a Confederate brigadier general in May 1861 and promoted to major general in February 1862, he had served in Virginia prior to his assignment to the Army of Mississippi in December 1862. Loring commanded a division under Generals Leonidas Polk, Joseph E. Johnston, and John Bell Hood. After the war, he accepted a general's commission in the army of the khedive of Egypt. Warner, *Generals in Gray*, 193–94.

27. Sherman was similarly impressed, writing his wife on May 9: "It was *Maj.* Grierson who made the famous Raid from LaGrange to Baton Rouge. You remember him at Memphis. I find that Regt. 6ᵗʰ Ills. down at the heels & brought it out. I hope Grierson will be rewarded, as the feint was a daring & successful one." Simpson and Berlin, *Sherman's Civil War*, 470.

7. The Siege of Port Hudson

1. Joseph E. Johnston (1807–91) was perhaps the South's most proficient defensive fighter. But his bitter public resentment toward President Jefferson Davis over his relative ranking in the hierarchy of Confederate generals sometimes impaired his judgment and actions. Dispatched from his sickbed by Davis to rescue Vicksburg during Grant's final offensive, Johnston wired from Jackson on May 13: "I arrived this evening, finding the enemy's force between this place and General Pemberton. I am too late." Johnston never felt strong enough to attack Grant and, after the fall of Vicksburg, abandoned Jackson on July 10, 1863. Symonds, *Joseph E. Johnston*, especially 204–18; Woodworth, *Jefferson Davis and His Generals*, 173–78, 200–221.

2. Grierson had his first opportunity to gauge the combat qualities of black troops during Banks's disastrous May 27 assault on the Confederate defenses at Port Hudson. "The negro Regiments fought bravely yesterday, charging up to the enemys [*sic*] works," he wrote Alice. "There can be no question about the good fighting qualities of negroes hereafter, that question was settled beyond a doubt yesterday." Ben to Alice, May 28, 1863, roll 4, Grierson Papers, TTU.

3. Grierson refers to the 2nd Massachusetts Light Artillery Battery, commanded by Capt. Ormand F. Nims. Whitcomb, *History of the Second Massachusetts Battery*, 47–52.

4. Grierson engaged Col. John L. Logan's Confederate cavalry and mounted infantry, who held the upper hand in the Clinton engagement. Cunningham, *Port Hudson Campaign*, 76–77. Lt. Perkins's death is described in Ewer, *Third Massachusetts Cavalry*, 332–33. The skirmishes between Grierson and Logan continued throughout the siege. The best account of the campaign and siege is Hewitt, *Port Hudson*.

5. Halbert E. Paine (1826–1905), a cousin of Gen. Eleazer A. Paine, was practicing law with Carl Schurz in Milwaukee when he accepted the colonelcy of the 4th Wisconsin Cavalry. Promoted to brigadier general on April 9, 1863, he lost a leg at Port Hudson. After his recovery, Paine served in the defense of Washington, D.C., during Jubal Early's raid and later commanded the District of Illinois. After the war, he served three terms in Congress as a Radical Republican, practiced law in the capital, and was commissioner of patents in 1878–80. Warner, *Generals in Blue*, 356–57; Hubbell and Geary, *Biographical Dictionary of the Union*, 389–90.

6. An 1836 West Point graduate and veteran of twenty-five years' service in the regular army, Thomas W. Sherman (1813–79) had a reputation as a tough discipli-

narian. Appointed brigadier general of volunteers in May 1861, he commanded land forces in the assault on Port Royal, South Carolina, and led a division of the Army of the Ohio in the Corinth campaign. Although he argued against the attack on Port Hudson, Sherman commanded the left wing of Maj. Gen. Nathaniel P. Banks's army and lost a leg in the May 27, 1863, assault on the Confederate stronghold. He returned to duty in March 1864 as a district commander in and around New Orleans. Sherman retired in 1870 as a major general in the regular army. Warner, *Generals in Blue,* 440–41; Hubbell and Geary, *Biographical Dictionary of the Union,* 474–75.

7. Vicksburg capitulated on July 4, 1863.

8. Reorganizing the Cavalry in West Tennessee

1. Banks endorsed Prince's scheme to construct parapets of cotton-filled barrels and dirt that overlooked the Confederate works. On May 25, 1863, Prince captured the steamers *Starlight* and *Red Chief,* along with twenty-five prisoners, on Thompson's Creek. Prince, "Cavalry Captured Navy"; Surby, *Grierson Raids,* 13–14; Cunningham, *Port Hudson Campaign,* 47.

2. An 1845 graduate of West Point, Charles P. Stone (1824–87) was in charge of security in Washington, D.C., during Lincoln's inauguration. Appointed brigadier general of volunteers in May 1861, he was made the scapegoat for the Union debacle at Ball's Bluff and imprisoned, without charges, for six months. At Gen. Banks's request, he was assigned to the Department of the Gulf during the Port Hudson and Red River campaigns. Stripped of his volunteer commission by Secretary of War Stanton, Stone resigned from the army in 1864. After the war, he served in the army of the khedive of Egypt and, upon his return to the United States, was engineer for the Statue of Liberty's foundation. Warner, *Generals in Blue,* 480–81.

3. William N. R. Beall (1825–83), an 1845 West Point graduate, commanded a brigade of Arkansas, Louisiana, Alabama, and Mississippi troops at Port Hudson. Imprisoned at Johnson's Island, he was released on parole in 1864 to sell cotton, the proceeds of which were used to furnish clothing and blankets for Confederates in Northern prisons. Warner, *Generals in Gray,* 21–22.

4. At Gen. Henry W. Halleck's urging, and reacting to pressure from wealthy Massachusetts mill owners to seize Confederate cotton, Banks left Alexandria, Louisiana, on March 26, 1864, to invade Texas via the Red River. The badly managed campaign ended on April 8 in a rout at Sabine Cross Roads, where Ransom was severely wounded (his fourth wound during the war). He returned to duty and died in the field six months later from a combination of dysentery and the effect of his wound. Johnson, *Red River Campaign;* Eddy, *Patriotism of Illinois,* 490–93.

5. Under the pretext of collecting Mexico's foreign debt, France invaded the country during the spring of 1862, deposed President Benito Juárez, and installed the Archduke Ferdinand Maximilian of Austria as emperor. Events in Mexico caused the Lincoln administration grave concern because of cordial diplomatic relations between the Confederacy and Napoleon III and the brisk blockade-running trade through the Mexican port of Matamoros at the mouth of the Rio Grande. Tyler, *Santiago Vidaurri and the Southern Confederacy.*

6. An engineer in civilian life, Grenville M. Dodge (1831–1916) participated as colonel of the 4th Iowa Infantry in the early fighting in Missouri. Promoted to brigadier general of volunteers in 1862 and major general in 1864, he commanded the XVI Corps during the Atlanta campaign. His most significant accomplishment was as the organizer and chief of Grant's secret service, "the largest and most extensive intel-

ligence network of the war." At the end of the war, he commanded the departments of Missouri and Kansas. As chief engineer of the Union Pacific Railroad, Dodge became one of Gilded Age America's most successful railroad builders and lobbyists. Warner, *Generals in Blue*, 127–28; Hubbell and Geary, *Biographical Dictionary of the Union*, 144–45; Hirshon, *Grenville M. Dodge*; Feis, *Grant's Secret Service*, especially 125–30, 142–70; quote on 149.

7. Eugene A. Carr (1830–1910) graduated from West Point in 1850 and served with the Regiment of Mounted Rifles and the 1st Cavalry on the frontier. He fought at the battles of Wilson's Creek and Pea Ridge (Elkhorn Tavern), where he earned the Medal of Honor. Commissioned colonel of the 3rd Illinois Cavalry in August 1861, and promoted to brigadier general of volunteers to rank from March 7, 1862, he commanded a division in the Vicksburg campaign, during Frederick Steele's operations in Arkansas, and in the advance on Mobile, Alabama. As major, lieutenant colonel, and colonel of the 5th Cavalry, Carr participated in the major Indian campaigns on the Great Plains, the Northern Plains, and the Southwest. He retired as brigadier general in 1893. King, *War Eagle*.

8. A native of New Hampshire, Lafayette McCrillis was living in Springfield when he enlisted as lieutenant colonel of the 3rd Illinois Cavalry on August 30, 1861. He was promoted to colonel on July 25, 1864, and mustered out on September 5, 1864. McCrillis died on November 30, 1876. Illinois Civil War Muster and Descriptive Rolls Database; Heitman, *Historical Register*, 1:661.

9. On September 19 and 20, 1863, Bragg's Army of Tennessee engaged Rosecrans's Army of the Cumberland along Chickamauga Creek in northwestern Georgia. The heavy fighting produced 20,000 Confederate casualties and 16,000 Union killed, wounded, and missing. Only Gen. George Thomas's determined stand saved Rosecrans from a complete rout as Federal troops fell back behind the Chattanooga defenses. Cozzens, *This Terrible Sound*.

10. Fifty-two-year-old John N. Niglas enlisted as surgeon of the 6th Illinois Cavalry at Springfield on October 1, 1861, and mustered out at the expiration of his term of service on February 16, 1865. Illinois Civil War Muster and Descriptive Rolls Database.

11. Union military reverses and the implementation of a conscription law in March 1863 had strengthened the voices of the Peace Democrats ("Copperheads"), especially under the leadership of Ohio congressman Clement L. Vallandingham. There was even talk of forming a "Northwest Confederacy" that would split off from the rest of the North and seek accommodation with the South. The fall of Vicksburg and Lee's defeat at Gettysburg eroded, but did not destroy, Copperhead sentiment. McPherson, *Battle Cry of Freedom*, 591–611. For a comprehensive study, see Weber, *Copperheads*.

12. Nine-year-old Willie Sherman, the general's favorite son, contracted typhoid fever and died at the Gayoso House in Memphis on October 3, 1863. Sherman, *Memoirs*, 1:375–76.

13. On October 11, 1863, Chalmers attacked Collierville, Tennessee, during a diversionary raid on the Memphis and Charleston Railroad. Sherman, who had been ordered to reinforce Rosecrans at Chattanooga, was at the depot. Hatch pursued the raiders, striking them at Wyatt on October 13. Despite what one historian describes as the absence of "the determination and energy to be expected of a topflight cavalryman," Hatch dispersed the Confederate cavalry, only to resume the pursuit when Chalmers launched another raid on Collierville three weeks later. Sherman, *Memoirs*, 1:374–81; Starr, *Union Cavalry*, 362–68.

14. Thomas and Burnside commanded the Army of the Cumberland at Chattanooga and the Army of the Ohio at Knoxville, respectively, under the overall command of U. S. Grant following Rosecrans's removal. Burnside's biographer gives the woefully inadequate former commander of the Army of the Potomac much of the credit for the Union victory at Chattanooga, arguing that by pinning down Gen. James A. Longstreet's army at Knoxville he deprived Bragg of 23,000 reinforcements that might have turned back the massive assaults of November 24–25, 1863. Marvel, *Burnside*, 294–325.

15. In late September 1863, Joseph "Fighting Joe" Hooker (1814–79) was sent by rail with the XI and XII Corps from the Army of the Potomac to reinforce the besieged Union army at Chattanooga. Hooker's successful assault on Lookout Mountain on November 24, popularly known as "The Battle above the Clouds," set the stage for the following day's advance on the Confederate center and right flank on Missionary Ridge that broke the siege and threw Braxton Bragg's army back into northern Georgia. Hebert, *Fighting Joe Hooker*, 250–65; McDonough, *Chattanooga*, especially 129–42.

16. Union forces turned back Gen. Robert E. Lee's invasion of the North at Gettysburg, Pennsylvania, on July 1–3, 1863. McPherson, in *Battle Cry of Freedom*, 665, agrees with Grierson's assessment. "Though the war was destined to continue for almost two more bloody years," McPherson writes, "Gettysburg and Vicksburg proved to have been its critical turning point."

17. Although virtually uneducated, Nathan Bedford Forrest (1821–77) emerged as the Civil War's most brilliant and successful cavalry commander. A wealthy Tennessee planter and slave dealer, he raised and equipped his own mounted battalion at the beginning of the war and fought in the major battles in northern Mississippi and Tennessee. Grierson had the opportunity to test Forrest's battlefield skills at Brice's Cross Roads and Tupelo. Forrest was promoted to major general on December 4, 1863, and to lieutenant general on February 28, 1865. He led a quiet life as a planter and railroad president after the war and reputedly organized the Ku Klux Klan. Hurst, *Nathan Bedford Forrest*; Wills, *Battle from the Start*; Wyeth, *That Devil Forrest*.

18. Joseph A. Mower (1827–70) had served as a private during the Mexican War and received a commission as second lieutenant in the 1st Infantry in 1855. He began the Civil War as colonel of the 11th Missouri Infantry and was promoted to brigadier general of volunteers on March 16, 1863. He compiled a distinguished record at Iuka and Corinth, during the Vicksburg and Red River campaigns, in Arkansas, and during Sherman's march to the sea and through the Carolinas. Mower was promoted to major general of volunteers in November 1864. After the war, he commanded the black 39th Infantry and, with consolidation of the 39th and 40th regiments, the 25th Infantry. He was in command of the Department of Louisiana when he died. Warner, *Generals in Blue*, 338–39; Nankivell, *History of the Twenty-fifth Regiment*, 2–15.

19. Andrew Jackson "Whiskey" Smith (1815–97) was an 1838 West Point graduate who had served in the Mexican War and saw frontier duty in California. At the beginning of the Civil War, he served as Maj. Gen. Henry W. Halleck's chief of cavalry. He was a division commander under Sherman and McClernand during the Vicksburg campaign and, after the Meridian expedition, participated in Nathaniel P. Banks's Red River campaign. Following his battles against Nathan Bedford Forrest at Tupelo and Oxford, in the fall of 1864 he crossed the Mississippi to operate against Sterling Price. Smith fought at Nashville and played an important role as commander of the XVI Corps in the capture of Mobile, Alabama. He was commissioned colonel of the 7th Cavalry in 1866, but resigned in 1869. Hubbell and Geary, *Biographical Dictionary of the Union*, 483–84; Warner, *Generals in Blue*, 454–55.

20. A businessman and politician, James M. Tuttle (1832–92) commanded the 2nd Iowa Infantry at Fort Donelson and a brigade under Maj. Gen. W. H. L. Wallace at Shiloh, which he led to safety from the Hornet's Nest after Wallace's death. Promoted to brigadier general of volunteers on June 9, 1862, he commanded the Third Division of Sherman's XV Corps that forced the hasty Confederate evacuation of Jackson, Mississippi. Tuttle three times ran unsuccessfully for the Iowa governorship during the war, before finally resigning his commission on June 14, 1864. Warner, *Generals in Blue*, 513–14; Hubbell and Geary, *Biographical Dictionary of the Union*, 542–43.

21. James C. Veatch (1819–95), an Indiana attorney, fought at Fort Donelson and commanded a brigade under Stephen A. Hurlbut at Shiloh. Promoted to brigadier general of volunteers on April 28, 1862, he participated in the Corinth campaign and afterward commanded the District of Memphis. Assigned to command a division of the Army of the Tennessee during the Atlanta campaign, Veatch apparently ran afoul of Maj. Gen. O. O. Howard and returned to desk work at Memphis in the fall of 1864. After February 18, 1865, he commanded a division in the Army of the Gulf and participated in the Mobile campaign. Warner, *Generals in Blue*, 525–26; Hubbell and Geary, *Biographical Dictionary of the Union*, 555–56.

22. Grierson appears to be saying that Waring's brigade was expected to march, *by way of* the Memphis and Ohio Railroad, from Union City, near the Tennessee-Kentucky border, and rendezvous with Smith at Collierville by the end of January. Sherman had instructed Smith to assemble his cavalry by February 1 and join him at Meridian, Mississippi, on the Mobile and Ohio Railroad, on or about February 10, tearing up tracks along the way. Drenching rain, muddy roads, and ice-clogged streams impeded Waring's 220-mile march. Smith waited for Waring and left Collierville on February 11. Sherman, who was forced to abandon the expedition and return to Vicksburg, called the delay "unpardonable." *O.R.*, Series 1, 32, part 1: 173–82 (quote on 174), 262–65.

23. An incomplete paragraph follows:

> Sometime previous to our starting on the W. Sooy Smith expedition, a bulky manuscript dropped in my office by accident and handed to my acting assistant adjutant general, S. L. Woodward, revealed the underhanded plottings of an insubordinate officer, Colonel Edward Prince of the 7th Illinois Cavalry. It was a letter addressed to W. Sooy Smith, written with the special request that it not be shown to myself or to General Hurlbut, in which the writer claimed that his "energy and vigilance" had accomplished the labor which gave me honors, and in bad grammar and worse taste, set forth that his, Colonel Prince's, "connection with the Cavalry Division and the 16th Army Corps, is loathsome in the extreme"; that at home he was accustomed to associate with honorable men and why should he not do so here; with other balderdash about blushing for the . . .

A handwritten notation states: "Remainder not found. This entire paragraph was cut out of the other copy."

9. The Meridian Expedition

1. The following paragraph was marked "omit" by Grierson: "A brigade of Infantry under command of Wm. S. McMillen, 95th Ohio Infantry, had been ordered to report to General Smith, to operate in conjunction with the cavalry and make a demonstration to Wyatt on the Tallahatchie River with a view to give the impression to the enemy

that a crossing would be made at that point. General Hurlbut with two divisions of his corps was absent from Memphis with General Sherman on the Meridian expedition and General [Ralph P.] Buckland was left in command at Memphis."

2. A former Mississippi legislator, congressman, and judge, Samuel J. Gholson (1808–83) rose from private to brigadier general in the Confederate army and commanded a cavalry brigade in James Chalmers's division under Nathan Bedford Forrest. Gholson lost an arm in the fight with Grierson's cavalry at Egypt, Mississippi, in December 1864. Warner, *Generals in Gray*, 103–4.

3. Jeffrey Forrest (1837–63) was the youngest brother of Gen. Nathan Bedford Forrest. Wyeth, *That Devil Forrest*, 6.

4. An 1854 graduate of West Point, as a brigadier general Stephen D. Lee (1833–1908) commanded a Confederate infantry brigade at Vicksburg. Captured and exchanged, he was promoted to major general and given command of the cavalry in the Department of Alabama, Mississippi, and East Louisiana. On June 23, 1864, Lee became the Confederacy's youngest lieutenant general and assumed command of John B. Hood's old corps in the Army of Tennessee. Warner, *Generals in Gray*, 183–84; Hattaway, *General Stephen D. Lee*.

5. Colonel W. W. Faulkner's 12th Kentucky Cavalry formed part of Lyon's brigade in Brig. Gen. Abraham Buford's Second Division of Forrest's Cavalry Corps. Luckett, "Bedford Forrest," 110.

6. Grierson is engaging in wishful thinking. By adroitly pulling back to a position behind Sakatonchee Creek, Forrest compelled Smith to either attack, retreat, or move southeast with Forrest in his rear. Smith chose the second course of action. As Grierson subsequently notes, his attack at the Ellis Bridge crossing of the Sakatonchee, west of West Point, was a holding action to allow the main body of the Union army to withdraw. Ballard, *Civil War Mississippi*, 83–84; Wills, *Battle from the Start*, 161–62; Hurst, *Nathan Bedford Forrest*, 147–55. See also Lee, "Sherman's Meridian Expedition."

7. Starr, *Union Cavalry*, 382, agrees that Grierson accurately characterized his role on the Meridian expedition as "a sort of supernumerary." Starr goes on to observe that Grierson's brief report "also gives the crystal-clear impression of his desire to place as great a distance as possible between himself and the failure of the campaign." He finds it curious, therefore, that Smith wrote "glowingly" to Sherman that "Grierson behaved nobly, and is a man of more capacity than either you or I have credited him with." As Foster, in *Sherman's Mississippi Campaign*, 147, points out, "Grierson remained convinced that he could have joined Sherman at Meridian had Smith not stopped the action the night of February 20. . . . Although Grierson was furious at Smith, he did not publicly chastise the General until after the war." In an astute assessment, Foster notes that the Meridian expedition's "short-term consequences were less important than the campaign's role in shaping Sherman's distinctive type of warfare" against Southern civilians and military infrastructure in order to "destroy the Confederates' ability and will to keep fighting." Ibid., 168.

10. Operations against Forrest

1. An Episcopal bishop, Leonidas Polk (1806–64) graduated in 1827 from West Point, where he formed a close friendship with future Confederate president Jefferson Davis. Early in the Civil War, Polk commanded Military Department No. 2, where he oversaw Confederate defenses along the upper Mississippi River and tested Kentucky neutrality. As a lieutenant general and second in command of the Army of Tennes-

see, he was the rallying point for senior officers disaffected with Gen. Braxton Bragg. Polk was killed by an artillery shot at Pine Mountain near Marietta, Georgia. Parks, *General Leonidas Polk*; Woodworth, *Jefferson Davis and His Generals*, especially 5–6, 36–45, 156–57, 238–41.

2. Richmond's Libby Prison consisted of three four-story warehouse buildings constructed by tobacco manufacturer John Enders Sr. between 1845 and 1854. They were leased by Maine ship chandler Captain Luther Libby, who closed down his business at the outbreak of the Civil War. The Confederates commandeered the buildings for use as a hospital and prison after the battle of First Manassas. Eventually, more than 50,000 Union prisoners passed through Libby Prison. Wiatt, *Libby Prison.*

3. John Hunt Morgan (1825–64) generated headlines with his raids into Kentucky, Tennessee, Indiana, and Ohio. Captured during his July 1863 excursion into Indiana and Ohio, Morgan escaped from the Ohio State Penitentiary and made his way back south. He was killed by a Union cavalry patrol at Greeneville, Tennessee, on September 4, 1864. Warner, *Generals in Gray*, 220–21; Ramage, *Rebel Raider.*

4. Joseph "Fightin' Joe" Wheeler (1836–1906) graduated from West Point in 1859 and was a second lieutenant in the Regiment of Mounted Rifles at the outbreak of the Civil War. He rose quickly in the Confederate service to major general at the age of twenty-six and commander of cavalry attached to the Army of Tennessee. Beginning in 1881, he served eight terms in the U.S. Congress and was appointed major general of volunteers during the Spanish-American War. He retired as a brigadier general in the regular army in 1900. Dyer, *Fightin' Joe Wheeler.*

5. On April 12, 1864, Forrest captured Fort Pillow on the east bank of the Mississippi River, about forty miles north of Memphis. According to testimony from survivors, the Confederates advanced on the garrison of approximately 560 officers and enlisted men (more than half of whom were African American troops) under a flag of truce and launched an assault with cries of "No quarter" and "Kill the damned niggers; shoot them down." A congressional committee investigating the matter concluded that many of the 170 black and 80 white casualties were inflicted after the Confederates had taken possession of the works and while the Union soldiers were attempting to surrender. The incident produced fierce debate, then and now. Fuchs, *An Unerring Fire*; Ward, *River Run Red*; Albert Castel, "The Fort Pillow Massacre: An Examination of the Evidence," in Urwin, *Black Flag*, 89–103; Derek W. Frisby, "'Remember Fort Pillow!': Politics, Atrocity Propaganda, and the Evolution of Hard War," ibid., 104–31.

6. Samuel Sturgis (1822–86) was an 1846 graduate of West Point who had served in the Mexican War (where he was captured near Buena Vista) and rose to captain of the 1st Cavalry by 1861. After fighting in Arkansas and Missouri, Sturgis was promoted to brigadier general of volunteers and led a division at Antietam and Fredericksburg. Sent west in the winter of 1863, he performed poorly against Forrest but nonetheless diverted the Confederate raid on Sherman's railroad supply line in the summer of 1864. Sturgis never shook the stigma of his defeat at Brice's Cross Roads, and many who served under him shared Grierson's opinion of Sturgis as at best incompetent and at worst a drunkard. After the war, Sturgis reverted to lieutenant colonel of the 6th Cavalry and in 1869 was promoted to colonel of the 7th Cavalry. He retired as governor of the Soldiers Home in 1886. Hubbell and Geary, *Biographical Dictionary of the Union*, 514–15; Starr, *Union Cavalry*, 254 n.13, 429, 432–34.

7. An officer of the Prussian Royal Horse Guard who was court-martialed for desertion and conspiracy, Joseph Kargé (1823–92) fled his native Poland and emigrated to

the United States in 1851. At the outbreak of the Civil War, he led the 1st New Jersey Cavalry in the Eastern theater and then recruited and commanded the 2nd New Jersey Cavalry in the West. On Grierson's and Washburn's recommendations, he was promoted to brevet brigadier general to date from March 13, 1865. After the war, Kargé occupied the chair of Continental Languages and Literature at the College of New Jersey (now Princeton University). Kajencki, *Star on Many a Battlefield*.

8. A Kentuckian, Abraham Buford (1820–84) graduated from West Point in 1841, served in the Mexican War, and was a planter at the outbreak of the Civil War. Appointed a Confederate brigadier general in September 1862, he participated in the Vicksburg campaign and then served under Forrest for the rest of the war. Warner, *Generals in Gray*, 39.

9. Philip D. Roddey (1826–97) was a former sheriff and Tennessee River steamboat operator. As colonel of the 4th Alabama Cavalry, he served under both Forrest and Joseph Wheeler. He was promoted to brigadier general in August 1863. Warner, *Generals in Gray*, 262.

11. Brice's Cross Roads

1. Bouton's Third Brigade consisted of the 55th and 59th U.S. Colored Infantry and Company F, 2nd U.S. Colored Artillery. Assigned to guard the Federal baggage train on the morning of June 10, Bouton's black soldiers, who wore badges that read "Remember Fort Pillow," acquitted themselves admirably and sustained heavy casualties in covering the Union retreat from Brice's Cross Roads. Bearss, *Forrest at Brice's Cross Roads*, 109–14, 135–36. A biographical sketch of Bouton is in ibid., 321.

2. Bearss, *Forrest at Brice's Cross Roads*, 71, observes that "This was not to be one of General Grierson's better days. . . . A bold commander, in view of Sturgis' orders and knowing that McMillen's footsoldiers were hastening to the front, would have attacked and recovered the initiative. Grierson was a raider and not a fighter, and he was faced by a man who knew that fighting meant killing." Forrest, knowing that the Union cavalry would be several hours in front of the infantry slowly advancing in the heat over muddy roads, planned to converge his scattered units on Brice's Cross Roads and "whip" the Federal horsemen, using the dense woods and underbrush to mask his numbers. He would then turn on the Union foot soldiers as they arrived, exhausted by their forced march, at the scene of the fighting. Ibid., 64.

3. Grierson exaggerates. Forrest states that he commanded approximately 3,500 cavalry at Brice's Cross Roads. *O.R.*, Series 1, 39, part 1: 225. His recent biographers place the number at 4,800 Confederates, arriving "piecemeal" on the battlefield. Hurst, *Nathan Bedford Forrest*, 184–97; Wills, *Battle from the Start*, 204–15. At the point of initial contact, Grierson may have faced as few as 800 Confederates. Forrest launched his main attack shortly after noon with three brigades, numbering about 2,000 men, reinforced by another brigade and artillery around 1:00 or 1:30 P.M. Stephen D. Lee judged that Forrest's skillful disposition of his troops "made the Federals believe he had a larger force than he really had." Leftwich, "Battle of Brice's Crossroads," 9; Luckett, "Bedford Forrest," 103–4; Lee, "Battle of Brice's Cross Roads," 35.

4. Waring, in *Whip and Spur*, 135–37, recalls that

during our last night's march [June 11], my brigade having the advance, and I being at its rear, Grierson ordered me to prevent any pushing ahead of the stragglers of the other brigades, who were to be recognized, he reminded me, by their wearing hats (mine wore caps). The order was peremptory, and was to be enforced even at the cost of cutting the offenders down. Grierson's adjutant was at my side; we were all sleeping more or less of the time, but constantly some hatted straggler was detected pushing toward the front, and ordered back—the adjutant being especially sharp-eyed in detecting the mutilated sugar-loaves through the gloom. Finally, close to my right and pushing slowly to the front, in a long-strided walk, came à gray horse with a hatted rider,—an india-rubber poncho covering his uniform. I ordered him back; the adjutant, eager for enforcement of the order, remonstrated at the man's disobedience; I ordered him again, but without result; the adjutant ejaculated, "Damn him, cut him down!" I drew my sabre and laid its flat in one long stinging welt across that black poncho: "——! Who are you hitting?" Then we both remembered that Grierson too wore a hat.

5. Sturgis reported the Union cavalry losses as 3 officers and 330 enlisted men and the infantry losses as 72 officers and 1,835 enlisted men. Moore, *Rebellion Record*, 166.

6. Proceedings of the Sturgis court of inquiry, including Grierson's testimony (199–203), are in *O.R.*, Series 1, 39, part 1: 147–217. After questioning Sturgis and senior Union officers, the board retired without making any recommendations. Hubbell and Geary, *Biographical Dictionary of the Union*, 515.

7. Grierson was correct. As the principal historian of the Union cavalry notes, Sturgis spent the remainder of the war "in limbo, 'awaiting orders.'" Starr, *Union Cavalry*, 438.

12. A. J. Smith's Operations in Mississippi

1. Kentuckian Hylan B. Lyon (1836–1907) graduated from West Point in 1856 and was an artillery lieutenant before the war. As lieutenant colonel of the 8th Kentucky Infantry, he was captured at Fort Donelson and imprisoned on Johnson's Island. After his exchange, he participated in the Holly Springs and Vicksburg campaigns. Promoted to brigadier general in June of 1864, he commanded a brigade of Kentucky mounted infantry under Forrest. He fled to Mexico after the war, returning to Kentucky in 1866. Warner, *Generals in Gray*, 197.

2. Skirmishes along the line of Union advance over the Pontotoc-Tupelo road, including Rucker's and Buford's attacks on the Federal wagon train at Burrow's Shop and Coonewah Crossroads, respectively, are described in Bearss, *Forrest at Brice's Cross Roads*, 179–89. Bearss points to confusion and breakdown of communication between Forrest and his senior field commanders that allowed Smith to get the jump on the Confederates. "Grierson's division had covered half the 18 miles separating Pontotoc and Tupelo before any orders from Forrest were received." Ibid., 181.

3. Grierson is confused. Col. Joseph J. Woods, 12th Iowa Infantry, commanded the Third Brigade, First Division, XVI Corps; Col. David Moore commanded the Third Division, XVI Corps. See *O.R.*, Series 1, 39, part 1: 255. Grierson several times here refers to the Second Division when he means the Third Division. Mower's First Division, with Woods's brigade anchoring its left flank, formed the right of the Union line; followed by Moore's Third Division holding the center; and Bouton's Colored Brigade on the left. Woods's brigade distinguished itself in repulsing Confederate assaults on the Union right and center on the morning of July 14. Bearss, *Forrest at Brice's Cross Roads*, 195–97, 206–10.

4. Grierson neglects to comment on Confederate reports that Union soldiers burned local homes on the evening of July 14, "showing preparation for retreat or movement in some direction." Lee, "Battle of Tupelo," 48.

5. Forrest placed the Confederate loss at Tupelo at 210 killed and 1,116 wounded, for a total of 1,326. A. J. Smith listed his casualties as 674 killed, wounded, and missing. *O.R.*, Series 1, 39, part 1: 256, 324. See also Lee, "Battle of Tupelo," 50–51.

6. Grierson's account appears to discredit Southern accusations that Edward Hatch looted and then torched the Thompson mansion. Kenner, *Buffalo Soldiers and Officers*, 35–36. A. J. Smith's culpability is assessed in Dimick, "Motives for the Burning of Oxford, Mississippi."

7. Charles Lever (1806–72) was a Dublin physician-turned-novelist whose military romances, particularly *Charles O'Malley, the Irish Dragoon*, were popular on both sides of the Atlantic in the mid-nineteenth century. Radbourne, *Mickey Free*, 25, 226 n. 4.

13. Reorganization and Controversy

1. An attorney, Ralph P. Buckland (1812–92) was commissioned colonel of the 72nd Ohio Volunteer Infantry in January 1862 and commanded a brigade at Shiloh. Promoted to brigadier general in November 1862, he participated in the Vicksburg campaign. He commanded the District of Memphis from January 1864 to January 1865, at which time he resigned his commission to take a seat in the U.S. Congress. Warner, *Generals in Blue*, 50–51. In an attempt to compel Smith to abandon his invasion of Mississippi, at dawn on Sunday, August 21, 1864, Forrest raided Memphis with the intention of seizing Buckland, along with Gen. C. C. Washburn and Gen. Stephen A. Hurlbut. The Confederate cavalry failed in their attempt, seized horses and prisoners, and retreated. Col. Matthew Starr of the 6th Illinois Cavalry was wounded during the fighting. *O.R.*, Series 1, 39, part 1: 468–69, 472; Wyeth, *That Devil Forrest*, 410–21; Wills, *Battle from the Start*, 238–39; Hurst, *Nathan Bedford Forrest*, 212–14.

2. An 1839 West Point graduate, Edward R. S. Canby (1817–73) was a veteran of the Second Seminole and Mexican wars. He repulsed the Confederate invasion of New Mexico and was promoted to brigadier general on March 11, 1862. Canby was assigned to staff duty in Washington, D.C., and commanded at New York City following the 1863 draft riots. On May 7, 1864, he was promoted to major general of volunteers and assigned to command the Military Division of West Mississippi. As commander of the Division of the Pacific, Canby was assassinated on April 11, 1873, during a peace conference with the Modoc Indians at the Lava Beds in northern California. Heyman, *Prudent Soldier.*

3. Called the "Christian General" because of his profound religious beliefs, Oliver O. Howard (1830–1909) graduated from Bowdoin College and West Point. He rose rapidly to major general of volunteers, despite lackluster performances at Chancellorsville and Gettysburg. Howard, who lost his right arm at Fair Oaks, Virginia, in 1862, redeemed himself in the West, where he assumed command of the Army of the Tennessee following James B. McPherson's death. After the war, Howard exercised his humanitarian impulses as commissioner of the Freedmen's Bureau, founder of Howard University, and an advocate of fair treatment for Native Americans. Carpenter, *Sword and Olive Branch.*

4. On July 17, 1864, thirty-three-year-old John Bell Hood (1831–79) replaced Joseph Johnston as commander of the Army of Tennessee. After the fall of Atlanta, Hood—an aggressive fighter who had lost the use of his left arm at Gettysburg and lost his right leg at the hip at Chickamauga—launched an ill-conceived invasion of Tennessee in the hope that Sherman would follow him north. Hood wrecked his army in suicidal assaults on Nashville and Franklin, forcing President Davis to replace him with Lt. Gen. Richard Taylor. McMurry, *John Bell Hood.*

5. On June 12, 1864, Robert E. Lee dispatched Jubal Early and his 8,000-man Second Corps of the Army of Northern Virginia to disperse Federal forces in the Shenandoah Valley and threaten Washington in an effort to divert troops from Grant's army, which was threatening Richmond and Petersburg. In the space of four weeks, Early defeated Gen. David Hunter and Gen. Lew Wallace and fired on the defenses of Washington, D.C. The raid created panic in the Union high command and compelled Grant to detach two infantry corps and two cavalry divisions to deal with the Confederate threat in his rear. An 1837 West Point graduate, Early (1816–94) was, in his biographer's estimation, "an anomaly"—irreligious, misanthropic, and "independent in thought to the point of eccentricity." Osborne, *Jubal*, xiii–xiv, 245–93; Vandiver, *Jubal's Raid*.

6. Grierson provides an optimistic assessment. On September 27, 1864, Forrest drove Rousseau into the fortifications at Pulaski, Tennessee, on the Nashville and Decatur Railroad. Forrest then moved east toward Tullahoma on the Nashville and Chattanooga Railroad, with Rousseau pursuing by rail via Nashville. Forrest's September 16 to October 6 raid forced Sherman to break up his railroad supply lines in Tennessee and strike out for Savannah, Georgia, subsisting off the land. Rousseau enjoyed a measure of revenge on December 7, when he foiled Forrest's assault on Murfreesboro during John B. Hood's Nashville campaign. Wyeth, *That Devil Forrest*, 423–51, 485–88.

7. An 1842 graduate of West Point, Napoleon J. T. Dana (1822–1905) had been severely wounded at Cerro Gordo during the Mexican War and resigned his commission in 1855 to engage in banking at St. Paul, Minnesota. He entered the Civil War as colonel of the 1st Minnesota Infantry. He commanded a brigade at Antietam, where he was again severely wounded. Promoted to major general of volunteers from November 29, 1862, he returned to duty in July 1863 and commanded a variety of districts behind Union lines, including Vicksburg. In December 1864, he was placed in command of the Department of the Mississippi. Warner, *Generals in Blue*, 111–12.

8. Joseph F. Knipe (1823–1901) served as an enlisted man in the Mexican War and was working for the Pennsylvania Railroad at the outbreak of the Civil War. Commissioned colonel of the 46th Pennsylvania Infantry, he received a wound at Cedar Mountain that plagued him throughout the Gettysburg campaign, by which time he had been appointed brigadier general of volunteers. Transferred to the Western theater, he was sent to Memphis to recruit and reorganize cavalry and was later appointed to command a division of Maj. Gen. James H. Wilson's cavalry corps. In early 1865, he was transferred to E. R. S. Canby's command for the expedition against Mobile. Knipe's intemperate protest over his demotion to brigade commander compelled Canby to relieve him. Warner, *Generals in Blue*, 272–73; Hubbell and Geary, *Biographical Dictionary of the Union*, 291–92.

9. Described by his admiring biographer as a glory-hunter "of the first magnitude" who was "often imperious and outspoken, to the extent that he alienated fully as many people as he attracted," James H. Wilson (1837–1925) graduated from West Point in 1860 and served on the staffs of McClellan and Grant, the latter of whom promoted him to brigadier general of volunteers and in February 1864 assigned him chief of the Cavalry Bureau in Washington, D.C. Wilson commanded a division of Philip Sheridan's cavalry during Grant's advance on Richmond, before being sent west as chief of cavalry in the Department of the Mississippi. He immediately cleaned house, replacing experienced commanders like Grierson and George Stoneman with younger and more energetic officers. In the spring of 1865, Wilson led 12,000 troopers on the largest cavalry expedition of the war, culminating in the capture of Selma,

Alabama. He resigned from the army in 1870 to work on various railroad enterprises and pursue a writing career. He returned to the army as a major general during the Spanish-American War and the Boxer Rebellion. Longacre, *From Union Stars to Top Hat,* especially 162–64, quote on 14; Jones, *Yankee Blitzkrieg.*

10. Albert G. Brackett (1829–96) served as a lieutenant in the 4th Indiana Infantry during the Mexican War and in 1855 was commissioned captain in the 2nd Cavalry. He was serving with the 5th Cavalry in October 1861 when he accepted the colonelcy of the 9th Illinois Cavalry. A major in the 1st Cavalry since 1862, after the war he became lieutenant colonel of the 2nd Cavalry and in 1879 was promoted to colonel of the 3rd Cavalry. He retired in 1891. Brackett's *History of the United States Cavalry* was published in 1865. Heitman, *Historical Register,* 1:237.

11. A Virginian, Frederick W. Benteen (1834–98) served the entire war with the 10th Missouri Cavalry, rising from first lieutenant to lieutenant colonel. He was appointed captain in the 7th Cavalry in the 1866 army reorganization, where his outspoken criticism of Lt. Col. George Armstrong Custer and his actions at the battle of the Little Bighorn became one of the sources of a controversy that continues today. Benteen was promoted to major of the 9th Cavalry in 1882 and retired in 1888. Mills, *Harvest of Barren Regrets*; Carroll, *Camp Talk*; Heitman, *Historical Register,* 1:212.

12. Samuel R. Curtis (1805–66) graduated from West Point in 1831 but resigned a year later to pursue civil engineering and the law in Ohio. At the outbreak of the Mexican War, he was adjutant general of Ohio before accepting the colonelcy of the 2nd Ohio Volunteers. After the war, Curtis moved to Keokuk, Iowa, where he was elected mayor and served three terms in Congress. He resigned to accept a commission as brigadier general of volunteers to rank from May 17, 1861. In recognition of his victory over Gen. Sterling Price at the battle of Pea Ridge, Arkansas, he was promoted to major general in March and became military governor of Arkansas in May 1862. That fall, he was assigned to command the Department of the Missouri, until a falling out with Gov. Hamilton B. Gamble forced his transfer to the Department of Kansas. In January 1865, he was given command of the Department of the Northwest. He died while serving on the commission to inspect the Union Pacific Railroad. Curtis has been described as "a colorless but complex man who became the most successful Union field commander in the Trans-Mississippi." Shea and Hess, *Pea Ridge,* quote on 7; Warner, *Generals in Blue,* 107–8.

13. Francis P. Blair Jr. (1821–75), son of the powerful editor of the *St. Louis Globe* and brother of Postmaster General Montgomery Blair, was a passionate Unionist, despite owning slaves. He took part in the mobilization of Missouri volunteers at the outset of the war, before leaving to take his seat in Congress, where he chaired the House Committee on Military Affairs. Appointed brigadier general of volunteers in August and a major general in November 1862, he commanded first a brigade and then a division at Vicksburg and Chattanooga and the XVII Corps during Sherman's march to the sea. A forceful personality with a profound abhorrence of racial equality, Blair provided a counterbalance to the Radical Republicans. He was the 1868 vice presidential running mate of Horatio Seymour and served as U.S. senator from Missouri. W. E. Parrish, *Frank Blair.*

14. Grant, in *Memoirs,* 2:518, writes:

The three expeditions which I had tried so hard to get off from the commands of Thomas and Canby did finally get off: one under Canby himself, against Mobile, late in March [1865]; that under Stoneman from East Tennessee on the 20th; and the one under Wilson, starting from Eastport,

Mississippi, on the 22d of March. They were all eminently successful, but without any good result. Indeed much valuable property was destroyed and many lives lost at a time when we would have liked to spare them. The war was practically over before their victories were gained. They were so late in commencing operations, that they did not hold any troops away that otherwise would have been operating against the armies which were gradually forcing the Confederate armies to a surrender.

For a modern assessment of Wilson's raid, see Jones, *Yankee Blitzkrieg*, especially, 185–89.

15. David S. Stanley (1828–1902) graduated from West Point in 1852 and served on the frontier. Commissioned brigadier general of volunteers in September 1861, he participated in the fighting from New Madrid and Island No. 10 to Iuka and Corinth. From November 1862 to September 1863, he was chief of cavalry for Maj. Gen. William S. Rosecrans's Army of the Cumberland. Promoted to major general of volunteers, he commanded the IV Corps in the Atlanta campaign. After the battle of Jonesboro, he was detached, with John M. Schofield's corps, to deal with Gen. John B. Hood's invasion of Tennessee. He was wounded at the battle of Franklin. After the war, Stanley was colonel of the 22nd Infantry until his promotion to brigadier general in 1884. He retired in 1892. In 1879, Grierson sat on a court-martial board called by Gen. Sherman to resolve a long-standing and acrimonious public fight between Stanley and Col. William B. Hazen. Stanley had accused Hazen of cowardice and misrepresentation of his Civil War record and of perjury in the impeachment trial of Secretary of War William W. Belknap, to which Hazen responded with charges of slander against Stanley. The board found Stanley guilty of a minor count of "conduct unbecoming" and issued a mild reprimand. Warner, *Generals in Blue*, 470–71; Kroeker, *Great Plains Command*, 154–69; Leckie and Leckie, *Unlikely Warriors*, 255.

16. One scholar views the situation between Wilson and Grierson quite differently. Starr, in *Union Cavalry*, 543, sees Grierson's motivation as a desire to maintain "his quasi-independent status in Memphis" and avoid being reduced to "a mere cog in a corps commanded by a man ten years his junior," who failed to show Grierson significant respect. In that light, Starr argues, "Wilson's order of December 13 removing Grierson of the command of the division was fully justified."

17. For an analysis of administrative problems in the West, see Keenan, *Wilson's Cavalry Corps*, 81–87. Keenan places blame for the fiasco on the logistical difficulty of bringing the cavalry back from Missouri and Arkansas, the jurisdictional dispute over which department exercised authority over which units, and Grierson's own "failure to appreciate the sense of urgency in Wilson's orders." Emory Upton (1839–81) graduated from West Point in 1861 and by 1864 had risen to brigadier general of volunteers in hard fighting in the Eastern theater. Upton was recovering from a serious wound at the battle of Opequan Creek, Virginia, on September 19, 1864, when he was assigned to command the Fourth Division in Wilson's Cavalry Corps. He reverted to the rank of captain after the war and became lieutenant colonel of the 25th Infantry in the 1866 army reorganization. Upton was commandant of cadets at West Point, 1870–75, and was perhaps best known for his book *Military Policy of the United States*. He committed suicide at the San Francisco Presidio. Ambrose, *Upton and the Army*.

18. John M. Schofield (1831–1906), the son of a Baptist minister, was raised in Freeport, Illinois, and graduated seventh in the West Point Class of 1853. He was commissioned a major in the 1st Missouri Volunteers and served as Nathaniel Lyon's adjutant

general and chief of staff until Lyon's death at Wilson's Creek. Thereafter, Schofield served as a brigadier general of Missouri militia and was eventually promoted to major general of volunteers. Schofield considered the repulse of Hood's army at Franklin, Tennessee, his proudest accomplishment. As commander of the Army of the Ohio, he participated in the Atlanta campaign. After the war, Schofield commanded the Department of the Missouri and the divisions of the Pacific and the Atlantic, was superintendent at West Point, and in 1888 succeeded Philip Sheridan as commanding general of the army. Schofield served as interim secretary of war after President Andrew Johnson's controversial removal of Edwin M. Stanton and presided over the Fitz-John Porter court of inquiry. A recent biographer characterizes him as a "political soldier," who contributed greatly to the professional independence of the U.S. Army. D. B. Connelly, *John M. Schofield*, especially xii; Schofield, *Forty-six Years in the Army*.

19. A historian of the Army of Tennessee describes Hood's frontal assault on the Union defenses at Franklin on November 30, 1864, as "less a battle than a slaughter." Of the 16,000 Confederates who went into action, Hood lost 6,200 (1,750 of them killed). Devastating as well, 12 general officers were killed, wounded, or captured, along with 54 regimental commanders. "In leadership, as well as in numbers, the army was destroyed at Franklin." On December 15–16, Maj. Gen. George H. Thomas's army rolled over Hood's Confederates entrenched at Nashville, sending the remnants of the Army of Tennessee reeling back across the Tennessee River. T. L. Connelly, *Autumn of Glory*, 503–12, quotes on 504, 506; Horn, *Decisive Battle of Nashville*.

14. Raid on the Mobile and Ohio Railroad

1. Richard Taylor (1820–79), the son of President Zachary Taylor, graduated from Yale in 1845 and was a Louisiana plantation owner and legislator before the war. One of the Western Confederacy's most capable army commanders, he repulsed Banks's Red River expedition in the spring of 1864, for which he was promoted to lieutenant general and given command of the Department of Alabama, Mississippi, and East Louisiana. In May 1865, he surrendered the last Confederate army east of the Mississippi. Taylor was also a talented writer, whose *Destruction and Reconstruction* stands at the summit of a tall mountain of Confederate memoirs. T. M. Parrish, *Richard Taylor*; Warner, *Generals in Gray*, 299–300.

2. Joel Elliott (1839–68) enlisted as a private in the 2nd Indiana Cavalry on September 13, 1861, and by October 1863 was a captain in the 7th Indiana Cavalry. After the war, he passed a qualifying examination and was commissioned a major in the 7th U.S. Cavalry. Elliott was killed while leading an attack on a Cheyenne village on the Washita River, November 27, 1868. Heitman, *Historical Register*, 1:402; Greene, *Washita*, especially 89, 122–23, 131–34.

3. Gholson lost an arm in the engagement. Warner, *Generals in Gray*, 104.

4. Grierson shipped these "galvanized rebels" to the prison camp at Alton, Illinois, with a recommendation for leniency. The judge advocate general disagreed, recommending that they be tried as deserters. By that time, the war had ended and the horrors of the Confederate prison camp at Andersonville were fresh in the public mind. Eventually, the former Union soldiers captured at Egypt Station were allowed to enlist, along with Confederate prisoners held in the North, in Companies C and D of the 5th U.S. Volunteers for service against hostile Indians on the Northern Plains. The two companies were mustered out on October 11, 1866. Dinges, "Making of a Cavalryman," 543–44 n. 44; Brown, *Galvanized Yankees*, 121–42, 214–15; Marvel, *Andersonville*, 223–24, 300 n.27. Although more destructive than Grierson's 1863

raid, the 1864 expedition produced far fewer strategic gains for the Union. Within days of Grierson's arrival at Vicksburg, the Confederates had repaired the rail line and locomotives were again carrying supplies to Hood's army. Bearss, in "Grierson's Winter Raid on the Mobile and Ohio Railroad," 37, concludes that "in part the inability of the Civil War cavalryman to exert himself thoroughly in wrecking a railroad had served to partially nullify the strategic effort of this brilliant raid carried out by Grierson in the final winter of the war."

5. Grierson refers to English essayist, poet, and playwright Charles Lamb (1775–1834). *Columbia Encyclopedia*, 6th ed., s.v. "Lamb, Charles."

15. A Visit to Washington

1. On February 3, 1865, President Lincoln and Secretary of State William H. Seward met with Confederate officials—Vice President Alexander Stephens, Senate President Pro Tem Robert M. T. Hunter, and Assistant Secretary of War John A. Campbell—on board the *River Queen* in Hampton Roads, Virginia, to discuss peace terms. The so-called peace commissioners, who in any event were not authorized to negotiate, returned to Richmond with the clear understanding that Lincoln would accept nothing less than unconditional surrender. McPherson, *Battle Cry of Freedom*, 821–25.

2. A graduate of Yale Law School, Brig. Gen. Alfred H. Terry (1827–90) captured Fort Fisher, guarding the approaches to Wilmington, Delaware, the Confederacy's last seaport, on January 15, 1865, for which he was promoted to major general of volunteers and brigadier general in the regular army. The fall of Fort Fisher intensified attacks on President Jefferson Davis in the Confederate Congress and led to the Hampton Roads peace conference. Terry retained his brigadier general's commission after the war, commanding the Department of Dakota during the Little Bighorn campaign. He retired in 1888. Warner, *Generals in Blue*, 497–98; Hubbell and Geary, *Biographical Dictionary of the Union*, 527–28; McPherson, *Battle Cry of Freedom*; Gragg, *Confederate Goliath*; Robinson, *Hurricane of Fire*.

3. An 1855 West Point graduate, William W. Averill (1832–1900) had campaigned against Indians in the Southwest, where he was wounded. As a brigadier general commanding cavalry during the Shenandoah campaign, Averill incurred the displeasure of Philip Sheridan, who removed him from command. Averill resigned on May 18, 1865. Eckert and Amato, *Ten Years in the Saddle*.

4. A Democrat, Edwin M. Stanton (1814–69) had served as attorney general in the Buchanan administration and on January 14, 1862, replaced Simon Cameron as secretary of war in Lincoln's cabinet. Described as "brusque to the point of rudeness," he improved the efficiency of the War Department and deflected criticism away from Lincoln for some of the North's more draconian war measures. Stanton became the central figure in President Andrew Johnson's impeachment proceedings, when the secretary refused to vacate his office without congressional approval. As president, Ulysses S. Grant appointed Stanton to the U.S. Supreme Court, but he died just days after the Senate confirmed the appointment. Hubbell and Geary, *Biographical Dictionary of the Union*, 499–500, quote on 409; Thomas and Hyman, *Stanton*, especially 360–93.

5. Nicknamed "Hancock the Superb," Winfield Scott Hancock (1824–86) played a significant role in the major events of the nineteenth century from the Mexican War to the Gilded Age. An 1844 West Point graduate, he served as a second lieutenant in the 16th Infantry during the Mexican War and rose rapidly in rank and respect during the major Civil War campaigns in the East, particularly in establishing the Union line

on the first day at Gettysburg and beating back Pickett's climactic charge. After the war, he oversaw the execution of the Lincoln conspirators, campaigned ineffectively against the Plains Indians, replaced Philip Sheridan as Reconstruction commander in Texas and Louisiana, commanded the Department of Dakota, put down the 1877 Pennsylvania railroad strike, and ran unsuccessfully as the Democratic presidential candidate against James A. Garfield in 1880. Jordan, *Winfield Scott Hancock.*

6. Republican senator from New Hampshire and vocal antislavery advocate, John P. Hale (1806–73) spent much of his time as chair of the Senate Naval Affairs Committee engaged in a vendetta against Secretary of the Navy Gideon Welles. Denied reelection in 1864, he accepted President Lincoln's appointment as minister to Spain. Hubbell and Geary, *Biographical Dictionary of the Union,* 225–26.

7. Military Governor Andrew Johnson had moved quickly to reestablish civil rule in Tennessee before leaving for Washington to become vice president, endorsing the actions of the January 1865 Republican-dominated state convention and setting February 22 and March 4 elections for the House and the Senate. Radical Republicans in both the House and the Senate, however, blocked seating the Tennessee delegation until after the state ratified the Fourteenth Amendment on July 19, 1866, but prior to the imposition of harsher criteria for readmission of former Confederate states. The fact that Tennessee thus avoided military reconstruction may actually have facilitated the outcome Grierson laments. Conservative Democrats ousted Republicans in Tennessee's 1869 elections. Alexander, *Political Reconstruction in Tennessee,* especially 18–32, 113–21, 238–45.

16. Final Operations

1. A watchmaker by trade, Thomas J. Lucas (1826–1908) had served as a lieutenant in the 4th Indiana Volunteers during the Mexican War. As lieutenant colonel and then colonel of the 14th Indiana Infantry, he saw hard service at Rich Mountain and during the Kentucky and Vicksburg campaigns, in the course of which he was wounded three times. He commanded a brigade during Banks's Red River campaign and was promoted to brigadier general of volunteers on November 10, 1865. His cavalry division raided into west Florida, south Georgia, and Alabama during the Mobile campaign. Warner, *Generals in Blue,* 285–86.

2. Nicknamed "the Bald Eagle," Louisiana-born Joseph R. West (1822–98) served in the Mexican War before migrating to California, where he owned the *San Francisco Price Current.* Commissioned lieutenant colonel of the 1st California Infantry in August 1861, he served under Brig. Gen. James Carleton in the Southwest, where he advanced to brigadier general of volunteers on October 25, 1862. West commanded a division during Nathaniel P. Banks's Red River campaign and at the end of the war commanded the cavalry in the Department of the Gulf. He was mustered out as major general of volunteers on January 4, 1866. West remained in Louisiana after the war, serving as U.S. senator from 1871 to 1877. Masich, *Civil War in Arizona,* especially 157 n. 7; Finch, *Confederate Pathway to the Pacific,* 147–49, 175; Hubbell and Geary, *Biographical Dictionary of the Union,* 580–81.

3. Canby reported the capture of 4,924 prisoners and 231 pieces of artillery. *O.R.,* Series 1, 49, part 1: 99.

4. The Confederates established the stockaded prison camp at Andersonville in east-central Georgia in February 1864. Some 41,000 captured Union soldiers were confined there, nearly one-third of whom died before the camp was evacuated in the spring of 1865. Marvell, *Andersonville.*

5. Democrat James L. Pugh (1820–1907) of Eufaula, Alabama, served in the U.S. Congress, 1859–61, and then resigned to enlist as a private in the Eufaula Rifles, 1st Alabama Regiment. He served in the Confederate Congress in 1862–65 and was a delegate to the Alabama state constitutional convention in 1875 and U.S. senator from Alabama, 1880–97. *Biographical Directory of the United States Congress.*

6. James H. Wilson's troopers captured Jefferson Davis and his entourage on May 10, 1865, near Irwinville, Georgia. Jones, *Yankee Blitzkrieg,* 170–79.

7. Gen. Simon B. Buckner formally surrendered the Trans-Mississippi Department to Canby at New Orleans on May 26, 1865. Edmund Kirby Smith, the department commander, was with a column of nearly 500 ex-Confederates, most from Jo Shelby's brigade, who crossed over the Rio Grande into Mexico on June 26. Kerby, *Kirby Smith's Confederacy,* 424–25, 428.

8. An 1853 West Point graduate, Philip H. Sheridan (1831–88) rose rapidly from first lieutenant to major general of volunteers, capturing Ulysses S. Grant's attention by his headlong charge that seized Missionary Ridge at the battle of Chattanooga. Assigned to command the cavalry of the Army of the Potomac, he devastated the Shenandoah Valley while Grant besieged Robert E. Lee's army at Petersburg. Promoted to lieutenant general in 1869, Sheridan commanded the Military Division of the Missouri during the Plains Indian wars and in 1884 succeeded William T. Sherman as commanding general of the army. Grierson privately harbored an intense dislike of Sheridan, whom he referred to as *"Sherry-dan,"* that dated back to the close of the Civil War. Hutton, *Phil Sheridan and His Army*; Dinges, "Benjamin H. Grierson," in Hutton, *Soldiers West,* 164.

9. At the close of the war, Grant pressured the Johnson administration to demand that the French withdraw from Mexico and, if they refused, to authorize Sheridan's army to unite with Benito Juárez and drive out the imperialists. Sheridan's very visible buildup of U.S. forces along the Rio Grande and shipments of arms to the Mexican Republican army helped convince the French to withdraw their support from Maximilian, who was captured and executed on July 19, 1867. Hutton, *Phil Sheridan and His Army,* 20–22; Tyler, *Santiago Vidaurri and the Southern Confederacy,* 152–55.

10. U.S. Supreme Court chief justice Salmon P. Chase (1808–73) was on the final leg of a fact-finding tour of the South to assist President Andrew Johnson in formulating Reconstruction policy. His entourage included daughter Janette Ralston "Nettie" Chase, newspaperman Whitelaw Reid, Baptist clergyman Dr. Richard Fuller, special treasury agent and aide Russell Lowell, Chase's close friend and political adviser William P. Miller, and Miller's son. Described by his biographer as "a moralist torn by ambition," Chase was a prominent antislavery Republican who had served as Lincoln's secretary of the treasury. He would eventually preside over Johnson's impeachment trial in the U.S. Senate. Niven, *Salmon P. Chase,* especially vi–vii, 382–93.

11. James W. "Tony" Forsyth (1835–1906) graduated from West Point and was assigned as a first lieutenant to the 9th Infantry, where he and Philip Sheridan served together in the Pacific Northwest. "Tall and thin with a ramrod straight, even imperious, military bearing that belied his warm, gregarious nature," according to Sheridan's biographer, "Forsyth was a 'champion story-teller.' He served Sheridan as aide-de-camp until 1873 and as military secretary until 1878, when he was promoted to lieutenant colonel, First Cavalry. . . . In 1886, he became colonel of the Seventh Cavalry and commanded the troops that brought the curtain down on the Indian wars with the terrible slaughter at Wounded Knee." Forsyth retired as a major general in 1897. Hutton, *Phil Sheridan and His Army,* 153–54; Warner, *Generals in Blue,* 156–57.

12. Another of the Union army's "boy generals," Wesley Merritt (1834–1910) commanded the cavalry of Philip Sheridan's Army of the Shenandoah during the climactic Appomattox campaign. Ending the war as a major general of volunteers, Merritt played an important role in the Plains Indian campaigns as lieutenant colonel of the 9th Cavalry and later colonel of the 5th Cavalry. As a major general in the regular army, Merritt commanded the American expeditionary force to the Philippines. Alberts, *Brandy Station to Manila Bay.*

13. Horatio G. Wright (1820–99) graduated second in the West Point class of 1841 and was an engineer officer until his appointment to brigadier general of volunteers in September 1861. Following service in Virginia, South Carolina, and Florida, he was assigned to command the Department of the Ohio, until May 1863. As major general of volunteers, he led a division in the Wilderness campaign and succeeded to command of the VI Corps after the death of Maj. Gen. John Sedgwick. He was dispatched to deal with Jubal Early's summer 1864 raid on Washington and returned to command the first troops to breach the Confederate defenses in the final assault on Petersburg. After a year in command of the Department of Texas following the Confederate surrender, he returned to engineer duty, including completion of the Washington Monument. Warner, *Generals in Blue,* 575–76; Hubbell and Geary, *Biographical Dictionary of the Union,* 605–6.

14. A New Yorker, Frank V. L. Eno was living in Missouri when he was commissioned captain and assistant adjutant general of volunteers on March 31, 1862. He was promoted to major on February 8 and mustered out on September 19, 1865. He died on March 8, 1887. Heitman, *Historical Register,* 1:407.

15. Alexander S. Asboth (1811–68) was a Hungarian exile who had served as chief of staff to Maj. Gen. John C. Frémont. Appointed brigadier general of volunteers on March 21, 1861, he commanded a division at Pea Ridge and later commanded at Columbus, Kentucky, and the District of West Florida. In 1866, Asboth was appointed U.S. minister to Argentina and Uruguay. He died in Buenos Aires of complications from a wound received two years earlier at the battle of Marianna, Florida. Warner, *Generals in Blue,* 11–12; Shea and Hess, *Pea Ridge*; Beszedits, "Hungarians in Civil War Missouri."

16. Charles R. Woods (1827–85) was an 1852 West Point graduate and veteran of frontier service. He led the 76th Ohio Infantry at Fort Donelson and Shiloh and commanded a brigade during the advance on Corinth, Mississippi. He fought in the Vicksburg campaign and was promoted to brigadier general of volunteers in August 1864. He commanded a brigade at Chattanooga and during the Atlanta campaign. Woods was advanced to division command for Sherman's march to the sea. He was appointed lieutenant colonel of the 33rd Infantry in 1866 and retired in 1874 as colonel of the 2nd Infantry. Warner, *Generals in Blue,* 571–72; Hubbell and Geary, *Biographical Dictionary of the Union,* 601–2.

17. Reconstruction Duty

1. Edith Clare, the Grierson's third child and only daughter, died of typhoid fever at Fort Concho, Texas, September 9, 1878. Leckie and Leckie, *Unlikely Warriors,* 253.

2. Andrew Johnson (1808–75), a War Democrat and former Unionist governor of Tennessee, set himself on a collision course with the Republican Congress—and in particular the Radical Republican faction—upon assuming the presidency after Lincoln's assassination. A proponent of leniency toward the former slaveholders, he vetoed key Reconstruction legislation and encouraged restoration of political power

to Southern leaders. Matters came to a head when Johnson removed Edwin Stanton as secretary of war, which Johnson's congressional opponents claimed violated the Tenure of Office Act. Articles of impeachment were handed down on February 28, 1868. Foner, *Reconstruction*, 176–84, 247–51, 333–36; Hubbell and Geary, *Biographical Dictionary of the Union*, 274–75.

3. Ben Grierson was largely indifferent to religion, to the consternation of his wife, Alice, a devout member of the Disciples of Christ, also known as the Christian Church. Early in their marriage, she often tried to convert him, but on this topic he largely ignored her. See Leckie and Leckie, *Unlikely Warriors*, 18, 28, 135. Nonetheless, Ben was extremely patriotic and, as he notes earlier, had acted on his political and ideological convictions when he volunteered to serve in the army in order to help restore the Union. Thus, while dismissive of religion for himself, he believed that if Southern Episcopalians were going to pray for their political leaders they should certainly pray for the president of the United States.

4. John Grierson remained in the quartermaster service but ran into trouble while in charge of the army depot at Mobile, Alabama. In November 1867, a court of inquiry was convened to investigate allegations of irregularities in his official conduct. The charges were eventually dropped, and he was mustered out on July 9, 1868. Heitman, *Historical Register*, 1:478; Leckie and Leckie, *Unlikely Warriors*, 153.

5. Grierson's transcription of his testimony, copied from the March 7, 1866, *New York Herald*, has been deleted here. Before the subcommittee, Grierson praised the freedmen for their intelligence, hard work, and remarkable patience and predicted that with the government's protection they would become loyal, educated, and self-sufficient citizens. At the same time, he harshly criticized Southern whites who "have no patriotism for the Union and are as much devoted to the lost cause or rebellion as they were during the war." In Grierson's opinion, stern measures at the end of the war would have stamped out disloyalty, but instead former Confederates had resumed positions of influence in business and local government and "would not fail to seize the opportunity to attempt again its [the Union's] destruction."

6. The lavish wedding of Kate Chase (1840–99), the vivacious daughter of Treasury Secretary Salmon P. Chase, and U.S. Senator William Sprague (1830–1915) on November 12, 1863 was a major social event in Washington. Unfortunately, the marriage ended tragically. Sprague, the handsome offspring of a wealthy manufacturing family, former Rhode Island governor, and hero of First Manassas, was an alcoholic philanderer and abusive husband. The couple divorced in 1882 after Kate had engaged in an affair with New York senator Roscoe Conklin. In a commentary on Victorian mores, Kate secluded herself at the Chase estate outside Washington, where she died impoverished at the age of fifty-eight. Sprague remarried and eventually moved to Paris, where he died at age eighty-five. Lamphier, *Kate Chase and William Sprague.*

7. On April 13, 1866, Ben wrote to Alice from Philadelphia: "I would have written you again from Washington, had it not been that my time was taken up constantly night & day for 3 or 4 days, with Gov. Senator Yates. . . . [H]e was on the road to destruction and I determined that he should be reclaimed & become a sober man. I believe I have succeeded. I locked him up in a room & never let him out untill [sic] he was perfectly sober. He at first fought against it very hard, but I had determined to win & he had to give up. . . . I do not think that he will ever drink again." Roll 6, Grierson Papers, TTU; Leckie and Leckie, *Unlikely Warriors*, 140.

8. Johnson's Reconstruction plan is outlined in Foner, *Reconstruction*, 176–227.

9. An 1843 graduate of West Point, James A. Hardie (1823–76) had a long and distinguished career beginning with the Mexican War and serving on the staffs of Generals John Wool, George B. McClellan, and William B. Franklin. He was promoted to colonel and inspector general in March 1864 and after the war was one of four inspector generals, with the rank of colonel. Warner, *Generals in Blue*, 204–5.

10. Congress passed the Civil Rights Bill in early April 1866, over President Johnson's veto. The law defined as citizens all persons born in the United States (except Indians) and spelled out rights to which they were equally entitled, regardless of race. Violations of the law would be prosecuted in federal court. Foner, *Reconstruction*, 243–51.

11. Grierson, of course, has the benefit of hindsight, but he articulates the views of the Radical Republicans that led to Johnson's impeachment trial in February to May 1868, where he was acquitted by a single vote. Foner, *Reconstruction*, 333–36.

12. An 1837 graduate of West Point, Edward D. Townsend (1817–93) transferred from the artillery to the adjutant general's department in 1846. At the outbreak of the Civil War, he served as adjutant general to Gen. Winfield Scott. After Scott's retirement, he became a senior assistant in the Adjutant General's Department and in 1863 was appointed acting adjutant general, an appointment President Grant made permanent in 1869. He retired in 1880. Heitman, *Historical Register*, 1:967; Edwards, *California Diary of General E. D. Townsend*, vii–ix.

13. On July 28, 1866, President Johnson signed an "Act to Increase and Fix the Military Peace Establishment of the United States." The law increased the infantry from nineteen to forty-five regiments and the cavalry from six to ten regiments. The artillery remained at five regiments. Four (later reduced to two) of the infantry regiments and two of the cavalry regiments would be composed of white officers and black enlisted men. Officers of the newly created regiments would be drawn from veterans of two years' "distinguished service" with the Civil War volunteers. Coffman, *Old Army*, 218–19; Utley, *Frontier Regulars*, 11–14.

Conclusion

1. Nelson A. Miles (1839–1925) rose from first lieutenant in the 22nd Massachusetts Infantry in 1861 to general-in-chief of the U.S. Army when he retired in 1903. Vain, egotistical, and opportunistic, he was also one of America's preeminent Civil War and frontier military officers. In 1888, Grierson succeeded Miles as commander of the Department of Arizona. Miles lobbied for Grierson's promotion to brigadier general in the regular army. Wooster, *Nelson Miles*; Dinges, "Benjamin H. Grierson," in Hutton, *Soldiers West*, 170–72.

Bibliography

Manuscripts

Benjamin H. Grierson Papers, Fort Davis National Historic Site, Fort Davis, Texas
Benjamin H. Grierson Papers, Illinois State Historical Library, Springfield
Benjamin H. Grierson Papers, Newberry Library, Chicago
Benjamin Henry Grierson Papers, Southwest Collection/Special Collections Library, Texas Tech University, Lubbock

Articles

Bayley, T. H., and Sir Henry Bishop. "The Mistletoe Bough." In Roy Palmer, ed., *Everyman's Book of British Ballads.* London: J. M. Dent and Sons, 1980. 30–31.

Bearss, Edwin C. "Grierson's Winter Raid on the Mobile and Ohio Railroad." *Military Affairs* 24 (Spring 1960): 20–37.

Beszedits, Stephen. "Hungarians in Civil War Missouri." <http://missouricivilwarmuseum.org>.

Dimick, Howard T. "Motives for the Burning of Oxford, Mississippi." *Journal of Mississippi History* 8 (July 1946): 111–20.

Dinges, Bruce J. "Grierson's Raid." *Civil War Times Illustrated,* February 1996: 50–64.

———. "Running Down Rebels," *Civil War Times Illustrated,* April 1980: 10–18.

Fisk, William L., Jr. "The Scotch-Irish in Central Ohio." *Ohio State Archaeological and Historical Quarterly* 57 (April 1948): 111–25.

Forbes, Stephen A. "Grierson's Cavalry Raid." *Transactions of the Illinois State Historical Society,* 1908: 99–130.

Lee, Stephen D. "Battle of Brice's Cross Roads, or Tishomingo Creek, June 2nd to 12th, 1864." *Publications of the Mississippi State Historical Society* 6 (1902): 27–37.

———. "The Battle of Tupelo, or Harrisburg, July 14, 1863." *Publications of the Mississippi State Historical Society* 6 (1902): 39–52.

———. "Sherman's Meridian Expedition and Sooy Smith's Raid to West Point." *Southern Historical Society Papers* 8 (February 1880): 49–61.

Leftwich, William Groom, Jr. "The Battle of Brice's Cross Roads." *West Tennessee Historical Society Papers* 20 (1966): 5–19.

Lott, Eric. "Blackface and Blackness: The Minstrel Show in American Culture." In Annemarie Bean, James V. Hatch, and Brooks McNamera, eds., *Inside the Minstrel Mask: Readings in Nineteenth-Century Blackface Minstrelsy.* Hanover, Conn.: Wesleyan University Press, 1996. 3–34.

Luckett, William W. "Bedford Forrest in the Battle of Brice's Cross Roads." *Tennessee Historical Quarterly* 15 (June 1956): 99–110.

Padgett, John B. "People, Places, and Events: A Faulkner Glossary." *Faulkner on the Web,* <http://www.olemiss.edu/~egjbp/glossary.html>.

Prince, Edward. "Cavalry Captured Navy." *National Tribune* (Washington, D.C.), April 28, 1904.

VandeCreek, Drew E. "The State Constitutional Convention of 1862." <http://dig.lib.niu.edu/civilwar/narrative3.html>.

Welter, Barbara. "The Cult of True Womanhood, 1820–1860." *American Quarterly* 18 (Summer 1966): 151–74.

Whiting, F. S. "Diary and Personal Recollection of the Second Grierson Raid through Tennessee and Mississippi, December 1864, and January, 1865, and the General Wilson Raid through Alabama and Georgia during the Months of March and April, 1865." In *War Sketches and Incidents as Related by Companions of the Iowa Commandery of the Military Order of the Loyal Legion of the United States.* 2 vols. Des Moines: P. C. Kenyon, 1893. 1:89–104.

Woodward, S. L. "Grierson's Raid, April 17th to May 2nd, 1863." Parts 1 and 2. *Journal of the U.S. Cavalry Association* 14 (1903–4): 685–710; 15 (1904): 94–123.

Books

Alberts, Don E. *Brandy Station to Manila Bay: A Biography of General Wesley Merritt.* Austin: Presidial Press, 1980.

Alexander, Thomas B. *Political Reconstruction in Tennessee.* New York: Russell and Russell, 1950.

Allardice, Bruce S. *More Generals in Gray.* Baton Rouge: Louisiana State University Press, 1995.

Ambrose, Stephen E. *Upton and the Army.* Baton Rouge: Louisiana State University Press, 1964.

Ballard, Michael B. *Civil War Mississippi: A Guide.* Jackson: University Press of Mississippi, 2000.

———. *Pemberton: A Biography.* Jackson: University Press of Mississippi, 1991.

———. *Vicksburg: The Campaign That Opened the Mississippi.* Chapel Hill: University of North Carolina Press, 2004.

Bearss, Edwin C. *Forrest at Brice's Cross Roads and in North Mississippi in 1864.* Reprint, Dayton, Ohio: Morningside Bookshop, 1987.

Bradley, George C., and Richard L. Dahlen. *From Conciliation to Conquest: The Sack of Athens and the Court-Martial of Colonel John B. Turchin.* Tuscaloosa: University of Alabama Press, 2006.

Brown, D. Alexander. *The Galvanized Yankees.* Urbana: University of Illinois Press, 1964.

———. *Grierson's Raid.* Urbana: University of Illinois Press, 1954.

Buel, Clarence C., and Robert U. Johnson. *Battles and Leaders of the Civil War.* 4 vols. Reprint, New York.: Thomas Yoseloff, 1956.

Carpenter, John A. *Sword and Olive Branch: Oliver Otis Howard.* Pittsburgh: University of Pittsburgh Press, 1964.

Carroll, John M., ed. *Camp Talk: The Very Private Letters of Frederick W. Benteen of the 7th U.S. Cavalry to His Wife, 1871–1888.* Mattituck, N.Y.: J. M. Carroll, 1983.

Carter, Arthur B. *The Tarnished Cavalier: Major General Earl Van Dorn.* Knoxville: University of Tennessee Press, 1999.

Castel, Albert. *Decision in the West: The Atlanta Campaign of 1864.* Lawrence: University Press of Kansas, 1992.

———. *General Sterling Price and the Civil War in the West.* Baton Rouge: Louisiana State University Press, 1968.

Chaffin, Tom. *Pathfinder: John Charles Frémont and the Course of American Empire.* New York: Hill and Wang, 2002.

Chase, Salmon P. *Diary and Correspondence of Salmon P. Chase.* New York: Da Capo, 1971.

Chepesiuk, Ron. *The Scotch-Irish: From the North of Ireland to the Making of America.* Jefferson, N.C.: McFarland, 2000.

Coffman, Edward M. *The Old Army: A Portrait of the American Army in Peacetime, 1784–1898.* New York: Oxford University Press, 1986.

Cole, Arthur C. *The Era of the Civil War, 1848–1870.* Vol. 3 of *The Sesquicentennial History of Illinois.* Springfield: Illinois Centennial Commission, 1919. Reprint, Urbana: University of Illinois Press, 1987.

Colley, Charles C. *The Century of Robert H. Forbes.* Tucson: Arizona Historical Society, 1977.

Connelly, Donald B. *John M. Schofield and the Politics of Generalship.* Chapel Hill: University of North Carolina Press, 2006.

Connelly, Thomas Lawrence. *Army of the Heartland: The Army of Tennessee, 1861–1862.* Baton Rouge: Louisiana State University Press, 1967.

———. *Autumn of Glory: The Army of Tennessee, 1862–1865.* Baton Rouge: Louisiana State University Press, 1971.

Cooper, William J., Jr. *Jefferson Davis, American.* New York: Alfred A. Knopf, 2000.

Cozzens, Peter. *General John Pope: A Life for the Nation.* Urbana: University of Illinois Press, 2000.

———. *No Better Place to Die: The Battle of Stones River.* Urbana: University of Illinois Press, 1990.

———. *This Terrible Sound: The Battle of Chickamauga.* Urbana: University of Illinois Press, 1992.

Cunningham, Edward. *The Port Hudson Campaign, 1862–1863.* Baton Rouge: Louisiana State University Press, 1963.

Cutrer, Thomas W. *Ben McCulloch and the Frontier Military Tradition.* Chapel Hill: University of North Carolina Press, 1993.

Degler, Carl. *At Odds: Women and the Family from the Revolution to the Present.* New York: Oxford University Press, 1980.

Dinges, Bruce J. "The Making of a Cavalryman: Benjamin H. Grierson and the Civil War along the Mississippi." Ph.D. diss., Rice University, 1978.

Doyle, Don Harrison. *The Social Order of a Frontier Community: Jacksonville, Illinois, 1825–1870.* Urbana: University of Illinois Press, 1978.

Duffy, James P. *Lincoln's Admiral: The Civil War Campaigns of David Farragut.* New York: John Wiley and Sons, 1997.

Dyer, John P. *Fightin' Joe Wheeler: From Shiloh to San Juan.* Rev. ed. Baton Rouge: Louisiana State University Press, 1961.

Ecelbarger, Gary. *Black Jack Logan: An Extraordinary Life in Peace and War.* Guilford, Conn.: Lyons, 2005.

Eckert, Edward K., and Nicholas J. Amato, eds. *Ten Years in the Saddle: The Memoir of William Woods Averill, 1851–1862.* San Rafael, Calif.: Presidio, 1978.

Eddy, T. M. *The Patriotism of Illinois: A Record of the Civil and Military History of the State in the War for the Union.* Vol. 1. Chicago: Clarke, 1865.

Edwards, Malcolm, ed. *The California Diary of General E. D. Townsend.* [Los Angeles:] Ward Ritchie, 1970.

Ellis, Richard N. *General Pope and U.S. Indian Policy.* Albuquerque: University of New Mexico Press, 1970.

Engle, Nancy Arlene Driscoll. "'We Can't Be the Women We Were Before': Mary Livermore and the Chicago Women in the Civil War." M.A. thesis, University of Central Florida, 1996.

Engle, Stephen D. *Don Carlos Buell: Most Promising of All.* Chapel Hill: University of North Carolina Press, 1999.

Ewer, James K. *The Third Massachusetts Cavalry in the War for the Union.* N.p.: Historical Committee of the Regimental Association, 1903.

Feis, William B. *Grant's Secret Service: The Intelligence War from Belmont to Appomattox.* Lincoln: University of Nebraska Press, 2002.

Fellman, Michael. *Citizen Sherman: A Life of William Tecumseh Sherman.* New York: Random House, 1995.

Ferri Pisani, Camille. *Prince Napoleon in America, 1861: Letters from His Aide-de-Camp.* Translated by Georges Joyaux. Bloomington: Indiana University Press, 1959.

Finch, L. Boyd. *Confederate Pathway to the Pacific: Major Sherod Hunter and Arizona Territory, C.S.A.* Tucson: Arizona Historical Society, 1996.

Foner, Eric. *Free Soil, Free Labor, Free Men: The Ideology of the Republican Party before the Civil War.* New York: Oxford University Press, 1970.

———. *Reconstruction: America's Unfinished Revolution, 1863–1877.* New York: Harper and Row, 1988.

Foster, Buck T. *Sherman's Mississippi Campaign.* Tuscaloosa: University of Alabama Press, 2006.

Fuchs, Richard L. *An Unerring Fire: The Massacre at Fort Pillow.* London: Associated University Presses, 1994.

Glass, E. L. N. *History of the Tenth Cavalry, 1866–1921.* Reprint, Fort Collins, Colo.: Old Army Press, 1972.

Gragg, Rod. *Confederate Goliath: The Battle of Fort Fisher.* New York: Harper and Row, 1991.

Grant, Ulysses S. *Personal Memoirs of U. S. Grant.* 2 vols. New York: Charles Webster, 1885.

Greene, Jerome A. *Washita: The U.S. Army and the Southern Cheyennes, 1867–1869.* Norman: University of Oklahoma Press, 2004.

Hallock, Judith Lee. *Braxton Bragg and Confederate Defeat.* Vol. 2. Tuscaloosa: University of Alabama Press, 1991.

Hamilton, James J. *The Battle of Fort Donelson.* South Brunswick, N.J.: Thomas Yoseloff, 1968.

Harrington, Fred Harvey. *Fighting Politician: Major General N. P. Banks.* Philadelphia: University of Pennsylvania Press, 1948.

Hartje, Robert G. *Van Dorn: The Life and Times of a Confederate General.* Nashville: Vanderbilt University Press, 1967.

Hattaway, Herman. *General Stephen D. Lee.* Jackson: University Press of Mississippi, 1976.

Hebert, Walter H. *Fighting Joe Hooker.* Indianapolis: Bobbs-Merrill, 1944.

Heitman, Francis B. *Historical Register and Dictionary of the United States Army, 1789–1903.* 2 vols. Reprint, Urbana: University of Illinois Press, 1965.

Herr, Pamela. *Jessie Benton Frémont.* New York: Franklin Watts, 1987.

Herr, Pamela, and Mary Lee Spence, eds. *The Letters of Jessie Benton Frémont.* Urbana: University of Illinois Press, 1993.

Hewitt, Lawrence L. *Port Hudson: Confederate Bastion on the Mississippi.* Baton Rouge: Louisiana State University Press, 1987.

Heyman, Max L., Jr. *Prudent Soldier: A Biography of Major General E. R. S. Canby, 1817–1873.* Glendale, Calif.: Arthur H. Clark, 1959.

Hicken, Victor. *Illinois in the Civil War.* Urbana: University of Illinois Press, 1966.

Hirshon, Stanley P. *Grenville M. Dodge: Soldier, Politician, Railroad Pioneer.* Bloomington: Indiana University Press, 1967.

Hollandsworth, James G., Jr. *Pretense of Glory: The Life of General Nathaniel P. Banks.* Baton Rouge: Louisiana State University Press, 1998.

Holzer, Harold, ed. *The Lincoln-Douglas Debates: The First Complete, Unexpurgated Text.* New York: HarperCollins, 1993.

Horn, Stanley F. *The Decisive Battle of Nashville.* Baton Rouge: Louisiana State University Press, 1956.

Hubbell, John T., and James W. Geary, eds. *Biographical Dictionary of the Union: Northern Leaders of the Civil War.* Westport, Conn.: Greenwood, 1995.

Hughes, Nathaniel Cheairs, Jr. *The Battle of Belmont: Grant Strikes South.* Chapel Hill: University of North Carolina Press, 1991.

———. *General William J. Hardee: Old Reliable.* Baton Rouge: Louisiana State University Press, 1965.

Hughes, Nathaniel Cheairs, Jr., and Roy P. Stonesifer Jr. *The Life and Wars of Gideon J. Pillow.* Chapel Hill: University of North Carolina Press, 1993.

Hurst, Jack. *Nathan Bedford Forrest.* New York: Alfred A. Knopf, 1993.

Hutton, Paul A. *Phil Sheridan and His Army.* Lincoln: University of Nebraska Press, 1985.

———, ed. *Soldiers West: Biographies from the Military Frontier.* Lincoln: University of Nebraska Press, 1987.

Johannsen, Robert W. *Stephen A. Douglas.* New York: Oxford University Press, 1973.

Johnson, Ludwell H. *Red River Campaign: Politics and Cotton in the Civil War.* Baltimore: Johns Hopkins University Press, 1958.

Jones, James Pickett. *Yankee Blitzkrieg: Wilson's Raid through Alabama and Georgia.* Athens: University of Georgia Press, 1976.

Jordan, David M. *Winfield Scott Hancock: A Soldier's Life.* Bloomington: Indiana University Press, 1988.

Jordan, Donaldson, and Edwin J. Pratt. *Europe and the American Civil War.* Boston: Houghton Mifflin, 1931.

Kajencki, Francis C. *Star on Many a Battlefield: Brevet Brigadier General Joseph Kargé in the American Civil War.* Rutherford, N.J.: Fairleigh Dickinson University Press, 1980.

Keenan, Jerry. *Wilson's Cavalry Corps: Union Campaigns in the Western Theatre, October 1864 through Spring 1865.* Jefferson, N.C.: McFarland, 1998.

Kenner, Charles L. *Buffalo Soldiers and Officers of the Ninth Cavalry, 1867–1898: Black and White Together.* Norman: University of Oklahoma Press, 1999.

Kerby, Robert L. *Kirby Smith's Confederacy: The Trans-Mississippi South, 1863–1865.* New York: Columbia University Press, 1972.

Kinchen, Oscar. *Confederate Operations in Canada and the North: A Little-Known Phase of the American Civil War.* North Quincy, Mass.: Christopher, 1970.

King, James T. *War Eagle: A Life of General Eugene A. Carr.* Lincoln: University of Nebraska Press, 1963.

Kionka, T. K. *Key Command: Ulysses S. Grant's District of Cairo.* Columbia: University of Missouri Press, 2006.

Kiper, Richard L. *Major General John Alexander McClernand: Politician in Uniform.* Kent, Ohio: Kent State University Press, 1999.

Kraditor, Aileen. *Means and Ends in American Abolitionism: Garrison and His Critics on Strategy and Tactics, 1834–1850.* New York: Pantheon Books, 1967.

Kroeker, Marvin E. *Great Plains Command: William B. Hazen in the Frontier West.* Norman: University of Oklahoma Press, 1976.

Lamers, William M. *The Edge of Glory: A Biography of General William S. Rosecrans.* New York: Harcourt, Brace, 1961.

Lamphier, Peg A. *Kate Chase and William Sprague: Politics and Gender in a Civil War Marriage.* Lincoln: University of Nebraska Press, 2003.

Lash, Jeffrey N. *A Politician Turned General: The Civil War Career of Stephen Augustus Hurlbut.* Kent, Ohio: Kent State University Press, 2003.

Leckie, Shirley A., ed. *The Colonel's Lady on the Western Frontier: The Correspondence of Alice Kirk Grierson.* Lincoln: University of Nebraska Press, 1989.

Leckie, William H., and Shirley A. Leckie. *The Buffalo Soldiers: A Narrative of the Black Cavalry in the West.* Rev. ed. Norman: University of Oklahoma Press, 2003.

———. *Unlikely Warriors: General Benjamin Grierson and His Family.* Norman: University of Oklahoma Press, 1984.

Leonard, Elizabeth D. *Yankee Women: Gender Battles in the Civil War.* New York: W. W. Norton, 1994.

Leyburn, James G. *The Scots-Irish: A Social History.* Chapel Hill: University of North Carolina Press, 1962.

Livermore, Mary Ashton. *My Story of the War: A Woman's Narrative of Four Years Personal Experience as Nurse in the Union Army, and Relief Work at Home, in Hospitals, Camps, and at the Front, during the War of the Rebellion.* Hartford, Conn.: A. D. Worthington, 1889.

Longacre, Edward G. *From Union Stars to Top Hat: A Biography of the Extraordinary General James Harrison Wilson.* Harrisburg, Pa.: Stackpole Books, 1972.

Marszalek, John F. *Commander of All Lincoln's Armies: A Life of General Henry W. Halleck.* Cambridge, Mass.: Harvard University Press, 2005.

———. *Sherman: A Soldier's Passion for Order.* New York: Free Press, 1993.

Marvel, William. *Andersonville: The Last Depot.* Chapel Hill: University of North Carolina Press, 1994.

———. *Burnside.* Chapel Hill: University of North Carolina Press, 1991.

Masich, Andrew E. *The Civil War in Arizona: The Story of the California Volunteers, 1861–1865.* Norman: University of Oklahoma Press, 2006.

Mayer, Henry. *All on Fire: William Lloyd Garrison and the Abolition of Slavery.* New York: St. Martin's, 1998.

McDonough, James Lee. *Chattanooga: A Death Grip on the Confederacy.* Knoxville: University of Tennessee Press, 1984.

———. *Shiloh: In Hell before Night.* Knoxville: University of Tennessee Press, 1977.

———. *Stones River: Bloody Winter in Tennessee.* Knoxville: University of Tennessee Press, 1980.

McFeely, William S. *Grant: A Biography.* New York: W. W. Norton, 1981.

McKinney, Francis F. *Education in Violence: The Life of George H. Thomas and the History of the Army of the Cumberland.* Detroit: Wayne State University Press, 1961.

McMurry, Richard M. *John Bell Hood and the War for Southern Independence.* Lexington: University Press of Kentucky, 1982.

McPherson, James M. *Battle Cry of Freedom: The Civil War Era.* New York: Oxford University Press, 1988.

———. *For Cause and Comrades: Why Men Fought in the Civil War.* New York: Oxford University Press, 1997.

McWhiney, Grady. *Braxton Bragg and Confederate Defeat.* Vol.1. New York: Columbia University Press, 1969.

Miller, Edward A., Jr. *Lincoln's Abolitionist General: The Biography of David Hunter.* Chapel Hill: University of North Carolina Press, 1997.

Mills, Charles K. *Harvest of Barren Regrets: The Army Career of Frederick William Benteen, 1834–1898.* Glendale, Calif.: Arthur H. Clark, 1985.

Monaghan, Jay. *Swamp Fox of the Confederacy: The Life and Military Services of M. Jeff Thompson.* Tuscaloosa, Ala.: Confederate Publishing, 1956.

Moore, Frank, ed. *The Rebellion Record: A Diary of American Events.* Vol.11. New York: D. Van Nostrand, 1868.

Morris, Richard B., ed. *Encyclopedia of American History.* Bicentennial edition. New York: Harper and Row, 1976.

Morsberger, Robert E., and Katherine M. Morsberger. *Lew Wallace, Militant Romantic.* New York: McGraw-Hill, 1980.

Nankivell, John H. *History of the Twenty-fifth Regiment, United States Infantry, 1869–1926.* Reprint, New York: Negro Universities Press, 1969.

Nevins, Allan. *Frémont, Pathmarker of the West.* New York: Longmans, Green, 1955.

Niven, John. *Salmon P. Chase: A Biography.* New York: Oxford University Press, 1995.

Official Army Register, 1912. Washington, D.C.: Adjutant General's Office, 1912.

Osborne, Charles C. *Jubal: The Life and Times of General Jubal A. Early, C.S.A., Defender of the Lost Cause.* Chapel Hill, N.C.: Algonquin Books, 1992.

Parks, Joseph Howard. *General Leonidas Polk, C.S.A.: The Fighting Bishop.* Baton Rouge: Louisiana State University Press, 1962.

Parrish, T. Michael. *Richard Taylor: Soldier Prince of Dixie.* Chapel Hill: University of North Carolina Press, 1992.

Parrish, William E. *Frank Blair: Lincoln's Conservative.* Columbia: University of Missouri Press, 1998.

Perry, James M. *Touched with Fire: Five Presidents and the Civil War Battles That Made Them.* New York: Public Affairs, 2003.

Peskin, Allan. *Garfield: A Biography.* Kent, Ohio: Kent State University Press, 1978.

Phillips, Christopher. *Damned Yankee: The Life of General Nathaniel Lyon.* Columbia: University of Missouri Press, 1990.

Portrait and Biographical Album of Champaign County, Illinois. Chicago: Chapman Brothers, 1887.

Radbourne, Allan. *Mickey Free: Apache Captive, Interpreter, and Indian Scout.* Tucson: Arizona Historical Society, 2005.

Ramage, James A. *Rebel Raider: The Life of General John Hunt Morgan.* Lexington: University Press of Kentucky, 1986.

Robinson, Charles M., III. *Hurricane of Fire: The Union Assault on Fort Fisher.* Annapolis, Md.: Naval Institute Press, 1998.

Rolle, Andrew F. *John C. Frémont: Character as Destiny.* Norman: University of Oklahoma Press, 1991.

Schofield, John M. *Forty-six Years in the Army.* Reprint, Norman: University of Oklahoma Press, 1998.

Shea, William L., and Earl J. Hess. *Pea Ridge: Civil War Campaign in the West.* Chapel Hill: University of North Carolina Press, 1992.

Sherman, William T. *Memoirs of Gen. W. T. Sherman.* 2 vols. New York: Charles L. Webster, 1891.

Simpson, Brooks D. *Let Us Have Peace: Ulysses S. Grant and the Politics of War and Reconstruction, 1861–1868.* Chapel Hill: University of North Carolina Press, 1991.

———. *Ulysses S. Grant: Triumph over Adversity, 1822–1865.* New York: Houghton Mifflin, 2000.

Simpson, Brooks D., and Jean V. Berlin, eds. *Sherman's Civil War: Selected Correspondence of William T. Sherman.* Chapel Hill: University of North Carolina Press, 1999.

Starr, Stephen Z. *Jennison's Jayhawkers: A Civil War Cavalry Regiment and Its Commander.* Baton Rouge: Louisiana State University Press, 1973.

———. *The Union Cavalry in the Civil War.* Vol. 3, *The War for the West, 1861–1865.* Baton Rouge: Louisiana State University Press, 1985.

Stewart, James Brewer. *Wendell Phillips, Liberty's Hero.* Baton Rouge: Louisiana State University Press, 1986.

Surby, Richard W. *Grierson Raids.* Chicago: Rounds and James, 1865.

Symonds, Craig L. *Joseph E. Johnston: A Civil War Biography.* New York: W. W. Norton, 1992.

Taylor, John M. *William Henry Seward: Lincoln's Right Hand.* New York: HarperCollins, 1991.

Taylor, Richard. *Destruction and Reconstruction: Personal Experiences of the Late Civil War.* Edited by Richard B. Harwell. New York: Longmans, Green, 1955.

Thomas, Benjamin, and Harold M. Hyman. *Stanton: The Life and Times of Lincoln's Secretary of War.* New York: Alfred A. Knopf, 1962.

Thomas, Wilbur. *General George H. Thomas: The Indomitable Warrior.* New York: Exposition, 1964.

Tucker, Spencer C. *Unconditional Surrender: The Capture of Forts Henry and Donelson.* Abilene, Tex.: McWhiney Foundation, 2001.

Tyler, Ronnie C. *Santiago Vidaurri and the Southern Confederacy.* Austin: Texas State Historical Association, 1973.

Underwood, Larry D. *The Butternut Guerillas: A Story of Grierson's Raid.* N.p.: Dageforde, n.d.

Urwin, Gregory J. W., ed. *Black Flag over Dixie: Racial Atrocities and Reprisals in the Civil War.* Carbondale: Southern Illinois University Press, 2004.

Utley, Robert M. *Frontier Regulars: The United States Army and the Indian, 1866–1890.* New York: Macmillan, 1973.

Vandiver, Frank E. *Jubal's Raid: General Early's Famous Attack on Washington in 1864.* New York: McGraw-Hill, 1960.

Wagner, Lavern J., ed. *Band Music from the Benjamin H. Grierson Collection.* Madison, Wisc.: A-R Editions, 1998.

Ward, Andrew. *River Run Red: The Fort Pillow Massacre and the American Civil War.* New York: Viking, 2005.

Waring, George E., Jr. *Whip and Spur.* Boston: James R. Osgood, 1875.

Warner, Ezra J. *Generals in Blue: The Lives of the Union Commanders.* Baton Rouge: Louisiana State University Press, 1989.

———. *Generals in Gray: The Lives of the Confederate Commanders.* Baton Rouge: Louisiana State University Press, 1959.

The War of the Rebellion: A Compilation of the Official Records of the Union and Confederate Armies [O.R.]. 70 vols. in 128. Washington, D.C.: Government Printing Office, 1880–1901.

Weber, Jennifer L. *Copperheads: The Rise and Fall of Lincoln's Opponents in the North.* New York: Oxford University Press, 2006.

Whitcomb, Caroline E. *History of the Second Massachusetts Battery (Nims' Battery) of Light Artillery, 1861–1865.* Concord, N.H.: Rumford, 1912.

Wiatt, R. W. *Libby Prison, Richmond, Virginia.* Official Publication No. 12. Richmond: Civil War Centennial Commission, 1961–65.

Wiley, Bell Irvin. *The Life of Johnny Reb and the Life of Billy Yank.* Indianapolis: Bobbs-Merrill, 1943. Reprint, Baton Rouge: Louisiana State University Press, 1979.

Williams, Frederick D., ed. *The Wild Life of the Army: Civil War Letters of James A. Garfield.* [Ann Arbor:] Michigan State University Press, 1964.

Williams, Kenneth P. *Lincoln Finds a General.* Vol. 4, *Grant Rises in the West: From Iuka to Vicksburg, 1862-1863.* Lincoln: University of Nebraska Press, 1997.

Williams, T. Harry. *P. G. T. Beauregard: Napoleon in Gray.* Baton Rouge: Louisiana State University Press, 1954.

Wills, Brian Steele. *A Battle from the Start: The Life of Nathan Bedford Forrest.* New York: HarperCollins, 1992.

Woodworth, Steven E., ed. *Grant's Lieutenants: From Cairo to Vicksburg.* Lawrence: University Press of Kansas, 2001.

———. *Jefferson Davis and His Generals: The Failure of Confederate Command in the West.* Lawrence: University Press of Kansas, 1990.

Wooster, Robert. *Nelson Miles and the Twilight of the Frontier Army.* Lincoln: University of Nebraska Press, 1993.

Wyeth, John Allan. *That Devil Forrest: Life of General Nathan Bedford Forrest.* New York: Harper and Brothers, 1959.

York, Neil Longley. *Fiction as Fact: The Horse Soldiers and Popular Memory.* Kent, Ohio: Kent State University Press, 2001.

Newspapers

Frank Leslie's Illustrated Newspaper
Harper's Weekly
Jacksonville (Ill.) Journal
Springfield (Ill.) State Journal
St. Louis Globe-Democrat

Electronic Sources

Appleton's Encyclopedia. <http://www.famousamericans.net>.

Biographical Directory of the United States Congress. <http://www.gpoacess.gov/serialset/cdocuments/hd108-222/index>.

The Columbia Encyclopedia, 6th ed. <http://www.bartleby.com>.

Illinois Civil War Muster and Descriptive Rolls Database. <http://www.cyberdriveillinois.com/departments/archives/datcivil.html>.

New Georgia Encyclopedia.< http://www.georgiaencyclopedia.org>.

Tennessee Encyclopedia of History and Culture. <http://www.tennesseeencyclopedia.net>.

Index

from, 56–57, 129–30, 138; life in Jacksonville, 28–29, 109; marriage, 6, 28; photographs of, following 186; in St. Louis, 8; visits Ben in Alabama, 351, 353, 355–56; visits Ben in Memphis, 99, 107–9, 115, 201–5, 211–12, 235, 257, 315; visits Ben in Missouri, 48–49; visits Ben at Paducah, 83–85, 386n. 26

Grierson, Benjamin H., 23, 132, 231, 317–18, 385n. 16, 410n. 15; as aide-de-camp to Prentiss, 36–37, 41, 46, 58–59; appointment to regular army, 336, 346–47, 349, 359–62, 416n. 7; in Arkansas, 120–21; attitude toward African Americans, 93, 101, 207–8, 351; birth of, 14–15; business affairs of, 29–30, 69, 86, 189–90; career in Ohio militia, 37–38; cavalry command positions, 3–4, 127, 129, 201, 212, 271, 292, 324, 342, 350, 369, 380n.19, 392n. 10, 417n. 1; cavalry preparations for Mobile campaign, 325, 327–28, 345; childhood of, 16–17; children of, 349, 415n. 1; as colonel of 6th Illinois Cavalry in Kentucky, 64–68, 72–73, 75–77, 81–82; correspondence with wife, 52, 61–62, 77, 86, 99, 103, 131, 136, 138, 145, 189, 194, 227, 386n. 25; and court martial of Thomas Worthington, 98–99; courtship, 24–28; death of, 2, 373n. 8; efforts to re-enlist soldiers, 225–27; family of, 5–6, 8, 21–22, 56–57, 108, 115, 202, 212, 315, 353, 355–56; injuries, 199–205, 212, 374n. 1; loss of cavalry command, 117–18, 127–28, 139, 197–98, 213–15, 235, 283–89, 299, 315, 346; meets with Frémonts, 44; meets with Grant and Lincoln, 318–22, 365–67; as member of Jacksonville volunteers, 36–37; military pay of, 63, 69–72, 76, 81–82, 100, 131, 144, 351–52; musical talents of, 19–21, 24–25, 27–29, 32–33, 37, 58, 375n. 9, 376n. 12; mustered, 57–58, 61, 63, 69; mustered out, 355–56, 366–68; in New Orleans, 324, 343–44; photographs of, following 186; raid through Mississippi, 146–47, 150–61, 163–64, 166–69, 171, 178, 181–82, 185–86, 195–96, 299, 326; relationship with Sher-

man, 75, 113, 349, 376–377n. 2; and removal of Frémont, 60–61; role in A. J. Smith's operations, 258–65, 267–69, 271–78, 280–81; role in Alabama, 330–37, 339–40, 344, 349–50, 352, 354–56; role at Brice's Cross Roads, 235, 240, 242–54, 405n. 2; role in march to Holly Springs, 123, 127, 132, 134; role in Meridian expedition, 213, 220–25; role in Missouri campaign, 42–44, 48, 54–55, 58; role in Mobile and Ohio Railroad raid, 298–99, 301–10; role in operations against Forrest, 207–11, 228–33, 401n. 17; role at Port Hudson, 182, 184, 188–93, 195, 198–99; reunification of cavalry under, 290–95; with 6th Illinois Cavalry in Tennessee and Mississippi, 87–90, 92–95, 100–3, 105, 107–9, 111–13, 116, 129–31, 391n. 8; as Superintendent of General Mounted Recruiting Service, 8; on use of troops after war, 343; at Vicksburg, 189, 199, 201, 412n. 4 (chap. 14); views on reconstruction, 353, 362–63; views on slavery, 161–62; visits home, 204, 356–57

Grierson, Benjamin Henry (uncle), 11
Grierson, Benjamin Henry, Jr. (son), 6, 21
Grierson, Benjamin Henry Jesse Francis Shepard. See Grierson, Francis
Grierson, Charles, 6, 70, 77–78, 83–85, 107–9, 115, 129, 145, 203–4, 386n. 26
Grierson, Edith Clare, 349, 415n. 1
Grierson, Elizabeth, 254; photograph of, following 186
Grierson, Francis, 374n. 14
Grierson, John (grandfather), 11
Grierson, John Charles (brother), 14, 16–17, 22–24, 54, 98, 388n. 8; assists in Ben's business affairs, 70, 189; correspondence with Alice Grierson, 103; correspondence with Ben, 47–48; in Memphis, 34–35, 95–96, 115, 201, 323; photograph of, following 186; promotion of, 326, 344; as quartermaster, 81, 108, 129, 254, 355, 416n. 4
Grierson, Joshua (uncle), 11
Grierson, Lillian King, 2
Grierson, Louisa (sister), 12, 18–19, 21, 29, 129. See also Semple, Louisa Grierson

6th Illinois Cavalry (*continued*)
Mississippi, 116–20; Grierson as commander, 79–80, 82, 391n. 8; Grierson joins, 2, 57–58; on Grierson's raid, 146–78, 181, 200–201, 326; in Kentucky, 63–68, 87; on Meridian expedition, 217, 218, 220; in Mississippi, 102, 123, 128, 134; operations in Tennessee, 87, 97, 99–104, 110, 115, 129–30, 200; petition for Grierson as commander, 77; photograph of, following 186; at Port Hudson, 188–96; in pursuit of Van Dorn, 123–26; role in A. J. Smith's operations, 273–74; Sherman's inspection of, 103–4; skirmish at Cockrum's Crossroads, 104–5; skirmish near Covington, 137–38; skirmishes near La Grange, 140–41; supply of, 111–12, 122, 147–48
6th Tennessee Cavalry, 208, 228
6th U.S. Cavalry, 404n. 6
Skelton, J. W., 274–75, 303, 310
Skinner, Lucius B., 195
Slack, James B., 87, 97, 108
Smith, A. J., 208–9, 258–59, 269–70, 283, 292–93, 331–32, 334, 339; Grierson's relationship with, 284–85; operations in Mississippi, 262–65, 271–82, 296, 406n. 2, 407n. 1; with Rosecrans in Missouri, 282–83; at Tupelo, 266–67, 407n. 5
Smith, C. F., 71, 384n. 12
Smith, J. Condit, 114, 115
Smith, Jason B., 146, 152
Smith, Morgan L., 104, 105–7, 287, 289–90, 296, 297, 323; career of, 389–90n. 16
Smith, William Sooy, 3, 139–40, 213–15, 234, 284, 395n. 12, 402n. 23; career of, 394n. 5; and Grierson's raid, 145–46, 151, 159; and Meridian expedition, 215–22, 227, 403nn. 6–7; photograph of, following, 186
Smithland, Ky., 72–76, 100
Snyder, Adam, 166
Snyder, John M., 68
Somerville, Miss., 125
Somerville, Tenn., 111–13, 125, 140, 207, 209, 230, 230, 233, 235
Somerville Branch Railroad, 207

Sooukatonchie River (Miss.), 306
Southern Railroad, 156, 158, 160
Spanish Fort, Ala., 329
Sprague, Kate Chase, 416n. 6
Sprague, William, 357, 416n. 6
Springdale, Miss., 123
Springfield, Ill., 5, 7, 27–28, 36, 41, 53, 57, 63–64, 66, 69, 70, 72, 76, 81, 144, 204, 229, 318, 349, 382n. 2, 400n. 8, 400n. 10
Spurlack, Alten, 169–70
Stacey, James D., 101–2
Stanley, David S., 298, 410n. 15
Stanton, Edwin M., 321–22, 358, 361–62, 399n. 2, 411n. 18, 416n. 2; career of, 412n. 4; and Grierson's promotion, 359–60
Stark's Landing, Ala., 330
Starkville, Miss., 151–52, 154, 307, 396n. 15
Starr, Matthew H., 98, 103, 208, 210, 220, 231, 394n. 2, 403n. 7, 407n. 1; in A. J. Smith's operations, 273–74; career of, 388n. 10; during Forrest's attack on Memphis, 279–80; on Grierson's raid, 155, 158–59; on Meridian expedition, 217–18
Steadman, George, 160–61
Steele, Frederick, 119–20, 122, 282, 332, 392n. 11, 400n. 7
Stephens, Alexander, 412n. 1
Stevens, Stoddard, 23
Stewart, John, 355
Stewart, Mathew, 278
St. Joseph, Mo., 53, 379n. 13
St. Louis, Mo., 41, 315, 380n. 21, 385n. 19; Frémont at, 44–46, 48, 52, 60–61; Grierson at, 1, 8, 47, 55, 204, 290–91, 294–95, 349, 369; Union cavalry at, 293
Stone, Charles P., 198, 399n. 2
Stones River, battle of, 143, 383nn. 7–8; 387n. 5, 390n. 2, 395n. 11
Strong, William K., 76
Stuart, David, 111
Sturgis, Samuel D., 3, 233–34, 287; career of, 404n. 6; operations against Forrest, 235–58, 264, 303, 404n. 6; 405n. 2; 406nn. 5–6; photograph of, following 186
Summerville, Tenn., 109

Bruce J. Dinges holds a Ph.D. from Rice University. He is director of publications at the Arizona Historical Society and editor of the *Journal of Arizona History*.

Shirley A. Leckie is professor emerita of history at the University of Central Florida. Her previous books include *Unlikely Warriors: General Benjamin H. Grierson and His Family* (1984, 1998), which she coauthored with the late William H. Leckie, with whom she worked on the 2003 revised edition of his *Buffalo Soldiers: A Narrative of the Black Cavalry in the West*; *The Colonel's Lady on the Western Frontier: The Correspondence of Alice Kirk Grierson* (1989), which she edited; biographies of Elizabeth Bacon Custer (1993, 1998) and Angie Debo (2000, 2002); and *Their Own Frontier: Women Intellectuals Re-Visioning the American West* (forthcoming in 2008), which she coedited with Nancy J. Parezo.